Successful Service Operations Management

2e

D0164617

■ **Richard Metters**
Goizueta Business School,
Emory University

■ **Kathryn King-Metters**
Department of Economics and Business,
Agnes Scott College

■ **Madeleine Pullman**
School of Hotel Administration,
Cornell University

■ **Steve Walton**
Goizueta Business School,
Emory University

THOMSON

SOUTH-WESTERN

Australia · Canada · Mexico · Singapore · Spain · United Kingdom · United States

THOMSON

SOUTH-WESTERN

Successful Service Operations Management, 2e

Richard D. Metters, Kathryn H. King-Metters, Madeleine Pullman, Steve Walton

VP/Editorial Director: Jack W. Calhoun	**Technology Project Editor:** Christine Wittmer	**Art Director:** Michelle Kunkler
Senior Acquisitions Editor: Charles E. McCormick, Jr.	**Web Coordinator:** Kelly Reid	**Cover and Internal Designer:** Lisa Albonetti Cincinnati, OH
Developmental Editor: Taney Wilkins	**Senior Manufacturing Coordinator:** Diane Lohman	**Cover Images:** © Tim Mosenfelder/Getty Images and Digital Vision
Senior Marketing Manager: Larry Qualls	**Production House:** DPS Associates, Cincinnati, OH	
Production Editor: Tamborah Moore	**Printer:** Edwards Brothers, Ann Arbor, MI	

ASIA (including India)
Thomson Learning
5 Shenton Way
#01-01 UIC Building
Singapore 068808

CANADA
Thomson Nelson
1120 Birchmount Road
Toronto, Ontario
Canada M1K 5G4

AUSTRALIA/NEW ZEALAND
Thomson Learning Australia
102 Dodds Street
Southbank, Victoria 3006
Australia
LATIN AMERICA

UK/EUROPE/MIDDLE
EAST/AFRICA
Thomson Learning
High Holborn House
50-51 Bedford Road
London WC1R 4LR
United Kingdom

Thomson Learning
Seneca, 53
Colonia Polanco
11560 Mexico
D.F.Mexico

SPAIN (includes Portugal)
Thomson Paraninfo
Calle Magallanes, 25
28015 Madrid, Spain

To our families, Alexandra, Tim, Vicki, Jacob, and Noah

Brief Contents

Contents

*PY and the Dome
included on the
Student CD.*

*SimQuick Example
included on the
Student CD.*

Six Sigma Tools supplemental material included on the Student CD.

PART 4

Matching Supply and Demand   233

Quantitative discussion of multiple products and shelf space limitations included on the Student CD.

Advanced queuing models material included on the Student CD.

PART 5

Tools for Managing Services   297

Mathematical solution methods for delivered services material included on the Student CD.

Mixed linear/integer programming for location selection material included on the Student CD.

DEA software information included on the Student CD.

Preface

The academic field of operations management has often been called production management or production and operations management because of its close ties to manufacturing management. Now, however, roughly 80% of the U.S. economy falls within the "services" domain, giving a new perspective to operations management. The future careers of business school students tend to be even more extreme in their tilt toward services. Further, even traditional manufacturers such as Ford and General Electric now derive large portions of their revenue from their service businesses, rather than from their physical products.

The challenge before the operations management community is to keep our field growing and relevant by embracing the service economy. This book is written in response to that challenge.

Many traditional operations management tools and techniques presented by textbooks with manufacturing examples are also valuable in services firms, such as project management, process analysis, or inventory management. However, even with these traditional tools, the context and emphasis of their application in a service business often differs radically from a manufacturer. Consequently, this book contains many topics found in general operations management texts, but discusses those topics exclusively from the viewpoint of a service sector manager.

Other tools and concepts, such as yield management, data envelopment analysis, experience management, and scoring systems, are used nearly exclusively in services. Not only are these topics not found in traditional operations textbooks, but the major case study writing institutions also ignore them, leading to a general dearth of teaching material for these topics. Here, we not only include explanatory material for these topics, but also provide original case studies to offer the decision-oriented learning environment favored by many students.

ORGANIZATION OF THE BOOK

The book is organized around both qualitative and quantitative themes, starting from a "top down" look at operations. The first half of the book is largely qualitative and presents conceptual frameworks to guide strategic operational decisions. The second half of the book is largely quantitative and focuses on using techniques to achieve the goals set forth in the strategically oriented material.

This book contains the following features:

- Learning objectives precede every chapter to keep students focused on key concepts.
- Nineteen original case studies are included.
- Boxed features throughout the text, called Service Operations Management Practices, provide practical contexts for theoretical points.
- Visit the textbook support site at http://metters.swlearning.com for additional support resources.
- The Instructor's Resource CD (ISBN 0-324-22441-9) includes answers to chapter-end problems, discussion of cases, and PowerPoint® presentations.

NEW FOR THE SECOND EDITION

Text Material on the Student CD

For the second edition the book has gained both quantitative and qualitative material. The material actually on the text pages is more qualitative, as a significant portion of the quantitative material has been moved to the Student CD. The quantitative material is still here! In fact, a significant amount of quantitative material has been added to the queuing, location, and DEA chapters, and it is now found on the Student CD.

New Chapters

New chapters have been added covering: "Outsourcing and Offshoring," and "Six Sigma for Service Process Improvement." Additionally, the "strategic planning" chapter has been completely reworked.

New Cases

The first edition had 10 cases, this edition has 19. Every chapter after Chapter 1 has a case study, either in the text or on the Student CD.

ACKNOWLEDGEMENTS

Special thanks go to Michael Ketzenberg, Colorado State University, for writing the chapter on project management. Sherry Oh, University of Calgary; Vicente Vargas, University of San Diego; Ken Klassen, Brock University; and John McClain, Johnson Graduate School of Management, Cornell University also provided valuable additions to this work.

We would also like to thank our publishing team at South-Western/Thomson Learning: Charles E. McCormick, Jr., Senior Acquisitions Editor; Taney Wilkins, Developmental Editor; Larry Qualls, Senior Marketing Manager; Tamborah Moore, Production Editor, and Crystal Bullen at DPS.

Reviewers

Finally, we would like to thank the following reviewers for contributing their wisdom:

Elliot Bendoly
Emory University

Ken Boyer
Michigan State University

David T. Cadden
Quinnipiac University

Alan R. Cannon
Appalachian State University

Barb Flynn
Wake Forest University

David Ho
Oklahoma State University

Edward Hufft
Alcorn State University

Kenneth J. Klassen
Brock University

Ted Klastorin
University of Washington

Matthew Macarty
University of New Hampshire

Renato de Matta
University of Iowa

Behnam Nakhai
Millersville University

Michael Pesch
St. Cloud State University

Britt Shirley
The University of Tampa

Timothy Vaughan
University of Wisconsin–Eau Clair

Rohit Verma
University of Utah

About the Authors

RICHARD D. METTERS

is Associate Professor of Decision and Information Analysis at the Goizueta Business School, Emory University. He has also taught at Vanderbilt University and Southern Methodist University, where he specialized in teaching service sector operations. He received his PhD from the University of North Carolina, his MBA from Duke University, and a BA from Stanford University. Prior to his academic career, he worked for Crocker Bank, Bank of America, and Citicorp.

He has published more than 20 articles in journals such as *Journal of Operations Management*, *Management Science*, *Operations Research*, and *Harvard Business Review*. Rich is on the editorial review boards of *Production and Operations Management*, and *Journal of Service Research*, and is an Associate Editor of *Decision Sciences*.

KATHRYN H. KING-METTERS

is an Adjunct Professor of Marketing at Agnes Scott College and a Management Consultant. She has also taught at the University of North Carolina at Chapel Hill and at Meredith College, where she specialized in teaching marketing, sales, and advertising. She received her MBA from the University of North Carolina at Chapel Hill, an MA from The Ohio State University, and a BS from East Stroudsburg University.

In addition to holding a variety of management positions at IBM, SAS Institute, and Berol Corporation, she ran her own management consulting company for five years specializing in entrepreneurial ventures and start-ups. Since that time she has consulted with Arthur Anderson, Scott, Madden & Associates, and J. D. Power & Associates. Her particular consulting interests are services operations, strategic analysis, strategic and operational planning, and customer service satisfaction.

MADELEINE PULLMAN

is an Associate Professor at the Cornell University School of Hotel Administration. She has also taught at Colorado State University, London Business School, and Southern Methodist University. She has a PhD in business, an MBA, and an MS in Mechanical Engineering from the University of Utah, and a BS in Energy Systems from Evergreen State College.

She has published case studies and articles in the *Journal of Service Research*, *Journal of Operations Management*, *Decision Sciences*, *Production and Operations Management*, *International Journal of Service Industry Management*, and many other journals. Her interests in service operations include teaching a course in the entertainment industry, as well as traditional service operations courses.

STEVE WALTON

is Associate Professor in the Practice of Decision and Information Analysis at Goizueta Business School, Emory University. He has also served on the faculty at Baylor University and North Carolina A&T State University. He received his PhD from the University of North Carolina at Chapel Hill, and his MS and BS from Clemson University.

Steve's teaching has been recognized with six teaching awards, including the university-wide Emory Williams Distinguished Teaching Award and the Marc Adler Prize for Teaching Excellence. His research interests include the application of Six Sigma to service operations, business-to-business electronic commerce and managing supply chains for both operational and environmental improvements. His research has been published in *Journal of Operations Management*, *International Journal of Operations and Production Management*, and several other journals.

Steve's consulting clients include The Home Depot, Delta Air Lines, McKesson Information Solutions, The Arthur M. Blank Family Office, Siemens Medical Systems, Synovus, Crawford & Company, Sigvaris, ZC Sterling, Great American Insurance Company, Atlanta Casualty Company, Kurt Salmon Associates, Crawford Long Hospital, and several technology startup companies.

Introduction: Services in the Economy

LEARNING OBJECTIVES *The material in this chapter prepares students to:*

- Understand how and why services dominate the U.S. economy.

- Define "operations."

- Delineate the differences between goods and services.

- Categorize services according to the "customer contact model" and the "service process matrix" and understand the managerial ramifications of those conceptual models.

Why study service operations?

Several reasons make services, and the *operations* of services in particular, worthy of study:

- Service firms constitute an overwhelmingly large percentage of the economy of every industrialized nation, the size will only increase, and it is by far the most likely economic sector in which business school graduates will be employed.
- Despite the size of the service economy, academic research has largely ignored services. The relative lack of attention given to services provides a competitive edge to those students who pursue its study.
- Many services have characteristics that are strongly different from goods. Consequently, specialized and different managerial techniques are employed in services than are employed in many manufacturing firms, and knowledge and experience gained from studying manufacturing settings does not always transfer to services.

This chapter sets the stage for the study of service operations. Here, we will discuss the what, why, and how of service operations: What services are, why service operations should be studied, and two different views of how to look at service firms in frameworks that can help in organizing thought.

THE IMPORTANCE OF THE SERVICE SECTOR

Economically, the term *services* is often defined not by what it is, but by what it is *not*. Historically, economic reports identify activities as "service producing" that are *not* "goods producing," which includes manufacturing and construction, and are *not* "extraction," such as agriculture, forestry, fishing, and mining. By this definition, "service producing" encompasses a wide variety of industries, including retailing, wholesaling, transportation, financial services, lodging, education, government, entertainment, and many others.

As defined above, services account for roughly 80% of the U.S. economy in both employment and gross domestic product. Unlike the manufacturing sector, services contribute positively to the balance of trade for the United States.[1] But it wasn't always the case. Figure 1.1 shows the radical shift in the U.S. economy over time. Even in recent times, the shift has been dramatic. The parents of students reading this book faced a very different economic structure from today's environment when looking for their first jobs.

A classic description of economic stages by Bell (1973) described the stages of economic growth as "preindustrial," "industrial," and "postindustrial." In 1800, the United States was in the position a great number of countries are in today, the "preindustrial society." The labor force was mostly engaged in the extraction industries, with agriculture the most prominent. At that time, more than 80% of the U.S. workforce was engaged in agriculture.

Government statistics report that the most prominent service occupations at the time were domestic servants and sailors. Because technology was extremely limited, much of the economy depended upon sheer brawn. According to Bell, the social ramifications of this type of economy are important. With a preindustrial economy, family relationships and traditions are important, while education and innovation are not important or even threatening. The quality of life depends largely upon nature, and upward mobility is difficult.

Figure 1.1 depicts 1900 to 1950 as being in the "industrial society," in which an important activity is goods production. To paraphrase Bell in a most unfair manner, it could be said that the quality of life in an industrial society is measured by accumulation of goods; "he who dies with the most toys, wins" representing the philosophy of the age. Industry focus is on maximizing the productivity of labor and machines to turn out more goods at a cheaper price. Extreme division of labor helps in accomplishing this task, and the assembly line epitomizes this way of thinking. Henry Ford's assembly line in the early 1900s purportedly cut the labor time required to assemble a car from 13 hours to $1\frac{1}{2}$ hours.

The social ramifications of an industrial society included the view of an individual laborer as merely a cog in a machine, where showing up for work before the whistle blows is of paramount importance—after all, a 200-person assembly line can't be held up for a late employee. Further, doing what they are told is also an important trait for workers. Frederick Taylor, in his notable experiments, developed a science of movement, in which the one best way to accomplish a task was discovered by management and implemented—exactly—by workers. If commodity goods are produced, a firm must get more output from less input, as that is the only way to increase profitability. Consequently, the pressure is on to squeeze wages and provide workers, who supply muscle rather than brains, with the minimum of accommodations.

---

1. In 2003, U.S. net exports of services exceeded imports of services by about $59 billion. For goods, imports outdistanced exports by $549 billion. Source: *http://www.census.gov/indicator/www/ustrade.html*.

FIGURE 1.1: *Historical U.S. Employment by Economic Sector*

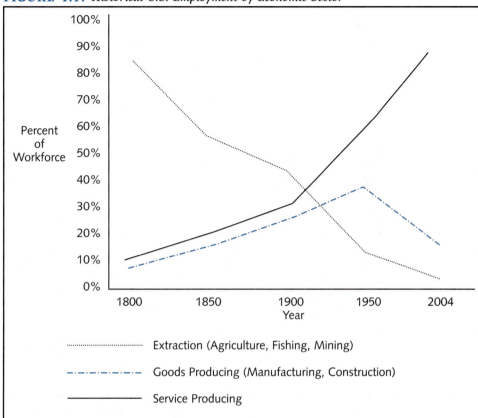

Extraction (Agriculture, Fishing, Mining)

Goods Producing (Manufacturing, Construction)

Service Producing

Sources: U.S. Department of Commerce. 1976. *Historical Statistics of the United States.* (Note: The 21% "unallocated" employment for the year 1800 was distributed evenly between sectors.) Bureau of Labor Statistics 2004. Accessed at *ftp.bls.gov/pub/suppl/empsit.ceseeb1.txt.*

The most egregious excesses of this era gave rise to strong labor unions as a counterweight to dehumanizing jobs. The poor working conditions in Birmingham, England, in the late 1800s also served as the inspiration for Karl Marx and his theories on Communism.

Since 1950, the United States entered the "postindustrial" era. From 1950 to the current time, service-producing industries increased, roughly, from 50% to 80% of the U.S. workforce. Bell stated that in the postindustrial society, services such as health, education, and recreation predominate. Taken a step further, recent arguments claim that a small subset of the service economy called "experiences" will be a dominant economic force (see Chapter 6). Information, rather than muscle, becomes the central figure in this economy, and organizations value workers more for their judgment, creativity, and theoretical reasoning than as mere executors of a plan.

Changes in job titles and characteristics reflect the changing nature of work done. According to government statistics, in 1900 "manual workers" outnumbered "white-collar workers" two to one. Today, the situation is entirely reversed, with twice as many white-collar workers as manual laborers.

The ramifications of this postindustrial society to service operations are twofold. The more obvious factor is that the economy is constructed of a far higher percentage of service-producing activity than in previous times, resulting in far more jobs in the service sector than in any other. Consequently, merely due to its sheer bulk, the service sector merits study.

However, the importance of studying the service sector goes well beyond its size. If Bell is right and the postindustrial service economy requires different managerial skills, different ways of thinking, and a break with the traditions of the industrial society, then new thinking and new methods are required to excel in the service economy. We cannot rely on merely adapting the old paradigms, forged in an industrial age, to manage this new economy.

THE IMPORTANCE OF STUDYING OPERATIONS IN SERVICES

The previous section attempted to answer the question "Why study services?" The question addressed by this section is "Why study the *operations* of services?"

To answer that basic question, we begin by defining *operations*. The classic textbook definition states that operations is the "transformation process" that turns inputs into outputs, that is, the act of combining people, raw materials, technology, etc., into useable services and products.

Although accurate, that definition is less than satisfying as it seems too ethereal. A working definition of who is in the operations function in a firm would be the people who actually make a product or perform a service. The operations function typically employs—by far—more personnel than any other functional area. A large firm may need a marketing department of 50 and a treasury department of five at the same time it may need an operational force of 5,000 to deliver its services. Examples of positions in the operations function of a firm include football players, airline pilots, bank branch managers, NYSE bond traders, and university professors (yes, even a finance or marketing professor is officially in the "operations" functional area of a university), as each position is actually performing a service.

Consequently, one very basic reason to study the operations of service firms is due to their sheer size. If one is to become a top manager of a service firm, knowing how to manage and what to expect from the largest group of employees in that firm is essential.

Another reason to study operations is related to the traditional definition of operations as a "transformation process." At its heart, operations means "getting things done"—the transformation processes that make products and perform services. Regardless of the functional area a person is in, he or she must still engage in processes to produce work. A marketer must organize people and resources across different departments or different firms to deliver an advertising campaign. Finance must execute trades. Accounting may carry out lengthy procedures covering days to close the books at month-end. Because all these tasks involve service processes, the study of service operations includes the study and improvement of all service processes, regardless of their functional area.

Historically, however, another, more abstract reason motivates the study of operations. It relates to the future of the economies of postindustrial nations. Figure 1.1 may depict "what" happened in the United States over the past 200 years, but it does not indicate "why." Answering the "why" question underlies the importance of the operations function. Figure 1.1 shows that more than 80% of the workforce in the United States was required in 1800 just to feed the population, but in 2004 it required only 2% of the workforce to feed not only the U.S. population but part of the rest of the world (the United States is a net exporter of agricultural goods to the rest of the world, with an expected net of $9.5 billion in exports in 2004).[2]

As the collective waistlines of America attest, the reason that fewer farmers are needed is not that we are eating less. Rather, the reason lies in increased productivity, where productivity is defined as outputs/inputs, which is the province of the operations function. The financing and marketing of farm products today is somewhat different from 200 years ago, but the actual day-to-day work done on a farm—the operations—is done far differently now and the productivity of farming has increased by orders of magnitude.

Because of improvements in the way agriculture was performed, wealth was created worldwide that allowed most human beings in industrialized nations to look beyond mere sustenance and accumulate goods. The same operational process improvements then moved the goods-producing sector forward. Just as in the agricultural sector, we are not consuming fewer manufactured goods now than in 1950, we're buying far more. The gross output of U.S. factories has doubled in the past 30 years (Geewax, 2003). Although other factors contributed, a primary reason that the percentage of workers employed in manufacturing in general is smaller today than in 1950 is because manufacturers became too good at their jobs. The labor hours required to produce basic goods is now a small fraction of what it was because of operational improvements, often related to adapting to better technology. This is not just happening in the United States. Although many people believe the United States is losing manufacturing jobs to countries such as China and South Korea, those countries are losing manufacturing jobs as well. China reports a decline in manufacturing employment of 15% between 1995–2002, and South Korea's manufacturing employment declined 12% during that time (Geewax, 2003). Worldwide, manufacturing jobs are being lost to productivity increases.

Baumol, Batey Blackman, and Wolff (1991) described the rise of services in similar, but negative terms: A relative "cost disease" in services arises because, even though more services are not being consumed, the low productivity in services makes it appear as though they are. The dramatic increases in productivity of agriculture and manufacturing mean that the same amount of food and manufactured goods purchased years ago cost far less today in real terms. Services, however, have not seen such productivity growth, so they cost relatively the same. Consequently, as a percentage of expenditures, services may look larger, even though as an economic sector it is staying the same. As a simple example, if $3 bought food, $3 bought goods, and $3 bought services, services would represent 33% of expenditures. If the same amount of food and manufactured goods now cost $1 each, services would represent 60% of expenditures, even though the amount spent on services stayed the same. This argument contains substantial flaws. It neglects the development of new services and the fulfillment of the new "quality of life" standards in the postindustrial era, which are met by services, rather than agriculture or manufacturing. However, it sets a "floor" below which the percentage of services in the economy is highly unlikely to go.

The "cost disease" argument presents both a picture of the future of services as well as a global reason for their study. Productivity improvements in agriculture and manufacturing continue. Consequently, low productivity improvements in services are likely to make the service sector an even larger portion of the economy, even if no net increase in services consumed occurs. On an individual basis, however, the

---

2. *Source: http://www.fas.usda.gov/cmp/outlook/2004/Feb-04/outlook-0204.html.*

productivity challenge is on. Managers of services need to take advantage of opportunities to replicate the productivity success stories of other sectors of the economy.

OPPORTUNITIES IN SERVICE OPERATIONS

From an academic perspective, exploring the field of services versus manufacturing is akin to following Columbus to the "new world" versus staying back in Europe. The vast and untapped opportunities to improve service businesses are just as great as the historic lack of effort in attacking them. For example, Geoffrion (1992) noted that of the manuscripts sent for publication in the prestigious academic journal, *Operations Research*, manufacturing-based manuscripts outnumbered services-based manuscripts by a ratio of six to one.

The attitude about services goes further than simply ignoring them. In fact, some researchers show an active disdain for the service economy. Cohen and Zysman (1987) wrote about the "myth" of the postindustrial economy, and Dertouzos, Lester, and Solow (1989) popularized the idea that only manufacturing matters to a modern economy. The arguments presented by these and other authors depict service businesses as a mere derivative activity of a manufacturing-based economy, which would surely dry up and fade away as manufacturing was withdrawn.

Although both time and the progress of the world economy show these sentiments to be greatly exaggerated, the bulk of academic training, work, and classroom teaching remains in manufacturing. This imbalance represents an enormous opportunity for students who wish to focus on the service sector as its issues create a heavier demand for knowledge about the service sector among potential employers.

CHARACTERISTICS OF SERVICES

Focused study of the problems of service firms is useful because services, in general, have different characteristics than goods. Consequently, analogies and conceptual models formed by a study of how goods-producing industries work may not always translate to service firms. Various characteristics have been listed over the years as to how services differ from goods. Some of the ways in which services are said to differ from goods include the following:

- Services are intangible whereas goods are tangible.
- Sources are simultaneously consumed as they are produced.
- Services often require closer proximity to the customer.
- Services cannot be inventoried.

Each of these characteristics makes management more challenging and requires a different mindset from traditional managerial practices. However, a closer look at these traditionally discussed differences indicate that they are only partially true.

Intangibility of Services

The results from a service may be an emotion from hearing a song or seeing a tennis match, but frequently no *thing* is left behind. However, most services come with "facilitating goods." For example, a playbill can remind one of a good performance, or a photograph of a friend on the roller coaster at the amusement park can serve as a physical reminder of a service. Of course, the results of many service firms are quite tangible: A car that runs again or a sack full of groceries both come from service-producing businesses.

Conversely, physical goods frequently have intangible aspects. For example, the U.S. government officially defines vodka as a "colorless, odorless, tasteless" alcoholic beverage, yet consumers gladly pay four times the price of a lesser brand for a premium brand. Even though distinctions regarding the quality of vodka brands may be debatable, an intangible feeling clearly can be derived from owning a premium car, a premium antique furnishing, or an original painting by a master, which goes well beyond the physical good.

Further, just as services have "facilitating goods," nearly every good has a "facilitating service" that is tangible. At a minimum, goods often must be transported to the customer, and transportation is a service.

Simultaneous Production and Consumption

Many services are "produced" by the seller and "consumed" by the buyer at the same time. Live performances of plays or music are the quintessential examples. Simultaneity of production and consumption makes quality control (Chapters 10 and 11) and matching capacity to demand especially difficult. Some services, however, such as computer system upgrading and janitorial work, are specifically designed to be produced while the customer is *not* there. Also, many manufacturers face similar managerial difficulties with rush orders that must be done immediately and to a customer's specification.

Proximity to the Customer

Many services must be physically close to the customer. For example, placing one giant McDonald's in the middle of Nebraska isn't a good business model. For this reason, large service firms operate hundreds or thousands of units, while manufacturers operate only a few. McDonald's and Dell Computer record roughly the same revenues, yet McDonald's operates a "few" more facilities than the six Dell plants worldwide. (A method for managing large numbers of units is explained in Chapter 17.) Also, even choosing where to locate a service requires totally different criteria than a manufacturing facility, because services generally must be close to the customer (Chapter 16).

Proximity is not always essential in services. For example, Internet-based services employ radically different strategies (Chapter 3) than services that are location-dependent. Many back-office services such as credit approval or insurance claim processing are performed halfway across the globe from the customer (Chapter 8). Also, manufacturers of products like cement and sheetrock must be close to the customer because the cost of transportation is large relative to the cost of the product.

Services Cannot Be Inventoried

The lack of ability to build inventory or use backorders seriously influences managerial choices. Imagine approaching a store clerk for help only to be told, "I'm busy now, I'll get back to you in four to six weeks." Consumers routinely wait that long for goods delivery, but services often must be provided in a very short time or suffer a lost sale. Consequently, many services manage waiting time (Chapter 14), rather than inventory. Of course, some exceptions are notable. Restaurant reservations are a clear example of a service that can be backordered.

For many service industries, such as retailing and wholesaling, managing physical inventory is a highly strategic endeavor. Chapter 13 is dedicated to the special inventory problems of these services. For other service firms, like hotels and airlines, effectively managing their "inventory" of hotel rooms and airline seats is essential, and is the subject of Chapter 12.

On the other hand, some manufacturers must more closely manage customer waiting time than inventory. Manufacturers of custom goods suffer some of the same problems of traditional services. If all finished goods are custom-made, finished goods inventory cannot be kept, and customers may make their purchasing decision based on waiting time.

The foregoing discussion is not meant to imply that goods-producing and service-producing industries do not differ. Clear differences distinguish the management problems of the Bolshoi Ballet from those of Bethlehem Steel. However, the differences between goods and services fall on a continuum. Some service firms and manufacturers may share many similarities at the same time that firms lumped together under the "services" umbrella exhibit extreme differences. A customer of a grocery store mainly buys goods, though a grocer is a service industry, whereas the customer of a nail salon is purchasing nearly 100% service. Naturally, such firms face different managerial challenges.

CLASSIFICATION FRAMEWORKS

A number of proposed service firm classification frameworks attempt to show where similarities among service firms may yield insights. Many service business managers seem to believe their problems are unique to their particular business, or at most their particular industry, and that they share little in common with other service industries. If this view is correct, then only individuals with vast experience within the firm or industry should be hired for management positions, and firms could at best only look at their direct competitors for help on ideas on how to improve.

The basis for academic study of the field of service operations lies in the opposite view: Commonalities can be found among the problems and challenges many businesses face. This view contends that methods, ideas, and people can span industries, and employees and ideas from other industries can bring a fresh, vital approach to a business.

To gain a perspective about which industries share certain characteristics, it is useful to classify service firms. Classification schemes provide a mental lens for viewing the commonalities between businesses that may also demonstrate vast differences.

A well-known classification scheme for service operations is called the Customer Contact Model[3] and is depicted in Figure 1.2. Here, services are classified according to the amount of customer contact. High contact services, or "pure services," include hospitals and restaurants, and a high percentage of their activity must take place in the presence of the customer. Low contact services—called "quasi-manufacturing" firms—include distribution centers, wholesalers, and back-office facilities such as the check-processing centers of retail banks, which require virtually no face-to-face contact with customers. Services with elements of both are termed "mixed services," and include the branch offices of banks and insurance firms.

The customer as the dominant force to be considered in designing service systems represents the central guiding principle in this view. This simple, yet powerful idea can be formulated as:

Potential Efficiency $= f\,(1 - \text{Customer Contact Time} / \text{Service Creation Time})$

3. The Customer Contact Model was proposed by Chase (1978). The discussion of this view is summarized from Chase (1978, 1981) and Chase and Tansik (1983).

FIGURE 1.2: *Customer Contact Model of Services*

High Contact			Low Contact
Pure Services	Mixed Services	Quasi-Manufacturing	Manufacturing
Medical Restaurants Transportation	Branch offices	Home offices Distribution centers	

Source: Chase (1978).

This equation indicates that the "potential" efficiency of a service is limited by the amount of time the customer is involved in the system. Note, however, that it is not necessarily desirable to maximize efficiency.

Several essential insights are associated with this line of thinking. Most obviously, firms with similar levels of customer contact may encounter similar problems, and could benefit from sharing "best practices" across industry boundaries. Further, this idea states that the high contact and low contact areas within a company should be managed differently. For example, contact-enhancing strategies, such as specifically hiring people-oriented workers and partitioning back-office, noncontact activities away from the customer's view, should be employed in the high contact areas. On the other hand, those pesky customers sometimes interfere with the efficiency of low contact facilities. In such cases, contact-reduction strategies, such as appointment systems or drop-off points such as Automated Teller Machines are appropriate. It is in the low contact facilities where traditional manufacturing techniques could be effectively borrowed to increase efficiency. Chapter 7 elaborates further on this view.

Another way to view services is provided by the Service Process Matrix proposed by Schmenner (1986) and shown in Figure 1.3. Schmenner differentiates service processes according to two major differentiating factors: the degree of interaction and customization and the degree of labor intensity.

FIGURE 1.3: *The Service Process Matrix*

	Degree of Interaction and Customization	
	Low	High
Low Degree of Labor Intensity **High**	**Service Factory** • Airlines • Trucking • Hotels	**Service Shop** • Hospitals • Auto repair • Other repair services
	Mass Service • Retailing • Wholesaling • Schools • Retail aspects of commercial banking	**Professional Service** • Doctors • Lawyers • Accountants • Architects

Source: Reprinted from "How Can Service Businesses Survive and Prosper?" by Roger Schmenner, *MIT Sloan Management Review*, v.27(3), p. 25, by permission of publisher. Copyright © 1986 by Massachusetts Institute of Technology. All rights reserved.

FIGURE 1.4: *The Service Process Matrix: Challenges for Service Managers*

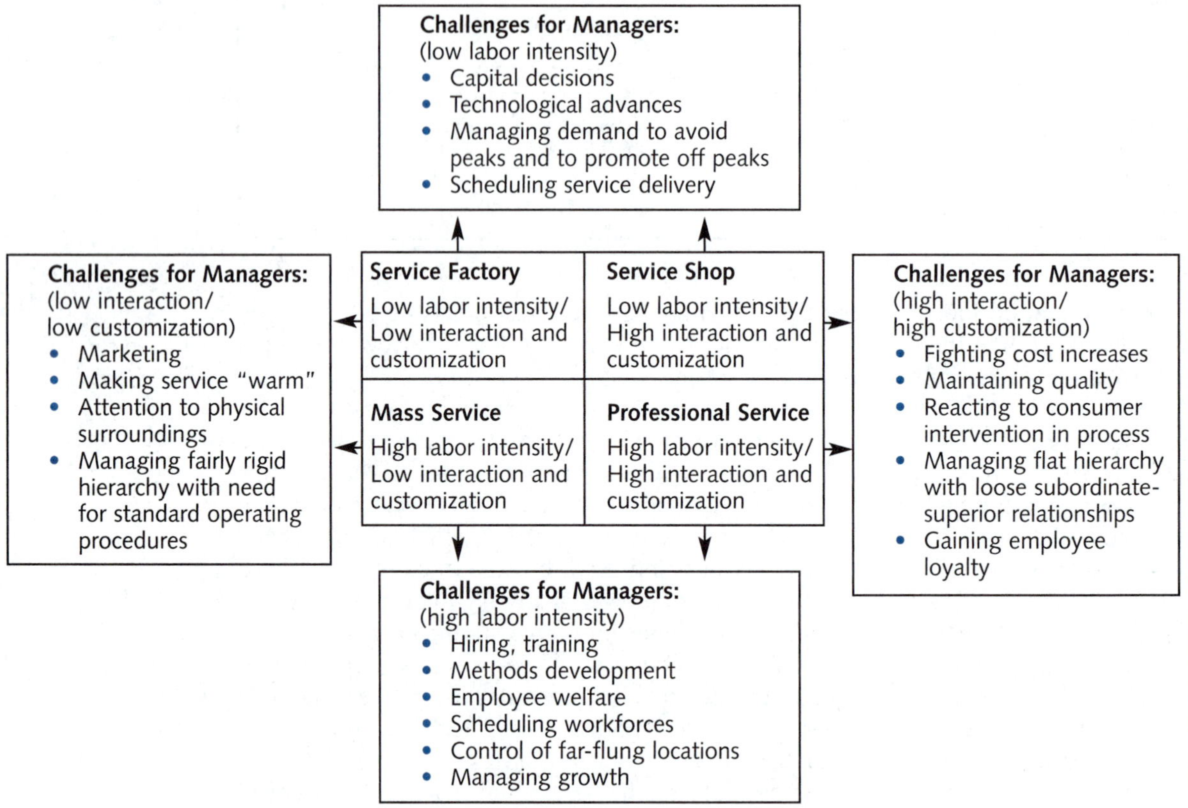

Challenges for Managers:
(low labor intensity)
- Capital decisions
- Technological advances
- Managing demand to avoid peaks and to promote off peaks
- Scheduling service delivery

Challenges for Managers:
(low interaction/ low customization)
- Marketing
- Making service "warm"
- Attention to physical surroundings
- Managing fairly rigid hierarchy with need for standard operating procedures

Service Factory
Low labor intensity/ Low interaction and customization

Service Shop
Low labor intensity/ High interaction and customization

Mass Service
High labor intensity/ Low interaction and customization

Professional Service
High labor intensity/ High interaction and customization

Challenges for Managers:
(high interaction/ high customization)
- Fighting cost increases
- Maintaining quality
- Reacting to consumer intervention in process
- Managing flat hierarchy with loose subordinate-superior relationships
- Gaining employee loyalty

Challenges for Managers:
(high labor intensity)
- Hiring, training
- Methods development
- Employee welfare
- Scheduling workforces
- Control of far-flung locations
- Managing growth

Source: Reprinted from "How Can Service Businesses Survive and Prosper?" by Roger Schmenner, *MIT Sloan Management Review*, v.27(3), p. 27, by permission of publisher. Copyright © 1986 by Massachusetts Institute of Technology. All rights reserved.

The *Service Factory*, has both low interaction and customization and low labor intensity. A quintessential example is a traditional commercial airline. Customization is quite low. If flights are scheduled for 10 A.M. and 6 P.M., they won't accommodate a customer who wants to go "around two-ish." Capital cost are enormous, with typical commercial jets costing as much as $50 to $100 million each.

Service Shops, such as hospitals, also experience high capital costs. Fortunately, hospitals can customize their services a bit more than the airlines do. *Professional Services*, such as lawyers, consultants, and accountants, combine highly customized service with a high labor intensity. Finally, *Mass Services*, like retailers and wholesalers, show higher ratios of labor to capital costs than do Service Factory firms, but do not offer highly customized services.

In theory, then, each quadrant faces managerial challenges unique to the processes within that quadrant (Figure 1.4). Both the Service Factory and Service Shop processes are capital intensive, so, of course, capital purchases and technology choices are highly important. The amount of capital goods cannot easily change and usually must be highly utilized to be profitable; therefore, the challenge to managers is to smooth out demand peaks that cannot be served.

Mass Service and Professional Service firms are more labor intensive. In these areas, hiring and training of labor is of greater importance. The list of challenges is likewise different for processes with varying degrees of interaction and customization. Service Factory and Mass Service firms, with low interaction and customization, are challenged to make their services feel "warm" to the customer. Service Shop and Professional Service firms' challenges are associated with high interaction and customization issues, such as quality control.

The lists of managerial challenges in Figure 1.4 would not surprise veterans of the industries listed. In many ways, the value of this view is similar to the Customer Contact Model discussed earlier: When service businesses are categorized according to problem similarities, techniques and solutions adapted from entirely different industries within the same quadrant may be effective in addressing these problems. Further, Schmenner poses another use for the service process matrix: Companies often change their positioning over time. When their positioning within the matrix changes, they face different challenges and should adopt different managerial responses. For example, a traditional hospital should be managed differently from a clinic that focuses solely on eye laser procedures, even though both are in medicine, and a traditional law firm should be managed differently from a legal services chain like Jacoby & Meyers that specializes in personal injury cases. Although simple enough in principle, such a transformation of internal processes and procedures is difficult to accomplish. The management team of firms that are changing position within the matrix typically have years of experience in the old framework, so they have deeply imbedded views on how to manage an operation in their field.

Summary

Over the years, the service sector has assumed a preeminent position in the U.S. economy. Both in overall employment and in trade with other countries, it far outdistances other sectors of the economy. This change did not take place in a vacuum. It is theorized that concurrently with the rise of the service economy came the "post-industrial society." In this new society different values and desires from consumers have accompanied the rise of the service sector and have changed the emphasis of management.

Physically, much of this economic change took place through the operations function. The enhanced productivity of agriculture means that only 2% of our nation's workforce is required for this sector that previously employed more than 80%. Likewise in manufacturing, the ever-increasing amount and variety of goods is produced by fewer and fewer laborers. The challenge of effectively using the operations function of the service sector, the subject of this text, is therefore laid before us.

Review Questions

1. In the economic sectors of extraction, goods-producing, and service-producing industries, how has the U.S. economy shifted since the nation began?
2. True or false: The decrease in farmers from more than 80% of the population to just 2% results from rising U.S. imports of farm goods.
3. Define *services* and *operations*.
4. In what ways is the postindustrial economy different from the industrial economy?
5. The "Customer Contact Model" and the "Service Process Matrix" may be true, but how can they be used in managerial decision making?

Selected Bibliography

Baumol, W., Batey Blackman, S., and E. Wolff. 1991. *Productivity and American Leadership*. MIT Press, Cambridge, MA.

Bell, D. 1973. *The Coming of Post-Industrial Society: A Venture in Social Forecasting*. Basic Books, Inc., New York.

Chase, R. 1978. Where Does the Customer Fit in a Service Operation? *Harvard Business Review*, 56, 137–142.

Chase, R. 1981. The Customer Contact Approach to Services: Theoretical Bases and Practical Extensions. *Operations Research*, 29(4), 698–705.

Chase, R., and D. Tansik. 1983. The Customer Contact Model for Organizational Design. *Management Science*, 29(9), 1037–1049.

Cohen, S., and J. Zysman. 1987. Why Manufacturing Matters: The Myth of the Post-Industrial Economy. *California Management Review*, 29(3), 9–26.

Dertouzos, M., Lester, J., and R. Solow. 1989. *Made in America: Regaining the Productive Edge*, MIT Press, Cambridge, MA.

Geewax, M. 2003. Factories Prosper as Jobs Vanish, *Atlanta Journal-Constitution*, December 21, 2003, p. Q1.

Schmenner, R. 1986. How Can Service Business Survive and Prosper? *Sloan Management Review*, 27 (3), 21–32.

Formulating Strategy

The first decisions of a service firm take place long before staff is hired, facilities built, or even a corporate logo designed. This section provides several frameworks for considering a service organization's basic strategic decisions:

- Who will be our customers?
- What can we offer potential customers that competitors do not?
- On which customer desires will we compete?
- How will the business grow?

The answers to these basic questions both limit and guide the decisions concerning facilities, people, and procedures that an operating system will eventually possess. Basic strategy becomes the blueprint for making the managerial trade-offs discussed later in this text.

Several conceptual models are presented in Chapter 2 to aid the strategy formulation process. Conceptual models of firm growth are also discussed, including the service life cycle, industry roll-ups, and franchising.

Due to the perceived necessity of competing for business on the Internet, Chapter 3 is devoted to business-to-consumer Internet strategies for service firms.

Increasing environmental regulation, environmental case law, the rise of environmental standards bodies such as ISO 14000, combined with a large population segment that is concerned with corporate response to environmental issues force firms to consider environmental planning in their basic strategic outlook. Specialized strategies concerning environmental issues are contained in Chapter 4.

Strategic Positioning and Service Strategy

LEARNING OBJECTIVES *The material in this chapter prepares students to:*

- Link the desires of targeted customers to operational tactics.

- Evaluate the strategic position of a service company.

- Identify the different operational requirements over the life cycle of a service.

- Choose an appropriate growth strategy.

- Make appropriate operational tradeoffs when pursuing a strategy.

Chapter 1 ended with a figure (Figure 1.4) that showed the wide array of challenges and tactical decision areas that have to be addressed to successfully manage a service organization. This figure begs two critical questions:

1. How does a service business decide which quadrant of the matrix to position itself in?
2. How does a service business decide how to balance the tradeoffs between the various "challenges for managers?"

These two questions in general form the basis for this section on "Formulating Strategy," and in detail form the basis for this chapter. For now, the short answer to the questions is, "A company has to consider both external issues (e.g., customer expectations, competitors, the government) and internal issues (e.g., capacity, location, inventory, quality) in order to intelligently decide how to position itself and how to set service strategies to balance the tradeoffs." But which is more important, external forces or internal competencies? And which comes first, "strategic positioning" or "service strategy?" Possibly more importantly, how does an executive make sure that strategic positioning, service strategy, and tactical execution are all consistent and working in the same direction? This chapter will explore these and other questions related to strategic positioning and service strategy.

As a starting point, Table 2.1 presents one way to think about how these pieces fit together. Understanding internal capabilities allows a company to identify its own "strengths and weaknesses," while examining external entities is an excellent way to identify potential "opportunities and threats." Taken together, a company can

TABLE 2.1: *Strategic Positioning and Service Strategy*

	External	Internal
Strategy	Strategic Positioning	Service Strategy
Execution	Frontroom Operations	Backroom Operations

evaluate how what it does relates to what competitors do and what the market values; i.e., SWOT (SWOT = Strengths, Weaknesses, Opportunities, and Threats) analysis. But, as we'll see in this chapter, companies will end up in very different strategic places depending on whether they start with SW or with OT.

A STRATEGIC HIERARCHY AND STRATEGIC CONSISTENCY

Strategic positioning, service strategy, and tactical execution form a hierarchy of strategic planning. That is, strategic positioning sets out a corporate-level set of objectives, goals, missions, etc.; service strategy takes these corporate-level strategies and refines them into a set of specific operational objectives, goals and missions; and tactical execution does just that, executes the service strategy. Specifically, strategic positioning determines how a company will compete, what markets it will serve, and how it will distinguish its service from its competitors. Service strategy translates these strategic positioning decisions into a clear operational plan. This operational plan would address at a high level issues like capacity, facility size and location, growth strategies, employee skill level, and how inventory would be used (if it could be used at all). Finally, tactical execution would take care of specific decisions like supplier selection and management, hiring, firing, training of staff, franchisee selection, determining amounts and location of inventory, and determining how many facilities there will be, where they will be, and how big each one will be. Figure 2.1 shows this hierarchy.

FIGURE 2.1: *The Strategic Planning Process for Services*

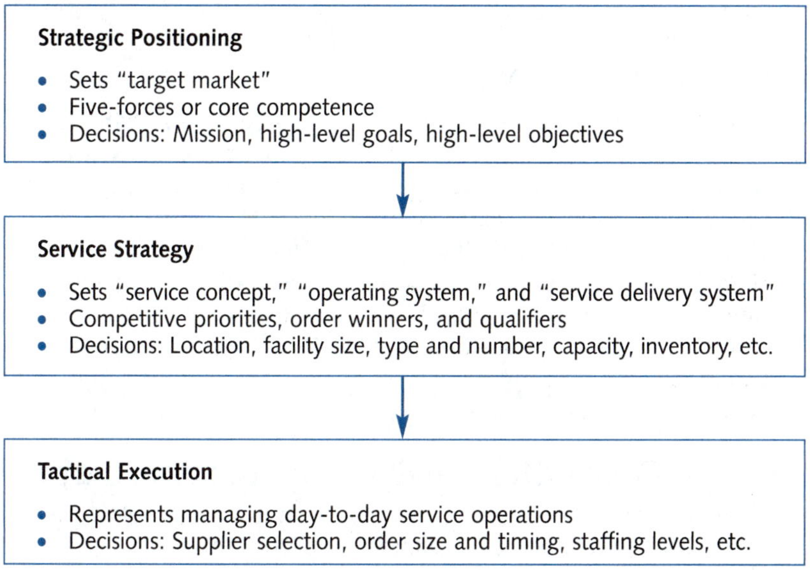

Strategic Positioning
- Sets "target market"
- Five-forces or core competence
- Decisions: Mission, high-level goals, high-level objectives

Service Strategy
- Sets "service concept," "operating system," and "service delivery system"
- Competitive priorities, order winners, and qualifiers
- Decisions: Location, facility size, type and number, capacity, inventory, etc.

Tactical Execution
- Represents managing day-to-day service operations
- Decisions: Supplier selection, order size and timing, staffing levels, etc.

Heskett, Sasser, and Schlesinger (1997) describe this hierarchy as "target market," "service concept," "operating strategy," and "service delivery system." Target market describes whom the firm will serve. For services this poses a real challenge because not all customers are equal. A customer that is not part of the target market distracts resources away from the group of customers the service is intended for. The service concept, stated from the customer's point of view, describes the reason that the customer would choose one service over a competitor's. The operating strategy, stated from the point of view of the company, describes how the company should be structured in order to meet the service concept. Finally, the service delivery system is the specific set of operational decisions that have to be made in order to provide the service.

Though it sounds obvious that all of the decisions made in this hierarchy should be consistent and support one another, in practice it is more difficult to accomplish. One company (for confidentiality reasons we must change the context of the process to "new loan type" to disguise it) decided to add a new loan product to serve the high-end mortgage market for extremely well-qualified buyers. Because this segment is quite small, the company chose to use relatively skilled workers in relatively small numbers. They put in place processes, procedures, and technology, then told the sales force that they would be compensated based on the total number of loan requests they generated. What happened? The strategic position was to target a small, specialized market. The service strategy entailed meeting the high customer contact needs of the market by using high-skilled labor and low capacity. The execution (i.e., what happened because of the sales compensation system) was to flood the process with potential borrowers that had no business being considered. This caused the process to choke on filtering out inappropriate loan risks, which in turn caused the process to be unable to meet the needs of the real target market. Failure to ensure strategic consistency caused the entire product line to appear to be unprofitable.

The best way to avoid these sorts of problems is to have a clear understanding of each of the three components of the strategic hierarchy, and a clear understanding of how they relate to each other. Service Operations Management In Practice: Two Different Strategies, Two Different Operating Systems compares how Delta Air Lines and Southwest Airlines approached strategic consistency and ended up in radically different places.

STRATEGIC POSITIONING

There are two dominant ways of thinking about strategic positioning, and they are nearly exact opposites. The first view of strategic positioning derives from Michael Porter's work (1979) on corporate strategy, "generic strategies," and industry analysis. This point of view starts with external conditions (OT in the SWOT vernacular) in order to set internal operations (SW). The second view, derived from C.K. Prahalad and Gary Hamel's work (1990) on core competencies of the corporation, begins with internal competencies (SW) and builds out to address external conditions (OT). Regardless of the approach taken, the objective of strategic positioning is to define the "target market" the company will serve, as well as to define the organization's strategy, including its mission and objectives.

Industry and Competitor Analysis Approach to Strategy

Porter's influential work in the area of strategy focuses on two related issues: what generic strategies are available for a company to choose from, and how external

SERVICE OPERATIONS MANAGEMENT PRACTICES

Two Different Strategies, Two Different Operating Systems

The impact of strategy on a company's operating system and financial performance simply can't be overstated. The following table compares Delta Air Lines to Southwest Airlines. Their strategic positions are very different, as are their operating systems (number of employees, number and types of planes, flight length, etc.). The impact of these differences is clearly seen when you consider that Delta lost almost twice as much money as Southwest earned in 2003.

Criterion	Delta Air Lines	Southwest Airlines
Strategy	Full-service airline serving as many routes as feasible	Limited service carrier serving smaller domestic markets
Generic strategy	Differentiation based on route structure and frequency of departures	Focus on short hop domestic travelers, cost leader
Core competence	"Fortress hub" in Atlanta with spoke route structure	Plane turn time at gate
Types of planes	737, 757, 767, 777, MD-11, MD-88, MD-90, ATR-72, CRJ-100/200, CRJ-700	737s only
Number of planes	838	388
Cities served	491	58
Flights per day	3,910 (including ASA and Comair)	2,800
Flights per plane per day	4.7	7.2
Average flight length (miles)	852 (excluding ASA and Comair)	558
2003 fuel use (gal)	2.4 billion	1.1 billion
Employees	60,000+	34,000
2003 revenue	$13.3 billion	$5.9 billion
2003 net income (loss)	($773 million)	$422 million
How they spell "airline"	"air line," with a space	"airline," with no space

forces like suppliers, customers, and competitors influence the choice of generic strategies. In this view, the three generic strategies a company might pick are *overall cost leadership*, *differentiation*, and *focus*. *Overall cost leadership* is self-explanatory, but *differentiation* and *focus* require a bit more explanation. *Differentiation* entails trying to serve the needs of a broad group of constituencies in the industry while having everyone in the industry perceive the specific bundle of product and service a company offers as unique, different from everyone else's. This can be accomplished through various mechanisms like having a unique brand image, distribution network, or service delivery system. What makes *differentiation* different from *focus* is that *focus* is not aimed at the needs of everyone in the industry, only the specific needs of a small, focused subset of the industry (hence the name). *Focus* as a generic strategy describes who the customers are, but the company can still choose to compete on *cost leadership* or *differentiation* within this market segment. Within an industry like hotels, Motel 6 and other discount properties compete on *cost leadership*. Frequent traveler programs, like Marriott's Rewards program create *differentiation*, and upscale hotels like The Ritz-Carlton Hotel Company focus on a particular market niche.

What makes Porter's point of view so powerful, though, is the technique for industry and competitor analysis he developed. Porter identifies "five forces" that have to be considered before a company can decide on its strategy. These forces are potential entrants, suppliers, buyers, substitute products, and current competitors. By looking outside the company to these external forces, a company can determine how to position itself in the industry. Table 2.2 shows how this industry and competitor analysis framework would ensure strategic consistency, starting with the five forces analysis and ending with internal operations management. In other words, all operational decisions are completely subordinate to the external strategic analysis conducted as part of the five forces analysis.

Core Competence Approach to Strategy

Prahalad and Hamel attack the question of strategy in nearly a completely opposite way from Porter. This "resource based view of the firm" looks at what resources and competencies the company possesses, then looks outward to find markets and opportunities to exploit. A core competency must meet three tests. It must:

1. Provide access to a wide array of potential markets,
2. Contribute to the customers' perceptions of the benefits of the end product or service, and
3. Be difficult for other competitors to imitate.

One of the classic examples of a core competency is Honda Motors and its competency with engines. Honda leverages its expertise to serve markets from cars to lawnmowers. However, it is a little harder to apply these three tests to services. For example, Southwest Airlines is known to have a competency in how it manages the

TABLE 2.2: *Industry/Competitor Analysis Approach to Strategic Consistency*

		External		Internal
Strategy	Step 1	Five Forces analysis	Step 2	Design the operating system
Execution	Step 3a	Manage interaction with external entities like customers and suppliers	Step 3b	Manage internal operations to meet objectives of operating system design

time an airplane is on the ground between flight segments. It clearly contributes to the customers' perception of value because it directly contributes to Southwest being able to price their tickets so cheaply (because the planes spend so little time on the ground, Southwest gets more flights per day out of each plane, which means fewer planes to serve the same number of passengers). This competency has proven to be quite difficult to imitate, but it is not so clear that it provides access to a wide array of potential markets. It does mean that Southwest could fly more routes if it were to choose to, but that is not the same as Honda making great minivans, racecars, lawnmowers, and tillers.

When doing strategic analysis and planning using the resource based view, the requirement of strategic consistency still stands. But the way that it is achieved is quite different from the way it is achieved under Porter's approach. Table 2.3 shows how the core competence approach ensures strategic consistency by starting with internal strengths and weaknesses, then determining external threats and opportunities.

SERVICE STRATEGY

Once the strategic position is determined, by whichever means, the next step is to determine the service strategy. Generally, service strategy involves setting the service concept, the operating strategy, and the service delivery system the company will pursue (what Heskett, et al. call the "strategic service vision"). The service strategy is critical because it links the company's strategic position with tactical execution. A significant portion of determining the service strategy is determining which "competitive priorities" the company will emphasize as order winners or as order qualifiers.

Competitive Priorities, Order Winners, and Order Qualifiers

One way to think about what matters to a target market and what a company will do to meet those market desires is to ask, "What characteristics must my service have just to be able to compete, and if I manage that, what characteristics should I emphasize to convince the customer to buy my service instead of my competitors'?" The set of operationally oriented dimensions that companies can compete on are called *competitive priorities*. It is generally acknowledged that there are five (some with subcategories): cost, quality (conformance or high-performance design), time (delivery speed, development speed, on-time delivery), service, and flexibility (volume flexibility, customization). We would argue that a sixth *competitive priority* is the natural environment (we will make this case in detail in Chapter 4). As examples, UPS and FedEx emphasize delivery speed and delivery reliability as important competitive priorities, while Southwest Airlines emphasizes cost.

TABLE 2.3: *Core Competence Approach to Strategic Consistency*

		External		Internal
Strategy	Step 3	Determine markets to be served by the core competence	Step 2	Determine core competence of the corporation
Execution	Step 4a	Manage interaction with external entities like suppliers	Step 1	Scan operating system for potential competencies
			4b	Manage internal operations to meet objectives of operating system design

Companies have to decide which competitive priorities to emphasize. The first step is to be sure to emphasize the competitive priorities that are order qualifiers. Order qualifiers are those competitive priorities that everyone in the industry must have just to be able to compete. In the fast food business, speed is a qualifier since every fast food joint gets the customer's food to them in a matter of a minute or two. For package delivery, quality is a qualifier since no one wants his or her package to be crushed. In general, being better at order qualifiers does not help a business. Using package delivery as an example, delivering a "more not crushed package" won't get a company more business.

Order winners, on the other hand, are those competitive priorities that an individual company emphasizes to cause a customer to choose it over its competitors. By letting customers configure their computers to match their own needs, Dell emphasizes customization as an order winner; people choose Dell because they can customize. People choose Southwest Airlines because it is cheap; the company emphasizes cost as an order winner.

Service Concept and Operating Strategy

The service concept can be broadly described as the set of competitive priorities that the target market values. The service concept focuses on the results that must be produced for the customer, ranging from fast and reliable delivery for UPS, to inexpensive and no-frills (i.e., not high-performance design) flights for Southwest, and on the elements of the service that will be offered. The service concept also describes how the target market, the employees of the service company, and the market as a whole would perceive the service elements.

The operating strategy, by comparison, describes the competitive priorities that the internal operations will emphasize (both order winners and qualifiers). The operating strategy details how the different business functions (e.g., marketing, strategy, finance, operations, etc.) will support the service concept. The operating strategy also defines the measures and systems that will be used to control the cost and quality of the service, and how the service is intended to stack up against competitors on these dimensions.

Coming back to the earlier point about strategic consistency, emphasizing a competitive priority in the operating strategy that is not valued by the customers as part of the service concept leads to what Hill (2000) describes as "mismatch." Car rental companies provide a good example of a mismatch between the service concept (i.e., customer desires) and the operating strategy (i.e., the company's operations). Most car rental customers want the rental transaction to be fast so they can get on with their travel plans; delivery speed is a critical competitive priority. Many car rental companies ask their counter agents to up-sell the type of car, offer insurance, and sell a pre-paid tank of gas; the company focuses on service as a competitive priority. The mismatch arises because the things the counter agent does to provide more service explicitly causes the company to perform poorly on the thing that the customer desires (speed). Once the service concept and the operating strategy are set and are consistent, the company can design the service delivery system.

Service Delivery System

Designing the service delivery system sets in place the physical and procedural assets that are needed to execute the service concept. Components of the service delivery system that must be considered are job responsibilities, technology requirements, equipment requirements, facility layout, management policies and procedures, service process designs, operating capacity, and quality management systems. The service delivery system should clearly position the service in a way that is different from competitors and hopefully in a position that is difficult for competitors to imitate. Finalizing the service delivery system completes the service strategy design, but that leaves tactical execution to get right.

TACTICAL EXECUTION

Tactical execution entails managing the service's day-to-day activities to meet the requirements of the target market segment. We will not explore this in too much depth now because it represents the bulk of the remainder of this book. Tactical execution includes tasks like managing staffing levels to meet capacity strategies, managing quality systems to continually improve the efficiency and effectiveness of the service delivery system, selecting the specific site for a new location, and determining what items to stock in inventory, and at what levels. The impact of tactical execution should not be taken for granted. First, it is much harder to execute well than most students think. Second, as a company executes its strategic service vision its competencies may change, and its markets will definitely change. So one critical component of execution is to develop appropriate strategic feedback loops that make sure that a company is not very efficient at delivering a service no one wants. As an example, Motorola launched a satellite phone system called Iridium. The handsets were of superior quality, the company had a market niche they intended to serve but no one wanted the service.

STRATEGICALLY PLANNING FOR SERVICE GROWTH

One strategic issue is so different from its counterpart in manufacturing it deserves special attention, and that is growth strategies. Manufacturing companies can grow by adding machines one at a time, by expanding an existing plant, by building a new plant, or by making an acquisition to add capacity. But because services entail significantly more customer contact, the location of the new service capacity matters in a way that it simply doesn't for manufacturing. Specifically, for service companies that operate in a multi-site environment, growth strategies have to reflect this difference in customer contact.

The Multi-Site Service Lifecycle

Like the more well known "product life cycle" discussed in many marketing courses, Sasser, Olsen, and Wycoff (1978) suggested that the service concepts of multi-site service firms follow a lifecycle. Figure 2.2 shows the cycle of growth for a successful firm (in fact, only a small percentage of firms make it out of each stage). Revenues start low in the "entrepreneurial" stage as the service concept and delivery system seek to define themselves. In "multi-site rationalization" firms move away from the owner's personality quirks and the specific limitations of their first location toward a "cookie-cutter" approach that can be replicated. Successful firms then move on to "growth," where the service concept is replicated over many units. The "maturity" phase maintains and extends the brand, and is the most profitable phase. Finally, because of competitive copying, changes in consumer tastes, or some other reason, a firm either enters decline or must rethink its service concept to progress to regeneration.

These stages matter because what would make an entrepreneurial firm successful would not help a firm in maturity. In other words, a firm's strategy will naturally

FIGURE 2.2: *The Multi-Site Service Firm Lifecycle*

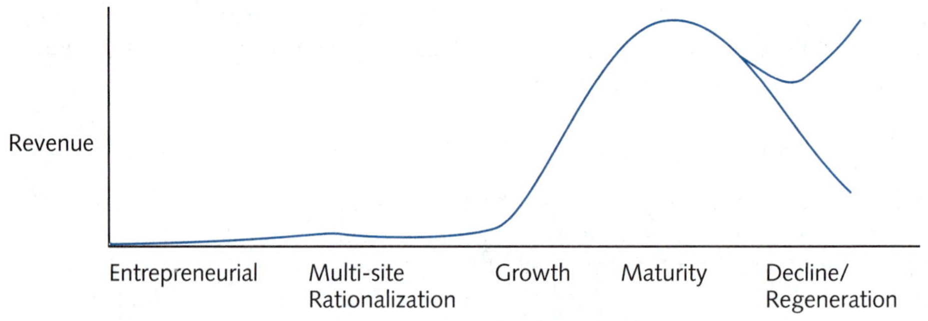

Revenue

| Entrepreneurial | Multi-site Rationalization | Growth | Maturity | Decline/ Regeneration |

Source: Adapted from Sasser, Olsen, and Wycoff (1978).

change over time, which means that its operational structures, marketing plans, and personnel may need to change as well.

In the entrepreneurial stage, the skills that matter are local marketing and public relations, and a charismatic founder who can personally motivate the few personnel at an initial site. In this phase, most personnel are probably underpaid relative to competitors in the mature phase, and they are often in serious jeopardy of seeing very few paychecks because most businesses in this phase fail. Yet, these people must find a way to innovate and develop the service strategy (i.e., the service delivery system and operating strategy around the service concept), or even change the service concept on the fly when trying to gain market acceptance.

In multi-site rationalization, the firm must select a dominant paradigm for marketing, operations, and human resources. It then must standardize its systems around this paradigm. The entrepreneur's motivation to go the extra mile must be replaced with procedures replicable by another employee far away who is just reading a manual. This stage requires developing training programs and accounting systems, and writing detailed procedures. Such development may mean taking much of the uniqueness and individual personality that characterized the entrepreneurial stage out of the various tasks.

The operations and design should already be set when the service enters the growth stage. Selling the service concept to wider consumer and managerial audiences becomes a critical skill. Wider-scale advertising becomes both feasible and more important than local public relations, and investors or franchisees must be found to fund the growth (a topic we will return to shortly).

During maturity, the managerial challenges involve maintaining market position and awareness and somehow keeping a well-known concept "fresh." Operationally, maintaining standards and operational control over less-than-inspired, geographically dispersed employees becomes paramount. The lower-level employees are no longer at the hub of an exciting new idea, but instead work at a safe job in perhaps a dull, established firm. Keeping employees motivated and vigilant is difficult.

Finally, when the service concept becomes stale, revising the service concept and operationally implementing such revisions over a large network that is comfortable with the old service concept again requires the personal charisma reminiscent of an entrepreneur. Understanding this lifecycle provides significant insight into how a service company might manage in the growth stage. Two dominant strategies a service firm might use are *industry rollups* and *franchising*.

Industry Roll-Ups

One strategy for growth that is peculiar to services is called an industry "roll-up." The technique is relatively recent, with quite a few roll-ups taking place in the late 1990s. The idea behind a roll-up is for a company to use its publicly traded stock to buy up dozens of small firms in a fragmented industry. Typically, a small, privately owned "mom and pop" firm trades its ownership of a single unit for shares of stock in a firm encompassing many units in the same industry. Although a few manufacturing-based roll-ups occurred, most roll-ups combine single-unit service firms. The precise number of roll-ups is unavailable because the practice does not have to be officially registered, but 86 are listed as still being publicly traded as of September 2000 (Ho, 2000).

Some people consider roll-ups to be financial tricks driven by Wall Street. A recent article in the *Los Angeles Business Journal* quotes a money manager who says, "I am very skeptical of these roll-up stories. A company needs to be more than a one-trick pony, and that is what a roll-up is. I like to see a company with a strategic vision or some unique creativity embedded in their culture." This may be a bit one-sided; like nearly every business concept, roll-ups are neither intrinsically good nor bad. It depends on how the roll-up fits into the strategic positioning of the firm. Table 2.4 presents a list of characteristics that make an industry a good target for roll-ups.

Operationally, roll-ups succeed because once-independent competitive units can share facilities, supplies, marketing expenses, and operational expertise. Successful roll-ups allow small operators to retain their local connections and personal touch while achieving economies of scale. A prominent example is Service Corporation International (SCI), which operates 4,500 funeral homes, cemeteries, and crematoriums. Customers usually don't see the SCI name, because the funeral homes retain their individual names. In this particular business, the back-office embalming operations of a single unit are not highly efficient due to queuing effects (discussed in Chapter 11). However, groups of funeral homes that use the same back-office facilities can be highly efficient.

TABLE 2.4: *Characteristics of Industries to Target for Roll-ups*

Characteristics	Comments
Favorable market conditions, not just fragmented	An industry should be growing enough in its own right to warrant consolidation. Stitching together a bunch of stagnant companies may show growth in the short term, but will be impossible to manage for growth when the roll-up stops.
Enough competitors that roll-up partners can be selectively chosen	In order to succeed, companies that are rolled up must be sufficiently compatible that managerial systems and culture can coexist, or be brought together. Buying a company just to buy a company is a recipe for failure.
Conviction that a real business can be built	In other words, roll-ups must add business value, not simply allow for consolidation. How will the new business be run? How will it compete? What is its strategic position? Service strategy?

Characteristics are adapted from *Roll-ups: Are they right for you? http://www.netpreneur.org/events/doughnets/990422/article.html,* accessed 4/29/04.

Prominent roll-ups have occurred in waste management (Waste Management, Inc.), general practice physicians (Physicians Resource Group), tow-truck operators (Miller Industries), video rental (Blockbuster, prior to being acquired by Viacom), and direct marketing firms (TeleSpectrum Worldwide). Recently roll-ups have begun in electronic commercial security systems and transportation/logistics services. In the case of commercial security systems, a few of the roll-up transactions have been fairly big (over $1 billion), but many are targeted at acquiring companies with sales between $5 and $10 million. One anonymous head of corporate development quoted by USBX Advisory Services called these smaller deals his "sweet spot."

Franchising

Franchising is a second strategy that can be used to facilitate multi-site service growth. Unlike roll-ups, which increase market coverage by buying up competitors, franchising increases market coverage by selling the right to operate to someone else. For example, McDonald's will sell the right to set up a new restaurant to an investor for an upfront "franchise fee." McDonald's will help set up the restaurant, provide equipment and production methods, and train the new owner. Then the restaurant pays a portion of its sales to McDonald's as royalties for using the McDonald's name and methods. Franchising is quite common; there are about 1,500 firms seeking to sell franchises (i.e., franchisers) and more than 300,000 franchised units in the United States. In fact, roughly one-third of all retail dollars spent are spent at franchises (most auto dealers are franchises).

Franchising provides a way for a service company to grow more rapidly than it could if it had to fund the expansion out of its own cash flow. Most service concepts cannot be patented, so a successful service concept can be more easily copied and implemented by a competitor than in a manufacturing setting, which means that quick expansion in services requires a physical presence to serve a geographic market. Obtaining the necessary capital from a bank to open multiple units of a new service firm quickly is nearly impossible. The loan "collateral" in a service business often consists of a real estate lease, specific décor that wouldn't fit other firms, and a good idea, none of which is worth much to a bank in a foreclosure sale if things go wrong. Franchising, however, is self-financing. Franchisees usually pay an up-front fee and a percentage of gross revenue, so a significant financial base for the franchiser is not necessary. (See Service Operations Management in Practice: "Is Opportunity Knocking for You?" to see Blockbuster's franchise pitch.)

Like every other strategy, franchising represents a series of tradeoffs. For example, paradoxically, franchised stores tend to be more profitable than company-owned stores, which tends to reduce the company's overall profit potential. In other words, franchising reduces the financial risk for the franchiser by shifting a portion of the risk onto the franchisee. So while the franchised store is more profitable, a significant portion of the profits of the store goes to the franchisees to compensate them for the risk shifted onto them, thus reducing the profitability of the franchiser. Table 2.5 presents several more pros and cons of franchising.

Some risks of franchising are just now being understood. These risks relate to the rise of the Internet. In 1999, the company-owned Internet presence of Toys "R" Us wanted to offer steep discounts to compete against other Internet toy sites. They were not allowed to because the discounts would have undercut the 700 franchised Toys "R" Us stores. Also in 1999, the franchisees of H&R Block sued the parent company over selling tax preparation software over the Internet and in retail stores, stating that such sales violated their contracts to exclusive areas. In both instances,

SERVICE OPERATIONS MANAGEMENT PRACTICES

Is Opportunity Knocking for You?

If you become a BLOCKBUSTER® franchisee, you will be in very good company. Today, we have more than 8,500 corporate and franchise stores in 28 countries. The BLOCKBUSTER franchising initiative is one of the fastest and most exciting ways to grow in attractive new markets and in under-served existing markets. Our franchisees get to associate with a world leader in home entertainment. In return, we're assured high-quality, on-site management to service BLOCKBUSTER customers.

Advantages to Affiliating with Blockbuster

- The power of a brand leader with nearly 100% awareness among active movie renters in the U.S.

- As one of America's major advertisers, BLOCKBUSTER supplements its national advertising with targeted marketing to millions of active BLOCKBUSTER members.

- Training, operations and marketing guidance from BLOCKBUSTER.

- Surprisingly simple store operation that doesn't require the operational nightmare of handling perishables, monitoring food preparation and managing dozens of employees.

Franchise Requirements

Financial requirements are a minimum net worth of $400,000 and a minimum liquidity of $100,000.

If you are interested in pursuing a Blockbuster franchise, please download our *Request for Consideration* document to get started with the approval process.

From: *http://www.blockbuster.com/bb/about/ franchisingops/0,7707,NT-ABT,00.html* Accessed 4/29/04

Internet technology would have been an excellent way to reach customers, but that channel was not available because of franchising choices.

Other operational constraints apply. McDonald's wanted to institute a new set of business practices, but its Franchising 2000 plan met with stiff resistance, which, of course, would have been less likely if McDonald's owned the stores and the managers worked for the company. One might think that a franchiser could merely point to a clause in the franchise contract that may allow it to make such changes, but both laws favoring the rights of franchisees and the ability of disgruntled franchisees to make life difficult for franchisers militate against a "command-and-control" relationship between these parties. Consequently, making major changes to a system requires a firm to negotiate and develop a consensus with its franchisees.

The challenge for franchisers is to provide continuing value to franchisees. That is, providing a continuing reason why a franchisee should give 7% of its gross revenue away. For many franchisees, the reason is simple: They derive most of their

TABLE 2.5: *Pros and Cons of Franchising*

Functional Area	Advantages	Disadvantages
Finance	Self-financing Can finance rapid growth Less risky to franchiser	Limits income of successful concept Shifts profits to franchisee
Operations	Entrepreneurial spirit of franchisees	Control more difficult Operational changes more difficult
Human Resources	Career path for store owners not needed Revenue maximizing incentives naturally aligned	Ability to influence behavior curtailed Profit maximizing incentives not aligned
Marketing	Ability to use national marketing media	Can limit marketing channels Local innovations blur marketing message Potential for brand shirking Special events more difficult

business from the national reputation of the franchiser. A lone McDonald's in a small town located on a busy interstate highway derives much of its business from customers who will visit it only once and visit it only because of the brand association. However, a franchisee of Novus Windshield repair (a system with more than 1,000 units) does not benefit as substantially from such an association. The initial franchise value is often quite high. The franchiser trains the franchisee to run the accounting system, provides manuals for how to perform the work, what standards are appropriate, how to do local marketing, and how to deal with suppliers, but after several years in business and an understanding of these one-time issues, what keeps franchisees from branching out on their own? The key for many franchisers is to set up a system that provides continuing value, as described in the Service Operations Management Practices: Franchising at Dunkin' Donuts.

Where Do We Go From Here?

The rest of this book explores in more detail the issues raised in this chapter (Table 2.6 shows how the rest of the book fits into the strategic framework developed in this chapter). The next two chapters examine two emerging strategic issues: the Internet and the natural environment. Both of these are topics that have recently gained added strategic importance. Part 2 of the book looks at issues related to designing the service delivery system, including the recently hot topic of global outsourcing and offshoring. Because service concepts and service delivery systems are not static, Part 3 presents ways to improve on a service delivery design, including showing how Six Sigma can be used in a service environment. Parts 4 and 5 demonstrate a set of powerful tools to match supply to demand and to conduct more detailed analysis of service systems.

As students work through this book, they should remember that every decision that is described in subsequent chapters must be consistent with the strategic positioning of the firm. One way to increase the chance of successfully managing service operations is to make sure that everything is aimed to a common goal.

SERVICE OPERATIONS MANAGEMENT PRACTICES

Franchising at Dunkin' Donuts

Dunkin' Donuts has more than 4,000 franchised units and a thorough program for its franchisees. Initial franchisee training begins with several weeks at Dunkin' Donuts University (DDU). Additionally, financial planning and accounting assistance is available, as well as production scheduling assistance, an applied sanitation program, a technical assistance program, and an A/V system for shop employees. Corporate headquarters also provides "mystery shoppers" for marketing grading. Various physical plant programs include "operation facelift" to help with signage, a landscaping program, line striping for parking lots, pavement sealing, and a remodeling program. To assist franchisees in helping each other, bimonthly meetings of local franchisees are held at company expense, as well as a national franchisee meeting (sorry, they have to pay their own way), and an advisory system. DDU also provides refresher courses on a variety of topics.

TABLE 2.6: *Service Excellence: Strategic Consistency and Tactical Execution*

	External	Internal
Strategy	**Topics** • Five forces • Core competence • Service strategy • Service lifecycle • Natural environment • Outsourcing and offshoring **Book Chapters** Chapters 1, 2, 4, 5, and 8	**Topics** • Capacity, location, and layout • Job design and staffing • Decoupling • Waste stream management • Technology infrastructure • Six Sigma **Book Chapters** Chapters 3, 4, 7, 9, 11, 14, and 16
Execution	**Topics** • Service experience • Customer selection • Supplier selection **Book Chapters** Chapters 6 and 18	**Topics** • Inventory • Waiting lines • Staff training and evaluation • Capacity and yield management • Project management • Internet security and reliability • Quality **Book Chapters** Chapters 3, 10, 12, 13, 14, 15, and 17

Summary

This chapter presented a hierarchical model of service strategy: strategic positioning, service strategy, and tactical execution. Regardless of whether the strategic position is determined by a five-forces approach or a core competence approach, the service strategy decisions of service concept, operating strategy, and service delivery system link the strategic position of the firm to its day-to-day tactical execution. One part of strategic planning that is quite different from manufacturing is planning for growth, because of the customer contact required by multi-site services. Firms that are aware of the multi-site service lifecycle can plan for growth using either a roll-up or a franchising approach.

Review Questions

1. What are the components of the strategic service vision?
2. For a service company like Delta Air Lines (or any other you choose) conduct a strategic analysis using both the five forces and core competence approach. How are the results different?
3. How does the service concept differ from the operating strategy?
4. How might the structure of a service firm change as it grows?
5. Imagine you run a very successful local landscaping company. You have grown as much as you can given capital limitations (i.e., you can't afford another truck). What growth strategies are available to you? Which do you prefer? Why?

Selected Bibliography

Galbraith, J. 1995. *Designing Organizations: An Executive Briefing on Strategy, Structure, and Process.* Jossey Bass, San Francisco.

Heskett, J. L., Sasser, W. E., and L. A. Schlesinger. 1997. *The Service Profit Chain.* The Free Press, New York.

Ho, R. 2000. Veteran of Roll-ups Brings His Skills to the Virtual World. *The Wall Street Journal* (September 26), p. B2.

Klassen, K., and T. Rohleder. 2001. Combining Operations and Marketing to Manage Capacity and Demand in Services. *The Service Industries Journal,* 21(2), 1–30.

Porter, M. E. 1979. "How Competitive Forces Shape Strategy," *Harvard Business Review,* March–April 1979.

Prahalad, C. K. and G. Hamel. 1990. "The Core Competence of the Corporation," *Harvard Business Review,* May–June 1990.

Sasser, E., Olsen, P., and D. Wycoff. 1978. *Management of Service Operations.* Allyn and Bacon, Inc., Boston.

CASE STUDY

Can You Manage a Football Team Like You Manage a Retail Giant?

Arthur Blank, co-founder of The Home Depot and owner of the NFL's Atlanta Falcons, was making a presentation on leadership to a group of undergraduate business students at Emory's Goizueta Business School. During the question and answer session after the presentation one student asked Blank what he thought about competitors and competitor analysis. He answered saying, "At The Home Depot we didn't focus a lot of our attention on our competition. We focused on what was the right thing to do for our customers. Then we did that to the best of our ability." Most of the class appreciated this answer, but one person raised his hand to follow up, "That's easy to do when you are the clear market leader, and so much bigger than your closest competitor. But what about with the Falcons? You have to deal with a salary cap, free agency, player injuries, revenue sharing, and you've only had 8 winning seasons since 1966. That's nearly 40 years!"

Questions:

1. Think about strategic analysis for a market leader versus less dominant companies. Is it different? In what ways?
2. Conduct a brief five forces analysis for both The Home Depot (*http://www.homedepot.com*) and for The Atlanta Falcons (*http://www.atlantafalcons.com*).
3. Conduct a brief core competence analysis for both organizations.
4. Which approach is more appropriate for which organization? Why?

CASE STUDY

PC Repair

Since the introduction of the IBM PC in 1981, the personal computer market experienced explosive growth. This growth in turn created an increasing demand for computer repair services.

Devise a business strategy for a firm specializing in computer hardware repair. Choose the dimensions on which you will compete and articulate an operations strategy that supports your selected business strategy. Identify the key tasks for operations to accomplish. What infrastructural, structural, and integration choices would you make in support of the operations strategy?

Some dimensions you may wish to consider include the following:

- Spare parts stocking policy: Carry ample supplies of all parts? Some parts? Order as needed?
- Capacity: Having capacity for peak demand will mean idle time and increased costs during low demand periods, but having capacity for average demand will mean backlogged customer orders.
- Facilities: The number, types, and locations.
- Specialization of labor.
- Production control: If a customer calls and wants to know when his or her computer will be ready, how will you be able to provide an answer?

This list is not meant to be exhaustive; it is meant to stimulate discussion of the critical dimensions of an operations strategy. Feel free to use your imagination and incorporate other dimensions as you see fit.

The following information from marketing should be useful in formulating a strategy. Market analysis identifies several distinct groups of customers, each with the same profit potential: small business users, recreational home users, and specialized users.

The small business PC market includes those who privately own PCs but use them for business purposes. These users exhibit two special attributes: They abhor any amount of downtime and can be greatly unsophisticated about their computers; that is, they want their PCs fixed immediately and don't care what you have to do to get it going. Due to their lack of sophistication, many of the problems they need fixed are routine.

Recreational home PC users are generally concerned foremost about cost and tend to be unsophisticated as well.

Specialized users are the smallest segment but represent large potential per unit revenue. They perform routine maintenance themselves and call a repair service only when difficult problems arise. They typically have unique machine configurations and time-consuming, difficult repairs that require exotic parts.

Internet Strategies

LEARNING OBJECTIVES *The material in this chapter prepares students to:*

- Understand the operational advantages and disadvantages of doing business over the internet.

- Choose an appropriate distribution and inventory strategy for a brick-and-mortar retailer who will also compete on the internet.

- Select an appropriate customer service strategy for the internet.

In early March 2000, the NASDAQ composite index hit a record high of 5,049, largely because of Internet-based companies. The hype leading up to that time touted e-commerce as a vastly superior way to do business, a true leap forward, that would challenge every rule and assumption of conventional business. A year later, after NASDAQ lost 60% of its value, many of the firms that spearheaded the Internet frenzy had folded. According to the U.S. Department of Commerce, total retail sales in the United States in the 4th quarter of 2003 amounted to $918 billion, with Internet sales comprising only $17 billion, or just under 2%.

As the Internet "bubble" burst, many "pure-play," or Internet-only firms, fell by the wayside. However, Internet strategies remain an important competitive strategy consideration—especially in the retail sector. Although still small when compared to the total economy, e-commerce retail sales[1] increased almost 220% from 1999 to 2003, far outpacing the annual 4% growth of retail in general. It is nearly impossible to find a large U.S. firm without an Internet presence to at least provide information. Further, the so-called "clicks-and-bricks" firms, or firms with a sales presence both on the Web and as a physical store, are now commonplace.

Operationally, Internet-based businesses face different structures, opportunities, and obstacles from those of traditional businesses. This chapter explores the inherently different ways to manage these different types of firms. Specifically, the operational

---

1. The definition of *e-commerce* sales is "sales of goods and services where an order is placed by the buyer or price and terms of sale are negotiated over an Internet, extranet, Electronic Data Interchange (EDI) network, electronic mail, or other online system. Payment may or may not be made online." (*Source: http://www.commerce.gov.*)

difficulties inherent in the now dominant mixed traditional and Internet format are explained. The focus is on the B2C or business-to-consumer, retail context.

INTERNET MARKETING AND OPERATIONS ADVANTAGES

The strength of the Internet hype was based on several factors. Some basic expected effects of the Internet were supposed to produce the following:

- **Better products and services:** Especially software and games which could be interactive when on the Web. Maps that are not just references to streets, but can be queried for useful information, like the closest gas station to your current position.
- **More intelligent products and services:** A key example of building more intelligent services is Amazon.com, which is able to link past purchase behavior with current book publishing to automatically send e-mails to customers who are likely to purchase a particular item.

A potential advantage that most directly concerns operations and is responsible for much of the anticipated advantage of the Internet over traditional retail business, however, is lower prices for standard products. For many reasons, discussed in the next section, it is assumed that Internet-based firms can operate with a far lower cost structure than traditional brick-and-mortar firms. Further, it is assumed that it is far easier to comparison shop on the Internet. With physical stores, just comparing prices can be costly in terms of time and effort. Driving to, parking at, and shopping through a few retail stores may take all day, but comparing the book prices for the same book at Amazon.com and BarnesandNoble.com takes only a few mouse clicks.

Because of this ease of comparison shopping on the Internet and the far better prices that the format is supposed to deliver, it could be reasoned that key marketing concepts such as store brand identity, loss leaders, store displays, and store ambiance could become far less relevant, and low prices could become the key order winner for consumers.

For example, a traditional marketing tactic is to advertise prices below cost on a few items in a store—the loss leaders—to bring consumers into a store, hoping that they will then buy several more profitable items while they are physically in the store, because it is too inconvenient to comparison shop in many stores. However, a consumer can easily pick only the sale items shopping over the Internet, because a competitor is merely a click away.

In similar manner, the entire marketing thrust of a store might be rendered less vital. Stores attempt to meet a target market through the products they display for sale. Limited store space means only products that appeal to the main target market make it to the shelf. Theoretically, retail space is unlimited on the Internet. Consequently, an Internet presence can provide for an unbundling between image and products carried. For example, Amazon.com could carry every book possible, not just a certain subset.

Further, the ambiance of a store, composed of the store layout, juxtaposition of displays, music, scent, and other items, can create a shopping experience (see Chapter 6). When this experience is reduced to pixels on a 17-inch screen and sound from two small speakers, the potential effect of such marketing is muted.

In summary, the presumed cost advantages of Internet-based over traditional businesses, combined with the presumed comparison shopping advantages of Internet-based businesses, were supposed to overwhelm traditional, brick-and-mortar stores.

DIFFERENTIAL COST DRIVERS OF INTERNET AND TRADITIONAL FIRMS

These presumptions turned out to be incorrect on several fronts. The customer experience of a physical store is not just a comparison-shopping inconvenience, but a value-added feature. A customer can experience goods and services with all their senses—get the feel of fabric or the scent of a new perfume. This material, however, is discussed in depth in Chapter 6. Consequently, this chapter will focus on the presumed cost differences between Internet and traditional firms.

The main cost differences between Internet-based and brick-and-mortar firms include the following:

- **Bricks:** The cost of building and maintaining physical stores. As this is a more obvious cost, it will not be discussed in detail.
- **Taxes:** Federal legislation allowed Internet sales an advantage over traditional retail sales by exempting Internet sales from sales taxes. It is unlikely that this will be a sustained advantage.
- **Inventory and Personnel:** When working appropriately, Internet firms enjoy a large advantage over traditional firms in both the inventory and personnel required to run the operations of the firm.
- **Logistics:** Generally, Internet firms have a significant disadvantage versus traditional firms in logistics.

Inventory

The potential inventory savings in e-tailing is a prime example of the textbook "square root law" of combining normal distribution variances taught in nearly every statistics course. To review this statistical logic, consider N stores with independent and identically distributed demand. That is, each of the N stores, on average, has customers that buy the same amount, and their activity is not related to each other (a busy day at one store does not mean either a busy or a slack day at another store). Let us also assume that demand is normally distributed. The question is, how much inventory should be at each store?

Given the preceding assumptions, the stocking level for any given store is related to the service level the store wants to provide (a more detailed discussion of this topic can be found in Chapter 13). If the store wishes to make sure that, say, 95% of the order cycles do not have a stockout, it should stock $k = 1.645$ standard deviations of demand over the average demand, or $k\sigma$ units of "safety stock," or stock that is not expected to sell, but is there just in case demand is heavy. Given N such stores, a specified service level of k standard deviations is achieved by stocking $k\sigma N$ units of safety stock.

However, a significant inventory advantage can be realized by replacing those N store locations with one central location. The variance of demand of the one central location is given by the formula:

$$\sigma^2 \text{ (central location)} = \sigma^2(\text{store 1}) + \sigma^2 \text{ (store 2)} + \sigma^2 \text{ (store 3)} + \ldots + \sigma^2(\text{store } N)$$

or

$$\sigma^2 \text{ (central location)} = N \sigma^2 \text{ (any one store)}$$

So, the standard deviation is,

$$\sigma(\text{central location}) = N^{0.5}\,\sigma(\text{any one store})$$

If one could replace those N stores with a single warehouse linked to a Web site, only $k\sigma\sqrt{N}$ units of safety stock are necessary, rather than $k\sigma N$, hence the name *square root law*. To put some numbers to this general theory, consider replacing a chain of 1,000 bookstores with a Web site. Given a 95% service level on the latest Grisham novel that sells a mean of 15 books, standard deviation of 3, at each store (distributed normally), would mean 15(1,000) = 15,000 books will be stocked to meet mean demand, and 1.645 × 3(1,000) = 4,935 books will be stocked just for safety stock in the retail chain, for a total of 19,935 books. Alternatively, 15,000 books will be stocked in addition to 1.645 × 3(31.6) = 156 books in safety stock, for a total of 15,156 in the Internet business.

However, this basic formula does not capture the true magnitude of the inventory benefits of an Internet-based facility. Retail demand for individual stock-keeping items often is characterized by a small mean demand with high variance, and often follows a different, more extreme, demand distribution than the normal distribution.[2] For example, 56% of dry goods at grocery stores average selling fewer than one unit per week (Kurt Salmon Associates, 1993), yet several units may be purchased in one day. These distinctions magnify the benefits substantially. For example, consider a book that sells an average of 0.5 per order cycle, with a variance of 6 in a 1,000-store system, with an appropriate demand distribution. To achieve a 98% service level (stockouts on 2% of order cycles), inventory of seven units should be stocked in each store, or 7,000 units chainwide. If those stores are replaced by a centralized inventory system, only 661 units are needed for a 98% service level.

Further, maintaining inventory record accuracy is a persistent problem for retailers (Fisher et al., 2000). Retailers hold more inventory due to the uncertainty of the actual inventory position. Record inaccuracy comes primarily from customer theft, customer misfiling, and shipment miscounts. The problems can be extreme, with one "very successful retailer . . . [who is] a leader in information systems" finding that store inventory records are inaccurate on 71% of their products (Raman, 2000, p. 100). This inventory inaccuracy also leads to the problem of "phantom stockouts," in which goods may be in the store, but due primarily to customer reshelving, those goods cannot be found. One bookstore chain found that 19% of their stockouts were of this phantom type (Raman, 2000). Inventory accuracy is far less of an issue with a single facility that does not need to accommodate customers.

Personnel

The personnel required to handle customers in physical stores versus a Web site also favors an Internet business. The results are similar to the inventory situation: Fewer personnel are needed in a centralized system, such as a Web site or a telephone bank, than in de-centralized physical locations to provide the same level of service. The specific mathematics of personnel requirements are different, and are covered in the additional CD-ROM material to Chapter 14.

The basic reasoning why fewer personnel are necessary lies in the variability of serving customers and the variability of how customers want service. On average, a store may need five clerks, but on a busy day may need seven, so seven are hired.

---

2. The negative binomial distribution is cited as a typical retail demand distribution rather than the normal distribution (Agrawal and Smith, 1996, Downs et al., 2001). For a detailed explanation, see Chapter 13.

However, because only five are needed on average, employee utilization is $5/7 = 71\%$. When all stores are combined into one Web site, the high demand times from one area can correspond to the low demand times from another, so that for 1,000 stores that need 5,000 employees on average, only 5,500 may be needed for a peak time, or 91% utilization.

Logistics

A major cost advantage of the traditional system is in product distribution. The operational differences stem from the basic traditional versus Internet distribution strategies shown in Figure 3.1. Traditional retailers often employ what is called an "arborescent" distribution strategy with truckloads or train carloads proceeding from central warehouses to regional facilities, then regional facilities sending pallet loads to retail outlets. Conveniently, customers themselves provide the last link from the retail stores to their homes. The term *arborescent* describes the tree-like shapes of the diagram. Its flow always goes from fewer and larger facilities to more numerous and smaller facilities, with facilities not normally sending product to another facility at the same level.

Within the prototypical Internet strategy, which is also the prototypical catalog merchant strategy, central facilities send one-off products directly to customers. This structure is subject to a severe disadvantage in distribution costs. The cost per unit of product of shipping train car or full truckloads of goods to a few hundred different retail store addresses is trivial compared to the cost of delivering individual units to a few hundred million different customer addresses. Further, returned items—or reverse logistics—are a far larger problem for an Internet provider than a traditional retailer. Returned items at a traditional retailer are a small percentage of sales, whereas return items from Internet merchants can approach 30%. At a traditional store a purchaser is able to view and touch the actual item before purchase, whereas in an Internet transaction, a 6-inch visual item display on a computer screen may not accurately characterize the item. Also, many returned items stay in traditional stores and go back on the retail shelf, but a wrong size or color for an Internet merchant must be mailed back to the merchant and placed back in the right spot in a vast warehouse.

This description, however, presents a best-case scenario of the typical Internet warehouse. Consider, for example, that Amazon.com sells several different types of items stored in different warehouses located in different parts of the country. The interface over the computer appears seamless, but an individual order may need to be combined from several different warehouses to the customer—and customers typically don't wish to pay multiple shipping charges.

STRATEGIES FOR MIXED TRADITIONAL AND INTERNET RETAILERS

It would seem clear that a pure Internet merchant would choose the Internet system in Figure 3.1 and a pure retailer would choose a traditional system. However, as noted previously, the combined Internet/traditional retailer appears to be emerging as the dominant business model. The inherent difficulty for the combined back office is that these two systems cannot be integrated easily.

Distribution centers for traditional retailers require wide aisle widths, so forklifts can easily pass, and the aisle heights reach as high as the forks on a forklift truck will go. Because of these heights, the floors sometimes are laid with the aid of lasers to eliminate small imbalances on the ground that can magnify into a dangerous

FIGURE 3.1: *Traditional Versus Digital Distribution Strategies*

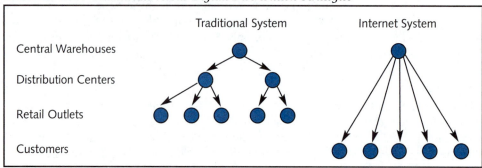

imbalance when loading cargo that is 40 feet in the air. They move product by the pallet load, where a forklift is most efficient. Packing materials tend to be "palletizers," which rotate large pallets with multiple hundreds of pounds of goods to wrap them in plastic wrap, which is then treated to tighten it. Forklifts then load the wrapped pallets on to trucks for delivery to a few stores.

An Internet-based business, however, usually runs a pick-and-pack operation, where aisles are narrow—only wide enough to accommodate a person—and short in height since humans have to reach for items. Items are stored on shelves in open boxes, because one item at a time will be taken, rather than a pallet load. Packing is for individual items, usually for pickup by a firm such as UPS. These items, and a host of others, preclude directly combining pick-and-pack operations with those that focus on delivering pallet-loads of goods.

A general way to think about the operational choices involved is captured with the inventory and shipping options on Figure 3.2. For inventories, firms can make a strategic decision to share inventory between their Web and traditional retail business (Integrated) or keep inventories segregated. In terms of shipping to customers, a general choice must also be made between shipping in bulk or shipping single items as they are ordered. Those not familiar with bulk shipping of Internet-ordered consumer items may be unaware of this option, but it is used by several firms.

FIGURE 3.2: *Inventory and Shipping Strategies for Combined Internet/Traditional Retailers*

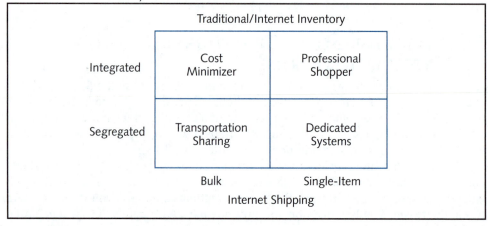

Firms apply several different strategies with no single strategy emerging as dominant. Some firms, such as JCPenney, fall in the Dedicated Systems category; corporate divisions are entirely separate, with separate warehouse systems for the retail side and the catalog/Internet side. The drawbacks of this solution include the excess inventories related to operating segregated systems and excess distribution costs. Approximately 60% of JCPenney's Internet customers pick up goods ordered online at a JCPenney-owned store rather than have them delivered to their home. Yet, those goods are still shipped from the Internet division warehouse rather than being pulled from the shelves of the store that hands over the product. Many other firms, such as Wal-Mart, Macy's, and Bloomingdale's, take this segregation strategy a step further by outsourcing all their Internet orders to third-party firms.

Another strategy that attempts to integrate back-office systems could be called the Professional Shopper strategy. According to Andersen Consulting, six retailers adopted this strategy (Andersen Consulting, 2000). Here, when an Internet order is placed, a store employee walks the aisles of a retail outlet and picks the order. The downside of this strategy is both the cost and filling an order completely. Cost-wise, Internet orders are doomed to be priced at retail plus shipping and handling. It also deprives firms of the basic inventory and personnel benefits of the Internet model already discussed. Further, due to the inventory accuracy problems discussed earlier, many orders may be incomplete. Even when the computer says two are on the shelf, no product may actually be there for the customer. A professional shopper cannot make the judgment for a customer as to whether that customer would like a close substitute or would prefer to do without the item entirely. This concern is real in some industries, such as the grocery industry, which averages 8%–10% stockouts. This strategy also limits the product breadth on the Internet to the same as in the retail store, negating one of the basic promises of Internet-based commerce.

Internet goods shipping can also take place in bulk. Although most Internet businesses package items one at a time and use a carrier such as UPS to deliver goods, others take a different approach. In the United States, Grolier and Fingerhut pick orders one at a time, but combine goods being sent to specific parts of the country on their own trucks. This option is more cost effective, but it is also more time consuming for the customer. When other businesses, such as Wal-Mart and Macy's, outsource their Internet business to these firms, these goods shippers have the opportunity to become Cost Minimizers.

Opportunities also exist for Transportation Sharing in firms such as JCPenney and 7-Eleven of Japan. Both firms serve as sites for customer pickup, so that individually picked Internet-ordered goods could arrive in the same transportation system as traditional goods. With more than 8,000 stores throughout Japan, a 7-Eleven is nearly always close by for picking up goods. Delivering goods to the so-called "last mile," or to the customer's home, is expensive, so transportation sharing systems show promise as a means to tackle this problem.

Both of the dimensions in Figure 3.2 are more complex than the figure can convey. Rather than being two discrete choices, they represent a spectrum of strategic choices as shown in Figures 3.3 and 3.4. Internet and traditional systems can share inventory at either the distribution center or retail store level; that is, the same distribution center that performs order fulfillment for the retail network can perform order fulfillment for Web orders. This level of integration gives the highest level of inventory cost benefit, but warehouses are typically not configured to do both store delivery and individual item pick.

FIGURE 3.3: *Inventory Segregation of Internet and Traditional Retail:*
Where Internet Order Picking Occurs

High					Low
Bulk distribution center	Break-bulk distribution center	Flagship retail store	Retail stores	Contiguous distribution center	Dedicated distribution center

FIGURE 3.4: *Options for Delivering Internet Orders*

Bulk Shipments			Individual Shipments
Customer pickup at retail store/Retail store order pick	Customer pickup at retail store/Delivery from distribution center	Bulk from distribution center to general area/ Individual delivery to home	Shipping direct to customer home

One choice between a completely segregated distribution center system and the integrated systems approach consists of contiguous Web and traditional retail warehouses. Inventory savings are realized through joint delivery of goods to the same location and the ability to stock the Web warehouse with a forklift from the other side of a wall, rather than with a truck from a supplier.

The choices for delivering Web-based orders can also be represented in a spectrum between bulk delivery and the last-mile delivery to customer homes. At one cost extreme, if customers pick up orders at the same retail establishment that orders were kitted from—a traditional call-in option used for years, and an option used by some Internet grocers now—the inventory was essentially delivered in bulk from the distribution center, and no additional delivery charge is needed.

CUSTOMER SERVICE AND THE INTERNET

Not only are businesses adapting distribution and inventory strategies for the Internet, but the rapid growth and development of e-commerce Web sites are significantly changing the face of customer service management. Today, companies that wish to integrate an Internet presence must perform customer service functions through multiple channels, including in-person, traditional mail, phone, Web sites, live online chat, and e-mail. The cost advantages of Internet transactions over traditional media are impressive. (See Table 3.1.) Although businesses are able to reduce their costs through self-service channels such as automated phone systems and their Internet sites, customers do not necessarily respond positively to these changes. Reports indicate that customer satisfaction with most services declined in the last five years. Companies dropped the ball when it came to satisfaction as they applied technology to handle calls and other Internet transactions more cost-efficiently without considering customer satisfaction issues in the process. Customers grow increasingly frustrated with automated phone systems and look to Internet services to address their pent-up demand for better customer service. But, much to their dismay, they often face new challenges with Internet sites. Many find the sites difficult to navigate, abandon their shopping carts before purchasing, have difficulty understanding new service concepts such as auction sites, encounter long response times and misunderstandings with e-mail queries, and attempt to solve problems with new e-businesses that have inadequate service delivery systems.

TABLE 3.1: *Cost of Service Transactions*

Process	Unit Cost	% of Telephone Cost
Traditional Means		
Letter	$12.45	451%
Telephone	2.76	100
Web		
Billing query—fully automated (occasional operator intervention)	0.27	10
Billing query through customer online account	0.14	5
Query that requires agent response back to customer	1.38	50
Operational update available through online access	0.14	5
Operational query that can have automated response (occasional operator intervention)	0.27	10

Additionally, many companies were caught completely unprepared for the tidal wave of e-mails they received after posting an e-mail address on their ads or products, as illustrated in the case discussed in Service Operations Management Practices: If You Build It, They Will Come. For most sectors, e-mail volume has grown faster than the staff hired to deal with it. After adding Internet customer service, Cisco found that the number of customer service transactions increased dramatically along with the need for staff; Amazon.com logs 20,000 customer service problems each day and uses real people to answer each individual e-mail.

Current measures of Internet customer service show dismal results. In terms of e-mail responsiveness, even though 47% of all e-mail inquiries receive a response within 24 hours, 37% never receive any response (Voss, 2000). The online shopping experience encounters similar problems. Two-thirds of all online shoppers abandon their shopping carts and the majority claim that the transaction was not completed due to lack of information. Finally, 90% of online shoppers claim that they would prefer some type of human contact (Durr, 2000). Currently only 1% of all e-retailers offers some type of live support (phone or live interactive text chatting), but this figure could rapidly increase as Web sites worldwide potentially sacrifice $3.2 billion in annual sales because they are not doing enough about customer support. Service companies venturing onto the Internet need to start by asking themselves the following questions about their Internet presence:

- Will customers buy anything or get all the information they need on the site?
- Will customers return?
- Will customers understand the business concept?
- Will the business be able to handle outbound and inbound (returns) volume?
- Will customers prefer self-serve or some kind of human contact?
- Will the Internet customer service be in-house or provided through a third-party vendor?
- What are the metrics and goals for customer service?

To address these questions, the next section covers the fundamentals of Internet service design.

SERVICE OPERATIONS MANAGEMENT PRACTICES

If You Build It, They Will Come

Wasatch Brewery in Park City, Utah, introduced an ad campaign for its beers tied into Utah's location for the 2002 Olympics. International periodicals covered their controversial introduction of Polygamy Porter and campaign slogans such as "when one is not enough." The brewery's Web site posted an e-mail address encouraging people interested in buying T-shirts and other merchandise to contact them. Soon after the press coverage, the business received hundreds of e-mails every day requesting merchandise. Unfortunately, the brewery never anticipated this kind of demand and was caught without a system in place to deal effectively with this volume of Internet sales or e-mail response.

INTERNET SERVICE DESIGN

Several key strategic design choices must be made when developing good customer service on the Web. They include product characteristics (customization level, complexity, customer knowledge, and capacity), process characteristics (technology and task), and touch points (customer, employees, and system interaction). Each of these decisions affects the final outcome measured by performance metrics (customer satisfaction, loyalty, market, and economic indicators) as shown in Figure 3.5.

Product

The product itself sets precedence for what type of activity will happen on the Internet site and the service design. First, the service provider must define the intent of the site. For example, a cell phone company must provide sales and information or troubleshooting services. A restaurant may use the Web as an information source (like the Yellow Pages) by providing only the current menu, reviews, and directions. On the other hand, the restaurant may want to extend interactive capabilities to build relationships with its client base and offer capabilities for making reservations, voting

FIGURE 3.5: *Service Design Model*

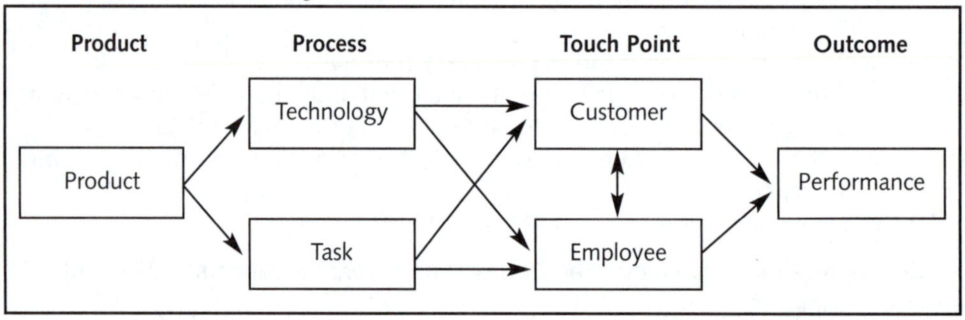

FIGURE 3.6: *Range of Internet Services*

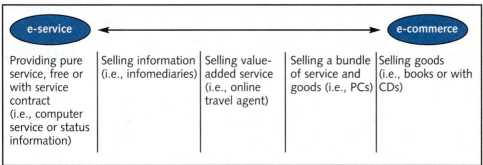

on favorite menu items, or viewing streaming video of its sushi bar. Thus Internet services can fall between pure e-service and e-commerce as shown in Figure 3.6. depending on the product offering. The corresponding Internet service design depends on the product's customization level, complexity, customer knowledge, and expected volume of interactions.

For certain services, it is important to convey a highly customized environment for each customer, and the customer must interact with a real person to close a sale. For example, Post Ranch Inn in Big Sur, California, uses its Web site to show pictures of the property and provide basic information such as room rates and amenities. Because of its highly unique lodging, however, customers must speak to an agent so the agent can fit the customer needs to an appropriate room. Car sales sites use phone agents to try to close deals and match clients to available models at dealerships in their geographic area.

Businesses expecting high volumes of customer service inquiries look to the Internet to alleviate some of the demand on phone and on-site transactions. Because of the available technologies, many Internet services can provide mass customization for this volume business. Businesses with sensitive material, such as financial services and banking (Fidelity or Bank One), use personalized pages to create trust. Those trying to create customer loyalty and increased sales with certain customer groups (Dell, eBay, or Amazon.com) create customized environments to stimulate impulse spending and suggest matching products using the customer's previous purchases or stated interests. In this case, the personalized pages provide only information that the customer (or customer segment) needs to see.

Product complexity and customer's product knowledge are both variables that influence the amount of customer interaction and Internet service design. When customers need to troubleshoot computers, software, or cell phones, the Internet site can provide in-depth service manuals/help sites for this equipment. Generally experienced users can decipher these manuals and self-serve, but the average layperson requires additional interaction with a service representative. For high-volume services, it is important to make the self-help as user-friendly as possible to capture the widest range of customers with varying degrees of product knowledge.

Processes

From a service operations perspective, two key design elements must be considered under processes: technology and task. Technology supports both front- and back-office operations. Here, we will restrict our discussions of task to the customer service support activities.

Technology

The five basic process technology systems that any Internet service should consider when dealing with the customer service side of the business are shown in Figure 3.7. The back-office technologies cover all the supporting processes such as transaction, distribution and fulfillment, information, and knowledge management systems. The front office requires the interaction technologies that may overlap with the back-office information systems.

In the previous section, we covered the distribution and fulfillment processes so here we limit discussion to the remaining systems. When designing an Internet presence, the *transaction system* provides a key ingredient because this process covers the money and product flows (billing, shipping, receiving, and returns). Once customers pay for the goods or service, they want to receive their product. And, if the product or service is unsatisfactory, they are equally interested in convenient return and payment credit. Billing security or the ability to have secure credit card transactions over the Internet, accurate status on product availability and receiving, prompt shipment

FIGURE 3.7: *Internet Service Processes*

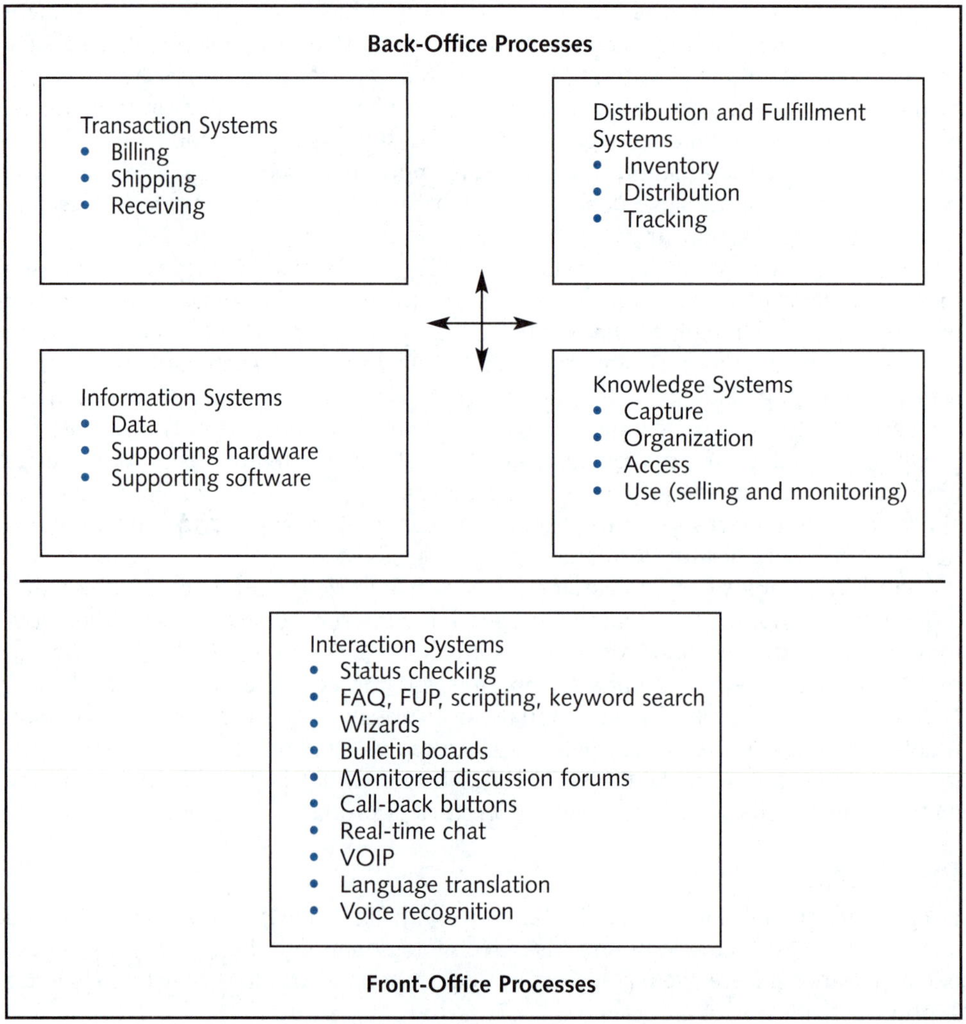

with tracking, and a convenient return and payment credit represent critical customer concerns. Ideally, both the customer service representative and the customer should be able to monitor the whole transaction cycle. A good example of this process can be found on the Amazon.com site (Figure 3.8). Much to the dismay of many e-commerce businesses, product returns are much larger than at their bricks-and-mortar counterparts at 30% compared to 5%, respectively. Many e-services subcontract the return cycle to third-party vendors to reduce reverse supply chain costs and tracking. These vendors perform these functions for less cost due to transportation and other overhead sharing, which creates economies of scope and scale.

The information system processes cover data management, the hardware and software systems, and integration of all the other systems that support front- and back-office operations. New customer service applications and hardware entering the market influence the interaction processes. Although current Enterprise Resource Planning (ERP) systems provide seamless integration of many of the other business processes, these new applications can be challenging to integrate.

The knowledge system process involves the capture, organization, access, and use of knowledge. The main focus of the knowledge system is customer relationship

FIGURE 3.8: *Amazon.com's Internet Order Tracking*

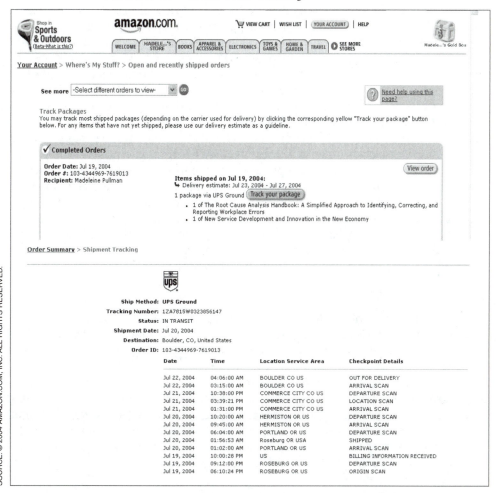

management (CRM), but it can also be used for new product development, quality monitoring, and improvement. Using the information gained through CRM, companies can choose how they interact with their customers. It allows them to build better relationships with customers than previously possible in the offline world. Amazon.com is the most visible Internet presence with its CRM program. Their system determines customer preferences and segments and automatically sends promotional e-mails and banners to the targeted customers about their interest areas. Well-managed knowledge systems permit firms to choose to whom they wish to offer specific services and at what quality level. As a selling tool, these systems encourage repeat customers and higher revenues per transaction at low interaction costs. Additionally, the knowledge management process monitors the customer interactions via Internet, phone, e-mail, and other channels to identify quality problems, problem resolution, sales strategies, and other patterns that could improve product and service offerings.

On the front office side, the customer interaction process is supported by a number of technologies. These interaction systems have exploded over the last three years with media for enhancing the customer experience. Simple phone interactions with customer service agents evolved into multiple options and supporting technologies. *Agent Supporting Technologies* include enhanced scripting capabilities such as Wizards, which create templates for customer interaction, and rapid search enhancements for Keywords, FAQ (Frequently Asked Questions), and FUP (Frequently Used Phrases). Additionally, *Content & Quality Supporting Technologies* provide agents with programs that automatically check for spelling, grammar, correct company identification, and "marketing image" language (for agents covering multiple vendor groups), e-mail-intelligent systems that route and track inbound mail, and translation software to interact with different language customers. *Customer Supporting Technologies* offer systems that help customers find information by themselves through searching enhancements, status checking, monitored discussion forums, and bulletin boards. The discussion forums and bulletin boards allow customers to answer queries for each other, and these methods help create a loyal community. *Interaction Technologies* cover all enhancements to real-time communication such as interactive voice response (IVR) in which a caller interacts with integrated database with digital or speech recognition; automated virtual representatives (vReps), computer-generated images on the Web site that answer customer questions in real time using natural language; voice over Internet phone (VOIP), the ability to communicate verbally through computers instead of phone line; call-back buttons; and, real-time chat, the ability to communicate in written text over an Internet site.

Task

When customers interact with an Internet service, their communication is generally task-specific. The task could be a simple inquiry or information search, purchase intent, problem solving, or complaint. Companies would like customers to perform all these tasks online without human interaction because it costs a fraction of traditional overhead. But, it is important to recognize that certain tasks or certain customer groups respond more favorably to real-time interactions. Most customers require speed, accuracy, and relevant information for all tasks. As we mentioned previously, 90% of all customers would prefer to interact with a human being. So how should the service provider reconcile the trade-off between customer preferences and cost? A look at the task and technology options that best satisfy the customer is the first step.

For example, sales are generally enhanced by live interaction. The agent can quickly focus on the customer needs and up-sell to more expensive products or additional services or accessories. Using live chat, an agent can actually communicate with up to four customers simultaneously due to time lags in writing and viewing text and Internet pages. Reviews of live chat show an increase in sales and customer satisfaction with e-services. Comparing live chat to unassisted Internet sales, Camera World realized 25% sales closure versus 3%, HomeTownStores.com experienced a 30% sales increase, and Consumer Financial Network's customer satisfaction index increased 5%. Similarly, simple inquiries can turn into sales opportunities more readily with real-time interactions.

Another important task is dealing with complaints. Complaints tend to be personalized. Generally, the customer can choose to e-mail the company, call on the phone, or use real-time Internet interaction. Without question, e-mail offers the least effective vehicle for customer complaint resolution. Normally e-mail is fraught with miscommunication and time lags. In addition, companies ignore nearly one-third of all e-mails. Customer anger with the company can escalate quickly, and those customers often tell every one of their friends and an Internet chat community about their negative experience with the company. The best vehicle for complaint resolution is verbal real-time interaction with a skilled agent. Good customer service agents listen to the tone of the client and can quickly deescalate anger and frustration.

Finally, it is important to give customers options for contacting the company instead of forcing them to self-serve. This way, they can choose the technology that they feel best fits their task. Experienced users and self-servers can use all the automated aspects of the Internet site, while the "high touch" users can interact with a real person.

Customer Contact Centers

Companies may address this new customer service demand via Web and call center integration, places where the customer can access a real person via a variety of means. These expanded call centers are known as customer contact centers (CCC). The customer contact center usually offers 24/7 support for multiple touch points with multimedia support. At a minimum, CCCs must now cover phone and e-mail with more advanced centers supporting online chat, bulletin boards, chat rooms, I-telephony, and other options. Similar to trends in call center management, the leading CCCs are outsourced or hosted by third-party vendors.

Traditional call centers employ a large number of agents to handle relatively few accounts. Thus the management benefits from cost saving labor-scheduling models that match labor supply to variable daily and weekly demand. These models assume that all employees perform the same general task of answering different types of phone calls with stochastic demand and service length and assume call center employees focus on one customer at a time and that all customers are responded to in real-time with minimal queue time.

The new multitouch point centers service a large number of accounts with a small number of agents. Depending on the account needs, vendors offer a variety of pricing and "pick and choose" service options.

Outcomes

We discussed the relationship between the various resources (employees, technologies, and processes) and the needs of the customer and clients. Ultimately, companies need to answer the following question: What are the issues that most affect both delivery of superior customer service and the bottom line? Clearly most companies want to maximize customer service, loyalty, and sales closure. Because Internet services are relatively new, only informal rules of thumb guide operations strategies. For example, "E-mails should be answered within 24 hours." Other important measures of performance include the following:

- Employee satisfaction
- Customer satisfaction
- Response time between chat or e-mail
- Form (greeting, language, offering additional help, proper template use)
- Employee knowledge of topic during interaction
- Customer regard
- Intention for repeat encounter

To ensure desirable outcomes, several important relationships must be considered. First, the outcomes should be measured. Every Internet service needs access to metrics such as average e-mail response time and the time for problem resolution. Second, it is important to match the employees to the task, support employees with training and technologies to improve their efficiency and effectiveness, and allow customers to choose low or high touch for their interaction with the company. Finally, global quality measures such as repurchase intent and customer satisfaction with the Internet presence should be constantly monitored for potential problems and continuous improvement.

Summary

Internet service providers must consider back-room supply chain management as well as front-room and Web site interaction with customers. In this chapter we covered emerging models for distribution and inventory in hybrid clicks-and-bricks services organization as well as the operations management issues found in the front room, the interaction with the site, and customer service support. Many Internet services perish during their first few years primarily from lack of a holistic understanding of the entire operation. Too much emphasis on the Web site or portal with too little emphasis on the supporting supply chain and customer service has caused the demise of many initially popular companies.

Review Questions

1. What are the myths and realities about Internet marketing and operational advantages?
2. How do the primary distribution systems and inventory costs differ between "bricks" and "clicks" firms?
3. Describe the four different strategies for mixed and traditional retailers.
4. What are the differences between "bricks" and "clicks" warehouse design?
5. How do the process characteristics of technology and task interact to affect customer service?
6. In what ways does a customer contact center differ from a traditional call-in center?

Selected Bibliography

Agrawal, N., and S. Smith. 1996. Estimating Negative Binomial Demand for Retail Inventory Management with Unobservable Lost Sales. *Naval Research Logistics, 43,* 839-861.

Andersen Consulting. 2000. Who Does the Best Job of E-Fulfillment? *Logistics Magazine* (November), 59-66.

Downs, B., Metters, R., and J. Semple. 2001. Managing Inventory with Multiple Products, Lags in Delivery, Resource Constraints, and Lost Sales: A Mathematical Programming Approach. *Management Science, 47*(3), 464-479.

Durr, W. 2000. Turning Browsers into Buyers Using Your Call Centers. *Call Center Solutions, 19*(3), 68-70.

Fisher, M., Raman, A., and B. McClelland. 2000. Rocket Science Retailing Is Almost Here. *Harvard Business Review,* 78(4), 115-124.

Kurt Salmon Associates. 1993. *Efficient Consumer Response: Enhancing Consumer Value in the Grocery Industry.* Author.

Raman, A. 2000. Retail Data Quality: Evidence, Causes, Costs, and Fixes. *Technology in Society, 22,* 97-109.

Voss, C., 2000. eService Key Trends. Working paper, London Business School, London, England.

CASE STUDY

PeopleSupport.com

PeopleSupport.com provides multitouch-point customer support for companies with an Internet presence (henceforth referred to as the "clients"). Using innovative chat technology, PeopleSupport.com gives customers the option of contacting a service representative directly via online chat, e-mail response, or traditional telephone support from their clients' Web sites. With the interactive chat option, customers click a "chat" button and are seamlessly connected via personal chat to an eRep (an online representative) who has the ability to "push" Web content, optimizing the interactive nature of the Internet. This live assistance function allows for crucial questions, potential objections, and various concerns to be addressed in real-time. If customers choose the e-mail option, PeopleSupport.com has the expertise to handle clients' inbound e-mail management needs including intelligent e-mail routing, escalation processes, and overflow or seasonal e-mail management programs. The e-mail response function blends e-mail routing and auto-suggest functions (searches for certain words in the customer email and provides suggested responses) with the ability to provide a personal touch to each reply. Currently, the company's business is 60% e-mail, 30% chat, and 10% phone interactions.

There are three ways that PeopleSupport.com generates revenue from clients. First, clients can choose to pay per session. Any time there is some interaction between the eRep and the customer, it is considered a session. Second, clients can pay per minute (measured by the length of chat, e-mail, or voice). Finally, clients can pay hourly for their own designated eReps. The dedicated model requires 12 to 16 employees per week to handle a 24/7 schedule. This method is usually appropriate for high volume companies (toys at Christmas) or complex product or information companies (cell phone troubleshooting).

PeopleSupport.com represents many different clients. A partial list of clients is shown in Table 3.2. The typical client uses PeopleSupport.com to handle all their Web-based customer service for e-mail and chat. The client and his or her PeopleSupport.com sales representative develop training materials, frequently used sentences, and other employee support materials. The average employee training time can take from three days for simple sites and products to more than three weeks for technically sophisticated products such as cell phone customer service. The company employs several hundred full-time-equivalent employees, approximately half of whom are dedicated to a specific client. The remaining employees are members of teams that represent between three and fifteen different clients at any given time.

Given this structure of multitask teams (an individual can do e-mail, phones, and live chat simultaneously) and multiclient mix teams, the company is able to keep level staffing patterns rather than the staggered shift schedules usually seen in call-in centers. For example, Vendor M's customers are predominately teenagers who use the live chat from hours after school until midnight, while Vendor C's customers call for car part information from early morning through traditional business hours.

CASE STUDY

TABLE 3.2: *Vendor Types*

Vendor	Products/Services	Touch Points
Vendor A	Technical software products	E-mail
Vendor B	Cell phone	E-mail & chat
Vendor C	Car parts	E-mail, chat, & phone
Vendor D	Car sales	E-mail, chat, & phone
Vendor E	Cooking products	E-mail, chat, & phone
Vendor F	PeopleSupport.com demonstration	E-mail, chat, phone, & Voice-IP
Vendor G	Movie studio merchandise	E-mail & chat
Vendor H	Shopping network	E-mail, chat, & phone
Vendor I	Toys	E-mail & chat
Vendor J	High end clothing	E-mail & chat
Vendor K	Retail auction site	E-mail & chat
Vendor L	Beauty products	E-mail & chat
Vendor M	Teenage info & products	E-mail & chat
Vendor N	Audio books	E-mail & chat
Vendor O	Financial services	E-mail & chat

Vendor E's customers (cooking products) generally use both live chat and phone support from 8 A.M. until 3 P.M. and then again during the after dinner hours.

Supporting technologies help those employees covering five to eight different businesses simultaneously. These technologies include appropriate scripts, frequently used sentences (FUSs), and frequently used paragraphs (FUPs) for a client's Web site. For example, the high-end Italian clothing client expects formal and respectful language interactions while the teenage surfing product client expects informal "surf culture" language appropriate for that product category. According to one eRep:

> *"FUP/FUS works best because you portray how the company wants to be represented rather than in your own words. This also eliminates typing out the same answer over and over again. However, they don't work with very specific answers and when you don't want to sound like you are a robot."*

This type of contact center with multiple customers and contact points has many advantages over a traditional call-in center because of the ability to create a more balanced employee schedule, offer more interesting and varied work to employees, and offer clients revenue generating rather than cost producing activities. On the other hand, the role of a contact center employee is much more complex than an in-house, call-center employee, thus hiring activities; team design and support; and employee scheduling, training, measuring, and monitoring are crucial to the client and customer experience. Many employees prefer to use the live chat function rather than the phone interaction as indicated by one employee:

CASE STUDY

"Customer service over chat is easier than phone. When customers are irate, it's easier to let it roll off your back. If you don't know the answer to a chat question, you can ask someone next to you which is hard with phone calls. About 75% of our work relates to complaints."

But the conflicting nature of covering multiple vendors and tasks is pointed out by another employee:

"If customers are looking for particular pants and they can't find them, we're supposed to sell them another type. But, I often forget because we're so used to dealing with complaints that it's hard to switch modes. The clothing and teenage products companies could benefit from more selling, but these companies don't give any incentives to the eReps and we get limited feedback or no feedback on our job performance from the clients. It seems like both companies aren't really interested in selling the product, just dealing with the complaints."

Questions:

1. Given the mix of clients currently using PeopleSupport.com, what kinds of employees (background and skill set) do you suggest that the contact center hire and which clients and tasks should they "bundle together" versus using a designated eRep?
2. What types of customer satisfaction measures should be monitored and rewarded given that customers contact the center for problem resolution, Web site help, or sales support? How could they actually measure these items? Which contact technologies are best for each customer purpose?
3. What are the advantages and disadvantages of using scripting in customer contact centers? How would you address these disadvantages?

Environmental Strategies

LEARNING OBJECTIVES   *The material in this chapter prepares students to:*

- Understand the business relevance of the environment to service companies.

- Describe the types of environmental issues that service companies face.

- Explain the role that service companies play in creating and mitigating environmental issues for both themselves and other companies.

- Evaluate the environmental impacts of a service company.

Until recently, a businessperson hearing the word *environment* in a sentence either thought about competitors and suppliers (i.e., "competitive environment") or got this nagging feeling that costs were about to go up (i.e., the Environmental Protection Agency). Business leaders and environmentalists have been opponents ever since Rachel Carson published *Silent Spring* in the early 1960s. (*Silent Spring* is an exposé about the effects of pesticides.) Yet since 1990, *Harvard Business Review* has published at least 15 articles about the role the natural environment plays in business specifically, or about "sustainability" in general. In fact, MBA programs are now ranked on how well they incorporate environment-business issues into their curricula. Every other year the World Resources Institute (WRI) publishes its *Beyond Grey Pinstripes: Preparing MBAs for Social and Environmental Stewardship*. Table 4.1 lists a few of the programs included in the 2003 rankings.

Most of this attention focuses on manufacturing companies. It is relatively easy to understand how Ricoh Electronics, DuPont, BMW, Kodak, Royal Dutch/Shell and other "smokestack" companies could hurt the environment. So when companies like these innovate in ways that improve both their business and the environment, it makes sense to everyone. For example, Royal Dutch/Shell developed an innovative approach to deal with carbon dioxide emissions that created a win-win situation with an important trading partner, which is described in Service Operations Management Practices: How Royal Dutch/Shell Relieved a Serious Gas Problem. As another example, by the end of 2001 all of Ricoh Electronics' manufacturing facilities in Europe and America reached the unprecedented goal of zero waste to landfills, or 100% resource recovery. Despite these

TABLE 4.1: *A Partial Listing of MBA Programs Ranked by the World Resources Institute*

University of North Carolina–Chapel Hill (Kenan-Flagler)	Harvard University
University of Texas–Austin (McCombs)	Northwestern University (Kellogg)
University of Pennsylvania (Wharton)	Stanford University
University of Michigan–Ann Arbor	Yale University
Cornell University (Johnson)	Dartmouth (Tuck)

Source: Adapted from *Beyond Grey Pinstripes: Preparing MBAs for Social and Environmental Stewardship*. The World Resources Institute, 2003.

manufacturing successes in the business-environment arena, little attention focuses on service companies and their impact on the environment.

Two separate issues need to be considered when thinking about services and the environment: the environmental impacts of service companies, and companies that offer environmental services. What immediately comes to mind is that without tangible products involved, no environmental issues exist. However, no process is 100% waste free, therefore services do create some environmental effects, and as will be shown, many services make a considerable impact.

Industries that focus on environmental services include waste disposal, cleaning services, environmental lawyers, and environmental consultants. These sorts of companies include ServiceMaster, Perma Fix Environmental Services, Allied Waste Industries, Inc., and the environmental law practices group at Skadden, Arps, Slate, Meagher & Flom, LLP, which, according to Hoovers.com, is the largest law firm in the country with more than 1,800 lawyers. Even the premier strategic consulting firm McKinsey & Company has an environmental service offering.

The big question remains: "Does all this focus on the environment really matter?" The next section is devoted to answering that question by providing the financial, strategic, operational, and marketing reasons why services need to understand the environment.

ENVIRONMENTAL MANAGEMENT AND PROFITABILITY

One could argue that companies of all types should manage environmental issues because it is the right thing to do. In other words, it is socially responsible. This view leads companies to evaluate their performance on measures beyond traditional financial dimensions. Companies like Anheuser-Busch, Dow Chemical, Lockheed Martin, Motorola, and Procter & Gamble now evaluate performance according to what John Elkington called the "triple bottom line" of financial, environmental, and social performance. The triple bottom line requires that companies track their performance on all three dimensions. Figure 4.1 shows some examples of triple bottom line performance metrics.

A triple bottom line focus can be a tough argument to make in a profit-driven world. *The Economist* calls this argument "the curse of the ethical executive," not to deride the importance of business ethics, but to point out that corporate social responsibility can negatively affect people's opinions about market capitalism as well as distract companies from their fiduciary responsibility of maximizing shareholder wealth. A more powerful argument demonstrates how services that successfully manage the environment end up financially more successful than those that don't.

Research demonstrates this real relationship between environmental and financial performance metrics. In other words, companies that manage their environmental performance well can achieve significant financial performance gains, while those that

SERVICE OPERATIONS MANAGEMENT PRACTICES

How Royal Dutch/Shell Relieved a Serious Gas Problem

At the [Royal Dutch/Shell] Scotford plant in Alberta, Canada, more than 60% of carbon dioxide emissions, which were previously vented into the atmosphere as a waste product, are now recycled. Carbon dioxide, blamed by some scientists for being a principal cause of global warming, is produced as a by-product of fuel combustion and some chemical processes.

The plant recently began selling carbon dioxide to a neighboring company, Air Liquide, which processes the gas so that it can be used to carbonate soft drinks. Shell will eventually sell 62,000 tons of carbon dioxide a year to Air Liquide. In return Air Liquide is now the sole supplier of steam and electricity to the Shell complex, making the deal a win-win situation for both companies.

Karl Blonski, Health, Safety and Environment, and Quality Manager at Scotford, says: "It's real synergy—Air Liquide will eventually buy much of our carbon dioxide and we are able to buy cheap, efficiently-produced electricity from them, which previously we bought from the Alberta Grid. It's a kind of partnership because we are reliant on each other and at the same time we are both reducing emissions and saving on energy."

Source: Adapted from Shell's Web site. For more information on this and other Royal Dutch/Shell environmental initiatives, go to http://www.shellchemicals.com/chemicals/magazine/article/ 0,1261,92-gen_page_id = 896,00.html or http://www.enn.com/news/enn-stories/2001/10/10302001/shell_45365.asp.

FIGURE 4.1: *Measuring the Triple Bottom Line*

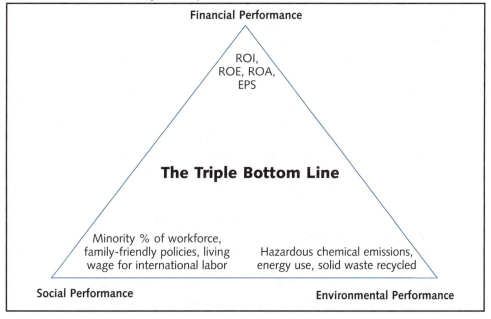

fail to adequately manage environmental performance can face equally significant financial losses. Some of the financial implications of poor environmental performance include fines assessed by government agencies such as the U.S. Environmental Protection Agency (EPA), costs of litigation to defend against these fines, and the damage to the company's brand from environmental issues.

Companies that violate state or federal laws face stiff penalties, and the likelihood of violating a law increases with every page of environmental legislation that is passed. From 1972 to 1992, for example, the total number of pages of legislation related to the environment went from zero to more than 160,000. The cost of noncompliance is also large. Delta Air Lines was fined over $1 million by the Georgia Environmental Protection Department not for actually spilling anything but for failing to accurately report what hazardous chemicals they had on site. Borden Chemicals and Plastics signed a consent agreement with the U.S. Department of Justice to pay a $3.6 million fine as part of a settlement that included charges of illegally exporting mercury waste to South Africa.

This amount, though, hardly approaches the value of the damage caused when part of the 137,500 gallons of the highly toxic liquid metal leaked from its barrels, contaminating both the surroundings and the workers near the Thor Chemical Plant in Cato Ridge, South Africa. This matter is the focus of several criminal and civil investigations in South Africa, though the statute of limitations in the United States expired January 27, 2001. Ciba-Geigy was fined an impressive $120 million to clean up a 1,500-acre Superfund site in Alabama. Investigations into Ciba-Geigy began in 1979, and the prosecution concluded in 1992. Litigation costs for environmental problems are significant. The Cato Institute estimates that half of all public expenditures for Superfund litigation is spent on lawyers and consultants, about $60 million for the Ciba-Geigy site.

The message then is that companies can improve their financial performance while improving their environmental performance. These financial gains come from cost reductions, quality and yield improvements, improved relationships with regulators, reduced insurance costs, and enhancements to the company's revenue streams and brands. Delta Air Lines achieved significant cost reductions when they pioneered the practice of using only one engine while taxiing. Company estimates show that this change reduced fuel consumption by 40 million gallons per year, a significant improvement since fuel is typically the second largest cost airlines face (after labor costs). For the quarter ending December 2003, Delta's average fuel cost was $0.85 per gallon, for a total savings of $34 million. Of course, fuel not burned does not emit residual pollution, which contributes to a substantial environmental gain in the form of energy conservation and pollution prevention, and results in a major financial payoff. In 1997 the National Resources Defense Council recognized Delta for this innovation.

Home Depot began its environmental efforts in 1990, on the twentieth anniversary of Earth Day. One of their initiatives commits them to the principles of sustainable forestry (see Service Operations Management Practices: Home Depot's Commitment to Sustainable Forestry) and to offer environmentally preferred products for sale in their stores. According to the Sierra Club, Home Depot is responding to consumer demand for wood not harvested from old-growth forests. So Home Depot uses its environmental efforts to meet customer desires while strengthening its position as a market leader and adding value to the company's brand through its responsible leadership.

United Parcel Service (UPS) partnered with The Alliance for Environmental Innovation, a joint initiative of the Environmental Defense Fund and The Pew

SERVICE OPERATIONS MANAGEMENT PRACTICES

Lawyers in Love

One of the chief reasons for Superfund's exploding costs is the litigious free-for-all engendered by the act. Superfund calls for retroactive liability, meaning that corporate practices that might have been safe, legal, fully permitted, or even required under the law years ago can now be punished retroactively. "Potentially Responsible Parties" (PRPs), according to the law, are those who (1) own or operate a site; (2) owned or operated a site at the time of the disposal of wastes; (3) arranged for disposal, treatment, or transportation of waste; or (4) accepted waste for transport. The courts have interpreted Superfund as calling for joint and several liability, meaning that any party that ever touched that waste—no matter how tertiary the involvement or how minor the amount—can be held liable for the full cost of remediation. Finally, these laws shift the burden of proof from the government to the accused and does not require the government to meet any significant standards for admissible evidence. For example, the vague recollections of a garbage hauler about customers 40 years in the past have repeatedly been accepted as dispositive by the EPA and the courts.

Typically, the EPA tries to hunt down one or two "deep pocket" corporations that can somehow be linked to the site and then hits them with the full cost of cleanup. Those companies then go about finding any party that might conceivably have had anything to do with the site and then sue that party under the joint and several liability standard to pay the bill. Not surprisingly, lawyers, consultants, private investigators, and administrative overhead consume vast quantities of Superfund dollars. Such "transaction costs" eat up 35% of corporate Superfund expenditures, 88% of insurance company Superfund expenditures, and 50% of public Superfund expenditures. Before 1980 only 2,000 attorneys specialized in environmental litigation nationwide. After 15 years of Superfund, that number has increased tenfold. Although not all of those additional 18,000 attorneys were created by Superfund, best guesses from practitioners indicate that about 75% were.

Source: From "Salting the Earth: The Case for Repealing the Superfund," by Jerry Taylor. Used by permission from the Cato Institute. This document can be found at http://www.cato.org/pubs/regulation/reg18n2d.html.

Charitable Trusts, to redesign much of their packaging. For example, the redesign made UPS's Next Day Air service packaging both lighter and reusable. The company estimates that this change saved UPS about $1.6 million per year since 1998, as well as conserved enough energy to light 20,000 light bulbs for a year, eliminated 550 tons of solid waste, and saved more than 2,200 tons of trees.

More generally, researchers found a significant positive relationship between environmental events, both positive and negative, and stock market performance (Klassen and McLaughlin, 1996). When companies are mentioned in the media for positive environmental events, their share price is stronger than the broader market. Conversely, share price is weaker relative to the broader market for companies associated with negative environmental events. For example, Alcan Aluminum was awarded Kentucky's 1998 Governor's Environmental Excellence for Industrial Environmental Leadership on October 27, 1998. For the two weeks following the report of the award ceremony

SERVICE OPERATIONS MANAGEMENT PRACTICES

Home Depot's Commitment to Sustainable Forestry

As a home improvement retailer, we have worked diligently to educate ourselves and our suppliers about important forestry issues. In fact, The Home Depot was the first home improvement retailer to pioneer the U.S. market for wood products certified under the principles of the Forest Stewardship Council (FSC). Our Timber Task Force is continually striving for improvements in forest management practices.

As members of the FSC, we helped lay the foundation for the Certified Forest Products Council, an organization that facilitates the increased purchase, use, and sale of third-party, independent, certified forest products. Over the last six years, we have introduced new FSC-certified products and other alternatives for you to choose from. For example, in most of our stores you'll find:

- Royal Mahogany Doors from a certified forest in Costa Rica.
- Premwood Doors, an alternative to lauan (light yellow to reddish brown wood often called Philippine mahogany) interior doors.
- FSC-certified dimensional lumber from one of our largest Canadian suppliers.
- Flooring underlayment made from recycled newspapers and gypsum sold as replacement to lauan flooring underlayment.

Rest assured, as more of these products become available, The Home Depot will carry them.

Source: From The Home Depot's Web site. Used by permission. This document can be found at http://www.homedepot.com.

(Monday, October 26, 1998 to Friday, November 6, 1998), the company's stock price increased 80% faster than the Dow Jones Industrial Average. On the other hand, on October 12, 2001, IBP, Inc., a meat packer owned by Tyson Foods Inc., agreed to pay $2.25 million to the EPA and $1.85 million to the state of Nebraska to settle charges that included emitting excessive hydrogen sulfide into the air and illegally discharging ammonia into a river near the company's slaughter and tannery operations in Dakota City, Nebraska, and disposing of spent stun-gun cartridges that contained lead into wastewater lagoons. The stock market reacted in the two weeks subsequent to this settlement announcement (October 11, 2001, to October 26, 2001) by taking more than 8% off Tyson's market capitalization, even though IBP is only one of Tyson's businesses. During those same two weeks the Dow rose by about 1.5%.

From a slightly different perspective, Hoover's estimate that, in the United States alone, the market for environmental services and equipment is worth about $200 billion per year. As a specific example, in February, 2004, the U.S. Air Force awarded a group of companies led by Tetra Tech, a leading environmental consultancy, a contract worth $200 million. The February 24, 2004 *Business Wire* reports that the firms will support the Air Force's Air Combat Command by providing consulting, engineering design, information management, and construction management over the life of the 7-year contract.

SERVICE OPERATIONS AND THE ENVIRONMENT

The service process matrix (discussed in Chapter 1) is a powerful tool for classifying both environmental services and the environmental issues service operations in general face. Figure 4.2a shows the service process matrix with several examples of environmental services, while Figure 4.2b shows it with several examples of environmental issues for services operations in general.

Environmental Services

The main product of environmental services alters the environmental performance of another company. As shown in Figure 4.2a, these sorts of services are represented in every quadrant of the service process matrix. Some of these services are fairly obvious; others are highly innovative.

Professional environmental services provide customized environmental products to clients using labor-intensive processes. Such services include environmental consultants and architects.

Boston Consulting Group (BCG), as a member of the World Business Council for Sustainable Development (WBCSD), undertook projects, several pro bono, with significant environmental implications. For example, BCG developed a five-year strategic plan for the World Wildlife Fund and developed a comprehensive environmental plan for eastern Germany.

PriceWaterhouseCoopers, another member of WBCSD, offers a wide range of environmental services. Their services range from tactical issues (e.g., raw materials'

FIGURE 4.2a: *Example Environmental Services*

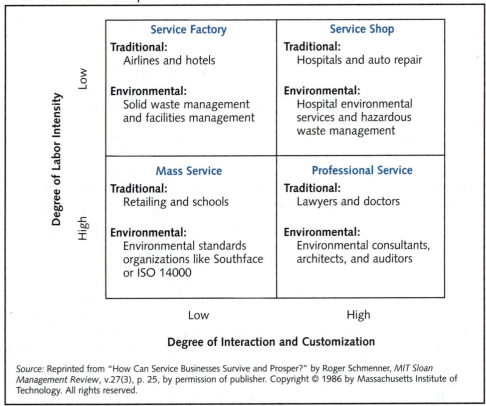

FIGURE 4.2b: *Example Environmental Issues for Service*

	Degree of Interaction and Customization	
Degree of Labor Intensity (Low → High)	**Service Factory** **Airlines:** Solid waste from cabin service, "blue water," fuel use, engine emissions, hazardous chemicals from aircraft maintenance **Hotels:** Solid waste from restaurant and room operations, energy use from lighting and climate control, water use from laundry	**Service Shop** **Hospitals:** Solid waste from rooms, biohazards, energy uses from lighting and climate control, water use from laundry, cleaning chemicals **Auto Repair Shops:** Hazardous chemicals to clean parts, waste oil, solid waste of replaced parts, hazardous chemical-soaked rags
	Mass Service **Retailing Operations:** Fuel and emissions from product distribution, urban sprawl from location decisions, solid waste from packaging **Schools:** Energy use from lighting and climate control, food waste, hazardous cleaning products, paper use from copiers, and printing	**Professional Service** **Consultants:** Fuel and emissions from travel, paper use, carbon dioxide emitted during client meetings **Dentists:** Biohazard waste, toner cartridges, paper, and other office waste
	Low	High

Degree of Interaction and Customization

Source: Reprinted from "How Can Service Businesses Survive and Prosper?" by Roger Schmenner, *MIT Sloan Management Review*, v.27(3), p. 25, by permission of publisher. Copyright © 1986 by Massachusetts Institute of Technology. All rights reserved.

use and waste disposal) to strategic issues (e.g., developing sustainable product strategies) to global issues (e.g., strategic advice related to global climate change and the "Kyoto Protocol," an international environmental agreement regarding global warming).

In addition to consultants, architects and builders offer important environmental services. Not surprisingly, the environmental performance of a building is primarily determined by decisions made in the design of the building. The U.S. Green Building Council developed the Leadership in Energy and Environmental Design (LEED™) program, which sets guidelines for designing and constructing environmentally friendly buildings. LEED emphasizes five design areas: (1) building site selection and erosion control, (2) water efficiency, (3) energy and atmosphere, (4) materials and resources, and (5) indoor environmental quality. Currently, 83 buildings in the United States are LEED-certified, but the standards are quickly gaining acceptance. Emory University, for example, is in the process of constructing three different buildings to the LEED standard. Estimates suggest that the operations of buildings constructed to this standard generally cost about half of those for non-LEED buildings (as low as $0.60 per square foot versus $1.50 per square foot). Productivity is also affected by building to this standard because it addresses indoor environmental quality and natural lighting. West Bend Mutual Insurance Company experienced a 16% increase in productivity when it moved into a LEED-certified building. Another environmental building design standard exists for residential buildings. An Earthcraft House™ must meet a similar set of requirements that LEED commercial buildings meet, and delivers similar cost savings. Southface Energy Institute designs and manages the Earthcraft House standards.

Environmental service shops also provide customized environmental services, but use processes with significantly lower labor intensity. Environmental service shops include the environmental services division in hospitals and hazardous waste management companies such as Perma-Fix. Massachusetts General Hospital's Environmental Services Department, for example, is responsible for services ranging from routine cleaning that frequently requires hazardous chemicals, to disposal of medical waste including sharps (e.g., needles) and chemotherapy waste, to ultrasonic cleaning of instruments and other objects. Another example of an environmental service shop is a company that provides chemical management. Interface-LLC is a relatively small chemical management company in Atlanta, Georgia, that does much more than just sell chemicals to the airline industry. Interface-LLC is an important business partner for Delta Air Lines, Northwest, and Comair because of the additional, environmentally oriented, value-added services it provides, such as compliance reporting data management and hazardous chemical inventory management. The case at the end of the chapter explores the relationship between Delta and Interface-LLC in greater detail.

Environmental service factories offer a fairly standard environmental service using processes with significant capital intensity (i.e., lower labor intensity). Environmental service factories often perform relatively low value-adding hygiene services like solid waste management or industrial site management. Even so, companies like the creatively named waste management company Waste Management can generate significant environmental opportunities. In December 2000, four Waste Management facilities were recognized by the EPA for innovative environmental programs such as using compressed natural gas as fuel for refuse trucks, a wetlands conservation program, and landfill gas recovery projects. Landfill gas, composed of about 50% methane and 50% carbon dioxide, is produced when organic waste decomposes in the absence of oxygen. The EPA estimates that about 6,000 landfills in the United States are currently producing methane, making it the largest source of human-made methane emissions in the country. Landfill gas poses an environmental risk, smells bad, and can blow up. It can seep underground, potentially onto adjoining property, and be ignited by things like furnace pilot lights.

Contracting for services provided by environmental service factories is risky though. Because of "joint and several liability" associated with some environmental legislation, a company that chooses its waste management provider poorly may face noncompliance penalties for things that happened after the waste leaves its facility. A manufacturer of high-end office furniture, located in North Carolina, was named a potentially responsible party for one of the top 100 Superfund sites in the country. The company is strictly liable for the 19 drums they disposed of during three years of doing business with a waste disposal contractor. Even in instances in which the company is not liable in a legal sense, public perception can hold a company liable for the actions of its contracted service providers. In the wake of the September 11th attacks, much of the public held the airlines responsible for the security breakdowns even though that responsibility had been outsourced.

Environmental mass services offer environmental services with little customization but with significant labor intensity. These services come in two types: physical services and informational services. Examples of physical environmental mass services include cabin cleaning and other ramp services for the airlines, residential pest control, and residential landscaping services. ServiceMaster Aviation Services group conducts cabin cleaning, lavatory servicing (i.e., blue water service), aircraft exterior cleaning, and maintenance for ground service equipment like trucks and baggage carts. TruGreen Chemlawn and Terminix, both ServiceMaster companies, use hazardous chemicals to deliver their relatively standard service to homeowners.

Informational environmental mass services generate environmental information content that other companies use, such as standards for evaluating environmental performance. Two such groups are CERES (the Coalition for Environmentally Responsible Economies) and Southface Energy Institute. The CERES Principles are a set of environmentally oriented practices that companies commit to as guiding business principles (see Table 4.2). American Airlines, Coca-Cola, Northeast Utilities, General Motors, and Wainright Bank are just a few of the companies that subscribe to the CERES Principles. A later section of this chapter will explore how companies use the CERES Principles in practice.

Services and Their Environmental Impacts

In addition to services that influence the environmental performance of other companies, many services create significant environmental impacts of their own. Many of these environmental impacts arise from activities behind the line of visibility that separates the back office from the front office. Even in those instances where customer contact determines the environmental direction a service firm takes, many of the environmental issues are still back-office issues. For example, many hotels now offer guests the choice to not have sheets and towels changed every day, which saves water, saves electricity, and reduces the amount of residual laundry soap discharged into the sewer system. Even though this decision belongs to the customer (i.e., high customer contact), its benefits are generated by changes in back-office behavior (i.e., laundry services). This same sort of discussion holds for ski resorts, restaurants, hospitals, and virtually all other services.

Professional services, including doctors, lawyers, and consultants, generate significant waste. Medical waste from dentists and doctors includes soiled or blood-soaked bandages, culture dishes and other glassware, used surgical gloves, used surgical instruments, needles, cultures, swabs used to inoculate cultures, and removed body organs. To give you a sense of the magnitude of this issue, the EPA estimates that more than 1 billion syringes and lancets are used annually in the United States just for the treatment of diabetes. In addition, virtually every professional service generates significant office waste, such as discarded paper and toner cartridges.

TABLE 4.2: *The CERES Principles*

• Protection of the biosphere	• Environmental restoration
• Sustainable use of natural resources	• Informing the public
• Reduction and disposal of wastes	• Management commitment
• Energy conservation	• Audits and reports
• Risk reduction	
• Safe products and services	*Source:* Adapted from the CERES Web site at http://www.ceres.org.

Environmental issues for service shops overlap somewhat with those of professional services. For example, hospitals generate many of the same waste streams as doctors and dentists. The American Medical Association estimates that hospitals generate approximately 2 pounds of infectious waste per patient per day. For a hospital like Mass General, with its 853 beds at about a 75% occupancy rate, it means 1,284 pounds of hazardous medical waste every day, or 468,660 pounds per year at this one hospital, not counting waste generated by outpatient services.

Another example of a service shop is an automotive repair shop. These operations work with refrigerants and hazardous cleaners. They also must dispose of worn-out parts, used motor oil, used antifreeze, and other hazardous wastes. Much used motor oil is disposed of improperly. In fact, 200 million gallons of used oil nationwide—20 times the oil that was lost in the *Exxon Valdez* spill—is improperly disposed of each year, nearly all by do-it-yourselfers. Moreover, 2 gallons of recovered motor oil delivers sufficient electricity to power an average American household for nearly a full day.

Service factories face an equally challenging set of environmental issues. Some of these environmental issues overlap with service shops. For example, transportation-oriented services deal with many of the same issues as automotive repair shops in the general maintenance and operation of their own fleet. UPS, for example, maintains a fleet of more than 80,000 motor vehicles that travel more than 2 billion miles per year. If it changes the oil every 2,500 miles, it means approximately 800,000 oil changes a year. These transportation-oriented services also deal with fuel use issues. In 2003, Delta consumed 2.37 billion gallons of fuel at an average cost of 81.78¢ per gallon, for a total fuel cost of more than $1.93 billion.

Cruise lines, hotels, and resorts present other examples of service factories with significant environmental impact. Many resorts and most cruises operate in environmentally sensitive areas, so their environmental impact is magnified. For example, Holland America Line and Royal Caribbean together paid nearly $10 million in fines for dumping "black water" and "gray water" overboard in Alaska's fjords. According to *The Economist*, only 1 in 80 black water samples (i.e., treated sewage) met federal standards. *The Economist* also reports that some gray water samples (from showers, dishwashers, and laundries) contained 50,000 times more fecal coliform than accepted standards (May 17, 2001).

Mass services share some environmental characteristics with service factories, particularly the transportation-intensive mass services such as retail operations with delivery models. Webvan, the now-defunct grocery delivery company, demonstrates quite a few of the environmental issues these companies face. Webvan's business model allowed customers to pick delivery times, forcing the company into inefficient routings. Unlike UPS, it could not optimize delivery routes. Switching to home delivery significantly increased both the volume of emissions generated (by at least a factor of 25) and of fuel consumed (by more than 50%, see Table 4.3). As another example of environmental issues at a mass service, consider Emory University. Emory recycles more than 125 tons of white paper and 100 tons of cardboard every year. In addition, 20,000 cars come to Emory's campus every day, all of which affect land use (through the 13,000 parking spaces on campus), fuel use, and air emissions.

Wal-Mart changed the design of their new facilities to include an innovative skylight/dimming system to reduce energy usage. This system dims the lights in the facility as more natural light comes through the skylight. The system can even turn off the lights on brighter days. Wal-Mart estimates that the "daylighting system" reduced electricity use by 250 million kilowatt hours per year, enough energy to power about

TABLE 4.3:   *Environmental Impacts of Webvan's Delivery Model*

Issue	Supermarket	Webvan	Difference
Number of households	10,000	10,000	0
Average round trip of complete route (miles)	5	62	+57
Number of trips per month	8	4	−4 trips
Percent of route dedicated to groceries	25%	100%	+75%
Grocery miles driven per month	100,000	89,067	−10,933
Fuel consumed (gallons)	3,994	6,177	+2,183
Carbon monoxide emission (grams)	340,000	10,022,300	+9,682,300
NOx emissions (grams)	40,000	3,879,600	+3,839,600
Particulate matter emissions (grams)	8,000	387,960	+379,960

Source: Galea and Walton. 2002. "Is E-commerce Sustainable? An Analysis of Webvan."

23,000 homes each year. Wal-Mart is also retrofitting the lighting in its stores with low-mercury fluorescent lights with electronic ballasts (the "starters" for fluorescent bulbs). They estimate that a retrofitted store saves 15% to 20% of its energy load.

ENVIRONMENTAL STRATEGIES FOR SERVICE OPERATIONS

The preceding discussion provides a framework for thinking about services and the environment. But a critical question remains unanswered: What strategies are available for service companies that want to improve their business performance by improving their environmental performance? These strategies are not service-specific; manufacturing companies could pursue similar initiatives. These initiatives can be broadly classified as either process- or product-focused. Process focused environmental strategies include process improvements, process certification, and implementing e-commerce models and methods. Product focused environmental strategies include redesigning the service offering, offering new value-added services, and "dematerializing" the product.

Process Opportunities

Process Improvement

Services can use any of the currently popular process improvement methodologies to improve their environmental performance. For example, any company that uses Total Quality Management (TQM) can easily adopt Total Quality Environmental Management (TQEM). Although they share many of the same characteristics, TQEM focuses the improvement effort on environmental performance. Companies adopting a Six Sigma approach to quality can extend that approach to include Six Sigma environmental management. Both TQEM and Six Sigma environmental management impose requirements of structured thinking, management by fact through data analysis, and systematic business process improvement.

Process Certification

Service companies can take three different approaches to process certification: self-certification, ISO 14000 certification, or subscribing to environmentally oriented standards, like the CERES Principles. Self-certification allows an individual company to audit its own and its suppliers' environmental performance. Delta Air Lines, like many companies, publishes an annual environmental report describing the results of its self-certification. The advantage of self-certification is that it is relatively inexpensive. The obvious disadvantage is that no independent third party examines the operations, data, and results.

Some companies choose to extend certification requirements to their suppliers. Disney, for example, maintains a "Code of Conduct for Manufacturers" that dictates business practices, social performance, and environmental performance requirements that all Disney suppliers must follow. The Code requires that all suppliers meet at least a minimum standard of compliance with all relevant environmental laws and regulations. The Code also allows Disney or "its designated agents" to monitor any supplier's process to confirm compliance to the Code. (See Disney's Web site for more details about the Code at http://www.disney.com.)

The most common third-party environmental certification is ISO 14000. ISO 14000 is a standard of the International Organization for Standardization, the same group that established ISO 9000. ISO 14000 requires companies to document the way they manage environmental issues. The standard looks at six major areas: environmental management systems, environmental auditing investigations, environmental labels and declarations, environmental performance evaluation, life cycle assessment, and terms and definitions. Companies that choose to pursue ISO 14000 document their processes in these six areas and in most cases hire an independent auditor to evaluate their performance relative to the documented processes.

Similar to ISO 9000, the benefits from becoming ISO 14000 certified vary widely depending on the company's commitment to the ideals of the standard, but companies can achieve significant results from getting certified. For example, the Saunders Hotel Group, owners and operators of two upscale hotels in Boston, earned ISO 14000 certification as part of their SHINE program (Saunders Hotels Initiatives to Nurture the Environment). Through SHINE, the company annually saves 4 million gallons of drinking water, eliminates 109 tons of trash, and saves 225,000 kilowatt hours of electricity, and realizes the associated financial benefits of such changes.

The most common environmentally oriented standard is the CERES Principles. Unlike ISO 14000, which does not define what should be considered appropriate environmental business practices, the CERES Principles describe a fairly detailed set of activities to which a company must commit, including adherence to "generally accepted environmental audit procedures." The standards provide a sort of seal of approval to companies that subscribe to the Principles. In subscribing to the Principles, the company publicly takes a pledge that affirms their "belief that corporations have a responsibility for the environment, and must conduct all aspects of their business as responsible stewards of the environment by operating in a manner that protects the Earth." The biggest complaint leveled at the CERES Principles is its extensive reporting and auditing requirements. Several service companies claim that the work required to translate their internal environmental reports into a format acceptable under the CERES Principles requires at least one new full-time employee. In fact, in the face of these reporting requirements, several companies agreed to follow all the principles except the reporting requirement.

E-Commerce

Service companies can use e-commerce to improve the environmental performance of their processes. The companies can migrate processes that are traditionally paper-based to an e-commerce model, use e-commerce to refine existing processes, or use e-commerce to develop new processes.

Most airlines and financial service companies transferred their traditionally paper-based processes to an e-commerce model that includes e-tickets and online statements. Most U.S. domestic tickets issued now are e-tickets. US Airways issues more than 90% of their tickets electronically, while American has quit issuing paper tickets altogether for directly booked domestic travel. Not only do e-tickets reduce paper use (which obviously reduces the airline's costs), but e-tickets also improve customer satisfaction. Surveys conducted by United Airlines suggest that 90% of customers using e-tickets prefer them to paper tickets.

E-commerce presents many opportunities to improve existing processes. As the case at the end of the chapter shows, the data transmission capabilities embodied in e-commerce played a prominent role in the process automation between Delta Air Lines and Interface-LLC. In many instances, electronically exchanged purchase orders enabled both trading partners to use the more timely and accurate information to reduce inventory and delivery cycle time.

The opportunity is unlimited for companies able to figure out how to use e-commerce to develop new processes that impact environmental performance. One example of such an opportunity is reverse logistics services. Most supply chains are designed to move materials and information forward, toward the end customer. Without an infrastructure in place to move failed products back for disposition, those products are usually thrown away. Yet, disposition could include returning the product to the manufacturer for rework, selling the product to a liquidator, or selling the various components through different channels. Each of these other disposition methods extracts residual value from the product for the company and decreases the amount of material going to the landfill. In the electronics and consumer products industry, a start-up company called 180Commerce developed a Returns Management Platform™, which provides the information infrastructure that allows manufacturing companies to offload the reverse logistics process to 180Commerce as their preferred service provider.

Product Opportunities

Product Redesign

In manufacturing, even though the design phase represents less than 10% of the total cost of a product over its lifetime, the decisions made in design commit the company to more than 80% of those lifetime costs. For example, the decision in design to use screws to attach two pieces of wood instead of glue affects issues such as the cost of raw materials, the type of tools and equipment needed, labor productivity, and types of product quality failures. The same holds true for services; the decision to design a high-contact service commits the company to a different set of costs than a low-contact service would entail. Changing the service design is, therefore, a high-impact way to improve the environmental performance of a service.

Design for the Environment (DFE) provides one approach to service process design/redesign to improve environmental performance. DFE's stated goal includes designing products and services with a favorable environmental footprint. For example, BMW designs its cars to be easily disassembled because of regulations in Europe that require car companies to take back their vehicles for disposition (disassembly, metal and component recycling, and shredding of the remaining automotive hulk).

One important tool often used as a part of DFE is lifecycle analysis (LCA). In this context, lifecycles mean something different from the stages of introduction, growth, maturity, and decline as studied in marketing classes. Instead, the lifecycle of a product focuses on an individual unit of a product from the moment it first begins to come into existence until when it reaches its final disposition. Table 4.4 shows some dimensions of a lifecycle analysis comparison of the decision of kegs or cans.

TABLE 4.4: *A Lifecycle Analysis of Kegs Versus Cans*

Kegs	Cans
Aluminum to make keg	Aluminum to make can
Soap and water used to clean keg before each refill	Packaging the cans come in (cases and plastic rings)
Transportation to return keg	Transportation to recycle cans
Plastic cups used	Additional ice needed to keep cans cold
Materials required to make pump	Number of cans needed to equal the volume of a keg

One essential question that comes up during lifecycle analysis is "How far back should I go?" When describing the environmental impacts of the kegs, do you need to include the energy used to mine the bauxite? Should it include scrap and waste generated in the smelting process? Questions like these are important because they lead the analyst to a deeper understanding of the full implications of a product or service. However, LCA risks falling into "analysis paralysis" because the method allows the analyst to determine how far back to go. In the end the analyst must strike a balance between completeness and usability.

Value-Added Services

A second way service companies can influence environmental outcomes is to redesign their service offerings to include value-added services along environmental dimensions. For example, UPS's Service Parts Logistics (UPS SPL) group manages critical repair component distribution systems for telecommunication and computer companies. They provide an extensive network of distribution centers and transportation carriers that allows them to stock components needed to repair their customers' electronic products and to deliver these critical parts as quickly as within one hour.

Interface-LLC is another service company that offers extensive value-added services. They provide the airline industry with inventory tracking and maintenance, compliance reporting data management, bar coding and e-commerce-oriented data transmission and management, and other valuable services.

Dematerialize

Companies can also improve their environmental performance by dematerializing their products. This strategy presents some challenges for services because their "products" are already intangible, but it is worth describing because it allows manufacturing companies to behave much more like service companies.

In many instances, consumers don't want a product; they want the functionality the product can provide. A creative company can find ways to decouple the functionality from the form of the product. For example, DuPont is best known as a manufacturer of chemicals. But in Europe, DuPont dematerialized one of their products, paint for auto manufacturing. When a company makes and sells paint, their goals revolve around making and selling more paint. But paint is generally a hazardous product. Most formulations of paint require solvents, which are volatile organic compounds. Consider then that if the company sells Ford the service of painting cars, it is now motivated to meet the painting quality requirements set by Ford while using as little paint as possible. Dematerializing the product removes the "moral hazard" associated with wanting to sell more of a hazardous product.

Summary

This chapter demonstrated the importance of the environment as a business issue, one that matters to both manufacturing and service companies. Even though most attention focuses on manufacturing companies, the dominance of services in the economies of most developed countries suggests that environmental management in services warrants more attention. By considering the location of a company in the service process matrix, one gains insight into the type of environmental issues a service company might face. The rewards for understanding how to manage environmental issues in services can be significant because environmental excellence can be used as a driver for company financial success. Services affect the environment directly as well as the environmental performance of other companies. Hence, service companies can embark on both process and product changes to improve their environmental performance. Methods available to improve environmental performance range from self-certification of business processes to implementing e-commerce models and dematerializing the product.

Review Questions

1. Describe the negative financial impacts that service companies face for failing to properly manage environmental performance. What specific financial impacts are services more likely to experience than manufacturing companies?
2. Aside from those listed in the chapter, describe an environmental service in each quadrant of the service process matrix. Name a company as an example of each service.
3. Describe the environmental impacts of a service company in each quadrant of the service process matrix.
4. Select a service offering and conduct a lifecycle analysis of the offering. How far back did you choose to go? Why?
5. Can video conferencing "dematerialize" business travel? Why or why not?

Selected Bibliography

Anonymous. 1994. The Challenge of Going Green, *Harvard Business Review*, 73(4), 37–50.

Carson, R. 1962. *Silent Spring*. Houghton Mifflin, Boston.

The Economist. 2001. The Things They Leave Behind. *The Economist* (May 17).

Elkington, J. 1997. *Cannibals with Forks: The Triple Bottom Line of 21st Century Business*. Capstone Publishing, Oxford, England.

Foster, S., Sampson, S., and S. Dunn. 2000. The Impact of Customer Contact on Environmental Initiatives for Service Firms. *International Journal of Operations and Production Management*, 20(2), 187–203.

Galea, C., and S. Walton. 2002. *Is E-Commerce Sustainable? An Analysis of Webvan. In Ecology of the New Economy: Sustainable Transformation of Global Information, Communication, and Electronics Industries*. Greenleaf Publishing, Sheffield, UK.

Hart, S. 1997. Beyond Greening: Strategies for a Sustainable World. *Harvard Business Review*, 75(1), 66–76.

Klassen, R., and C. McLaughlin. 1996. The Impact of Environmental Management on Firm Performance. *Management Science*, 42(8), 199–214.

Magretta, J. 1997. Growth Through Global Sustainability: An Interview with Monsanto's CEO, Robert Shapiro. *Harvard Business Review*, 75(1), 78–89.

Porter, M., and C. van der Linde. 1995. Green and Competitive. *Harvard Business Review*, 73(5), 120–134.

Reinhardt, F. L. 1999. Bringing the Environment Down to Earth. *Harvard Business Review*, 77(4), 149–158.

Walley, N., and B. Whitehead. 1994. It's Not Easy Being Green. *Harvard Business Review*, 72(3), 46–52.

Chemical Management at Delta Air Lines

What would happen if a company bought chemicals "the same way we bought widgets," as one Delta Air Lines manager put it? In Delta's case, you end up with no centralized way to reconcile purchased amounts, usage, air emissions, and disposal amounts. And you risk fines in excess of $1 million from the Georgia Environmental Protection Division (EPD). Prior to implementing an innovative chemical management program with Interface-LLC, chemical management at Delta meant each group in the company that used chemicals could buy them when they needed them at the lowest unit cost they could find. One example of what happens under this sort of purchasing policy was that acetone (a solvent used to clean parts during aircraft maintenance and repair) was purchased in 55-gallon drums even though the mechanic needed only a few ounces at a time. The time required for a mechanic to transfer the acetone into smaller containers was never considered as a cost of using the chemicals.

Other chemicals approved for use on aircraft have shelf lives of between 6 and 24 months, often less time than the chemicals were held in inventory. Chemicals not used by their expiration date had to be disposed of as hazardous waste. Tracking the chemicals purchased and used was difficult and extremely labor intensive. These and other critical factors were not included in Delta's purchasing decisions. This case looks at what Delta did to design and implement a chemical management system that avoided costs of nearly $1 million from reduced inventories, lowered insurance premiums, and fewer instances of expired shelf life materials in fiscal years 1996 and 1997, and continues to pay off (with projected savings of $500,000 per year).

From 1994 to 1997, Delta Air Lines undertook a reengineering effort they dubbed "7.5." Like so many efforts of this type, 7.5 was designed to reduce Delta's cost measure (cost per available seat mile, or CASM) from 10.8 cents to 7.5 cents. To meet this goal, Delta reduced head count through early retirement and refocused on core businesses by outsourcing ancillary services. In 1994, the Georgia Environmental Protection Agency alleged that Delta's chemical management system was inadequate and levied a fine of more than $1 million on Delta. The EPD cited the chemical management system's weaknesses in tracking, managing, and reporting chemical usage and disposition in Delta's Technical Operations center at Hartsfield International Airport in Atlanta. These two seemingly unrelated events of 7.5 and the EPD fine set the stage for Delta's innovative response: They devised a new way to manage chemicals that improved operational performance, reduced chemical usage, and met all reporting requirements from the EPD.

Prior to 1995, integrated chemical management did not exist at Delta. For example, systems were in place for chemical purchasing but these systems were not integrated with point of use monitoring. This limitation prevented individual managers from reconciling chemicals purchased and used with chemicals disposed of. Myles

CASE STUDY

Craig, who started working at Delta while he was in college and took a full-time position in 1980, had some ideas about how this situation might be changed but felt like he needed more information. Craig decided to benchmark against other companies, intentionally avoiding other air carriers. He visited Saturn Automotive, GE Engines, Ford Motor Company, General Motors, and Boeing to understand the different methods these companies were applying to chemical management. Craig used the best attributes of each system as the basis for the system he designed at Delta.

Delta set three main goals for the chemical management system Craig was developing: (1) to manage chemicals better than they currently did, (2) to capture all required and relevant data concerning chemical use, and (3) to accomplish these tasks at a lower cost. These goals focused internal attention on the critical issues of service levels, systems performance, and cost. It became clear that Delta needed a more integrated chemical management system.

Part of this integrated view was to move from making purchasing decisions based on unit cost to making these decisions on total cost of ownership. "Total cost of ownership" is the idea that a company pays more than just the per-unit purchase price when it buys materials and supplies. Total cost of ownership would include costs of procurement, handling, warehousing, environmental fees, late deliveries, poor quality, incomplete deliveries, inventory costs, and so on. Table 4.5 shows some of the total cost components Delta considered when redesigning the chemical management program.

Chemicals at Delta

In 1994, chemical management at Delta was a complex task because of the sheer scale of operations, the number of suppliers they dealt with, and the decentralized use of chemicals bought through a centralized purchasing process. To provide a sense of the scale, Table 4.6 shows the four main ground-based activities and example waste streams and chemicals used in each activity. Managing chemicals was complex in part because it was difficult to monitor and manage what was in these waste streams. The addition of the wrong thing into a waste stream could make an otherwise harmless waste stream hazardous, which meant additional disposal costs.

Delta spends between $15 and $16 million on chemicals annually, including $1.8 million per year for cabin cleaning chemicals like window cleaner and gum remover. They buy approximately 1,500 different stock-keeping units (SKUs), 1,000 of which are routine stock items, and 500 are rare use or special order items, ranging from epoxies and baking soda to plasma-spray compounds for refinishing specialty aircraft components. Per-unit costs range from $0.67 for a container of cleaner to about $10,000 for a three-pound container of brazing powder, used for the metal build up on landing gear components. Thirty percent of these SKUs have a limited shelf life, ranging from 6 to 24 months. Upon expiration, most of these products become hazardous waste. The materials' cost for expired chemicals alone

CASE STUDY

TABLE 4.5: *Example Total Cost of Ownership Components*

Component	Examples
Quality	Labor cost of conducting incoming materials inspection, return of out-of-date chemicals, replacement of defects not detected until later in the maintenance process
Delivery	Process disruptions from not having the right chemical to degrease a part during maintenance
Inventory	Storage space required to stock chemicals, insurance costs for holding significant quantities of hazardous chemicals, labor cost to stock chemicals
Compliance	Record-keeping and reporting requirements, potential EPA fines for failure of various noncompliance opportunities
Material cost	Unit price for chemical material purchase
Inventory carrying cost	Generally 11% (Interface-LLC) to 18.5% (Delta) of unit price; cost to handle, label, and shelve material until it is requested
Labor cost	Cost of Delta mechanic to transfer contents of larger container to smaller container, relabeling, etc. to meet application need and OSHA Employee-Right-to-Know or HAZCOM requirements
Safety/risk cost	Assigned costs (relative to potential for occupational exposure down the road, immediate risk to Delta property, as well as future liability for any cleanups from mishandling/mismanagement) associated with handling and exposure to chemicals based on health and flammability rating as well as studied number of transfers
Disposal cost	Extra costs associated with disposal of expired unused material

was about $250,000 in 1996. All of the chemicals bought were stored in general use at the Technical Operations Center in Atlanta, which required that significant space be set aside for inventory.

Prior to implementing the chemical management program, Delta's chemical vendor database included 350 different suppliers. Many of the chemicals could be sourced through distributors, which would reduce the number of suppliers Delta needed to manage. However, the main result of this supply base reduction would be to add another layer of administration that had to be paid for their services. For this reason, Delta chose to buy many chemicals from the manufacturer, which bypassed intermediaries, but kept the vendor base large.

Decentralized usage of chemicals caused the centralized chemical buying process to work poorly. Automotive mechanics working on ground service equipment, for example, often found it was easier to make a trip to a local hardware store

CASE STUDY

TABLE 4.6:   *Waste Streams at Delta Air Lines*

Activity	Description	Waste Streams	Chemicals
Airport Customer Service (ACS)	Provides baggage handling, cabin cleaning, security	Garbage and trash from cabin services, "blue water" from lavatories	Deicing chemicals, cabin cleaning chemicals like gum remover and window cleaner
Line Maintenance	Conduct repairs to aircraft on the ramp	Replaced parts, tires, oil, and hydraulic fluid	Solvents like acetone, degreasers, and engine oils, paint, primer, sealant, hydraulic fluid
Hangar Maintenance	Conduct major repairs, maintenance, and overhauls	Solvents, oils, paints, plating shop waste, paint strippers	Solvents and cleaners like acetone and methyl ethyl ketone engine oils, paint, primer, sealant, hydraulic fluid
Ground Service Equipment	Provide and maintain the vehicles and equipment for ACS	Solvents, oils, paints, paint strippers	Solvents like acetone, degreasers, and engine oil

to buy more carburetor, glass, or upholstery cleaners than it was to process a purchase order, resulting in many "maverick buys" of chemicals and making it difficult for a manager to track chemical use, quantities, and locations throughout the maintenance facility. It also meant that Delta lost its leverage as a large buyer. As one manager put it, "Maverick buying is like stepping over a dollar to save a nickel."

The regulatory requirements for holding large quantities of chemicals were significant. For example, the Community Right to Know Act set a threshold of 10,000 pounds of hazardous chemicals; any facility that purchased or stored more than that had to report to the EPA. The Occupational Safety and Health Administration required that Materials Safety Data Sheets be available for any hazardous material the employees used. The Clean Air Act demanded that companies track and report on emissions from certain chemicals used in their operations. Delta's large chemical inventory required that they comply with these and other regulatory requirements, each with its own set of data collection and reporting requirements.

A New Way to Manage Chemicals

Carroll Rushing, a long-time supplier to Delta, approached Craig with a way to completely change the chemical management system. Craig worked with Rushing to create a new company, Interface-LLC. According to the original agreement, reached in late 1995, Interface-LLC would purchase Delta's inventory of

CASE STUDY

chemicals and move them off-site to a nearby location owned by Interface-LLC. Interface-LLC would then act as the "gatekeeper" of chemicals and sell the chemicals back to Delta using Delta's existing information infrastructure along with new environmental chemical tracking software developed for Delta and implemented by Interface-LLC. Although the process sounds inefficient, it turned out to be a great start to a successful program. Moving the chemicals out of Delta's stores freed up 30,000 square feet of space to be used for maintenance in one of its buildings at the Technical Operations Center, at a value of $30 per square foot. It also immediately solved Delta's conflicting desires to simplify the supplier base and minimize intermediaries in transactions. Delta suddenly went from 350 suppliers to one.

As part of the 1995 agreement, Interface-LLC absorbed all of Delta's existing supplier-negotiated contracts. Interface-LLC also agreed to deliver all routine orders in three hours, and all expedited deliveries in two hours. They also agreed to a 95% fill rate (fill rate is the proportion of orders a company receives that can be met with inventory on hand). Interface-LLC opened a small distribution center a mile and a half from Delta's Technical Operations Center in Atlanta. Delta transmitted orders to Interface-LLC through Delta's existing requisition system (a database management system), fax, Electronic Data Interchange, or a Web-based electronic catalog.

Implementation of the system took about six months of bumps and headaches to debug. One unexpected issue that arose was the resistance within Delta to give up responsibility for the tasks of chemical purchasing and management. Continued operational successes eventually won over the skeptics by clearly demonstrating the value that could be gained by the new program. According to Craig, "We overcame their concerns by improving upon service levels. We lowered costs and improved performance. Bottom line, it was a culture change for Delta to handle chemicals in a modern way."

These operational improvements, though, were only a part of the total benefit Interface-LLC was able to generate for Delta. Interface-LLC offered other value-added services including streamlining MSDS management, bar coding and tracking chemicals delivered to shops throughout the operation, development of an "approved chemical" list, and negotiating with chemical manufacturers. Interface-LLC also extended the scope of the chemical management program to include sourcing safety products. Because the structure of the contract allows for joint cost savings, Interface-LLC is motivated to continue to find innovative ways to save Delta money. For example, when grease was bought in 5-gallon buckets, 35% of the grease ended up as waste. Interface-LLC was able to shift the purchase to 14 oz. tubes, finding ways to increase efficiency through better packaging.

The chemical management program also provided Interface-LLC with a new tool to win business. Interface-LLC was now able to approach other airlines and clearly demonstrate the success of their chemical management system. Interface-LLC now

CASE STUDY

services Northwest and Comair in addition to Delta. Interface-LLC is also in the process of negotiating several other chemical management contracts.

Questions:

- What strategic risks and opportunities does Delta face in entering into this relationship with Interface-LLC? What risks and opportunities does Interface-LLC face?
- What product- and process-oriented environmental strategies are available to Interface-LLC as they continue to expand their service offerings? To Delta?
- If you were in charge of the chemical management program at Delta, what changes would you make to further improve environmental performance? If you were in charge of the chemical management program at Interface-LLC, what changes would you make to further improve environmental performance?

Designing the Delivery System

The idea seems simple and obvious: The service delivery system—the equipment, facilities, type of personnel, procedures—should be designed to meet the overall corporate strategic directives. Even though it is simple and clear to state, it often proves difficult to perform in practice. Everywhere one looks one can find service firms that profess to stress one attribute but design processes to support another. Two of the examples cited in the chapters ahead include a doughnut retailer that builds a business on freshness and taste, yet decides to centralize all baking in a metropolitan area to cut costs, and a bank that advertises personal service, but all telephone calls to local branches are routed to a nationwide call center hundreds of miles away.

This section provides conceptual tools for integrating the service delivery system with the overall corporate strategy.

Chapter 5 concerns the genesis of strategic linkage to the service delivery system, the new service development process. The chapter contains both concepts and mathematical models to assist in this process.

Chapter 6 considers the management of the apparent next logical development of the service economy, the "experience" economy, wherein customers pay not merely for a transaction, but for the emotion or intensity of feeling an experience generates.

The growth of service firms that can take advantage of scale economies and the rise of electronic transmission of information in the last few decades mean a disassembling of the processes previously performed in a front office. The number of traditional service procedures that take place in geographically distant back offices where the customer is never seen continue to increase dramatically. A strategic template that guides when to decouple service functions and how to do so is contained in Chapter 7 and 8.

New Service Development

The material in this chapter prepares students to:

- Understand the new service development process.

- Choose appropriate tools for making decisions in new service design.

- Understand the different design attributes and their strategic implications.

Services are now the dominant economic sector in most modern Western economies. With trends of increasing globalization and new technologies, contemporary businesses realize that in order to survive, they must continuously develop new services and products. A *new service* is defined as an offering not previously available to customers. It can be the result of additional offerings, radical changes in the service delivery process, or incremental improvements to existing service packages or delivery processes that the customer perceives as new (Johnson et al., 2000). So, for example, the majority of Internet service activity that emerged over the last five years falls under this definition. On one end of the continuum, we see incremental additions from existing catalog companies like Lands' End that supplemented their mail-order catalog with a new Internet catalog and ordering processes. At the other end, companies like eBay developed a radical new service innovation, the online auction. In this chapter, we first give a broad overview of the actual process of new service development. Then we cover three key aspects of new service development: service innovation, service system design, and service system design tools.

NEW SERVICE DEVELOPMENT PROCESS

In the past, new service developers often did not follow the traditional new product development path, but instead developed their own ad hoc processes. They took this approach for several reasons. Due to the intangible nature of services, it is difficult to prototype and field test a new concept. Additionally, most service firms lack formal research and development departments (Gadrey et al., 1995). Even though providers are often slow to adopt formal new service development processes, the successful service providers are more likely to emulate new product development methods (Griffin, 1997). Generally, a formalized service development process consists of four key steps: design, analysis, development, and full launch (Johnson et al., 2000).

The process could be conceptualized as a sequence from design through launch or a full cycle if a continuous improvement approach is included. In actuality, the process tends to be nonlinear and iterative. Design and analysis are *planning* activities, while development and launch are *execution* activities. The design stage covers the formulation of a new service objective and strategy, idea generation and screening, and concept development and testing. The analysis stage includes business analysis and project authorization. The development stage addresses the complete service design and testing, process and system design and testing, marketing program design and testing, personnel training, service testing and pilot run, and test marketing. The launch is the full-scale launch and postlaunch review.

At the heart of the model sits the service delivery system: the people, technology, and systems that go into designing and delivering the new service. Organizations that continuously develop successful new services tend to organize their people into cross-functional teams, provide them with appropriate tools and resources for planning and execution, and develop an organizational context that facilitates the entire process so that products can be developed quickly and effectively. In the next section, we will look at how this model can contribute to new service innovations.

SERVICE INNOVATION

Lovelock (1984) first classified new services as shown in Table 5.1. In the new service development process, it is important to differentiate between the radical and incremental innovations. Radical service innovations require a different process and design approach than incremental innovations. A radical innovation is either new to the world or new to the market. Recent radical innovations include online auctions such as eBay and Priceline.com or facilitating services such as Century 21 Realty; both of these concepts bring together buyers and sellers and provide information and advice for both parties. Usually, the radical innovation is developed through some form of the new service development cycle. After the innovation is launched, its development process becomes the foundation for further incremental innovation. Firms that continuously cycle through the process steps can build service innovation competence.

Innovative service firms utilize "enablers" who facilitate the new service development cycle. These enablers reduce the development cycle time and allow service developers to design service delivery systems that meet the customer needs. For example, United Airlines made successful use of 22 cross-functional teams in the design of the Shuttle by United flights. After the Shuttle was operational, these enablers facilitated incremental improvements through periodic design/development team "huddles" (Kimes and Young, 1997).

The incremental or radical nature of the service innovation will dictate where the firm should devote resources. Incremental innovations usually involve some minor adjustment to the existing service delivery components (people, systems, and technology). Hence, fewer resources and less effort are devoted to the planning side and more devoted to the execution side of the process cycle. For example, if McDonald's wants to offer a new sandwich, the delivery system designers would consider not only how the new item would be made in the kitchen, but the assembly technique, cooking equipment, additional labor and inventory requirements, marketing plan, and information system adjustments for inventory and pricing as well.

Radical service innovations imply increased risk and resource investments. Here a large amount of planning is needed to flesh out the idea along with committing substantial resources to the new service development process. Similarly, the execution side must be equally supported with significant effort and resources. Consider the planning

TABLE 5.1: *New Services*

New Service Category	Description	Example
Radical Innovations		
Major innovations	New service for markets as yet undefined; innovations usually driven by information and computer-based technologies	Online auctions such as eBay and Priceline.com; facilitating services such as Edward Jones Financial
Start-up business	New services in a market that is already served by existing services	Travelocity, Internet travel planning, allows automated travel agency service
New services for a market presently served	New service offerings to existing customer of an organization (although the services may be available from other companies)	Free-standing bank branches or kiosks in supermarkets or other retail establishments
Incremental Innovations		
Service line extension	Augmentations of the existing service line such as adding new menu items, new routes, and new courses	Southwest Airlines adding Fresno as a new destination; McDonald's adding a new sandwich
Service improvement	Changes in features of services that currently are being offered	Delta Airlines' and British Airlines' use of ATM-like kiosks to distribute boarding passes to passengers
Style changes	The most common of all "new services"; modest forms of visible changes that affect customer perceptions, emotions, and attitudes, on-site with style changes that do not change the service fundamentally, only its appearance	Funeral homes that offer abbreviated ceremonies that celebrate life instead of mourning death, on-site full-service flower shops, and a brighter appearance

involved with eBay online auction activities and the flawless execution that was required when the product was launched. With issues of trust, product and money exchange, and valid and timely site information, eBay required substantial efforts and investment in all aspects of the process cycle to successfully launch the radical new service concept.

SERVICE SYSTEM DESIGN

The initial part of the planning cycle tackles the development of a service concept and operating strategy (see Chapter 2 for in-depth discussion of strategic service vision). Once these elements are formulated, the next stage covers decisions related to the service process or delivery system design to produce the service concept. Good service product and process design provides the key to success for a company. Surprisingly, even the smallest service design detail can affect the bottom line as shown in Table 5.2. Even an interaction detail such as wait-staff introducing themselves increased their tips by a whopping 53%.

All service design factors should relate to the service strategy and concept. Generally, the key factors include location, facility layout, product design, scheduling, worker skills, quality control and measures, time standards, demand/capacity planning, industrialization level, standardization of service offering, customer contact level, front-line personnel discretion, sales opportunity, and customer participation.

TABLE 5.2: *Summary of Study on Employee Actions and Restaurant Tipping*

Tip-Enhancing Action	Average Tip		Percentage Increase in Tip
	Control Without Treatment	Experimental With Treatment	
Introducing self by name	15%	23%	53%
Squatting next to table:			
• Waiter	15%	18%	20%
• Waitress	12%	15%	25%
Smiling	$0.20	$0.48	140%
Wearing a flower in hair	$1.50	$1.75	17%
Entertaining customer			
• Tell a joke	16%	19%	40%
• Give a puzzle	23%	22%	18%
Suggestive selling	$1.25	$1.53	23%
Repeat order to customer	1.36 DG	2.73 DG	100%
Touching customer			
• Study 1	12%	17%	42%
• Study 2	11%	14%	27%
• Study 3	14.5%	17.7%	22%
• Study 4	11.5%	14.8%	28%
Forecasting good weather	19%	22%	18%
Writing "thank you" on check	16%	18%	13%
Drawing a picture on check			
• Waiter drawing a smiley face	21%	18%	–
• Waitress drawing a smiley face	28%	33%	18%
• Bartender drawing a sun	19%	26%	37%
Using credit card insignia			
• Restaurant	16%	20%	25%
• Café	18%	22%	22%
Calling customer by name	14%	15%	10%
Giving customer candy			
• Study 1	15%	18%	18%
• Study 2	19%	23%	21%

Source: Lynn, M., "Seven Ways to Increase Server Tips" *Cornell Hotel and Restaurant Administration Quarterly*, June 1996, pp. 24-29.

* Dollar amounts are per person. With regard to suggestive selling, the tip is 15% of total check. DG = Dutch Guilders

For example, a "bricks" book retailer such as Borders would design the service system completely different from a "clicks" book retailer such as Amazon.com as shown in Table 5.3. These distinctions are discussed in more detail in the following section.

Facility location decisions for services are usually based around proximity to the customers. Companies like Starbucks and Mailboxes, Etc. want extensive customer coverage and locate near their key target markets, primarily lively residential or small business neighborhoods. On the other hand, back-office services such as Internet services, call-in centers, and processing centers should locate closer to key employee groups and other important resources such as telecommunications and transportation infrastructure.

Facility layout depends on the presence of the customer at the location. If the customer is not present in the service (back-office operations) then layout decisions are based on operational efficiency. But when the customer is physically present, the layout decisions revolve around how the surroundings affect the customers and employees. Mary Jo Bitner (1992) coined the term *servicescape* to refer to a service's physical surroundings and how they affect people in a retail setting. The layout is crucial to

TABLE 5.3: *Service Decision Factors for "Bricks" Versus "Clicks" Book Retailers*

Design Factor	"Bricks" Book Retailer	"Clicks" Book Retailer
Facility location	Multiple locations close to customers	Centralized location
Facility layout	Facility accommodates customer's needs and enhances shopping experience	Facility accommodates back-office tasks such as shipping, receiving, information systems management, and call-in center
Product design	Store design emphasizes book shopping experience with best-seller tables, cozy furnishings, and entertainment	Web site is designed to emphasize book shopping while facility is customer-free and oriented toward inventory and distribution
Scheduling	Workers are scheduled to meet peak customer demands on basis; lumpy schedules	Workers are scheduled to meet completion dates or daily requirements; flat schedules
Worker skills	People oriented with knowledge of books	Technology and task oriented
Quality control, measures, time standards	More difficult to measure and develop standards, oriented toward variable customer beliefs	Easy to measure Web site-related quality and time issues
Demand/capacity planning	Capacity must match peak demand on hourly basis	Capacity must match peak demand on daily or weekly basis
Industrialization level	Low substitution of technology for people	High substitution of technology for people
Standardization	Store look is generally standardized; customer interaction is customized by personnel	Customer Web page is customized, all else is standardized
Customer contact time	High	Low
Frontline personnel discretion	High employee discretion in their interaction with customers	Minimal employee discretion in interaction with customers (often scripted)
Sales opportunity	More opportunity for selling additional books and merchandise (coffee, pastries, music)	Less opportunity for selling additional merchandise
Customer participation	Mixed self-serve and assisted sales	Mostly self-serve

enhancing the customer experience (see Chapter 6 for extensive coverage of experience design) and to the service functionality. The layout in large grocery stores, like Safeway, and superstores, such as Wal-Mart, emphasizes strategic product placement and customer flows through their stores to maximize sales and convenience.

Product and process design covers both the tangible and intangible aspects of the service offering or package. For example, a restaurant's product design includes the physical environment, menu offerings, customer interaction level, music, and many other factors. A franchised fast-food service follows a well-defined product design that is ubiquitous for each location. The customer expects to find a standardized product at each McDonald's that includes a similar process design, such as the service transaction and short waiting time, in addition to the Quarter Pounder™.

Scheduling addresses how the workers are assigned to the service. When the customer is part of the service interaction, then employees are scheduled to meet immediate demand generally creating a "lumpy" schedule for businesses facing variable demand. Customers who are not physically present, as with Internet services, can interact either automatically with technology or through chat, phone, and e-mail. Here, the employee schedule is level because the responses may not need to be immediate or demand can be spread across time zones and activities.

Quality control, measures, and time standards should focus on customers' needs and how well the service addresses those needs. For example, the significant quality measures for Internet retail services are shown in Figure 5.1. Customers' number one concern is quality of customer service followed closely by on-time delivery. Quality control systems for these businesses monitor customer interaction with employees to ensure that employees are friendly, accurate, and provide quick problem resolution. Each company establishes its own measures for "friendliness," such as appropriate greeting, closure, addressing customer by name, and so on. Time standards that apply to an e-service would be length of time for delivery, customer's time in phone queue, e-mail response time, length of time for order assembly, and problem resolution time.

Demand/capacity planning depends on the type of service and the immediacy of matching supply to demand. Many services, such as restaurants, hotels, and airlines, use reservation or yield management (see Chapter 12) to match their capacity to demand. Still others attempt to match employee capacity to customer demands to reduce queues using scheduling techniques (see Chapter 14). Other capacity issues include technology capacity, ability to handle unusual spikes in demand, seating capacity, ability to shift demand, and use of self-service.

Customer contact level refers to physical presence and length of time that a customer spends with a service provider. This interaction can happen in several ways. In a *direct contact* service, the customer is physically present and interacts with a service provider such as in a medical clinic or hairdresser. The customer is not physically present or interacting in real-time with an *indirect contact* service, such as e-mailing or live chat with a service. Finally, some services can be executed with *no contact* with the service provider, such as an ATM interaction.

FIGURE 5.1: *Quality Standards and Customer Satisfaction with e-Service*

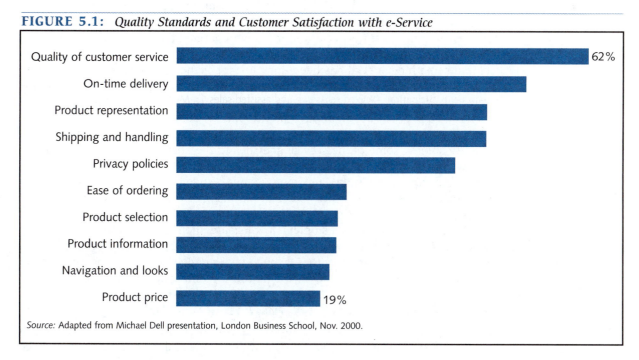

Source: Adapted from Michael Dell presentation, London Business School, Nov. 2000.

Industrialization level refers to the substitution of technology for people. Today, all businesses make efforts to increase their industrialization level. Whether done through automated phone answering systems with simulated voice or through soft systems such as visual inventory reordering cards, the goal is to reduce the use of service employees and direct customer contact, the most costly and fallible side of a service encounter.

Front line personnel discretion denotes the flexibility of the service employee while interacting with a customer. For many customer service centers, the use of formalized dialog sequences or "scripting" limits the employee discretion. This practice encourages consistency and quality or promotes a certain marketing message or image. Highly personalized services such as boutique hotels and luxury product retail give the personnel high flexibility during their customer interaction to encourage customer loyalty and sales. For example, Joie de Vivre Hotel Chain has a dream-maker program. Here, the employee can create a customized welcome gift for VIP customers. In one example, an employee called the VIP's assistant to find out the guest's favorite snack foods and made a special welcome gift basket filled with these items.

Worker skills depend on the service strategy and concept, customer contact level, and industrialization level. Generally speaking, in high customer contact services with high-quality expectations, the workers require strong people skills. In low contact services, however, the workers require technology skills or dexterity and memory skills for back-office tasks such as check or package sorting by codes.

Sales opportunities coincide with high customer contact and employee discretion. When a customer directly interacts with an employee and the employee has a high level of discretion, the opportunity to close the sale or upsell increases. Good sales employees quickly determine customers' needs and solutions to appeal to and satisfy those needs. This phenomenon is particularly apparent with online retail shopping. Here two-thirds of all consumers abandon their electronic shopping carts. But, when companies implement live chat (the ability to type questions to a service representative and get real-time responses), their sales closures rise dramatically. Companies like Cameraworld.com went from 3% to 25% sales closure after implementing live chat.

Standardization of service offering is the level of uniformity provided in the service. Standardized services such as fast-food or hotel franchises reduce costs, provide the customer with a certain expectation or known commodity, and are easier for management to control the process and duplicate for growth. But, customers do like to feel that something special has been done just for them, so many services offer customization to appeal to these people. Increasingly, technology allows for mass customization so that the entire standardization/customization continuum can be covered by a provider appealing to a broad range of customers.

Customer participation refers to the substitution of consumer labor for provider labor. By shifting some of the service activities to the customer, the service provider can save money, increase efficiency, and place some of the responsibility for service quality and experience in the customer's hands. Customers can participate in small tasks such as bussing their own tables at Starbucks. Other companies ask the customers to completely self-serve, such as Smith and Noble, a window treatment provider that requires the customers to measure their own windows, order, and install the treatments themselves. The company will not take a verbal order but must see the dimensions in writing either through fax or online ordering. This requirement makes the customer responsible for the measuring and installation errors.

SERVICE SYSTEM DESIGN AND INNOVATION

Service system designers face unique challenges relative to product designers because the service customer buys a package of goods and services usually provided in the same environment. This package consists of different features or attributes. First, a *supporting facility* generally must be in place before a service can be offered. For example, Texaco must have a site and building or leased space for the gas station. Second, *facilitating goods* such as a product or other tangible features are part of the service. In the gas station example, facilitating goods would include gas, groceries, and fast food. Third, *sensual* and *psychological benefits* are associated with the services. These benefits could include sights, smells, and sounds or feelings of status, privacy, or security. The gas station should be designed for cleanliness and comforting smells as well as creating a feeling of security for the road-weary traveler.

Additionally, today's services may actually bundle several services together in one supporting facility. Therefore, it is important to differentiate between the *core* and *ancillary* services. For example, contemporary gas stations offer gas as their core service and ancillary services such as a convenience store facility, an ATM, and perhaps several fast-food vendors such as KFC, Subway Sandwiches, and Taco Bell under one roof. It is important for service designers to consider the right mix of services that complement the core service and address the target market's needs and the core service strategy. In many businesses, the ancillary services become major sources of revenue or key attributes in the customer's choice of a particular core service over competitors. Las Vegas casinos aggressively pursued celebrity chef restaurants such as Emeril's and Wolfgang Puck's to fill their retail eating space. Many customers now choose their gaming location based on the choice of restaurants in the facility.

How does the service system design contribute to innovative new services? Most recently, the emergence of the Internet as a significant process technology enables delivery of many new service products, both incremental and radical innovations. The interaction of design factors of customer contact, industrialization, and standardization play an important role in new service innovations (see Figure 5.2). In face-to-face delivery systems, new technologies improve the service standardization or consistency for incremental innovations. For example, handheld wireless order pads in London's Wagamama Restaurants are an incremental innovation that helps the restaurants reduce order time and errors along with improved inventory management. Internet technologies can assist services wishing to increase their industrialization level and move completely away from face-to-face delivery to technology-based self-service. Typical examples of this type of technology-driven service innovation are online book and CD sales, travel agencies, and many other retail businesses. Finally, we see that radical service innovations shift the paradigm from face-to-face customer interaction and low standardization to self-service and high standardization, usually through information and computer-based technologies.

FIGURE 5.2: *Industrialization and Standardization Effects on Service Innovations*

Industrialization Level	Standardization Level	
	Low	*High*
Low (Face-to-Face Delivery)	*Current Service* Shop at store Take computer to repair center	*Incremental Service Innovation* Trunk shows at home "House call" computer repair services
High (Technology-based Self-Serve)	*Technology-Driven Service Innovation* Body-scanning technology Computer Diagnostics via phone menus	*Radical Service Innovation* Shop on-line for made-to-order clothing

SERVICE SYSTEM DESIGN TOOLS

New service designers rely on several tools to develop and analyze their concepts. All of these tools recognize the importance of the customer in the system. The first tool, service blueprinting, maps the customer's processes and examines interactions in different steps in the service encounter. The second tool, customer utility models, generates the attributes that are important to a customer and then analyzes the potential customer satisfaction level, revenues, and profits from a new service design in a competitive market.

Service Blueprinting

Service blueprinting is a design tool based on the process flow diagram (discussed in Chapter 9, Analyzing Processes). Not only is the diagram useful for analyzing and improving existing processes, but, it creates the map of a new process. Several key points differentiate the blueprint from a standard process flow diagram as illustrated in Figure 5.3, a blueprint for an Espresso & Coffee Shop, similar to Starbucks.

First, a clear delineation separates the front office or high-contact area from the back office or low customer contact area. A "line of visibility" divides these two functional areas and the processes occurring in each. When developing a new service, designers must think about who will perform that task, what processes will happen in front of the customer and what is behind the scenes, when the process occurs and in what sequence, and why the process is placed in that sequence and visibility area. For example, espresso shops could pregrind espresso beans behind the scene, but the act of grinding them within the customer's view shows the customer the freshness of the drink and creates a certain sensory experience.

Second, designers can determine standard or maximum execution times, materials, and the exact details of a particular step. In the example shop, the designer can dictate the exact sequence with which the employee takes the customer's money and creates change during the purchase transaction. The diagram addresses the materials required for each process and where the purchase and ordering responsibility occurs. The espresso shop uses coffee, flavoring, cups, and lids as the materials in its process. The shop may sell other merchandise such as mugs, coffee-making machines, books, and CDs, but these items belong to another design element, not the drink-making design.

FIGURE 5.3: *Service Blueprint for Espresso and Coffee Shop*

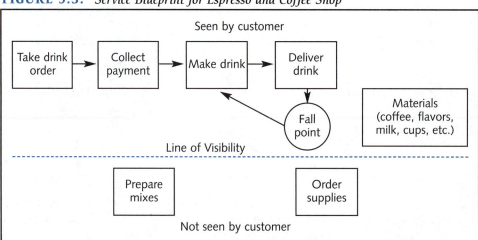

Third, designers can examine potential failure points and come up with strategies for preventing or recovering from failure. The mistake-proofing strategy, or *poka-yoke* (which is Japanese for avoiding mistakes), can be an integral part of the design. Poka-yokes are generally warning, physical, or visual contact methods. They cover the task to be done, the customer treatment, and the tangible or environmental features of the service. (See Chapter 10 for more on poka-yokes.) The espresso shop example shows a fail point at drink delivery. Here the customer may receive a drink that does not match what was ordered. Poka-yoke design elements to prevent this failure include the following: The employee marks the drink specifications on the paper cup as the customer orders, the employee then repeats back what the customer ordered (i.e., "decaf, skim milk, large latte"), the customer confirms or corrects the order at this point, and when the drink is finished the employee again repeats the order just completed.

Customer Utility Models

Commercial success often depends on a favorable market response to a new service configuration. In turn, that response depends on the customer's perceived utility or benefit provided by the service's price and nonprice attributes and that of competing brands. Tools such as conjoint analysis (CJA) are now widely used to assess the perceived utility of new service design and to predict the market's sensitivity to changes in the levels of key price and nonprice attributes.

One of the more tantalizing promises of consumer utility measurement is the ability to optimize the design of a service (i.e., specify a level for each price and nonprice attribute). Typical objectives include maximizing customers' aggregate utility, market share, expected customer satisfaction, or expected contribution to profits. Drivers of service customer satisfaction and utility are often linked to interactions with service delivery personnel. The importance of these interactions on customer satisfaction suggests that certain process attributes, such as employee recruiting, training, and retention efforts, should be explicitly modeled in any service design decision.

Customers develop service attribute expectations from marketing messages and previous experience. To design a new service, managers must determine which attributes are important to customers, whether the service is capable of delivering the attributes according to expectation, the cost of taking an attribute to a different level, and the customer's subsequent perception of the delivered service or satisfaction.

Satisfaction with the quality of a service affects customer loyalty and repurchase intent, and thus the utility of the service for customers. Service quality can be determined along five principal dimensions. The first four address the service process: reliability, responsiveness, assurance, and empathy. The remaining dimension covers the goods content or tangible aspect of the service. These dimensions can be mapped to specific attributes of the service design (Easton and Pullman, 2001). In general, increasing the intensity of a service quality attribute affects one or more of the following service delivery expenses: (1) direct labor expenses, (2) expenses for consumables, or tangibles, (3) hiring costs, and (4) training costs. In Table 5.4, we identify specific service attributes likely to influence perceptions for each dimension of service quality and suggest mechanisms for varying the intensity of these attributes.

Options for improving perceived service *reliability* often result in increased labor expenses and training costs. For example, the perceived reliability may depend on whether the service begins and ends at the expected times. To improve reliability, designers might choose to increase the length of appointment blocks, train and equip service workers to better meet temporal service performance expectations, or simply add more service capacity during periods of high utilization.

TABLE 5.4: *Nonprice Service Attributes and Cost Implications*

Service Quality Attribute	Examples	Potential Actions to Intensify Attribute	Increased Operating Cost Implications
Reliability	• Service begins on time • Accurate records and billing • Predictable treatment	• Decrease service rates • Increase preventative maintenance • Increase training in standard operating procedures • Increase service level	• Labor schedule costs: labor required/period • Training costs: function of number of employees and training intensity
Responsiveness	• Prompt service • Availability (hours of operation) • Willingness to help customers • Ability to compensate for service breakdowns	• Reduce waiting time • Increase hours of operations • Increase training • Increase selective hiring • Increase gratis consumables and refunds • Improve explicit benefits for guarantees of service quality	• Labor schedule costs: labor required/period, shift premiums • Training costs: function of number of employees and intensity • Hiring costs: function of number of screened candidates • Consumable cost: function of number of service failure, type of failure, and effective recovery cost
Assurance	• Employee knowledge, courtesy, and confidence • Employee competence	• Increase training • Increase selective hiring • Increase incentives and wage rate	• Training costs: function of number of employees and wages • Hiring costs: function of number of screened candidates • Labor schedule costs: higher wage rates
Empathy	• Provision of caring attention to customers • Employee approachability and sensitivity to customers' needs	• Increase training • Increase selective hiring • Increase incentives and wage rate	• Training costs: function of number of employees and wages • Hiring costs: function of number of screened candidates • Labor schedule costs: higher wage rates
Tangibles	• Product characteristics • Specifications • Packaging Appearance of: • Physical facilities • Equipment • Personnel • Communication materials	• Improve product and package • Increase preventative maintenance • Increase training • Improved consumables	• Overall product cost • Labor schedule costs: higher wage rates and number of shifts • Training costs: function of number of employees • Consumable costs: quality of facility, product, and employee uniforms

Source: Easton and Pullman (2001).

Perceptions of *responsiveness* may be enhanced by reducing queue times. Because service demand can vary significantly from hour to hour and service outputs can rarely be stored for later use, it is usually necessary to adjust service capacity to match temporal demand. Service capacity is adjusted through employee scheduling decisions after target response times and the predicted service demands for each period are converted to employee requirements. Due to hours-of-work constraints, the number of workers scheduled for duty at a particular time often exceeds the prescribed capacity level. Thus, the incremental cost of a modest improvement in responsiveness may range upwards from zero (when sufficient slack already exists) to the combined wages for several additional employees.

Perceptions of *empathy* and *assurance* are influenced by the ability of service providers to convey knowledge, courtesy, impressions of caring, and approachability during each service encounter. To increase the intensity of these attributes, designers may invest in more sophisticated screening methods for hiring decisions, train and empower employees to interact effectively with anxious or potentially angry customers, and increase the amount of time spent with each customer. Each activity affects labor-related expenses such as recruiting, hiring, training, and labor schedule costs.

Enhancing the *tangible* attributes of a service generally increases costs for consumables and, in some cases, capital requirements and maintenance expenses. In the hospitality industry, the service good content relates to food, hotel rooms, and other amenities. Generally, increased consumable expenses such as packaging, ingredients, or interior design elements can improve perceptions of the tangible attributes. Similarly, these improvements affect labor costs. For example, to improve customer perceptions of bathroom cleanliness a national hotel chain considered several ideas to improve perceptions. It could instruct its staff to spend more time on each bathroom, assign additional personnel to clean bathrooms, or increase the amount of training on how to clean a bathroom. Compared with the status quo, each alternative increased recurring training costs and labor expenses.

In order to design services in a competitive market, designers need to determine (1) important service attributes along with customer's preference model for them, (2) the attributes that are appropriate for standardization for all segments or customization for a specific segment, (3) the practicality and economic feasibility of different attributes and attribute levels, and (4) the market share or profit implications of their chosen design. The overall utility model is shown in Figure 5.4.

To evaluate a new service using the utility model, conjoint analysis (CJA) and discrete choice analysis (DCA) are used to model customer utility (preferences) in response to experimentally designed profiles of service attributes. Recent studies demonstrate that market utility models developed from carefully conducted DCA experiments can be used to effectively predict market share for various types of products and services.

Discrete choice experiments involve careful design of service profiles (a specific service) and choice sets (a number of services) in which two or more service alternatives are offered to decision makers who are then asked to evaluate the options and choose one (or none). Based on the experimental design, the decision makers' choices (dependent variable) are a function of the attributes of each alternative, personal characteristics of the respondents, and unobserved effects captured by a random component (for example, unobserved heterogeneity or omitted factors).

For example, to design a new restaurant in an international airport terminal, the following steps are required:

1. Identification of important attributes
2. Specification of attribute levels

FIGURE 5.4: *Utility-Based Service Design Process*

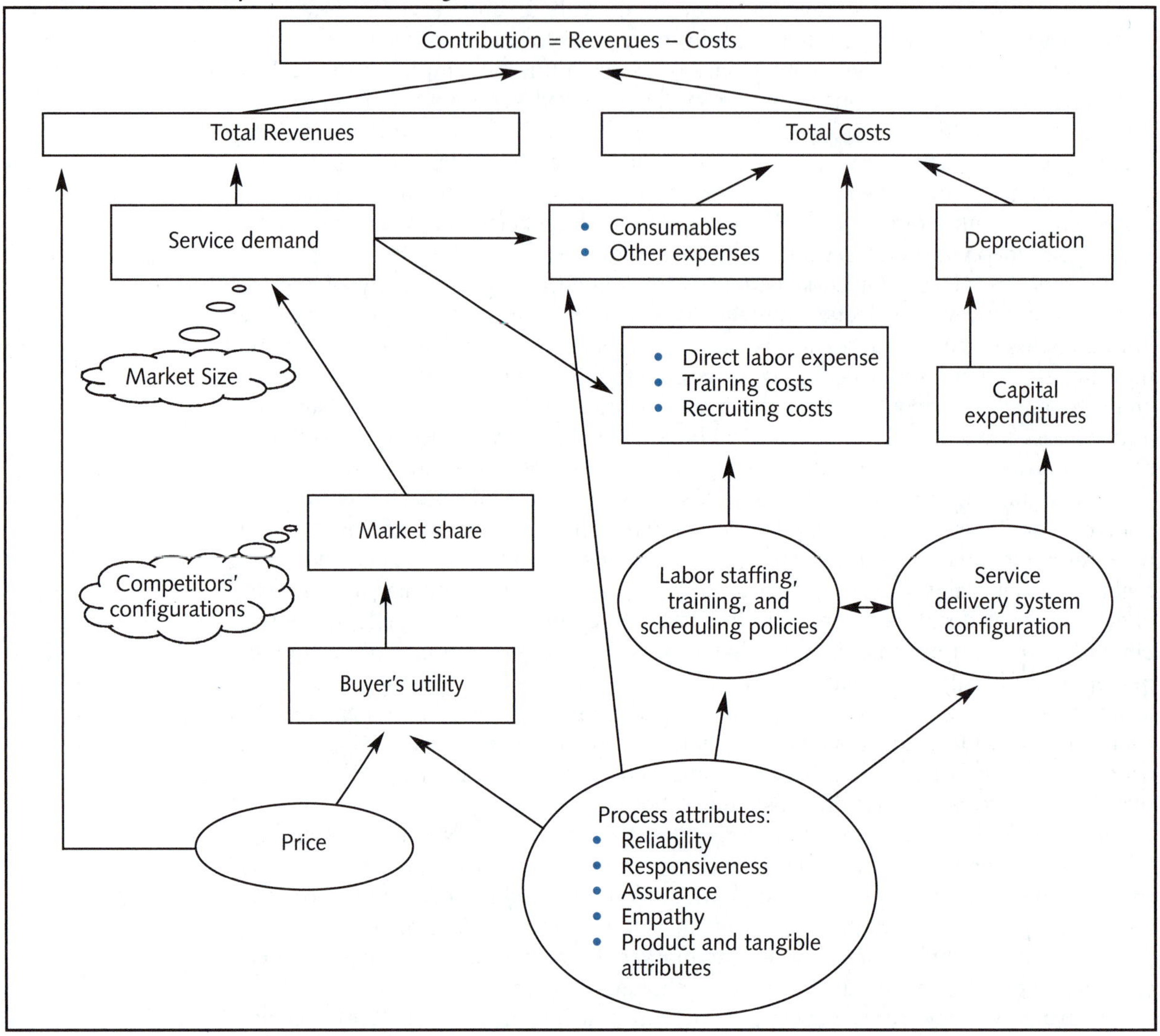

3. Experimental design
4. Presentation of alternatives to respondents
5. Estimation of choice model

Table 5.5 highlights the appropriate attributes and the potential level of each attribute for the restaurant. In this case, restaurant brand name, menu variety, food price, wait time to order and to serve, menu languages, and pictorial displays of menu items are the important attributes. Because each attribute can be assessed on several potential levels such as price range or waiting times, respondents are provided with a number of choice profiles (16 to 32 profiles) similar to Table 5.6. From their responses, a choice model is built for customer segments or an aggregate customer group. This choice model can be used to predict sample customers' utility, market share, and potential profit for a new service design. Verma, Thompson, and Louviere (1999) provide a guideline for designing and conducting DCA studies for services.

TABLE 5.5: *Attributes and Levels for International Terminal Restaurant Design*

Attributes and Levels	Restaurant #1	Restaurant #2	Restaurant #3	Restaurant #4
Brand name				
Level 1	Local chain	Local chain	Generic food items	Local chain
Level 2	McDonald's	Pizza Hut/Dominos	La Prefreda/Goya	Subway/Boston Market
Variety				
Level 1	Burgers, fries, ice cream	Pizza	Hot dog, fries, nachos + Burritos, tacos	Sandwich, soup, ice cream + Udan noodle soup, salads
Level 2 (add to Level 1 items)	+ Chicken nuggets and salads	+ Lasagna, pasta	+ Tamales, enchiladas	+ Sushi, simple Asian dishes
Level 3 (add to Level 1 & 2 items)	+ Special burgers and sandwiches	+ Salads, soups		
Wait-before-ordering				
Level 1	0–2 mins	0–2 mins	0–2 mins	0–2 mins
Level 2	3–4 mins	3–4 mins	3–4 mins	3–4 mins
Level 3	5–6 mins	5–6 mins	5–6 mins	5–6 mins
Service time				
Level 1	0–2 mins	0–2 mins	0–2 mins	0–2 mins
Level 2	3–4 mins	3–4 mins	3–4 mins	3–4 mins
Level 3	5–6 mins	5–6 mins	5–6 mins	5–6 mins
Menu language				
Level 1	English	English	English	English
Level 2	+ Spanish	+ Spanish	+ Spanish	+ Spanish
Level 3	+ Japanese	+ Japanese	+ Japanese	+ Japanese
Picture display				
Level 1	No	No	No	No
Level 2	Yes	Yes	Yes	Yes
Price: meal + drinks				
Level 1	$ 4	$ 4	$ 4	$ 4
Level 2	$ 7	$ 7	$ 7	$ 7
Level 3	$10	$10	$10	$10

TABLE 5.6: *Restaurant Sample Choice Set*

CHOICE SET #11	Restaurant #1	Restaurant #2	Restaurant #3	Restaurant #4
Brand name	McDonald's	Local restaurant	La Prefreda/Goya Products	Subway/Boston Market
Variety	Burger, fries, ice cream	Pizza, lasagna, pasta, salads, and soups	Hot dogs, fries, nachos, burritos, tacos, tamales, and enchiladas	Sandwich, soup, ice cream, Udan noodle soup, and salads
Wait time (before ordering)	5–6 mins	0–2 mins	3–4 mins	0–2 mins
Service time	0–2 mins	3–4 mins	5–6 mins	3–4 mins
Menu language	English	English, Spanish, and Japanese	English and Spanish	English and Spanish
Picture display	Yes	No	No	No
Price (meal + drinks)	$4	$4	$10	$7

I would purchase food from

Source: Pullman, Verma, and Goodale (2001)

SERVICE OPERATIONS MANAGEMENT PRACTICES

New Service Design for Snowbird Ski Resort

Snowbird Ski Resort competes against six other contenders in a regional market. Most western resorts face varying constraints on capacity due to environmental regulations that limit their acreage and parking areas, surrounding public lands, natural rugged terrain, and snow-making capability. On the other hand, to be a contender in this market, a resort must continually improve the facility by installing chair lifts, adding trails, and keeping up with the latest snow-making technology. Half of the other competitive resorts made investments in facility improvements during the last five years. Snowbird observed a decline in ticket sales, which management attributed to their competitors' improvements. Therefore, resort management, considered service design changes and wanted to determine the most profitable option.

Following the sequence outlined in Figure 5.5, the design team held focus groups to determine the most important attributes for a ski resort. They then developed a choice model questionnaire with these attributes and two to three different levels for each attribute with 16 choice sets. A sample choice set is

FIGURE 5.5: *Service Design Process with Customer Utility Models*

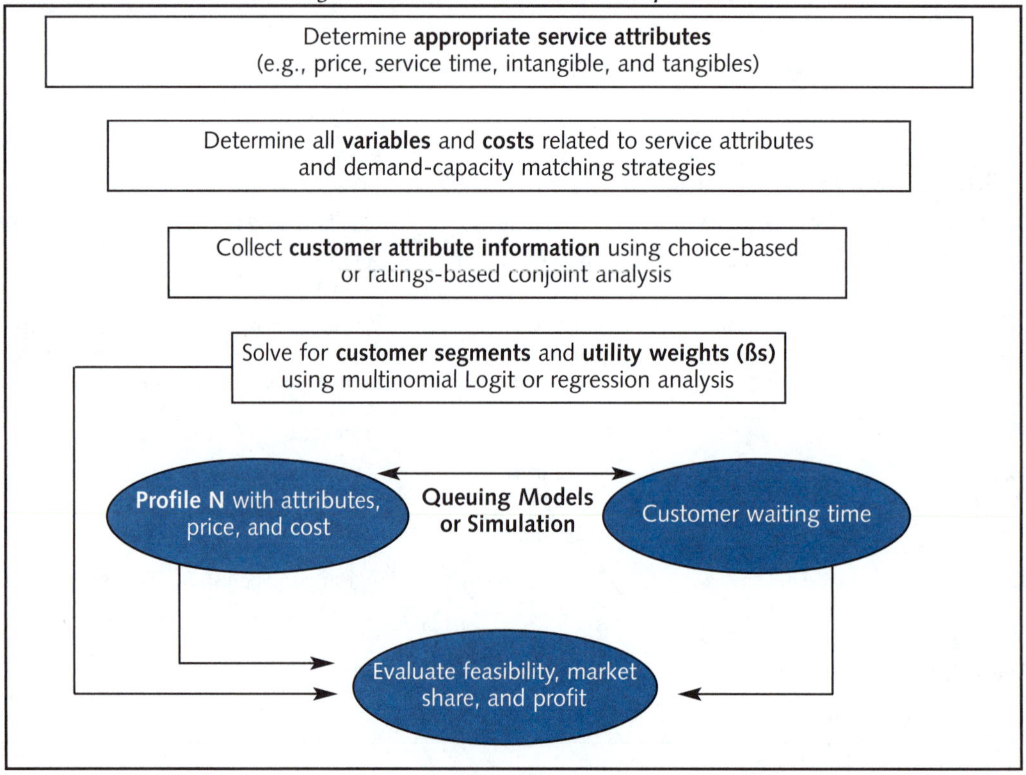

- Determine **appropriate service attributes** (e.g., price, service time, intangible, and tangibles)
- Determine all **variables** and **costs** related to service attributes and demand-capacity matching strategies
- Collect **customer attribute information** using choice-based or ratings-based conjoint analysis
- Solve for **customer segments** and **utility weights (ßs)** using multinomial Logit or regression analysis
- **Profile N** with attributes, price, and cost
- **Queuing Models or Simulation**
- Customer waiting time
- Evaluate feasibility, market share, and profit

SERVICE OPERATIONS MANAGEMENT PRACTICES

shown in Figure 5.6. The questionnaires were completed by 276 regional skiers and the resulting model (Multinomial Logit) is shown in Table 5.7. For this customer group, the beta coefficients indicate that skiers want decreased prices and waits in line but increased lift capacity to high-speed quads, more facilities, and more beginner and intermediate level runs.

The design team looked at several options to address these preferences: lower ticket prices, off-peak pricing to shift demand, adding a number of new lifts and runs, adding new terrain, and installing real-time queue information signage. Each of these options car-

ried some level of fixed and variable cost. Finally, through a complete resort simulation with many different scenarios, the design team determined the various relationships between design changes, waiting time, and overall customer preference or market share for each scenario. Using this information, the team found that by installing two new lifts and the queue information signage, the resort could increase its market share by 3%, adding 80,000 skier-day sales (tickets) per year and increasing profits by 20% (including the new investments). (For more information on this project see Pullman and Moore, 1999.)

FIGURE 5.6: *Choice Set for Ski Resort Design*

Ski Area A	Features	Ski Area B
Rugged terrain, sparsely forested, dramatic rock peaks	**Physical Setting**	Rugged terrain, sparsely forested, and dramatic rock peaks
40 minutes drive from home	**Distance**	40 minutes drive from home
70 inches	**Snow Base**	70 inches
12 inches new powder	**New Snow**	12 inches new powder
3,250 feet	**Vertical Drop**	3,250 feet
Groomed trails with glades and bowls	**Type of Runs**	Groomed trails only
35 ski runs	**Size of Area**	35 ski runs
25% Advanced, 50% Intermediate, 25% Beginner	**Challenge**	25% Advanced, 50% Intermediate, 25% Beginner
Ski shops, restaurants, nightlife, boutiques, lodging	**Facilities**	Ski shops, restaurants, nightlife, boutiques, lodging
$50 per day	**Ticket Price**	$20 per day
30 minutes at peak time	**Lift Line Wait**	30 minutes at peak time
Mostly triples and quads	**Type of Lifts**	Mostly triples and quads
Not allowed	**Snowboards**	Not allowed

Suppose these two ski areas described were the only ones available for your next ski outing. Please check (✓) one box below to indicate what you would most likely do:

	I would choose Ski Area A.
	I would choose Ski Area B.
	I would do something else and not ski.

Source: Pullman and Moore (1999).

SERVICE OPERATIONS MANAGEMENT PRACTICES

TABLE 5.7: *Customer Utility Model for Ski Resort Design*

Variable	Beta Coefficient
Intercept	0.2435
Drive time	−0.1414
Snow base	0.0896
Lift line wait	−0.1909
New snow	0.0308
Vertical drop	0.0086
Number runs	0.0068
Price	−0.0697
Difficulty level 1	0.0463
Difficulty level 2	0.0876
Difficulty level 3	−0.0464
Setting level 1	0.2080
Setting level 2	0.0834
Setting level 3	−0.0754
Terrain level 1	0.0167
Terrain level 2	0.0238
Terrain level 3	0.0433
Facility level 1	−0.0492
Facility level 2	0.0835
Facility level 3	0.0784
Lift types level 1	0.0258
Lift types level 2	0.0279
Lift types level 3	0.0601
Allow snowboarding	−0.0279

Summary

New service design poses many challenges for firms due to the intangible nature of service encounters, inability to prototype and test new concepts, and a propensity to use ad hoc methods. Innovations come through both incremental and radical new services. The two approaches may require different design processes but generally address the same significant factors such as level of customer contact and industrialization. We introduced several design tools that assist designers in evaluating service concepts for improved efficiency, customer satisfaction, quality, market share, and profitability.

Review Questions

1. What is the difference between incremental and radical new service design?
2. Where should management allocate effort and resources in incremental and radical new service design processes?
3. How can service blueprinting be used in new service design?

4. What are failure points in a coffee shop? What types of poka-yokes can one use to eliminate these failures?

5. How are customer utility models used in service design? How do they differ from other approaches such as service blueprinting?

Selected Bibliography

Bitner, M. 1992. Servicescapes: The Impact of Physical Surroundings on Customers and Employees, *Journal of Marketing*, 56 (April), 57–71.

Easton, F., and M. Pullman. 2001. Optimizing Service Attributes: The Seller's Utility Problem, *Decision Science*, 32(2), 1–25.

Gadrey, J., Gallouj, F., and O. Weinstein. 1995. New Modes of Innovation: How Services Benefit Industry, *International Journal of Service Industry Management*, 6(3), 4–16.

Griffin, A. 1997. PDMA Research on New Product Development Practices: Updating Trends and Benchmarking Best Practices, *Journal of Product Innovation Management*, 14, 429–458.

Johnson, S., Menor, L., Roth, A., and R. Chase. 2000. A Critical Evaluation of the New Service Development Process: Integrating Service Innovation and Service Design. In J. Fitzsimmons and M. Fitzsimmons (Eds.), *New Service Development*. Sage Publications, Thousand Oaks, CA.

Kimes, S., and F. Young. 1997. The Shuttle by United, *Interfaces*, 27(3), 1–13.

Lovelock, C. 1984. Developing and Implementing New Services. In W. George and C. Marshall (Eds.), *Developing New Services*. American Marketing Services, Chicago.

Lynn, M. 1996. Seven Ways to Increase Server Tips, *Cornell Hotel and Restaurant Administration Quarterly* (June), 24–29.

Pullman, M., and W. Moore. 1999. Optimal Service Design: Integrating Marketing and Operations Elements for Capacity Decisions, *International Journal of Service Industry Management*, 10(2), 239–260.

Pullman, M., Verma, R., and J. Goodale. 2001. Service Design and Operations Strategy Formulation in Multicultural Markets, *Journal of Operations Management*, 19(2), 239–254.

Verma, R., Thompson, G., and J. Louviere. 1999. Configuring Service Operations in Accordance with Customer Needs and Preferences, *Journal of Service Research*, 1(3), 262–274.

CASE STUDY

New Service Design Experiments at Bank of America

Companies that develop new products have many options available for developing and testing new ideas. Products like cars or food can be put through a series of lab or field-based tests, evaluated by sample populations, and refined before a major market rollout. On the other hand, services require real customers to interact with the concept at the point of purchase for evaluation and refinement. Putting out a "prototype" service is riskier on many levels. A new concept that does not work could harm customer satisfaction and perceptions of the brand. Service prototype experiments are difficult to monitor and evaluate due to variation between or among customers and employees; many other factors operating in a real environment can obscure the variable of interest. Over the last few years, Bank of America has taken on this new service development challenge and developed a series of formal experiments to create new retail banking services by turning a number of their branch offices into "laboratories."

Bank of America Experiment Designs

Bank of America's Innovation and Development (I & D) Team reconfigured 20 of their 200 Atlanta bank branches into three alternative models; *express centers*, efficient, modernistic buildings where consumers could quickly perform routing transactions; *financial centers*, spacious, relaxed outlets where customers would have access to trained staff and advanced technologies for stock trading and portfolio management; and *traditional centers*, familiar branches that provide conventional banking services supported by new technologies and redesigned processes.

After generating a list of more than 200 potential experiments, the I & D team categorized each idea according to priority based on projected impact on customers, alignment with bank strategy and goals, and funding requirements. To plan and execute each experiment quickly, the bank created a prototype branch to rehearse steps of an experimental process and work out problems before going live with real customers. The team required that every experiment minimize the effects of noise (those variables not being tested), have a high likelihood of providing attractive returns, and run for 90 days before adjusting or discontinuing. The performance data for each experiment (at test locations and control branches) were analyzed to determine whether the experiment had enhanced customer satisfaction, revenue generation, productivity, or any other relevant measure of performance. In addition, cost-benefit analysis was required to ensure that the performance gain outweighed the expense of the new process or technology.

Example of a Waiting Time Experiment

For one of their first experiments, the I & D team chose to focus on waiting processes. From initial survey results, they found that customers who waited in line for two

CASE STUDY

minutes felt like it was a two minute wait, but if they waited for five minutes, they felt like it was a ten minute wait. The team felt that if people are entertained in line by offering television monitors above the rows of tellers in the lobby then the customer's perception of wait time could be reduced and satisfaction improved.

The team installed monitors set to CNN in one traditional center; another traditional center with a similar clientele was used as a control branch. The team then carefully measured actual versus perceived waiting time at the two branches. The degree of overestimation of wait times dropped from 32% to 15% at the test branch, while the control branch actually saw an increase in overestimates wait times, from 15% to 26%. In addition, the team had to justify spending $22,000 to upgrade a branch. From statistical analysis of the project and prior studies on their customer-satisfaction index, the group estimated that the reduction in perceived waiting time would translate into a 5.9% increase in overall banking-center customer satisfaction (or about $84,000 increase in annual revenue for a branch with a 10,000 household customer base.) Thus, any branch with more than a few thousand households in its customer base could recoup the up-front cost in less than one year. After the success of the initial experiment, the team launched a second phase to evaluate the impact of more varied television programming, different sound levels, and advertising.

Challenges

Using a live setting for new service experiments is not without its challenges. Customers can get confused by unfamiliar processes. Employee time is taken up with many more meetings and training sessions. Employee routines are disrupted by ongoing experiments and often their incentive programs such as sales bonuses can be affected by participating in "experimental roles" rather than their selling roles. At Bank of America, customers often loved a new "experimental" service, thus branch managers at these locations wanted the service to be continued regardless of the financial implications. These are challenges that any service can expect to encounter when using live setting experiments. But, as Bank of America's efforts suggest, the challenges can be met and the bank achieved important current and future benefits by applying a systematic approach.

Source: From Thomke, Stefan (April, 2003). R&D Comes to Services: Bank of America's Pathbreaking Experiments, *Harvard Business Review*.

Managing Service Experiences

The material in this chapter prepares students to:

- Understand the need for services that deliver an experience.

- Understand the components or elements of experience.

- Use different models for designing and evaluating the experience.

In today's economic environment, customers face an enormous amount of service offerings both in the physical locations and through other channels such as the Internet. With this glut of information, organizations must "battle for the eyeballs," and customers' attention. Not only is it difficult for service providers to get the customers' attention for their offerings, but keeping their attention can be even more challenging. Generally, those companies that can grab the attention and hold it will be winners. Along a similar vein, author Jeffrey Gitomer (1998) stated that a merely *satisfied* customer is still likely to shop around, the next time he or she needs to buy a service, for a better price or more convenient offering. A *loyal* customer is more likely to come back to a specific supplier, and moreover, is likely to recommend the service to others. Thus, it becomes imperative to look at ways to create a loyal customer rather than just a satisfied customer. Providers must transform a vanilla "me too" service into a memorable event that the customer will want to repeat again and recount to all their friends. In other words, companies must create or stage an "experience." Not only should the experience be memorable, it should also be designed to increase customer loyalty by letting customers build on their encounters with the provider through time. In this chapter, we discuss what it takes to create such an experience.

EXPERIENCE ECONOMY

Pine and Gilmore (1998) describe the changing competitive environment as an "experience economy." They argue that as services and products become more like commodities, experiences emerge as the next step in the progression of economic value (see Table 6.1 for the full progression). An experience differs from a normal service in

TABLE 6.1: *Pine and Gilmore's Economic Progression*

Economy	Agrarian	Industrial	Service	Experience
Time	\--->			
Economic offering	Commodities	Goods	Services	Experiences
Economic function	Extract	Make	Deliver	Stage
Nature of offering	Fungible	Tangible	Intangible	Memorable
Key attribute	Natural	Standardize	Customized	Personal
Method of supply	Stored in bulk	Inventoried after produced	Delivered on demand	Revealed over time
Seller	Trader	Manufacturer	Provider	Stager
Buyer	Market	User	Client	Guest
Factors of demand	Characteristics	Features	Benefits	Sensations

Source: Reprinted by permission of Harvard Business School Press. From *The Experience Economy* by B. Joseph Pine II and James H. Gilmore, Boston, MA, 1999, p. 6. Copyright ©1999 by B. Joseph Pine II and James H. Gilmore. All rights reserved.

that companies use services as a stage and goods as props with the goal of engaging individual customers in a way that creates a memorable event for which the organization can charge "admission." The customer or "guest" must be drawn into the offering such that they feel a sensation. A typical example is a Disney theme park with its different "lands." Each land has a specific theme, all the characters are costumed and act the part, the rides fit with the theme, and all souvenirs and merchandise are developed accordingly. Disney wants all guests to feel the Disney "magic" so any items or behavior that might detract from the theme's "magic" are minimized (trash removal and security, employees acting out-of-character, food delivery trucks, etc.).

Many trend watchers agree that creating experiences will become a priority for most businesses, and it will create opportunities for new service innovations. For example, prominent entertainment consultant Michael Wolf believes that businesses need to incorporate the "e-factor" (entertainment factor) into their offerings to be competitive as well as have an understanding of the "fun-focused consumer." Themed restaurants like Hard Rock Café, retailing environments such as Mall of America, and tourist destinations like Las Vegas reinventing themselves with rides, celebrity restaurants, and other nongambling attractions, all incorporated the e-factor to differentiate themselves. But entertainment is just one facet of experience (the fun side). Although much can be learned from the industry that demonstrates the skills and talents for engaging people, service developers must understand all facets of experience.

Experiences have different facets. Some play heavily on emotions while others could be as simple as accomplishing a task in a new way. Often people want to collect experiences (traveling to multiple countries, seeing all the current movies, or visiting shows in local museums). Experiences are not always positive, however; they may be intentionally negative or emotionally upsetting (horror movies, drinking or smoking prevention programs, and other self-help programs).

In a recent study, respondents were asked about a recent purchase (of more than $100) they had made with the intention of advancing their happiness and enjoyment in life. Typically respondents made purchases for experiential services such as travel, spas, restaurants, admission to concerts or ski slopes while material purchases were items like clothing, jewelry, televisions, stereos or computer equipment (Van Boven and Gilovich, 2003). As shown in Table 6.2, respondents felt more positively about

TABLE 6.2: *Evaluation of Recent Experiential and Material Purchases*

Evaluation	Type of Purchase	
Scale = 1 (not at all) to 9 (extremely)	Experiential	Material
How happy does thinking about it make you?	7.51	6.62
Contributed to your overall business life?	6.40	5.42
Money well spent?	7.30	6.42
Better spent on something else?	3.77	5.52
Anticipated happiness of other people's purchase	6.78	4.25

Source: Van Boven and Gilovich (2003)

experiential purchases than material ones on a number of criteria including antici-
pating how happy others might be with that type of purchase.

Popcorn and Marigold (1996) predicted many trends for the next decade and
indicated that for a new service to be successful, it should address several of these
trends. Many of their trends address different experiential issues:

1. **Cocooning:** Our desire to build ourselves strong and cozy nests where we can
   retreat from the world and enjoy ourselves in safety and comfort. The nesting
   trend is apparent in the boom in home stores such as Crate & Barrel or Pottery
   Barn; home entertainment rooms and equipment; and home crafts such as
   cooking or building craft television shows, magazines, and associated products.
2. **Clanning:** Our need to associate with like-minded individuals and to identify
   ourselves with a particular group that shares our outlook and values. This
   type of behavior is addressed by special interest chat rooms and Web sites,
   lifestyle publications, coffee shops, niche hotels, and resorts.
3. **Fantasy adventure:** Our need to seek out risk-free fantasy and adventure
   experiences as a break from the mundane day-to-day activities. Examples of
   products and services oriented toward this behavior include computer games,
   location-based entertainment like theme parks, television shows such as
   Survivor, and adventure travel.
4. **Pleasure revenge:** Another form of escape comes in the form of sensual and
   pleasurable activities that provide a feeling of compensation for all of life's
   struggles. Typical examples of this trend are evident in the growth of massage
   therapy and spas.
5. **Small indulgences:** The trend toward people rewarding themselves regularly
   with small affordable luxuries such as ubiquitous Starbuck's latte coffee drinks
   (sold at a premium over regular coffee), dining out, and gourmet food items.
6. **Anchoring:** This term refers to the increasing tendency for people to seek fulfillment in spiritual values and looking back to the past to recapture what was
   comforting and reassuring then. Stores like Restoration Hardware with retro
   furnishings and accessories; New Urbanism housing developments such as
   Seaside and Celebration, which draw inspiration from historical Southern
   towns and traditional neighborhoods of the 1920s and 1930s; and themed
   restaurants such as Johnny Rockets that replicate 1940s American diners complete with jukeboxes, hand-formed hamburgers, and malts.
7. **Egonomics:** This reaction to the standardization imposed by the computer age
   manifests itself through various avenues of self-expression and personal statements. Interactive Web and television activities, installation art and music
   gatherings such as the Burning Man Event, paint-your-own ceramics shops,
   and online publications create avenues for addressing this need.

Thus, a look at hedonics or the more general study of sensation-seeking customers is essential to developing experiences that cater to a wide variety of situations. In the next section, we will consider what it takes to move a service beyond the mundane to one that creates a memorable experience.

CREATING SUCCESSFUL AND SATISFYING EXPERIENCES

Generally defined, an experience occurs when any sensation or knowledge acquisition results from a customer's interaction with different elements of a context created by a service provider. Successful experiences are those that the customer finds unique, memorable, and sustainable over time; would want to repeat and build upon; and enthusiastically promotes via word of mouth. But experiences are inherently emotional and personal, so we must acknowledge that many factors are beyond the control of management (personal interpretation of a situation based on cultural background, prior experience, mood, sensation-seeking personality traits, and many other factors). Thus, the service designer is designing *for* experience just as the manager manages an environment *for* experience. In this section, we describe the key dimensions within management control during experience creation: specifically, engagement, context, and time. These dimensions build upon each other as show in Figure 6.1.

Engagement

In order to feel the sensation or acquire the knowledge, the customer must become engaged in creating the experience. Engagement happens through two channels: the personal level (active or passive customer participation) and the environment level (absorption or connection) (Pine and Gilmore, 1998). Figure 6.2 illustrates these four realms of experience. In *passive* participation, customers do not directly influence the performance. Generally, they are observers or listeners such as in a university lecture or a symphony environment. On the *active* end of the continuum, the customers can affect the performance or event. They actively contribute to their experience; participative examples include skiing or golf.

On one end of engaging in the environment, the customer can be completely *immersed* either physically or virtually in part of the experience. The customer "goes into" the experience when playing a computer game like "Myst" or becoming part of

FIGURE 6.1: *Model for Building Memorable Experiences*

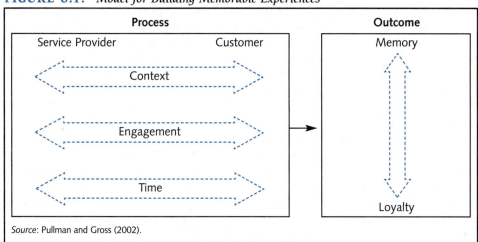

Source: Pullman and Gross (2002).

FIGURE 6.2: *The Process of Customer Experience*

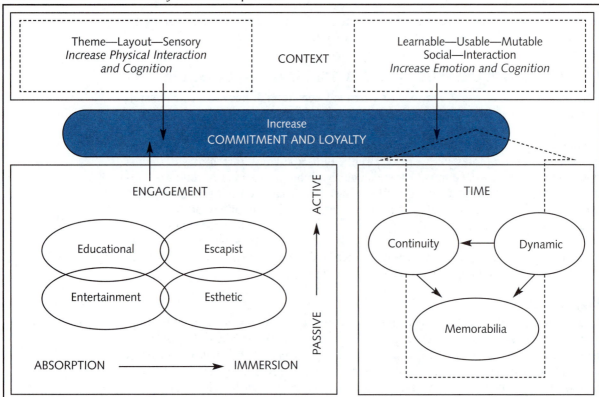

a skit or game at a Club Med, for example. On the *absorption* end of the continuum, the experience "goes into" the customers when they watch a TV show. Any type of experience exhibits some combination of the two dimensions as shown in Table 6.3. For example, traditional *entertainment* like TV or theatre is an absorbing passive experience because the customer is not part of the show and does not participate in the show. But *escapist* experiences involve greater immersion and active participation. The customer is part of the performance and can affect its outcome. Typically, these experiences provide a respite from real life. Examples would include casinos, chat rooms, and simulator rides and simulated environments. A person might feel alienated in his or her life and want to interact with a community of like-minded individuals. Typical *educational* experiences tend toward absorption with active participation by engaging the mind and body. Students absorb the events unfolding in front of them and tend to acquire more knowledge when they interact (actively) with the instructor, fellow students, and teaching materials. Finally, *esthetic* experiences allow individuals to immerse themselves in an event or environment but have little effect on it (passive participation). These experiences can be natural, such as standing on the rim of the Grand Canyon or viewing the Northern Lights, or artificial environments such as Disneyland Park or the spectacular water show at the Bellagio Hotel in Las Vegas.

The richest and most satisfying experiences encompass aspects of all four realms in the middle of the framework, otherwise known as the "sweet spot." To improve the engagement level of the experience, service designers should ask themselves the following questions (Pine and Gilmore, 1999):

TABLE 6.3: *Environment Relationship Versus Participation Examples*

		Environment Relationship	
		Absorption	**Immersion**
Participation	**Passive**	*Entertainment* Television Circus Theater Video/DVD	*Esthetic* Grand Canyon Cathedral Bellagio Water Show
	Active	*Educational* Training Discussion Laboratory	*Escapist* Myst computer game *Terminator 2* ride Chat rooms *Survivor* Show participant

- What can be done to improve the *esthetics* of the experience? What will make guests want to come in, sit down, and hang out (or stay on your Web site)? What will make the environment more inviting, interesting, and comfortable?
- What can be done to improve the *escapist* aspect of the experience? How can the guests get further immersed? Do they have the sense that their real lives are left behind? What can they do to become active participants in the experience? For an example of attempts to move from *entertainment* toward *escapist* (more active participation and immersion) see Service Operations Management Practices: Getting the Potatoes Off the Couch.
- What can be done to increase the *educational* aspects of the experience? What do you want your guests to learn? What information or activities will help to engage them in exploration of knowledge and skills? How can you get them actively engaged in learning? How can you get them to continue to come back and learn more? Increase their depth and breadth of knowledge?
- What can be done, in terms of *entertainment*, to get the guests to stay? How can you make the experience more fun and enjoyable? How can you connect emotionally with the customers? What would increase the thrill, surprise, and delight?

Attempts to improve experiences by combining aspects of different realms contribute to the evolution of service concepts.

Eatertainment combines a restaurant with theme park-like entertainment elements. Dave & Buster's and Chuck E. Cheese's are current successful models of this concept. While Chuck E. Cheese's targets kids with games and food, Dave & Buster's combines its full-service restaurants and bars with an extensive assortment of games oriented toward teens and adults. From traditional pub games such as darts and billiards to state-of-the-art computer simulation games such as motorcycle or snowboard courses, the choices appeal to a wide variety of ages. The management of Dave & Buster's claims that their success can be attributed to emphasizing high-quality food and service standards in addition to acquiring the newest games and maintaining them in top condition. This dual emphasis was not apparent in the less successful contenders such as Planet Hollywood or Rainforest Café, which appeared to sacrifice food quality and did not consider ways to enhance the initial service experience.

SERVICE OPERATIONS MANAGEMENT PRACTICES

Getting the Potatoes Off the Couch

Recently, TV shows actively involve people in the outcome of shows by allowing them to vote online or via telephone (drop-dialing or premium-rate phone lines allow both the show and telephone company to collect revenues). Viewers like voting because they feel it gives them a say in the show's outcome. Recent successful models include *Survivor*, *Big Brother*, and *Who Wants to Be a Millionaire?* In the U.K. *Big Brother* version, more than 20 million people voted on household evictions, bringing in $3 million in revenues. Also, the *Big Brother* Web site showed every room in the house, 24 hours a day, giving viewers a sense of total immersion. (*Vickers*, 2001)

Entertailing or *shoppertainment* combines a retail environment with theatre or theme park-like elements. In an increasingly competitive market, new mall and store designers turn to "fun" or designing stores that are visually exciting, selling concepts and ideas rather than boxes on the shelf. On the single store level, Toys "R" Us designed an indoor playground in their new Times Square location complete with a 60-foot Ferris wheel, 4,000-square-foot Barbie mansion, and 20-foot animatronic T-Rex dinosaur.

Similarly, this concept is integrated into many new mall developments and specific retail shops. The new Grapevine Mills shopping center in Texas installed large suspended televisions, oversized steel Texas-themed sculptures (50-foot footballs and state flags), and virtual reality simulators to entertain customers. Xscape, outside of London, integrated indoor skiing, rock climbing, mountain biking, and off-road car driving into an all outdoor equipment retail mall. Both of these malls found that the average visitor stays 3.5 to 4 hours rather than the traditional 45 minutes and spends almost twice as much per capita on merchandise and services.

Volkswagen recently opened the world's largest theme store, Autostadt, a $400 million, 62-acre factory/car dealership/theme park in Wolfsburg, Germany. Its 20-story glass and steel towers house hundreds of shiny new cars, ready for delivery. When one orders a Beetle, it drops down like a candy bar from a vending machine. Other attractions include a virtual reality ride through a giant engine and pavilions devoted to other VW brands such as Audi, Bentley, and Rolls Royce.

Safeway modified its food court concept in certain locations. It is more than a "fresh-to-go" concept with a nice assortment of premade foods; it includes entertainment. The initiative is a key factor in grocers' strategy to keep customers off the Net and lure them away from other leisure activities. In-store entertainment includes tossing noodle dishes in woks, making pizzas, and sliding them in and out of stone-baking ovens in full view of customers. The cooking staff attends a three-day course with actors to help them interact with customers with such tricks as juggling balls of pizza dough. On Valentine's Day, two women were sent to the store to play Cupid with customers as they waited in long queues. If "customer A" liked the look of "customer B," customer A wrote his or her phone number on a Valentine card, which the

Safeway employee ferried across to the object of affection. If the object responded negatively, "customer A" was consoled with chocolates or a balloon.

Edutainment combines playing and learning for parents who want to add substance to the cotton-candy experience. This concept is extremely popular with both for-profits and nonprofits. Several museums took advantage of the *Jurassic Park*-driven dinosaur rage by theming their exhibits along those lines. Additionally, historic, botanic, or national park sites are trying to enhance their experiences. Bonfante Gardens in Gilroy, California, created a 28-acre nonprofit theme park dedicated to trees, flower, and other flora. It offers 40 rides, shows, and attractions for the 12-and-under set with such attractions as a garlic bulb ride and a singing fruits and vegetables revue ("We're good for you!" they chirp). Instead of signs identifying every bush and flower, volunteers offer "moments of learning." Four learning sheds house video presentations that cover the birds and the bees and their impact on trees. In addition to the usual merchandise, such as T-shirts and mugs, the park runs a nursery with trees, shrubs, and other plants for sale.

The Great Wall of China Mutianyu site (north of Beijing) is trying to attract more visitors with fun. The Wall is an ancient monument built by a series of emperors to repel foreign invaders. It is studded with parapets and extends as far as the eye can see. But now it holds a curious blend of cultural history and theme-park style entertainment. To get off the Great Wall, one has two options: a ski lift or toboggans with a mile-long aluminum track that starts at the wall and winds its way through the woods to the parking lot in the valley. To go even one better, at the Jin Shanling site two hours from Beijing, a developer is putting the finishing touches on a terrifying-looking ride in which people hurtle down into that valley buckled into a skimpy harness that slides on a wheel down a cable stretched high above the ground.

Sometimes these concepts fail when designers stress the entertainment aspect at the expense of the core activity (e.g., poor food quality at Planet Hollywood). Care should be taken to ensure that the core activities such as eating, shopping, or learning, are not marginalized for the sake of entertainment. If done well, the experience should enhance the other activity. In Table 6.4, one can see a comparison of a winning and losing concept (Hard Rock Café versus Planet Hollywood).

Context

Context is the physical setting, particular selection and arrangement of products, the world of objects and social actors, and the rules and procedures for social interactions with other customers and service facilitators (Gupta and Vajic, 1999). In a service setting, context refers to the place where the customer consumes the service and everything that the customer interacts with in that setting. Bitner (1992) referred to this context as the "servicescape" and indicated that the organization should consider environmental dimensions, participant mediating responses (cognitive, emotional and physiological), and employee and customer behaviors. In particular, a provider should design a setting in which the meaning of the experience is created in a favorable way for individual customers. For example, Starbucks creates a "contemporary bohemian" context with a specific layout of comfortable living room furniture, bistro tables, and work areas; food goods such as freshly roasted coffee and baked goods; ambient sound with custom eclectic music mixes and guest artists; and learning elements such as selected books and magazines. The locations are chosen in specific trendy and young professional neighborhoods. This context encourages lingering over coffee, reading, working, interacting, or socializing with other patrons from that neighborhood. On the surface it would appear that getting people in and

TABLE 6.3: *Comparison of Two Themed Restaurant Experiences*

Dimension	Hard Rock Cafe	Planet Hollywood
Engagement: Entertainment and Food: • Get guests to stay/return • Make experience fun • Connect emotionally with customers • Increase thrill, surprise, delight	• Offers high-quality American diner/pub food • Has 100 cafes in 40 countries • Appeals to international music enthusiasts • Connects with irreverent, rebellious customer group • Keeps the legends and adds new talent constantly • Refreshes concept constantly and adds new features: hardrock.com, performances, CDs, and hotels	• Offered low-quality eclectic food, i.e., Cap'n Crunch chicken strips • Had 80 restaurants predominately in the United States • Appealed to celebrity seekers • Connected with tourists (not locals) seeking stars when stars are available • Depended on star availability at cafe • Kept a stable of celebrity stock-holders who may or may not be in favor • Difficult to refresh concept with-out constant major investments in hot stars • Added concept with sports stars
Context: • Theme • Learnable and usable • Mutable • Layout • Sensory • Social interaction	• "Authentic keeper of the rock music experience" • Updates atmosphere, locations, food, and music constantly • Allows different customers to create use environment and choose music • Designs layout for dining, drinking and/or concert • Offers high-quality multisensory experience • Encourages social interaction and fan building	• "Tribute to Hollywood" • Offered easy-to-understand concept but not well executed • Did not offer mutable stars; once stars have passed prime or do not want to visit sites, they lose appeal • Designed layout for dining and viewing memorabilia • Offered poor-quality food experience and unpredictable star-viewing experience • Offered limited interaction depending on location and time
Time: • Memorabilia • Continuity • Dynamic	• Offers constantly refreshed rock music memorabilia, live concerts of new and legendary artists • Provides customers with many opportunities to enhance initial experience through ongoing activities and international locations • Controlled expansion of concept over 30 years with careful location and relocation analysis	• Offered Hollywood memorabilia but no updating of merchandise • Found it difficult to attract contemporary stars, so lost key demographic customer; suffered from "graying of celebrity stable" • Provided limited reason to enhance initial experience • Hyper-speed expansion over 8 years and self-cannibalization

out quickly would provide higher revenues than having customers taking up a table for an hour drinking an espresso drink. But this ambiance sets them apart from other coffee vendors and successfully contributes to the Starbucks experience. Not only does the experience create long-term customer loyalty, but customers also buy the context elements (music, books, and coffee accessories).

Context is defined by six dominant elements: theme, learnable and usable, muta-ble, layout, sensory, and social interaction.

Theme

The experience should have an explicit or implicit theme. A coherent theme ties together all elements of the context into a unified story that captivates the customer.

Good themes alter the customer's sense of reality by affecting the experience of space, time, and matter, but also fit the character of the organization staging the experience. For example, the Venetian Hotel in Las Vegas has interiors, furnishing, and merchandise with an Italian theme. The hotel was built with a series of canals, and gondoliers take guests on boat rides through the hotel. The staff is dressed in traditional Italian costumes. Customers get the sense that they could be in Venice at the turn of the century surrounded by Doges Palace, Piazza San Marco, and the Rialto Bridge. Other themes are more subtle, such as "a sense of home," which can be cued by small touches such as baking cookies or apple pie aromas, cozy furnishings, stuffed animals on beds, and other homey accessories.

Learnable and Usable

The context should be designed so that the experience is easy to learn and use. The elements of the context should communicate their purpose and operations, as well as support different personal styles and different knowledge, skills, and strategies for problem solving. For example, Flat Top Grill Restaurant offers a concept in which customers put together a personalized meal of raw meats and vegetables at a large "salad bar," then take this meal to chefs who stir-fry the food on a big steel grill. In this environment, customers need to understand how to build a combination and which sauce to apply. The restaurants help the customers "learn" by posting suggestions in front of each sauce and by suggesting combinations on a big board over the bar. In addition, a service staff person explains the concept and sequence of events to each table.

Mutable

Because experiences should be inherently personal (to be meaningful), a good experience context has mutability. Mutability means incorporating flexibility in the system to allow different customers to create their own use environment during their interaction with the service. It is nearly impossible to force all customers to interact with a setting in an identical manner to create an experience. Each customer may need to use tools and interact with other customers or employees differently.

For example, at the popular new surf camps north of San Diego, customers are adventure seekers ranging from CEOs and celebrities to teenagers. At the weeklong camps, the diverse group sleeps in tents, eats together, and takes surfing lessons together. After initial group lessons, customers pick the type of wetsuit and surfboard to use each day; they can choose to surf alone, with any of the instructors, or with any of their fellow campers; and they can choose where and when to go out surfing. The instructors closely monitor each camper and intervene if they feel that they can improve the customer's experience (either socially or athletically). The instructors make sure that each camper leaves feeling as though he or she succeeded at having fun with the sport. It may require teaching one individual completely different skills from the other campers. The organization hires a diverse staff so that most campers find someone with whom they can relate.

Layout

Physical layout and organization of objects (tools, equipment, utensils, accessories, and other paraphernalia) should encourage active participation. The theme should be reflected in the arrangement of these objects and the organization of space. Layout should satisfy accessibility and visibility criteria, promote participation, and avoid chaos. The facility design, displays, and equipment should help the customer through the experience. The objects should be located according to their function and frequency of their use, bearing in mind that each customer uses tools in different ways.

SERVICE OPERATIONS MANAGEMENT PRACTICES

Developing a Theme and Creating Context: Joie de Vivre Approach

Joie de Vivre is San Francisco's fastest growing independent hospitality company and features 20 boutique hotels. Each carefully designed property celebrates the San Francisco Bay Area through its unique visual style, one-of-a-kind amenities, and highly personalized service. Joie de Vivre Hospitality sets itself apart within the hospitality industry by taking a themed approach to its businesses through the creation of a "refreshment identity" or crafted experiences for each guest. Chip Conley, founder of Joie de Vivre says it best, "Our goal is to create landmark hotels full of soul and personality!"

To design a context, Chip and his team first find a magazine that serves as a metaphor for what that hotel will be about. For example, the Hotel Rex is themed around *The New Yorker* magazine. The team then identifies five adjectives that will speak to their potential guests. These words build the context for all aspects of the hotel from the in-room directories, lobby, and room interiors, to the staff's dress and demeanor. For the Rex, the descriptors are worldly, sophisticated, literate, artistic, and clever. The resulting hotel is described as follows:

The Hotel Rex was inspired by the arts and literary salons of 1930s San Francisco. The

clubby lobby showcases period furnishings, original portraits, and walls of antiquarian books. Guestrooms feature the work of local artisans and an impressive selection of contemporary amenities. Hotel staff dresses as intellectuals with all black clothing and European-styled eyewear. (Conley, 2001)

Another one of their properties, Hotel Bijou, is themed around *MovieLine* magazine. Here the adjectives are dramatic, nostalgic, fun-loving, classic, and informal. This hotel is described as follows:

The Hotel Bijou celebrates San Francisco's rich cinematic history. Each room is named for a film shot in the city. It has "Le Petit Theatre Bijou" in the lobby showing double features of San Francisco motion pictures each evening. There is a candy counter at the Front Desk (because what movie palace experience would be complete without Jujubes?) and a hotline in their lobby with a direct link to the San Francisco Film Commission. There, guests can find out where all the current filming is in the city and even become an extra in one.

Source: Conley, 2001 and http://www.jdvhospitality.com

Designers of Ikea stores carefully addressed these layout issues. Each store contains a play center with activities for kids at the entrance to the store. Here parents can deposit the kids and then browse through the store comfortably. Conveniently located restaurants and sitting areas invite customers to relax and think about big (or little) purchase decisions. Pads and pencils for sketching and planning are located in highly visible and easy-to-use locations.

On the other hand, the Millennium Dome, an ill-conceived museum-theme park concept in London, suffered from tremendous layout problems, which led to unanimously poor experiences for the initial visitors. The most popular attraction, the Body, located at the entrance of the building presented visitors with giant queues as soon as they entered the Dome. Because the encompassing theme was not clear, people had no idea what to do with themselves after going to the popular Body attraction. Should they go to World Religion, the Circus, or Journey? None of the attractions fit together into a coherent story and lacked any obvious flow. Not only was the map of the place impossible to read, but signs to various attractions were not visible either. Bathrooms and retail shops were difficult to find; some restaurants and facilities had too much business during peak hours while others had none. When a new operations manager corrected these layout problems (through signage, new maps, customer helpers/guides, and flow management), the customer satisfaction index went up 30%.

Access your Student CD now for the PY and the Dome case study.

Sensory

Sensory stimulants not only increase *immersion* in an experience but support and enhance the theme. Popular sensory items are bakery smells, misting, lighting, and pyrotechnics; the more engaged senses the better. For example, going to a contemporary movie theater is a totally different sensory experience than staying at home and watching the video. The theater offers enhanced visual effects (consider the difference between watching an IMAX film over a typical movie), surround sound, comfortable stadium seating, and smells and tastes of popcorn and other treats. Today, several of the most successful theme park rides have addressed full sensory experiences. One of the best examples is Universal Studio's ride, *Terminator 2*. At different parts of the ride, real actors merge into simulated characters, metallic or smoke smells permeate the air when appropriate, the seats tilt and jolt, and ice crystals or fog surround the customers when ships take off. One really feels as though one is part of the action.

Most people, regardless of their age, would agree that Disney's *The Lion King* theatrical performance was a truly memorable experience. The play designers created this experience by immersing the audience in the performance. Characters dance and sing among the audience. The Conga drum players sit above the stage so that the audience can really see and feel the beat. The costume designer builds costumes from unique puppetry, creating half-human/half-puppet characters, shifting the audience's sense of reality, helping to fully engage the audience's senses throughout the performance.

Social Interaction

If social interaction were not important for an experience, then everyone would stay home watching TV or surfing the Internet rather than go to the World Series, attend a concert, or throw a party. Organizations need to look at how their experience design helps or hinders social interaction. For new customers who encounter difficulties in understanding the procedures or rituals of new experiences, assigned guides explain, enable customers to learn by doing, facilitate, or encourage customers to engage in novel activities and social interaction. Recall that in inherently personal experiences, we expect each customer to interact with facilitators and other customers differently. Thus, employees need to be well trained and be given autonomy to respond to specific needs. It requires skilled people who can dynamically personalize each event according to the needs, the responses, and behavioral traits of the guests.

Disney spends many months training employees on magic and how to connect emotionally with guests. Similarly, Cruse Lines and Club Med train their employees to look for different ways to get customers socially involved. On the other hand, they also must understand when to leave people alone who really don't want to interact and would rather lie on lounge chairs reading their books. Rather than using rigid scripts, the employees need to dynamically select sentences and individual props in response to statements, questions, and the body language of the guests.

Time

Experiences are an emergent phenomenon. They should be designed for enhancement over time, with new and constant learning. Good experiences are hard to copy and discourage switching. If all activities within the time frame of the experience are carefully orchestrated, they stay in the customer's memory, but the customer must also discover ways to build on his or her experience(s) with the organization. Management needs to consider three key elements in relation to time: memorabilia, continuity, and dynamic.

Memorabilia

Memorabilia serve several purposes for experience design. First, a physical reminder of an experience extends the memory of it long after the actual encounter occurred. Second, it generates dialog about the experience, encouraging word-of-mouth. Third, it provides additional revenue to the organization and free advertising. It is important to tie the memorabilia in with the theme of the organization. Of course typical approaches include photos of the guest doing the activity (eating dinner at Benihana, running in a marathon, shaking hands with a VIP), T-shirts, mugs, pens, and other overly used trinkets. Creative organizations use different approaches such as promoting exclusivity by making memorabilia scarce or by forming a members-only goods club. Groundswell Surf Camp puts both videos and photos of guests on their Web site, changing the content throughout the year. Former guests can periodically check the site for their own or friends' photos and view current surfing footage to relive the memories.

Continuity

Continuity describes the time aspects of experience as they relate to the individual. Experiences are inherently personal on emotional, physical, intellectual, or even spiritual levels; a rich experience modifies the person who has it and the quality of subsequent experiences. It fosters growth, arouses curiosity, and carries a person to a new and stronger place in the future. Customers move through different stages with a service as long as their service experience remains satisfactory. For personal experiences, customers cannot be expected to open up and fully engage on their first encounter. It may require a number of encounters for customers to reveal themselves. Over a period of time, trust and bonding needs to develop between the provider, customer, and even fellow customers. Service providers need to examine ways to build an experience for a customer over time. Computer game makers, such as the developers of "Myst," carefully design the experience to engage users in a long-term, unfolding experience.

Dynamic

There is a preferred or most desirable pattern for good experiences to reveal themselves over a specific time frame. Like good plays, movies, and musical scores, they begin at a low-level, increase in intensity to reach a climax, and then gradually subside. Each individual brings a different desire and capacity for expending their emotional resources over that duration. Organizations such as Outward Bound or National Outdoor Leadership School rely on long duration trips (two- to six-week trips) with varying intensity of challenging tasks (climbing Mount McKinley or sea kayaking in

SERVICE OPERATIONS MANAGEMENT PRACTICES

Using Time to an Advantage in Cruise Lines

A more desirable pattern for staging an experience over time has several key principles (Chase & Dasu, 2001):

1. **Finish Strong:** The end is far more important than the beginning because customers have a preference for improvement over time. So try to design an experience that ends on a high note.

    On a cruise trip, each day ends on a high note using activities such as shows, contests, raffles, etc. At the end of the cruise, the captain has a special celebration dinner and guests received special keepsakes upon reaching home port.

2. **Get the Bad Experiences Out of the Way Early:** If a service has to have a low point, such as paperwork or payment, then it's best to get this out of the way early so the rest of the activities are on the upswing from that point.

    For a cruise ship, liability papers and pre-billing are arranged in advance so that customers can forget about those painful activities during their vacation.

3. **Segment the Pleasure; Combine the Pain:** Put different pleasurable activities in a sequence together because it makes the experience seem longer. On the other hand, all negative activities should be combined to minimize their impact.

    Cruise lines pack many events into one short vacation. Guests feel like the trip had a longer vacation because they did so many different activities (cooking courses, yoga, dancing, educational side trips, etc.)

4. **Build Commitment through Choice:** People are happier and more comfortable when they feel they have some control over the process, particularly an uncomfortable one.

    Cruise ships offer different rooms for different prices. By clearly showing guests what they will actually get for their money in terms of amenities, the guests can choose to pay more for more services and space.

5. **Give People Rituals and Stick to Them:** People find comfort, order, and meaning in repetitive, familiar activities so deviations from expected rituals can cause dissatisfaction with the whole experience. Whether it is offering an afternoon tea or wine hour with snacks or decoratively arranging flower petals on a turned down bed at night, once a guest expects a certain delightful ritual, the service should stick with it or build on that theme.

    Many cruise ships offer the Captain's dinner and midnight buffets, which have now become expected rituals for those lines.

Baja) followed by a calmer and often festive situation. The students are eventually put in stressful situations such as surviving alone in the woods for several days with limited food and tools. Although this test is harder for some than others, the leaders carefully monitor the pre- and postsurvival periods to ensure that the individual actually saw the benefits of the "awful experience." Most graduates express fond (and long-term) memories of their ordeals and feel that they altered their lives in positive ways. See the "Using Time to an Advantage in Cruise Lines" feature.

EVALUATING SERVICE EXPERIENCES

The designer or manager should have a good idea about the current or desired experiential world of the customer. Understanding the customer's experiential world can be determined only by observing and/or interacting with the customer while he or she goes through the process. Because of the emotional nature of experiences, it is very difficult to use standard survey techniques to understand a service experience. As alternatives, there are several methods for understanding the customer's experiential perspective: Observation or video taping the environment, customer personal documentation of their interaction with the service, in-depth interviews, and experiential blueprinting.

Observing the Experiential Environment

Because an experience extends over time and can involve different segments and interactions, it is important to follow customers around while they interact with the experience and observe their behavior. This trailing can be done with hidden cameras or by intercepting customers while they participate in experiences and asking them what they like, dislike, or would like to change. Several health care providers have installed hidden cameras in the emergency rooms and were surprised to see that customers waiting to be served were left alone for several hours with no interaction from a human—an experience which did not jibe with the HMO's caring and trust themes.

Customers' Personal Documentation of Their Interaction with the Service

Another research tool for evaluating experiences over time is the personal diary. By asking a set of respondents to document in words, photographs, or videos, the things that they react to or notice during an extended service experience, the provider can learn many things about its current design. By allowing the respondents the flexibility to convey what they see and feel either visually or in words, a provider can get a more accurate picture of how different employee and customer interactions, usage, process flows, design features, and other elements are interpreted by the customer.

In-Depth Interviews

Similar to the above methods, an in-depth interview of a customer in the natural experience environment or with realistic prototypes can reveal the potential improvements or reactions to new service designs. By using a relatively unstructured interview, this format allows respondents to reveal their own ideas without leading questions. The interviewer can probe ideas to determine how to improve or why the respondent does not like a concept. For example, interviewers might ask, "What about this hotel makes you want to return (or not)?" "What about the room makes it comfortable?"

In addition, improvements or wish lists can be generated which provide new service design ideas.

Experiential Blueprinting

A basic process design tool from Chapter 5 (service blueprinting) can be modified to evaluate experience design. Here the researcher looks at every experiential aspect (or clues) of the process and evaluates it for conformance to key themes, sensory impact, resource requirements, and improvements (are we getting "bang for the buck?"). For example, an experiential blueprint for guest arrival at a hotel

FIGURE 6.3:   *Clue for Designed Experience*

Senses	Impact (high, medium, & low)	Resources needed to maintain Clue ($, time, logistics) Who is responsible?	How does the clue align or not align with above metaphor or descriptive words?	What can the business do to change or improve this clue for better alignment?
Taste				
Touch				
Smell				
Sight				
Hearing				

Clue Description:
Intended Experience or Emotion Connection from this Clue:

would start with the airport transportation and proceed through all the steps until the guest is settled in his or her room. At each step, a clue design form is filled out (see Figure 6.3) to address all the criteria. For example, Figure 6.4 shows a clue design form for the fresh baked chocolate chip cookies at Double Tree Inns. Obviously, one can imagine that the clue design card for the water fountains at the Bellagio Hotel in Las Vegas would be quite different and involve many other resources and responsible parties. This type of blueprinting and clue design form is useful for designing new experiences so that the managers are aware of the importance of simple things (such as lighting the candles in the lobby at night and changing the music to convey a different mood).

FIGURE 6.4: *Clue Design for Double Tree Chocolate Chip Cookie*

Clue Description: Double Tree Hotel Chocolate Chip Cookie
Intended Experience or Emotion Connection from this Clue: Home or Comfort

Senses	Impact (high, medium, & low)	Resources needed to maintain Clue ($, time, logistics) Who is responsible?	How does the clue align or not align with above metaphor or descriptive words?	What can the business do to change or improve this clue for better alignment?
Taste	High	$: Ingredients & labor Time: Constant baking Resp.: Front desk and baker	The cookie aligns well with a sense of home. It creates an image of "mom baking cookies for you after school" and other comfortable connotations. The smell of home baked goods reminds people of childhood and home.	Must produce high quality home made cookies throughout the day. Currently, the clue is well aligned. It is a well made and tasty cookie, always warm and fragrant. It is essential to deliver it hot to the guest, not over-baked, stale, or crumbling. The package should prevent guests from getting chocolate on their hands or clothes.
Touch	Low	$: Labor Time: Fresh as possible Resp.: Front desk and baker		
Smell	High	$: Labor and equip Oven near front desk and fan for circulation Resp.: Front desk cooks constantly		
Sight	Med	$: Labor Resp.: Front desk and baker		
Hearing	None			

Summary

The chapter outlined the importance of developing services with an experience focus in today's competitive market. We extensively covered the most important elements in a generic sense (applicable to both for-profit and not-for-profit industries). Pine and Gilmore (1998; 1999) state that experiences should be designed for people to pay admission for the experience element too, not just the accompanying product.

Review Questions

1. What are the critical elements of a good experience at a mass venue such as a baseball game or theater?
2. Describe how a theme restaurant with which you are familiar creates an experience.
3. Using the elements of context, describe how Borders designs an experience. How does Amazon.com attempt to compete on the same elements of experience?
4. How is the Internet limited in terms of creating experience?
5. What resources are needed to create experiences at theme parks today?

Selected Bibliography

Bitner, M. 1992. Servicescapes: The Impact of Physical Surroundings on Customers and Employees. *Journal of Marketing*, 56, 57–71.

Cain, J. 1998. Experience-Based Design: Toward a Science of Artful Business Innovation. *Design Management Journal* (Fall), 10.

Caves, R. 2000. *Creative Industries: Contracts Between Art and Commerce*. Harvard University Press, Cambridge, MA.

Chase, R. and S. Dasu. 2001. Want to Perfect Your Company's Service? Use Behavioral Science. *Harvard Business Review*. June. 79–84.

Conley, C. 2001. *The Rebel Rules: Daring to Be Yourself in Business*. Simon & Schuster/Fireside.

Gitomer, J. 1998. *Customer Satisfaction Is WORTHLESS: Customer Loyalty Is Priceless*. Bard Press, Austin, TX.

Gupta, S., and M. Vajic. 1999. The Contextual and Dialectical Nature of Experiences, pp. 33–51. In Fitzsimmons and Fitzsimmons (Eds.), *New Service Development*. Sage Publications Inc., Thousand Oaks, CA.

Hirschman, E., and B. Holbrook. 1982. Hedonic Consumption: Emerging Concepts, Methods, and Propositions. *Journal of Marketing*, 46(3), 92–101.

Pine, B., and J. Gilmore. 1998. Welcome to the Experience Economy. *Harvard Business Review* (July–August), 97–105.

Pine, B., and J. Gilmore. 1999. *The Experience Economy*. Harvard Business School Press, Boston.

Popcorn, F., and L. Marigold. 1996. *Clicking—16 Trends to Future Fit Your Life, Your Work and Your Business*. HarperCollins, New York.

Pullman, M., and M. Gross. 2003. Welcome to Your Customer Experience, Where 'You Can Check Out Anytime You'd Like, But You Can Never Leave.' *Journal of Business and Management*, 9 (3) 215–232.

Schmitt, B. 2003. *Customer Experience Management*. John Wilkey and Sons, Inc. New Jersey.

Van Boven, L. and T. Gilovich. 2003. To Do or to Have? That is the Question. *Journal of Personality and Social Psychology*, 85 (6), 1193–1202.

Vickers, A. 2001. Drop Everything, New Media. *The Guardian*, Monday, March 10, 50.

Wasserman, V., Rafaeli, A., and A. Kluger. 2000. Aesthetic Symbols as Emotional Cues, pp. 140–165. In S. Fineman (Ed.), *Emotion in Organizations*. Sage Publications Inc., London.

Wolf, M. 1999. *The Entertainment Economy—How Mega-Media Forces Are Transforming Our Lives*. Times Books, Random House, New York.

CASE STUDY

PY & the Dome

Access your Student CD now for the PY & the Dome case study.

The Millennium Dome, built in London, England, cost over a billion dollars of public funds and took six years to build. It was planned to be the largest tourist attraction in England, both figuratively and literally. It was forecast to have 12 million visitors per year, far beyond the volume of any other attraction in England. Further, it was so large physically that it could be seen from space.

It opened on New Year's Eve, 1999, to celebrate the new millennium. But the opening was a spectacular failure of service operations. Attractions broke down, waiting lines were hours long, and some displays just mystified the public. Less than two months after the opening, the leadership was sacked and PY Gerbeau was put in charge.

Access your student CD to see the project that was the talk of English talk shows for years: The Millennium Dome.

Questions:

1. Acting as PY, what strategy will you implement to show results to your sponsors and the media in 10 days? Prioritise the activities and specific actions plans, who will implement the steps, what they are supposed to do, determine how they will measure performance, how the costs will get covered, etc.
2. Does the Dome work as an "experience?" Why or why not? What would you do to improve the "experience" at this point?
3. Give your expectation of yearly attendance and how you expect to achieve these figures. How much revenue can the Dome expect to bring in with your attendance figures and strategy changes?

The Front-Office, Back-Office Interface

LEARNING OBJECTIVES   *The material in this chapter prepares students to:*

- Make appropriate decisions on job content for front-office and back-office jobs.

- Choose a back-office strategy.

- Understand the trade-offs of possible strategies.

- Understand the implementation issues involved in implementing back-office changes.

Applied for a loan recently in Tennessee? If it was with Bank of America, the loan decision was probably made in Tampa, Florida, by a lending officer you will never see nor know the name of. Your insurance claim was probably processed in India, as described in the Service Operations Management Practices: The Way-Back, Back Office: Offshoring. This chapter discusses the strategic decisions and operational management behind decisions involving back-office work. The pertinent issues are especially obvious when deciding to move work to a distant location. Many changes often need to be made: The nature of the work, compensation systems, and intrafirm relationships are likely to be different.

Service firms can be distinguished from manufacturers by the relatively high level of customer contact involved. Despite all the activities in a service firm that require the presence of the customer, a host of activities can or must be performed without the customer present. In banking, insurance, educational institutions, and other similar industries the application approval process usually occurs without the customer present and is often conducted by employees the customer may never speak to or see. Also, many physical products associated with a service firm are prepared outside of the customer's view. Examples include such diverse industries as food services, printers, or professional services like architecture and law. We label the work performed in service firms that does not require the presence of the customer as *back-office* work, and work that does require the customer as *front-office* work.

Throughout the service economy there has been a shift in where, how, and by whom such back-office work is performed. In many industries work that does not

SERVICE OPERATIONS MANAGEMENT PRACTICES

The Way-Back, Back Office: Offshoring

Your New York Life Insurance claim may be processed in Ireland. The Montreal telephone directory: Typed in Asia. Globalization of services is not new, but through modern communications networks, foreign locations can produce services that are timely inputs to domestic-end services. Several factors influence back-office service functions to move to foreign lands:

- *Technology*. Modern communications systems allow low-cost, rapid, reliable transmission of large amounts of data.
- *Cost*. The cost per verified keystroke is one-third the U.S. rate in places such as the Caribbean, China, India, and Ireland. Generous tax laws in some nations increase the financial attraction.
- *Language*. Many citizens in these countries grow up learning English. Although they do not understand U.S. idiom, they know more than enough to process insurance claims.
- *Flexibility*. Some foreign operations offer flexible labor practices (of course, many nations have far more rigid labor laws than the United States). Outsourcing services to a foreign subcontractor can allow for seasonal production that would be costly domestically.
- *Time-zone differences*. Otherwise known as playing "beat the clock," a U.S. worker can pass information to India at 5:00 P.M. and have tasks completed by 8:00 A.M. the next day in the United States.

The topic of offshoring is the subject of Chapter 8.

Source: Adapted from Wilson (1995).

require customer contact has been "decoupled" from front-office jobs. "Decoupling" means that separate job descriptions with different employees are formed around the back-office work, and those employees are often removed from the physical sites that deal with customers.

In general, many industries have been racing headlong toward more and more decoupling in recent years. This chapter describes what is happening in practice and explores the fit between a decoupled service delivery system and the firm service concept. Four decoupling strategies are also developed and illustrated.

CURRENT PRACTICE

A number of reasons explain the exodus of low-contact tasks from the point of service. A few examples are described here for the purpose of motivating the discussion.[1]

Consider the historical development of processing deposits in retail banks as an example of a decoupled activity. Some time ago, when one presented a check to a bank teller for deposit, the teller inspected the items, verified the deposit total, and

---

1. The following articles written by practitioners solely about retail banking are all supportive of decoupling, with some considering it the only real strategic option for the industry: Burger, 1988; Cronander, 1990; Gilmore, 1997; Pirrie et al., 1990; and Reed, 1971. (John Reed went on to become CEO of Citibank.)

gave a receipt. Then, during downtime or after closing, checks and deposit slips were encoded by branch personnel with dollar amounts. At the other end of the transaction, when checks written by a customer were presented for payment, clerks or bank tellers in a branch sorted the checks by customer, compared bank statement information against the checks, and stuffed and mailed statements on a monthly basis. The physical processing of exception items, such as stop payments and overdrafts, were also handled at the branch. The only activities still handled now at the branch level for most banks include inspecting items and giving receipts—even verifying deposit totals is performed centrally.

Postal facilities face a problem similar to that of banks: mail must be sorted in a similar fashion to checks. Due to extensive automation and decoupling the U.S. Postal Service successfully met a steadily increasing mail volume with a relatively constant labor force. From 1970, when the extensive push for postal reorganization began, to the present day, mail volume increased well over 100% whereas personnel increased less than 5%.

Other paper-processing industries experienced similar migrations of work content away from branch facilities. In a manner somewhat parallel to the decoupling described in the postal and banking industries, many firms decoupled their mail and accounts receivable processing functions to reduce costs. Governmental offices must by nature be dispersed throughout various regions, yet back-office record keeping is becoming more decoupled. Hospitals also engaged in decoupling and centralizing of back-office management. "Shared Service Centers" comprising decoupled general corporate functions such as human resources and corporate treasury and finance appear to be in vogue. As an example, the accounting, payroll, human resources, and other record-keeping functions for the *New York Times* newspaper are conducted in such a shared service center located in Virginia.[2]

The Internet and other modern communication advances are pushing traditional paper-processing industries even further toward decoupling. As noted in the Service Operations Management Practices: The Way-Back, Back Office: Offshoring, the ability to electronically move information, rather than mailing paper, allows decoupling on an unprecedented scale.

The ability to move operations from the front-office to the back-office and centralize those service activities appears to be held back merely by lack of imagination, and perhaps a supportive consumer market. For example, some medical diagnoses now are made in telephone call centers by nursing staff. With the aid of technology such as two-way television and electronic stethoscopes, patients in remote locations can be "seen" by physicians in central locations. In another example, the so-called "local" (and to customers, supposedly "live") television weather report for 50 stations across the United States is actually performed and taped in Jackson, Mississippi (Thomas, 1994). Though the weather forecaster cannot look out the window to determine accuracy, the broadcasts are convincing as local phenomena, at times even including taped rehearsed banter that appears to the viewing audience to be spontaneous live repartee between a weather forecaster and a news anchorperson.

THEORY IN SERVICES DECOUPLING

The theory behind decoupling relates back to the customer contact model of services by Richard Chase (1978; 1981) discussed in Chapter 1. The idea is that if a service

---

2. Examples of decoupling in each of the areas mentioned are contained in: Connors, 1986; Greene, 1990; Keith and Hirschfield, 1996; Queree, 1994; and Sharp 1996.

requires some high-contact elements and others that are low contact, those activities should be separated into different jobs done by different personnel. Several basic reasons are cited for this approach.

Efficiency

Decoupling improves efficiency on several fronts. First of all, production can flow far more smoothly when tasks are taken away from customer contact areas where customers' requests could potentially interrupt those tasks. Secondly, when one performs a small number of tasks over and over again, that person becomes highly proficient and efficient in performing those tasks. This same basic logic led to the efficiencies of the assembly line: Utilize division of labor to achieve efficiencies. Thirdly, these segregated, specialized tasks can now be centralized to achieve scale economies. These types of changes should lead to both improvements in conformance quality and cost, just as they did in manufacturing.

This general theory indicates that workers should not be segregated solely by job duties; they should be separated geographically as well. The cost benefits from separating the low-contact activities stem from their greater *potential* efficiency over high-contact activities. The way to achieve this potential efficiency is to physically buffer the low-contact activities from customers, essentially by sealing them off from the environment of random customer arrivals and nonstandard customer demands. In practice, many large back-office operations of service firms are housed in unmarked buildings so that public contact is channeled to appropriate venues. The cost benefits that accrue to this policy include highly efficient labor practices in low-contact areas and facility location costs reduced by locating low-contact facilities away from higher-priced retail settings.

Worker Personality Type

The argument that the two basic types of activities—contact and noncontact—should be segregated is based on differing sets of worker skills and orientations required by the two types of activities: Public relations and interpersonal attributes for high-contact purposes and technical and analytical attributes for low-contact purposes.

Conformance Quality

Conformance quality refers to the service being the same tomorrow as it was yesterday and getting reliable results from a process. When complex jobs are decoupled, and a single individual performs only one task, that task inherently experiences less variance.

Given the advantages of cost, conformance quality, and a better fit for personnel, back-office service decoupling appears to be an obvious recommendation. Both academic and practitioner literature converge on decoupling as a clear strategy to improve services.

LINKING DECOUPLING TO SERVICE CONCEPT

However, back-office decoupling often conflicts with the service concept of a firm. It is necessary to balance the potential operational cost savings against marketing losses stemming from a change in the nature of the service. To organize the discussion of how decoupling supports or conflicts with various service concepts, we adopt the framework of four general strategies mentioned in Chapter 2: Cost, Quality, Response time, and Flexibility.

Decoupling and Cost

Cost reduction is one of the basic arguments for decoupling, but increases in costs can also occur. More obvious cost increases include increased transportation costs and the substantial implementation costs. Cost increases also can come from increased idle time in high-contact workers, overlap of duties stemming from decoupled operations, and the reduction of duties without the reduction of personnel from high-contact units.

Idle Time

Personnel staffing in high-contact facilities is not usually based on average workload but instead in accordance with peak demand. The most fundamental results from waiting line theory (see Chapter 14) indicate that to offer any reasonable level of customer service, the number of service personnel must be large enough to more than accommodate the average customer arrival rate, which directly implies some idle time for high-contact personnel. Note that this time is considered idle only in the sense that it lacks direct contact with customers. If workers perform noncontact duties, the idle time can be filled. Of course, these activities are the most likely candidates for decoupling.

The amount of idle time depends on both the service level desired and the facility size. Obviously, better service levels for customers—smaller waiting times—require more employee idle time, but the effect of facility size on idle time is also important.

Well-established theory makes plain that the same customer service rate can be achieved with higher personnel utilization rates (or less idle time) in larger facilities. The basic lesson from centralizing waiting lines (see Chapter 14) is that relatively fewer personnel are needed to achieve the same system performance. In a decentralized system, some service personnel may be swamped with customers waiting while other personnel stand idle. When all work is centralized this variation cannot occur. Consequently, smaller facilities generally suffer from idle time problems more than larger facilities. Therefore, to realize the best worker efficiency and the lowest waiting times for customers, it is far better to have a few large facilities than several smaller ones. Although this objective can be accomplished easily in, say, large telephone call centers where customers from around the world can be effectively handled at one location, it is more difficult in service encounters that must be accomplished face-to-face. This distinction is becoming increasingly important as some industries move toward smaller, more numerous "kiosk" facilities to increase customer convenience.

Duty Overlap

When duties belonging to one employee are segregated and divided among several employees, identical information may be processed multiple times in a firm. Unlike the physical goods in manufacturing, a service "assembly line" working on documents or listening to a customer must usually repeat some steps of previous employees. Loan officers in banks with decoupled loan processing still review an application for correctness and completeness, then send it to the loan processing center where the first step is usually, once again, to review the application for correctness and completeness. The more steps are segregated, the more this overlap takes place.

Duty Reduction Without Personnel Reduction

The cost justification for the decoupling of facilities is usually based in part on an estimate of the work content removed from a high-contact office and the cost benefits accruing to the associated personnel reduction. The promised personnel reduction at the high-contact facility, however, may not occur due to three reasons:

1. *The necessity of keeping high-contact workers for customer service requirements.* Customer service standards dictate high-contact personnel requirements, so any reduction in the work content of high-contact workers below the amount of idle time built into the system will not produce any personnel reduction.
2. *Employee integrality.* Any personnel reduction due to the withdrawal of work content must be rounded down for each high-contact facility affected. That is, if one-fourth of a person's worth of work is transferred out, no gain is made—an entire person's worth of work must go to realize a true savings.
3. *Managerial philosophy in laying-off employees.* Concerns regarding morale and appropriate management technique often motivate practitioners to effect personnel reductions through attrition rather than layoffs, which may or may not actually occur, or may occur over such a length of time that the profitability of the project is affected.

Decoupling and Quality

Decoupling works well to increase conformance quality. Consolidating the performance of a task from many individuals to a few reduces the variability of the system. But true quality requires more than conformance.

Aspects of quality such as the dependability and accuracy of a service provided can be hindered by decoupling. At Bank of America in the late 1980s lending for automobiles and repossession of autos for loans in default were separate, decoupled activities. As a result of miscommunications, several "accidental repossessions" of automobiles of customers who were not in default on their loans occurred each month. It is difficult to imagine an accidental repossession taking place if the process were not decoupled and the same individual solicited the loan, received the payments, and made the collection calls if payments were not received.

Presumably, by specializing tasks according to worker skills and orientation, high-contact workers who demonstrate interpersonal and public relations skills should contribute greater courtesy and helpfulness along with the benefits resulting from personal charisma. On the other hand, decoupling decreases the span of involvement of the front-office service provider and increases the number of management layers involved in service provision. This dilution of responsibility may limit the ability or desire to respond to nonstandard customer requests, empathy for the customer, and the overall knowledge of the front-office worker.

Decoupling and Delivery Speed

Decoupling contributes to individual task speed from the task specialization and learning curve effects recognized since the times of Frederick Taylor and Henry Ford and from any automation that takes place. Task speed, however, is distinct from process speed. The time relevant to a customer is the time from service request to service provision, a process comprising many tasks as well as the waiting times and hand-offs between tasks. It is the waiting times and hand-offs between processes which can be negatively affected by decoupling.

One of the basic purposes of decoupling is diametrically opposed to obtaining quick delivery speed. Centralizing buffers the back-office from disruption and allows for smooth workflow, which reduces costs by allowing capacity, or personnel, to be held at average demand rather than peak demand. Because holding inventory ahead of time in such services is not possible, it is specifically designed to backlog customer orders. The decoupled portion of the service is similar to a manufacturing bottleneck: It is operationally desirable to have an inventory of work available to the bottleneck so that production is maximized. If the decoupled service is not behaving as a bot-tleneck, it is not serving its purpose of cost minimization.

A more insidious delivery speed problem stems from benign neglect, rather than design. Decoupled back-office services depend on high-contact workers to collect accurate and complete information, yet high-contact workers are usually rewarded for sales. Consequently, the focus of the high-contact worker is not on collecting information that streamlines back-office work, which may add time or require rework at the decoupled facility. Back-office rework reduces the capacity available at the bot-tleneck, which in turn leads to longer delivery lead time or the necessity of increas-ing capacity and reducing the financial advantage of decoupling.

Decoupling and Flexibility

The need for standardization in the name of cost reduction and the multiple chan-nels a customer request must go through once decoupling takes place contributes to the potential homogenization of the service. If high-contact workers see a customer need that requires bending the rules, they may need to obtain consent from multiple people in different physical facilities. Additionally, the workers in the decoupled facil-ity who must agree to the change are unlikely to know the customer. It is such dis-tance from the customer, combined with services standardization, that leads to such celebrated gaffs as a governor of the Federal Reserve Board being denied a Toys "R" Us credit card (Wessel, 1995).

Interviews with back-office personnel indicate that another side of this issue is also problematic. In an environment where high- and low-contact work is performed in separate facilities, high-contact workers may be willing to promise customers any-thing to get their business, even if they are aware that the back-office cannot provide the service. The high-contact worker thereby appears to give good service to the cus-tomer on the front end, and when the service is not delivered appropriately, blame can be shifted to the low-contact facility.

LINKING DECOUPLING AND FIRM STRATEGY

Figure 7.1 identifies four strategy types based on the characteristics of the level of decoupling and the general strategic focus of operations. Strategic focus is collapsed into the two dimensions of service and cost. In this conception, a number of various possible operational perspectives, such as flexibility, delivery speed, and quality, are included in the service strategic focus. Although they remain distinct operational advantages, achieving them requires similar choices with respect to decoupling. The four quadrants of Figure 7.1 represent distinct decoupling strategies that can be attained within a given industry, though not every quadrant may be relevant for every industry. Each of the four quadrants is characterized by an idealized set of opera-tional, marketing, and human resource policies (Table 7.1) and provides a distinct set of competitive advantages. Firms from several industries that share similar char-acteristics with the profile of these categories are included in Table 7.2.

It is helpful to consider an organizing example when discussing these strategies. Here, we use the context of retail bank lending. Consequently, an understanding of the retail lending process is helpful before proceeding. The activities involved in retail lending are generically described in Figure 7.2. All the activities in Figure 7.2 above the "Line of Customer Visibility" must occur with the customer present, but those below do not require the presence of the customer and are candidates for decoupling.

TABLE 7.1: *Consistent Functional Choices for Decoupling Strategies*

Management Practice	Cost Leader	Cheap Convenience	Focused Professionals	High Service
Level of Decoupling	High	Low	High	Low
Competitive Advantage	Low costs	Locational convenience at low cost	Provide experts: Back-office experts support front-office experts	Premium level of personalized service
Reason to Decouple	Scale economies	Maintain cost competitiveness	Quality control; disaggregation of high- and low-contact activities	Centralize only when it is cost prohibitive not to
Activities to Decouple	All back-office work	Due to small office size, only centralize back-office work in excess of front-office idle time	Back-office activities "regionalized," not decoupled	Activities requiring expensive capital goods
Operational Strategic Focus	Cost minimization; conformance quality	Cost minimization; Conformance quality	Maintain sufficient flexibility, response time, or service quality	Maximize flexibility, response time, or service quality
Product Line	Narrow	Very narrow	Broad	Very broad
Training	Narrow, focused on task within process; low cross-training	Broad; all employees should be able to perform each function	Narrow, but focused on an entire process rather than a task within a process	Broad, but with specialization across functions
High-Contact Worker Responsibility	Service customer requests; low off-site responsibilities	Service customer requests; low off-site responsibilities	Increasing number of customers largely through off-site activity	Increasing customer relationship depth; high off-site responsibilities
High-Contact Worker Compensation	Salary/hourly	Salary/hourly	Commission on sales	Salary with commission on unit performance
Purpose of Automation	Standardize activity; labor replacement	Reduce job complexity	Enhance marketing	Enhance service, maintain competitive costs

FIGURE 7.1: *Back-Office Decoupling Strategies*

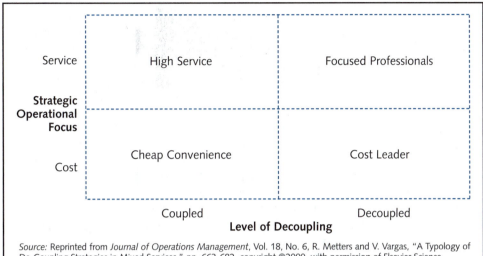

Source: Reprinted from *Journal of Operations Management*, Vol. 18, No. 6, R. Metters and V. Vargas, "A Typology of De-Coupling Strategies in Mixed Services," pp. 663-682, copyright ©2000, with permission of Elsevier Science.

TABLE 7.2: *Decoupling Strategies of Sample Firms*

Industry	Cost Leader	Cheap Convenience	Focused Professionals	High Service
Personal investing	Charles Schwab (discount stock brokerage)	Edward D. Jones (full-service stock brokerage)	Merrill Lynch (full-service stock brokerage)	American Express Financial Advisors, Inc. (financial planner)
Real estate	For Sale By Owner		Re/Max	
Insurance	GEICO		State Farm	
Legal representation	General Counsel Associates	Jacoby & Myers	Traditional law firm	
Medical	Shouldice Hospital	MedPartners	Columbia/HCA	The Tennessee Birth Place (birth center)
Photo refinishing	Kodak	Moto Photo		
General merchandise	Wal-Mart	Dollar General	Amway; Avon (network marketing)	
Retail doughnuts	Dunkin' Donuts			Krispy Kreme
Grocers	Food Lion (supermarket)	Convenience stores		

Source: Reprinted from *Journal of Operations Management*, Vol. 18, No. 6, R. Metters and V. Vargas, "A Typology of De-Coupling Strategies in Mixed Services," pp. 663-682, copyright ©2000, with permission of Elsevier Science.

FIGURE 7.2: *Activities in Processing a Retail Loan*

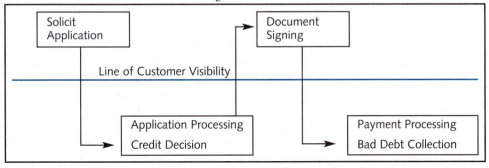

Retail lending involves customers seeking a loan for themselves personally, rather than for a business. Typically, the purpose of the loan is to purchase a large capital good, consolidate debts, or finance a vacation. After a loan interview, a significant amount of work is required that a customer does not need to be a part of before monies are disbursed. Due to the ubiquitous marketing of "15-minute" loan decisions, a general misunderstanding surrounds the work required in lending. In reality, quick loan approvals are only "conditional" approvals, and a number of activities must take place prior to loan closing. For virtually every loan, applicant credit history must be checked, employment and income must be verified in writing, a host of legal documents must be prepared, and a loan approval decision must be made. For loans involving collateral, the value of the collateral item requires inspection and appraisal, and the collateral ownership and various insurance coverages need verification. Customer contact again is required for signing documents. Also, significant post-loan processing includes insurance documentation updating, files and collateral documents maintenance, payoff quotations, and, in some cases, contacting delinquent borrowers and initiation of repossession/foreclosure, most of which is performed without face-to-face customer contact.

The specific decoupling strategies indicated in Figure 7.1 are now described in greater detail.

High Decoupling, Cost Emphasis: Cost Leader

For the cost leader the operational imperative is to reduce costs. Decoupling contributes to the pursuit of scale economies. The cost leader aggressively tracks technological innovation in the attempt to substitute automation for labor. Duties for high-contact personnel include a sufficient amount of back-office work content to avoid excessive idle time, but all other back-office functions are decoupled. Accordingly, compensation for high-contact personnel is not primarily commission based, because customers are attracted by broad-based marketing rather than through the efforts of high-contact personnel.

This focus on cost is a common strategy across many industries. Discount stock brokers, such as Charles Schwab, operate in a similar fashion to the retail insurance firm GEICO: They focus on cost reduction by eliminating the localized high-contact commission-oriented personnel that formerly dominated the industries to which they belong. General Counsel Associates provides low-cost corporate legal services by focusing solely on routine legal matters that require little customer contact, and they employ only seasoned lawyers who are well down the learning curve in such matters. Dunkin' Donuts, with more than 5,000 locations, achieves cost reductions in many areas by cooking doughnuts in centralized facilities that provide product for many outlets in a given metropolitan area. Some real estate firms augment their normal commission-based operations by selling space on the local multiple-listing service and offering a limited amount of counseling for a fixed fee. Other firms, such as For Sale By Owner in Dallas, Texas, provide a kit and a listing service to help homeowners sell their own homes.

AmSouth Bank is a typical example of this strategy in retail banking. At AmSouth a telephone call to a local branch is automatically routed to a decoupled, geographically distant call center that oversees several branches. Loan operations are heavily decoupled as well, with all 250 branches throughout several states faxing loan applications into a single service center. At the loan service center incoming faxes go to whomever is available. Job duties are highly specialized with little cross-training. For example, specific jobs are assigned to those who do data entry, appraisal ordering, disclosure construction, and underwriting. This decoupled system is highly efficient for standard customers, but can bog down with special requests. Consequently, special requests are not encouraged. Branch personnel complete only a few lines on the form to request special considerations.

For cost leaders, technology is used primarily to save labor. They centralize document preparation, electronically transmitting documents to branch locations for the closing of the loan. The task of loan approval at cost leader banks is also geared toward replacing labor with technology. A loan application may be taken verbally and entered into a computer by a customer service representative in the presence of the customer. But the branch is linked by satellite to national headquarters, where a computer statistically assesses the borrower's demographic characteristics and credit history via an electronic link to a credit bureau. Within seconds the computer informs the customer service representative whether the loan is approved. (Note that loan approval does not mean loan closing. Documentation, such as home appraisals and title searches, still must be conducted.)

From the perspective of the customer, a significant service downside accompanies such an automated system. Mistakes can be made. A significant percentage of credit bureau records are inaccurate. Some are obviously inaccurate, such as a 25-year-old applicant having a 30-year credit history or a credit record showing simultaneous home loans in several states for an applicant of modest means. In such a totally automated system, the physical credit record is not viewed by a person who could determine accuracy, only the computer-generated overall score is seen, which may be far better or worse than the applicant's actual credit record deserves.

Another downside involves personnel development. As one loan officer states, "There are no tough decisions to make." Loan officers never develop the ability to judge good credit risks and thereby the ability to more profitably focus their marketing efforts. Further, the product line is also truncated. The only collateralized loans handled by the central facilities generally are home, auto, and boat loans. If one wanted to use such high-value items as furniture, musical instruments (e.g., a grand piano), jewelry, coins, stamps, antiques, or art, as loan collateral, one would have to seek out another bank.

The jobs of the personnel at cost leader banks are different from employees at other banks. Rather than seek out business, these personal bankers tend to stay inside the branch and serve customers who walk in. Consequently, it is appropriate to receive the bulk of their income by straight salary. A large commission would not be appropriate, because customers are brought in due to overall bank reputation or advertising, but a small commission is helpful in motivating employees to service and cross-sell customers.

Low Decoupling, Cost Emphasis: Cheap Convenience

For the cheap convenience decoupling strategy, back-office work remains coupled for precisely the reason that cost leaders choose to decouple: Cost. Large numbers of small service units dot the landscape to enhance customer convenience while providing a limited product line at a low cost in what might be called a "kiosk" strategy. As discussed earlier, due to the smaller number of employees per unit, these firms suffer more potential idle time in high-contact facilities. Consequently, it is desirable to maintain a sufficient amount of back-office work in the front-office to fill this idle time, helping to keep costs low. Employees of cheap convenience firms should be cross-trained so that, ideally, any employee can handle any task. Correspondingly, it is difficult to have a broad, complex product line. Emphasis is placed on employee utilization and conformance quality. High-contact workers should be paid on a salaried or hourly basis.

In a number of service industries, firms compete in this part of the matrix. Edward Jones, a rapidly growing stock brokerage firm based in St. Louis, operates more than 8,800 offices, most with only one broker (up from 304 offices in 1980). The product line is somewhat abbreviated: Jones does not sell penny stocks, derivatives, or commodities. In the medical field, the strategy of Phycor and Med-Partners is to purchase the practices of individual physicians and put those physicians on salary. The cost of photo developing at Moto Photo, a chain of one-hour photo developers, is substantially higher than the cost leader strategy of mailing in film to be developed, but response time and geographic convenience provide a strategic advantage for their service. Similarly, Dollar General and 7-Eleven, both with thousands of sites, compete against the traditional cost leader firms in their industries by offering more numerous, convenient, small footprint stores.

The National Bank of Commerce (acquired in 2004 by SunTrust) applies this concept to retail banking. Largely, their branches are located within grocery stores, each with two or three employees working at any time. Cross-training levels are high. Aside from part-time employees, any branch employee can take a loan application or cash a check. Only retail products, however, are available at the vast majority of branches. Corporate customers are seen only in a few locations. Consequently, cross-training is limited to retail products.

Some portions of the lending process are decoupled. For some loans, such as auto and personal loans, preprocessing and loan approval are performed in the branch. For home equity loans, some portions of the work, such as arranging for an appraisal, are performed centrally. For all loan types, problem loan collection, insurance updating, and repossession/foreclosure are handled in a decoupled facility in Memphis, Tennessee. Employees are basically salaried with a small amount available in incentives for loans booked.

High Decoupling, Service Emphasis: Focused Professional

Operationally, this decoupling strategy divides high- and low-contact activities, segregating and centralizing low-contact activities, but with a primary goal of supporting the front-office, rather than cost control. Employee tasks are segregated according to personality type and abilities that conform to the worker suitability arguments discussed earlier. Employees are specialists and are paid for task performance. Consequently, commission-based pay is common. The goal for back-office operations is primarily to assist the high-contact workers in providing customer service and secondarily to control costs. Product ranges must be broad enough to meet the service objectives.

Traditional stock brokerages, real estate, insurance, and law firms are organized in this fashion. High-end retail outlets such as Brooks Brothers and Neiman Marcus use similar commission-based pay scales. Network marketing firms such as Amway also display some of these characteristics.

Union Planters Bank provides an example of a focused professional firm. Their loan officers are compensated largely by the amount of successful loan applications generated and are expected to spend 25% of their time outside the branch soliciting customers. All back-office work, however, is performed at regional loan operations centers, staffed with 20 to 30 full-time equivalents, that support 20 to 30 branches each. At the regional office, preprocessors are designated contacts for a subset of the branches served, maintaining a consistent face to the internal customer. Groups organized by function also serve as input, underwriting, and document processing teams. All employees are cross-trained to permit Union Planters to mitigate any back-office bottlenecks.

For the focused professional decoupling strategy, back-office activities are decoupled primarily to facilitate task focus and to ensure consistency of quality, with cost considerations being secondary. In the case of Union Planters Bank, back-office activity of a relatively small number of branches is decoupled by region, providing "more intimacy in decision making" in the words of a competitor. Because the focus of the back-office is to provide support for a more flexible system, rather than as cost control, it is far more imperative that the front and back office communicate well in a focused professional firm. In cost leader firms the front- and back-office employees may never know each others' names, but as one lender described his relationship with his back-office point person, "I send her flowers on her birthday and candy at Christmas."

In such firms, a potential danger results from the separation of high-contact worker pay from overall corporate results. In this scheme, the individual high-contact service provider no longer is charged with responsibility for an entire process, which can motivate individual service providers to act in ways that will benefit them to the detriment of the process as a whole.

Two examples of this problem can be taken from financial services industries. In banks where decoupled loan underwriting takes place, the job of the branch lender is to solicit applications, and they are often paid based on the volume of accepted loans. These lenders no longer have to collect on delinquent accounts or take the blame for an approved loan that results in losses to the bank. Quite the contrary, the only side of the loan equation they see is the customer who wants the money. Once the customer gets a loan, the loan officer need not interact with the customer again. Due to the combination of the change in the nature of their work and their reward systems, it is tempting for these loan officers to advocate strongly for every loan application. Discussions with lenders indicate that it is not uncommon for loan officers to polish applications to a high gloss prior to sending them to the underwriting department and to plead their customers' cases if the underwriters are reluctant regardless of the quality of the applicant. The life insurance industry faces a similar problem, known in the industry as "white sheeting," where brokers omit negative health information about customers on applications in order to maximize commissions.

Low Decoupling, Service Emphasis: High Service

A high service firm provides an exceptional level of personal service commanding a premium price. Maximizing flexibility and responsiveness are the key operations tasks. The competitive goal is to get beyond a transaction orientation and into a relationship orientation. At the extreme, the relationship with the customer may be so well established that needs/wants are anticipated prior to a customer's request. Marketing relies more on word-of-mouth and community outreach than mass mailings with discount offers or television advertising.

For this strategy, back-office operations are decoupled only where overwhelming advantages are provided by a technology that requires scale economies to be effective. Further, task separation is minimized. For the high-contact worker to have maximum flexibility and responsiveness, fewer layers of management, fewer workers to coordinate, and as deep a knowledge as possible about the customer are desirable. A broad, complex product line is needed to accommodate the range of customers' needs. Workers are primarily dedicated to customers, not products, so workers need a broad skill range. The general strategy here demands local, decoupled decision making to react to local conditions.

For the personal investing industry, financial planning firms represent this quadrant. A typical brokerage would not advise purchasing real estate; it receives no commission for the transaction. Financial planners, however, cover more than stocks and bonds. In medicine, focused firms are increasing along two dimensions: cost leaders and high service. The well-known Shouldice Hospital Corporation cut its costs and turnaround time by focusing solely on simple hernia operations requiring a standardized procedure. In contrast, birthing centers increase the turnaround time of patients and focus on individualized patient desires. As a foil to cost leader Dunkin' Donuts policy of decoupled cooking, Krispy Kreme makes doughnuts on each retail site, and lights up a neon sign that can be seen from passing traffic stating "hot doughnuts now" when each batch is ready.

In a high service bank each branch is like a bank unto itself. For retail lending, the branch loan officers personally handle virtually all aspects of retail loan processing (Figure 7.2) from soliciting applicants to collecting bad debts. The authority to approve the loan resides in the same person who solicited the application, the same person who must initiate foreclosure/repossession if loan payments are not made. This personal touch stands in marked contrast to the task of loan approval at cost leader banks where the goal is to displace labor with technology. The goal at high service banks is to develop and maintain a strong personal relationship that can last several years. High-contact service personnel are expected to know their customers' names and preferences. Community involvement plays an important role in attracting new customers. Pay for loan officers is largely salary based, but significant bonuses can be awarded based on overall branch performance. These banks also pay for officer memberships in local community organizations. Most branches are "full service," meaning that each branch can perform commercial and retail activities, whereas their more decoupled competitors are often dedicated units to either commercial or retail activity.

A study by Leath (1998) indicated that these banks enjoy an advantage in response time due to their coupled nature. Because hand-offs between departments are not necessary, work can proceed unimpeded for an important customer.

OPERATIONAL IMPLEMENTATION

The previous sections detail the potential advantages and disadvantages of decoupling, and provide a construct for aligning human resource, marketing, and operations decisions. The extent to which a firm can benefit from decoupling back-office activity depends on how it is implemented. Here, we explore three issues in implementation: (1) strategic congruence, (2) designing back-office jobs to assist the interface between front and back offices, and (3) the speed of implementation.

Strategic Congruence

It is not unusual for different functions in a service enterprise to have different strategic outlooks, such as a revenue maximization orientation for one area versus a cost minimization orientation in another. These differing views must be reconciled, though, for a firm to succeed.

Strategic congruence presents an especially vexing problem for organizations with decoupled activities. As a back-office area is decoupled, it may be tempting to manage the decoupled activity for cost control, ignoring the effects of such management on the rest of the business. Given the necessarily myopic views of the differing factions of product managers, program administrators, and functional area managers that persist in any large organization, strategic congruence is difficult to attain. By its nature, decoupling creates more departments and requires more administrators, which makes achieving a congruent strategic framework among tactical decisions more difficult.

As a broad example of mismatched strategies, a cost leader discussed earlier, AmSouth Bank, advertises itself as "the relationship people," even though all local calls to a local branch are automatically switched to a decoupled call center—which is often located in a different state—and local branch personnel have no lending authority.

Compensation also presents a difficult issue. For cost leaders, employees largely service walk-in traffic and are not expected to become prominent community members who bring in business by force of personality. Consequently, commissions are largely a function of random daily traffic and the economic status of the local community. Commissions do serve a purpose in these institutions: They give an incentive to adequately perform duties and to sell more products to a customer who walks in. Accordingly, commissions should be a relatively small percentage of salary.

Back-Office Job Design

The linkages between front- and back-office activities require attention. Reward systems must encourage coordinated action, rather than focusing myopically on the task in that particular office. This prescription extends to management as well as labor. For example, management and labor in back offices can have peer evaluations by front-office personnel included in their performance review.

It is generally believed that internal motivation, job satisfaction, and effectiveness are linked to the knowledge of the results of work activities, the degree to which a task seems to be an identifiable unit, and the responsibility that an individual feels for the outcome of his or her work (Hackman and Oldham, 1980, p. 90). Certain managerial choices within the back office affect these issues. One can choose to structure a department where contact from front-office personnel is taken by any available worker. Alternatively, a specific back-office worker can be assigned as a contact person for each front-office worker. Worker assignment helps build long-term relationships between front- and back-office personnel, assists in reducing the amount of overlap work due to differing personal styles, and provides more personal responsibility to the back-office worker. Given a long-term relationship with a specific front-office worker, back-office workers are no longer just processing paper for a customer they may never meet, they are meeting an obligation for someone with whom they have a relationship. These benefits, however, may come at the expense of flexibility to pool common back-office capacity or an increased variability in processing times because peak demands are less easily shifted among back-office personnel under such a plan.

It is appropriate at focused professional, high service, and cheap convenience firms for their high-contact workers to maintain specific contacts at low-contact facilities. For cost leaders, though, the best structure for the smoothest flow of work and, therefore, the lowest costs does not commonly include any personal liaison between the front and back office. This separation makes two processes difficult: communicating nonstandard transactions and following up for customers when problems occur.

Another choice available is the level of specialization within the back office. High levels of job specialization may be related to high task efficiency, but, as argued previously, may lower both task speed (due to duty overlap) and overall process speed (due to queuing between tasks) and may lead to the need for increased levels of supervision. Conversely, when workers take responsibility for an entire process, it reduces all of these factors. According to Hammer (1990, p. 113–114), "The fact that a worker sees only a piece of the process calls for a manager with a broader vision . . . [when workers] provide end-to-end management of the process, . . . the need for traditional managers [is reduced]." Further, having responsibility for an entire process helps employees see their duties as an identifiable unit, which provides a more intrinsic motivating influence.

Implementation Speed

For firms that desire to move toward decoupling, two opposing forces affect the speed with which it is done. From both a financial perspective and presenting a consistent face to the customer, it is best to decouple and centralize quickly and completely throughout a network. Having a positive net present value on decoupling projects may depend on the timing of personnel reduction.

But an opposing force argues for gradual implementation. One of the benefits of dividing front- and back-office work is that many workers are intrinsically better suited to one or the other. It is reasonable to assume that many workers who are currently employed in the front office are there because they favor interpersonal skills over technical ones. Decoupling activity means shifting staff from the front office to the back office, either by moving current workers with mismatched skills or by wholesale layoffs and new hires. Neither prospect is particularly attractive.

As an example of such a dilemma, in 1983, Crocker Bank, then the thirteenth largest U.S. bank, began centralizing many branch loan and deposit functions. At the time, more than 100 trainees were going through an 18-month program to become branch operations managers, essentially a back-office position, but one that physically takes place in the branch. Because of the decoupling taking place, it was clear that no new operations managers would be needed, so all the trainees were immediately switched to a front-office retail lending training program. Either these trainees had highly malleable personalities or, more likely, they were poor candidates for new retail lending positions.

Summary

The decoupling of back-office service activity provides a strategy recommended by researchers and heavily used by practitioners for some time. Much of this decoupling is pushed by technological advance and results in far higher productivity. Advantages from decoupling include both financial advantages from labor specialization and the pooling effect of combining the work from many individual units. Further, advantages associated with a better fit between job descriptions and worker personality types can be realized.

Many disadvantages, however, are also possible. Decoupling should lower costs and increase productivity, but due to increases in idle time, increases in total work needed to be done due to duty overlap, the lack of actual personnel reduction that takes place, and self-serving behavior, these supposed advantages may not occur. Further, the key competitive strategies of quality, delivery speed time, and flexibility may be impaired.

The disadvantages of decoupling can be exaggerated by improper implementation and a lack of strategic focus. Here, four general strategies use decoupling to achieve different strategic purposes.

Review Questions

1. What are the main reasons service firms decouple back-office tasks from the front office?
2. Why should decoupled back-office tasks be centralized?
3. What service concepts does decoupling support or not support?
4. How can decoupling add to a firm's cost structure?
5. How does a decoupled system affect delivery speed?
6. How does the speed of implementation of a decision to decouple make a difference to a firm?

Selected Bibliography

Burger, K. 1988. Leveraging Bank's Operations Dollars Powers Superregional Growth. *Bank Systems and Equipment*, 25(5), 68–71.

Chase, R. 1978. Where Does the Customer Fit in a Service Operation? *Harvard Business Review*, 56(6), 137–142.

Chase, R. 1981. The Customer Contact Approach to Services: Theoretical Bases and Practical Extensions. *Operations Research*, 29(4), 698–705.

Connors, J. 1986. Massachusetts Department Centralizes Records System. *Office*, 103(6), 126–128.

Cronander, J. 1990. Centralization versus De-centralization: What to Do with Back Office Operations. *Texas Banking*, 79(10), 29–33.

Gilmore, D. 1997. Lending and Centralization: Is This the Future? *Real Estate Finance Journal*, 12(4), 89–90.

Greene, J. 1990. De-coupling Paying Off at Not-for-Profits. *Modern Healthcare*, 31–32.

Hackman, J., and R. Oldham. 1980. *Work Redesign*. Addison-Wesley Publishing Co., Reading, MA.

Hammer, M. 1990. Reengineering Work: Don't Automate, Obliterate. *Harvard Business Review*, 68(4), 104–112.

Keith, D., and R. Hirschfield. 1996. The Benefits of Sharing. *HR Focus*, 73(9), 15–16.

Leath, J. 1998. Study Identifies Best Practices in Core Processes of Consumer Lending. *Journal of Retail Banking Services*, 20(1), 35–39.

Metters, R., and V. Vargas. 2000. A Typology of De-coupling Strategies in Mixed Services. *Journal of Operations Management*, 18(6), 663–682.

Pirrie, D., De Feo, J., Scott, I., Abramson, F., Comber, S., Myhill, S., Berry, J., Legg, S., and G. Lockhart. 1990. The Bank of the Future: Lloyds Bank; Barclays; Bank of Scotland; TSB Bank; The Toral Bank of Scotland; Birobank; Abbey National; National Westminster Bank; Midland Bank. *Banking World*, 8(12), 19–31.

Queree, A. 1994. Shared Financial Services. *Corporate Finance*, 113, 37–39.

Reed, J. 1971. Sure It's a Bank But I Think of It as a Factory. *Innovation*, 23, 19–27.

Sharp, J. 1996. Service from Afar. *Editor & Publisher*, 129(29), 30–31.

Thomas, E. 1994. You May Not Know Your Weatherman Is in Jackson, Miss. *The Wall Street Journal*, (November 2), A1.

Wessel, D. 1995. A Man Who Governs Credit Is Denied a Toys "R" Us Card. *The Wall Street Journal* (December 14), B1.

Wilson, M. 1995. The Office Further Back: Business Services, Productivity, and the Offshore Back Office. In, P. Harker (ed.), *The Service Productivity and Quality Challenge*. Kluwer Academic Publishers, Boston.

The "Future Bank"

For a big bank, it was a big change. In describing the plan to enact "Future Bank," a different vision of retail banking, John Georgius, president of First Union Bank, said, "This is massive. This is a huge, fundamental change to what we do."

Georgius's points of comparison come from presiding over other "massive" changes at First Union. Largely, banks were required by law to operate in just one state of the United States before the industry was deregulated in the mid-1980s. After interstate banking laws were changed First Union took full advantage, buying 70 banks in 10 years. First Union grew from being the third largest bank in Charlotte, North Carolina, into the sixth largest bank in the United States by 1998. The biggest acquisition was in November 1997, buying Philadelphia-based CoreStates for $16.5 billion, history's largest bank merger at that time.

In 1998, First Union decided to challenge banking tradition by turning the retail bank branch on its head with the Future Bank concept. The point was to get bankers out of the branch and selling—developing an aggressive, sales-oriented culture at First Union. Bankers will be changed from salaried decision makers sitting behind a desk to a commission-only salesforce that cold-calls customers. First Union's product line also escaped the bounds of traditional banking products to include products such as mutual funds and insurance.

The plan to reach customers through a variety of methods does not include the large, monolithic, marble-halled, downtown bank branches of old. Its methods combined Internet banking, minibranches, and a call center two-thirds the size of the Pentagon. "Future Bank" was set on an expedited timetable to achieve company-wide implementation by January 1999. The stock price responded highly favorably to the changes, increasing 151% from January 1995 to March 1998.

As to infrastructure, the Future Bank integrates the back-office functions into the branch. Job duties in the branches are altered significantly. Customers entering a branch are met by "greeters," rather than the traditional method of a customer trying to figure out where to go themselves. The job of the greeters however, is not just to provide warm and fuzzy service, but to save the bank money and help integrate the back-office by directing customers away from branch personnel and toward automatic teller machines (ATMs), or to connect them by phone to the call center. It is estimated that ATMs handle transactions for $0.27 while tellers cost $1.25 per transaction.

To change the traditional culture of the branch from waiting until customers walk in to being more proactive, branches receive several hundred names every day of prospects and suggestions on what products to sell to them individually.

The Future Bank compensation structure differs significantly from a traditional bank. Everyone in the branch is on a commission system based heavily on sales. The variable portion of pay accounts for 40% of pay for branch staff. Naturally, with the immense changes, old job descriptions were out and new ones created. Current

CASE STUDY

employees were invited to apply for the new jobs they felt best fit with their talents. First Union also recruited heavily from outside the banking industry, hiring those with a knowledge of how to sell, rather than a knowledge of banking. "There will be a fair number of people who decide they do not want to sell," Georgius said, "but our company has got to move on."

An example of the way Future Bank is supposed to work is personified in the way Barbara O'Connor now makes her living. "A key to Future Bank is people like Barbara O'Connor. She has an office at a First Union branch, but her real office is her car. Working from a notebook computer, she scans names and prepares presentations as she drives to offices and homes around Atlanta. She books appointments on her cell phone. Banks have always had some employees catering to the rich, but her target market is people with about $75,000 in income whom she can persuade to consolidate their financial affairs at First Union. When she hooks a prospect, she turns new customers over to a service representative who does actual banking tasks, freeing her to hunt for new money. O'Connor draws no salary and is paid purely on commission, with no limit to the amount she can earn."

Source: D. Greising (1998), "Fast Eddie's Future Bank," *BusinessWeek*, March 23, 75–76.

Questions:

- What implementation difficulties lay ahead for First Union?
- How will consumers react? Which consumer markets are being approached/ withdrawn from by this strategy?

Offshoring and Outsourcing

LEARNING OBJECTIVES *The material in this chapter prepares students to:*

- Understand the size and extent of offshoring and outsourcing.

- Know the risks and benefits of offshoring and outsourcing.

- Decide what activities in a firm should be offshored or outsourced.

The hype: 3,400,000 white collar jobs with $151 billion in annual wages will leave the United States for low-wage countries by 2015. A Silicon Valley venture capital firm partner states "In a couple of years, 90% of all start-ups will have some connection to India or China." The Gartner Group forecasts that offshore BPO (Business Process Outsourcing) will have an 80% compound annual growth rate through 2007. "Any job that is English language based . . . can be done in India," claims Scott Bayman, CEO of GE India.[1]

The offshoring of white collar jobs seems especially unnerving to many people in developed nations. When manufacturing jobs fled to low-wage countries, solace could be taken in the prediction that a new age of the "service economy" was being entered, and that shedding low-wage, dull, routine jobs was a precursor to a new economy filled with high-wage, interesting, innovative jobs that required educated workers. With the offshoring boom, however, some of those high-wage jobs are moving offshore. Some high-end consulting firms are getting their client presentation PowerPoint slides made overseas. Stock research for U.S. investment banks is being done in India. Even white collar jobs at venerable U.S. firms seem to be at risk. An internal IBM memo leaked to *The Wall Street Journal* indicated that up to 4,700 white collar jobs with annual salaries of $75,000–$100,000 were to be offshored to workers in India whose expected salary range was $10,000–$20,000 per year (Bulkeley, 2003). Those losing their jobs would be required to train their replacements in the United States for several weeks. They would then have 60 days to find another job within IBM, or face unemployment.

How can developed countries compete when someone in a lesser developed nation will do the same job for one-tenth the salary? The issue has gotten the attention of the U.S. Congress, which is considering several laws restricting offshoring (see Service Operations Management Practice: The Empire Strikes Back). This mood seemed to be perfectly captured by the *BusinessWeek* magazine cover page: "Is Your Job Next?" (February 3, 2003).

---

1 *Sources:* Hilsenbath (2004), Geewax (2004), *The Wall Street Journal* 2004, Knowledge@Wharton, 2003a, Clott (2004), p.166, respectively.

SERVICE OPERATIONS MANAGEMENT PRACTICES

The Empire Strikes Back

The U.S. Congress is considering many laws that have an impact on offshoring. The names of these acts are:

- Defending American Jobs Act
- U.S. Workers Protection Act
- USA Jobs Protection Act
- Jobs for America Act
- Trade Adjustment Assistance Act (1974) extension to services

(Currently, the Trade Adjustment Assistance Act provides training to manufacturing employees who are laid off because their jobs are sent overseas. Currently, this act applies only to manufacturing jobs, not service sector jobs.)

At least 36 States are considering over 100 laws banning or restricting offshoring in some form. Many of these laws are probably unconstitutional, as they usurp foreign affairs powers from the federal government, or otherwise illegal, as they violate existing international treaties, but they are politically popular to propose to angry, unemployed constituents.

The effects of these possible laws are:

- End corporate tax structure favoring offshoring
- Require a three month lay-off notice if offshoring
- Require informing customers of where work is processed
- Ban sending private information (financial, medical, or other personally identifiable information) overseas
- Eliminate corporate tax deductions for expenses of offshoring jobs
- Bar federal loans, grants, or contracts to a firm if it lays off more U.S. than non-U.S. workers, and
- Bar federal contracts to offshore locations unless the activities were previously performed offshore.

Source: (Phillips, 2004, Klinger and Sykes, 2004)

This chapter examines the phenomenon of offshoring and a term offshoring is frequently confused with: Outsourcing. We detail what types of activities are currently outsourced or offshored. The ethics of offshoring and outsourcing are explored, with a focus on who profits from these activities and the governmental responses that have occurred. Finally, a road map is developed to help sort out what types of activities should be offshored, kept on shore, outsourced, or in-sourced.

OUTSOURCING

The words "offshoring" and "outsourcing" are frequently used interchangeably, but actually have very different meanings. *Outsourcing* refers to hiring another company to perform a task that is currently performed internally. The vast bulk of outsourcing is done "onshore," so it is a separate decision from offshoring. Typically, outsourced activities are deemed not central to the mission of a company, or activities that outside vendors can perform more efficiently, with better response time, and/or at better quality. For example, many firms outsource peripheral functions such as their cafe-terias, janitorial duties, copy centers, trucking, building maintenance, payroll, etc. These activities are usually seen as not being the core, central activities of the firm doing the outsourcing. Further, it is reasonable to assume that a firm that runs, say, hundreds of cafeterias as their main business could run a cafeteria more effectively than a firm that only runs one cafeteria, where the cafeteria is merely a side busi-ness. Examples of this type of outsourcing include outsourcing payroll to ADP, or document processing to Xerox.

Another main reason for outsourcing is to gain expertise in technically advanced areas. The Information Technology (IT) area in many firms is outsourced due to this issue. IT physical technology and software changes rapidly. Many firms feel that small, in-house units have a hard time keeping up with the latest technology. It is believed that firms that dedicate themselves to these tasks, such as EDS, Computer Sciences Corp., IBM, or Perot Systems can be more innovative in this area because they are specialized firms. Even relatively large firms have outsourced IT. An early leader in this thinking was Eastman-Kodak, a Fortune 200 firm, that outsourced vir-tually all its IT functions in 1989. Virtually all firms outsource much of their legal work for this reason, as well. Although large firms will have in-house lawyers on their payroll, they outsource much of the more difficult work to established law firms.

Activities that have a high degree of variance are also good candidates for out-sourcing. That is, if one day 50 employees are needed and the next day only 10, then to provide good service 50 people should be on the payroll. An outsourcer, however, can utilize the benefits of centralization (see Chapter 14). That is, the day that one of their clients needs 50 people is often the day another client only needs 10, and vice-versa, so an outsourcer can save substantial money by staffing for the average demand level, rather than staffing for peak demand. For example, Intuit outsources its sales and product service processes, even though they are considered "core" processes. Intuit's main products are tax and accounting related (e.g., the tax soft-ware "Turbotax®"), which have very heavy seasonality. According to their Operations SVP, "If we did not outsource these contacts, we would spend more of our time hir-ing, training, and laying off seasonal employees than executing for our customers" (Adsit 2003, p.99).

Potential outsourced activities would follow the logic introduced in Chapter 7 on decoupling of services. If an activity can be reasonably decoupled, then it is a *candidate* for outsourcing. For example, in the auto loan process for the mythical Bank of A, repossessing autos for unpaid loans is a portion of the process. We examine three basic choices—though more than three choices exist—Bank of A has in determining who does repossession work that are of interest for this chapter: (A) have a Bank of A employee who has substantial contact with the customer do the repossessing, (B) have a decoupled unit within Bank of A do it, or (C) contract out the whole, messy business to the third party provider, such as "Repos 'R' Us." (A summary of these choices and what one should be looking for in terms of activity characteristics is in Table 8.1.)

A business would consider several factors to determine which choice to make. As noted in the last chapter, scale is important. If this activity takes place infrequently, a dedicated unit (option B) is too expensive. Outsourcing (option C) can be used for infrequent jobs (a firm "outsources" the job of taking someone to the airport to a taxi-cab company), but is usually not appropriate for more frequent activities. Going through the search for a repossession firm, creating a contract with service level met-rics, monitoring the service provider to make sure it does the job properly, and enforcing a contract is simply too much effort for any gain involved. For example,

TABLE 8.1: *Activity Characteristics to Consider for Outsourcing*

| | Outsourcing Choice | | |
| | In-Sourcing | | |
Activity Characteristic	Coupled (Choice A)	Decoupled (Choice B)	Outsourced (Choice C)
Scale	All	Moderate or High	Low or High
Expertise needed	Customer specific	Firm specific	Process oriented
Strategic importance			Low
Demand			High Variability

Source: Reprinted with permission from *Journal of Marketing*, published by the American Marketing Association, A. Parasuraman, Valarie A. Zeithaml, and Leonard L. Berry, Fall 1985/Vol. 49, p. 47.

experts recommend that accounts receivable departments should be kept in-house if there are fewer than 50 jobs to be outsourced (Gattenio, 2004).

If the scale is sufficient, either options B or C may be considered—but with the disadvantages detailed in Chapter 7, which are summarized briefly here. Because options B and C move the activity away from the central point of customer contact, there can be some problems.

The goals and measures of a dedicated back-office unit may be different from what a front-office considers good service. It is natural for dedicated or outsourced units to have a cost focus, as they are often measured by productivity. So, rather than staffing sufficiently to handle all the work on a heavy day, it may staff to an average workload and let service requests gather dust on heavy days.

There may be a problem with "organizational commitment." That is, workers that do not have contact with the customer are unlikely to have as much empathy with the customer as those who do, leading to less of a desire to provide flexibility for non-standard customer requests or situations. Further, since outsourced workers do not work directly for the outsourcing firm, there is a chance they will be less loyal to that firm, and less likely to burn the midnight oil to help the firm thrive. These and other reasons discussed in Chapter 7 often cause firms to keep potentially outsourced activities in-house, and in the front office.

As noted in Chapter 7, scale and technology are intertwined. Some technology operates efficiently only at a scale that precludes keeping work in-house. For example, many small banks outsource the check processing function to larger banks, as the most efficient check sorting machinery is very costly and operates efficiently only at high volume.

There are also qualitative differences between outsourcing and having dedicated internal units (Table 8.2). Outsourcers could be considered experts at their particular task, so they can often perform tasks more cheaply and at better quality than dedicated internal units. But outsourcing generally is more risky. Outsourcing suffers more acutely from contract risk, firm risk, pricing risk, information privacy risk, and strategic competence risk.

Contract Risk

The relationship with an outsourcing firm is governed by a contract, whereas the relationship of an internal unit can be influenced in more informal ways. That is, an

TABLE 8.2: *Risks and Benefits of Outsourcing*

Benefits	Risks
Access to expertise	Contract appropriateness
Pooling effect on variability	Outsource firm (solvency, strikes)
Lower costs	Future pricing
Higher quality	Information privacy
	Competitive advantage
	Firm specific risks
	Loss of firm knowledge
	Loss of career paths
	Organizational identification
	Loss of customer empathy
	Loss of employee-firm identification

outsourcer may contractually live up to the specified Service Level Agreements in the contract, but if not all the actual desired services were specified in the contract, or if business conditions change and different levels of service are desired, conditions cannot be as easily altered with an outsourcer.

Outsource Firm Risk and Pricing Risk

Once a task is outsourced it can be expensive and difficult to change outsourcers or to bring the task back in-house. Both *firm risk* and *pricing risk* speak to this issue. *Firm risk* is the risk that the outsourcer may collapse financially, forcing a company to find a new solution on short notice. It's the unsettling feeling that "(i)f the vendor goes bankrupt, all I can do is try to hire its former employees" (Barthelemy, 2003, p.88). Outsourcing firms may experience labor strikes, so even if the client firm typically enjoys good labor relations, they can still be shut down. *Pricing risk* is the risk that a company can become so tied into a particular outsourcer that the outsourcer can drastically increase prices in the future, or not cut prices when prices in the rest of the industry are falling, leaving a company with few options other than to pay.

Competitive Advantage and Information Privacy Risk

Several risks relate to the competitive environment. Depending on the task outsourced, sensitive company information is shared with an outsourcer. A risk exists that the outsourcer could share or sell this information to competitors. Finally, there is a competitive risk of mediocrity endemic to outsourcing. By outsourcing a process to a firm that performs that process for many other firms, one is essentially giving up trying to be better than the competition at that process. Consequently, outsourcing is generally restricted to processes that are not seen as being at the strategic core of a firm.

Firm Specific Risks

If a firm outsources a task, the institutional knowledge associated with that task also leaves. There are no longer personnel on hand who know entire processes, which can lead to breakdowns as processes change. That is, there's no one with the knowledge to say, "if we do it that way, it causes a problem in the next process." Another firm-specific risk is that of dwindling career paths. Outsourcing creates flatter corporate hierarchies, with fewer rungs on the corporate ladder to climb.

OFFSHORING

Offshoring is a decision independent from outsourcing, but highly intertwined with decoupling (Chapter 7). Offshoring can be defined as performing work for customers in one country in a different country. The offshored unit can be either "captive" (owned by the same firm that did the work onshore) or outsourced. For example, General Electric, American Express, British Airways, Swissair and many other firms have captive call centers in India (*The Economist*, 2003b). The workers in India handle callers from the United States (offshoring), but are employees of the American firm.

Most service jobs can never be offshored. Serving a meal, making a bed, fixing a flat tire on the highway, and the vast bulk of service jobs must be done in person. However, the scope of jobs that are able to be offshored is wide. Basically, any task that is either transmitted electronically or can be shipped is a candidate for offshoring. "Transmitted electronically" encompasses data sent via computer, voice and video communication, as well as scanned documents. Currently, offshored activities range from mundane data entry to high level product design (Table 8.3).

Some especially embarrassing incidents of offshoring include New York City parking tickets being processed in Ghana (Worth, 2002), and New Jersey's welfare help line being answered in India (*The Economist*, 2003b). Due to public outcry, both of these activities were brought back to the United States.

Manufacturing offshoring has occurred in substantial numbers for quite some time, but services offshoring has a more recent feel, and has increased rapidly since 2000. However, services offshoring has existed in small amounts for several decades: American Airlines began processing airline tickets in the Caribbean in 1983.

By the mid-1990s it is estimated that 10,000 workers in the Caribbean, 3,000 in Ireland, and 10,000–20,000 in Asia were performing offshored service work for U.S. firms (Wilson, 1995). Largely, this was processing paper work. Paper was physically flown in and dumped in the in-boxes of workers, who might turn around the work in a few weeks. The main task these workers performed was factory-like keypunching of data that was not time sensitive. The reason for moving this work offshore was the enormous cost advantage: At the time, the price per 1,000 verified keystrokes was $1.50–$3.50 in the United States, but only $0.90–$1.25 in the Philippines (Wilson, 1995).

Technology, however, transformed the type of work that could be done, and the response time in which it could be been done. Voice communication technology has

---

TABLE 8.3: *Activities Often Offshored*

Professional judgment:
   medical diagnosis (e.g., radiology), computer programming, product design, architecture, legal services, tax preparation, document editing, securities research, consulting presentation preparation

Communication oriented:
   call centers, customer contact centers

Back-office transaction processes:
   human resource department activity (medical reimbursements, payroll, benefits),
   finance department activity (accounts receivable, accounts payable),
   loan administration (initial mortgage application processing, payment processing, collateral tracking, loan payoffs, collections),
   insurance (new account setup, policy issue, address/beneficiary information change, claims processing: examination, capture, settlement, and correspondence),
   data entry (credit card receipts, warranty cards, medical transcription, etc.)

changed most abruptly, so call centers provide a good example of the explosiveness and suddenness of the technological impact. In the past, it was operationally infeasible to locate a call center overseas. In 1966, there were so few telephone connections between the United States and Europe that only 138 simultaneous trans-Atlantic conversations were possible (Frank and Cook, 1995, p.48). A story told is that some Citibank employees would be "dedicated dialers," repeatedly trying to connect with their European offices. Once a connection was made, giving it up was unthinkable—employees would read the paper to one another over the phone rather than stop the call. The first trans-oceanic fiberoptic cable, in 1988, could by itself carry 40,000 conversations, but it was still cost prohibitive to call overseas. In the late 1990's, however, the amount of fiberoptic cable was increased, and the call carrying capacity of any one fiber was drastically increased by the technological advances of multiplexing (putting multiple calls on the same line) and optical switching (replacing old electronic telephone switching equipment with light-based switches). Between 2001 and 2002, the capacity of fiber-optic lines from the United States to India increased nearly seven fold. As of early 2004, the cost of a trans-oceanic line capable of handling 128 simultaneous calls had plummeted to $11,000/month, one-fourth of what it was only two years prior (Drucker, 2004). Within the short span of a couple of years, the entire cost structure of the call center industry has changed. Third-world labor has always been drastically cheaper than in developed countries, but the technology cost barrier has crumbled.

Technology has also had a profound impact on paper-based offshoring. As noted previously, offshoring paper-based work such as accounts receivable, payroll, etc., involved actually physically transporting the original documents overseas, which resulted in time delays. They were then keypunched into a computer system, and the data relayed back by satellite. Now, original documents are scanned in the home country, and the scanned images can be sent electronically overseas, reducing both shipping costs and response time. This was not a welcome strategy prior to 2000 because the bandwidth available to move these images overseas was highly restricted.

A substantial portion of offshore services involves computer programming, and "technology" played an important role there, as well. In the late 1990's, it was feared that many older computer codes would cause substantial problems for businesses when the year 2000 occurred. Although computer RAM and hard disk space is rarely a constraint today, it was a major problem at the dawn of the computer era. To save space, a significant amount of software written through the 1980's assumed that any yearly date would begin with 19 and required only the last two digits as input. Of course, in the year 2000, these programs would view the year as either 1900 or 19100. It was feared that this problem would create havoc throughout computer systems, so the old computer code had to be rewritten. There was too much work to do for domestic programmers, so much of this task was sent out to places like India. The results of this collaboration of necessity helped convince developed nations that lesser developed nations could produce timely, accurate, and cheap code, and writing code continues to be the largest outsourced task today.

QUANTIFYING OFFSHORING

The precise extent of services offshoring can only be guessed at. No government collects authoritative numbers, and many companies are very secretive about their offshoring practices, as they are worried about domestic customer backlash.

The estimates of how many jobs have been lost in the United States due to outsourcing: 400,000 by Forrester Research (Vina and Mudd, 2003), 200,000 by the

Information Technology Association. How many people are in India and the Philippines answering telephone calls from the United States?: 250,000, according to the Technology Marketing Corporation, 55,000 according to Warburg-Pincus (*Knowledge@Wharton*, 2004b), while another source cited 160,000 (Basu, 2003). The total number of jobs in India doing offshore work? NASSCOM says 171,000 (Vina and Mudd, 2003), *Fortune* magazine quoted 350,000 (Fox, 2003).

In terms of dollar impact, the numbers are equally diverse. McKinsey Global Institute (2003) stated that $30–$35 billion/year is offshored from the United States, with Ireland the leader at $8.3 billion and India in second at $7.7 billion. Infosys (2002), a billion-dollar-per-year Indian firm, estimates there are $10.2 billion offshored to India alone. The Gartner Group estimated world-wide offshore Business Process Outsourcing activity at $1.3 billion, but Giga Information Group estimated Indian BPO alone at $1.5 billion (*Knowledge@Wharton*, 2004c).

OFFSHORING AND COMPETITIVE CAPABILITIES: COST

While the extent of offshoring is debatable, there are clear reasons to offshore. The reason that gets the most attention is comparative labor rates. While a call center employee in the United States might make $25,000/year, a call center employee at ExlService in India, a leading offshore BPO firm, averages $4,000/year (2002 wages).

However, the differential wage rates are misleading, as there are other costs involved. At a wage rate of $4,000/year, employees cannot afford cars, so it is not unusual for employers to provide free transportation to and from work. There are usually no restaurants nearby work, and even if there were, due to time zone differences Indian call centers serving the U.S. market must work during the middle of their night, so "lunch" is at midnight. Consequently, free or highly subsidized employee cafeterias are common. While terrorism is a concern worldwide, both the Philippines and India have had numerous terrorist attacks on their soil. Expenses related to security can be high. On a visit to an Indian call center the author of this chapter had his car searched for bombs merely to enter the parking lot, then had to pass through several heavily armed guards to enter the facility. In lesser developed countries, infrastructure is not as well developed, leading to higher costs. For example, it is not unusual for electrical or telephone service to shut down. In response, offshore service providers often purchase their own electrical generators and have duplicative technology for telephone access.

Training is much more extensive and expensive, especially in call centers, where an offshore employee must interact in real time with someone from another culture. American Express puts their Indian employees who speak to U.S. customers through 3–4 months of training. On average, English-speaking Indians speak English faster than the typical American, and they speak English with an accent that creates difficulties for Americans. Consequently, a common part of training is both slowing down their speech and accent neutralization. It also greatly helps to know not merely the language of a customer, but the local idiom of that language. Some firms require or encourage call center employees serving the United States to watch episodes of popular TV shows to keep up with trends and speech patterns. The expense of training is vital due to turnover: While turnover appears to be quite a bit less in India than the United States, 30% is not uncommon, meaning that the percentage of time in training is a significant portion of their total employment.

Differential tax rates also drive offshoring, as many countries have provided specific tax advantages to attract offshoring. Ireland attracted a large amount of offshoring due in large part to the tax advantages provided. The standard U.S. corporate tax rate is 35%. The standard tax rate in Ireland is 43%, but BPO firms get a preferential rate of 10% until 2010. Jamaica has a 34% tax rate normally, but the "Digiport" BPO free trade zones are tax free. Mauritius offers personal tax holidays to key employees involved in BPO. In general, corporate tax rates in many areas of the world are less than in the United States. and Europe. Offshoring tax policy has become a minor issue in the 2004 U.S. presidential race. As of the writing of this book, the U.S. tax code favors offshoring over keeping work domestic. U.S. corporations are allowed to defer taxes on offshore units until the money is repatriated back to the United States, thereby giving firms an interest free loan on taxes owed if they offshore work.

OFFSHORING AND COMPETITIVE CAPABILITIES: NON-COST ISSUES

Pro-offshoring Arguments

Besides clear cost advantages, another reason often cited for offshoring work is higher quality. Most of the jobs developed countries offshore are considered undesirable in the home countries. Call center work in the United States is generally not considered glamorous, and generally attracts workers who don't stay long. Most BPO offshoring involves data entry: Entering accounts payable/receivable into a computer system, typing handwritten medical records, and the like. Domestically, employee turnover for these jobs often reaches 100%, and the jobs have little status.

In other countries, however, that is not the case. In India, call center operators brag about having 20 to 100 applicants for every job and being able to hire college graduates for these positions. This work is seen as "professional," and has a much higher status than in the United States. Because these jobs garner higher esteem in other parts of the world, companies can get higher quality workers who pay more attention to detail. One British bank reported call center agents in India process 20% more transactions, with 3% higher accuracy, than their counterparts in Britain (Agrawal et al., 2003). A "prominent financial services company" in the United States offshored and outsourced their call center to the Philippines and reported a combined 25% reduction in call handling time with an increase in customer satisfaction levels (Hagel, 2004).

The quality differential is marketed heavily for computer programming projects. There is a process certification for software developers called CMM (Capability Maturity Model). The highest rank is CMM level 5. Fifty of the 74 CMM Level 5 firms in the world are in India (*http://www.sei.cmu.edu/cmm/high-maturity/HighMatOrgs.pdf*).

A possible advantage in some businesses can involve response time. One can exploit time zone differences to get work done more quickly, known as playing "beat the clock." A request e-mailed at the end of the normal work day in the Western Hemisphere will arrive at the beginning of the normal work day in the East. So, by the time the normal work day starts again in the West, a number of work hours can be dedicated to the request.

Anti-offshoring Arguments

Thus far, only issues favoring offshoring have been expressed. However, there are many factors that militate against offshoring. Projects that require constant communication or refinement, seasonal or temporary services, services of insufficient size, services where local knowledge or tacit knowledge are important, where cultural differences are salient, or where cultural biases are present are poor candidates for offshoring.

Offshoring shares many of the negative elements noted in Table 8.2. Even if the offshore unit is not outsourced, the physical distance can create problems: There may be an increased risk of loss of customer empathy and loss of career paths. In addition to the risks noted in Table 8.2, country risk needs to be considered when offshoring. The managerial concerns are summarized on Figure 8.1.

Communication Requirements

The prior section ended with a possible increase in productivity and response time: Play "beat the clock" and magically get work done while you sleep. If this sounds like an ad from a late night infomercial, it's because it can have a similar result. Frequently, a substantial amount of communication is required to get a job done correctly. The initial charge is either too vague, has some errors or omissions, is misinterpreted by the receiving party, or, as more facts are found, turns out to be wrong. For tasks that require a substantial interplay between customer and service provider time zone differences can cause problems.

FIGURE 8.1: *Choices for Electronically Transmitted Services*

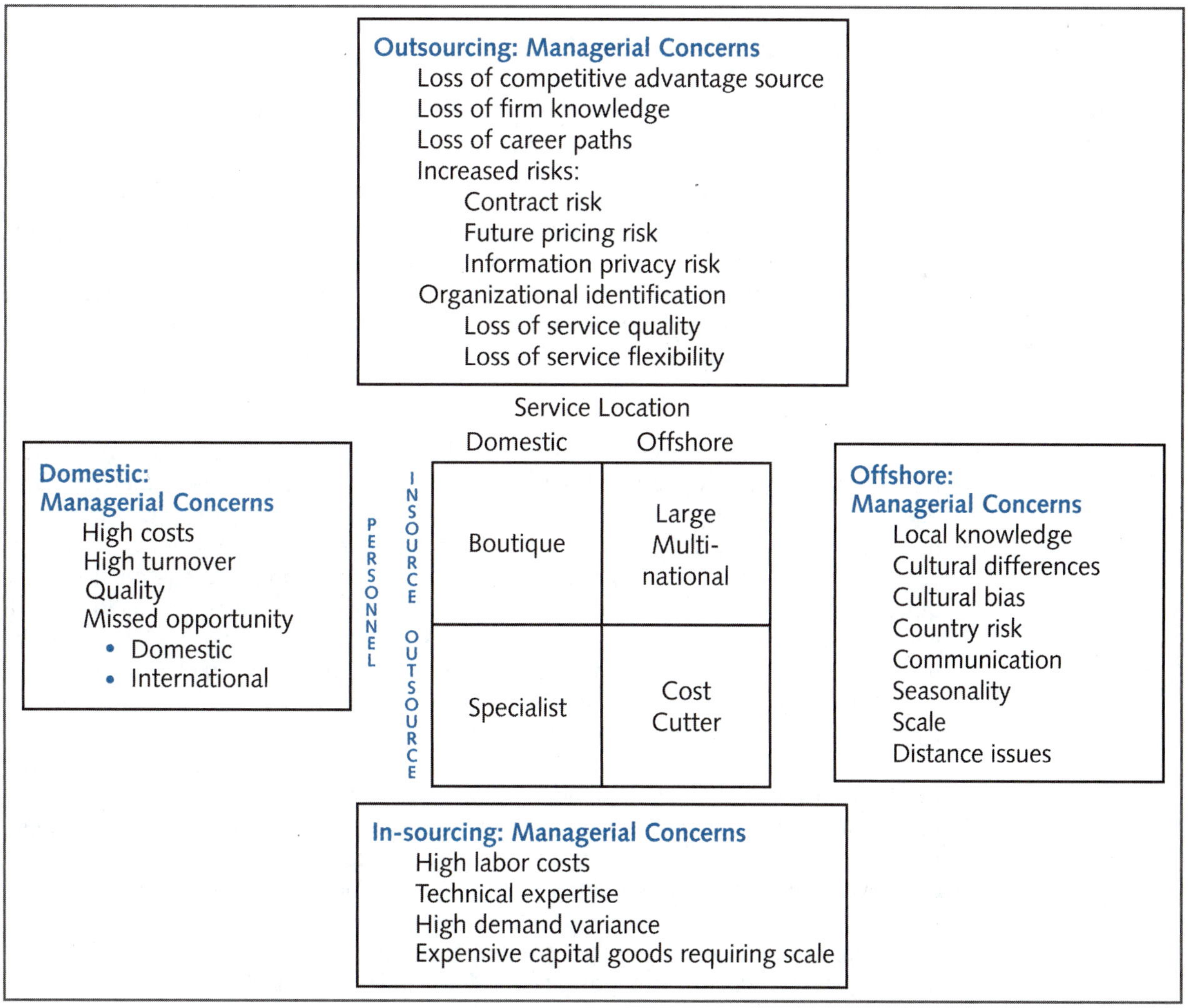

Outsourcing: Managerial Concerns
- Loss of competitive advantage source
- Loss of firm knowledge
- Loss of career paths
- Increased risks:
  - Contract risk
  - Future pricing risk
  - Information privacy risk
- Organizational identification
- Loss of service quality
- Loss of service flexibility

Service Location

	PERSONNEL	INSOURCE / OUTSOURCE	Domestic	Offshore
INSOURCE			Boutique	Large Multi-national
OUTSOURCE			Specialist	Cost Cutter

Domestic: Managerial Concerns
- High costs
- High turnover
- Quality
- Missed opportunity
  - Domestic
  - International

Offshore: Managerial Concerns
- Local knowledge
- Cultural differences
- Cultural bias
- Country risk
- Communication
- Seasonality
- Scale
- Distance issues

In-sourcing: Managerial Concerns
- High labor costs
- Technical expertise
- High demand variance
- Expensive capital goods requiring scale

SERVICE OPERATIONS MANAGEMENT PRACTICES

Who's Offshoring Where?

The choice of offshoring destination differs dramatically by country of origin. Below is a list of common offshoring destinations. For the most part, this is language oriented. Unlike manufacturing offshoring, services offshoring generally requires a detailed knowledge of the offshoring country's language. For example, former colonial relationships often result in a large pool of indigenous population who know the language of the colonial power—a talent which can land offshoring jobs. There may also be a "cultural proximity" element: Those cultures that are most alike do more business.

Offshoring country	Offshoring to
U.S.	India, Philippines
United Kingdom	India
Spain, Portugal	South America
Germany, Switzerland, Austria	Eastern Europe (Hungary, Czechoslovakia)
Finland	Estonia
France	Rumania, Mauritius
Italy	Serbia
Japan	North East China

Beyond the time zone issue, any geographic separation makes work that requires constant communication difficult. One way to adapt to this is to have employees of the outsourcing firm physically in the building with the firm doing the outsourcing. This is very common in services outsourcing in general, such as copy centers, janitorial, etc. This technique allows for a job to be outsourced, but not offshored.

Cultural Bias

An important political issue is customer tolerance to offshoring. This is a political issue that is of great concern to many customers, just as the "made in America" campaigns caused customer anger at foreign manufactured goods years ago. There may be entirely xenophobic reactions by customers hating all offshoring, or customer objections might have an underlying racial element. For example, a customer may be quite angry at the thought of offshoring to India, but if the call is answered in Ireland, it's "OK." Some have posited that a relative lack of "cultural openness" explains the relatively small amount of offshoring from the main European countries, although a significant amount of European business is involved in offshoring (see Service Operations Management Practice: Who's Offshoring Where?).

A great deal of training in some call centers is devoted to hiding the fact that the service provider is offshore. Instead of answering the phone, "hello, this is Akbar, you have reached New Delhi," some call centers have required their workers to assume names common to the population calling them and to adopt fake home towns in the country of interest, so "Akbar from New Delhi" becomes "Chip from Chicago" (Landler, 2001).

There is little evidence on the extent of customer resistance and cultural bias, but there is one experiment to report. The online lender E-Loan, Inc., gave customers a choice: Have your loan handled now, in India, or request your loan be processed in the United States, and wait as long as two days more: 86% of their customers chose India (Drucker and Brown, 2004). On the other hand, Dell Computer's move back to the United States from India may be related to this issue, or it may be due to higher quality of its U.S. employees (*The Economist*, 2003a).

Cultural bias works in both directions. Many developing countries have cultural norms and mores that are in conflict with working for Western corporations. Specifically, women who dress appropriately for office work are viewed as promiscuous in some countries (Freeman, 2000), and some Indians see call center work as destructive to traditional family values there (Abraham, 2004). Some types of work are simply inconsistent with certain cultures. As an extreme case, can one imagine offshoring the Victoria's Secret call center to a traditional Muslim country?

Country Risk

If international relations between countries become tense, governments may impose trade constraints, which could effectively shut down a business if all its back-office operations were being performed in that country. Some of the bills being considered in the U.S. Congress at the writing of this book could shut down the medical transcription offshoring industry and the offshoring of many financial processes due to data privacy concerns.

Country risk also includes economic factors. For example, while Indian labor is certainly cheaper than U.S. labor, it has been reported that the offshoring boom is increasing Indian call center wages by 10–15% per year. Also, exchange rate changes can turn long-term commitments sour.

Both the increased distance and different legal systems involved in offshoring heighten contract risk. Contracts must be written that are binding in both legal systems. But there is a deeper issue: Even if the offshore firm clearly breaks a contract and owes penalties, what is the probability a firm can win a legal dispute against a foreign firm in the foreign country? The level of trust with a foreign firm has to be higher than the level of trust with a domestic outsourcer.

Further, there are idiosyncratic country risks that need to be taken into account. Just as anyone setting up a facility on the San Andreas fault in California needs to have an earthquake contingency plan, setting up operations offshore means developing contingency plans based on the specific threats to that location.

Cultural Differences

Potentially more important are the cultural and language differences between customers, domestic employees, and offshored employees. Although offshored workers assisting U.S. customers generally must understand the English language, there may be differences between how the workers and customers use language, leading to problems. In the United States, the word "turnover" means employees leaving, but means "gross revenue" to most other English speaking people around the world. The abbreviation "4 2nate" for the word "fortunate" is readily translatable for a native English speaker, but may cause problems for a worker that mentally translates "4" and "2" into their native language and then wonders who "Nate" could be and what he wants 42 of? Training in the idiom of the customer is important, but no reasonable amount of training can cover all situations.

Cultural problems also manifest themselves in terms of behavior, specifically humor or rudeness. What is merely "direct" in one culture is "rude" in another.

Consequently, offshore workers may be angering customers without realizing it. Often, humor doesn't travel well between cultures. While this is unimportant for transaction-oriented work, it can be important for more high-level or high-communication oriented work. Situations where establishing a good rapport with the customer is important, such as outbound sales or collection calls, could be affected.

Cultural differences may hamper the empathy between employees and customers. It is conceivable that workers making $300/month may feel little connection with, and may even resent, customers from another, more wealthy, part of the world making $3,000/month who complain about not having enough money.

Local Knowledge/Tacit Knowledge Requirement

Other types of services where offshoring makes little sense are services where local knowledge or tacit knowledge are key. This type of knowledge has long been the "official" reason for giving travel agents free trips to resorts. Someone who has actually "been there and done that" is a better resource than someone looking at a description on a computer screen. Local knowledge can allow someone to say "I've seen a lot of people wearing that color in downtown Chicago this year," or "if you're rafting the Stanislaus River this May, you might also want a wet suit—the water is about 36 degrees." Offshore employees just wouldn't make the sale.

Lack of Scale, Seasonality, and New Businesses

In the discussion on outsourcing, it was noted that scale is helpful—outsourcing small tasks is more trouble than it can possibly be worth. Offshoring is even more extreme. Starting up an offshore destination often involves hiring an intermediary between the domestic and offshored workers, having executives travel and observe the offshore destination, and having a team "qualify" potential offshore suppliers. For these reasons, there is a large fixed cost to starting an offshore operation. This large fixed cost cannot be overcome unless the size of the job to be offshored is sufficiently large.

A similar problem with overcoming setup costs accrues to seasonal tasks and start-up operations. Seasonal work, like staffing retail oriented call centers during the Christmas season, is difficult to do in offshore environments due to the length of training offshore workers require. Similarly, start-up operations are usually both small and uncertain—their operations may change significantly, or even be shut down. The higher fixed cost of operating offshore is difficult to justify in these cases.

Losses Due to Distance

The physical distance and crossing of national borders necessary in offshoring exacerbate some problems inherent to outsourcing. When customers are 12,000 miles away, it may be easier to feel less empathy for them. Career paths also lose out in offshoring. Domestic junior people may not want to start for a firm at the bottom, if the bottom means moving to a third-world country and being paid $300/month. Consequently, domestic employees may never experience those jobs. Conversely, once an offshore employee has reached the peak position in what is offshored, she or he faces moving to a different country to advance. While some will jump at the opportunity, others will not.

THE ETHICS OF OFFSHORING

Is offshoring good or bad for the offshoring country? Should the government get involved?

Typical arguments proposed against offshoring manufacturing tasks in the past decades don't seem relevant to the services debate. It was often said that other countries prevailed in the manufacture of steel or textiles because they ignored environmental concerns or exploited child labor—but these aren't genuine concerns for much of services offshoring. The call center employees are college graduates, not 10-year-olds, and how much industrial pollution does typing data into a computer cause?

The traditional pro-offshoring argument is that it fuels economic growth and is beneficial to all countries. Economic offshoring arguments date from the theories of Ricardo in the early 1800's: International trade benefits everyone. The consulting firm McKinsey and Co. (McKinsey Global Institute, 2003), has estimated the economic benefit of offshoring services to other nations for the United States For every $1 offshored, they claim the United States benefits $1.12–1.14. The breakdown is as follows:

Immediate benefits:
  $0.58 cost reduction to a U.S. firm,
  $0.05 other countries buying more U.S. goods,
  $0.04 repatriation of profits from captive offshore units of U.S. multinational firms, and delayed benefits
  $0.45 – 0.47 in redeployed U.S. labor (workers whose jobs are offshored taking other jobs).

This calculation seems to make an obvious case for offshoring, but it neglects an important fact—the pain of offshoring is not distributed equally. Specifically, the $0.45 – 0.47 in "redeployed labor" is calculated thusly: 72% of offshored process dollars is labor, and 69% of those who lose their jobs are re-employed. Of those re-employed, they average making 96% of their former wage: 72% × 69% × 96% = $0.48 in eventual benefit (the $0.45–0.47 is "conservative"). This means, of course, that $100 – 69 = 31$% of workers whose jobs are outsourced remain unemployed, an unacceptable proposition if millions of jobs are outsourced quickly. In their report, McKinsey called for "retraining" for those whose jobs are offshored. But the operative question seems to be "retraining to do what?" Concerns over unemployment have led to a number of potential laws being discussed in the U.S. Congress (see Service Operations Management Practices: The Empire Strikes Back).

The subject of international political relationships becomes important for offshoring. Some trade relationships that have been highly important historically include Japan's lack of access to oil in World War II, as Japan had no domestic supply. An argument against offshoring "key" industries is that a country may need them in a time of crisis and not have access to them. Considering political risk, does the United States, as a nation, want to have the ability to program its computers in foreign hands? Should a potentially hostile nation, or at least a nation whose self-interest will not always coincide with the interests of the United States, have access to (or control of) the detailed medical records or financial records of millions of its citizens? Would detailed knowledge of bank accounts, credit records, welfare rolls, and other back-office data, help a hostile group find citizens to bribe or inflict harm on the United States?

Given the potential of international disputes leading to trade sanctions, does the United States want large portions of its back-office work to be performed in countries that may no longer be able to trade with the United States? Or, alternatively, will offshoring help the international situation? Does the intertwining of economies lead to better understanding, more tolerance of differences, or a lesser chance of hostile action?

While there are many opinions regarding these questions, facts are in short supply.

IMPLEMENTING OFFSHORE OPERATIONS

Merely transplanting operations performed in one country to another does not take full advantage of the possibilities. Copying an operation in a lower wage country will reduce labor costs, but more benefits can be extracted if different work is done, or work is performed in different ways.

Consider the "collections" function. Collections refers to getting customers who are behind in their payments to pay up. Often this is not just making a phone call. A firm frequently has to invest many hours in skip-tracing customers, meaning finding out where a customer now lives. If a firm is paying a collections clerk $4,000/year the firm will have a far lower threshold of customers to collect from than if it is paying a clerk $30,000/year. That is, a firm can chase down debtors with far lower outstanding debt.

The lower labor costs might also cause competitive priorities to change. Figure 8.2 depicts a typical relationship between cost and "service" in a waiting line operation such as a call center. Here, "service" is defined by how quickly the average call is answered. Because of the variability of incoming calls—sometimes 20 at once, sometimes none for long stretches—and the variability of time spent by an operator answering calls, getting close to an average of immediate response is immensely costly (see Chapter 14). Since the low-cost country labor is less expense, getting to any particular level of quality costs less money. So, it might be the case that the optimal trade-off of response time versus cost reduces both cost and response time in a low-wage environment.

Due to the different ratio of capital and labor costs, it makes sense to organize activities differently offshore. For example, in call centers in the United States, labor is the main cost driver, whereas in India, the cost of the technology and the telecommunications cost for the call itself is a far higher percentage of overall costs. In the United States, it makes sense to have added technology that enables a call center operator to make online, real time changes to a system with a customer waiting on the telephone line. In a more capital-intensive environment, it makes more sense to reduce the time using the telephone line and make changes off-line.

For basic data entry work, labor cost is still the predominant concern in developed countries, so there is generally one shift. If the role of capital and labor costs are reversed, it might make sense to have work shifts around the clock to minimize machinery costs (Agrawal et al., 2003).

FIGURE 8.2: *Cost Versus Service in High- and Low-wage Countries*

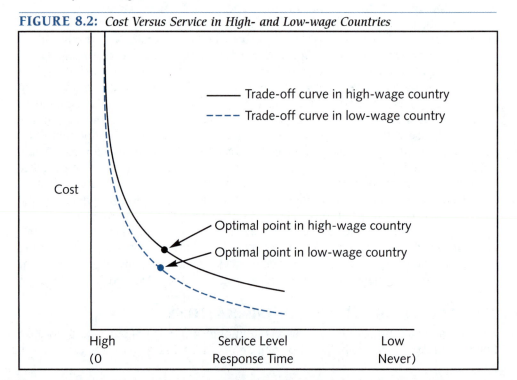

Summary

The terms "outsourcing" and "offshoring" are used interchangeably by some, but they are very different concepts, with very different risks and benefits.

The vast majority of outsourcing is domestic, rather than offshore. Services outsourcing is commonplace and used by many businesses to cut costs or keep up with technological advance. However, it should not be entered into blindly. While there are many situations that call for outsourcing, there are also many situations that are best served by keeping tasks in-house.

Services offshoring, while still small, has received enormous attention. This attention derives from labor rate differentials and the range of services moving offshore. White-collar, professional work, thought by workers in developed countries to be their exclusive domain, is now being offshored to less-developed nations. And those offshore workers have salaries as little as one-tenth of the workers they are replacing. A prevailing feeling among many is that no job is safe.

However, there are many risks and downsides to offshoring. The loss of local and tacit knowledge, the cultural conflict, and the additional country risk associated with offshoring argue that many information-oriented jobs will remain onshore.

Review Questions

1. What is the difference between offshoring and outsourcing?
2. What are the main benefits of outsourcing?
3. What activities should a firm not outsource?
4. Why are firms offshoring service work?
5. What are the risks involved in offshoring?

Selected Bibliography

Abraham, M., 2004. Call Centers Fuel Social Change in Traditional India, *Reuters*, June 9.

Adsit, D., 2003. Executive Commentary, *Academy of Management Executive*, 17(2), 99-100.

Agrawal, V., D. Farrell and J. Remes, 2003. Offshoring and Beyond, *McKinsey Quarterly*, 2003 Special Edition, Issue 4.

Barthelemy, J., 2003. The Seven Deadly Sins of Outsourcing, *Academy of Management Executive*, 17(2), 87-98.

Basu, M., December 17, 2003. Call Centers Mushroom in India: Hello, Y'all, *Atlanta Journal-Constitution*, A1.

Bulkeley, W. December 15, 2003, IBM to Export Highly Paid Jobs to India, China, *The Wall Street Journal*, B1.

Clott, C., 2004. Perspectives on Global Outsourcing and the Changing Nature of Work, *Business and Society Review*, 109(2), 153-170.

Drucker, J., March 11, 2004. Global Talk Gets Cheaper, *The Wall Street Journal*, B1.

Drucker, J. and K. Brown, March 9, 2004. Press 1 for Delhi, 2 for Dallas—Latest Wrinkle in Jobs Fight: Letting Customers Choose Where Their Work Is Done. *The Wall Street Journal*, B1.

The Economist, November 29, 2003a. Lost in Translation, p.58.

The Economist, December 13, 2003b. Relocating the Back Office, pp.67-69.

Fox, J., November 24, 2003. Where Your Job Is Going, *Fortune*, p.86.

Frank, R. and P. Cook, 1995. *The Winner Take All Society*, The Free Press, NY.

Freeman, C., 2000. *High Tech and High Heels in the Global Economy*. Duke University Press, Durham NC.

Gattenio, C., May 14, 2004. Panel Discussion: When Does Outsourcing Make Sense? Presentation at The Hackett Group 14th Annual Best Practices Conference, Stone Mountain, GA.

Geewax, M. May 18, 2004. Offshoring Picks Up Steam, *Atlanta Journal-Constitution*, D1.

Hagel, J., 2004. Offshoring Goes on the Offensive, *McKinsey Quarterly*, 2004(2), 83–91.

Hilsenrath, April 12, 2004a. Behind Outsourcing Debate: Surprisingly Few Hard Numbers, *The Wall Street Journal*, A1.

Hilsenrath, May 17, 2004b. Forrester Revises Loss Estimates to Overseas Jobs, *The Wall Street Journal*, A8.

Infosys, 2002. Presentation at Bangalore corporate campus, January, 2002.

Klinger, S. and L. Sykes, May 10, 2004. Legislation that Bans or Severely Restricts Outsourcing Raises Serious Policy Questions, May Violate the U.S. Constitution and Risks Jeopardizing U.S. Obligations Under International Trade Agreements, *Legislative and Public Policy Advisory*, Alston & Bird, LLP, Atlanta, Ga.

Knowledge@Wharton, March 28, 2004a. Business Opportunity vs. Backlash: Perspectives on BPO.

Knowledge@Wharton, March 28, 2004b. How Warburg Pincus Views Prospects and Perils in Outsourcing Deals.

Knowledge@Wharton, March 28, 2004c. Mauritius Calling: We Want Your Call Centers. [Giga quote].

Landler, M., March 21, 2001. Hi, I'm in Bangalore (But I Can't Say So), *New York Times*, A1.

The Wall Street Journal, April 2, 2004, p.B1.

McKinsey Global Institute, August 2003. *Offshoring: Is It a Win-Win Game?* San Francisco, Ca.

Phillips, M., March 5, 2004. Outsourcing Fears Land in Congress's Lap, *The Wall Street Journal*, A4.

Vina, G. and T. Mudd, November 5, 2003. Call Centers Migrate to India, and North of England Loses Jobs, *The Wall Street Journal*, B4A.

Wilson, M. 1995. The Office Farther Back: Business Services, Productivity, and the Offshore Back Office. Chapter 7 in Harker, P. (ed.) *The Service Productivity and Quality Challenge*, Kluwer Academic Publishers.

Worth, R. July 22, 2002. In New York Tickets, Ghana Sees Orderly City, *New York Times*, A1.

Offshoring a Call Center for Everdream[2]

Finding the right talent for its call center has been a perennial challenge for Everdream, an IT services provider, even though it's based in Fremont, California in the heart of Silicon Valley. The company, which offers an outsourced hosted solution for desktop management, is constantly searching for employees with technical savvy who are also willing to work in an entry-level call center support position. "While these are entry-level positions, we need people who know their way around operating systems and who also know how to treat our customers with the proper level of courtesy and care," says CEO Gary Griffiths.

The company pays about $30,000 a year to entry-level employees in its Charlotte, North Carolina facility and $38,000 at its California-based headquarters call center.

Griffiths says the company began to consider an offshore option in 2002 because it was worried about scalability. "We were concerned about our ability to grow at the rate we thought was necessary. Even though America was in the midst of a so-called jobless recovery, we couldn't find the right talent quickly enough," he explains. Of course, the reduced labor costs of an offshore provider were an enticement, too. But Griffiths says scalability was the primary driver.

The top-down initiative was also a product of outsourcing thinking: Everdream's management felt the company was a technology company, so it would be better off outsourcing its own call center operations to a call center expert.

In October 2002, the company issued a Request for Proposal (RFP) to 12 companies. Everdream explored all its options, looking at onshore, nearshore and offshore companies. Candidates were based everywhere from Bangalore, India to close by the Charlotte center in Florida.

Choosing Costa Rica over India

"We decided early on that we were not comfortable going to India," says Griffiths. First, he felt the distance from California was just too great, since Everdream employees would be onsite during the transition phase "when we handed over the crown jewels." Second, Everdream grilled its prospective suppliers by asking them how they would handle specific situations. "Based on those responses, we didn't feel the Indian suppliers could maintain the quality levels we required," says Belle Kulick, Everdream's Vice President of Operations, who was aware of what the company's customers expected.

After extensive due diligence, Everdream selected a call center supplier in Costa Rica—the executives felt comfortable in the Central American country. Other technology companies like Intel and Microsoft were already outsourcing to Costa Rican suppliers. The Costa Rican team to be assigned to Everdream had just finished

2. Reprinted with permission of the Everest Group and Outsourcing Journal, http://www.outsourcing-center.com. Original article: Rosenthal, B., "Why a Silicon Valley Supplier Brought Its Offshore Call Center Home," *Outsourcing Journal*, May 2004 issue.

CASE STUDY

working on a Toshiba account. "We thought once we got the Costa Rican operation working, we could expand our offshore presence to India or the Philippines," Griffiths says.

Opening a captive operation in a foreign country "was never an option," according to the CEO. If the company went the offshore route, it wanted an outsourcing partner already on the ground. Realistically, that was not an option anyway since Everdream was only outsourcing 40 jobs; it planned to keep a small U.S. presence as it experimented with this new way of doing business.

After selecting the partner in January, 2003, Everdream began its pilot in February. Thirteen employees and a trainer from the Costa Rican supplier flew to California for three months of training. Then those people, who now formed the core Everdream team, went back to Costa Rica. In addition to manning the call center, their job was to train two more classes to handle Everdream's work.

Everdream trainers from California accompanied the supplier's workers when they returned to their home base. The American employees remained at the supplier's site for 90 days to help the new team become operational.

Problems Training the B Team

The problems arose when the core team attempted to train the B and C teams. "We knew the initial 13 were the cream of the crop. But we didn't anticipate the wide gap in knowledge between them and the other people assigned to our account," reports Griffiths. Unfortunately, offshoring didn't solve the scalability problem.

In its American centers, Everdream figures new agents need eight weeks of training before they're ready to answer customer questions solo. "We expected an intensive learning curve in Costa Rica," says Kulick. But the offshore employees who weren't trained in California couldn't perform at the expected level. So Everdream employees held a second training session for the Costa Rican team. Over time Everdream realized "they were never able to get to that next level we required," she reports.

Because the team could not reach the needed knowledge levels, the Costa Rican office needed twice as many agents to handle the same number of calls as the California office. "The lack of productivity wiped out the cost savings," Griffith calculates.

During the RFP process, the due diligence team had investigated these skill levels. The Costa Rican supplier demonstrated that most of its employees had college degrees. But the American company discovered "their degrees apparently aren't equal to ours," Kulick notes.

CASE STUDY

A Mismatch of Corporate Cultures

Everdream also discovered there was a mismatch in corporate cultures between it and the service provider. The Costa Rican company was used to answering calls about a specific product or operating system that had easy-to-use documentation. It was simple to script responses in a cookbook fashion.

On the other hand, Everdream's slogan is: "Any problem. Any time. No excuses." Its employees have to know about several different applications and operating environments. The wide variety of questions they receive daily makes it impossible to script support responses. "We give our employees a high level of autonomy to solve problems. We expect them to think out of the box," says Griffiths.

In the end, Everdream realized each company had a different management philosophy. "They were a call center company and we are an outsourcing services company," he explains. "Our customers pay us money because they want premium service."

Meanwhile, Kulick noticed that Everdream's customer satisfaction ratings, always at 96% or higher, had fallen to less than 90 percent. "That was a disaster," says Griffiths. That's when both parties agreed the arrangement was not working. In March 2004, Everdream moved its work back to the United States and began looking for those hard-to-find people in Charlotte and the Silicon Valley.

While Everdream is back to square one in dealing with its scalability challenge, Griffiths says his team learned a lot from its offshore experience. First, he's not giving up on outsourcing if he can find the right partner. But for now, he's going to stay stateside. Everdeam would consider outsourcing a call center to a supplier in a U.S. city where labor costs are lower than Silicon Valley.

Second, the experience was a useful exercise in learning exactly what the company is about. Future training for any new provider would focus more heavily on the key business fundamentals management had to dissect in explaining its business to an outsider.

"Our board says offshoring was a worthwhile experience. We learned what our customers truly value about us. Now we have a clearer idea of what our customers want. And we know more about our business than we ever did," concludes Griffiths.

Questions:

- Is Everdream's position on offshoring to India reasonable?
- What offshoring or outsourcing lessons from Everdream's experience can be used by other firms?

Improving the Delivery System

Operating systems must be constantly maintained and updated. Technological changes, competitive changes, service-product changes, and customer taste changes all conspire to create an environment where the operation cannot be "left alone." Even where all of the elements above are stable, operations will deteriorate over time unless it is given care and attention.

There are specific techniques and mental models for the care and attention of service operations that are covered in this section: Process analysis, service quality management, and applying six-sigma methodologies to the service sector.

Analyzing Processes

LEARNING OBJECTIVES   *The material in this chapter prepares students to:*

- Diagnose and fix problems in processes.
- Create process flow diagrams and Gantt charts.

- Identify bottlenecks in processes.
- Understand the procedures behind simulating services.

- Run a service simulation.
- The simulation software SimQuick is described on the Student CD.

Regardless of the functional area, be it marketing, finance, operations, or any other, the actual work done can usually be described as a group of processes. If resources are used to produce outputs, then generally a process has been used. Examples of processes include scheduling a media campaign, writing a contract, executing a trade, approving a loan, and billing a customer.

This chapter looks at the process of analyzing and improving processes. The first half of the chapter will demonstrate two simple visual tools that help in improving processes: process flow diagrams and Gantt charts. The second half discusses the more complex task of simulating processes. The Student CD makes use of process simulation software.

THE NEED FOR PROCESS ANALYSIS IN SERVICES

The simple tools introduced in this chapter are well known to manufacturers. A formal responsibility of many industrial engineers is to maintain process flow diagrams for any complex manufacturing processes. In services, however, this aspect is quite often neglected—to their detriment. Within many service firms a single process can involve several different departments. Because of the lack of a formal description of a process, these different departments are often unaware of how their actions impact other parts of a service. We provide some examples of these complex service processes.

Consider a New York City cop who gets a flat tire on his patrol car. Although police are allowed to carry lethal weapons, have wide latitude in investigating criminal activity, and can pass physical tests of endurance and strength, they evidently cannot be trusted to change a tire. In the mid-1990s, the following process was necessary (*New York Daily News*, 1996):

1. Officer fills out a tire replacement request (TRR) form.
2. Tire Integrity Unit reviews the TRR.

3. Officer picks up tire at an approved vehicle maintenance facility.
4. City-approved vendor replaces tire.
5. Used tire is returned to the police garage.
6. Precinct commander signs off on TRR.
7. Tire Integrity Unit compares original and signed TRR forms and files them.

The estimated annual police officer salaries spent for tire changing amounted to $500,000.

On a more serious note, consider the arrest-to-arraignment system in New York City in 1988 (Larson, Cahn, and Shell, 1993):

1. Arrest is made and detainees are placed in patrol car by arresting officer (AO).
2. Detainees are transported to precinct by AO (average time: one hour after arrest).
3. Prisoner searched, fingerprinted, and arrest report generated.
4. Detainees are transported to central booking by AO and placed in a large holding cell (average cumulative time: five hours).
5. Detainee searched and given a bail interview. Fingerprints faxed to state capital for positive ID and return of detainee's rap sheet (average cumulative time: 15 hours).
6. AO gives a statement to an Assistant District Attorney (average cumulative time: 14 hours). (AO must be present and wait—often for several hours—for an available Assistant District Attorney.)
7. The last of steps 5 and 6 completed and additional paperwork performed (average cumulative time: 18 hours).
8. Detainee transported back to precinct holding cell. Arraignment scheduled. Detainee transported to courthouse holding pen (average cumulative time: 39 hours).
9. Detainee arraigned and bail set (average cumulative time: 44 hours).

It is generally considered unreasonable to hold a defendant more than 24 hours without a court hearing to determine probable cause, but in New York the average was 44 hours. However, 44 hours was only an average—many people were held far longer. Because of the cumbersome nature of this process some detainees were being held more than 100 hours—while making new friends in crowded holding cells—before arraignment.

The Los Angeles Police Department also went through a thorough process analysis. A few of the less productive processes included work scheduling: Each month, each officer spent three hours requesting days off for the next month. Also, forms were required from so many different entities that arresting a juvenile drunk driver required manually writing the suspect's name 70 times (Bailey, 1996).

Hopefully, readers will have little experience with the aforementioned institutions. However, one is likely to encounter insurance companies and retail banks. Table 9.1 demonstrates the relative back-office productivity of three firms with a similar customer

TABLE 9.1: *Productivity in the Insurance Industry*

Firm	Percentage of General Expenses/Premiums
Connecticut Mutual	20.5
Phoenix Mutual	15.7
Northwestern Mutual	6.9

Source: Van Biema and Greenwald (1997).

mix. Northwestern Mutual is credited with spending approximately one-third the amount of money on comparable processes that Connecticut Mutual spends. Possible results of this process efficiency include far more profitability at Northwestern Mutual if prices are the same, or an ability of Northwestern Mutual to charge significantly less for their products than the competition.

The amount of time required to open a checking account at a retail bank is illustrated in Table 9.2. Virtually all the large banks in the United States were included in this study, comprising approximately 75% of the banking assets in the country. If one were to try to open an account during a lunch hour, the best bank in the study would detain a customer only 24 minutes. Going to the slowest bank in the study on a lunch hour, however, would constitute an effective diet plan, as the 59 minutes required at the bank could send an employee on a lunch hour running back to work hungry. This disparity is especially surprising in the retail banking industry, because many employees move from bank to bank, which eliminates "trade secrets." To find out how a competitor opens accounts, a bank can simply send in an employee or hire a "mystery shopper" to do so.

The question is begged: How does this happen? Clearly, there is no centrally planned "evil genius" who gloats with the thought of LAPD officers writing a suspect's name 70 times, or who desires to hold detainees in New York holding cells for four days. In large part, processes become this way due to a slow, incremental buildup of process steps over time combined with the ignorance of some departments about the pressures they put on other groups. Departments frequently only know what their part of the process is and not what other parts of the process even do. This departmental myopia is compounded by the lack of anyone being in charge of a process. Instead, employees are usually in charge of a functional area, and many functional areas must get along for a process to work.

For example, in the New York arrest-to-arraignment system, the problem only became known when the *New York Times* ran a front-page article entitled, "Trapped in the Terror of New York's Holding Pens." Data did not exist on the total time detainees spent in the system, because no one was in charge of the system as a whole. Fixing the system required coordinating the NYPD, NYC Department of Corrections, District Attorney's offices, New York State Office of Court Administration, the State Department of Criminal Justice, the Legal Aid Society, the Criminal Justice Agency, and various bar associations. Solving the problem involved, first, describing the entire process, the topic of this chapter. As will be shown later, once a process is properly described in the visual format of process flow diagrams, departments realize more easily the totality of the issues, and the process flow diagram can become a central document for improvement. In this specific case, a number of changes were made, resulting in cutting the average time to 24 hours and saving approximately $10 million per year for the system in reduced overtime pay and other costs.

TABLE 9.2: *Retail Banking Processes*

Time required to open a checking account with a $500 cashiers' check and no prior banking relationship

	Activity Time	Customer Time (in minutes)
Best Bank	27	24
Average	54	42
Worst Bank	70	59
Worst 20 Banks	≥ 60	≥ 48

Source: Frei and Harker (1999).

In the more mundane case of retail banks opening new accounts, many of the banks were unaware of their own processes and purchased the information that researchers gathered from the banks' own systems!

PROCESS FLOW DIAGRAMS

The first step in analyzing and improving processes is to build a process flow diagram. This simple-to-construct, simple-to-understand visual tool describes a process. The standard tools of the trade are the symbols shown in Figure 9.1. Process flow diagrams are common; many appear in prior chapters of this book. Arrows are typically used to show direction of flow of products, information, customers, or whatever is of interest. Diamonds are used to denote decisions; one arrow often enters a diamond, then two or more arrows exit the diamond to denote decision results. Activities are represented by rectangles and inventory or delays are often represented by inverted triangles. Figure 9.1 shows only the most common images used. A more robust set of icons is standard equipment in many word-processing packages.

Process flow charts technically describe processes. However, they serve three primary "soft" managerial functions beyond technical description that will be described here.

Use 1: Process Communication

The process flow chart is the language used to communicate processes. Merely constructing a process flow chart can be enough to get a process improvement project underway. Consider Figure 9.2, a diagram of the steps involved in ordering inventory for the emergency room of a West Texas hospital. Figure 9.2 is in absurdly small print, since the original, normally-sized, document occupies six pages. The managerial purpose behind the original construction of Figure 9.2 was to communicate a feel, rather than precise process steps—to let hospital management know that, due to interdepartmental meddling, the inventory ordering process had become absurdly complex. The sheer bulk of unfolding the six-page document had the desired effect, and drew managerial attention to the problem.

Figure 9.3 also serves that purpose. This figure describes the check-out process at a Blockbuster Video store. This potentially simple process became the complex network shown as more and more marketing programs were added (see the Service Operations Management Practices: Blockbuster Video Links Process to Profits).

FIGURE 9.1: *Most Common Flowchart Tools*

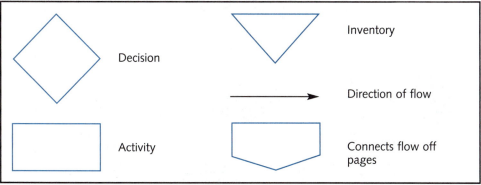

FIGURE 9.2: *Sample Inventory Ordering Flowchart*

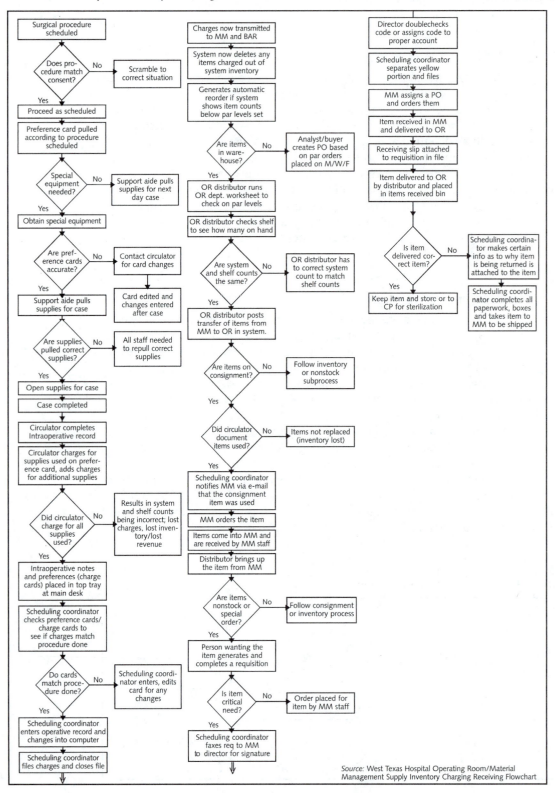

Source: West Texas Hospital Operating Room/Material
Management Supply Inventory Charging Receiving Flowchart

SERVICE OPERATIONS MANAGEMENT PRACTICES

Telecommunications Operation Without True Communication

In the early 1990s when AT&T wanted to increase the efficiency of its lockbox operation (processing incoming payments), the company decided to start by documenting its current process. Representatives of the two separate operations were selected to the newly formed "process team" and brought together at an off-site location. Many of the employees on the team had been processing the incoming payments for this company for more than 20 years.

Chaos erupted when two employees almost came to blows over how one particular process was supposed to flow. It turned out that these two employees, who sat literally only three feet apart for more than 20 years, carried out the same process *differently* for all those years!

It should also be noted that using the precise and correct symbols in describing a process is not always necessary—the key point is whether the nature of the process is communicated. For example, Figure 9.2 is not technically correct. It contains actions that seemingly end the process, because they have no arrows extending outward, but really are imbedded actions in the process. Often the most significant benefit of creating a process flow diagram is simply drawing attention to a process.

To demonstrate the next two managerial uses of process flow charts, consider the simplified process depicted in Figure 9.4, the back-office processes involved in creating an insurance policy. First, a lengthy, handwritten information form filled out by the salesperson/customer is reviewed for accuracy and entered into a computer system (30 minutes). The information is fed to an underwriter, who is responsible for assessing risk, pricing, and determining whether the insurance company should accept the policy (40 minutes). Finally, the policy writer converts the information into a formal, written policy for the customer (10 minutes). Let us assume that an individual worker is at each station and that each activity takes specialized training and cannot be performed by the other workers. The overall time the process takes, from beginning to end, is 30 + 40 + 10 = 80 minutes. Some call this time the *throughput time*, others call it *cycle time*. In this text it will be referred to as throughput time.

The comparison of throughput time to the actual time taken brings us to our second "soft" use of process flow charts.

Use 2: Focusing Managerial Attention on the Customer

In Figure 9.4 the throughput time is 80 minutes, but the actual elapsed time for the customer is a week. Though this particular example is fictitious, it is representative. It is not unusual for the so-called value-added time that a service firm actually works for a customer to be 5% or less of the total time it takes for the customer to be served (Blackburn, 1991). Reasons for this discrepancy between throughput time and actual

FIGURE 9.3: *Check-out Process at Blockbuster Video*

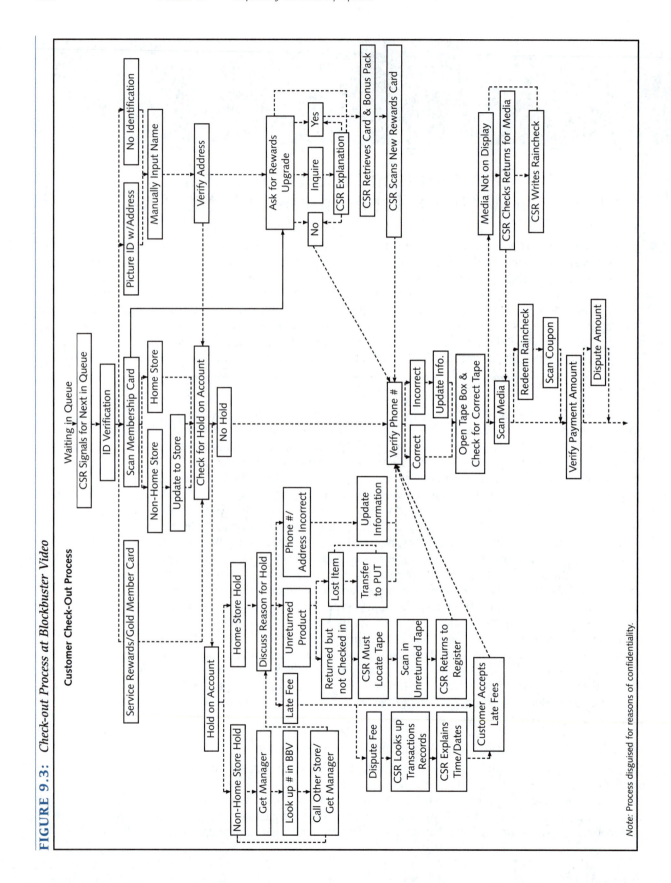

Note: Process disguised for reasons of confidentiality.

FIGURE 9.3: *Check-out Process at Blockbuster Video (continued)*

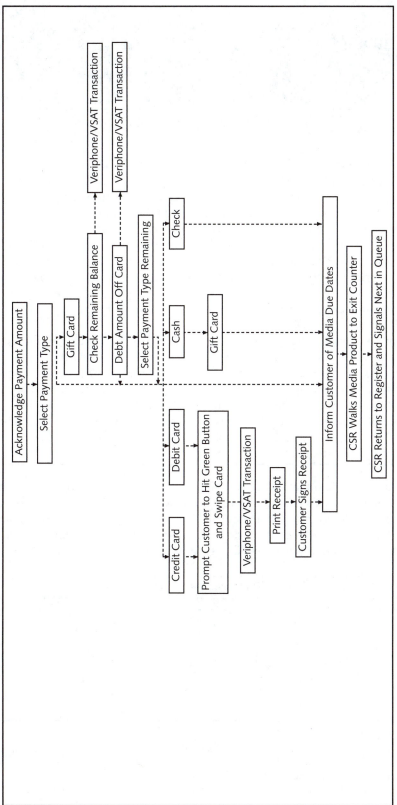

Source: S. Evangelist, B. Godwin, J. Johnson, V. Conzola, R. Kizer, S. Young-Helou, and R. Metters, "Linking Marketing and Operations at Blockbuster, Inc.," *Journal of Service Research,* 5(2), 2002, copyright © *Journal of Service Research.*

SERVICE OPERATIONS MANAGEMENT PRACTICES

Blockbuster Video Links Processes to Profits

The nightmare conversation for management at Blockbuster Video: "Let's go to Blockbuster and rent a movie." "Ugh, remember the line at the checkout last Friday? I bet we were there 30 minutes." "You're right, it's too much of a hassle. Let's see what's on the tube instead."

The check-out process at a Blockbuster Video store would seem simple. You give them the cash, they give you the movies, right? Well, not exactly. Due to different marketing programs (e.g., Rewards™ program, "raincheck" program for movies not in stock), different payment methods (e.g., gift cards, credit cards, debit cards, cash, checks), and holds on accounts for various reasons (e.g., late fees for forgotten movies), the check-out process has become amazingly complex (Figure 9.3). Because of the complexity, it takes longer to check out each customer. The reason it took 30

minutes to check out is that you were 15th in line, and the reason 15 customers were in line in the first place is because the customers in front of them took so long to check out.

With the help of marketing models from Walker Information and analysis from IBM, Blockbuster was able to link the time it takes at the check-out counter to customer loyalty, and link customer loyalty to repurchase behavior, then link repurchase behavior to financial results.

How much did they increase profits by using process analysis? Sorry, that answer is confidential, but now every marketing program that impacts the check-out counter is added to Figure 9.3. The times for these programs are assessed, and their effects on profitability become part of the program justification.

elapsed time include unbalanced work flow (no work comes in for a week, then three weeks' of work comes in on one day); batching of work, which makes the first customer's information wait until all customers in the batch are finished; inefficient hand-offs between departments, where work sits in in-boxes or e-mail systems for days before it is touched, just to name a few.

FIGURE 9.4: *Idealized Back-Office Insurance Policy Process*

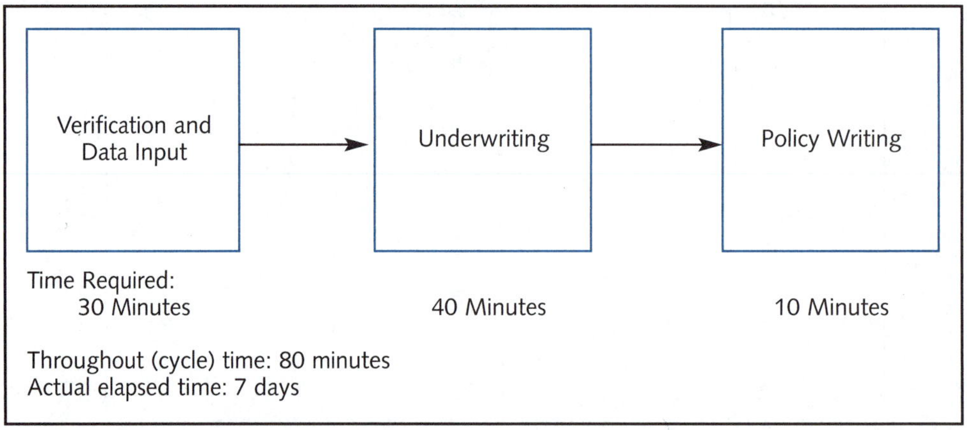

Verification and Data Input → Underwriting → Policy Writing

Time Required:
30 Minutes   40 Minutes   10 Minutes

Throughout (cycle) time: 80 minutes
Actual elapsed time: 7 days

Typically, departmental managers and workers focus on how to make their own tasks more efficient and do not consider the effect of their actions on the whole process. However, laying out the entire process in the customer's time frame, rather than their own, refocuses efforts toward the customer. This beneficial effect is also seen in the description of the NYPD arrest-to-arraignment process discussed earlier, where the times given in the steps were in terms of customer time, rather than activity time.

Use 3: Determining What to Work On and When to Stop Improving Process Steps

Suppose one were to suggest an improvement to the process in Figure 9.4. By changing the input automation, the data entry stage will take only 20 minutes, rather than 30. The change will be costly to install, but it will cut the work time of that station by one-third. Although such a labor savings sounds seductive, it should not be implemented in this case. In fact, the only changes that should be considered are changes to the underwriting process. To show why, let us start out by determining the capacity of this system. How many policies can be finished in a typical eight-hour day? A naïve calculation would state that because the throughput time is 80 minutes to finish one, and 8 hours = 480 minutes, then 480/80 = 6 policies per day can be finished. A Gantt chart, however, shows that the six policies per day solution is not a good one (see Figure 9.5, part A). A Gantt chart delineates the responsibilities of each person or piece of equipment in the specific time frames they are needed. The times that are actually being worked are in the rectangular boxes, while the spaces between the boxes represent idle time for that person. Part A shows that if a new policy is worked on once an old policy is finished, six policies a day may be done, but a lot of idle time also occurs. Physically, better solutions to the problem come from squeezing the idle time out and getting the rectangular boxes closer together. The best solution is shown in Figure 9.5, part B, where 12 policies per day can be written. In this solution, all three workers are working simultaneously on different policies. Note that even in this best solution, the data entry and policy writing jobs still have blank space, or idle time. (It may appear from the picture that only 11 policies could be written, because the underwriter has to wait 30 minutes for the first policy, and 11 more would take 30 + 11(40) = 470 minutes. However, on a daily basis the underwriter would start work in the morning on the last policy finished by data entry the night before.)

The capacity of the system is directly related to the length of the longest activity. In this case underwriting is the longest, requiring 40 minutes. This longest activity is usually called the *bottleneck*, because the bottleneck process regulates the flow of a service system like the neck of a bottle regulates flow of a liquid. The bottleneck process time and capacity are related by the following simple equation:

$$\text{Capacity} = 1/\text{Bottleneck time}$$

In this case, the bottleneck is 40 minutes, so

Capacity: Policies/Day = 1 policy/40 minutes × 480 minutes/day = 12 policies/day.

The bottleneck time is also referred to as "cycle time" or, less frequently, "takt time." Here, we will refer to it as cycle time.

A Gantt chart is a good visual style to see how bottlenecks affect capacity, but simple numerical calculations are an alternative means. To determine system capacity, take the smallest capacity of any process. For this example,

Input: 1 policy/30 minutes × 480 minutes/day = 16 policies/day

Underwriting: 1 policy/40 minutes × 480 minutes/day = 12 policies/day

FIGURE 9.5: *Gantt Chart of Insurance Process*

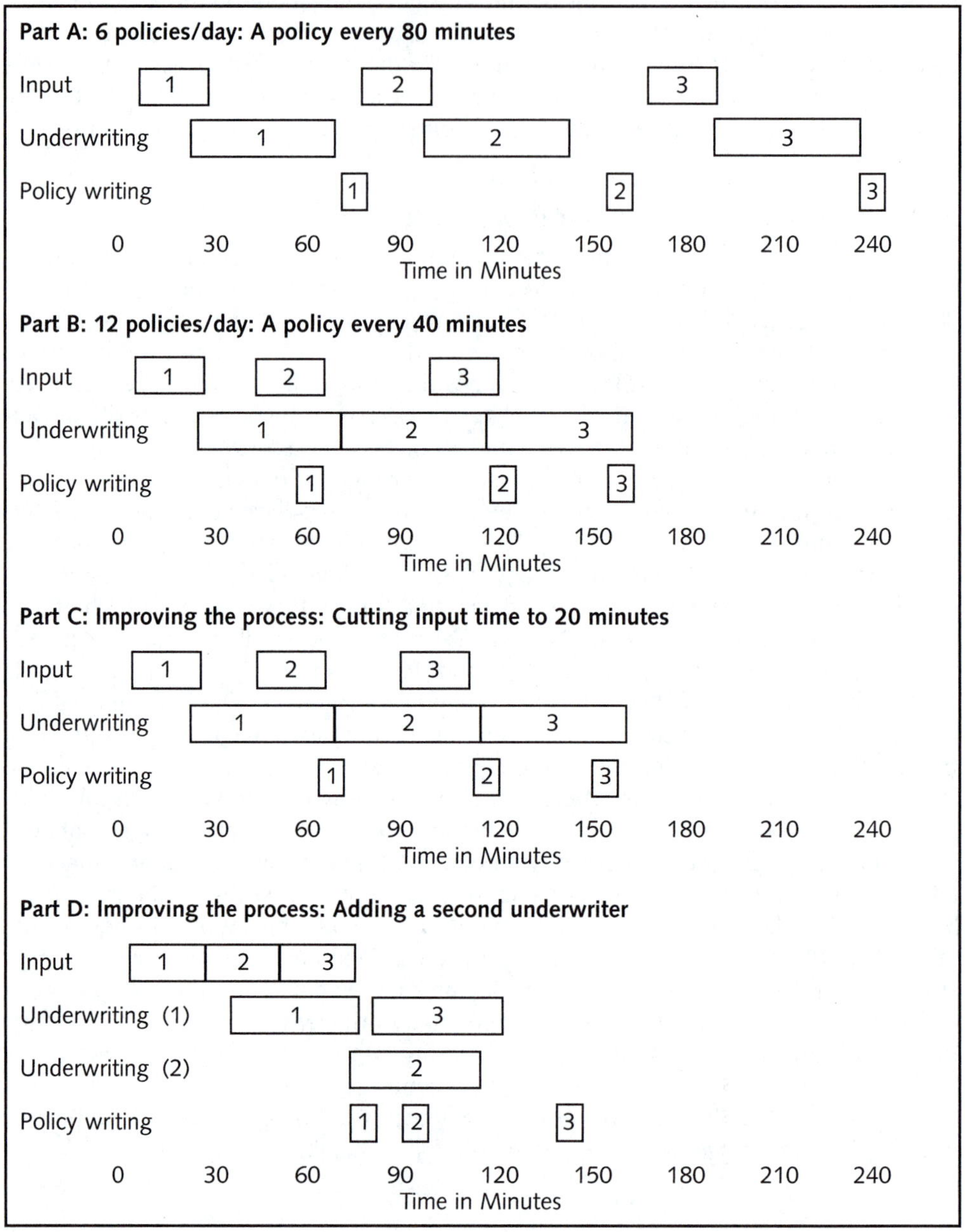

Part A: 6 policies/day: A policy every 80 minutes

Input: 1, 2, 3

Underwriting: 1, 2, 3

Policy writing: 1, 2, 3

0　30　60　90　120　150　180　210　240
Time in Minutes

Part B: 12 policies/day: A policy every 40 minutes

Input: 1, 2, 3

Underwriting: 1, 2, 3

Policy writing: 1, 2, 3

0　30　60　90　120　150　180　210　240
Time in Minutes

Part C: Improving the process: Cutting input time to 20 minutes

Input: 1, 2, 3

Underwriting: 1, 2, 3

Policy writing: 1, 2, 3

0　30　60　90　120　150　180　210　240
Time in Minutes

Part D: Improving the process: Adding a second underwriter

Input: 1, 2, 3

Underwriting (1): 1, 3

Underwriting (2): 2

Policy writing: 1, 2, 3

0　30　60　90　120　150　180　210　240
Time in Minutes

Policy writing:　1 policy/10 minutes × 480 minutes/day = 48 policies/day

so underwriting is the bottleneck.

Besides determining capacity, the bottleneck is important because it indicates what to work on and what to leave alone. To get back to improving the system by reducing data input time, consider Figure 9.5, part C, a Gantt chart mirroring a 10-minute reduction in input time. Here, a policy still exits the system every 40 minutes. All that is accomplished by reducing the input task time is that idle time in the input position has increased.

To improve the system one must attack the bottleneck process. Here, it might be wise to hire a second underwriter. Logic might dictate that if capacity with one underwriter is 12 policies per day, then capacity with two underwriters would be 24 policies per day. However, the reality is different. Figure 9.5, part D shows what happens when two underwriters are on the job. The capacity of the underwriting function is now 24 policies per day, but underwriting is no longer the bottleneck. Now, data input is the bottleneck at 16 policies a day. So, by doubling the capacity of the bottleneck, an improvement of 4/12 or 33% is garnered. In fact, any improvement beyond cutting the time per policy down below 30 minutes is wasted. In other words, useful improvement reaches a limit, a time to stop improving, and that limit can only be found by considering the process as a whole.

Consider multiple improvements. Now that data input is the bottleneck process, it might be time to go back to the original improvement envisioned. If the process includes two underwriters and the data input process only takes 20 minutes, the capacities of the processes are:

Input: 1 policy/20 minutes × 480 minutes/day = 24 policies/day

Underwriting: 2 policies/40 minutes × 480 minutes/day = 24 policies/day

Policy writing: 1 policy/10 minutes × 480 minutes/day = 48 policies/day

so underwriting and data input are jointly the bottleneck and the system capacity is 24 policies per day.

PROCESS SIMULATION

Simulation is a useful tool for analyzing and improving service processes. Unlike tangible products, usually service designers cannot build a prototype of a service and use this model in field tests to understand the service's performance. Likewise, if one considers making some changes to a service process and would like to measure performance improvements (i.e., worker or technology utilization, waiting time, capacity planning, or scheduling), it is difficult to run pilot tests on the service due to disruptions to the real business, employee reactions, and other implementation costs. As an alternative, simulation allows designers to develop and perform experiments on a model of a real system.

Simulation offers several other advantages. First, it often leads to better understanding of a real system and is far more general than mathematical models such as waiting time theory (see Chapter 14). Second, it allows compression of years of experience into just a few seconds or minutes of computer time. Third, simulation can answer what-if questions and can be used to analyze transient (nonsteady state) conditions. On the other hand, it may take multiple simulation runs and scenarios to evaluate a service system, with no guarantee of an optimal solution.

Most simulation models are built on a computer either with commonly available programs, such as Microsoft Excel, or more specialized simulation packages such as SimQuick, ServiceModel™, MedModel™, or Crystal Ball™. The process example described in this chapter uses an Excel-based simulation. An example of process improvement with SimQuick is covered on the CD. More advanced process modeling requires specialized packages.

Access your Student CD now for the simulation example with SimQuick.

Steps for Conducting a Simulation Study

A good simulation project should include five crucial steps as shown in Figure 9.6. The five steps are: (1) plan the study, (2) define the service system, (3) select appropriate software and build the model, (4) validate the model and run experiments, and (5) analyze and report results.

Plan the Study

To build a simulation model, the modeler must *define* the objective and constraints of the project. Can the existing system be modeled? What is the objective of the study? What are the essential aspects of the process that need to be included in the model? Typical objectives involve performance and capacity analysis such as average waiting time for customers at a ski resort, throughput time for an insurance claim, or average employee utilization at different stages of a process. Models can also be used for capability and sensitivity analysis of service systems or for comparison studies. For example, one may want to evaluate how one service process design performs compared to another. Typically one evaluates an existing process or proposed new system and then makes changes to the model with the goal of reducing customer waiting time or throughput and increasing or balancing employee utilization throughout a process.

FIGURE 9.6: *Major Phases in a Simulation Study*

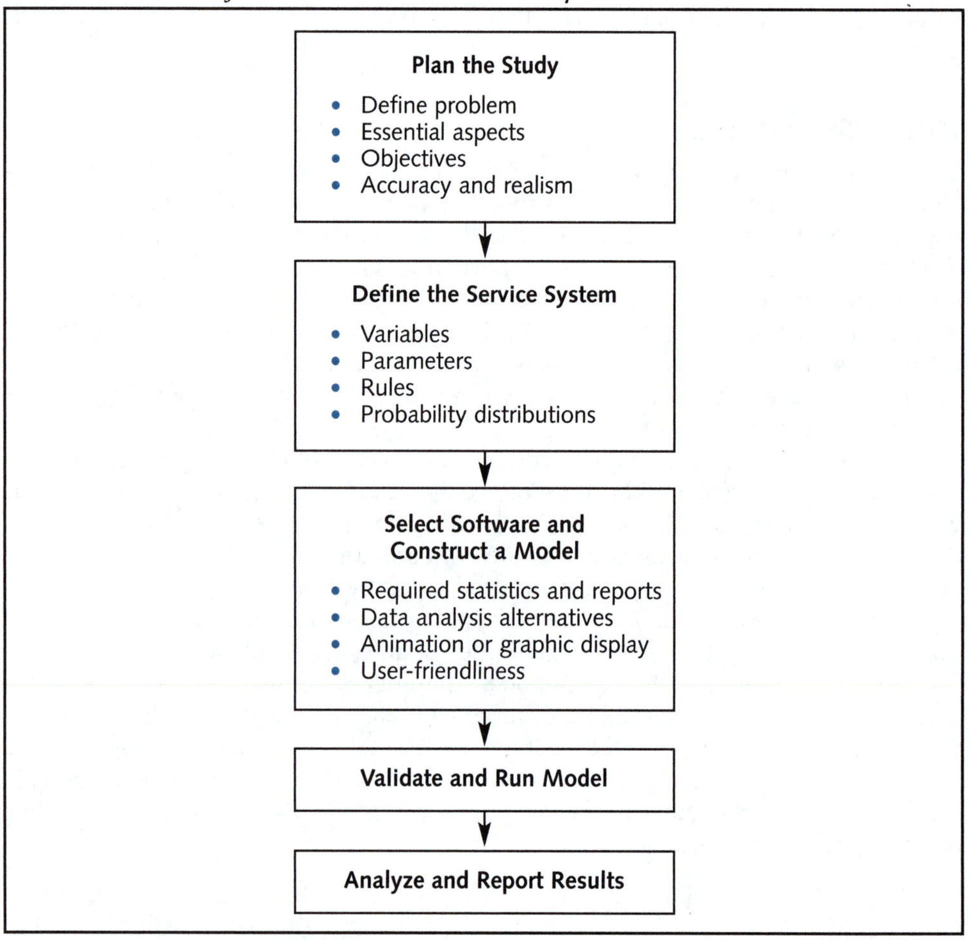

Plan the Study
- Define problem
- Essential aspects
- Objectives
- Accuracy and realism

Define the Service System
- Variables
- Parameters
- Rules
- Probability distributions

Select Software and Construct a Model
- Required statistics and reports
- Data analysis alternatives
- Animation or graphic display
- User-friendliness

Validate and Run Model

Analyze and Report Results

Several trade-offs occur in the planning state. Increasing the accuracy and realism of a model will increase its complexity, level of detail, and software required to model the system, which in turn requires more development time, expertise, and money. Depending on the financial implications of the model results, these increases may be justified. For example, simulations of work distribution and policies for a large call-in center may justify the building of detailed realistic models due to the potential for increases in customer satisfaction, investments in costly technology, or substantial labor cost reductions. On the other hand, evaluations of replacing several employees with an automation technology may require only a simple simulation.

Define the System

Once the modeler identifies the objectives of the project, the service system can be defined in detail. During this phase, one must determine the relevant variables, variable characteristics, and system rules, and collect data that emulate the input variables in the model. The first step is to *specify* variables, parameters, rules, and probability distributions. What variables within and outside of management's control need to be addressed in the model? For example, daily customer demand is often uncontrollable while the number of employees scheduled, their break times, seating capacity, and hours of operations can be controlled by management. For certain processes, the customer or employee must go through a fixed sequence of activities. This sequence is one of the parameters of the system. The previously mentioned process flow diagram is a useful tool for specifying the sequence. What are the rules of the system? Although some processes operate according to rules like first-come, first-served, other systems might include high-priority customers or paperwork that preempts other items. Finally, those variables not under management's control usually behave according to some probability distribution. From historic records, the modeler can construct empirical frequency, normal, exponential, or any appropriate distribution of the variable's behavior. Often, models of new services must rely on best-guess estimates of variable behavior. An example of the data collection for improving queue lines at Snowbird Ski resort is illustrated in the Service Operations Management Practices: Example of Data Collection for Snowbird Ski Resort Improvement.

Select Appropriate Software and Build the Model

After all pertinent information is obtained the appropriate software should be selected. As mentioned previously, the required software will depend on the modeler's needs, time, and programming skills to realistically replicate the service. In addition, desirable features for software include the following capabilities:

- Generates standard statistics such as worker utilization, wait time, and throughput or cycle time.
- Allows a variety of data analysis alternatives for both input and output data.
- Provides animation for graphic display of the customer or product flow through the system.
- Demonstrates user-friendliness for both clients and consultants (templates, control panels, and standard or custom output reports).

Usually, a model is built progressively by adding layers of detail to a simple structure. With this method, the modeler can debug each stage and compare the elementary model with the existing system or similar systems before adding more complex elements. By using a progressive or incremental expansion approach, the modeler can begin building the system while data collection occurs.

SERVICE OPERATIONS MANAGEMENT PRACTICES

Example of Data Collection for Snowbird Ski Resort Improvement

For a simulation study on ski lift waiting time and process improvement at Snowbird Resort in Utah, the research team required extensive data collection. Snowbird's eight ski lifts all experience queuing; movement between queues is probabilistic based on ski terrain ability levels. At most resorts, terrain is classified as beginner, intermediate, and advanced. Figure 9.7 illustrates the ski resort network configuration. The data collection phase involved many steps, but one of the biggest challenges was obtaining estimates of (1) daily network flow patterns for different customer classes, and (2) time for travel between lifts as a function of customer class.

To estimate network flow, the probability of customers going between lifts as a function of their ability or customer class, a survey was administered to 500 randomly selected skiers during their lunch breaks or after skiing. The survey asked skiers to outline their previous choices of lifts and connecting runs for either the morning or the afternoon period. This information was summarized to develop an empirical frequency distribution matrix for the probability of each customer class skiing between lifts at the existing resort. A sample matrix for beginners is provided in Table 9.3.

For estimating the travel time between service facilities, data were collected on 10 different days during the ski season. The observers averaged 10 observations per day for a total of 100 observations. Skiers were observed on two of the eight possible lifts each day. The observer randomly selected a customer departing a lift and followed the

FIGURE 9.7: *Ski Resort Service Network Configurations*

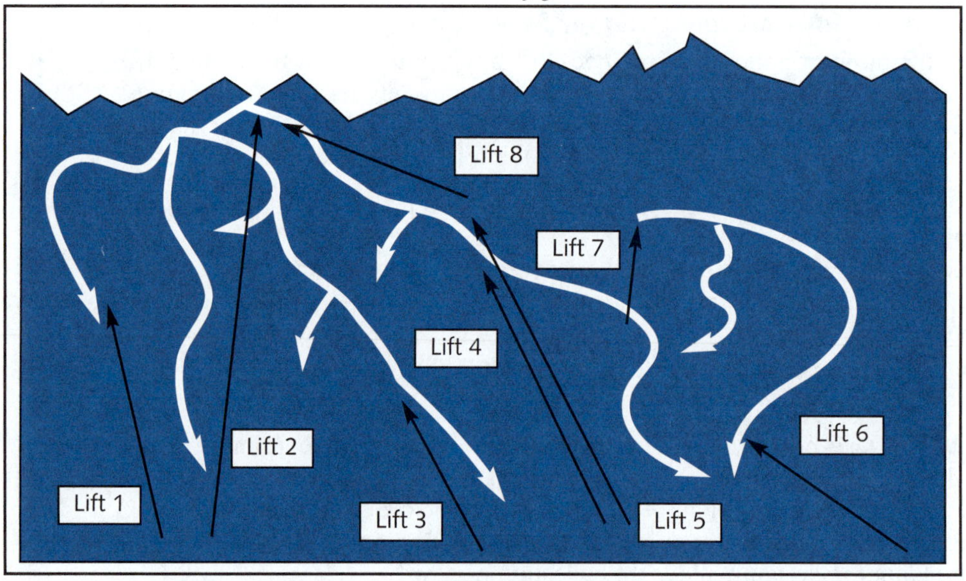

SERVICE OPERATIONS MANAGEMENT PRACTICES

customer until arrival at the next lift. The observer noted skier ability (beginner to advanced), run choice, weather and ski terrain conditions, and time for travel between facilities. Additionally, a group of expert skiers provided information on the minimum times possible between facilities. The data were used to form a truncated normal distribution equation for the time between each lift. For example, the time to ski from the top of lift 2 to the bottom of the same lift provided a mean of 20 minutes and a standard deviation of 2 minutes.

The research team then used these data as part of a large model simulating the waiting line characteristics of the resort. Because of the available data, the researchers and managers could evaluate the performance of the resort when the marketing programs attempted to lure more beginning skiers or operations wanted to change the lifts from old two-seat chairs to new high-speed quad (four-seat) chairs.

TABLE 9.3: *Empirical Probability Distribution for Beginner Skier*

From Lift	To Lift							
	1	2	3	4	5	6	7	8
1	45	5	20	15	10	5	0	0
2	30	15	20	15	10	5	2.5	2.5
3	0	0	50	20	20	10	0	0
4	0	0	10	35	35	10	10	0
5	0	0	10	30	35	10	10	5
6	0	0	0	30	30	40	0	0
7	0	0	15	20	20	20	20	5
8	0	0	16	17	17	10	15	25

Validate the Model and Run Experiments

During the building stage, the model should be periodically validated to see how it corresponds to the real system. *Validation* generally refers to testing the model to make sure it adequately represents the real system. The modelers should constantly ask themselves whether the results appear reasonable and address any discrepancies between the real system and the model.

Once the model is validated, then the experimental process can begin. During this phase, a number of scenarios are developed to address changes to the variables of the system. For each scenario, the modeler must determine the appropriate run length (length of the simulation run), number of replications of each run, random number streams (different or the same for each run), whether start-up bias is present, and if so how to create similar initial conditions for each scenario, and termination conditions for each run. Possible experiments might address changes to parameters, variables, decision rules, starting conditions, or run length.

It is important to run the simulation for long enough that the system achieves steady state so that if the simulation experiment is repeated the results remain constant. For businesses that will experience start-up bias (i.e., when the doors open and queues take some time to form), the simulation data are not collected until enough time passes to allow for steady state to occur. For example, if the simulation is run for 2,000 hours then the first 200 hours of data may not be used in the final statistics.

For certain environments, it is important to capture the start-up conditions or fluctuations in queue patterns throughout a day or week. If so, these experiments are repeated multiple times with different random number streams. Again, depending on the environment, it may be necessary to capture several thousand repeated simulation runs' worth of statistics and collect mean, standard deviation, and confidence interval statistics for different periods of the day. In this case, it is necessary to collect a sufficiently large sample for statistical hypothesis testing. For more details on simulation experiments, refer to Law and Kelton (1991).

Analyze and Report Results

The final results will lead to conclusions about the service system. These conclusions depend on the degree to which the model reflects the real system (validity) and the statistical design of the simulation. To support the conclusion-generating process, many simulation packages come with analysis and results reporting capabilities. But keep in mind, the only true test of a simulation is how well the real system performs after the results of the study are implemented.

MANUAL SIMULATION EXAMPLE

To illustrate the general concepts behind simulation, we will use a wholesale bakery example.

Albert's Wholesale Bagels receives a delivery of fresh dough once every day from a central bakery. The management wants to insure that Albert's never runs out of dough but would like to examine the trade-off between spoilage of excess dough versus good customer service. Albert collected historic data for the previous six months and the resulting discrete probability distributions are provided in Table 9.4.

The daily supply delivery varies according to demand from other shops but ranges between 4 and 9 batches. Every day, Albert receives between 1 and 5 orders from customers. Each customer order requires from 1 to 4 batches of dough. Using this information, we will simulate daily performance of the system.

Step 1:

We begin by using random numbers to simulate daily delivery quantities as shown in Figure 9.8. Assume, we pick a two-digit random number from a hat of all possible

TABLE 9.4: *Empirical Frequency Distributions for Albert's Wholesale Bagels*

Delivery Quantities		Customer Order Distribution		Demand Per Customer Order	
Batch/Day	Probability	Orders/Day	Probability	Batch	Probability
4	0.15	1	0.25	1	0.40
5	0.20	2	0.25	2	0.30
6	0.25	3	0.30	3	0.20
7	0.15	4	0.15	4	0.10
8	0.15	5	0.05		
9	0.10				

FIGURE 9.8: *Using Random Numbers to Simulate Delivery Quantities*

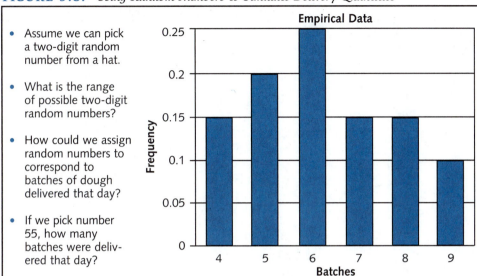

- Assume we can pick a two-digit random number from a hat.

- What is the range of possible two-digit random numbers?

- How could we assign random numbers to correspond to batches of dough delivered that day?

- If we pick number 55, how many batches were delivered that day?

two-digit numbers: 100 possible two-digit numbers ranging from 00 to 99. In Excel, we can generate a list of random numbers between 0 and 1 by entering the formula = RAND( ) in any cell. Then, we use only the first two digits of each number. Alternatively, we can use Excel's Random Number Generator as follows:

- Go to **Tools**
- Select **Data Analysis**
- Select **Random Number Generators**
- In **Number of Variables**, type 1
- In **Number of Random Numbers**, type in the number needed for your problem (Ex.: 30, 100)
- In **Distribution**, select Discrete
- In **Output range**, indicate the cell location where you want your list of random numbers to appear on the spreadsheet.

The results are shown in Table 9.5.

Step 2:

To simulate the number of batches in the daily delivery for day 1, we use the first random number in Table 9.5 and determine its corresponding delivery amount as shown in Table 9.6. The first number, 55, corresponds to a delivery of 6 batches. Assuming that the bakery started with 0 batches, 6 batches are now available for customer orders as shown in Table 9.7.

Step 3:

To simulate the number of orders received from customers on day 1, we use the second random number in Table 9.5 and determine its corresponding customer orders as shown in Table 9.8. The second number, 36, corresponds to 2 customer orders as shown in Table 9.7.

Step 4:

To simulate each of the two customers' demands, we use the third and fourth numbers in our random number list (Table 9.5) and their corresponding demand from

TABLE 9.5: *Random Number Examples*

#	Random Numbers between 0 and 100			
1	55	25	45	
2	36	26	34	
3	99	27	8	
4	21	28	20	
5	88	29	10	
6	50	30	53	
7	50	31	9	
8	11	32	40	
9	34	33	24	
10	39	34	3	
11	64	35	85	
12	21			
13	51			
14	30			
15	30			
16	40			
17	66			
18	97			
19	87			
20	96			
21	3			
22	13			
23	48			
24	12			

Table 9.9. The first customer's random number is 99, which corresponds to a 4-batch order; the second customer's random number is 21, which corresponds to a 1-batch order. The results are shown in Table 9.7, and we see that at the end of the day, 1 batch of dough remains in inventory.

Step 5:

Repeating steps 2 through 4 for subsequent days, the results are shown in Table 9.7 for two additional days.

TABLE 9.6: *Random Numbers and Batches Delivered*

Delivery Amount	Probability	Random Number
4	0.15	00–14
5	0.20	15–34
6	0.25	35–59
7	0.15	60–74
8	0.15	75–89
9	0.10	90–99

TABLE 9.7: *Albert's Bagel Shop Simulation*

Day 1

Batches Delivered	Random #	Amount	Batches Remaining
	55	6	6
Customer Order Amount	Random #	Amount	
	36	2	
Customer 1 Demand	Random #	Amount	
	99	4	2
Customer 2 Demand	Random #	Amount	
	21	1	1

Day 2

Batches Delivered	Random #	Amount	Batches Remaining
	88	8	9
Customer Order Amount	Random #	Amount	
	50	3	
Customer 1 Demand	Random #	Amount	
	50	2	7
Customer 2 Demand	Random #	Amount	
	11	1	6
Customer 3 Demand	Random #	Amount	
	34	1	5

Day 3

Batches Delivered	Random #	Amount	Batches Remaining
	39	6	11
Customer Order Amount	Random #	Amount	
	64	3	
Customer 1 Demand	Random #	Amount	
	21	1	10
Customer 2 Demand	Random #	Amount	
	51	2	8
Customer 3 Demand	Random #	Amount	
	30	1	7

TABLE 9.8: *Random Numbers and Customer Orders*

Customer Order	Probability	Random Number
1	0.25	00–24
2	0.25	25–49
3	0.30	50–79
4	0.15	80–94
5	0.05	95–99

TABLE 9.9: *Random Numbers and Customer Demand*

Customer Demand	Probability	Random Number
1	0.40	00–39
2	0.30	40–69
3	0.20	70–89
4	0.10	90–99

Summary

As both consumers and providers of services we are involved in processes several times each day. Often, these processes are needlessly complex or do not suit the purposes of the business for a variety of reasons. The subject of this chapter, process analysis, is the starting point in process improvement.

Usually, the first step in process analysis is a simple process flow chart. Complex process analysis of the sort done by Blockbuster or analyses accomplished through such simulation packages as SimQuick begin with process flow charts. However, this simple tool provides sufficient reasons for its use. The process flow chart and Gantt chart are easy-to-use, visually oriented tools that can accomplish the basic goals of communicating what a process is across departments or to upper management. They help in focusing managerial attention on the customer, and they aid in determining what to work on and when to stop improving process steps.

To understand processes of sufficient complexity, though, or to determine what the effect of changes might do to that process, requires simulation. The basic steps and expected outcomes of simulation were presented in this chapter. Thanks to modern computing power, a number of user-friendly yet powerful simulation tools are available. This chapter demonstrated improving processes by using Excel. The simulation software SimQuick is covered in the CD.

Review Questions

1. Why are visual tools helpful when attempting to change an interdepartmental process?
2. What are the benefits of creating process flow diagrams?
3. How are Gantt diagrams helpful?
4. What is the relationship between the time it takes to perform a bottleneck process and system capacity?
5. What are the main steps in constructing any process simulation?

Problems

9.1   Complete the spreadsheet simulation problem for seven days at Albert's Wholesale Bagels. What are your conclusions about the existing system?

9.2   You decide to change the delivery system for Albert's Wholesale Bagels and deliver on average two fewer batches per day. The resulting probability distribution follows:

Batch/Day	Probability
2	.15
3	.20
4	.25
5	.15
6	.15
7	.10

Redo the simulation with the same random number set. Does your change improve the performance of the system?

9.3   Using SimQuick, set up a two-agent call-in center problem as described in the chapter and run it for 120 time units and 20 simulations. Add another agent and repeat the process. What changes does the additional agent make in the service levels of the organization?

9.4   Using SimQuick, set up the two-agent call-in center problem with automation handling 40% of all calls as described in the chapter. Run this simulation for 120 time units and 20 simulations. Next, repeat the experiment with 50%, 60%, and 70% of customers using the automation. At what point can you eliminate an agent?

Selected Bibliography

Bailey, J. 1996. The LAPD Is Treated to a Business Analysis, and It Comes Up Short. *The Wall Street Journal* (June 11), A1.

Blackburn, J. 1991. *Time-Based Competition*. Business One Irwin, Homewood, IL.

Evangelist, S., Godwin, B., Johnson, J., Conzola, V., Kizer, R., Young-Helou, S., and R. Metters. 2002. Linking Marketing and Operations at Blockbuster, Inc. *Journal of Service Research*, 5(2).

Frei, F. and P. Harker. 1999. Measuring the Efficiency of Service Delivery Processes. *Journal of Service Research*, 1(4), 300–312.

Hartvigsen, D. 2004. *SimQuick: Process Simulation with Excel*, 2nd ed. Prentice Hall

Larson, R., M. Cahn, and M. Shell. 1993. Improving the New York City Arrest-to-Arraignment System. *Interfaces*, 23(1), 76–96.

Law, A., and W. Kelton. 1991. *Simulation Modeling and Analysis*, 2nd ed. McGraw-Hill, New York.

Van Biema, M., and B. Greenwald. 1997. Managing Our Way to Higher Service-Sector Productivity. *Harvard Business Review*, 75(4), 87–95.

CHAPTER 10

Service Quality

> *"Quality cannot be seen as separate from overall performance or the bottom line."*
>
> Curt W. Reimann, Director, Baldrige Quality Award

Quality is an increasingly important element that differentiates between competing services. Unlike tangible goods, though, many services are not easily measured or tested for quality. Often, one cannot even assess their quality until after consuming them. All across the service economy, however, leading companies are obsessed with service excellence. They use service to increase productivity. They use it to be different and to earn their customers' loyalty. They seek some shelter from price competition through quality service. Companies ranging from The Ritz-Carlton Company, Southwest Airlines, Land's End, Nordstrom, and The Walt Disney Company actively market themselves based on excellent service.

In manufacturing, companies may focus on Total Quality Management (TQM) and gurus such as Deming, Juran, and Crosby. TQM involves "managing the entire organization so that it excels on all dimensions of products and services that are important to the customer" (Chase, Acquilano, and Jacobs, 2001). TQM took hold in the United States after competition from the Japanese's excellent manufacturing quality hit U.S. companies hard in the late 1970s and 1980s. Consumer confidence in U.S. goods' quality diminished and caused a quality revolution across U.S. industry. The movement affected service organizations when consumers demanded quality in everything they purchased—both goods and services.

As the U.S. economy shifts ever more to one dominated by services and consumers demand more and better quality of their service providers, managers strive to provide "customer delight" with their services by adopting parts of the quality movement so effectively utilized by manufacturers. In fact, in a recent Gallup survey, executives ranked the improvement of service and tangible product quality as the single most critical challenge facing U.S. business.

Improving the quality of services is more difficult than improving the quality of products because of the temporary nature of a service. An unsatisfactory or defective product can be replaced or repaired. However, a delivery of an unsatisfactory service is something that cannot be undone, so it is vital to deliver a satisfactory—or preferably superior—service the first time (Pegels, 1995, p. 34).

The primary rule of total quality management is to know your customer. A good example of this axiom can be found in excellent companies like The Ritz-Carlton, Southwest Airlines, and The Walt Disney Company. Each prides itself on exceeding customer expectations and works diligently to create and maintain a culture of service quality. They have each developed extensive databases of customer information so that they can analyze how successful their service has been, where it might be improved, and how to predict what these same customers may expect in the future. They have processes in place to solicit feedback from employees and clients alike on how their service is working and where it might be improved. These companies are never satisfied with their current level of service and have processes in place for continual improvement.

Gradually, the TQM movement has shifted to one of return on quality (ROQ). With TQM, the drivers are too often defined internally. With ROQ, the customers set the parameters and the marketer selects those quality improvements that lead to the greatest return on investment.

WHY DOES QUALITY MATTER?

Evidence abounds in the business press and trade magazine articles that high quality and profitability go together. The American Customer Satisfaction Index (ACSI) is a quarterly survey conducted by the University of Michigan in Ann Arbor. The Michigan economists began watching customer satisfaction levels in 1994. From 1994–1998, the quality of service got worse each year. Then, it began to rise.

The overall ACSI reflects changes in the nation's quality of economic output, as experienced by the household users of that output. The economy's ability to create increasing consumer utility is central to economic health and real economic growth. Consumer utility, or satisfaction, is the ultimate standard for productive growth, not only because consumer spending makes up two-thirds of GDP but also because this is the fundamental premise of a market economy: Companies compete for the satisfaction of their customers. If they succeed, they are rewarded with more repeat business and lower price elasticity. Economic growth at the expense of customer satisfaction, which occurred in 1995–1996, is not sustainable, as it has a negative effect on demand. Rather, the continued improvements in ACSI contribute to upward shifts in consumer demand, which translate into GDP growth.

"A person who has a good purchase experience is more inclined to spend again," said Claes Fornell, director of the University of Michigan's National Quality Research Center, which compiles and analyzes the data. "Sustainable economic growth ultimately links to the availability of goods, services, and experiences for which people are willing to repeatedly open their wallets" (ACSI Web site, 2004).

"This is a healthy increase in Americans' satisfaction with their buying experiences, and is the continuation of a two-quarter upward movement," stated Fornell, who heads the Index at the University of Michigan. "Positive consumption experiences contribute to increased consumer demand and stimulate household spending. Based on the economy's customer satisfaction performance in the first quarter, we can expect a fairly strong increase in household spending. Since consumer spending accounts for two-thirds of the Gross Domestic Product, it is vital to economic growth."

"Every . . . industry has major players that have been taking deliberate, specific steps to better match product, service, and process quality with the customer's definition of how things should be," according to Jack West, past president of the American Society for Quality Control. "In a tough economy, many companies recognize that improving quality and delivering better experiences for customers is the way to stimulate spending."

The performance of e-commerce is impressive, also, especially given that the data also show customer expectations to be among the highest of any industry measured. Some companies, the ASCI reports, have mastered the considerable advantages of the Internet—so much so that they are producing among the most satisfying shopping and consumption experiences of any category of goods, services, and channels used by American consumers.

"E-commerce is getting better and better at first determining what constitutes an excellent experience in the minds of customers and then quickly delivering," said Larry Freed, an online satisfaction expert and CEO of ForeSee Results. "The barriers to making improvements are definitely lower on the Internet, and companies like Amazon.com, barnesandnoble.com, and eBay are showing they know how to use that advantage effectively."

DEFINING SERVICE QUALITY

Quality is much easier to define when manufacturing tangible products. Manufacturing quality may simply involve conformance to specifications. A manufacturer can evaluate the level of a product's quality based on what was produced relative to the design specifications. A defect means a product failed to meet those specifications. The specifications come from product engineers who may be designing the product based on what market research data show that customers want or from some other type of communication that indicates customer wants and needs.

In services, evaluating the level of quality is much more elusive. Quality specifications, for services, come from multiple simultaneous sources, including the company and the individual customers. The company presents specifications as standard operating procedures. Customers present specifications based on their personal expectations for what their service experience will be. Misalignment between company and customer specifications for the service process leads to dissatisfaction, even when the process goes exactly as it was designed. The misalignment of specifications can be avoided through communication. However, if the service performance does not address individual customer needs, the customer will not require the service (Sampson, 1999).

Understanding how this process works requires understanding the difference between quality and value. Service quality is often defined as the satisfaction of expectations. The expectations, of course, are subjective and based on cognitive or formal descriptions of the service process and outcome. Service value is the satisfaction of needs. Needs are the changes that customers perceive will increase their "happiness" or decrease their "happiness." When expectations for a service provider appear to fill customer needs, customers will consider purchasing the service, otherwise they will not. For example, the same waiter who is considered witty and urbane by some diners may seem outrageous and rude to others, even though the base service is identical.

A variety of available tools can help determine customer expectations, including customer satisfaction surveys, customer perception surveys, focus groups, complaint analysis, employee research, similar industry studies, and transaction analysis.

The true key to delivering quality service comes in identifying and understanding what dimensions of quality are important to *your* customers. High quality does not have to carry a high price. Even low-cost services can be viewed as high quality when they meet the needs and expectations of the customer and the customer values the service.

Definitions of Service Quality

Many definitions attempt to describe what constitutes quality service. Some proponents of quality service state that quality can be defined only by customers and occurs when an organization supplies goods or services to a specification that satisfies the customer's needs. Others simply define quality as the satisfaction of customer expectations.

Rust, Zahorik, and Keiningham (1994) claimed that customer satisfaction and delight are both strongly influenced by customer expectations and that the term *expectations* as used by behavioral researchers is not as precise as the usage by mathematicians, which is "what is likely to happen, on average." They found a bewildering array of "expectations" that reflected what might, could, will, should, or better not happen as shown in Figure 10.1.

They define the *will expectation* as coming closest to the mathematics definition. It is the "average level of quality that is predicted based on all known information." It represents the expectation level most often meant by customers and used by researchers. When someone says that the "service exceeded my expectations," what they generally mean is that the service was better than they had predicted it would be (Rust et al., 1994).

The *should expectation* is what the customer feels he or she deserves from the transaction. The *ideal expectation* is what would happen under the best of circumstances and is useful as a barometer of excellence. The *minimally acceptable* level (the threshold at which mere satisfaction is achieved) is the other end of the scale along with *worst possible* (the worst outcome that can be imagined).

FIGURE 10.1: *The Expectations Hierarchy*

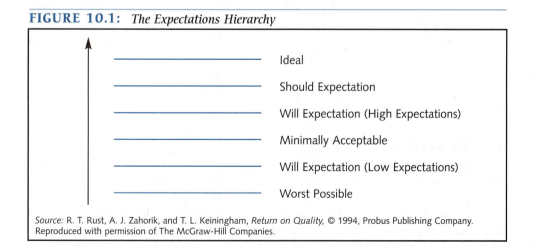

Source: R. T. Rust, A. J. Zahorik, and T. L. Keiningham, *Return on Quality,* © 1994, Probus Publishing Company. Reproduced with permission of The McGraw-Hill Companies.

Most quality definitions fall short, however, of reflecting all the various perspectives of the various stakeholders. The following categories of quality definitions reflect five different perspectives (Haksever et al., 2000; Garvin, 1988):

1. *Transcendent.* According to the transcendent view, quality is innate excellence and can be recognized only through experience. In other words, "You cannot define quality but you know it when you see it." It, however, provides little practical guidance to managers in the quest for quality.

2. *Product-based.* Product-based definitions rely on measurable quantities to define quality. For goods, the measures may include length of useful life, amount of a desirable ingredient (e.g., "100% cotton") or amount of a desirable output (e.g., "45 miles per gallon"). For services an example might be the length of time before a service is provided. Because it is based on measurable quantities, this definition allows an objective assessment of quality. The disadvantage of a product-based definition is that it assumes all customers desire the same attributes and hence fails to account for differences in tastes and preferences of individual consumers.

3. *User-based.* This approach to defining quality begins where the product-based definition ends; it defines quality from an individual consumer's perspective. The "fitness for use" definition of quality is consistent with this approach. In other words, it is based on the premise that "quality is in the eyes of the beholder." For example, a tastefully prepared and presented meal that takes 30 minutes to deliver to a customer's table may be seen as a sign of poor quality if the meal is for lunch and the customer is in a hurry. The subjectivity of this approach leads to two problems: (1) how to decide which attributes should be included in a good or service to appeal to the largest numbers of customers, and (2) how to differentiate between attributes that provide satisfaction and those that imply quality.

4. *Manufacturing-based.* Manufacturing-based definitions view quality as an outcome of engineering and production processes. According to this approach, quality is "conformance to requirements." In other words, how well does the output match the design specifications? For example, if an airline service specifies arrival within 15 minutes of the schedule, the level of quality in terms of this specification can easily be determined by comparing actual flight arrivals with the schedule. The disadvantage of this approach is that, unless specifications are based on customers' needs and preferences, quality becomes an internal issue that helps simplify production control but fails to deliver what customers want.

5. *Value-based.* This approach incorporates value and price into the definition of quality. Quality is defined as a balance between conformance or performance and an acceptable price to the customer.

The various departments within a company each use different perspectives in their definition of quality and their subsequent measurement of the quality they produce. Marketing, for example, will be much more focused on the user-based definition.

MEASURING SERVICE QUALITY

Clearly, quality is something customers expect and something they value when they purchase a service. But how do we define and then measure these expectations in order to meet them?

Companies utilize a wide variety of measures by which to judge their success in creating customer satisfaction and service quality. Though there are more than 50 national and international awards and standards for quality, most of them are for manufacturing quality, not service quality. A few of them, though, directly assist companies to identify their quality processes, measure them, and improve them.

The Malcolm Baldrige National Quality Award is the United States' highest honor for quality and performance excellence. It focuses mainly on outputs and the financial perspective of customer satisfaction. The Baldrige Award is weighted towards results.

The International Organization for Standardization's (ISO) standards identify and detail the processes in place to ensure quality in doing business. They are output oriented and are focused on all of the company's processes, not a single measurement. The ISO standards identify what a company's processes are and then measure if they match the processes the business actually performs.

Six Sigma is a useful tool for measuring service processes. It uses a strategic approach to improve business performance by reducing process variation. It is covered in depth in Chapter 11.

The Malcolm Baldrige National Quality Award

Arguably, the most prestigious U.S. quality award is The Baldrige. It is awarded by the President of the United States to businesses—manufacturing and service, small and large—and to education and health care organizations that apply and are judged to be outstanding in seven areas: leadership, strategic planning, customer and market focus, information and analysis, human resource focus, process management, and business results.

In the early and mid-1980s, many industry and government leaders saw that a renewed emphasis on quality was no longer an option for American companies but a necessity for doing business in an ever expanding, and more demanding, competitive world market. But many American businesses either did not believe quality mattered for them or did not know where to begin. The Baldrige Award was envisioned as a standard of excellence that would help U.S. organizations achieve world-class quality.

Malcolm Baldrige was Secretary of Commerce from 1981 until his death in a rodeo accident in July 1987. Baldrige was a proponent of quality management as a key to this country's prosperity and long-term strength. He took a personal interest in the quality improvement act that was eventually named after him and helped draft one of the early versions. In recognition of his contributions, Congress named the award in his honor.

Congress established the award program to recognize U.S. organizations for their achievements in quality and performance and to raise awareness about the importance of quality and performance excellence as a competitive edge. The award is not given for specific products or services. Three awards may be given annually in each of these categories: manufacturing, service, small business and, since 1999, education and health care.

While the Baldrige Award and the Baldrige recipients are the very visible centerpiece of the U.S. quality movement, a broader national quality program has evolved around the award and its criteria. A report, *Building on Baldrige: American Quality for the 21st Century,* by the private Council on Competitiveness, said, "More than any other program, the Baldrige Quality Award is responsible for making quality a national priority and disseminating best practices across the United States."

The U.S. Commerce Department's National Institute of Standards and Technology (NIST) manages the Baldrige National Quality Program in close cooperation with the private sector. The 2003 Baldrige Award winners for service were Boeing Aerospace Support in St. Louis, MO, and Caterpillar Financial Services Corporation, in Nashville, TN.

The ISO 9000 and ISO 14000 Standards

The ISO 9000 and ISO 14000 standards established by the International Organization for Standardization are implemented by some 610,000 organizations in 160 countries. ISO 9000 has become an international reference for quality management requirements in business-to-business dealings, and ISO 14000 is well on the way to achieving as much, if not more, in enabling organizations to meet their environmental challenges.

The ISO 9000 family is primarily concerned with "quality management." This means what the organization does to fulfill the customer's quality requirements and applicable regulatory requirements while aiming to enhance customer satisfaction and achieve continual improvement of its performance in pursuit of these objectives. The ISO 14000 family is primarily concerned with "environmental management." This means what the organization does to minimize harmful effects on the environment caused by its activities and to achieve continual improvement of its environmental performance.

The vast majority of ISO standards are highly specific to a particular product, material, or process. However, the standards that have earned the ISO 9000 and ISO 14000 families a worldwide reputation are known as "generic management system standards." "Generic" means that the same standards can be applied to any organization, large or small, whatever its product, including whether its "product" is actually a service, in any sector of activity, and whether it is a business enterprise, a public administration, or a government department. "Generic" also signifies that no matter what the organization's scope of activity, if it wants to establish a quality management system or an environmental management system, then such a system has a number of essential features for which the relevant standards of the ISO 9000 or ISO 14000 families provide the requirements. "Management system" refers to the organization's structure for managing its processes—or activities—that transform inputs of resources into a product or service which meet the organization's objectives, such as satisfying the customer's quality requirements, complying to regulations, or meeting environmental objectives.

The prime objective of these standards is customer orientation: the ISO 9000:2000 series focus on satisfying the customers (whatever they are called or designated) of the organization in the case of ISO 9001, and on satisfying all interested parties (society in the broadest sense, shareholders, etc.) in the case of ISO 9004 and ISO 14001. All organizations have customers or interested parties, or both, and are therefore potentially concerned with this series of standards. An organization wishing to build up its quality management system should therefore start by taking into account the needs and expectations of its customers.

This system will be constructed around the normal operation of the organization, which will have to identify the processes and then control these processes through its management system to ensure the sustained satisfaction of its customers (ISO 9001) and interested parties (ISO 14001). The concept of process, already present in the ISO 14001 standard, makes a noted entry in the new version of ISO 9001/ISO 9004. Process is the basic concept that reverses previous trends and, rather than encouraging organizations to adapt their management system to a standard, enables the standards to be adapted to any type of organization, provided the latter's general operation is effective and efficient. Therefore, there can be as many quality management systems or environmental management systems (according to the ISO 9000 and ISO 14000 models) as there are organizations. ISO 9001:2000 states, for example, that the documentation implemented by the company should be adapted to the organization and not to the structure of the model.

GAPS IN SERVICE QUALITY

Parasuraman, Zeithaml, and Berry (1985) recognized the idea that service quality is a function of the expectations-performance gap and conducted a broad-based exploratory study in the early 1980s. Their research results began to appear in 1985 and continue today with expansion into e-SQ, or electronic service quality.

Parasuraman and colleagues (1985) conducted studies in several industry sectors to develop and refine SERVQUAL, a multiple-item instrument to quantify customers' global (as opposed to transaction-specific) assessment of a company's service quality. Their model is also commonly known as the Gaps model.

Their scale involved expectations-perceptions gap scores along five dimensions: reliability, responsiveness, assurance, empathy, and tangibles (Parasuraman et al., 1985).

1. *Reliability.* Reliability involves consistency of performance and dependability. It means that the firm performs the service right the first time and that it honors its promises. Specifically, it involves accuracy in billing, keeping records correctly, and performing the service at the designated time.
2. *Responsiveness.* The willingness or readiness of employees to provide service. It involves timeliness of service, including mailing a transaction slip immediately, calling the customer back quickly, and giving prompt service (e.g., setting up appointments quickly).
3. *Assurance.* This dimension relates to the knowledge, competence, and courtesy of service employees and their ability to convey trust and confidence. Competence means possession of the required skills and knowledge to perform the service. Courtesy involves politeness, respect, consideration, and friendliness of contact personnel. It also includes trustworthiness, believability, and honesty of service employees.
4. *Empathy.* The caring and individualized attention provided to customers includes the approachability and ease of contact with the service providers and their efforts to understand the customers' needs.
5. *Tangibles.* Tangibles include the physical evidence of the service, such as physical facilities, appearance of service providers, tools or equipment used to provide the service, physical presentation of the service, and other customers in the service facility.

When Zeithaml, Parasuraman, and Berry asked more than 1,900 customers of five nationally known companies to allocate 100 points across the five service quality dimensions, they averaged as follows: reliability 32%, responsiveness 22%, assurance 19%, empathy 16%, and tangibles 11%. Though customers consistently reported that their most important quality dimension was reliability, this area seems to be where many service companies fail.

The SERVQUAL model conceptualizes service quality on the basis of the differences between customers' expectations with respect to the five dimensions and their perceptions of what was actually delivered. When a difference exists, it is characterized as a "gap." This model was fashioned after remarkably consistent patterns emerged from the study's interviews. Though some perceptions about service quality were specific to the industries selected, commonalities among the industries prevailed. The commonalities suggested that a general model of service could be developed.

The most important insight obtained from analyzing the responses was that "a set of key discrepancies or gaps exists regarding . . . perceptions of service quality and the tasks associated with service delivery to consumers. These gaps (Figure 10.2) can be

FIGURE 10.2: *Service Quality Model*

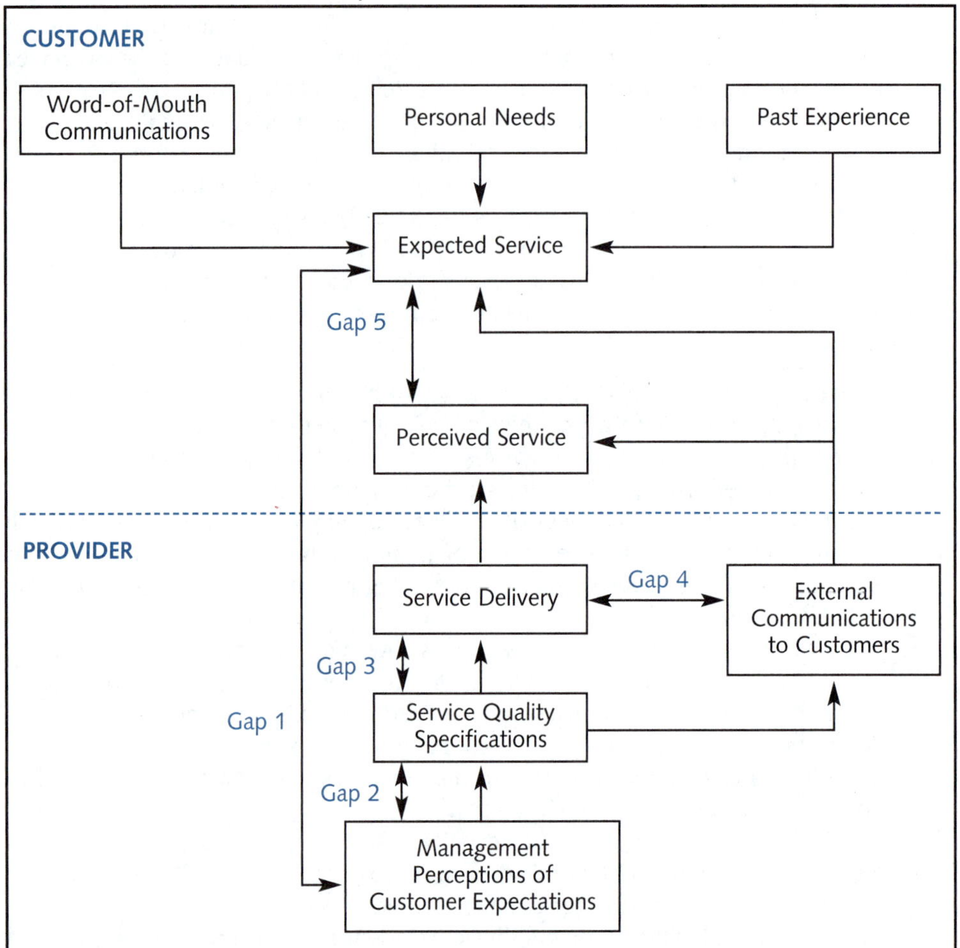

Source: Reprinted with permission of The Free Press, a Division of Simon & Schuster, Inc. from *Delivering Quality Service: Balancing Customer Perceptions and Expectations* by Valerie A. Zeithaml, A. Parasuraman, and Leonard L. Berry. Copyright © 1990 by The Free Press, p. 46.

major hurdles in attempting to deliver a service which consumers would perceive as being of high quality" (Parasuraman et al., 1985). The service-quality shortfall perceived by customers is defined as Gap 5 and the shortfalls within the service provider's organization are defined as Gaps 1 through 4.

Gap 1: Consumer expectation–management perception gap. Service firm executives may not always understand what features connote high quality to consumers in advance, what features a service must offer in order to meet consumer needs, and what levels of performance on those features are needed to deliver high-quality service. Lack of a marketing research orientation, inadequate upward communication from contact personnel to management, and too many levels of management separating contact personnel from top managers are some of the reasons for this gap.

Gap 2: Management perception–service quality specification gap. A variety of factors—resource constraints, market conditions, or management indifference—may result in a discrepancy between management perceptions of consumer expectations and the actual specifications established for a service. This discrepancy is predicted to affect quality perceptions of consumers. A key way in which this gap can surface is poor understanding of the system being designed (i.e., poor understanding of basic process design principles).

Gap 3: Service quality specifications–service delivery gap. Even when guidelines exist for performing services well and treating consumers correctly, high-quality service performance may not be a certainty. Executives recognize that the service quality perceived by consumers and employee performance cannot always be standardized.

Gap 4: Service delivery–external communications gap. External communications can affect not only consumer expectations about a service but also consumer perceptions of the delivered service. Alternatively, discrepancies between service delivery and external communications—in the form of exaggerated promises or the absence of information about service delivery aspects intended to serve consumers well—can affect consumer perceptions of service quality. Promising more than can be delivered raises initial expectations but lowers perceptions of quality when the promises are not fulfilled.

Gap 5: Expected service–perceived service gap. Judgments of high and low service quality depend on how consumers perceive the actual service performance in the context of what they expected. The quality that a consumer perceives in a service is a function of the magnitude and direction of the gap between expected service and perceived service.

It is important to note that the gaps on the marketer side of the equation can be favorable or unfavorable from a service quality perspective; that is, the magnitude and direction of each gap affect service quality. For instance, Gap 3 will be favorable when actual service delivery exceeds specifications; it will be unfavorable when service specifications are not met.

Parasuraman and colleagues found in their focus groups that, regardless of the type of service, consumers used basically similar criteria in evaluating service quality. These criteria fall into 10 key categories as presented in Table 10.1.

A consumer's view of service quality is elaborated in Figure 10.3. It reveals that perceived service quality is the result of the consumer's comparison of expected service with perceived service. The comparison and the perceived service evaluation are not unlike that performed by consumers when evaluating goods. What differs with services is the *nature* of the characteristics upon which they are evaluated.

SERVQUAL results can be used to identify which components or facets of a service the company is particularly good or bad at, relative to customer expectations. It can be used to monitor service quality over time, to compare performance with that of competitors, or to measure customer satisfaction with a particular service industry generally.

An organization or industry group can use the information collected through SERVQUAL to improve its position by acting upon the results and ensuring that it continuously surpasses customers' expectations. Additionally, the expectations-perceptions results, along with the demographic data, may facilitate effective customer segmentation.

It is important that service providers decide upon a target level of service quality and then communicate the level of service offered to both consumers and employees. This quality goal allows employees to know what is expected of them, and customers will have an idea of the level of service they can expect.

The SERVQUAL model highlights the difficulties in ensuring a high quality of service for all customers in all situations. More specifically, it identifies gaps where a

TABLE 10.1: *Determinants of Service Quality*

Reliability involves consistency of performance and dependability. It means that the firm performs the service right the first time. It also means that the firm honors its promises. Specifically, it involves:
- accuracy in billings;
- keeping records correctly;
- performing the service at the designated time.

Responsiveness concerns the willingness or readiness of employees to provide service. It involves timeliness of service:
- mailing a transaction slip immediately;
- calling the customer back quickly;
- giving prompt service (e.g., setting up appointments quickly).

Competence means possession of the required skills and knowledge to perform the service. It involves:
- knowledge and skill of the contact personnel;
- knowledge and skill of operational support personnel;
- research capability of the organization, e.g., securities brokerage firm.

Access involves approachability and ease of contact. It means:
- the service is easily accessible by telephone (lines are not busy and they don't put you on hold);
- waiting time to receive service (e.g., at a bank) is not extensive;
- convenient hours of operation;
- convenient location of service facility.

Courtesy involves politeness, respect, consideration, and friendliness of contact personnel (including receptionists, telephone operators, etc.) It includes:
- consideration for the consumer's property (e.g., no muddy shoes on the carpet);
- clean and neat appearance of public contact personnel.

Communication means keeping customers informed in language they can understand and listening to them. It may mean that the company has to adjust its language for different consumers—increasing the level of sophistication with a well-educated customer and speaking simply and plainly with a novice. It involves:
- explaining the service itself;
- explaining how much the service will cost;
- explaining the trade-offs between service and cost;
- assuring the consumer that a problem will be handled.

Credibility involves trustworthiness, believability, honesty. It involves having the customer's best interests at heart. Contributing to credibility are:
- company name;
- company reputation;
- personal characteristics of the contact personnel;
- the degree of hard sell involved in interactions with the customer.

Security is the freedom from danger, risk, or doubt. It involves:
- physical safety (Will I get mugged at the automatic teller machine?);
- financial security (Does the company know where my stock certificate is?);
- confidentiality (Are my dealings with the company private?).

Understanding/Knowing the Customer involves making the effort to understand the customer's needs. It involves:
- learning the customer's specific requirements;
- providing individualized attention;
- recognizing the regular customer.

Tangibles include the physical evidence of the service:
- physical facilities;
- appearance of personnel;
- tools or equipment used to provide the service;
- physical representations of the service, such as a plastic credit card or a bank statement;
- other customers in the service facility.

Source: Parasuraman, Zeithaml, and Berry (1985), p. 47.

FIGURE 10.3: *Determinants of Perceived Service Quality*

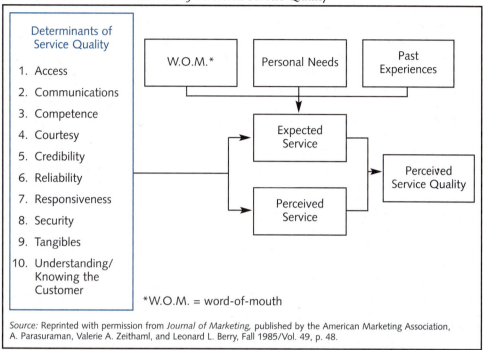

Source: Reprinted with permission from *Journal of Marketing,* published by the American Marketing Association, A. Parasuraman, Valerie A. Zeithaml, and Leonard L. Berry, Fall 1985/Vol. 49, p. 48.

shortfall between expectation of service level and perception of actual service delivery may occur (Palmer and Cole, 1995, pp. 153–154). The culmination of these four gaps in service quality results in Gap 5: the potential discrepancy between the expected and the perceived service from the customer's standpoint.

SERVICE QUALITY DESIGN

It is often important to design certain fail-safe techniques into a service to ensure the safety of service providers and consumers. Fail-safe constructs procedures that block mistakes from becoming service defects. Developing a service blueprint enables a company to identify potential areas where service failures can occur. Similar to the design process utilized in manufacturing, a service blueprint generally consists of four stages: direction, design, testing, and introduction (Scheuing and Johnson, 1989, pp. 25–34). During the design phase, the company can create fail-safe procedures or devices to signal potential mistakes and allow for their correction immediately.

FOOLPROOF SERVICE USING POKA-YOKE[1]

The quality assurance challenge for services is to achieve zero defects in the day-to-day provision of services. The late Shigeo Shingo, (known as "Mr. Improvement" in Japan), conceived of the idea of fail-safing or mistake-proofing to prevent the inevitable mistake from turning into a defect.

Shingo, an industrial engineer at Toyota, is credited with creating and formalizing Zero Quality Control (ZQC), an approach to quality management that relies

---

1. Baka/yoke is an early term, which was later replaced by poka-yoke. Baka/yoke is translated as fool-proofing. Shigeo Shingo changed the term to poka-yoke (mistake-proofing) when a worker was offended by the implication that she was a fool (Myers, 1995).

heavily on the use of poka-yoke (pronounced POH-kah YOH-kay) devices. J.P. Lafferty (1992) observed that, "Shingo brought his Poka-Yoke devices to America in the mid-80s . . . Unfortunately; the reception to Shingo's methods in this country is similar to our response to Dr. W. Edwards Deming in the 50s. It took us 30 years to become convinced Deming was right about statistical control. Must we wait 30 more to believe Shingo?" Fortunately, since his remark in the early 1990s, service quality and poka-yoke designs have both come a long way . . . for the better.

Although widely used in manufacturing operations, poka-yoke is less well known in services. A poka-yoke (from the Japanese *yokeru*, meaning "to prevent," and *poka*, meaning "inadvertent errors") is a simple, built-in step in a process that must be performed before the next stage can be performed. In essence, it is a device or procedure that signals a mistake is about to be made. Done well, a fail-safing procedure is also usually fairly simple and inexpensive to develop.

In services, hospitals use task poka-yokes in their medical processes. Indentations on trays that hold surgical instruments mean that all the instruments needed for a given operation will be nested on the tray. It is immediately evident not only if an instrument is missing, but also which specific instrument is missing before the patient's incision is closed.

Encounter poka-yoke devices and procedures can be used to warn and control customer actions to prevent customer errors during the encounter. Examples of this type of poka-yoke include frames in airport check-in for passengers to gauge the allowable size of carry-on luggage, locks on airplane lavatory doors that must be turned to switch on lights (and at the same time activate the "Occupied" sign), height bars at amusement rides to assure that riders meet or do not exceed size requirements, and beepers to signal customers to remove their cards from the ATM. Another hospital innovation involves electronic order entry. Doctors enter orders for prescriptions, X-rays, and lab tests into a computer system, which instantly checks the order for possible problems such as drug interactions or allergies.

Figure 10.4 illustrates how fail-safing can be incorporated into a design design. The figure shows a blueprint of an automotive service operation and how poka-yoke can be used to prevent service failures and create a robust service.

MEASURES OF CUSTOMER SATISFACTION

Good customer service and high customer satisfaction requires the commitment of management, supervisors, and front-line employees to create and maintain a strong business philosophy. These factors are influential in any business. Mastering these aspects means becoming more competitive in the marketplace today.

Excellent companies know their customers; they know their customers' needs and requirements. Although each company may approach it in different ways, they usually go to great lengths to gather this information. This information allows them to design effective and efficient services and delivery systems that satisfy customers, to position and market services effectively, and to forecast and manage demand.

L.L.Bean is often thought of as synonymous with great customer service and customer satisfaction. It displays a poster prominently all around its Freeport, Maine, facilities, which defines the customer (Figure 10.5).

Rust, Zahorik, and Keiningham suggested that service operations measure their quality management success by calculating their Return on Quality (ROQ). Figure 10.6 shows the steps involved in determining a company's ROQ. These steps can be broken down into four main sections: (1) exploratory research, (2) quantitative research, (3) impact of quality on satisfaction, and (4) market share and profit impact.

FIGURE 10.4: *Fail-Safing a Typical Automotive Service Operation*

Failure: Customer forgets the need for service.
Poka-Yoke: Send automatic reminders with a 5% discount.

Failure: Customer cannot find the service area or does not follow proper flow.
Poka-Yoke: Contact method—clear and informative signage directing customers.

Failure: Customer has difficulty communicating problem.
Poka-Yoke: Joint inspection—service advisor repeats his or her understanding of the problem for confirmation or elaboration by the customer.

Failure: Customer does not understand the necessary service.
Poka-Yoke: Preprinted material for most services, detailing work, reasons, and possibly a graphic representation.

Failure: Bill is illegible.
Poka-Yoke: Top copy to customer or plain paper bill.

Failure: Customer not located.
Poka-Yoke: Contact method—issue beepers to customers who wish to leave facility.

Failure: Feedback not obtained.
Poka-Yoke: Motion step—customer satisfaction postcard given to customer with keys to vehicle.

Process flow: Customer calls for service appointment → Service department schedules appointment → Customer arrives with vehicle → Greet customer → Obtain vehicle information → Customer specifies problem → Problem is diagnosed → Cost and time estimate is prepared → Customer approves service → Waiting room or service shuttle provided → Schedule work → Retrieve parts from stockroom → Perform required work → Work verified → Customer pays bill → Vehicle cleaned → Customer invoice prepared → Vehicle is retrieved → Customer departs

Failure: Customer arrival unnoticed.
Poka-Yoke: Contact method—use bell chain to signal arrivals.

Failure: Customers not served in order of arrival.
Poka-Yoke: Place numbered markers on cars as they arrive.

Failure: Vehicle information incorrect and process time consuming.
Poka-Yoke: Maintain customer database and print forms with historical information.

Failure: Incorrect diagnosis of the problem.
Poka-Yoke: High-tech checklist such as expert systems and diagnostic equipment.

Failure: Incorrect estimate.
Poka-Yoke: Checklists itemizing costs by common repair types.

Failure: Service shuttle is inconvenient.
Poka-Yoke: Fixed value method—seating in available shuttles is allocated when scheduling appointments. Lack of free spaces indicates that customers needing shuttle service should be scheduled for another time.

Failure: Parts are not in stock.
Poka-Yoke: Contact method—limit switches activate signal lamps when part level falls below order point.

Failure: Vehicle not cleaned correctly.
Poka-Yoke: Successive check-person retrieving vehicle inspects, orders a touch-up if necessary, and removes floor mat in presence of customer.

Failure: Vehicle takes too long to arrive.
Poka-Yoke: Motion step method—when cashier enters customer's name in order to print the bill, information is electronically sent to runners, who retrieve vehicle while the customer is paying.

Line of Visibility

Source: Reprinted from "Make Your Service Fail-Safe," by R. Chase and D. Stewart, *MIT Sloan Management Review*, Spring 1994, pp. 347–357, by permission of publisher. Copyright © 1994 by Massachusetts Institute of Technology. All rights reserved.

FIGURE 10.5: *Sign Prominently Displayed at L.L.Bean in Freeport, Maine*

What Is a Customer?

- A customer is the most important person ever in this office . . . in person or by mail.
- A customer is not dependent on us . . . we are dependent on him.
- A customer is not an interruption of our work . . . he is the purpose of it. We are not doing him a favor by serving him . . . he is doing us a favor by giving the opportunity to do so.
- A customer is not someone to argue or match wits with. Nobody ever won an argument with a customer.
- A customer is a person who brings us his wants. It is our job to handle them profitably to him and to ourselves.

Source: Courtesy of L.L.Bean, Inc.

FIGURE 10.6: *Steps Involved in Determining Return on Quality (ROQ)*

Determine customer needs from the service

↓

Relate customer needs to internal business processes

↓

Collect data on customer satisfaction with business processes

↓

Relate customer satisfaction with various processes and customer retention

↓

Determine the shift in customer satisfaction with the firm or a business process resulting from the quality improvement effort

↓

Estimate the customer retention rate after the quality improvement effort

↓

Estimate the market share impact corresponding to the new retention rate

↓

Determine the profit impact resulting from the change in market share, plus any cost savings, minus the cost of the quality improvement effort

Source: R. T. Rust, A. J. Zahorik, and T. L. Keiningham, *Return on Quality,* © 1994, Probus Publishing Company. Reproduced with permission of The McGraw-Hill Companies, p. 8.

The central chain of events that leads from quality to profits can be summarized as follows: Service performance impacts customer satisfaction, which impacts customer retention, which changes market share, which impacts profits. Figure 10.7 illustrates this quality-to-profits sequence.

This chain of events, however, focuses on customer retention and does not include three sources of profits generated by quality improvement: (1) cost reductions due to increased efficiency, (2) the attraction of new customers resulting from positive word-of-mouth, and (3) the ability to charge higher prices (Rust, 1994, p. 8).

Based on the concept that the primary purpose of every business is performing a service for customers, the service always centers on meeting customer needs. Thus, a mission of management is to identify and fulfill customer needs. To do so, companies must find out what the customer needs are, whether they are being met, and how to meet them better.

Thinking of a company as a service designed specifically to fulfill customer needs is not the natural way for most managers to view their organizations. It is essential, however, if they are to understand how customers perceive their firms. As a result, managers need to understand what is meant by "service performance," and then use that understanding to determine the actual benefits their companies offer to customers.

Common measurement tools used by market researchers to reveal service performance levels include customer satisfaction surveys, customer perception surveys, focus groups, complaint analysis, employee research, similar industry studies, and transaction analysis.

ACHIEVING SERVICE QUALITY

Costs of Service Quality

A lot of confusion surrounds the issue of whether quality costs money or saves money. In one sense, quality means the features of a service that make people willing to buy it. So it is income-oriented and affects income. To produce features, ordinarily you

FIGURE 10.7: *Chain of Events Leading from Quality to Profits*

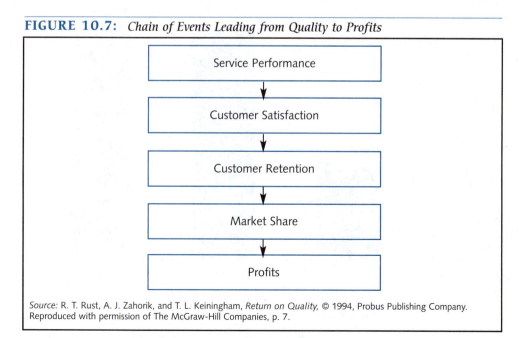

Source: R. T. Rust, A. J. Zahorik, and T. L. Keiningham, *Return on Quality,* © 1994, Probus Publishing Company. Reproduced with permission of The McGraw-Hill Companies, p. 7.

must invest money. In that sense, higher quality costs more. Quality also means freedom from trouble, freedom from failure, which is cost-oriented. If things fail internally, it costs the company. If they fail externally, it also costs the customer. In these cases, quality costs less (Stewart, 1999).

Many executives still do not agree that investments in quality pay off in terms of service improvement and profits. Indeed, many companies waste money annually in the name of quality improvement that fails to lead to increased quality or profits. The thing that actually does pay off is improving service in the eyes of the customers. Quality becomes a profit strategy when service improvements lead to perceived service improvements (Zeithaml et al., 1990, p. 9). Studies show that, in the long run, the most important single factor affecting a business unit's performance is the quality of its products and services relative to those of competitors.

Quality service pays off, in the final analysis, because it creates *true* customers who are glad they selected a firm after the service experience, who will use the firm's services again, and who will sing the firm's praises to others. The essence of services operations is service or, more directly, the *performance* of that service. When everything comes together to produce customer delight, profits result (see Figure 10.8).

Roland Rust and colleagues (1994) summarized the facts around the costs involved with attaining and then keeping quality customers:

- It costs five times more money to acquire a new customer than to retain a current customer.
- Increasing the length of a customer relationship increases the lifetime value of the customer.
- Longer-term customers tend to purchase more.
- Familiar customers may be more efficient to deal with.

FIGURE 10.8: *The Delighted Stayed*

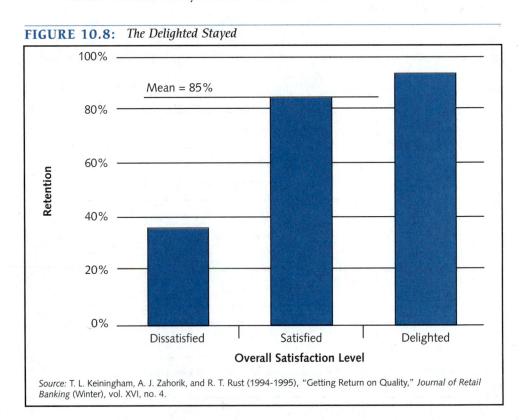

Source: T. L. Keiningham, A. J. Zahorik, and R. T. Rust (1994-1995), "Getting Return on Quality," *Journal of Retail Banking* (Winter), vol. XVI, no. 4.

SERVICE OPERATIONS MANAGEMENT PRACTICES

Develop a Culture to Achieve Customer Satisfaction

Having a good customer service and customer satisfaction requires the commitment of management, supervisors, and front-line employees to create and maintain a strong business philosophy. These are all influential factors of any business. Mastering these aspects means becoming more competitive in the marketplace today.

Source: Reprinted with permission of Service Quality Institute (© 2004), John Tschohl, 9201 East Bloomington Freeway, Minneapolis, MN, USA 55420–3437. Phone (952) 884-3311, http://www.customer-service.com.

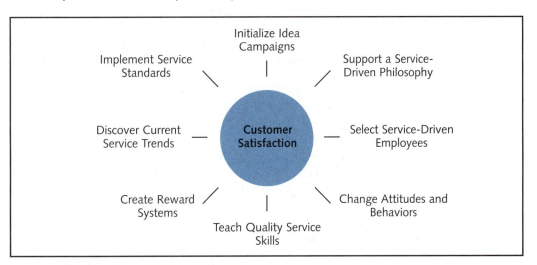

Profits Tied to Quality

Quality service, in and by itself, cannot guarantee higher profits or a better bottom-line number. Failure to link a company's quality program to the bottom line through cost reductions or revenue increases could, in fact, lead to corporate failure. Research evidence shows a relationship between quality and profits. Buzzell and Gale defined this relationship by calculating return on sales (ROS) and return on investment (ROI) as percentages. They found that inferior quality resulted in an 8% ROS and 18% ROI. Superior quality, however, resulted in 12% ROS and 32% ROI (Buzzell and Gale, 1990, p. 107).

Cost reductions from improving processes to do things right the first time were the basis for the initial enthusiasm for quality improvement processes in the manufacturing sector. To implement such a program, though, everybody in the organization must be convinced that things must to be done right the first time. W. Edwards Deming suggested that the cost of quality is the cost to the company of doing things wrong. He insisted that management is responsible for 85% of a company's quality problems; workers are responsible for only 15%. Some estimate that product (service) design is itself responsible for 50% or more of a firm's quality problems (Buzzell and Gale, 1990).

Rust and colleagues (1994) stated that the resources spent to provide quality on a consistent basis can be known collectively as the "cost of quality" and that spending usually occurs in four areas:

1. Prevention of problems
2. Inspection and appraisal to monitor ongoing quality
3. The cost to redo a defective product before it is delivered to the customer (also known as internal failures)
4. The cost to make good on a defective product after it reaches the customer (also known as external failures)

They also concede that identifying and estimating these costs can be difficult, particularly in a service setting.

DEVELOPING A CULTURE OF SERVICE QUALITY

Companies who regularly deliver quality service usually have a corporate culture that encourages and supports quality throughout the company. Starting at the very top and moving down through the ranks to the newest employee, these companies not only "talk the talk" but also enthusiastically "walk the walk" together as a team. It's just part of how they go about doing their daily business. Their names have become synonymous with quality. They include such giants as Boeing Aerospace Support, The Ritz-Carlton Hotel Company, Southwest Airlines, and The Walt Disney Company.

Boeing Aerospace Support won the Baldrige Award in 2003 for quality service. Boeing Aerospace Support (AS) is part of the Boeing Company, the largest aerospace company in the world. Boeing Airlift and Tanker Programs received the 1998 Baldrige Award in the manufacturing category. As evidenced by these two separate groups within The Boeing Company winning Baldrige Awards, the culture at Boeing clearly fosters quality results.

The Ritz-Carlton Hotel Company won the Baldrige Award in 1992, the first organization in the hospitality industry to do so. Using the extensive feedback of the Baldrige evaluators, they again won the prestigious award in 1999, becoming only the second American company to earn the Baldrige twice.

Southwest boasts the best on-time record, best baggage handling, and fewest customer complaints in the airline industry and won the industry's Triple Crown award for Best Airline five times in a row from 1992-1996.

So, what is so special about the culture at these companies that makes them consistently able to provide not just good service, but outstanding service? A closer look into some of these outstanding companies reveals that they all have **H.E.A.R.T.** in their corporate culture. They live and breathe the philosophy of:

Hire the right people.

Educate and train them well.

Allow them to fix anything.

Recognize and reward them regularly.

Tell them everything, every day.

Hire the Best

Hire the right people and treat them with respect. Analysis of successful service companies show cultures that value each employee. This respect is evident from the first encounter with potential employees. Potential Disney "cast members" first arrive at a special whimsical building built specifically to introduce their culture from the first moment an applicant arrives. They consider the casting process itself to be a process of entertainment and make it a pleasurable experience.

At The Ritz-Carlton the motto, "Ladies and Gentlemen Serving Ladies and Gentlemen" extends to every person, both employees and guests, at every encounter. Potential applicants are treated with respect, as equals, by everyone they meet.

Quality cultures recognize that you must hire the best people you can find who already support your corporate values and then train them for the skills you need. Find people with the right spirit, are other people oriented, are outgoing, and work hard.

Educate and Train Them Well

A common theme at companies with a quality culture is an excellent ongoing training program. New hires are immediately immersed in the company's culture, learn its values, and become a valued team member. "Walt Disney established Disney University when he realized the need for a structured learning environment to teach the unique skills that are required of Disney cast members. It was the first corporate university and remains one of the largest corporate training facilities in the world" (Paton, 1997). Every new cast member attends a class there on "Disney Traditions."

The Disney Institute provides business professionals with a unique opportunity to benchmark the "Disney approach" to business and management issues. Program offerings include people management, quality service, loyalty, and organizational creativity. In addition to taking classes at The Institute, training is also provided via satellite from some of America's top business schools to Disney's front-line supervisors and mid- to upper-level managers.

The Ritz-Carlton's "7 Day Countdown" for new hires includes two days devoted entirely to orienting employees to the Ritz-Carlton culture and values. The remaining five days involve more specific skills training and trial runs of service delivery. Every day, all Ritz-Carlton employees worldwide meet at the beginning of each shift for a daily "Line Up" to discuss one of the 20 Key Principles employees must follow. They discuss the same one again 20 days later.

The Ritz-Carlton Leadership Center, launched in 2000, has shared the secrets of their culture with thousands of leaders from diverse industries such as Healthcare, Automotive, Financial, Banking, Hospitality, Food Service, and Retail. The Center offers benchmarking workshops and seminars including Legendary Service at The Ritz-Carlton, Creating a Dynamic Employee Orientation, and Selecting and Retaining Highly Effective Performers.

The common theme here? Every new hire at these companies, from management on down to the basic entry positions, attends these "culture and values" classes together. While all these values seem idealistic, they are exactly the kind of values on which the actions of the most admired and successful companies are based. A company must be a place where people feel they are part of something bigger than themselves. They must identify their personal successes on the job with that something. Loyalty breeds loyalty, it moves everyone away from a "blame the person" mentality to a "blame the process and let's fix it" approach to problems and improvement.

Since about 80 to 95 percent of all problems, depending on whether you believe Juran or Deming, are due to variation in processes, it just does not make a lot of sense to blame individuals for problems. But the best reason for fostering a heavy process orientation? It is the most *realistic* position you can take. It affirms that improvement happens when people understand, measure, and reduce variation or reengineer those processes to be more efficient and effective at delivering value for customers.

Allow Them to Fix Anything

Quality cultures require the empowerment of employees to do whatever is required to create a satisfactory customer service experience. At Southwest, every employee is given the general guidelines of their responsibilities and role in the company, then expected and encouraged to go outside those guidelines fearlessly.

Each Ritz-Carlton employee is informally allotted $2,000 to spend on solving a particular customer's complaint. This "resolution" includes such things as subtracting the cost of a room or a meal from the bill. More importantly, though, each incident must be reported by filling out a QIA, a Quality Incident Action, with the aim of preventing similar problems in the future.

Disney has a program they call "Take Five" in which cast members take five minutes out of their day to proactively do something special for a guest. The cast members look for opportunities for magic moments—those little things that happen for guests that are utter surprises (Emory, 2001).

At retail giant Lands' End, its Eight Principles of Doing Business are clearly spelled out for all of its customers and employees on its web site. These principles describe how at Lands' End the philosophy is to "believe that what is best for our customer is best for all of us. Everyone here understands that concept. Our sales and service people are trained to know our products, and to be friendly and helpful. They are urged to take all the time necessary to take care of you" (Lands' End Web site, 2004).

Lands' End believes that a guarantee is a reflection of the quality of not just its products, but also its people. The company philosophy is that a guarantee makes everyone try harder to get it right the first time, then attend to the problem (not the terms of the guarantee) if something goes wrong.

Recognize and Reward Them Regularly

Rewards are a key element in developing a quality culture, both on an individual and team basis. Set up recognition programs for people and teams. Most such recognition should be more symbolic than material. It should reward behaviors and actions that support the cultural values of "we're all in this together" or open communication or process improvement and so on. The Ritz-Carlton's Daily Line-Up gives management an opportunity to "nourish" their employees while repeating the corporate services standards. Top performers are also regularly rewarded with dinners, gift certificates, gift coupons, or weekend stays at the hotel.

Celebrate everything, together. Celebration encourages creativity, creates a mini-vacation, transcends routines, leads to unconventional thoughts, raises self-esteem, motivates, creates memories, and bonds relationships. On-the-spot type rewards (i.e.: dinners, gift certificates) can be given to employees when something extraordinary occurs.

Disney cast members are rewarded daily for guest service, performance, behavior, and longevity. In addition, cast members can treat themselves to a getaway at Mickey's Retreat, a cast-only resort.

Other ways to introduce and reinforce culture include legends and symbols. Legends, found in every company, are stories that capture the culture and the acts of certain people that demonstrate a commitment to the company's cultural values. These may be formal or informal stories passed around the company. Whichever they are, they help people understand what the company is about and what they are supposed to do. Symbols are like a brand name. In one way or another they say what the company is all about. People around the world recognize Mickey Mouse and the quality customer service he represents.

The legend behind The Ritz-Carlton begins with the celebrated hotelier César Ritz . . . the "king of hoteliers and hotelier to kings." César was a Swiss sheepherder's son who had been fired from four jobs before he opened a hotel under his name in Paris in 1898. Ritz, who by some accounts coined the phrase "the customer is never wrong," formed a philosophy of service and innovations that redefined the luxury hotel experience in Europe.

Symbols for a culture can be an animal, a phrase, anything that people can use to represent the culture. One travel agency has adopted the salmon as their corporate symbol, because of its can-do behavior, famous for swimming upstream. They have salmon awards and use this symbol in many different contexts to reinforce their values. You can work with others in your company to come up with one that exemplifies what makes your culture special (Woods, 1996).

Tell Them Everything, Every Day

In a large, widespread organization, communication is vital. Create processes that solicit and reward complaints and feedback. When you create an environment where there is no fear of retribution, employees will communicate system failures or problem opportunities before they impact your customer service. This gives you the opportunity to improve the system, or to fix a mistake or defect. This also gives you a vehicle to receive suggestions for improvements from the people closest to your customers.

Be honest and consistent with communication while assuring that everyone has access to all the information they need. The Ritz-Carlton was a leader in developing databases that track information on their repeat customers. A complete guest file is readily available to all Ritz-Carlton employees during a guest's stay that includes guest preferences. Staff members are encouraged to update these files with current information if they note a guest making a special request or having a fondness for a certain food or drink. If a guest moves the room furniture during a visit, for example, the furniture is placed in that position for him or her on all future visits.

Employees at Boeing AS are encouraged to "shamelessly share" information across businesses, sites, and functions. A continuous flow of information also comes from a wide range of sources, including meetings, roundtable discussions, online newsletters, and functional and business councils.

The company-wide belief that every cast member has valuable information to share is given life through Disney's ongoing employee communication efforts. Cast members receive a biweekly newsletter with company information and updates available in English, Spanish, and Haitian Creole. They can find updated information online via the Disney intranet as well, which contains everything a cast member could need, from the current Disney stock price to the day's weather forecast. Cast members get consistent feedback on their own performances as well, participating in beginning, mid- and end-year reviews on how well they meet Disney's quality standards (Blassingame, 2003).

Business leaders have a powerful influence on the development of whatever the culture is in their company. You might not be very aware of your culture, or you may just think of it as "the way we do things around here." But each company does have a culture, and it probably reflects its leader's values for good or bad. People adopt the behaviors and attitudes of their leaders toward their work.

IMPLEMENTING QUALITY SERVICE

Designing Fail-Safing into Service

We already discussed one method of ensuring proper service, that of designing poka-yoke devices to help fail-safe a service. Companies often use software, procedures, or gimmicks whose purpose is to make the quality way of delivering the service the only way the service gets delivered. The good part of these devices is that they involve relatively little capital goods investment. An example is the fast-food restaurants' use of a french-fry scoop for quick action and proper portion control. Software often prompts for the next piece of data or buzzes when the wrong piece of data has been entered.

Other fail-safing devices relate to customers and affect their behavior. Reminder cards for appointments, special uniforms or other clues so customers know whom to ask for help, and directions mailed ahead of time.

Sometimes things work even when they don't. Service failure can also be something that merely degrades a service, rather than stopping it entirely. An escalator doesn't really "break;" it becomes stairs. You rarely see an 'Escalator Out of Order' sign. You might see an 'Escalator Temporarily Stairs. Sorry for the inconvenience' sign, though. Contrast this with elevators which, when broken, are useless. Other examples of items with built-in recovery failure modes are:

- Radio-operated car keys which can also be used in the physical lock.
- Magnetic stripes on keycards (of any sort, such as library cards) which can also be used by manual entry of their ID numbers.
- ISBNs given as both barcodes and numerals, so that people wanting to read the number without a scanner can do so.

Service Guarantees and Refunds

Many firms meet the quality challenge by offering *service guarantees* to their customers. Guarantees can be a powerful marketing tool to increase sales, but the primary objective of a guarantee should be to foster repeat business. They can even work to create and define specific service "niches," such as FedEx's guarantee of overnight delivery. Market leaders can establish the new "rules of the game" for niches they create and develop. Guarantees can take many forms. Domino Pizza's former guarantee of 30 minutes delivery or L.L.Bean's policy of "no questions asked returns" are two well-known examples.

A good service guarantee should be identified and clearly defined as part of the initial design of a service. Unfortunately, many service guarantees don't really do the job they are designed to do because they are limited in scope or are difficult to use. Often a guarantee will be offered with conditions that negate the guarantee. Airlines, for instance, guarantee on-time arrivals *except* when the delay is weather-related or air-traffic delays occur.

Christopher Hart (1988) studied service guarantees and indicated they work best when they include the following characteristics:

- *Unconditional:* Customer satisfaction without exceptions
- *Easy to understand and communicate:* Written in simple, concise language that pinpoints the promise
- *Meaningful:* Important to customers and financially significant without being overly generous
- *Easy to invoke:* No red tape or runaround to hurdle, no guilt involved
- *Easy to collect:* The procedure needs to be quick and hassle-free

SERVICE OPERATIONS MANAGEMENT PRACTICES

Keep Those Customers Coming Back!

It is an old marketing maxim that it costs roughly five times more to obtain a new customer than it does to keep an existing one. This seems so absolutely sensible that it almost does not bear repeating. Yet every one of us can cite dozens of examples—from our own experiences—where a business' actions do not support this truth. Businesses that spend heavily to attract new customers can sometimes seem oblivious to the needs of customers they already have.

Businesses that operate in the virtual world face special problems when it comes to improving their existing "customer care." Online shoppers may not receive the visual and "in-person" clues that let traditional shoppers know they are important. To help online merchants build a better shopping environment for their valuable existing customers, the Better Business Bureau OnLine (BBBOnLine) Update offers the following tips:

- **Always say "thank you."** Most of us have placed an online order at one time or another. And we almost always receive an e-mail acknowledgement of that order. But how many times does a company send a follow-up e-mail after the order has been delivered? This second e-mail can not only thank the customer for his or her patronage, but can also ask the customer to let you know if she has experienced any problems or has any suggestions to make her next shopping experience better.
- **Reward loyalty.** Companies in the travel industry recognize this with "frequent flyer/driver/guest" programs. Give your better customers advance notice of sales—or special sale prices available only to "gold" customers—or "points" that repeat customers can earn toward discounts or gifts. These can help encourage and retain repeat customers.

- **Forge a customer bond.** Since you will never get to meet your online customers the way you could meet customers who visit a physical place of business, finding substitute ways to build a bond with online customers is critically important. Some online merchants have created regular monthly or quarterly newsletters to keep in touch with customers. The best of these are more than just electronic marketing brochures. Often written by the owner or manager of the business, they strive to create a personal relationship. Weblogs (blogs) that allow direct conversation between a business and its customers are increasingly popular. The point is not what the site is marketing, but how you can help the customer connect—and remain connected—with your business.
- **Do not get too creative.** Your Web site is your storefront. Customers get used to the way your site is laid out. Avoid changing your site just for the sake of change. Unless the changes really enhance the ease of the customer's shopping experience, you may frustrate your best customers.
- **Find a way to reward referrals.** One of the best types of new customers (and the least expensive to acquire) is a new customer referred from an existing customer. Find a way to reward existing customers for making referrals.
- **Solicit problems.** A customer who has one unsatisfactory experience with your business may become a former customer. Do not wait for a customer to tell you he has a problem. Actively seek out customer problems and suggestions. Provide ways for your customers to let you know how you could have done a better job. Then, meet or exceed their expectations!

(BBBOnline, 2004)

Hart gave five reasons why a guarantee provides a powerful tool in achieving marketing and service quality:

1. It forces the service to focus on the customers' definition of good service, rather than the expectations of management. If a company identifies the wrong things to guarantee, it will be worthless to its customers.
2. It sets up clear performance standards, which boost employee performance and morale. Employees take pride in good service and a great reputation.
3. It generates reliable data (through payouts) when performance is poor. When a payout causes financial pain, it will be easier to ensure that every necessary step will be taken to correct and prevent future such occurrences.
4. It forces an organization to examine its entire service delivery system for possible failure points. Continual review of the service goals will ensure an ongoing process improvement all through the company systems. A guarantee provides customers an easy method of giving feedback on possible failure points so that management can direct attention to remedying them as quickly as possible.
5. It builds customer loyalty, sales, and market share. A good guarantee reduces the risk of the purchase decision for customers, and it generates more sales to existing customers by enhancing loyalty.

Some service firms will not benefit from a guarantee when they already have a reputation for sterling service. These types of firms usually instill a mission of absolute customer satisfaction in all of their employees and empower them to make amends as needed. Hotels such as The Ritz-Carlton and the Four Seasons Hotels are good examples. Guests at these hotels don't need a guarantee, because it is assumed that the service will be absolutely terrific. When it is not, employees go out of their way to make it right for the guest.

Lands' End is so confident it can deliver the products and service its customers want that it has instituted a guarantee program that is more than a marketing tool, it's a philosophy. The company's GUARANTEED. PERIOD.® Program promises customers a full refund if they aren't satisfied with their purchases, even if it's been worn and washed, with no questions asked and no exceptions. Lands' End offers other valuable services, as well. If, for example, a child loses a mitten during the same season it was purchased from the company, the Lost Mitten Club will replace it at half the price of a pair and Lands' End will pay for the shipping. If customers lose their luggage belt or button, the company offers free replacements.

The downside of guarantees, of course, is their implication that the service may fail. A guarantee might actually make customers more aware of service defects. It might also entice some customers to cheat. Great service providers, however, live by the philosophy that only 1% of their customers will cheat, which should not prevent them from providing great service to the other 99%. Many also believe that customers resort to cheating only when they feel they are not receiving value for their money.

SERVICE RECOVERY

All service providers experience moments of service failure at some point. Equipment failure, delivery delays, severe weather, or human frailties (no-shows, forgetful or careless employees) can affect a service profoundly.

For consumers, the coming years are going to be bleak, according to Gartner Research. "Through 2007, more than 75% of businesses will fail to fully meet expectations for customer service excellence—and, as a consequence, they will experience 100% turnover of their customer base every five years, on average. Although customer service and support, as a high-level concept, is discussed endlessly, businesses are failing to deliver sustained innovative processes at the point of customer interaction," said Michael Maoz, vice president and research director for Gartner.

Many Customer Relationship Management (CRM) software systems are available to businesses today that allow them to track and manage information about their customers' buying behaviors, predict possible future behaviors, and assist them to interact positively with their customers when a service failure occurs. Many of these programs, however, fail to roll customer feedback into forward-looking product and marketing plans. A bad purchase experience can alter customers' future buying decisions—leading them to take their business elsewhere. Yet, many current CRM systems do not indicate that there was a customer service problem until long after the situation occurred.

Predictive analytics (predicting the needs of your customers) depends on many data points, and thus is effective for industries with a high volume of transactions per customer, such as telecommunications or consumer goods. In low-volume, high-ticket areas, though, a company cannot gather enough data to make predictive analytics work. The same goes for many business-to-business relationships.

Mike Trotter, executive director of Purdue University's Center for Customer Driven Quality, agreed that enterprises do not solicit enough feedback from customers. "Most organizations," he told CRMDaily, "are not in touch enough with their customers. They see surveying customers as a necessary evil." He asserted that companies that understand the sometimes intangible benefits of customer input are, not surprisingly, also known as leaders in the customer loyalty realm. That's why companies like Schwab are doing such a good job of retaining customers. Shortly after they finish a customer transaction, they're sending out a follow-up to say, "How'd we do?" (Hill, 2002).

The most important step in service recovery is to find out as soon as possible when a service fails to meet customers' expectations. Customers who are dissatisfied but have no way of communicating their dissatisfaction to the organization may never come back. Worse yet, they will probably relate the bad experience to everyone they know. It is, therefore, imperative that companies facilitate customer feedback and find opportunities to correct any failure situations and create a "delighted" customer.

This feedback procedure needs to be part of the initial service design process. A key consideration focuses on empowering front-line personnel to remedy the situation immediately. These front-line emissaries need to be able to express empathy while taking concrete steps to assist the customer. All attempts to rectify the situation should occur at the time and place most critical from the *customer's* perspective.

Recovering from service failures does not happen automatically; an organization must carefully prepare for it. Hart, Heskett, and Sasser (1990) recommended the following approach:

1. *Measure the costs.* The old adage, "What gets measured gets managed," is the principle here. Service failures cost both the customer and the service organization. (See the Service Operations Management Practices: Keep Those Customers Coming Back.)
2. *Break the silence and listen closely for complaints.* Many customers do not complain if they are not happy with a product or service. Consider the most frequently given reasons found by Technical Assistance Research Programs (TARP), a Washington, D.C.–based research and consulting organization:

   • It's not worth the time or effort.
   • No one would be concerned with my problem or interested in acting on it.
   • I don't know where to go or what to do.

SERVICE OPERATIONS MANAGEMENT PRACTICES

Empathy + Responsiveness = Quality Service Recovery

Due to massive thunderstorms across the eastern seaboard, airlines canceled flights and held flights at every airport on a Sunday afternoon in August 2004. When a mother and daughter arrived at Philadelphia's airport to catch a flight home to Atlanta, they discovered US Airways canceled their flight while they were en route to the airport. They were told they would be put on the next available flight out, but probably not until the next morning.

An empathetic and efficient ticket agent, though, turned around what could have easily been a nightmare. When David Chaplin couldn't figure out how to get them back in time for the daughter's first day of school the next morning, he sought his manager's advice and assistance. Together the agent and manager identified two passengers on the last flight out who would be missing their connections in Atlanta anyway and changed their flights. The mother and daughter finally made it back to Atlanta much later that evening in this textbook example of quality service and excellent service recovery.

Clearly, if a service organization does not know about service failures, it cannot do anything about them. Using toll-free 800 numbers for complaints or suggestions; offering rewards for suggestions; conducting regular surveys, focus groups, and interviews of lost customers all can offer new information to uncover and thus prevent service problems.

3. *Anticipate needs for recovery.* A plan and a procedure for each potential failure must be developed, and employees must be trained in these procedures. Managers who understand the service and its delivery system can anticipate where failures may occur and make plans for recovery.

4. *Act fast.* A service organization that acts quickly to correct the situation will probably impress the customer and make her or him forget the incident. Long, drawn-out processes and weeks of waiting will not help the customer forget the failure easily even if it is eventually resolved satisfactorily.

5. *Train employees.* Effective service recovery is not possible if the employees who handle complaints are not prepared for occasional service failures. Preparation involves training and empowerment. Training should include developing good communication skills, creative thinking, quick decision making, and developing an awareness of customers' concerns. One of the most effective training methods is stimulated situations and role-playing.

6. *Empower the front line.* Quick and decisive action to remedy a service failure is not possible without empowered employees. Many rules and limits on authority are established because of a fear that employees will "give away the store," which is not likely to happen with a well-trained and motivated employee. Losing customers, however, is much more likely if their problem is not solved.

7. *Close the loop*. Recovery and complaint handling must achieve closure. If the condition that led to the problem cannot be remedied, the customer must be given an explanation. If the complaint leads to a change in the service or the delivery system, the customer should be told so.

Summary

As services constitute a larger and larger percentage of the economy, service quality becomes a competitive tool. Improving this quality, however, is more elusive due to the temporary nature of a service. As the TQM movement shifts to a focus on return on quality, customers set the parameters for quality service based on their needs.

Service quality is often defined as the satisfaction of expectations based on a customer's need for the service. A customer's expectations can reflect his or her "expectations" of what might, could, should, or better not happen. Service quality definitions often do not reflect the perspectives of all the various stakeholders, though.

SERVQUAL, also commonly known as the Gaps model, conceptualizes service quality on the basis of the differences between customers' expectations, with respect to five dimensions, and their perceptions of what was actually delivered. When asked which of SERVQUAL's five dimensions (reliability, responsiveness, assurance, empathy, or tangibles) was most important, customers consistently chose reliability, the area where many service companies fail.

Service design can greatly affect the quality of a service. Creating a service blueprint can identify where service failures may occur. Designing fail-safing techniques and poka-yoke devices into the service can often block mistakes before they become service defects.

The cost of quality is often seen as an added expense in the design of additional features. It can also be seen as freedom from a service failure that can cost a company. Service quality generally pays off in the final analysis, because it creates loyal customers. Scientific study links quality with profits.

Implementing quality service can include offering service guarantees and refunds. A good guarantee should be identified and clearly defined as part of the initial service design. Service recovery is another critical part of delivering quality service. All services experience moments of failure, and the response to that failure creates either a delighted customer or a lost customer. Organizations must, therefore, prepare carefully for their service recovery response.

Review Questions

1. What is the difference between customer *expectations* and customer *needs*? Between service *value* and service *quality*?
2. Choose a local company known for its quality service. Would you evaluate its quality processes using the Baldrige Award criteria or the ISO standards? Both? Why?
3. Which of the five different perspectives on quality definitions do you agree with most? Why?
4. How does a poka-yoke improve quality? Give two examples.
5. What is a "Gap" in service quality? How can a company utilize SERVQUAL to improve its service quality?

6. List and evaluate the H.E.A.R.T. processes of developing a culture that nurtures service quality.

7. Identify a Web site that you feel offers great customer service. Why do you think it does a great job? How could they improve their service?

8. Evaluate the following situations for how well the service provider responded. What did they do well? How could they have improved their response? Would you patronize the provider again? Have you had similar experiences?

a. **Faulty Elevator:** Washington, D.C. area Metro riders had developed a certain complacency about the train system's hit-and-usually-miss maintenance service when they read in the local media about the plight of one customer in a wheelchair. The man found himself stuck in the subway system because the elevator he needed to take to his exit was broken at his downtown stop—as were the elevators at the next two stops. Frustrated by his predicament, he let loose a string of obscenities as he made his third fruitless attempt to leave the system—for which he was promptly ticketed $25 by a nearby Metro officer. Eventually, the man found a working elevator and wound up taking a taxi to his destination. Complaints poured in about his treatment and about maintenance in general. And Metro officials *were* sorry. So sorry, in fact, that the Metro police chief personally drove to the passenger's home in Maryland to reimburse him for the ticket and taxi ride.

b. **Book Order:** The first order the customer ever placed with Amazon.com was for a travel guide to Hong Kong, requesting it be sent overnight as she was about to make an unplanned trip to the city. Though she was billed for overnight express, the book was shipped by regular mail. Amazon credited her the shipping charge, but she complained in an e-mail to its customer service department, that really wasn't the point. She had wanted a travel guide for her first—and maybe only—trip to Hong Kong. A customer service rep answered back offering an apology and—to the customer's complete shock—a few suggestions of sights to see. It wasn't the same as having the actual travel guide, she acknowledged, but she hoped it would help.

c. **Frequent Flyer:** The executive flew every month or so from San Diego to San Francisco to meet with clients. She recently discovered, however, that Southwest has a much lower fare between San Diego and San Jose than United does between San Diego and San Francisco, so she switched. After two or three months of her absence, United flagged her account for a special offer or communication.

d. **Lost Baggage:** Upon his arrival in Chicago O'Hare's airport, the weary traveler went to collect his suitcase. But it never appeared. After filing a lost bag report, he was told that when his bag was found, it would be delivered to his hotel. When he asked how soon that might be, he was told most bags are located and delivered within 24 hours. "That just won't do!" he exclaimed. "I just completed a training session for this client in a Florida location where we all wore business casual outfits, like the one I am currently wearing. I have to make a presentation to the client's executive board tomorrow morning at 8:30 A.M. I must have my suit for that presentation!" The claim's manager replied, "If you're such a hot-shot consultant, that shouldn't be a problem."

Selected Bibliography

Armstrong, L., and W. Symonds. 1991. Beyond 'May I Help You.' *BusinessWeek/Quality*, 100–103.

Blassingame, K.M. 2003. Working their Magic: Disney Culture Molds Happy Employees, *Employee Benefit News* (September 1, 2003), http://www.benefitnews.com/detail.cfm?id=4954

Buzzell, R., and B. Gale. 1990. *The PIMS Principles*. The Free Press, New York, 107.

Chase, R. Acquilano, N., and R. Jacobs; 2001. *Operations Management*. McGraw-Hill, Irwin, Boston.

Chase, R., and D. Stewart. 1994. Make Your Service Fail-Safe, *Sloan Management Review* (Spring), 35–44.

Emory, C. 2001. The Disney Institute Approach to Human Capital: An Interview with Larry Lynch LiNE Zine Spring 2001. http://linezine.com/4.1/interviews.

Garvin, D. 1988. *Managing Quality*. The Free Press, New York, 40–46.

Haksever, C., R. Render, R. Russell, and G. Murdick. 2000. *Service Management and Operations*. Prentice Hall, Upper Saddle River, NJ, 7.

Hart, C. 1988. The Power of Unconditional Service Guarantees. *Harvard Business Review* (July–August), 55–60.

Hart, C., J. Heskett, and W. Sasser, Jr. 1990. The Profitable Art of Service Recovery. *Harvard Business Review* (July–August), 148–156.

Hill, K. 2002. Factoring in the Voice of the Customer, *CRM Daily*, April 11: 7:46 A.M.

Keiningham, T. L., A. J. Zahorik, and R. T. Rust (1994–1995), "Getting Return on Quality," *Journal of Retail Banking* (Winter), 16(4).

Lafferty, J.P. 1992. Cpk of 2 Not Good Enough For You? *Manufacturing Engineering*, (October), 10.

Myers, M. 1995. Baka/yoke-ing Your Way to Success, *Network World*, (September 11), 39.

Palmer, A., and C. Cole. 1995. *Services Marketing: Principles and Practice*. Prentice Hall, Upper Saddle River, NJ, 109.

Parasuraman, A., V. Zeithaml, and L. Berry. 1985. A Conceptual Model of Service Quality and Its Implications for Future Research. *Journal of Marketing* (Fall), 41–50.

Paton, S.M. 1997. Service Quality, Disney Style, *Quality Digest* (January), http://www.qualitydigest.com/jan97/disney.html

Pegels, C. 1995. *Total Quality Management*. Boyd & Fraser Publishing, Danvers, MA, 31.

Rust, R., A. Zahorik, and T. Keiningham, 1994. *Return on Quality*. Probus Publishing, Chicago, 7–8.

Sampson, S. E. 1999. *Understanding Service Businesses*. Brigham Young University, Salt Lake City, Utah, 330–331.

Scheuing, E., and E. Johnson. 1989. A Proposed Model for New Service Development. *The Journal of Services Marketing*, 3(2), 25–34.

Stewart, T. 1999. *Fortune* (January 11), 168, 170.

Woods, J.A., 1996. *The Six Values of a Quality Culture*. CWL Publishing Enterprises.

Zeithaml, V., A. Parasuraman, and L. Berry. 1990. *Delivering Quality Service, Balancing Customer Perceptions and Expectations*. The Free Press, New York, 46.

CASE STUDY

The Ritz-Carlton Hotel Company

The company now known worldwide as The Ritz-Carlton Hotel Company began with celebrated hotelier César Ritz' opening, in 1898, of the first Ritz Hotel in Paris. Ritz' philosophy of service and innovations redefined the luxury hotel experience in Europe. His policy of maintaining the privacy of his guests attracted the elite to his hotels. Guests now routinely expect nothing less than the finest service, food, and accommodations at every Ritz-Carlton property.

Headquartered in Chevy Chase, Maryland, The Ritz-Carlton Hotel Company, L.L.C., has 59 hotels worldwide (35 city hotels and 24 resorts), employing over 25,000 people. Its name is synonymous with luxury and excellent service. The company has expanded from luxury hotels to include such innovative new businesses as The Ritz-Carlton Club for fractional home ownership, a Club and Golf Division, and The Residences at The Ritz-Carlton.

César Ritz's vision of a great hotel was one with excellent personalized service that satisfied the most discerning guest. In order to ensure that every guest receives impeccable service, Horst Schulze, The Ritz-Carlton's president and COO for nearly 20 years, believed it was necessary to establish standards to focus employees on the core company values. His focus was on creating a high-performance environment through leadership systems and processes where passionate employees could take ownership of their work. Believing in the importance of system and process development, in the early 1980's he helped to create The Ritz-Carlton Hotel Company's "Gold Standards."

The Gold Standards, the foundation of The Ritz-Carlton Hotel Company, encompass the values and philosophy by which the company operates. These standards include The Credo, The Motto, The Three Steps of Service, The Basics, and The Employee Promise.* Together they create a culture of excellent service quality in every aspect of customer service at a Ritz-Carlton property.

By living these standards in everything they do, Ritz-Carlton employees walk and talk the company's culture of quality service to each other and to each guest they encounter.

THE CREDO

The Ritz-Carlton Hotel is a place where the genuine care and comfort of our guests is our highest mission.

We pledge to provide the finest personal service and facilities for our guests who will always enjoy a warm, relaxed, yet refined ambience.

The Ritz-Carlton experience enlivens the senses, instills well-being, and fulfills even the unexpressed wishes and needs of our guests.

---

* All the Gold Standards can be found in their entirety on the company Web site: http://www.ritzcarlton.com.

CASE STUDY

Before opening a new property, a common procedure is to hold a job fair. Individuals who show up arrive first at a "Warm Welcome" station where they are greeted by several employees who wish them luck and escort them to a Registration Area. During this time it is common for the company to have musical entertainers, beverages, and snacks available while a Ritz-Carlton video is running. On the video will be current employees describing their experiences at the company.

THE MOTTO
We Are Ladies and Gentlemen Serving Ladies and Gentlemen.

Various screening levels must be met before someone is offered employment. Upon leaving, each individual will be personally escorted again to an area where he or she is thanked for applying, often given Ritz-Carlton chocolates, and escorted out of the building.

Regardless of whether someone is hired or not, all applicants are treated equally well. Each is made to understand that he or she is valued as a person. This type of attitude permeates every part of the Ritz-Carlton culture.

Once hired, employees come back for a Seven Day Countdown. The first two days of this Countdown are devoted entirely to orienting employees to The Ritz-Carlton culture and values. The remaining days are devoted to specific skills training and trial runs of service delivery.

The first day of orientation can be likened to a pep rally for the company, its culture, and its values. Over and over the new employee is sincerely welcomed as a new member of The Ritz-Carlton family by the scores of current employees and managers involved in the training. The new employees learn about the company's history, philosophy, and values.

THREE STEPS OF SERVICE
1. A warm and sincere greeting. Use the guest name, if and when possible.
2. Anticipation and compliance with guest needs.
3. Fond farewell. Give them a warm good-bye and use their names, if and when possible.

The company philosophy emphasizes that the employees are not servants. Their profession is service. As their motto states, they are all Ladies and Gentlemen, just as the guests are. Guests and employees alike should be respected as such. Each

CASE STUDY

employee of The Ritz-Carlton believes this motto deeply as a promise by the organization that everyone should be respected as a lady or gentleman. It is also a demand on all employees, especially managers and leaders, to believe and to live by the company's Employee Promise.

THE EMPLOYEE PROMISE

At The Ritz-Carlton, our Ladies & Gentlemen are the most important resource in our service commitment to our guests.

By applying the principles of trust, honesty, respect, integrity, and commitment, we nurture and maximize talent to the benefit of each individual and the company.

The Ritz-Carlton fosters a work environment where diversity is valued, quality of life is enhanced, individual aspirations are fulfilled, and The Ritz-Carlton mystique is strengthened.

Once employees have been trained in the company culture and in specific job skills, they start their new jobs each day with the daily "lineup." Each day, at the beginning of each shift, at every Ritz-Carlton hotel around the world, staffers are supposed to discuss the same Ritz-Carlton basic, one of the 20 key principles employees must follow. They do this together in each department with their managers. They discuss this same basic again 20 days later with the purpose being to keep the Ritz-Carlton philosophy front and center in each employee's mind. At this gathering, they also discuss hotel goings-on, particular guests' likes and dislikes, special needs, and any of their own concerns.

By using identical training and orientation programs at every new hotel and with every new employee, The Ritz-Carlton aims to maintain its high level of prestige as the epitome of luxury hotel accommodations internationally. At the same time, The Ritz-Carlton is expanding into uncharted areas with some of its new innovations. One of these, The Residences at the Ritz-Carlton, is promising to redefine the concept of an elegant lifestyle. In addition to spaciously proportioned condominiums, owners will enjoy all the legendary amenities and service points that have been a hallmark of The Ritz-Carlton from its beginning. These will include a dedicated concierge, gourmet dining, butler service, and the prestige of living at The Ritz-Carlton.

The Residences are already available in many key Ritz-Carlton destinations, including Berlin, Boston, Georgetown, New York, and Grand Cayman. They each have unique features to entice buyers to purchase. For example, The Residences in

CASE STUDY

Boston offer spectacular one- to four-bedroom condominiums with incredible views, access to a 100,000-square-foot sports and spa facility, and fronts Boston Common.

The Residences are a new service concept from operating a hotel property. The service challenges will be many and varied and not the same types Ritz-Carlton employees have come to expect and to manage. They have the potential to erode the prestige of The Ritz-Carlton or to enhance it. Only time will tell. (http://www.ritzcarlton.com/corporate/residential/default.asp)

Questions:

1. How does the training of Ritz-Carlton employees instill a culture of quality?
2. What is The Ritz-Carlton really selling?
3. What unique challenges might the employees of a Ritz-Carlton Residence experience? How will the service need to expand or change to meet the needs of owners versus guests?
4. How could less expensive hotels incorporate some of the Ritz-Carlton Hotel Company's quality standards into their company culture at a reasonable cost to their customers?
5. Does excellent service have to cost extra to the company or the customers?

Six Sigma for Service Process Improvement

LEARNING OBJECTIVES   *The material in this chapter prepares students to:*

- Describe the history and importance of Six Sigma.

- Describe the importance of variation to managers and executives.

- Explain the core concepts of Six Sigma.

- Explain whether Six Sigma is a fad, and whether it matters if it is a fad.

- Understand and use the tools included in the Supplementary CD.

Saying "Six Sigma" to an executive always elicits a powerfully emotional response. Some executives will swear that Six Sigma is the only reason their company is successful, while others will swear with equal passion that Six Sigma would be the death of their company if they were to adopt it. If a person talked to a hundred executives, they would be convinced that Six Sigma was the best thing that ever killed a company. Until relatively recently, service companies were insulated from this paradox because many people thought that Six Sigma could only be used in manufacturing companies. Recent history, though, has shown that this point of view is just wrong (companies like The Home Depot, Delta Air Lines, Bank of America, Wells Fargo, Wipro Technologies, Quest Diagnostics and others have adopted Six Sigma). This chapter will explain where many quality problems come from, what Six Sigma is, its history, whether it is a fad, and how it has been applied to service companies of all kinds. The chapter does not go into detail on the tools of Six Sigma, but the supplemental material included on the CD specifically explains and demonstrates these tools.

WHAT CAUSES MOST QUALITY PROBLEMS?

Chapter 10 explained service quality, SERVQUAL, and service recoveries. But it left open the question of what causes quality problems and how to keep these problems from happening in the first place. Equally important, why do managers and executives have such a hard time spotting quality problems until they become plain silly? (Remember the examples presented in Chapter 9 of the NYPD changing tires or the New York City arrest-to-arraignment process?) Chapter 9 pointed out one reason:

processes evolve over time; assumptions become embedded in the process; and managers stand so close to the process that they don't think to question these assumptions. One company we have worked with had an insurance policy approval process that required a manager to sign off on every policy before it went into force. Of course, the managers were so busy that getting a signature often added days to the cycle time to complete a policy request. A manager once explained that they required the manager's signature because "it has always been done that way." After doing a little analysis, the company discovered that when they first began selling this particular type of insurance, the only people that sold it happened to be managers, so every request was signed by a manager because of a quirk in staffing (not a policy decision).

A second reason why managers do such a bad job of recognizing quality problems before they get to be silly is that every person suffers from a predictable set of mental "biases" that makes it hard to process new information. Table 11.1 shows a few of these biases. Consider one classic experiment where people were asked about brands of pasta. They were asked things like "Have you seen advertisements for this brand?," "Have you bought this brand?," "Did you enjoy it?" The trouble was that some of the brands were made up, but still some respondents clearly remembered having these imaginary pastas for dinner, and liking them very much. But there is another, more compelling reason why managers have such a hard time spotting the source of quality problems.

Kirk Kirkpatrick, a Senior Vice President at Bank of America, says, "Managers are trained to manage based on the average, but our customers feel variation and they hate it." The implications of this statement are profound. Managers evaluate employee performance and award bonuses for achievements that are virtually always described as averages (average ticket size, average time on hold, average utilization, average airplane load, and the list goes on). But by definition an average distills a set of customers into a single number, the expected value for some arbitrary next customer. Customers, on the other hand, simply don't care what the

TABLE 11.1: *Mental Biases*

Bias Name	Explanation
Halo effect	If a person is good at one thing, he or she must be good at another. Studies have shown that attractive people are more likely to get promoted than ugly people.
Availability	Because I have seen it, it must happen a lot. When surveyed, people generally respond incorrectly that tornados kill more people than lightning because they see the devastated mobile home parks on the news.
Spurious awareness	I think I know things that really are not so. The pasta example described in the chapter.
Anchoring	People are very suggestible; they latch onto information early (anchor on a fact), then fail to update when new information is available.
Recency	People tend to pay more attention to what has happened recently, even if it is not representative of what usually happens.
Selective perception	People tend to give credence to what confirms their beliefs and discount things that contradict their beliefs.
Memory/hindsight	People remember things differently than they actually happened. Everyone has a friend that says after a big upset, "I knew they would win!"
Confirming evidence	When given information, people tend to see things that support their positions, while discounting things that conflict with their positions.

average number of people bumped from a flight is, they care whether they get bumped and how long they have to wait for the next flight.

Consider a specific example: "time to answer" is a widely used metric for call centers. A call center might have an average time to answer of 40 seconds, and for now let's assume that the target time to answer is also 40 seconds. But again, the customer doesn't see himself as an arbitrary next caller. He sees himself, rightly, as an individual needing service from our call center. Table 11.2 shows two different scenarios, each with an average time to answer of 40 seconds, but with wildly different customer service impacts. In Scenario 1, all of our customers are happy with our service. They don't love it, but they don't hate it. On the other hand, in Scenario 2, three people love us, one thinks we're ok, and two people despise us. But because both have an average time to answer of 40 seconds, right on target, management would view these two scenarios as the same. They would award the same bonus to the two managers even though one has lost the company a third of the customers who used the service. At the same time, the company would probably be fretting over the poor customer retention numbers, but have no clue what was driving the loss of customers.

So, quality problems come from the fact that managers don't understand variation well, they are distracted by their own, often unfounded, assumptions, and they are susceptible to an array of mental biases that cause them to overvalue what they think they know. So managers need a structured way to think about their business that pinpoints the impact of variation, allows them to bring assumptions to the surface so they can be evaluated, and forces them to step beyond the mental biases every person faces. The quality movement as it has developed over the past nearly 70 years provides these tools. The latest approach in the quality movement is Six Sigma as a method to reduce variation.

VARIATION

Every day we deal with variation, often without even realizing it. Those days that you are late to class because all of the stoplights conspired against you, and then there was no parking available is an example of two different instances of variation. You could talk about the average amount of time spent waiting at stoplights on the ride to class, but you know each day will be different (variation). Or you could talk about the average number of open parking places at 10:00 A.M. when you get to campus, but again you know it will be different every day. Stated directly, nearly every phenomenon has an average value that can be thought of as describing the "central tendency" of the phenomenon, and variation is the idea that any individual probably doesn't fall on that measure of the center, but has some "dispersion around the mean."

TABLE 11.2: *Two Different "Time to Answer" Scenarios*

Time to Answer in Seconds, Scenario 1	Time to Answer in Seconds, Scenario 2
40	80
40	10
40	20
40	90
40	10
40	30
Average: 40	Average: 40
Standard Deviation: 0	Standard Deviation: 35.77

Figure 11.1 graphically shows the distribution of the call center data from Table 11.2; the distance between each phone call and the mean represents the variation. In Scenario 1, the central tendency is obviously 40 seconds, and there is no dispersion around that number (i.e., every caller waited exactly 40 seconds before being connected with a customer service representative). But look at Scenario 2. Again the mean time to answer is 40 seconds, but not a single customer waited 40 seconds. Table 11.3 presents the deviations each customer felt. Mathematically, each deviation is found by subtracting the mean $\overline{X}$ from each individual observation (each one is called an X_i, with i ranging from 1 for the first caller up to 6 for the last), or:

$$X_i - \overline{X} \text{ for } i = 1 \text{ to } 6$$

Unfortunately, if one wanted to find the average deviation, it would be zero because the sum of the deviations around the mean by definition is zero. To keep the deviations from canceling each other out, square each deviation before adding them. For rather arcane statistical reasons, divide by 5 instead of 6 to get the average. In general, divide by $(n - 1)$; the reasons for this are beyond the scope of this book, but trust us—it works to make the average of the squared deviations a better estimate of what we want to know. But now when the squared deviations are averaged, they are in a completely different scale than the original data (40 seconds for the average, 1280 seconds^2 for the average squared deviations). In order to get the average deviation back into the correct scale, take the square root of 1280 seconds^2, which turns out to be 35.77 seconds, and is called the "standard deviation," the most common and useful of the measures of variation. The Greek character "sigma" (σ) is used to represent standard deviation, which is calculated as:

FIGURE 11.1: *Service Design Process with Customer Utility Model*

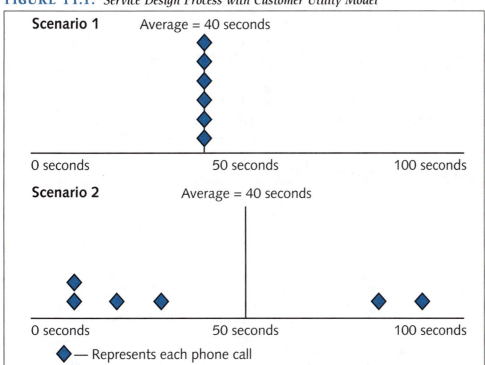

TABLE 11.3: *Deviations from Time to Answer*

Time to Answer in Seconds, Scenario 2	Deviation from the Mean (observation minus the mean)	Squared Deviations
80	80 − 40 = 40	1600
10	10 − 40 = −30	900
20	20 − 40 = −20	400
90	90 − 40 = 50	2500
10	10 − 40 = −30	900
30	30 − 40 = −10	100
Average: 40	Sum of the deviations = 0	Sum of squared deviations = 6400

$$\sigma = \sqrt{\frac{\sum_{i=1}^{n}\left(X_i - \overline{X}^2\right)}{n-1}}$$

Many different "distributions" exist, but the most commonly used distribution is the normal distribution, or the bell curve. The next section serves as a refresher for those who have previously studied the normal distribution. If you have never studied the normal distribution, you may need to consult a statistics book for more details. If you are quite familiar with the normal distribution, feel free to skip the next section.

The Normal Distribution

The normal distribution is shown on the back leaf of this book, and the picture of the distribution is recreated in Figure 11.2. While we commonly say "the normal distribution," implying that there is only one of them, there are in fact lots. The normal distribution is really a family of distributions, the particular member of the family determined by two pieces of information, the mean and the standard deviation. For every normal distribution, the mean defines the center point of the distribution. For the specific normal distribution shown in Figure 11.2, the mean is zero. Then the standard deviation determines the width of the normal distribution. A higher standard deviation (i.e., more dispersion from the mean) would lead to a wider and flatter normal curve, while a lower standard deviation would lead to a thinner and taller curve. But what does the normal curve tell us?

All probability distributions describe the chance of things happening, and the way the normal curve does this is by the "area under the curve." Take the easiest example;

FIGURE 11.2: *The Normal Distribution*

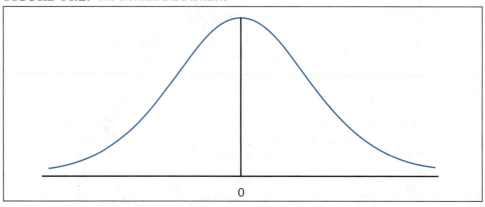

0

what is the chance you are below average? The mean of the normal distribution defines the middle point, so by definition half of all observations will be above the mean and half will be below. Put another way, the probability of being below the mean is 50%. Since the total area under the curve of the normal distribution is 1, or 100%, and the mean cuts the distribution precisely in half, the chance of being below average is precisely 50%.

The normal distribution is far more powerful than this simple example implies though. Most people have referred to the table on the back leaf of the book as a z-table without really understanding what z means, what to do with it after we find it, and why it is so helpful. These three points are critical. Recall that we calculate z as:

$$z = \frac{x - \overline{X}}{\sigma}$$

But again, what does it mean? Think about the numerator; it tells how far an individual observation is from the mean, in whatever units the original data are in. Using the call center data again, what if we wanted to know how strange it was that someone had to wait up to 60 seconds to be helped. The numerator would yield (60 minus 40) 20 seconds. This is to say; the thing that we are interested in is 20 seconds above the mean. Now consider what happens when we divide this result of 20 seconds by the standard deviation. We end up with a ratio that tells us how many standard deviations from the mean that 20 seconds is (20 divided by 35.77), 0.56 standard deviations. In other words, the 60-second cutoff we are interested in is 0.56 standard deviations above the mean of 40 seconds. z always tells us the number of standard deviations the thing of interest is away from the mean. Table 11.4 shows six more calculations of the number of standard deviations that some point of interest is from the mean.

The second point people often miss is what do we do with z when we find it? z is the linchpin to the normal table (a portion of which is recreated in Table 11.5). To find out how unusual it is that someone waits up to 60 seconds when she calls our call center, we need to find the probability that someone waits less than 60 seconds; the notation for this is $P(X < 60)$. The same question can be stated in terms of number of standard deviations. We have calculated that 60 is 0.56 standard deviations above the mean, so we can write the question as $P(z < 0.56)$. We will use the z table to find this probability. Look at the picture of the normal curve on the back leaf. The gray bar on the normal curve tells us that the table gives the area from the mean up to whatever z value we look up. For our example this would be, in words, the chance that someone waits between 40 and 60 seconds, in notation $P(40 < X < 60)$ or in terms of number of standard deviations $P(0 < z < 0.56)$. To use the table, find the first two digits in the column marked z (so find 0.5). Next, find the hundredths place digit in the row across the table (so find 0.06). Read to the intersection of this column

TABLE 11.4: *A Few Examples of Calculating z*

Point of Interest	Mean	Numerator	Standard Deviation	z
15	30	−15	5	−3
15	30	−15	10	−1.5
15	30	−15	20	−0.75
200	100	100	20	5
200	100	100	100	1
200	100	100	200	0.5

TABLE 11.5: *A Portion of the Normal Table Applied to the Call Center*

z	0.00	0.01	0.02	0.03	0.04	0.05	0.06	0.07	0.08	0.09
0.0	0.0000	0.0040	0.0080	0.0120	0.0160	0.0199	0.0239	0.0279	0.0319	0.0359
0.1	0.0398	0.0438	0.0478	0.0517	0.0557	0.0596	0.0636	0.0675	0.0714	0.0753
0.2	0.0793	0.0832	0.0871	0.0910	0.0948	0.0987	0.1026	0.1064	0.1103	0.1141
0.3	0.1179	0.1217	0.1255	0.1293	0.1331	0.1368	0.1406	0.1443	0.1480	0.1517
0.4	0.1554	0.1591	0.1628	0.1664	0.1700	0.1736	0.1772	0.1808	0.1844	0.1879
0.5	0.1915	0.1950	0.1985	0.2019	0.2054	0.2088	0.2123	0.2157	0.2190	0.2224
0.6	0.2257	0.2291	0.2324	0.2357	0.2389	0.2422	0.2454	0.2486	0.2518	0.2549
0.7	0.2580	0.2612	0.2642	0.2673	0.2704	0.2734	0.2764	0.2794	0.2823	0.2852
0.8	0.2881	0.2910	0.2939	0.2967	0.2995	0.3023	0.3051	0.3078	0.3106	0.3133
0.9	0.3159	0.3186	0.3212	0.3238	0.3264	0.3289	0.3315	0.3340	0.3365	0.3389

and row to find the probability. In this case it is 0.2123, which means the chance that someone waits between 40 and 60 seconds is 21.23%.

This doesn't answer the original question though. What is the chance someone waits no more than 60 seconds? We have both pieces calculated; we just need to put them together. We found the chance of being below the mean is always 50% by recognizing that the normal distribution is symmetric about the mean, in the notation of our example, $P(X < 40) = 0.5000$. We found the chance of the wait being between 40 and 60 seconds to be 21.23% by using the z table, in notation $P(40 < X < 60) = 0.2113$. If we add these together we have the chance of being either below 40 seconds or between 40 and 60 seconds. Which, of course, is the same as being below 60 seconds. So, $P(X < 60) = 0.5000 + 0.2123 = 0.7123$, or 71.23%. Table 11.6 presents a few more examples of using z scores to find probabilities.

Now why is this helpful? Being able to transform any question about a normal distribution into a standard measure like number of standard deviations away from the mean allows us to apply a single method for dealing with normal distributions to any normal distribution we might come across. The process of finding z, or transforming a normal variable into the standard normal (which by definition has a mean of zero and a standard deviation of one), allows us to use the normal table regardless of the context we find ourselves in.

Consider a different service example. Virtually all retailers track the amount spent by a shopper in an individual visit to the store, or "average ticket." The Home Depot recently announced that for the first quarter of 2004 the average ticket was

TABLE 11.6: *More Examples of Using the z Table*

Mean	Standard Deviation	Find...	z Values	z Notation	How to Find Probabilities	Probabilities
50	10	$P(50 < X < 75)$	0 and 2.5	$P(0 < z < 2.5)$	Directly from z Table	0.4938
100	18	$P(87 < X < 105)$	−0.72 and 0.28	$P(−0.72 < z < 0.28)$	$P(0 < z < 0.72) = 0.2642$, so by symmetry $P(−0.72 < z < 0) = 0.2642$ $P(0 < z < 0.28) = 0.1103$	0.3745
20	4	$P(X < 11)$	−2.25	$P(z < −2.25)$	$P(0 < z < 2.25) = 0.4878$ so by symmetry $P(−2.25 < z < 0) = 0.4878$ so, $P(z < −2.25) = 0.5$ $−0.4878 = 0122$	0.0122

$55 dollars. They did not announce the standard deviation so for this example let's assume a standard deviation of $15 dollars. What percentage of customers who buy from The Home Depot will spend between $40 and $70? In notation, we want to find $P(40 < X < 70)$. We can translate each of these two points of interest into z values:

$$z = \frac{40 - 55}{15} = -1 \quad \text{and} \quad z = \frac{70 - 55}{15} = 1$$

So in terms of z we want to find $P(-1.00 < z < 1.00)$. Looking in the z table in the back of the book, in the row marked 1.0 and the column marked 0.00, we find a z value of 0.3413. Remember that based on the structure of the table this is the probability of being between the mean and 1.00, or $P(0 < z < 1.00)$. Because the normal distribution is symmetric about the mean, the probability of being between −1.00 and 0 is exactly the same, 0.3413. So the chance of being between −1.00 and +1.00 standard deviations from the mean is 0.3413 + 0.3413 = 0.6826. Translating this result back into the language of retail sales, there is a 68.26% chance that a customer that buys from The Home Depot will spend between $40 and $70.

Common Cause and Special Cause Variation

One additional distinction concerning variation is critical from a business practice point of view. That distinction is between common cause and special cause variation. Conceptually, common cause variation is the variation we expect in a process, and special cause variation is the unexpected variation. For example, when ordering a pizza at midnight, let's say it usually takes between 35 and 45 minutes to be delivered, so we're not surprised if tonight's pizza takes 38 minutes. That's just the way it usually is; that's what is common. Hence the name common cause variation. On the other hand, it rarely takes 2 hours for the pizza to arrive. That would be unexpected, something special must have happened. Hence the name special cause variation.

From a business perspective, common cause variation reflects the choices management has made in terms of people, processes, technology, training, staffing, etc. Think back to our comparison of Delta Air Lines with Southwest Airlines in Chapter 2. Southwest is able to turn their aircraft in about 16 minutes. One description has it that two-thirds of the flights turn in 15 minutes and the remainder turn in 20 minutes (Heskett and Hallowell). Because of the decisions made by management, the variation in Southwest's turn time is quite small. They would consider the variation in turning a plane to be routine if the plane turned anywhere between 15 and 20 minutes. On the other hand, if the plane turned in the industry average 55 minutes, Southwest would be unpleasantly surprised and feel like its service system had failed. In this instance, common cause variation would be reflected in any aircraft turn that took place between 15 and 20 minutes, and special cause variation would be any flight that turned in under 15 minutes (special cause variation helped in this instance) or over 20 minutes (special cause variation hurt here).

So which type of variation is more important for managers to get rid of? Because special cause variation is in a sense an accident, management's first job is to get rid of special cause variation. This is analogous to a doctor in an emergency room stopping a patient's bleeding. It doesn't fix the underlying problem, but it stabilizes a patient's condition enough that the doctor can begin to find and fix the main problem. Once the process is "in control" (i.e., special cause variation is taken care of), the only way to improve the performance of the process is to reduce the common cause variation. Remember that common cause variation is what it is because of the decisions management has made, so reducing common cause variation can be done by changing the people, processes, technology, etc. that management has put in place.

One Really Important Property of Standard Deviation

The preceding work with z and the discussion of common versus special cause variation should have emphasized an unexpected but extremely important property of standard deviation to you. That is, while standard deviation by definition measures dispersion around the mean, or the effect of randomness on an individual observation, it is surprisingly predictable in how it behaves. As we just demonstrated, in every instance with the normal distribution, 68.26% of all occurrences take place between the mean $\pm 1\sigma$ (calls that are answered between 5 and 75 seconds, retail purchases between \$40 and \$70). If we make the not at all unreasonable assumption that we want to define a performance standard for our business, choosing to accept $\pm 1\sigma$ as our standard means that 68% of our service encounters will meet our standard, while $1 - 0.6826 = 0.3174$ or 32% of our service encounters will not. Setting our performance standards at $\pm 2\sigma$ (look up 2.0 in the first column in the z table, find 0.00 in the top row, read to the intersection of the row and column to find 0.4772, then double this because the normal distribution is symmetric) yields a success rate of about 95% and a failure rate of 5%. What happens at $\pm 3\sigma$? 4σ? 5σ? Wait for it . . . 6σ?

SIX SIGMA

Six Sigma was developed at Motorola in the late 1970s and early 1980s. Mikel Harry and Richard Schroeder describe how an executive stood up in a meeting in 1979 and declared, "the real problem at Motorola is that our quality stinks." In the time spent developing the approach, they estimated that there was an opportunity to return over \$800 million per year to the bottom line by improving quality. This represented the amount being spent to correct quality problems. Harry and Schroeder claim that within 4 years of implementation, Six Sigma had saved Motorola \$2.2 billion. Since then it has spread to other big manufacturing companies like General Electric (a total of \$900 million saved in the two years of 1997 and 1998), and AlliedSignal (\$2 billion saved in direct cost from 1994 to 2000), Polaroid (adds 6% to the bottom line each year) (Harry and Schroeder, 2000). And now a second wave of companies is adopting Six Sigma, many of them service companies. Interestingly, some manufacturing companies are aiming Six Sigma's methods at service processes inside their company, like information technology services.

Though it was formalized at Motorola, Six Sigma is in fact the culmination of years of development and evolution in the area of quality. In a nutshell, Six Sigma is a strategic approach to improving business performance by deploying a structured methodology to reduce process variation. It is comprised of several key components. Table 11.7 presents these components with explanations.

One characteristic of Six Sigma, how processes behave and process variation, can be traced back to Walter Shewart's work in the late 1930s. Many of the ideas associated with the strategic nature of quality and applying a structured approach to improvement can be traced back to the 1950s and the work of Deming and Juran. Ishikawa deployed many of the tools used in Six Sigma in the mid-1970s. Six Sigma's view of the cost of poor quality derives in part from Crosby's work in the late 1970s. But when taken all together, and with one or two evolutionary additions, Six Sigma embodies an approach that can dramatically improve business performance. The next sections explain the key ideas of Six Sigma.

TABLE 11.7: *Key Components of Six Sigma*

Component	Explanation
Management support	The approach is resource intensive, requiring training and time away from a person's normal job to execute
Project based	Teams select a problem to fix, then use a project-based approach to devise the solution
Metrics	Metrics define what matters to an organization, provide a baseline of current performance and allow for benchmarking of targeted performance
Structured approach	Teams follow "D-M-A-I-C" methodology for problem solving
Tools oriented	Teams use tools like flow charts and histograms as needed

Process Capability

But why is it called Six Sigma? The short answer to the question is that when we go ± 6s from the mean, the chance of making a defect is 3.4 per million opportunities. But to understand this in practice requires an understanding of "process capability," which in effect describes the likelihood of a process making a product or service that does not meet the specifications set by management. Go back to our call center that had a mean time to answer of 40 seconds, with a standard deviation of 35 seconds. In that instance, the target value set by management was also 40 seconds. Assume that management has set a target margin of error for answering calls to be ± 10 seconds. In other words, management wants calls to be answered between 30 and 50 seconds (i.e., 40 ± 10 seconds). How will this process behave compared to what management wants of it? How likely is it that this process can meet management's expectations? What percentage of calls will be answered between 30 and 50 seconds? Applying the z table methodology, the question can be written as $P(30 < X < 50)$ or $P(-0.28 < z < 0.28)$. Finding $z = 0.28$ in the table returns a probability of 0.1103, so the probability of a call being answered between 30 and 50 seconds is 22%. Hence, 78% of calls will be outside the range set by management; this process is not capable of meeting management's requirements.

Access your Student CD now for tools for determining process capability.

But management wouldn't necessarily care if the call was answered quickly, so the real question is what percentage of calls can be answered in less than 50 seconds [i.e., $P(X < 50)$ or $P(Z < 0.28)$]? The answer to this question is that 61% of all calls will be answered in less than 50 seconds (0.5000 for all calls below the average of 40 seconds + 0.1103 for the calls between 40 and 50 seconds). In the parlance of Six Sigma, this process would be capable at the 0.28σ level, and would generate 39 defects per hundred opportunities, or more commonly, 390,000 parts per million defective (PPM). This is pretty bad.

This 0.28σ capability level reflects the short-term capability, before time has a chance to really mess things up. In order to achieve the same level of performance in the long-term, the process has to be considerably better. In fact, research has shown that in order for a process to deliver 390,000 PPM in the long term, it must be better than the short-term capability by 1.5σ. In other words, for this call center to reliably provide time to answer service of less than 50 seconds in the long term, we need to be capable at the 1.78σ level!

But here is where it gets interesting. We have determined that for our current process, we are operating at a short-term 0.28σ capability, resulting in 390,000 PPM defective. And we have determined that we need to improve our capability to 1.78σ in order to deliver 390,000 PPM performance in the long term. Two questions need to be considered: What will be our short-term PPM performance if we achieve a 1.78σ capability, and how will we make such an improvement? The first question is statistical, and can be answered easily using the z table (look up 1.78 in the table and add 0.5000), 96.25% of calls will be answered within 50 seconds, yielding 37,500 PPM. The answer to the second question drives Six Sigma as a business practice: the only way to get this done is to find out why the standard deviation is so high (35.7 seconds), and find ways to reduce the standard deviation. Table 11.8 presents short- and long-term defect rates in PPM for various sigma levels of capability. Notice that in order to achieve comparable PPM performance in the long term as in the short term, a process' capability must be 1.5σ higher than its short-term capability.

The Cost of Poor Quality

Access your Student CD for tools for determining cost of poor quality.

One of the most compelling arguments in favor of a quality approach like Six Sigma is that the costs of poor quality are quite high, and that avoiding those costs would naturally improve business performance. Harry and Schroeder argue that in many companies that have not adopted a real quality approach, the cost of poor quality ranges between 20 and 30 percent of sales. To put this in context, salaries represent by far the largest single cost for the airline industry, often twice as much as the cost of fuel, which is the second largest cost. Salaries represent about 25 to 35 percent of sales in the airline industry. When GE began their Six Sigma initiative, they calculated that their cost of poor quality was about $5 billion per year (Harry and Schroeder, 2000).

But what comprises this cost of poor quality? There are two broad categories: failure costs and prevention/appraisal costs. Products that fail in front of the customers (i.e., external failures) incur costs for such things as warranties, returns, litigation, lost goodwill, and lost value of the brand. Products that fail internally incur costs such as scrap and rework. A common misconception is that service companies cannot suffer from scrapped products, or incur rework costs. Consider the service of processing a request for insurance coverage (a request for a quote). If the insurance company were to misplace the request, enter incorrect information into the policy quote, fail to get the driving record of the potential insured, or make any other of a host of "defects" one of two things will happen. First, customers will become so annoyed that they will withdraw their request. In this instance all of the time invested in generating the quote is lost, scrapped. The second possibility is that the company realizes the mistake and hurries to correct it, rework.

Prevention and appraisal costs are those spent to either avoid a defect or to find the defect after it happens. Prevention costs include employee training, supplier

TABLE 11.8: *Capability and PPM for the Short- and Long-Term*

Sigma Level	Short Term % Acceptable	ST Parts Per Million Defective	Long Term % Acceptable	LT Parts Per Million Defective
1.000	0.8413	158655.3	0.3085	691462.5
1.500	0.9332	66807.2	0.5000	500000.0
2.000	0.9772	22750.1	0.6915	308537.5
2.500	0.9938	6209.7	0.8413	158655.3
3.000	0.9987	1350.0	0.9332	66807.2
3.500	0.9998	232.7	0.9772	22750.1
4.000	1.0000	31.7	0.9938	6209.7
4.500	1.0000	3.4	0.9987	1350.0
5.000	1.0000	0.3	0.9998	232.7
5.500	1.0000	0.0	1.0000	31.7
6.000	1.0000	0.0	1.0000	3.4

certification and management, and process improvement initiatives. Appraisal costs include all of the inspection costs, like hiring inspectors, designing sampling plans, etc.

Two competing views of the cost of poor quality are shown in Figure 11.3. In the traditional view, the company attempts to achieve a balance between failure costs and prevention/appraisal costs. The minimum total cost of poor quality is found at the place where the two curves intersect. This quality level represents the company's "acceptable quality level," or AQL, and it is by definition something other than perfect quality.

The second view of the cost of quality says that if we focus on removing the "root cause" of the defect then the cost of poor quality will eventually go down as we get rid of the big causes for defects. Under this view, a company would strive for improved quality because it is cheaper than having poor quality.

FIGURE 11.3: *Two Views of the Cost of Poor Quality*

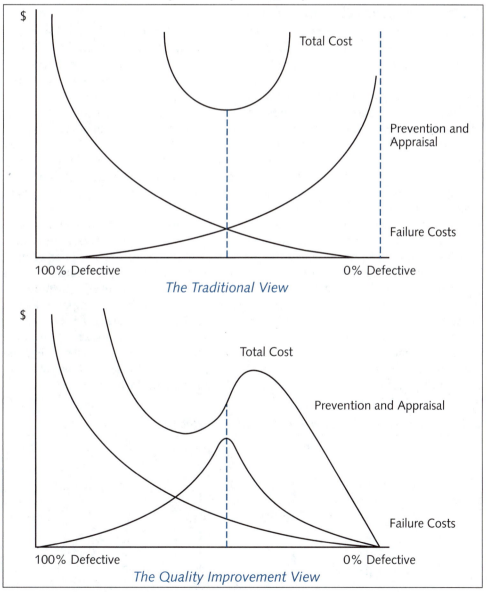

Historically, companies have set AQL at 95% (i.e., the boundary of common cause variation was at $\pm 3\sigma$). That left the remaining 5% of variation to be special cause. From a customer's perspective, this meant that there would be 5 defects for every 100 opportunities to make a defect. The problem is that if you expect defects, you are going to get them. There is an apocryphal story about a computer manufacturer buying components from a Japanese semiconductor company. The American computer manufacturer sent the purchase order with all the usual information, including the quality limit of 5%; if more than 5% of the items in the lot were defective, the computer company would reject the entire lot. When the order arrived, there were two boxes, one big one full of chips and a small one full of chips. And there was a note that said, "We didn't know why you wanted 5% defective, but since you ordered them we set our machines to make them for you. We put them in the small box so you wouldn't confuse them with the good chips."

Metrics and Strategic Consistency

Chapter 2 described how strategic consistency is conceptually easy, but is difficult to do. Six Sigma uses metrics as its approach to ensure strategic consistency. This is accomplished through a series of linked metrics that start at the highest level of the company and flow down to the individual processes within the company. Figure 11.4 shows the measures used by Six Sigma and their relationship to one another.

Top level indicators (TLIs) are those measures that would be reported to the executive suite. An organization should define between 4 and 6 TLIs, 2 or 3 should reflect financial objectives, and the remaining should reflect customer service objectives. Examples of TLIs include earnings per share growth, return on investment, return on assets, net sales to budget and same store/same month sales growth ("comps"). Examples of customer service TLIs include customer retention rate, customer complaints, and service acceptance.

Where TLIs define what matters to the business as a whole, outcome measures define what matters to an individual process. So, for example, the aircraft turnaround process at Southwest might define the percentage of planes turned in under 20 minutes as an outcome measure. A call center might monitor percentage of calls answered in 50 seconds, or percentage of calls dropped as outcome measures. But both TLIs and outcome measures suffer from the problem that a company doesn't know how they are performing on the measure until it is too late to fix. Companies need something to monitor while the process is being executed to make sure they are on track to meet their objectives. These are called "process measures." Process measures are those things a business might monitor during the game, if you will. For the call center, it could monitor the time on hold for any individual call.

FIGURE 11.4: *The Measurement Structure of Six Sigma*

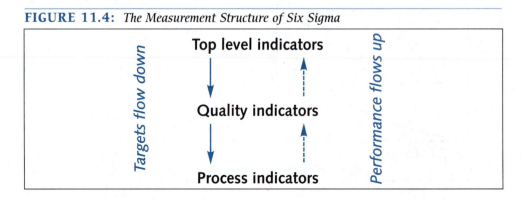

The Six Sigma measures ensure strategic consistency by requiring that the measures specifically relate to each other. The definition of any metric is driven by the measures above it. In other words, when a company decides on a process measure, it should be able to describe how succeeding on that process measure improves its outcome measures, and how being better at those outcome measures improves its top level indicators. With the measurement structure in place, the Six Sigma approach would require evaluating potential projects based on their ability to drive top level indicators. Some projects will be selected that drive almost exclusively at financial performance metrics, efficiency and cost-oriented projects. Other projects will drive at customer service metrics, effectiveness projects. Most will address both, so the challenge becomes selecting projects while balancing the sometimes conflicting goals of efficiency and effectiveness.

D-M-A-I-C

"DMAIC" (which has unfortunately been turned into a word, pronounced "duh-MAY-ick") is the acronym frequently used for the structured methodology Six Sigma uses to drive down common cause variation. The acronym stands for Define, Measure, Analyze, Improve, and Control. DMAIC provides the roadmap for how to execute a Six Sigma project. The purpose of this methodology is to provide a way to improve business level performance. In other words, DMAIC feeds into the measurement structure described in the previous section. Figure 11.5 graphically shows this relationship.

The Define step requires that the project team describe in detail what project they are considering. They must determine what process they intend to improve and determine how the current process works. This involves several steps. First the team must create a process map or flow chart that shows the main activities that take place to accomplish the process (all of the tools mentioned in this chapter are shown in detail in the supplementary materials included on the CD). Figure 11.6 presents an example process map. Second, the team defines the process and outcome metrics for the process, keeping in mind the link between these metrics and the TLIs. Third, the team has to define the project plan (schedule, resources, timelines, etc.) for the improvement project.

FIGURE 11.5: *DMAIC and the Measurement Structure*

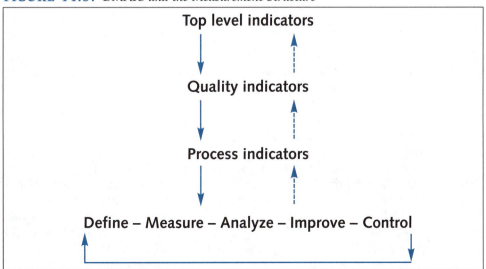

Top level indicators

Quality indicators

Process indicators

Define – Measure – Analyze – Improve – Control

FIGURE 11.6: *An Example Process Map*

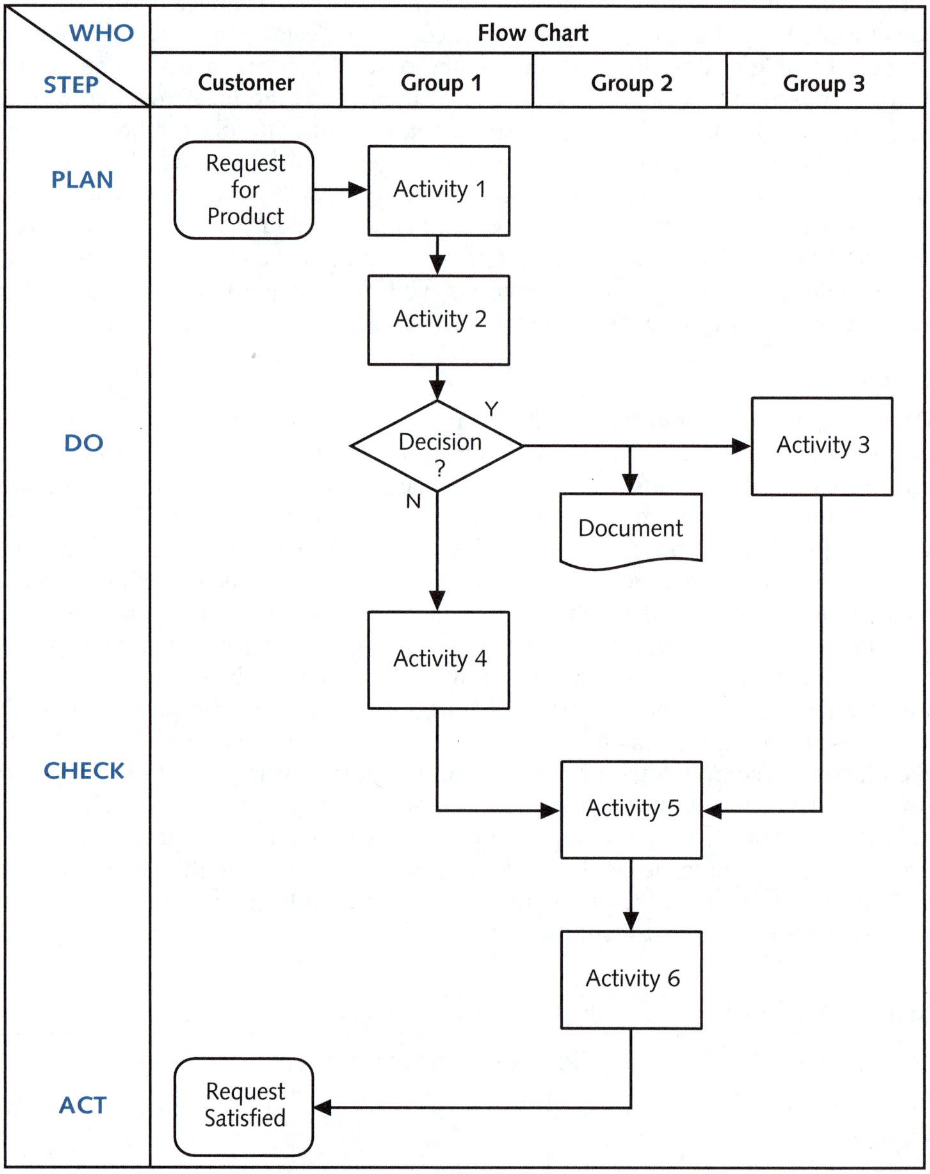

WHO / STEP	Flow Chart			
	Customer	Group 1	Group 2	Group 3
PLAN	Request for Product →	Activity 1		
		Activity 2		
DO		Decision ? (Y/N)	Document	Activity 3
		Activity 4		
CHECK			Activity 5	
			Activity 6	
ACT	Request Satisfied ←			

Note: Chart created using the QI Macros for Excel, available at http://www.qimacros.com.

Access your Student CD now for tools for constructing process maps.

The Measure step involves determining how the process currently performs on the outcome and process measures. The team must determine the baseline perform-ance of the process. While this sounds easy, companies often run into the problem that they don't have the data. Companies have access to data that they have histor-ically used to manage the process, but often find that after they have defined metrics that drive to the TLIs, they do not have data for these new metrics. Because of this, companies frequently have to gather new data to baseline their process. Next, the team determines how they want the process to perform after the improvement. Often through benchmarking against other companies or similar processes, the team will set a target performance level for the process. Third, the team measures the cost of poor quality. By identifying the types of failures that might occur and the costs associated with avoiding or mitigating these failures the team can estimate the cost of poor quality, which in turn helps team members estimate the business benefit associated with their project.

The Analyze step involves the work of determining the root cause of the problem. This work begins by analyzing the failure types identified in the Measure step. Generally, the failures identified are symptoms of a broader problem, so the first priority is to move past the obvious symptoms to get to the underlying "root cause." Fishbone analysis is one tool to help the team conduct this root cause analysis. This sort of analysis is also called "the 5 whys" because it requires the team to continue to ask "why does that happen" at least 5 times to drive past the obvious. Figure 11.7 shows a generic fishbone diagram.

The fishbone diagram suggests possible things that might be causing the quality problem. The next step of the Analyze step is to formulate theories about why these causes exist and test those theories (very much like the scientific method of devising and testing hypotheses). Data must be used to test the theories.

After developing, testing, rejecting, revising and retesting theories until one proves to be the root cause, the project moves to the Improve step. Improve involves devising ways to remedy the root cause. Usually there are multiple ways to get rid of the root cause, so the project team evaluates these alternatives to select the one most effective at removing the root cause. Much like the theory testing of the Analyze step, the Improve step is iterative. A solution is devised, and tested in a small scale pilot study. The results of the pilot study lead the solution to be refined until it works as needed. Then the solution is ready to be rolled out across the process.

But the work is not done. One of the most critical steps is to control the new process. This step is often not given the attention it deserves. The Control step is about devising the management control techniques that will ensure the process continues to perform to the new level achieved because of the Six Sigma project. This involves determining how the process will be monitored, who will be responsible for

Tools for constructing fishbone diagrams are included on your Student CD.

FIGURE 11.7: *An Example Fishbone Diagram*

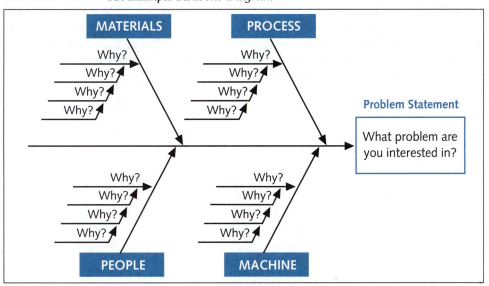

Note: Chart created using the QI Macros for Excel, available at http://www.qimacros.com.

monitoring and reporting process problems, what performance levels will be considered acceptable (common cause variation for the new process) and what will be considered out of control. Whenever possible the Control phase would include devising methods to foolproof the process so that it is as difficult as possible to get it wrong.

Six Sigma, then, is about process capability, the cost of poor quality, a hierarchy of metrics to drive strategic consistency, and DMAIC as a way to execute improvement projects. When we put all these pieces together we end up with a very powerful approach to improving process quality, and hence business level performance.

So, Is Six Sigma a Fad?

Why is it that some companies are dead-set against Six Sigma if it is as logical as the preceding discussion suggests? In fact one of the companies we have worked with forbade us from using the phrase "Six Sigma" when we met with a group of their managers. The main reason why is that many companies are convinced that Six Sigma is just another in a long string of management fads. The list of fads these managers have lived through is extensive (zero defects, TQM, ERP, CRM, 360 evaluations, self-directed work teams, etc.). And each time a company goes through a fad, it instills significant cynicism in the organization. Which then begs the question, is Six Sigma a fad?

There are two schools of thought. One side would argue that it is a fad. Companies are adopting Six Sigma without knowing what they are getting into. They are hiring consultants, going through a flurry of training, then abandoning the approach when it doesn't yield results in the first 30 days. Consultants are suggesting that Six Sigma is right for every company and that everyone should implement it in more or less the same way. Any time an approach is seen as a one-size-fits-all, quick fix to all that ails you, it has become a fad.

The other side would argue that Six Sigma really has delivered tremendous benefits to many companies, and if some companies implement it badly, then that's not Six Sigma's fault. But this is not convincing.

The fact of the matter is that it does not matter at all whether Six Sigma is a fad or not. Because the tools and approaches have proven effective over decades of use, the tools and mindset cannot be a fad. What might be a fad is the use of terminology like greenbelt (one who has received basic training in Six Sigma), blackbelt (one with more training who manages greenbelts) or master blackbelt (one who has more training still, and manages blackbelts). It might be a fad to use DMAIC as a word, but that doesn't minimize the strength of the approach.

Summary

This chapter presented an overview of variation and the impact that variation can have on process performance. The chapter describes the main points of Six Sigma: process capability, the cost of poor quality, a hierarchy of metrics to drive strategic consistency, and DMAIC as a way to execute improvement projects. It also addressed the issue of whether Six Sigma is a fad, and argued that it doesn't really matter whether it is a fad or not. The tools are so well proven and the approach so sound that it deserves attention even if it might be a fad. Many of these tools are explained in detail in the supplemental materials on the CD ROM.

Review Questions

1. An upscale hotel has been measuring the frequency with which customers try to check in to the hotel but find that their reserved rooms are unavailable. The hotel has gathered data and found that on average 18 guests are unable to check in because their rooms are not ready (with a standard deviation of 4 guests). What is the chance that more than 24 guests will be unable to check in for this reason? If management is willing to tolerate 15 guests per night as the maximum number of guests inconvenienced in this way, what is the capability of this process?
2. For the hotel described in question #1, what are some examples of the cost of poor quality?
3. Explain the difference between common cause and special cause variation.
4. Diagram the relationship between top level indicators, outcome measures and process measures. Explain how this relationship enforces strategic consistency.
5. In your opinion, is Six Sigma a fad? How might a manager mitigate the impression in a company that Six Sigma is a fad?
6. Explain the DMAIC approach.

Selected References

Harry, M. and R. Schroeder, *Six Sigma: The Breakthrough Management Strategy Revolutionizing The World's Top Corporations*, Doubleday Publishing, New York, NY, 2000.

Heskett, J.L. and R.H. Hallowell, Southwest Airlines 1993 (A), *Harvard Business School*, 1993.

Quality Improvement Pocket Guide, The Juran Institute, 1993.

CASE STUDY

ZC Sterling and Six Sigma in Financial Services

Every year for a decade, ZC Sterling, a part of the Zurich Financial Group, has held a conference for its major clients at a nice resort. In 2003, the Viewpoints conference was held at the Montage Resort and Spa in Laguna Beach, California. Bill Krochalis, a co-founder of the company and its current CEO, was preparing for a presentation in which he was going to pitch ZC Sterling's commitment to "an approach based on Six Sigma principles." Krochalis was not sure how the audience would respond. While Bank of America and ABN AMRO were represented in the audience (two companies that were actively engaged in Six Sigma), other participants were much less sure about what Six Sigma might mean for their company.

About ZC Sterling's Business

ZC Sterling is a service provider to the mortgage industry. In its words:

We were the industry's first provider of hazard insurance outsourcing services. Since then, the organization has grown to become one of the largest hazard insurance outsourcers. And now, as a member of the Zurich Financial Services Group, ZC Sterling leads the field in providing outsourced insurance, real estate tax, and customer care solutions for the mortgage industry . . . ZC Sterling achieved this growth with a winning philosophy and an innovative, collaborative approach that keeps its customers first in mind—and first in the minds of their customers. President and CEO of ZC Sterling, Bill Krochalis explains, "Our client partners are first in every way. Their business strategies, goals, and needs shape the way we do business—every day. It's as simple as that" (from the company Web site, http://www.zcsterling.com).

This focus on their customers coincided nicely with the underlying vision of Six Sigma, with its top level indicators focused at both financial and customer service performance.

Preparing for the Viewpoints Presentation

As Krochalis prepared himself for the presentation, he was "worried about what I am about to get myself into. I know we have a great message and we have great people, but how will it be received by our clients?" Some clients had already approached ZC Sterling about partnering for specific projects. One client, ABN AMRO, actually included ZC people in one of their Six Sigma projects. This partnership with ABN AMRO helped keep ZC Sterling on track as they learned more about Six Sigma.

But for every company like ABN AMRO or Bank of America, there were quite a few companies that held a different view of Six Sigma. A significant number of people believed that Six Sigma didn't apply to service companies. Since it came from

CASE STUDY

manufacturing, they were unsure how it would help their business. Others knew how expensive it was to implement; the newspapers are full of stories about General Electric spending over $200 million to train their employees. The overriding concern was that Six Sigma was a fad, and like every other fad before it, after a little while it would be forgotten so any effort spent doing Six Sigma would be wasted.

All of these things worried Krochalis. Before he could pitch Six Sigma as an initiative to his clients, he had to have the capabilities in his company to support it. That meant adopting Six Sigma or something like it at ZC Sterling. But in the history of the company, ZC Sterling had never fallen for a fad. A great deal was at risk if Krochalis really pressed the issue for Six Sigma and it turned out to be a fad that didn't last. The over 1,000 employees had a great deal of trust in senior management because they had never taken the company down the blind alley of "management by fad." Krochalis knew that this trust was critical to the success of ZC Sterling, wasn't to be taken lightly, and had to be reciprocated, "You wouldn't make the bets we make on people unless you have a lot of trust in training and empowerment."

Krochalis saw quite a few significant risks in adopting Six Sigma, aside from the time and cost required to train people in the Six Sigma approach. First, by definition Six Sigma is a distraction and a disruption of what the company does. It has to be this way because Six Sigma focuses on changing processes, but that doesn't make the change easy to do. Second, there is an implied criticism of operations when you take on process improvement. It is as if the company is saying to operations, "You haven't really been getting it right, so now we're going to come fix things for you." Third, the employees might perceive Six Sigma as "additive," in other words the work required of the employee will increase but no work or responsibility will be taken away to offset for the new work. Some call it "mission creep." In Krochalis' words, "This is something that is hard for Operations to put into place on their own. You need someone above to keep a holistic view of the issue. Otherwise, you'll get malicious compliance." He feared all the ways that people could obey the letter of the Six Sigma law, so to speak, while completely violating the spirit of the process.

But there was a significant upside as well. The partnership with ABN AMRO was a great nudge toward acquiring the skills of Six Sigma. It helped ZC Sterling learn a common language and approach that ABN AMRO and other big clients used routinely. Also, this could be a way to differentiate ZC Sterling further. For their big clients, ZC could partner for Six Sigma projects. For the smaller clients, ZC could bring their Six Sigma skills to bear on a client problem to devise a customer-driven solution.

By the time Krochalis was preparing for Viewpoints, ZC Sterling had adopted an approach based on Six Sigma principles. Blair Schrum, one of the Product Line Executives, describes it as, "We chose to soften the message, not the approach. We use all of the steps of DMAIC, and we use the discipline to systematically attack process problems. But we did not want to be distracted by phrases like 'greenbelt' or

CASE STUDY

'blackbelt'." ZC Sterling applied the approach to their internal processes, which were at the time organized functionally. For example, the mail was sorted, routed, and opened in an assembly line fashion. The study found that this was not effective from the client's point of view because no one had ownership of the client's incoming mail. Based on its analysis, ZC Sterling chose to break the functional organization, and organize around business product lines. This led to redundant processes across the businesses, but the gain in client effectiveness more than offset the loss of efficiency. As well, there was growing excitement among the employees; people were beginning to ask, "I've heard about the Six Sigma training. Can I get plugged in?"

Time to Make the Presentation . . .

Everything had gone well so far at Viewpoints, but the time for the presentation was coming up fast. The panel discussion that was designed to help the participants understand Six Sigma in general was just wrapping up, and it was time for Krochalis to make the pitch. He felt like he needed to explain what it means to be doing Six Sigma, but this was potentially risky if the clients already thought Six Sigma was a fad. As he walked to the stage to start the presentation he had two other driving fears: would ZC Sterling end up more under the thumb of their larger clients if they partnered more closely with these big companies for Six Sigma projects, and would ZC Sterling be able to handle the requests for projects after he had announced the initiative?

Questions:

1. What do you see as the strengths of how ZC Sterling has chosen to position Six Sigma? What weaknesses do you see?
2. How would you resolve the tension between the needs and expectations between ZC Sterling's smaller clients and their larger clients?
3. If you were Krochalis, what would be your next steps for positioning Six Sigma to the employees at ZC Sterling? For positioning it to your clients?

Matching Supply and Demand

The management of capacity in service firms frequently presents a more difficult and more expensive problem than in manufacturing. To determine capacity in many manufacturing firms, one usually considers long-run average demand. Inventory is frequently used to compensate for annual seasonality or short-term fluctuations in demand. In services, however, although the long-run average must be considered, the short term is vital as well. Because of the perishable nature of service sector "inventory" such as airplane seats or hotel rooms, capacity plans must consider demand by day of the week and even time of day—a level of detail that manufacturers usually find irrelevant.

Further, capacity planning mistakes are often more costly in services. When caught short on capacity many manufacturers simply "back-order" a customer's request. In many services, though, back orders simply cannot exist—quite literally, "the ship has sailed" for a cruise operator. Not having what the customer wants when she arrives can mean either a one-time lost sale to the competition, or possibly the defection of the entire stream of future sales of that customer and whoever else she chooses to tell about her experience.

Many strategic and tactical decisions must be made concerning services capacity. A "one-size-fits-all" strategy will not work. Even though it may be in the strategic interest of one airline to tightly match capacity to demand by heavily overbooking flights, another airline might be most profitable flying at far below capacity on average. Many of the qualitative aspects of these topics were covered in Chapter 2. This part of the book looks at putting those general strategies into action.

Yield Management

- Understand the need for overbooking.

- Use three different methods to calculate an overbooking level.

- Determine how to allocate service capacity among customer groups.

- Understand the intricacies of pricing for a capacity constrained service.

CAPACITY STRATEGIES

Capacity planning for many service firms can be far more difficult than for manufacturers. Manufacturers can set capacity by looking at long-run average demand. For many service firms, however, long-run averages become somewhat meaningless when capacity must react to general seasonality, daily demand variations, and time-of-day demand fluctuations. If the average manufacturer found out that most end consumers bought its product between 2 P.M. and 3 P.M., this knowledge wouldn't change its capacity strategy at all, but it would be important information for many service firms.

Capacity decisions in service firms are not only more complex than in manufacturers, but can be more important as well. Manufacturers deal with short-term imbalances in production and demand by either carrying inventory or creating a backorder list for later shipment. In most services, the "inventory" of capacity is employee time, or a fixed asset not being used, such as a hotel room or an airplane seat, so excess inventory cannot be stored for later use. Backorders quite often cannot occur: Imagine a sales clerk at a department store stating that he will be able to speak with a customer by next Tuesday. Consequently, a temporary imbalance in supply and demand can result in either idle employees and resources if demand is smaller than supply, or lost sales to the competition if demand is larger than supply. (Service firms that can use physical inventory are discussed in Chapter 13.)

These factors turn simple tactical decisions into strategic ones. Consider this simple example of the basic strategic direction for service capacity. An ice cream parlor experiences the following demand for ice cream cones:

Weekdays	100 – 300
Saturday	500 – 1,500
Sunday	500 – 1,100

For the manufacturer supplying the cones, capacity is a simple matter: It calculates average weekly demand:

$$5(200) + 1,000 + 800 = 2,800 \text{ cones}$$

It makes 2,800/7 = 400 cones every day, and carries a small inventory of extra cones for the busier days. For the service provider who fills cones as customers walk in, however, simple arithmetic no longer applies. A strategic decision must be made. The ice cream parlor manager may use one of the four basic strategies outlined next.[1] When considering these strategies, assume that one employee can make 100 cones per day.

1. **Provide: Ensure sufficient capacity at all times.** To carry out a provide strategy, one would want to always have enough people to handle the maximum demand, so the firm would have 15 employees working on Saturday, 11 on Sunday, and 3 the rest of the week. It is usually difficult to employ significant numbers of part-timers, so this strategy would employ enough full-time employees to meet those numbers. This strategy is associated with a high-service quality generic strategy, but it is also high cost, and would result in significant idle time for employees. Businesses with these characteristics include high-margin sales (e.g., jewelry, luxury automobiles) and those with wealthy individuals as clients (e.g., chauffeuring, private banking). Also, firms that compete on delivery speed (often called "time-based" competitors) should adopt this approach.

2. **Match: Change capacity as needed.** This strategy would use ten employees on Saturday, eight on Sunday, and two the rest of the week, with the excess Saturday and Sunday employees strictly part-timers. This approach balances service quality and costs and is representative of a large number of firms, including most mid- and low-priced restaurants and telemarketing firms.

3. **Influence: Alter demand patterns to fit firm capacity.** Here, pricing, marketing, or appointment systems flatten demand peaks to conform to capacity. It is most common in high capital-intensive services such as airlines and hotels, but highly paid professionals such as medical doctors and lawyers also commonly use it.

4. **Control: Maximize capacity utilization.** If only full-time employees could be used, five days per week, this strategy would have just two employees whose schedules overlapped on weekends. The generic strategy behind this option is to compete on cost by driving employee idle time to zero. It is often used in the public sector (e.g., driver's license bureaus) and low-margin services, as well as situations where high-priced employees want to maximize their utilization. Many physicians deliberately schedule patient appointments so tightly that a crowd is always in their waiting room. This strategy is willing to sacrifice sales at busy times to ensure the service functions efficiently all the time.

To assist in crafting these strategies, a host of specific tactics can be used to manage supply and demand (an in-depth discussion of these issues can be found in Klassen and Rohleder, 2001). Supply management tactics include the following:

---

1. Crandall and Markland (1996).

- **Workshift scheduling.** The unevenness of customer demand throughout a day means utilizing creative work schedules, such as nonuniform starting times, and workdays that have variable work hours. Work scheduling software is available to help construct flexible solutions within a match strategy.
- **Increasing customer participation.** A traditional method for a control strategy cuts total labor by encouraging customers to participate in serving themselves. For example, many fast-food restaurants use a semi-control strategy in which customers pour their own fountain drinks and procure their own condiments.
- **Adjustable (surge) capacity.** "Surge" capacity means capacity that can be available for a short period of time. By cross-training personnel for different jobs, a company can flexibly shift personnel temporarily to increase the capacity of any one position. Because cross-training is expensive to undertake, and cross-trained personnel are more expensive to retain, it is an appropriate approach within a provide strategy.
- **Sharing capacity.** Capacity can often be shared between departments or between firms for personnel or equipment that is needed only occasionally. For example, small business incubators often contract with dozens of businesses to share the same secretarial, accounting, and office management team.

Several tactics can be used to manage demand as well.

- **Partitioning demand.** It is not unusual for some components of demand to be inherently random, while some are fixed. This approach melds the more malleable demand around the tendencies of the random demand. That is, if it is known that more walk-in business generally comes in from 11 A.M. to 1 P.M., then schedule appointments either before or after that time. This approach works primarily for provide and match strategies.
- **Price incentives and promotion of off-peak demand.** This highly common method works in an influence strategy, which many of us see in our telephone bills. It is also commonly used in restaurants ("early bird" specials), hotels (both off-season and day-of-week pricing), resorts, and so on.
- **Develop complementary services.** The way to avoid the inevitable seasonality of many services is to couple countercyclical services together: Heating and air conditioning repair, ski slopes in winter and mountain bike trails in the summer. Unfortunately, this approach remains only a theoretical construct for most services.
- **Yield management.** Yield management combines three techniques: (1) overbooking, (2) assigning capacity amounts to different market segments, and (3) differential pricing in different market segments. It is used extensively by many industries and is the subject of the remainder of this chapter.

YIELD MANAGEMENT

Consumers encounter examples of what is called *yield management* constantly. A little knowledge about how these systems work can make life easier, or at least less expensive. Some practical examples of dealing with a yield management system include overbooking at a car rental agency. Even though you "confirmed" your reservation, it still pays to show up early in the day to get a car; sometimes those who show up late are out of luck. If you are a little more flexible about which days you fly, an airplane ticket may cost several hundred dollars less. The airline flight you are trying to book a seat on may be full today, but be patient and keep trying; tomorrow a seat may be available, even without others' cancellations. A hotel that says no room is available for you on Thursday night may suddenly find a room for Thursday if you add that you are staying Friday.

These situations occur because of yield management systems. The application of yield management practices often leave customers and employees puzzled. This chapter introduces the reasoning and techniques of yield management. Even if you do not work in an industry where yield management is practiced, this material will at least help you be a better consumer.

The term *yield management* itself is a bit of a misnomer because these techniques are not directly concerned with managing "yield" but are really concerned with managing revenue. Consequently, the set of techniques described in this chapter is sometimes called *revenue management* or *perishable asset revenue management*.

The purpose of yield management techniques is to sell the right capacity to the right customer at the right price. Not every firm can use these techniques, but many capital-intensive services can and do use them heavily. The main business requirement for using the techniques of this chapter is having limited, fixed capacity. Many other business characteristics make yield management more effective:

- Ability to segment markets
- Perishable inventory
- Advance sales
- Fluctuating demand
- Accurate, detailed information systems

These characteristics increase the complexity of a business and the profit potential from applying yield management.

Industries that currently fully utilize yield management techniques are transportation-oriented industries, such as airlines, railroads, car rental agencies, and shipping; vacation-oriented industries, such as tour operators, cruise ships, and resorts; and other capacity-constrained industries, such as hotels, medicine, storage facilities, and broadcasting (selling commercial time). Many other industries can partially use these techniques.

Yield management is a relatively young science. Airlines are credited with the invention of most of these techniques, especially Sabre, formerly with American Airlines (see the Service Operations Management Practices: Yield Management Increases Revenue $1 Billion/Year at American Airlines). However, the airlines did not develop most of these systems until a few years after the industry was deregulated in 1978, and the techniques only began to spread to other industries in the 1990s.

A yield management system consists of three basic elements:

1. Overbooking (accepting more requests for service than can be provided)
2. Differential pricing to different customer groups
3. Capacity allocation among customer groups

Each of these elements will be discussed in turn, then some practical implementation issues will be addressed.

OVERBOOKING

The need for overbooking is clear. Customers are fickle and do not always show up, so firms that overbook make far more money than those that don't. American Airlines

SERVICE OPERATIONS MANAGEMENT PRACTICES

Yield Management Increases Revenue $1 Billion/Year at American Airlines

It can be challenging to turn a profit in the airline business, with margins usually in the 1% to 5% range. Once flights are scheduled, costs are essentially fixed, and they can only hope to fill part of the plane with customers who aren't as fussy about price. Yield management got its start at American Airlines when the industry was deregulated. New startups PeopleExpress and World Airways were offering one-way fares from New York to San Francisco for $99—less than half the regulated fare. With their higher operating costs, the traditional airlines like American couldn't exist at such prices, because even a full load of $99 passengers would mean losses. Through its Sabre unit, American responded by inventing yield management. They matched the low fares, but allowed only a portion of their planes to be filled by them, while the newcomers sold every seat for the same price.

In a few years most of the upstarts were out of business, and yield management became more sophisticated. The founder of PeopleExpress, Don Burr, claimed that the superior yield management abilities of their competitors caused their demise (Cross, 1997, p.125). American estimates that its yield management system currently adds $1 billion per year in revenue. For American, whose annual profits are rarely above that figure, yield management is the difference between profitability and bankruptcy.

The CEO of American Airlines, Bob Crandall, said that "Yield management is the single most important technical development in transportation management since . . . deregulation" (Cross, 1997, p.127).

Source: Adapted from Cook (1998).

estimated that their overbooking system garners them an additional $225 million in profit annually (Smith, Leimkuhler, and Darrow, 1992).

If airlines did not overbook, planes that are now full would fly an average of 15% empty. "No-shows cost the world's airlines $3 billion annually, even after efforts to minimize the revenue loss by overbooking" (Cross, 1997, p. 146). No-shows for restaurant reservations average about 10%, with some reporting 40% no-shows during the Christmas holidays. It has been reported that rental car no-shows in the Florida market reached 70% of reservations. Of course, the alternative to overbooking is to simply charge the customers whether they show up or not. Unfortunately, that approach failed in restaurants and auto rental businesses, and other businesses discarded it out of hand. Consumer resistance was high: Imagine missing your plane flight due to traffic, only to be told, "The seat you paid for is in the sky, the ticket you have is worthless. The next flight out will cost you another $500, even though they have empty seats on that one." So the question for many businesses is not *whether* to overbook, but rather, *how much* to overbook.

To demonstrate some mathematical methods to help determine the level of overbooking, consider the following example.

EXAMPLE 12.1: *The Hotel California*

The Hotel California found that it frequently turned down a customer in the lobby because a room was reserved for a customer who never showed up. The manager, felt that the hotel's policy of overbooking should be examined.

The average room rate was $50 per night, but the hotel could not collect the room rate from the no-show customers. If no overbookings were allowed, each no-show would in reality cost the hotel $50. If it overbooked too much and filled up early in the night, customers with reservations who arrived later to find no rooms available would be most unhappy. About 10% of those customers did not cost the hotel any money; they merely muttered menacingly and walked out. Another 10% were satisfied with being "walked" (or transferred) to another hotel at no cost to the Hotel California. The remaining guests were so upset by this situation that the hotel had to repair broken lobby furniture at a cost of $150.

The hotel's no-show experience is summarized in Table 12.1. What should the overbooking policy be? We will discuss three approaches to answering that question.

OVERBOOKING APPROACH 1: USING AVERAGES

In Table 12.1 the average number of no-shows is calculated by

$$0(0.05) + 1(0.10) + 2(0.20) + 3(0.15) + \ldots + 10(0.05) = 4.05.$$

Since the average number of no-shows is four, it might seem reasonable to take up to four overbookings.

This approach offers the advantages of being intuitive and easy to explain. It is also usually better than doing no overbooking at all. It fails, however, to weigh the relevant costs, which presents a significant disadvantage. For instance, if the cost of a disgruntled customer is nothing, then the best policy would be to overbook 10 every night to ensure that the hotel is full. That is, if all the customers who had reservations and didn't get rooms simply left at no cost to the hotel, the hotel would just be concerned about losing the potential $50 of a paying guest. Likewise, if all the disappointed customers reacted by telling Norman's mother on him—the equivalent of an infinite cost to Mr. Bates—Norman would never overbook.

OVERBOOKING APPROACH 2: SPREADSHEET ANALYSIS

The two costs to consider here are:

C_o = Overage (customers denied advance reservation with rooms left unoccupied, often called "spoilage" in industry)

C_s = Stockouts (customers with reservations are turned away because no rooms are left, called "walked" customers in the hotel industry and "spill" by the airlines)

In this case, C_o = $50, the cost of the room, and C_s = 0.2($0) + 0.8($150) = $120.

TABLE 12.1: *Hotel California No-Show Experience*

No-Shows	% of Experiences	Cumulative % of Experience
0	5	5
1	10	15
2	20	35
3	15	50
4	15	65
5	10	75
6	5	80
7	5	85
8	5	90
9	5	95
19	5	100

One way to put the relevant costs into the picture is to use the spreadsheet shown on Table 12.2 (This spreadsheet is also on the CD included with this text.)

This spreadsheet calculates the expected cost for every possible scenario. For example, if no overbooking is done, then the column labeled "0" shows that on the 5% of days when there are zero no-shows, there's no cost at all, but on the 10% of days when there is one no-show, the cost is $50. The total cost at the bottom sums up 0.05($0) + 0.10($50) + . . . + 0.05($500) = $203. The overbooking level with the lowest expected cost is to overbook two rooms, with an expected cost of $137.

The advantages of this method are that it incorporates relevant costs and can be spreadsheet based and fairly easy to figure out. Also, as will be seen shortly, if the costs and revenues are uncertain or not quite as easy to figure out as in the Hotel California example, then this method can be readily adapted. Two disadvantages of this method, though, are that it requires accurate data and it is a "brute force" type of technique that does not increase a manager's intuition about the problem.

Access your Student CD now for Table 12.2 as an Excel spreadsheet.

TABLE 12.2: *Hotel California Overbooking Cost*

| No-Shows | Probability | Number of Reservations Overbooked | | | | | | | | | | |
		0	1	2	3	4	5	6	7	8	9	10
0	0.05	$ 0	$120	$240	$360	$480	$600	$720	$840	$960	$1,080	$1,200
1	0.10	$ 50	$ 0	$120	$240	$360	$480	$600	$720	$840	$ 960	$1,080
2	0.20	$100	$ 50	$ 0	$120	$240	$360	$480	$600	$720	$ 840	$ 960
3	0.15	$150	$100	$ 50	$ 0	$120	$240	$360	$480	$600	$ 720	$ 840
4	0.15	$200	$150	$100	$ 50	$ 0	$120	$240	$360	$480	$ 600	$ 720
5	0.10	$250	$200	$150	$100	$ 50	$ 0	$120	$240	$360	$ 480	$ 600
6	0.05	$300	$250	$200	$150	$100	$ 50	$ 0	$120	$240	$ 360	$ 480
7	0.05	$350	$300	$250	$200	$150	$100	$ 50	$ 0	$120	$ 240	$ 360
8	0.05	$400	$350	$300	$250	$200	$150	$100	$ 50	$ 0	$ 120	$ 240
9	0.05	$450	$400	$350	$300	$250	$200	$150	$100	$ 50	$ 0	$ 120
10	0.05	$500	$450	$400	$350	$300	$250	$200	$150	$100	$ 50	$ 0
Total Cost		$203	$161	$137	$146	$181	$242	$319	$405	$500	$ 603	$ 714

OVERBOOKING APPROACH 3: MARGINAL COST APPROACH

Using a little algebra, this method comes at the problem mathematically by noting that one would like to keep accepting bookings until the expected revenue is less than or equal to the expected loss from the last booking. Mathematically, increase bookings until

$$E(\text{revenue of next booking}) \leq E(\text{cost of next booking})$$

which is the same as

Revenue of filling a room $\times$ Probability of more no-shows than overbooked rooms $\leq$ Cost of dissatisfied customer $\times$ Probability of fewer or the same number of no-shows than overbooked rooms

Or, in the mathematical terms used previously,

$$C_o \times P(\text{Overbookings} < \text{No-shows}) \leq C_s \times P(\text{Overbookings} \geq \text{No-shows})$$

which can be converted to

$$C_o \times [1 - P(\text{Overbookings} \geq \text{No-shows})] \leq C_s \times P(\text{Overbookings} \geq \text{No-shows})$$

or equivalently,

$$C_o - C_o \times P(\text{Overbookings} \geq \text{No-shows}) \leq C_s \times P(\text{Overbookings} \geq \text{No-shows})$$

Adding $C_o \times P(\text{Overbookings} \geq \text{No-shows})$ to both sides and dividing both sides by $(C_o + C_s)$ leaves the basic overbooking formula: Accept bookings until

$$C_o /(C_s + C_o) \leq P(\text{Overbookings} \geq \text{No-shows}) \qquad (12.1)$$

In the preceding problem, this calculation leads to

$$\$50/(\$120 + \$50) = 0.29$$

Looking at Table 12.1, the smallest number of overbookings at which $P(\text{Overbookings} \geq \text{No-shows})$ is 2, where the cumulative probability of no-shows reaching this level is 0.35.

This basic formula is easy to remember and apply, even to informal data. For example, C_o, the lost potential revenue, may be easy to figure in most circumstances, but C_s is not, and usually must be estimated. Also, the cumulative probability distribution of no-shows is often not accurately known. So a general feel that, say, a complaining customer is three times as costly as the potential revenue means that a manager would only want to overbook until $P(\text{Overbookings} \geq \text{No-shows})$ is about $1/(1 + 3) = 25\%$. So, if the average number of no-shows is about 15 with a standard deviation of five, using the traditional z-score calculations from standard statistics texts, about 12 overbookings might be appropriate.

Although this formula is simple to use, it presents a significant drawback. Equation (12.1) implicitly assumes a linear cost of dissatisfied reservation holders; that is, if only one customer in your hotel lobby or airport lounge is dissatisfied and will cost \$300 to placate, then 20 dissatisfied customers will cost 20 $\times$ \$300 = \$6,000 to satisfy. Unfortunately, that answer is not always the case. As shown in Figure 12.1, the cost curve for overbooking can increase per person with the number of unhappy customers. A roomful of 20 unhappy customers is far more of a problem than 20 instances of a single unhappy customer. Although this formula does not account for this contingency, the spreadsheet method can easily be programmed with it in mind.

FIGURE 12.1: *Actual Versus Linear Overbooking Cost Curve*

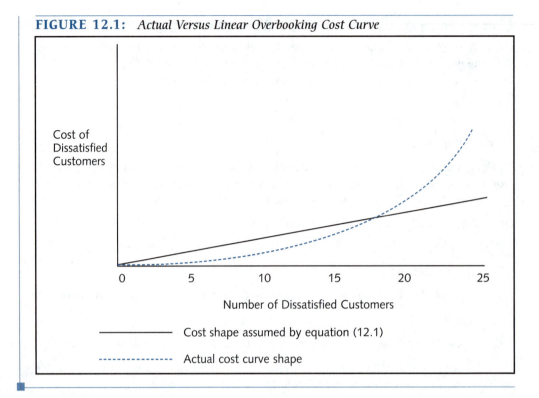

Cost of Dissatisfied Customers

Number of Dissatisfied Customers

——————— Cost shape assumed by equation (12.1)

- - - - - - - - - Actual cost curve shape

Dynamic Overbooking

The overbooking decision is often not a one-time, "static" decision. Rather, it is a decision that is "dynamic," which here just means that it changes over time. In a typical situation for a firm that takes reservations a long time in advance, the dynamic overbooking curve is shaped like Figure 12.2.

When the event is still a long time in the future, the allowed number of overbookings for it is at a peak. As the event nears, the number of allowed overbookings drops. This practice reaches its logical conclusion at the time the event takes place, when allowed overbookings drop to zero. For example, if three people are running to the plane for the final boarding and only two seats are available, the third person will not be sold a seat that cannot possibly be used.

ALLOCATING CAPACITY

A difficult problem that afflicts many firms is allocating capacity among their customer groups. That is, when to say "no, we're full" to one customer while holding open capacity in hopes that a more profitable customer will arrive later. For airlines and hotels, especially, reservation activity follows Figure 12.3: High-revenue customers tend to make reservations fairly close to the event, while low-revenue customers often make reservations months in advance. In the airline industry, the price-conscious vacationers make reservations months in advance, while the high-paying business travelers may make reservations close to the event. For hotels, price-conscious group business may make reservations a year in advance, while more highly profitable transient business may simply walk in the door that day. For the sake of simplicity, this chapter will focus on segmenting capacity between just two

FIGURE 12.2: *Dynamic Overbooking*

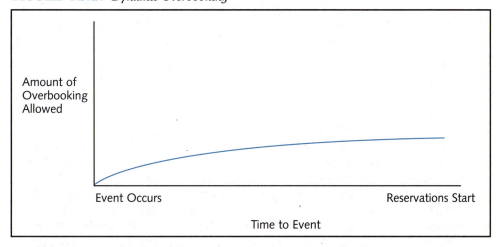

customer groups. The real problem, however, is far more complex. A modern airline can have 10 different customer segments on the plane, each of which requires a capacity allocation decision (Cross, 1004).

The situation depicted in Figure 12.3 is complex because one cannot simply let all reservations be taken first-come, first-served. Doing so would cause a firm to turn away a substantial portion of their most profitable customers while filling up on the less profitable ones. Also, most firms cannot simply say "no" to lower-revenue business, because they cannot fill their capacity solely with high-revenue business. Consequently, the firm must decide ahead of time at what point to shut off the low-revenue business in anticipation of the high-revenue business booking later.

FIGURE 12.3: *Cumulative Reservation Activity*

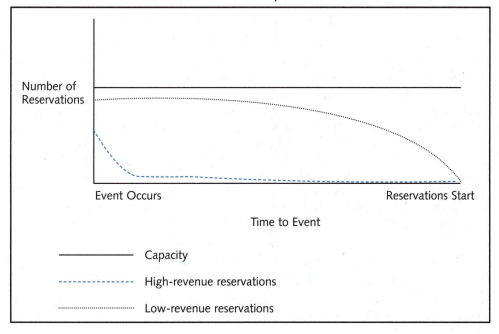

The general methods used to solve this problem can be classified as follows:

- Nested versus distinct
- Static versus dynamic

To demonstrate the differences in these methods, let's first describe an example problem.

EXAMPLE 12.2: *Chancey Travel*

Chancey Travel is offering a cruise to the Antarctic and wants to fill the 100 cabins available. Its primary market is Premium customers. Premium customers pay $12,000 for the trip, and the variable costs of serving these customers amounts to $2,000 per trip, as they are pampered endlessly and plied with Godiva chocolate three times a day. According to market analysis, the demand from Premium passengers is uniformly distributed between 51 and 100, which means a 2% chance that 51 Premiums will sign up, a 2% chance that 52 will go, and so on up to a 2% chance that the entire boat can be filled with 100 Premiums. This means that if the entire boat were reserved for Premiums an average of 75 Premiums would be on board. Premiums come from the idle rich, who tend to make their decisions at the last minute.

Because the probability that the entire boat cannot be filled with Premiums is substantial, another market is sought. Market research discovered customer interest in a "rough" experience to Antarctica, but these consumers were more price sensitive. These Discount customers paid $2,500 for the trip, but the marginal cost of serving them was $0: heat was turned off to their cabins (hot water bottles were available for a proper deposit), and they received no food (they had to catch penguins with their own equipment). Demand was such that the ship could be entirely filled with Discounts, and these customers were willing to book far in advance.

The dilemma for Chancey Travel is: How many cabins should be reserved in hopes of Premium customers? Several methods for arriving at an answer are discussed here.

CAPACITY ALLOCATION APPROACH 1: STATIC METHODS: FIXED NUMBER, FIXED TIME RULES

We begin with static or one-time decision rules. Basic fixed number and fixed time rules are the easiest to implement. A fixed time rule means simply that a firm will accept discount bookings until a specific date. No limit is set on the number of discount sales. The motivation for this type of rule is the transparency to the customer and the ease of implementation, but it is clearly not close to being optimal. A fixed number rule for the problem may be to, say, reserve exactly 75 slots for Premium customers and exactly 25 slots for Discount customers. The amounts reserved for each group can be viewed as a quota. Although a step up from the fixed time rule, it too presents certain problems. For example, if 75 Premiums and 20 Discounts are currently signed up, and a Premium customer wants to pay, this type of rule states that the Premium customer must be turned away because the Premium slots are already filled.

CAPACITY ALLOCATION APPROACH 2: NESTED STATIC METHODS

To get around the somewhat absurd problem of turning down more profitable customers in hopes that less profitable ones will appear later, so-called nested methods are used. Let's still assume that, because an average of 75 Premium bookings is expected, we want to reserve 75 slots for Premiums. Instead of the remaining 25 slots being given to Discounts, the remaining 25 are sold on a first-come, first-served basis. In this manner, the 75 slots for Premiums can be thought of as a "protection level;" that is, at least 75 rooms are protected just for Premiums, but they can get more. In this nested system other groups are not allowed into the "nest" of 75 protected rooms, but the protected group can venture outside that number.

Our use of 75 as a hypothetical number for the rooms protected for the Premiums does not offer the best strategy, however. To show how some basic calculations can lead to a better strategy, the expected marginal seat revenue (EMSR) heuristic is introduced here (Belobaba, 1989). The EMSR heuristic provides a basic logic for determining how much protection to give different customer levels. The EMSR heuristic is no longer widely used in industry. However, the methods that are used currently in industry are both highly complex and proprietary.

The EMSR heuristic allocates capacity one unit at a time. For this problem, allocating the 1st through 51st rooms is fairly simple—they should all go to Premiums, since we are certain that at least 51 Premiums will show up. For deciding whether to protect the 52nd room we compare the expected marginal revenue from each group and assign the room to the group that provides the most expected revenue. For allocating the 52nd room, we are 98% certain a Premium customer will request it, so the calculations are as follows:

$$\text{Premium: } 98\%(\$12,000 - \$2,000) = \$9,800 \text{ expected revenue}$$

$$\text{Discount: } 100\%(\$2,500) = \$2,500 \text{ expected revenue}$$

Because $9,800 > $2,500, the room is reserved for Premiums. For allocating the 53rd room, the following calculation applies:

$$\text{Premium: } 96\%(\$10,000) = \$9,600 \text{ expected revenue}$$

$$\text{Discount: } \$2,500 \text{ expected revenue}$$

Again the room is reserved for Premiums, because $9,600 > $2,500. This process continues until we reach the 88th seat:

$$\text{Premium: } 24\% (\$10,000) = \$2,400 \text{ expected revenue}$$

$$\text{Discount: } \$2,500 \text{ expected revenue}$$

Because $2,400 < $2,500, the protection level for Premiums stops at 87. The EMSR heuristic therefore states that we should allocate 87 rooms Premium, 13 rooms Discount. Note, however, that on an average boat, this allocation would result in 75 Premium passengers, 13 Discount passengers, and 12 empty rooms. This result explains why, when one is allocating capacity as best as one can, it frequently results in unused capacity.

This procedure can be summarized in a rule similar to the overbooking formula given in equation (12.1) earlier. Set the protection level of Premiums at the smallest number where:

$P(\text{Premium demand} \geq \text{Protection level}) \leq \text{Discount revenue/Premium revenue} \quad (12.2)$

Here, Discount revenue/Premium revenue = $2,500/($12,000 − $2,000) = 0.25, and there is a 26% chance that Premium demand is greater than 87.

To see how to use this from a different perspective, consider Premium demand for Chancey Travel to be normally distributed, with a mean of 70 and a standard deviation of 20. Let's make Discount revenue $3,000, instead of $2,500. So, Discount revenue/Premium revenue = 0.3, and we are searching for the 30th percentile of demand.

This is a one-tailed look-up of an "area of the standard normal distribution" table (located at the back of the book). So one desires to look up 0.5 − 0.3 or 0.2 in the body of the table, which yields a z-score of 0.515. Applying this z-score to the problem data, mean = 70, std dev = 20, 70 + 0.515 × 20 = 80 seats should be protected for the Premium passengers.

This approach is not limited to just two customer categories. The protection level for each customer category can be calculated by comparing the revenue associated with each successive customer class.

CAPACITY ALLOCATION APPROACH 3: DYNAMIC METHODS

The previous methods describe one-time decisions made in advance. However, in many cases, a better but more complicated method is available. The probability distribution used previously (uniform distribution between 51 and 100) is a forecast. But forecasts become more accurate as the event gets closer in time, and early activity tends to be a good predictor of what will eventually unfold.

For example, consider Table 12.3, which tracks the applications to a well-known Southern MBA program. Although only a small percentage of total applications arrive before December 1, the amount received by that date is a good predictor of the eventual number.

Applying that notion to yield management means that the type of analysis done with the EMSR heuristic earlier is constantly reassessed. In Figure 12.4, if we are continually forecasting demand from early reservations history, reservation activity 35 days before the event may look as though we are on the "low" demand curve for high-revenue customers. Consequently, the floodgates are opened up to lower-revenue customers. However, 30 days before the event, reservation activity looks as though a "medium" number of high-revenue customers will be forthcoming, so the protection level for high-revenue customers is increased. Finally, Figure 12.4 shows that 20 days before the event, high-revenue customer class reservation activity is such that the entire service capacity can be taken up with high-revenue customers, so all lower-revenue customer classes are cut off from further reservation activity. Of course, this scenario can happen in reverse order as well, with more and more capacity being allocated over time to lower-revenue customer classes. Consequently, as a discount-seeking consumer, one may find a flight to be "full" one day, yet be able to get a reservation the next day for the same price due to this constant reevaluation.

To be done accurately, this type of nonstop capacity allocation requires immense amounts of data regarding customer behavior. For example, Delta Air Lines forecasts passenger demand on 16.5 million future combined flight/customer classifications

TABLE 12.3: *MBA Program Applications*

| Year | Number of Applications Received By: | |
	December 1	June 1
1	57	852
2	89	931
3	110	1,023

FIGURE 12.4: *Dynamic Capacity Allocation*

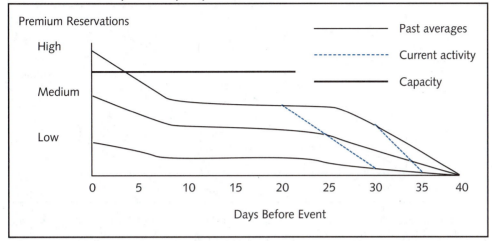

every day. The database for this forecast requires 2 terabytes of data (Cross, 2004). Unfortunately, such data do not exist for many firms. Also, events unknown to any computer model may cause reservation activity to suddenly drop or pick up, such as competitor pricing changes, new competitors coming on line, or such things as sporting events and conventions being scheduled where they did not exist before. Because of these difficulties, computer models help, but the final decisions on capacity allocation for many industries is still manual, performed by managers with an intuitive sense of the risks.

Complexities of Capacity Allocation

So far we considered allocating capacity for single events. However, the situation is often more complex. For example, consider a low-revenue customer booking a hotel room for a Thursday night versus booking for both Thursday and Friday nights. If the hotel has mainly a business clientele, then Thursdays tend to be fairly full of high-revenue customers, but on Friday night the hotel is relatively empty. Consequently, allowing a low-revenue customer to take up a valuable Thursday room might be unprofitable, but if the low-revenue customer also uses a Friday room that would ordinarily go unoccupied, the profitability changes. Consequently, the protection level of the high-revenue customer class for a Thursday night depends on the lower-revenue customer length of stay.

In the jargon of the hotel yield management industry, a "bid price" strategy is used to decide whether to accept such reservations; that is, the actual price of the lower-revenue customer is compared to the expected revenue over the course of the proposed length of stay.

PRICING

Thus far we assumed prices are exogenous, or outside of our control, which of course is not the case. This section discusses the difficult topic of setting prices in a yield management system.

The general idea in yield management is to break up a market into a number of different customer segments and charge different prices for each segment. Figure 12.5 shows the traditional supply and demand curves seen in every introductory economics class.

FIGURE 12.5: *Traditional Supply and Demand Equilibrium*

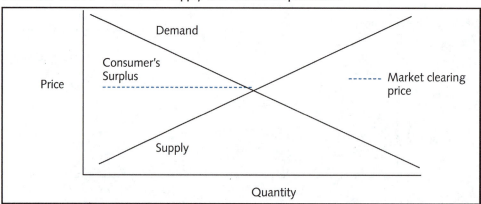

The market-clearing price creates "consumer's surplus" for customers who would have been willing to pay more and economic rent for suppliers whose costs are lower. The idea of yield management is to segment different customer categories with separate market clearing prices, so that high prices are charged to those who would be willing to pay them and low prices are charged to those who would ordinarily not use the service if the single market clearing price were in place. Figure 12.6 shows a general representation of three markets for airline seats.

Customer class 1 (first-class passengers) wants premium service and flexibility, and cares little about cost; customer class 2 (business class) values the flexibility of making last-minute changes over price; customer class 3 (often vacationing families) makes plans well in advance and are highly sensitive to price. The consumer surplus from each group is the area formed by the triangle of the market price (dotted line), demand curve, and the vertical line extending from the dotted line to the customer class bar. Two important economic effects come into play here: Large portions of consumer surplus are shifted to the supplier, and bringing on customers who would not ordinarily use the service can expand the market itself.

The magnitude of pricing differences can be enormous. Table 12.4 shows a snapshot of some airline fares. Here, premium first-class and business class are not considered—just full coach fare versus discounts on that same coach seat—and the cheapest prices are 11% to 13% of the cost of a full coach fare.

FIGURE 12.6: *Supply and Demand Equilibrium in Yield Management*

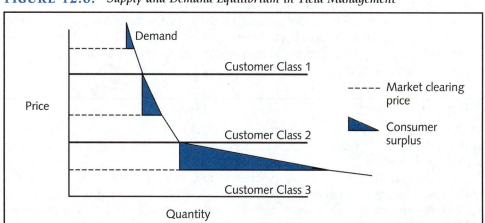

TABLE 12.4: *Airline Prices for an Identical Seat*

| City Pair | Airline | Ticket Prices | | |
		Full Coach	Advance Purchase 7 Days	Cheapest Fare
Washington, D.C.–Nashville	USAir	$ 811	$761	$251
Newark–Salt Lake City	Continental	$1,317	$571	$257
Dallas–Cleveland	American	$ 639	$471	$304

Source: Airline Web sites, March 2004.

Several difficulties can arise in creating these customer segments. Foremost, price discrimination, per se, is illegal in the United States. A business cannot simply tell some customers they must pay more for a good or service than others, just because the business knows that a customer will pay. Some types of customer segmentation are illegal in the United States, as well, such as segmenting customers according to race or ethnic origin and charging differential prices. This regulation does not apply in some other countries, however, and "ethnic pricing" of airfares is not an uncommon practice (Mitchener, 1997).

Consequently, it is up to the imagination of the marketing department to determine a legal and enforceable method for segmenting markets. For example, airlines want to charge higher prices to price-insensitive business customers and lower prices to price-sensitive vacationers. However, these markets can only be attacked indirectly, by segmenting pricing on how far in advance one makes a reservation.

The yield management issues of overbooking and capacity allocation lend themselves well to numerical analysis once pricing is set, but determining the best overall combination of prices, capacity allocation, and overbooking is difficult. In practice, marketing usually sets prices in coordination with company policy and competitive response, and the operations area sets capacity allocation numbers after pricing is determined. To show why pricing is so tricky in the yield management environment, consider the following example.

EXAMPLE 12.3: *Pricing and Capacity Allocation*

Consider a one-time event in which, miraculously, perfect economic information is provided on two groups of customers: Premium and Discount. For the Premium customers, the more that is charged, the fewer will attend, according to Table 12.5.

Consider three scenarios: (1) a service facility not facing a capacity constraint; (2) a capacity of only 100 customers, and Discount customers pay $50; and (3) again a capacity of 100 customers, but Discount customers pay $75. In scenario (1), the best price to charge premium customers is $90, resulting in a total of $10,800 in revenue, based on traditional economic logic. In a situation in which demand responds disproportionately to price cuts, prices should be low (high price elasticity, in economic-speak). Capacity restrictions and different customer classes, however, turn the traditional economics of price elasticity on its head. In scenario (2), high price elasticity still remains with the Premium customers, but one cannot take advantage of it, because the sheer number of potential customers overwhelms capacity. The best price to charge Premiums is $100, resulting in $10,000 revenue from dedicating the facility just to Premium customers and ignoring the Discount market. However, if the Discounts pay a bit more, as in scenario (3), the best price to charge Premiums is $110, resulting in more revenue by adding Discount customers.

TABLE 12.5: *Pricing and Capacity Allocation Example*

Premium Demand Information:			
Possible unit prices	$ 100	110	90
Associated demand	100	80	120
Scenario 1:			
Unlimited capacity, only Premium customers*			
Premium price	$ 100	110	90
Premium demand	100	80	120
Total revenue	$10,000	8,800	10,800
Scenario 2:			
Capacity of 100, Discount class unlimited demand at $50*			
Premium price	$ 100	110	90
Premium demand	100	80	100
Premium revenue	$10,000	8,800	9,000
Discount revenue	$ 0	1,000	0
Total revenue	$10,000	9,800	9,000
Scenario 3:			
Capacity of 100, Discount class unlimited demand at $75*			
Premium price	$ 100	110	90
Premium demand	100	80	100
Premium revenue	$10,000	8,800	9,000
Discount revenue	$ 0	1,500	0
Total revenue	$10,000	10,300	9,000

*Optimal solution in blue.

The overall lesson for pricing in yield management environments: Traditional reasoning regarding price elasticity does not apply, and pricing depends on the relative demand/capacity relationships that must be judged on an individual case-by-case basis.

IMPLEMENTATION ISSUES

Although yield management systems enjoy success in a number of different industries, some practical problems must be addressed in both customer relations and employee relations.

Alienating Customers

The chapter began with some examples of yield management practices that can alienate customers. From the customers' viewpoint, many of the rules for getting into a specific fare class seem ridiculous. The idea that they are told a service is full to capacity when they then find out it is not is unbelievable to many consumers. Further, pricing issues can create significant ill will among customers. The general public seems to accept the idea that one person may pay a different rate for an airline seat than another, although many people still get quite angry when they find out. That feeling, however, has not spread to other industries. If someone overhears the person in front of her in line getting a better room rate at a hotel, she will often *demand* that rate, even though the rate of her own customer class would have been perfectly fine with her before she knew about the better rate. A key in many industries is—to be blunt—to keep customers ignorant of the rates available to other customer classes.

Customer Class "Cheating"

If customers become knowledgeable about a system, they can manipulate it to their own benefit. For example, as stated previously in this chapter, business-oriented hotels are more willing to bargain with customers who are providing revenue on otherwise empty weekend nights. Consequently, one tactic used by some customers is to make a hotel reservation for three nights, Thursday through Saturday, then stay only Thursday night, their true original intention. Another tactic works in reverse: If a hotel is booked solid during weekdays, make a reservation for only Saturday night, then refuse to leave the hotel for several days. In many states, laws preclude evicting such guests. Even if the law allows, hoteliers find the process of evicting a paying customer both embarrassing and poor public relations, because it often must be done in front of other guests.

The complexity of airline customer class regulations created a veritable cottage industry of customer cheating. A number of firms specialize in the illegal (by airline rules) buying and selling of frequent flyer miles, and a few travel agents find sophisticated methods to avoid airline regulations as an added service to their customers. The airlines invest substantial sums in information systems to keep customers obeying the rules. For example, customers used to be able to avoid the expense of an expensive, mid-week round trip by purchasing two overlapping round-trip tickets with Saturday night stopovers and throwing away the other half of both tickets. Many airlines now, however, have the capability of detecting such abandoned tickets and require the customer to pay the appropriate price or lose the privilege of flying with that airline.

The solution to this type of problem usually requires both employee vigilance and investments in software.

Employee Empowerment

Strategic decisions must be made concerning how much power is given to employees to make decisions. If a system is seen as reducing employee discretion, employees can often make up for this perceived indignity by sabotaging the system. In the hotel industry, for example, a significant degree of responsibility for assigning the proper customer class and room rate resides in the clerk who sits at the front desk. If a system lacks enough structure, clerks may whimsically decide whether a customer gets a higher or lower rate depending on their mood rather than the customer's true class. However, a system with too much structure can lead to a loss of bargaining power by clerks, which can result in needlessly empty rooms. Consequently, it is important for anyone with such responsibility to understand the overall managerial goals of such a system.

Cost and Implementation Time

Fully implementing a yield management system for a large firm is not a simple matter. No off-the-shelf software can be purchased at the local mall to address yield management issues. The leading companies providing yield management software are Sabre, PROS Strategic Solutions, Manugistics, VeriTec Solutions, Opus 2 Revenue Technologies Inc., and VeriProfit, Inc. Implementation costs for such software can run several million dollars and it can take from several months to two years to implement the software. Further, once a system is running, training and system updating are also costly.

Summary

Yield management systems are used in a wide variety of industries that have limited capacity. Such systems can potentially make a significant difference in profitability for firms that use them well.

Three basic components of a yield management system are overbooking, capacity allocation, and pricing. For overbooking and capacity allocation, numerical methods presented in the chapter can help to solve those problems. However, a practical answer to the pricing problem still remains out of reach. Examples were used to show how the environment of a yield management system, with customer classes and capacity restrictions, can turn normal pricing decisions around.

Finally, a yield management system is not just a computer program. It is a system that must be implemented with flesh-and-blood employees and customers. These human elements of the system must be attended to carefully because poor employee or customer education as to the limits and nature of such a system may lead to its circumvention in a variety of ways.

Review Questions

1. A specific problem of yield management techniques noted in the chapter demonstrated that an optimal solution to a particular problem involving a 100-seat plane gave an average of 13 seats to discounters, 75 seats to premium passengers, and an average of 12 seats were unoccupied. Explain in words, not numbers, how it is possible for the best solution to leave seats unoccupied on average.
2. If the average number of no-shows are, for example, 12, why isn't the best overbooking number necessarily 12?
3. What are nested capacity allocation methods and why are they used?
4. Why can't the standard formula for overbooking be used in all cases?

Problems

12.1. The Greybeard Busing Company is assessing its overbooking policy for the Miami–Fort Myers run. The number of customers who don't show up after reserving a ticket is uniformly distributed from 1 to 10 (10% chance of 1 no-show, 10% chance of 2, etc.). Tickets cost $25, and if the particular bus run is full, a passenger with a reservation is given passage on a rival bus line, a cost of $60. What should Greybeard's overbooking policy be?

12.2. It's normal for an airline to overbook a flight by 20% or so, but Amtrak will overbook its long-distance trains only by 5% to 10%, even though they have even more no-shows than the airlines do. What reasons would Amtrak have for overbooking so little?

12.3. The Kaluauluauhala Resort rents weekly condominiums by the Hawaiian shore, nearly all to families from Japan and the U.S. mainland. It is the only resort on the west side of the island. These condos rent for $1,500 per week, and guests typically spend another $500 (in terms of profit for the firm) during their stay. A guest who doesn't show up is subject to a cancellation fee of $750. If no condo is available for a guest with a reservation, he has to be transported either to the other side of the island or to another island to a similar resort and Kaluauluauhala picks up half the cost of the other resort (about the same as Kaluauluauhala's price, so the customer receives a "half-price" vacation) and the average $200 transportation charge.

No-shows by customers average three each week, evenly distributed between 0 and 6. What should the resort's overbooking policy be?

12.4. Consultant Air focuses business on high-paying McKinsey consultants, but to fill planes, it also carries the general public. It is flying a 100-seat jet from Atlanta to San Francisco and the consultant demand is normally distributed with mean 60 and standard deviation 10. Consultants pay $1,200 per ticket, the general public pays $150. Of course, the general public must book a flight several weeks ahead of time, while the consultants book flights at the last minute. How many seats should be opened up for the general public? On average, assuming 0 no-shows, how full will the plane be under this plan?

12.5   In addition to the customer classes in the previous problem, Consultant Air added a third class, "normal business people," who pay $500 per ticket. Demand from these customers is normally distributed with mean 20 and standard deviation 5. How does this class of customers change the solution to the previous problem?

12.6. Assume the curves shown in Figure 12.7 represent only the highest, lowest, and average demand for full-fare flights. Other curves are also possible. You are now four weeks before the flight and have received 30 reservations. Assuming a 150-seat plane, what should your capacity allocation policy be?

12.7. The curves for problem 12.6 really represent averages rather than exact relationships. If the final boarding numbers represented by the curve are an average result, where the actual boarding passengers are normally distributed about that average with a standard deviation of 10, what should your nested capacity allocation policy be? Assume prices of $1,000 per seat for premium, $400 for discount.

FIGURE 12.7: *Dynamic Capacity Allocation*

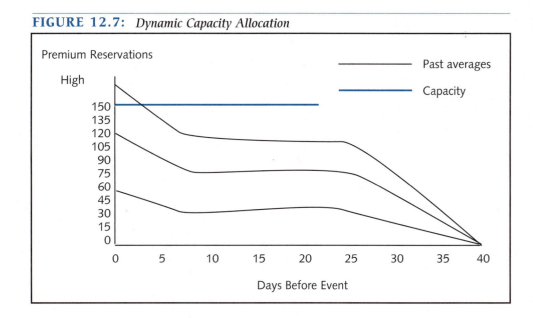

12.8. Rene was adamant. "If we have to tell customers we overbooked and there's no seating available, they are going to be extremely angry. I'll bet it costs us $150 per couple in goodwill each time." Tom replied, "No way, it doesn't cost us a penny. We're so popular now it doesn't matter if one potential customer doesn't come back. What matters is getting the most profit out of each seating. We prep everything ahead of time, so it costs us $50 per couple for food whether they show up or not, and we charge $150 per couple. At that rate of profit I don't want to see a single empty table."

The restaurant Chez Rogat was run by two Owen grads. They had two seatings each night, 6:00 P.M. and 8:30 P.M., for their 30-table restaurant. They prepared the same meal for everyone at each seating. Due to their popularity, they always had more reservations than they could handle and reservations were made far in advance. They had few no-shows, but did have some. They had about an equal chance of either 0, 1, 2, or 3 couples as no-shows at any given seating.

Given their costs, calculate an overbooking policy for Chez Rogat. Would you recommend any other capacity management strategy?

Selected Bibliography

Belobaba, P. 1989. Application of a Probabilistic Decision Model to Airline Seat Inventory Control. *Operations Research*, 37(2), 183–197.

Cook, T. 1998. SABRE Soars. *OR/MS Today* (June), 26–31.

Crandall, R., and R. Markland. 1996. Demand Management: Today's Challenge for Service Industries. *Production and Operations Management*, 5(2), 106–120.

Cross, R. 1997. *Revenue Management*. Broadway Books, NY.

Cross, R. 2004. February 10 presentation at Emory University.

Mitchener, B. 1997. "Ethnic Pricing" Means Unfair Air Fares. *The Wall Street Journal* (December 5), B1.

Smith, B., J. Leimkuhler, and R. Darrow. 1992. Yield Management at American Airlines, *Interfaces*, 22(1), 8–31.

CASE STUDY

Yield Management at MotherLand Air

MotherLand Air is an airline dedicated to the betterment of the proletariat, with original operating principles based upon the strong political beliefs of its founder, Al Niemi. Al started this airline for the selfless purpose of exposing Dallasites to the glories of communist ideals. His own vacation in North Korea convinced him that the communist economic system held ultimate truths, and he reasoned that his colleagues would be likewise convinced if only they would visit the motherland. Consequently, he leased a Boeing 747 and initiated direct service from Dallas to Pyongyang three days a week.

Al was philosophically against such capitalist notions as differential pricing for customers. He believed that all comrades were equal and should pay the same fare. Consequently, MotherLand Air was started as a one-price airline offering round-trip service for $400. Unfortunately, his 400-seat 747 was flying at far less than capacity seating on most trips and MotherLand was highly unprofitable.

Al was stunned that more travelers did not desire the icy North Korean air in their lungs, but he knew he had to adapt or shut down. He began to see wisdom in the old saying, "We are all equal, but some are more equal than others." Accordingly, he tried to salvage MotherLand by utilizing differential pricing. He segmented his customers into three different customer categories—"capitalist class" business flyers (who paid full coach fare), "comrade class" discount tickets, and "party member class" deep discount tickets—based on length of stay and flying days and time of year. He charged $1,000 for business flyers, $400 for discount tickets, and $100 for deep discount tickets.

This move improved his revenue significantly. He typically sold from 30 to 50 full-fare seats (Table 12.6), 70 to 100 discount seats (Table 12.7), and 100 to 150 deep discount seats on each trip.

TABLE 12.6: *Full Coach Fare History: Net Reservation Activity*

			------------------Weeks From Event---------------		-----Months From Event------					
Obs.	Boarded	1	2	3	4	5	6	7	2	3	4	5	6
1	34	53	51	37	28	23	16	15	13	8	9	6	5
2	26	40	40	29	18	16	14	12	10	6	7	5	5
3	27	42	39	30	22	15	15	13	10	7	6	6	4
4	36	43	40	28	21	17	11	10	11	6	6	5	4
•													
•													
•													
39	33	42	37	34	18	17	13	11	10	7	7	5	4
40	40	56	51	38	29	23	15	14	14	12	8	7	7

CASE STUDY

TABLE 12.7: *Discount Fare History: Net Reservation Activity*

| | | |------------Weeks From Event------------| | | | |------Months From Event-----| | | |
Obs.	Boarded	1	2	3	4	5	6	7	2	3	4	5	6
1	87	88	90	92	90	84	76	71	59	47	36	24	14
2	81	85	87	88	87	81	75	67	60	46	34	21	12
3	65	70	71	73	70	69	67	62	53	41	29	22	16
4	57	57	58	59	62	58	55	47	38	31	23	16	11
•													
•													
•													
39	100	101	103	105	104	102	95	85	71	57	44	32	21
40	105	111	113	115	114	110	104	93	79	65	50	32	19

Unfortunately, even with his new pricing scheme he was still not able to attain profitability, but a solution became clear. Since his 747 was never full, he negotiated a change in his lease for a much cheaper and more fuel-efficient 100-seat plane that would allow him to become profitable.

At this point, however, he needs assistance. He could fill his planes with deep discount and discount flyers, but it would be unprofitable to do so. Further, he had no experience with overbooking policies and was unsure whether he wanted to pursue one. Consequently, Al needs expert service operations consulting to maximize revenue.

Seating Allocation

Seating allocation must come in a "nested" form. For example, in Table 12.8 no deep discount, up to 50 discount and deep discount, and up to a combined 120 full coach, discount and deep discount seats are set aside six months prior to departure. Implicitly, for a 100-seat plane this allocation contains 20 overbooked seats.

Demand history from 40 flights on the larger planes is contained on Tables 12.6 and 12.7 and is available on the text CD. For example, in the Full Coach Fare History, Observation 1 indicates that 5 reservations were obtained 6 months before the flight, 6 reservations obtained 5 months before the flight, and so on, and of the 53 reservations in the system the week before the flight, 34 actually boarded the plane. Demand history for the deep discount tickets is not necessary because 100% of them are taken as soon as they are offered.

The demand history given can be used to determine threshold curves for each class of passenger. The purpose of developing threshold curves is to predict the eventual number of reservations just prior to boarding.

The costs involved in overbooking depend on the number of people not seated for the flight. The revenue from the ticket sales is subtracted (for simplicity, assume revenue of $1,000 for each person not seated), and Al estimates the per passenger

CASE STUDY

TABLE 12.8: *Game Tracking Sheet*

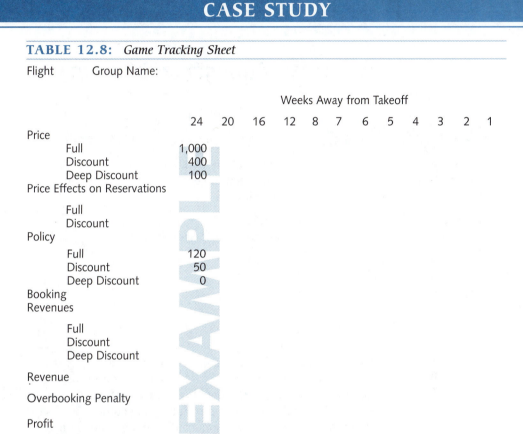

Flight   Group Name:

	Weeks Away from Takeoff											
	24	20	16	12	8	7	6	5	4	3	2	1
Price												
Full	1,000											
Discount	400											
Deep Discount	100											
Price Effects on Reservations												
Full												
Discount												
Policy												
Full	120											
Discount	50											
Deep Discount	0											
Booking												
Revenues												
Full												
Discount												
Deep Discount												
Revenue												
Overbooking Penalty												
Profit												

penalty cost of leaving passengers stranded as $200 times the number stranded squared. So leaving one person stranded costs $200, two people costs $800, three people costs $1,800, and so on.

Pricing

Currently, ticket prices start at $1,000, $400, and $100 for the three fare classes. Prices can be raised by 10% to $1,100 or $440, lowering demand by 15%, or prices can be lowered by 10% to $900 or $360, increasing demand by 15%. Prices on deep discount tickets cannot be changed.

Assignment

As a consultant, you advise Al Niemi concerning overbooking, seating allocation, and pricing for the three classes of passengers. Your group must indicate a policy prior to receiving any reservations. Once all policies are in, the reservation information for the six-month-out time frame will be given. At this point, you may alter your policies. Iterations of receiving reservation information and altering policies proceeds until plane departure, as depicted in Table 12.8.

Inventory Management in Services

LEARNING OBJECTIVES *The material in this chapter prepares students to:*

- Know how service inventory issues differ from manufacturing inventory issues.

- Conceptually understand how limited capacity and substitution effects change traditional inventory decisions.

- Find numerical solutions to simple inventory problems.

- Additional material on the Student CD prepares students to find numerical solutions to more complex inventory problems.[1]

Inventory in services? A hallmark of many service firms is their lack of inventory. With simultaneous production and consumption in many services, inventory is not stored. As discussed in Chapter 1, the core of the definition of services is intangibility. For many of the service firms that typical consumers visit every day, however, the facilitating goods that supplement the service can be inventoried and the amount and type of inventory represents a vital strategic decision. Many service sector firms, in fact, use inventory methods as a source of competitive advantage.

Inventory decisions are vital for four broad types of services:

1. Retail (e.g., grocers, auto parts, consumer electronics, department stores)
2. Wholesale
3. Field service (e.g., computer repair, copier repair)
4. Military (e.g., number/type of goods to be put in a tank, submarine, or soldier's pack)

For each of these general service sectors, inventory is a major cost. More than just the cost, inventory entails a basic strategic trade-off: In the retail, field service, and military sectors, space is limited, making it especially valuable. Given any specific store size, more inventory of one item means that the item takes up more shelf space, which in turn means less shelf space available for other items. The strategic choice, then, comes down to a lot of inventory of a few items *or* a little inventory of a lot of items.

---

1. The subject of services inventory poses both qualitative and quantitative problems. This chapter has quantitative content, but the focus is on a qualitative understanding of the issues. More quantitative material is available on the Student CD.

Beyond a general strategic direction, properly managing inventory is vital. "Recent studies indicate that 20% of customers leave video rental stores without the movie they would like to rent, 10% of items in grocery and convenience stores are out of stock, and 35% of women fail to buy apparel that they are shopping for because of stockouts of their size" (Narayanan, 2003, p.1). Inventory stockouts mean lost revenue, so properly managing inventory can substantially change profitability.

SERVICES VERSUS MANUFACTURING INVENTORY

This chapter presents the inventory problems specific to services. Inventory chapters are common in typical operations management textbooks, but much of that material focuses on manufacturing inventory problems, whose characteristics are fundamentally different from service sector problems. These differing characteristics include: setup/ordering costs, number of products, limited shelf space, lost sales versus back orders, product substitution, demand variance, and information accuracy.

Setup/Ordering Costs

A typical textbook manufacturing inventory problem entails large, costly setups. For example, the setup for changing the outer width of steel pipe manufactured by the Siderca plant of Techint Group costs $1 million so the width is not changed often. Because of these large expenses, a significant amount of manufacturing inventory work involves "rationalizing" large setup costs by determining how long one product should be produced before switching to another. The trade-offs between setup costs and other inventory costs are the main concern of such common inventory techniques as the Economic Order Quantity (EOQ), Wagner-Whitin algorithm, and various lot-sizing methods found in most textbooks.

Although these techniques are somewhat applicable in services, in most service inventory environments setup/ordering costs for all products combined can be substantial, but the added cost of ordering any one product can be trivial. For example, in the inventory-intense grocery business, the combined warehousing and distribution function is listed in company annual reports as 20% to 30% of cost of goods sold, but the added cost of a store manager deciding to order or not to order a given product is essentially zero.

A look at the typical services inventory system shows why. Often, a manager or clerk scans a computerized printout once every ordering period and notes any changes to the orders recommended by the computer. This revised list is often sent by computer to a distribution center, where order pickers roam warehouses, pick cases of product, and load them on a truck. When the truck arrives at a retail store, product is moved to store shelves. Altogether, it is an expensive process. The decision to order or not order any given product, however, barely nudges those costs. A few seconds of managerial time is required to place the order, the warehouse order picker picks just one more product on their list, the truck rolls regardless, and the store stocker takes at most a few more minutes to stock another product.

Consequently, here we will be concerned only with inventory techniques that are applicable to situations without ordering or setup costs.

Number of Products

A manufacturing firm may sell a few hundred, or even a few thousand products. (*Note*: Individual products are generally called stockkeeping units, or SKUs, in these businesses, and they will be referred to as SKUs in this text.) Even this amount is dwarfed by the number of SKUs sold by such services as supermarkets (an average of 40,000 SKUs in a store), auto parts stores (up to 60,000 SKUs), bookstores

(200,000 SKUs) or department stores (approximately 400,000 SKUs), many of which are ordered weekly or several times per week. What this scale of operation means is that, although manufacturers may have the luxury of pondering over production decisions, the managerial time spent on the ordering decision of any one SKU by a service firm must be short.

Limited Shelf Space

Shelf space presents a key consideration in many services, which is the primary reason why this chapter appears in this section of the textbook. Retail stores—even Wal-Mart Supercenters—are too small to carry all the different items that might sell, and are certainly far too small to carry all the items product manufacturers would like them to carry. A key decision is how to allocate that limited space among products.

Lost Sales Versus Back Orders

Manufacturers often cannot immediately ship items, because they are not in inventory. It is common for manufacturers to quote a lead time or place a requested item on back order and then fill the order weeks later. Although back orders may also occur in some service firms, a more common result is a lost sale. Imagine a supermarket clerk telling you to come back in two weeks for those lasagna noodles you want to serve tonight. Even though this distinction may not seem large in analyzing what to do, it actually complicates theory greatly and makes stocking out a much more expensive proposition.

Product Substitution

In many service inventory situations retailers carry nearly identical products from many manufacturers, so service inventory models need to consider the effects of customer's substitution behavior when faced with product stockouts. In other words, the stocking levels of products should not be considered in isolation of each other; groups of substitutable products have to be considered as a whole.

Demand Variance

The unpredictability of demand is often greater in services, especially for SKUs in a given store with a small average number of units sold. For example, more than 50% of dry goods SKUs in supermarkets sell fewer than one unit per week on average. However, on a given day an interested customer may clean out the entire stock. This high variance makes inventory decisions tougher to figure out and makes an inventory model—versus back-of-the-envelope guesses—more important. Consider the extremes: If precisely 50 units are sold every day, the decision on how much to stock is simple—stock 50. But if some days nothing is sold, other days a few, and occasionally 100, then a mathematical inventory model is useful.

Information Accuracy

Throughout the economy, millions of dollars are spent by manufacturers and service firms alike on information systems to track inventory. Service firms, however, must deal with an aspect that most manufacturers do not: customers! It would be reasonable to think that a grocery store would keep track of inventory through the computer by noting sales through the scanners at the checkout register. Unfortunately, grocers still must track inventory by physically walking the aisles to see how much is on the shelf. When customers or employees steal goods, they inconveniently don't scan them. Also, when someone picks up a jar of salsa in aisle 9 and changes his mind and deposits it in aisle 12, or breaks the jar in aisle 14, one less salsa sits on the shelf, but not in the computer system. Customer misshelving is perhaps worst in retail bookstores, where a book taken out of, say, the "history" section is reshelved by the customer in the "political science" section. The problem is magnified for these retailers because books do not look out of place in the wrong section, unlike a bottle of ketchup next to a gallon of milk in a grocery store, so it will not automatically be corrected by employees. For the purposes of a bookstore inventory system, the customer might as well have just burned the book—it won't be found by employees or other customers again until the annual physical inventory.

These problems receive serious attention in many businesses. Many U.S. retailers attach 3-inch-long plastic antishoplifting devices to dresses and suits. At Lojas Renner, the largest department store chain in Brazil, those tags are even attached to socks! As one otherwise highly successful Wal-Mart store manager said concerning the annual physical inventory, "[I]f inventory came out really bad, I was afraid they would ask for my keys" (Helliker, 1995).

The Need for Inventory Science

The conditions noted in the previous section make the services inventory problem different from the manufacturing inventory problem, so the inventory formulas normally found in textbooks dedicated to manufacturing problems are not especially helpful. The question is, "so what?" It may not seem like a major concern, since, clearly, grocers and department store managers used their own intuition and "gut feel" when ordering inventory throughout the history of commerce.

However, services need inventory models because the "common sense" inventory replenishment rules learned through years of practical experience are no longer good enough, and the computer power is now available to lend some science to the issue. The combination of time-based logistics practices, technological innovations, and changes in manufacturer product strategies radically altered the business environment for services, which impacts inventory decisions. According to Southland Corporation (1997 annual report), in a description of its new inventory information system, claims that "[r]etailing is evolving from an art to a science." The revival of Southland Corporation's 7-Eleven stores from near bankruptcy to a thriving enterprise, growing at more than a store per day, resulted primarily from advances in logistics and inventory management. See the accompanying Service Operations Management Practices: IBM Service Logistics' "Optimizer" for the value these methods can bring to another significant services inventory problem.

A basic thrust of time-based competition is to compress the amount of time required in the product delivery cycle. Time-based competitive practices began in the manufacturing sector, but they are used in services as well. Such practices are called *efficient consumer response* in the grocery industry and *quick response* in the apparel and general merchandise industries. These movements provide the central organizing principles for logistics planning in many firms in these industries.

These back-room advances significantly affect the practice of front-room inventory replenishment. Replenishment decisions can now be made far more frequently, reducing the need for inventory.

Technological innovations play a large role in the institution of time-based practices and the reduced need for retail inventory. Bar coding, scanner technology, and electronic data interchange all combine to reduce the uncertainty of inventory position, make the inventory ordering process less costly, and reduce the order fulfillment cycle time.

SERVICE OPERATIONS MANAGEMENT PRACTICES

IBM Service Logistics' "Optimizer"

IBM faces a very challenging service inventory problem. IBM office equipment is everywhere, and it is indispensable. When an IBM mainframe computer goes down, customers cannot be served, product orders cannot be entered, Web sites crash, and payroll will not run, just to name a few problems. Consequently, fast service is job 1. Fast service doesn't mean, "We'll overnight the part to you and get you running tomorrow." It means, "We'll have you back up and running in two hours."

How does that happen? It happens by placing the right amount of inventory in the right places. IBM services more than 1,000 products, and those products use a collective 200,000 different parts, and most of the 1,000 products have several common parts. For fast service, IBM operates two central warehouses, 21 field distribution centers, 64 parts stations, and 15,000 "outside locations," which often means an inventory of parts is maintained at the customers' locations. Clearly, IBM cannot stock all the possibly needed parts at every location, because the cost would be immense. Furthermore, "common sense" and "good judgment" are not enough when the problem is this large and complex.

A combined team from IBM, Stanford University, and the University of Pennsylvania developed inventory heuristics to maintain current service levels and cut $500 million of inventory out of the system. During implementation, IBM strategically chose to increase service levels, which still allowed them to cut $250 million in inventory.

Source: Cohen et al. (1990).

On another front, manufacturer strategies make service inventory decisions more complex and more important. Retail shelf space remains limited while the number of products increased sharply in recent years. For example, in the grocery industry the average supermarket can stock approximately 40,000 SKUs, but manufacturers list a few hundred thousand SKUs for consideration.

Generally, service inventory policy addresses three decision areas:

- *Assortment:* Deciding which products should be stocked
- *Allocation:* How much shelf space to give each product in the assortment
- *Replenishment:* When and how much to reorder

Assortment and allocation are usually decisions made by marketing. Assortment decisions are made by company buyers based on what products the buyers think will sell, and allocation decisions are often made on the relative sales between products in a category: If Heinz sells twice as much as Hunt's, then Heinz gets twice the shelf space within the ketchup category.

In the next several pages we describe some mathematical ways of addressing services inventory problems.

THE "NEWSVENDOR" MODEL: UNCERTAIN SALES, NO ORDERING COSTS, AND LOST SALES

We start with the simplest of inventory models for uncertain sales: The "newsvendor" model. This model tells us how much inventory to order if the number of customers purchasing product any day is uncertain, no ordering costs are involved, and if no more product is available, then customers simply don't buy anything. The classic teaching example is selling newspapers.

EXAMPLE 13.1:   *The Newsstand*

Although you were top academic achiever in your class, you studied so hard you had no time for interviewing and found yourself jobless at graduation. Knowing a good opportunity when it presents itself, the newspaper vendor at 5th and Broadway sold you his newsstand. His parting advice was, "Always buy 150 papers every day, that way you'll never disappoint your customers," which you followed for the first 20 days.

The cost of a newspaper to you is $0.30, and they are sold for $0.50. Excess papers have no value and unsatisfied customers harbor no ill will if you are out of newspapers; you just do not make the sale that day.

Sure enough, you never ran out of papers by buying 150 every day, but the business was hardly profitable. The amount sold each day can be found in Table 13.1. (Data for all tables in this textbook can be found on the accompanying CD.) Over the course of 20 days, you paid for 150 papers × 20 days × $0.30/paper = $900 and received 90 papers × 20 days × $0.50/paper = $900 from customers, earning no net profit overall.

What can you do to make more from this opportunity? Some notation will help in solving this problem:

C_o = the cost of overage, or ordering another unit that isn't sold, which here is $0.30 (if any value remains, usually called *salvage* value, that value is subtracted from C_o)

C_s = the cost of stocking out, or not getting the profit from selling a unit, which here is $0.50 – $0.30 = $0.20

y = inventory order

d = units demanded

$E(\bullet)$ = an expected value

$P(d \leq y)$ = probability demand d is less than or equal to y

One way to think through solving this problem is through a method called *marginal analysis*; that is, thinking about the marginal impact of incrementally increasing y, the inventory position, until the expected revenue from inventory is less than the expected cost. Starting from the lowest logical number, if 53 papers are stocked, then 53 will be sold every day with probability = 1.00, and no papers will be left over, so the profits for the 20 days in Table 13.1 will be 53 × 20 × $0.20 = $212 (see Table 13.2).

That stocking level, however, leaves a lot of customers unhappy. If 62 papers, the next logical number, are stocked, then 95% of the time those marginal, 62 – 53 = 9, papers will be bought, and 5% of the time, when demand is only 53, they will be thrown out. So those marginal papers contribute [0.95($0.20) – 0.05($0.30)]

TABLE 13.1: *Newsstand Example*

Demand	P (demand ≥ amount in first column)
53	1.00
62	.95
71	.90
71	.90
78	.80
81	.75
82	.70
85	.65
86	.60
88	.55
90	.50
92	.45
95	.40
95	.40
96	.30
97	.25
98	.20
118	.15
125	10
137	.05

Average demand = 90
Standard deviation = 20

× 9 papers × 20 days = $31.50, and bring the total profit for stocking 62 to $212 + $31.50 = $243.50 (see Table 13.2). We keep increasing the number of papers until the marginal contribution turns negative. We can take a short cut in this process by analyzing this problem algebraically. We increase y as long as:

$$E(\text{revenue of next unit of inventory}) \geq E(\text{cost of next unit of inventory})$$

which is the same as

$$\begin{array}{c}(\text{Profit from selling a unit}) \times (\text{Probability that the unit will sell}) \geq \\ (\text{Cost of leftover inventory}) \times (\text{Probability that the unit will not sell})\end{array}$$

In the mathematical terms used previously,

$$C_o \times P(d < y) \leq C_s \times P(d \geq y)$$

which can be converted to

$$C_o \times [1 - P(d \geq y)] \leq C_s \times P(d \geq y)$$

or equivalently,

$$C_o - C_o \times P(d \geq y) \leq C_s \times P(d \geq y)$$

Adding $C_o \times P(d \leq y)$ to both sides and dividing both sides by $(C_o + C_s)$ leaves the basic newsvendor formula: Find the largest inventory number for which

$$C_o/(C_s + C_o) \leq P(d \geq y) \tag{13.1}$$

In this problem, equation (13.1) yields $0.30/$0.50 = 0.60 ≤ P(d ≥ y), and in Table 13.1 demand is greater than or equal to 86 with a probability of 0.60. Table

Access your Student CD now for Table 13.2 as an Excel spreadsheet.

TABLE 13.2: *Marginal Analysis of the Newsstand*

Amount Ordered	53	62	71	78	82	85	86	88	90	95	98	125
Demand for Papers												
						Daily profit						
53	$10.60	$7.90	$5.20	$3.10	$1.90	$1.00	$0.70	$0.10	-$0.50	-$2.00	-$2.90	-$11.00
62	$10.60	$12.40	$9.70	$7.60	$6.40	$5.50	$5.20	$4.60	$4.00	$2.50	$1.60	-$6.50
71	$10.60	$12.40	$14.20	$12.10	$10.90	$10.00	$9.70	$9.10	$8.50	$7.00	$6.10	-$2.00
71	$10.60	$12.40	$14.20	$12.10	$10.90	$10.00	$9.70	$9.10	$8.50	$7.00	$6.10	-$2.00
78	$10.60	$12.40	$14.20	$15.60	$14.40	$13.50	$13.20	$12.60	$12.00	$10.50	$9.60	$1.50
81	$10.60	$12.40	$14.20	$15.60	$15.90	$15.00	$14.70	$14.10	$13.50	$12.00	$11.10	$3.00
82	$10.60	$12.40	$14.20	$15.60	$16.40	$15.50	$15.20	$14.60	$14.00	$12.50	$11.60	$3.50
85	$10.60	$12.40	$14.20	$15.60	$16.40	$17.00	$16.70	$16.10	$15.50	$14.00	$13.10	$5.00
86	$10.60	$12.40	$14.20	$15.60	$16.40	$17.00	$17.20	$16.60	$16.00	$14.50	$13.60	$5.50
88	$10.60	$12.40	$14.20	$15.60	$16.40	$17.00	$17.20	$17.60	$17.00	$15.50	$14.60	$6.50
90	$10.60	$12.40	$14.20	$15.60	$16.40	$17.00	$17.20	$17.60	$18.00	$16.50	$15.60	$7.50
92	$10.60	$12.40	$14.20	$15.60	$16.40	$17.00	$17.20	$17.60	$18.00	$17.50	$16.60	$8.50
95	$10.60	$12.40	$14.20	$15.60	$16.40	$17.00	$17.20	$17.60	$18.00	$19.00	$18.10	$10.00
95	$10.60	$12.40	$14.20	$15.60	$16.40	$17.00	$17.20	$17.60	$18.00	$19.00	$18.10	$10.00
96	$10.60	$12.40	$14.20	$15.60	$16.40	$17.00	$17.20	$17.60	$18.00	$19.00	$18.60	$10.50
97	$10.60	$12.40	$14.20	$15.60	$16.40	$17.00	$17.20	$17.60	$18.00	$19.00	$19.10	$11.00
98	$10.60	$12.40	$14.20	$15.60	$16.40	$17.00	$17.20	$17.60	$18.00	$19.00	$19.60	$11.50
118	$10.60	$12.40	$14.20	$15.60	$16.40	$17.00	$17.20	$17.60	$18.00	$19.00	$19.60	$21.50
125	$10.60	$12.40	$14.20	$15.60	$16.40	$17.00	$17.20	$17.60	$18.00	$19.00	$19.60	$25.00
137	$10.60	$12.40	$14.20	$15.60	$16.40	$17.00	$17.20	$17.60	$18.00	$19.00	$19.60	$25.00
Total Profit for 20 Days	$212.00	$243.50	$270.50	$284.50	$290.00	$291.50	$291.50	$290.50	$288.50	$279.50	$269.00	$144.00

13.2 shows that an order quantity of 86 is the most profitable amount, earning $291.50.

A few aspects of this problem are worthy of additional attention. First is the similarity of this math to the overbooking problem discussed in Chapter 12: Understand one of these situations, and you will understand the calculations behind the other.

Notice how the overall profitability differs little with orders anywhere between 82 and 88 in Table 13.2. This property is particularly important for this type of inventory problem. About the optimal solution you will notice is a "bowl" effect, where profits are close to optimal if the order quantity is close. This bowl effect is important because C_o and C_s are often estimates, rather than precise cost figures. Consequently, even if those estimates are off a bit, a solution close to optimal will still result. This bowl shape for the cost curve provides a major advantage in using a mathematical model. If one were to guess, based on intuition, one could easily make a significant mistake and end up far from optimality. These mathematical models, even without precise cost estimates, will generate a close-to-optimal solution. The bowl shape is so shallow that in this problem an order quantity of 85 provides the same profit as 86: Either solution is correct.

Finally, in the example given, the calculated answer of 0.60 corresponded directly to a number in Table 13.1. If the number does not correspond exactly, the optimal answer is the inventory position where the probability is "greater than" the result of the calculation. As an example, consider the situation if papers sold for $100, but cost $99—generally not considered a good profit margin. Common sense dictates that one would stock only what one is absolutely certain of selling, which would be 53 papers here. The ratio $C_o/(C_s + C_o) = 0.99$, and the lowest probability greater than or equal to 0.99 would be 1.00, representing an inventory position of 53.

This general formula can be used with general probability distributions as well as with actual data. For example, if data are normally distributed, one can use the z-score as taught in statistics classes. For example, the data in Table 13.1 appear to be normally distributed with a mean of 90 and standard deviation of 20. Looking for a probability of 0.60 corresponds to a z-score of approximately 0.25 in standard normal tables. So the typical z-score calculation of

$$\text{Order quantity} = \text{Mean} \pm z(\text{standard deviation})$$

would be $90 - 0.25(20) = 85$. (*Note:* In most examples of z-score arithmetic, when one is looking for less than 50% under the distribution, then one is *adding z* times the standard deviation to the mean. Here, we are looking for more than 50%, so it is appropriate to subtract. The business reason is that the costs of having too much inventory are greater than the profits gained, so one would stock *less* than the average demand.)

PRODUCT SUBSTITUTION AND DEMAND VARIANCE

The gross profit margins of many service sector inventory items are considerably larger than the preceding newspaper example. For example, the difference between selling price and purchase price of an average dry grocery item in a grocery store is approximately 40% of the selling price. Further, the cost of overage between order cycles continues to decrease for many items due to improved logistics. It is fairly common in service inventory systems to take delivery of a given product several times per week. Consequently, for any individual inventory decision, the cost of over-ordering nonperishable goods is just the cost of holding that item on the shelf until the next order cycle, which comes up in a few days.

Consider a mythical product with the preceding characteristics that sells for $10. The cost of a stockout results in C_s = $4 in lost profit as well as some additional cost for disappointing the customer. This "disappointment" cost is real. Customers who routinely see favorite products out of stock will take future business to a competitor. However, it is difficult to put a solid number on disappointment for each individual stockout. For this example, let us say customer disappointment costs an additional $2, so C_s = $6. Let us say that deliveries are made weekly and that the annual cost attributed to holding an item is considered to be 25% of the item cost. Therefore, the cost of overage, C_o = $10 × 0.25/52 = $0.05.

For this typical retail item, then, $C_o/(C_s + C_o)$ = 0.008, which means that one should stock to ensure only a 0.8% chance of demand exceeding the stock on the shelf. To put it another way, the newsvendor model suggests stocking in this example so that customers are served 99.2% of the time. These extreme stocking levels near 100% are not unusual in clothing stores and for dry goods at supermarkets (see the Service Operations Management Practices: Think Mom Buys Too Much?). Asymmetric penalties for missing the optimal target reinforce this high service level; that is, the cost penalty for carrying too much inventory over the optimal target number is relatively light compared to the financial penalty for holding too little. Just as Table 13.2 provided information concerning costs around the optimal order quantity for example 13.1, Figure 13.1 provides a typical profit curve for ordering a service inventory item. Stocking too few items that customers want to buy often results in angry customers and negative profits. After the newsvendor solution is achieved, the profits decline only slightly with the amount ordered, because the holding costs are relatively small.

Consequently, if one were only concerned with satisfying the demand for a single product in a store not subject to capacity restrictions, Figure 13.1 would depict the results of potential choices. However, other considerations enter in. First, we consider product substitution.

When consumers are faced with a stockout of their preferred product, a substantial percentage simply buy a competing brand. Although this tendency may be of great concern to product manufacturers, product substitution makes the stockout somewhat "revenue neutral" from the perspective of service sector inventory. The level of substitution differs drastically depending on the product category and ranges from 40% to virtually 100%, according to research. Physically, what this situation

FIGURE 13.1: *Profit Curve for Typical Service Inventory Form*

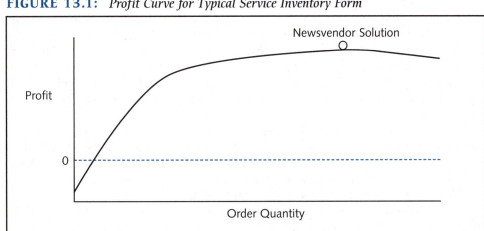

SERVICE OPERATIONS MANAGEMENT PRACTICES

Think Mom Buys Too Much? Look Who She's Buying From!

Ever look in the kitchen pantry and see enough cans of tuna to feed the world's hungry for a year? A study of a representative store at one of the leading U.S. grocers in terms of both sales and profits found something similar. Although deliveries from the main warehouse to the store took place five times a week, the average amount of inventory in the store section studied was enough to last a month. For one product in particular, the supermarket shelf held enough to last for six months.

How does this inventory overload happen? Several reasons: Unreliable sales data from creaky information systems that don't tie together can keep the person who makes the order from really knowing the situation; the need to purchase case-packs of 12 at a time, even though only two units sell per month, creates extra inventory everywhere; a reward system that punishes employees who let stockouts occur, but ignores employees who create excess inventory.

The entire industry knows it has an inventory problem. The industry-wide movement of Efficient Consumer Response (ECR, as it's known in the grocery biz) is based on tackling it. To the grocery chain that can solve its inventory problems will go some big rewards: Dominating market share and vastly increased profits.

Source: Ketzenberg et al. (2000).

---

means is that service firms are not negatively affected by occasional stockouts of certain products. For inventory policy, the substitution factor changes the calculation of the stockout cost in equation (13.1). For example, if consumer substitution were 90%, the real value of C_s would be 0.10($6) = $0.60, rather than $6, and the service level would be set at 92.4%, rather than 99.9%.

The difference between a 92.4% service level and a 99.9% service level may not sound like much, but it represents a significant difference in the amount of inventory ordered because of the high variance of service sector demand. As an example, typical demand for a service sector inventory item can be described by the negative binomial distribution, with a variance higher than its mean. Although it is not vital that you understand the intricacies of the negative binomial distribution, the shape of the distribution is important and is replicated graphically in Figure 13.2 and tabulated in Table 13.3, for a product with a mean demand of 2 and variance of 10.

For this example problem—and for most service inventory problems—we are concerned with a tail of the distribution, or service levels over 90%. Because that particular area is difficult to see on Figure 13.2, it is shown in greater detail in Figure 13.3. Without considering substitution, one should order enough inventory to reach the 99.9% of demand, or 22 units. Including substitution, one should order up to the 92.4% of demand, or 7 units. Including the substitution effect in this case cuts the amount of stock to buy from 22 to 7 units, a nearly 70% reduction.

Access your Student CD now for Excel worksheets of Table 13.3, Figure 13.2, and Figure 13.3.

FIGURE 13.2: *Negative Binomial Distribution (mean = 2, variance = 10)*

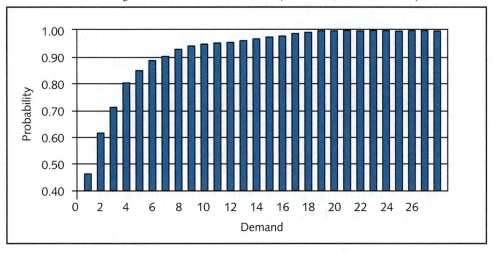

TABLE 13.3: *Probability Distribution (mean = 2, variance = 10)*

Amount	Probability Demand = Amount	Probability Demand ≤ Amount
0	0.447	0.447
1	0.179	0.626
2	0.107	0.733
3	0.072	0.805
4	0.050	0.855
5	0.036	0.891
6	0.026	0.918
7	0.020	0.937
8	0.015	0.852
9	0.011	0.963
10	0.008	0.972
11	0.006	0.978
12	0.005	0.983
13	0.004	0.987
14	0.003	0.990
15	0.002	0.992
16	0.002	0.994
17	0.001	0.995
18	0.001	0.996
19	0.0008	0.997
20	0.0006	0.998
21	0.0005	0.998
22	0.0004	0.999

Without considering substitution: order 22
Considering substitution: order 7

FIGURE 13.3: *Negative Binomial Distribution with High Service Levels*

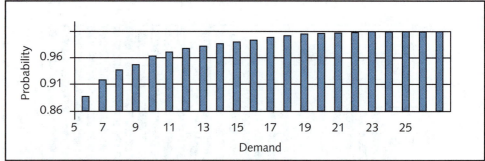

MULTIPLE PRODUCTS AND SHELF SPACE LIMITATIONS: A QUALITATIVE DISCUSSION

*Access your Student CD now for a **quantitative** discussion on multiple products and shelf space limitations.*

The numerical examples 13.2 and 13.3 on the Student CD provide some solid numbers to the inventory problems in the service sector. One purpose of showing detailed, quantitative calculations is to lead to a more strategic discussion. As noted in the introduction to this chapter, service inventory problems are difficult due to such factors as the enormous number of SKUs, high demand variance, and other factors. Because of these difficulties, services historically took a less than scientific view of inventory management.

The most prevalent method of ordering inventory in services could be called the "weeks of demand" method. That is, a manager has a gut feel that, say, three average weeks worth of demand should be on the shelf. So, if demand in the past five weeks has been 100, 150, 50, 75, 125, this method indicates that 3 × 100 = 300 units should be available. While this method has an intuitive appeal and is easily implemented, it can be substantially outperformed by other methods. In other words, "opportunity knocks" for changing the way services treat inventory.

One way to get a better inventory policy is to consider the demand variance of different items. Suppose Item A demand looks like this: 500, 0, 250, 100, 400; and Item B demand is more like this: 250, 250, 250, 250, 250. Clearly, one policy of "three weeks of demand" is not appropriate for both products. The higher variance of Item A means that it should have an overall higher inventory level than Item B.

Another consideration should be the relative product profitability. Suppose Items C and D both cost $10, but Item C sells for $100 and Item D sells for $10. It would be wise to have a higher service level on Item C that Item D. That is, get the best "bang for the buck" in inventory decisions. A similar problem occurs in repair businesses like computer and copier repair. Companies usually send out a technician with a van full of equipment to fix a computer or copier, but a van is only so large and can't possibly hold all the spare parts that may be needed. A customer is equally disappointed if a repair is not made because an expensive part or a cheap part is not on hand. Consequently, the parts to load in the van are the cheap ones. While this sounds trivial for a single van, firms like IBM and Xerox have a thousand or more mobile repair units servicing the United States alone.

Access your Student CD now for these tables and examples in the quantitative discussion of multiple products and shelf space limitations.

The qualitative solutions for these problems presented here are a bit vague when it comes to the detail needed for implementation. The basic lesson is that there are substantial gains to be made by managing product inventories individually, considering such differences as demand variance and product profitability. Specific methods for doing this are on the Student CD.

Practical Methods to Reduce Stockouts, Shrinkage, and Inventory Inaccuracy

Revenue Sharing

A major cause of stockouts at the retail level is the low and uncertain margin that retailers get for selling a product compared to the high price they must pay for the product from the manufacturer. Years ago, a movie video would cost a video rental store perhaps $60 to purchase, then the store could rent it out as many times as possible. The number of rentals is guesswork, but that $60 was clearly money out the door. Quoting the CEO of Movie Gallery, the third largest video rental chain, "Out-of-stocks were the single biggest problem in our industry. Between 20% and 25% of the people coming in to rent a video would leave without their intended title. Some of those found another movie to rent, but some proportion of them went away disgruntled. Under revenue sharing, only about 5% of video rental customers leave without their intended title" (Narayanan, 2003, p. 5).

"Revenue sharing" refers to charging a lower up-front price to the retailer, but sharing in the retailer's revenue. For the movie rental industry, this change meant the price for getting videos from Hollywood dropped from about $60 to about $8, but their rental revenue dropped from about $5/rental to $2.50/rental. The net effect of revenue sharing was that stores stocked more copies of each movie, and more customers got what they wanted. In the terms of the newsvendor model described earlier in the chapter, the cost of overage is reduced severely, while the cost of stocking out is reduced relatively mildly. Consequently, the optimal amount to order increases.

Markdown Money

Another type of incentive to give to retailers is "markdown money," which is sometimes called "price protection." Once it is determined that a product is not selling well, retailers often severely mark down the price on the remaining items to get some return for their dollars. Marking down the price below their own cost still makes sense—it's better to lose 80% of your money than 100%. Markdown money helps alleviate the downside of ordering too much product. The manufacturer agrees to pay a percentage of the markdown amount for the units that have their prices cut. With this downside protection, retailers are willing to order more product, and thereby take less of a chance of a stockout. Again, in terms of the newsvendor vocabulary, the cost of overage is reduced, so the optimal decision is to order more.

Phantom Stockouts

"Phantom stockouts" are situations where customers cannot locate the products they want, even though they are in a store. For the supermarket industry, the sales lost due to products that were in storage areas but not on the selling floor was estimated to be $560 – $960 million/year (Andersen Consulting, 1996). At Borders (bookstores), an average of 5,792 titles are in the store, but not in the selling area where a customer could find them (Ton and Raman, 2004). "One in six customers who approached a salesperson for help failed to find and purchase the title for which he or she was searching, not because the title was out-of-stock but rather because it was misplaced in a backroom, in other storage areas, or in the wrong aisle or location" (Ton and Raman, 1999).

Phantom stockouts hurt a business in several ways. Of course, the immediate sale is not made. Additionally, labor requirements are increased, as customers ask employees for help; forecasting accuracy and reordering policies are weakened, since the computer assumes product is sitting on the shelf and no one wants it. Customers walk away from the firm believing the employees are incompetent—the computer tells them the product is in the store but they can't find it.

Ton and Raman found that phantom stockouts were associated with having too much stuff. The more product variety was in a store, and the greater number of units of each product, the more phantom stockouts would occur. More to the point, just highlighting the problem and recognizing that it is a factor to be managed can help to reduce it. In the grocery industry it is common for manufacturers to hire full-time personnel to do retail audits. These personnel travel from store to store to make sure the manufacturer's product is actually on the shelf, rather than rotting in a back room.

Inventory Inaccuracy

The inventory records of many service firms are highly inaccurate. One particular "large, public retailer with highly modern operations including electronic point-of-sale scanning and automated replenishment systems in each of its nearly 1,000 stores and all of its warehouses" had discrepancies between what the computer thought it had and what it really had for 65% of all products (DeHoratius and Raman, 2003). Further, the average error was large—averaging being off by 5 units for SKUs that average only 15 units of inventory. Inventory inaccuracy isn't caused just by customers. For one new Borders store that customers had never entered, the inventory system had the wrong quantities for 29% of the SKUs (Raman, DeHoratius and Ton, 2001).

Inventory record inaccuracy has many costs. Increased labor cost is high among them. For example, computerized grocery store inventory records are so inaccurate that stores pay employees to wander the aisles and manually order products, rather than rely on their inventory system to tell them when to order. The other costs associated with inventory inaccuracy are the same as those associated with phantom stockouts, such as an inability to properly forecast demand. Further, many systems approaches such as Enterprise Resource Planning systems, Collaborative Forecasting and Replenishment systems, and Distribution Requirements Planning systems rely on accurate inventory information to work. If inventory records are not accurate, the recommendations and orders these systems place can be destructive.

DeHoratius and Raman (2004a) say that the most important aspect of inventory inaccuracy is to get managers to understand that it exists. In accordance with a Six-Sigma approach (Chapter 11), once it is visible it can be worked on. Some fixes are relatively easy, once known. For example, at H.E.Butt grocers, it was noticed that one store in particular sold enormous quantities of hard-boiled eggs—according to the computer. Consequently, more such eggs were ordered. When investigated, it was found that since hard-boiled eggs were priced at exactly 50 cents, when a cashier came upon an item he didn't know the inventory code for, he simply rang up an equivalent number of eggs to get close to the right price. So, a $4 mystery vegetable became eight eggs on the computer system. Once the problem was known, all it took was informing the cashiers they were causing problems elsewhere in order to get them to stop.

Shrinkage

Inventory shrinkage can be a significant problem for services. "Shrinkage" refers to lost, stolen, or damaged goods. The conundrum for service firms is that goods have to be available to see and touch for customers to make purchase decisions, but this also provides customers an opportunity to steal or damage products.

Most of the methods for reducing shrinkage are quite clear and will not be discussed here. Instead, the focus here is a cautionary tale of focusing too much on shrinkage.

The incentive for managers to reduce shrinkage at Bryn Mawr Stereo was powerful: Every dollar of shrinkage was a dollar that was taken out of their paychecks (DeHoratius and Raman, 2004b). With such an incentive, management took reducing shrinkage very seriously—too seriously. The focus on preventing theft and miscounts led to an atmosphere of "sales prevention." All small items that could be easily stolen were put behind lock and key. If insufficient employees were around to safeguard the store, the manager just closed the store down. Instead of helping and informing customers, managers personally counted shipments in the back room to make sure they were getting exactly what was on the invoice.

When a new incentive system was put into place, store performance changed dramatically. The new incentive system based manager pay on store profitability. Since the focus was no longer solely on shrinkage, the amount of shrinkage rose from a monthly average of $123 to $676. But the incentive system got managers out of the back room and helping customers, so sales jumped from $156,000 to $190,000 per month, and overall per store profit increased $5,000/month.

Summary

Yes, the service sector does have inventory—lots of it. It represents a major cost to service firms and, more importantly, a vital part of its strategic decisions.

Because of the high number of SKUs, product substitutability, high demand variances, the prevalence of lost sales rather than back orders, and the limited resource of space, service sector inventory problems are challenging and require solution methods different from many manufacturing inventory problems.

The good news is that inventory management can be a source of competitive advantage in the service sector. Consequently, both a quantitative study of inventory methods, as well as a good feel for what constitutes appropriate inventory policies are areas worthy of study.

Inventory models can harness the power of the computer to overcome the now less-effective common sense approach of yesteryear. Simple models, like the newsvendor model, allow retailers to offer the greatest possible customer satisfaction for the least cost. Product substitution tactics can also be employed to further lessen the impact of inventory stockouts.

Another exciting development in services inventory management is the use of modeling methods to address the cost and space limitation issues. Various methods can be used to make inventory management more rigorous, including weeks of sales, constant K, constant service, and marginal analysis. Qualitative judgment can then improve on the quantitative methods used just by applying the intuition gained by studying your results.

Review Questions

1. In what ways are service sector inventory problems different from typical manufacturing inventory problems?
2. How does consumer product substitution affect the amount of inventory a firm holds?
3. In practice, businesses often stock inventory in terms of the number of weeks of demand. For example, if average demand is 2 units per week, stock three weeks' worth, or 6 units. Discuss two problems with this policy.

Problems

13.1. Sales of hot dogs at the corner of Polk and Castro follow the following pattern: 30% of the days, 80 are sold; 40% of the days, 90 are sold; and the remaining days, 100 are sold. If 90 are stocked each day by the vendor, what demand fill rate is the vendor targeting?

13.2. For the information in problem 13.1, how much should be stocked to have a fill rate of 98%?

13.3. Due to long lead times, fashion goods must usually be purchased by retail stores long before the season begins, and "hot" items quite often cannot be ordered again during the season once their popularity becomes evident.

     The new, trendy aluminum foil dress is creating a buzz. Getting a consensus of opinion as to potential sales, the predicted average sales are 5,000 dresses per store chainwide, but with a high variance. Assume potential sales are normally distributed with a standard deviation of 1,500. The dresses cost $40 and can be sold for $120. Unsold dresses can be sold at the end of the season to discount stores for $10. How many should be ordered?

13.4. Sales are brisk at the Christmas tree lot, but a tough decision must be made: It's two weeks until Christmas, and one final truckload of trees will arrive today. Currently, 100 trees remain on the lot. Sales for the 14 days until Christmas are normally distributed with a mean of 400, variance of 2,500. The average tree costs $30 and is sold for $70. Leftover trees have no value. How many should be purchased?

13.5. Dunkin' Donuts joined many other service providers by centralizing manufacturing. Doughnut making in a geographic area is now done centrally for many stores, and the doughnuts are trucked to stores in the early morning. Imagine the decision of the franchisee: Jelly-filled, sprinkle doughnuts cost $0.10 from the central facility, and sell for $0.60 each, and demand the past 10 days has been 50, 38, 27, 45, 62, 44, 44, 29, 31, 39. Day-old doughnuts are thrown out (hopefully). How many should be ordered?

13.6. Consider the stocking level of a single item: Waist 36, inseam 34, green plaid pattern #7, Johnny Miller actionwear slacks. Deliveries are weekly, and the store wishes to provide 98% service (fill rate). Shockingly, demand for this item is 8 per week, with a variance of 60, corresponding to the product Nega-Byno-Meal in the chapter example 13.2 on your Student CD. The pants cost the store $25 each. How much should be stocked, and how much will it cost, given each of the following strategies discussed in the chapter (weeks of sales, constant K, and marginal analysis)?

13.7. The rack of waist 36, inseam 34, Johnny Miller actionwear slacks can barely keep up with demand, and choices must be made. Consider just one other product in addition to the product in the previous problem: Green plaid pattern #8, which also costs $25 each, and also has demand of 8 per week, but the variance is 10. Only 25 total pairs of pants fit on the rack. How many of each should be chosen to provide the best service?

13.8. A distributor of Lincoln Electric motors typically carries inventory of 200 different motor types in its warehouse. Consider just three of these motors, one each corresponding to the distribution in example 13.3 on your Student CD (the negative binomial distribution). Each motor has a mean demand of 10, variance 20, but Motor 1 costs $20, Motor 2 costs $50, and Motor 3 costs $100. How much of each motor should be stocked to provide 90% service at the lowest cost?

Selected Bibliography

Agrawal, N. and A. Smith, 1996. Estimating Negative Binomial Demand for Retail Inventory Management with Unobservable Lost Sales, *Naval Research Logistics*, 43, 839-861.

Andersen Consulting 1996. *Where to Look for Incremental Sales Gains: The Retail Problem of Out-Of-Stock Merchandise.*

Cohen, M., Kamesam, P., Kleindorfer, P., Lee, H., and A Tekerian,1990. Optimizer: IBM's Multi-echelon Inventory System for Managing Service Logistics, *Interfaces*, 20(1), 65-82.

DeHoratius, N. and A. Raman, 2003. Building on Foundations of Sand? *ECR Journal*, 3(1), 62-68.

DeHoratius, N. and A. Raman, 2004a. Inventory Record Inaccuracy: An Empirical Analysis, Working Paper, Harvard Business School.

DeHoratius, N. and A. Raman, 2004b. Retail Performance Improvement Through Appropriate Store Manager Incentive Design: An Empirical Analysis, Working Paper, Harvard Business School.

Downs, B., Metters, R. and J. Semple 2001. Managing Inventory with Multiple Products, Lags in Delivery, Resource Constraints, and Lost Sales: a Mathematical Programming Approach, *Management Science*, 47(3), 464-479.

Helliker, K., 1995. Retailing Chains Offer A Lot of Opportunity, Young Managers Find, *The Wall Street Journal*, August 25, p. A1.

Ketzenberg, M., Metters, R., and V, Vargas, 2000. Inventory Policy for Dense Retail Stores, *Journal of Operations Management*, 18(3), 303-316.

Narayanan, V. 2003. How to Induce Retailers to Reduce Stockouts, Harvard Business School case 9-103-080, Cambridge, Ma.

Raman, A., N. DeHoratius, and Z. Ton, 2001. The Achilles' Heel of Supply Chain Management, Harvard Business Review, May.

Sherbrooke, C., 1992. *Optimal Inventory Modeling of Systems*, Wiley, New York.

Ton, Z. and A. Raman, 1999. Borders Group, Inc. *Harvard Business School* case 601-037.

Ton, Z. and A. Raman, 2004. The Effect of Product Variety and Inventory Levels on Misplaced Products at Retail Stores: A Longitudinal Study. Working paper, Harvard Business School.

Zipkin, P., 2000. *Foundations of Inventory Management*, Irwin McGraw/Hill, Boston.

CASE STUDY

K's Grocery[1]

The inventory decisions at K's grocery are made to be simple. An employee with a hand-held electronic ordering device walks down the aisle and notes whether a product has a full amount of inventory on the shelf. If not, the amount needed to fill the shelf is punched into the ordering device and the employee moves on. As an example, consider the 64-ounce bottle of Wesson Vegetable Oil. The product has three "facings," where facings are the slots allocated to a product on a shelf—the number of product containers facing a customer. On any one facing, 4 units of the 64 ounce bottle can fit in the depth of the shelf, so the 3 facings can hold a total of $4 \times 3 = 12$ units of product. Thus, the ordering policy for an employee is to order up to 12 units. If there are 8 units on the shelf, she orders 4 more.

The price the grocer pays for the 64 ounce bottle of Wesson Vegetable Oil is $2.00 and she sells it for $2.80, an average dry goods mark-up for grocery stores. Ordering is done twice a week, late in the day on Thursday and Monday. Ordering takes such a small amount of time per product that it can be considered "costless." The product is delivered and on the shelf by the next morning. The historical demand in the last 10 weeks for the Friday-Monday time frame is: 5, 7, 10, 9, 6, 7, 8, 7, 6, 8. The historical demand in the last 10 weeks for the Tuesday-Thursday time frame is: 7, 4, 1, 6, 6, 4, 5, 7, 5, 6. If there is a stockout, there's a 70% chance that a customer will just buy a different brand of oil. The other 30% of the time the sale is lost. When a sale is lost, not only does the grocer not get the profit margin, but there's also a penalty for disappointing a customer—disappoint a customer enough with stockouts of his or her favorite brand, and that customer is lost for life. Though it is hard to know exactly what the real penalty cost is, assume it is 50 cents for every lost sale. The product doesn't go "bad," so the cost of overstocking is the cost of any investment for the firm, which is approximately 15%/year of the money paid for the item.

Questions:

1. In terms of inventory related costs only, what is the optimal inventory policy, if 100% of the stockouts are lost sales?
2. In terms of inventory related costs only, what is the optimal inventory policy, given the substitution effect listed?
3. The product currently has 3 facings. If equally profitable products are available, with the same demand, how many facings should the 64 ounce bottle get? How does that decision change as the substitution percentage increases?
4. What should K's grocery do?

1. Adapted from Ketzenberg, 2000.

Waiting Time Management

LEARNING OBJECTIVES *The material in this chapter prepares students to:*

- Know why waiting lines are often mismanaged.

- Conceptually understand the nonintuitive nature of waiting lines.

- Find numerical solutions to simple waiting line problems.

- Understand the cost trade-offs involved in the strategic decision of centralizing versus decentralizing service providers.

- Provide strategies to reduce customers' perceived waiting

time or reduce the psychological cost of waiting.

- Additional material on the Student CD prepares students to find numerical solutions to more complex waiting line problems.[1]

Three primary reasons explain why waiting time management is worth studying:

1. The pervasiveness of waiting lines
2. The importance of the problem
3. The lack of managerial intuition surrounding waiting lines

PERVASIVENESS OF WAITING LINES

Waiting lines are ubiquitous in services. Certainly, waiting lines are a common enough problem in services that require a high degree of customer contact. We experience those lines as consumers constantly in restaurants, retail stores, and banks, among many other services. Waiting lines are also an important factor in services without face-to-face contact. A large purchaser of waiting line software is the call center industry. An estimated 4 to 6.5 million people in the United States work in a call center where the largest expense is personnel, at $100 to $200 billion annually. The techniques in this chapter enable you to determine how many people to hire and when to schedule their work time to provide the lowest customer waiting times for the least cost.

---

1. The subject of waiting time management poses both qualitative and quantitative problems. Although the chapter contains quantitative content, the focus will be on a qualitative understanding of the problems and some simple math to provide managers with a reasonable approximation of the results of their decisions. More quantitative material is available on the Student CD.

Waiting lines don't occur only in high-contact situations, however. Banks use the information in this chapter to determine how many ATMs to put in place. Back offices of banks, insurance agencies, package delivery firms, payment processing centers, and other services generally do not have customers physically walking in the door. Still, they must complete their work in a timely manner, and the amount of work that comes in daily can be highly variable. Consequently, even back-office services need the material in this chapter.

This chapter is also applicable to the "waiting lines" of e-mails to be answered, phone calls to return, or tasks in an in-box to be done. Regardless of what form the work may come in—face-to-face contact, information on a screen, or paper on the desk—anyone who cannot say to her customers, "I'll get to you when I feel like it," can benefit by knowing the principles behind waiting lines.

IMPORTANCE OF THE PROBLEM

Frequently, the amount of waiting time a customer endures is THE customer service standard. Waiting time often comes at the beginning of the service process and can have a "halo" or "pitchfork" effect on how customers view the rest of the service encounter; that is, whether customers view the rest of the service with either a favorable or highly critical eye depends on how they view their up-front wait. Especially in professional services, a customer often cannot tell whether his lawyer, doctor, or dentist did a good job. Results may be evident, but even the best doctors doing their best work may not be able to restore perfect health to a patient. Likewise, great lawyers lose some cases. However, one thing that customers can determine for themselves is whether they have been waiting an unreasonable amount of time, and that aspect can color the customers' perception of the entire service.

This material can be important because of the strong link to personnel requests. Analysis of this kind must be performed to obtain accurate numbers on how many people should be working in a service. As an example in the next few pages will show, if staffing needs are projected based on the total workload, without including waiting line math, a service will be chronically understaffed.

In addition to deciding how many people to hire, the material here presents a strong link to what those people should do. As will be shown, the level of service desired interacts with job descriptions and affects actual job content.

LACK OF MANAGERIAL INTUITION SURROUNDING WAITING LINES

Lastly, this material is important to study because it is not obvious. It is one of those topics where diligent, intelligent managers who work hard will arrive at drastically wrong answers if they fail to consider this material.

QUALITATIVE UNDERSTANDING OF WAITING LINES

Many people misunderstand why waiting lines form. It is often assumed that waiting lines form only because there's too much work for employees to do in an aggregate sense—for example, giving someone 15 hours of work to do in an eight-hour work-day will result in seven hours of the work waiting at the end of the day. However, waiting lines also form when there appear to be more than enough people to handle the tasks in aggregate. This brings us to basic rules of waiting lines.

Rule 1: Waiting Lines Form Even When Total Workload Is Less Than Capacity

If only six hours of work is given to someone working an eight-hour day, waiting lines will still occur, which is an exceedingly important lesson to learn when deciding how many people should staff a service. The reason is variance: Customers do not arrive in uniform time intervals, and the time it takes to serve them is often highly variable.

To put some numbers to this idea, take the *waiting line pop quiz*.

Question: How long is the waiting line if a customer arrives exactly every 15 seconds and can be served in exactly 14 seconds?

Answer: No waiting line forms at all. This scenario is like an assembly line in a manufacturing plant, where the worker has one second every 15 to relax, put his or her feet up, and read the newspaper.

Question: How long is the waiting line if a customer arrives not exactly every 15 seconds, but 15 seconds on average, and can be served in, on average, every 14 seconds (and the arrivals and service times correspond to probability distributions discussed later)?

Answer: The length of the waiting line will average 13 people. The number of people in line will bounce up and down, with no one utilizing the system 7% of the time, but 13 will be the average number waiting. (The calculations needed to determine this answer will be shown later.) Even though a customer may arrive on average every 15 seconds, on some occasions five customers may arrive in a 15-second span while at other times no customers may arrive for a few minutes. Further, on those occasions when five customers arrive in a short span, the first customer waited on sometimes takes 90 seconds to satisfy, causing a great deal of waiting for everyone else, even though enough capacity appears to be available, in aggregate.

Rule 2: Waiting Lines Are Not Linearly Related to Capacity

This second rule of waiting lines defies managerial common sense, because nearly everyone not trained in the mathematics of waiting lines assumes a linear relationship exists between capacity and waiting lines. To visualize this concept, consider the next *waiting line pop quiz*:

Question: If one bank teller is working and the average number of customers in line is 12 (point A on Figure 14.1), what would be the average number of customers in line when a second bank teller is hired?

Answer: In dozens of presentations to undergraduates, MBA students, and executives, the overwhelming response is that, of course, the line would be cut in half when capacity is doubled. Increase from one to two employees, and the line will drop from 12 to six (point B on Figure 14.1). Unfortunately, this linear "natural" response is dead wrong. As will be demonstrated numerically later, doubling capacity usually causes waiting lines to decrease by more than 90%, and the line will drop from 12 to about one (point C on Figure 14.1). The good news about Figure 14.1 is that adding just a bit of capacity can solve many waiting line situations. The bad news about Figure 14.1 is that this relationship is not as well known in the business world as it should be.

Top management, however, is generally more interested in profit and loss than waiting time statistics. The relationships in Figure 14.1 drive the ultimate dollar relationships in Figure 14.2. The cost of adding capacity is easy for managers to see and tends to be linear: If one employee is $25/hour, two employees are $50/hour, and so

FIGURE 14.1: *Waiting Line Math*

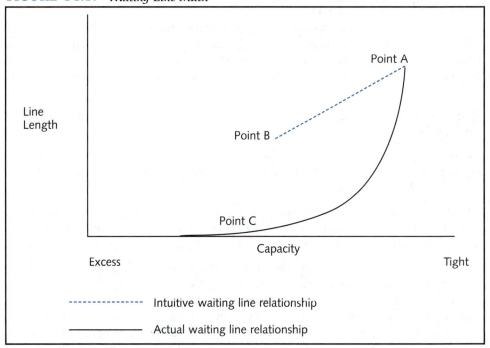

FIGURE 14.2: *Economics of Waiting Lines*

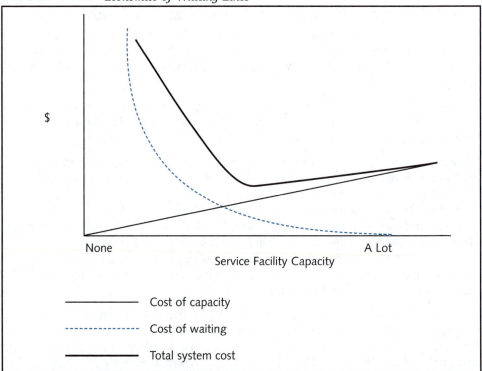

SERVICE OPERATIONS MANAGEMENT PRACTICES

Answering the Phone at L.L.Bean

"I've been on hold forever—think I'll try Lands' End instead."

Most of L.L.Bean's business comes through a telephone call center, and a large portion of that business comes in the concentrated time period six weeks prior to Christmas. If customers get busy signals, or stay on hold too long, many of them will take their business elsewhere. Because of their staffing plans, in some time slots 80% of the incoming calls received a busy signal, and customers who got through were on hold 10 minutes waiting for an agent. Lost sales were approaching $500,000 on some days, and because they were calling on "toll-free" numbers, L.L.Bean was paying $25,000 per day in telephone charges to keep their customers on hold.

Of course, it is not profitable to employ enough staff to answer every call. As the numbers in this chapter show, to do so would mean lots of employee idle time when calls are running low. L.L.Bean implemented a queuing and staffing model based on the economics of lost sales, telephone charges, and salaries to employees. This model shifted their staffing schedules to give them the right number of people at the right time to reach the level of service they were seeking.

The results: The percentage of callers giving up dropped 81% and the average time on hold decreased 83%. L.L.Bean increased profits by $9 million a year due to this study, and the study cost only $40,000.

Source: Condensed from Quinn, Andrews, and Parsons (1991).

on. The cost of waiting can be internal or external: Your own employees waiting in line—while collecting pay—or customers sitting on hold and eventually hanging up. This cost is nonlinear and rises in the same manner as the line length in Figure 14.1. For an example of a firm that went through the process of finding the best balance between the profits lost from customers waiting and the costs of hiring more people, see the Service Operations Management Practices: Answering the Phone at L.L.Bean.

To see how Figures 14.1 and 14.2 can possibly be right, and to demonstrate the two rules of waiting lines, we introduce Example 14.1.

EXAMPLE 14.1: *Teller Staffing at Feehappy Bank and Trust*

As the new manager of the Wilmington branch of Jones B&T, Katrina must decide how many tellers she should staff. The target market for Wilmington is the high net worth customer. Jones charges high fees but promises superior service, so waiting times must be kept short. To make the problem simpler to solve, assume that the branch is open from 8:00 A.M. to 4 P.M. weekdays, no work occurs before opening or after closing, and that the workers refuse to take any lunch breaks. (To see how normal employees may change this analysis, see the case study on teller staffing at the end of the chapter.)

To figure out how many tellers to staff, a study was conducted to determine what amount of work needed to be performed. Table 14.1 shows the various transactions performed by the tellers, the amount of time they take, and what percentage of total transactions this category represents. The expected transaction time, calculated from Table 14.1, is $10(0.05) + 25(0.05) + \ldots + 3(0.35) = 5$ minutes. Consequently, a teller could be expected to perform an average of 12 transactions per hour.

Table 14.2 shows how many customers enter the branch by time of day. In this table three particular days are surveyed and the average number of customers is in the far right column. We make the simplifying assumptions that every day is the same in terms of incoming customers and that each customer makes one transaction.

In aggregate, Table 14.1 shows that each worker should be able to help 12 customers per hour, and Table 14.2 shows that an average of 180 customers per day come by: This means that there are $180/12 = 15$ hours of work to do in an eight-hour workday. If only all the bank customers would drop their work off in the morning and kindly say to the tellers, "Please handle this whenever you can find the time," the work could be inventoried, only two tellers would need to be hired, and each teller would even be able to relax for a half-hour per day.

Unfortunately, as we will show, two tellers would result in quite poor service. Two different sources of variance cause the "two teller" or manufacturing-based solution to be a bad one.

TABLE 14.1: *Work Content at Jones*

Work Content for the Average Customer

Transaction	Average Minutes	Percentage of Transactions
Cashiers' check	10	5%
Open checking account	25	5%
Deposit/cash back	2	25%
Straight deposit	1	10%
Corporate deposit	8	10%
Balance inquiry	1	5%
Dispute	15	5%
Other	3	35%

Average transaction: 5 minutes

Transactions performed in an hour by one teller: 60/ 5 = 12

TABLE 14.2: *Customer Arrivals at Jones*

Time	May 1	May 8	May 15	Average Number of Transactions
8:00-9:00 A.M.	6	12	9	9
9:00-10:00 A.M.	4	11	12	9
10:00-11:00 A.M.	18	24	39	27
11:00-Noon	52	28	28	36
Noon-1:00 P.M.	40	60	35	45
1:00-2:00 P.M.	31	25	25	27
2:00-3:00 P.M.	25	10	19	18
3:00-4:00 P.M.	5	7	15	9
Total:	181	177	182	180

180 transactions × 5 minutes/transaction × 1 hour/60 minutes = 15 hours of work/day

15 hours of work = 1.875 workers

TABLE 14.3: *Variance of Customer Arrivals During the Day*

Workers Handle 12 Transactions per hour

Time	Number of Transactions	Workers Needed
8:00-9:00 A.M.	9	1
9:00-10:00 A.M.	9	1
10:00-11:00 A.M.	27	3
11:00-Noon	36	3
Noon-1:00 P.M.	45	4
1:00-2:00 P.M.	27	3
2:00-3:00 P.M.	18	2
3:00-4:00 P.M.	9	1

SOURCE OF VARIANCE 1: WITHIN DAY VARIANCE

Table 14.3 shows how many tellers are needed at different times of the day. As with many other retail firms, lighter traffic characteristically occurs early in the morning and toward the end of the day, with heavy traffic at traditional lunch hours. Although only one worker might be able to handle the early customers, the noontime rush requires at least four tellers. Given this typical intraday pattern, the best solution for Feehappy would be to hire only one full-time employee and a host of part-time workers, one of whom works only from noon to 1:00 P.M. every day. Unfortunately, such a plan is not realistic, and intraday variance often requires that more workers be available than are needed for that time slot's average.

SOURCE OF VARIANCE 2: SERVICE TIME AND CUSTOMER ARRIVAL TIME VARIANCE

Table 14.4 shows an extreme case of service time and customer arrival variance. On an average day, between 11:00 A.M. and noon, 36 transactions would occur, taking five minutes each, requiring 36 × 5/60 = 3 workers. This number of transactions establishes only an average. Consider the day May 1 in Table 14.2: 52 transactions took place on that day and time. What if those transactions included more time commitment transactions, such as more account openings, than average? For Table 14.4, we assume that the average transaction time took seven minutes rather than the usual five. In that case we would need 52 × 7/60 = 6 workers. Therefore, we would need six workers to do the work that could be done by only two workers if we could inventory the work.

However, the crush of customers in aggregate may not be the sole cause of a need for more employees. Table 14.5 gives some specific numbers to the example in

TABLE 14.4: *Variance of Transaction Times and Number of Customers*

Average day, 11:00 A.M. to Noon
  36 transactions × 5 minutes/transaction = 180 minutes of work
  180 minutes of work = 3 workers

May 1, 11:00 A.M. to Noon
  52 transactions: 6 accounts opened, 4 disputes . . .
    (higher than average transaction time)
  52 transactions × 7 minutes/transaction = 364 minutes of work

  364 minutes of work = 6 workers

TABLE 14.5: *A Tale of Two Tellers*

One Teller Scenario

Arrival Time	Transaction	Transaction Time	Waiting Time	Leaves Teller
08:00	Balance inquiry	1	0	8:01
08:04	Deposit/cash back	2	0	8:06
08:08	Open account	25	0	8:33
08:19	Cashier's check	10	14	8:43
08:25	Other	3	18	8:46
08:29	Deposit/cash back	2	17	8:48
08:46	Straight deposit	1	2	8:49
08:52	Other	3	0	8:55
08:54	Other	3	1	8:58
Total		50	52	

Two Teller Scenario

Arrival Time	Transaction	Transaction Time	Waiting Time	Leaves Teller 1	Leaves Teller 2
08:00	Balance inquiry	1	0	8:01	
08:04	Deposit/cash back	2	0		8:06
08:08	Open account	25	0	8:33	
08:19	Cashier's check	10	0		8:29
08:25	Other	3	4		8:32
08:29	Deposit/cash back	2	3		8:34
08:46	Straight deposit	1	0	8:47	
08:52	Other	3	0		8:55
08:54	Other	3	0	8:57	
Total		50	7		

Figure 14.1 (the example of doubling capacity from one to two tellers). The first series in Table 14.5 demonstrates *Rule 1: Waiting lines form even when total workload is less than capacity.* Table 14.5 shows that even though only 50 total minutes of work is being done in an hour, horrendous lines can still form. Consider an average 8:00–9:00 A.M. time period, where the average number of customers show up with average transactions, or nine customers with a little more than five minutes per transaction. One would think that with only 50 minutes of actual work to do in an hour, a single teller should be able to handle the job, but Table 14.5 shows that the "one teller scenario" results in a total of 52 minutes of waiting for customers. The second series on Table 14.5 demonstrates *Rule 2: Waiting lines are not linearly related to capacity.* As promised by Figure 14.1, doubling the number of tellers to two doesn't just cut the waiting time in half, but cuts waiting time from 52 minutes to just 7. However, the trade-off for better customer service means a steep price in productivity. The one teller scenario pays for 60 minutes and gets 50 minutes' worth of work, or a productivity rate of 83%, while the two teller scenario operates at only 42% productivity.

QUANTITATIVE METHODS: SINGLE SERVER MODEL

Although the preceding tables and figures contribute to an intuitive understanding of waiting lines, they do not solve the basic question of Example 14.1: How many tellers should be hired? How often will customers be spaced the way they are in Table 14.5, and how frequently will the customer arrivals be like Table 14.4?

To start, we make some simplifying assumptions about the system we are facing.[2] Given these assumptions, only two basic quantities must be known to calculate how many tellers we need:

$$\lambda \text{ (lambda)} = \text{ Arrival rate (example: people per hour)}$$

$$\mu \text{ (mu)} = \text{ Service rate (example: people per hour)}$$

Once these basic quantities are calculated, all the basic service information such as the average time in line, average line length, and so on, can be calculated for this system according to the calculation in Table 14.6.

For Jones B&T at 8:00–9:00 A.M., $\lambda = 9$ people per hour, and $\mu = 12$ people per hour, so with a single teller the average time in line would be $\lambda/[\mu(\mu - \lambda)] = 9/36 = 1/4$ hour or 15 minutes. Adding a second teller requires some mathematics that are a bit more complicated, but consider a similar idea that is roughly equivalent: Hire a teller that is twice as fast as a regular teller. With this "super teller" the average time in line would drop to $9/[24(24 - 9)] = 9/360$ hour, or 1.5 minutes, a 90% decrease from the original solution.

As for the general number of tellers to staff, it depends on the desired service level. If the four-teller equivalent were hired, average wait times would be 18.8 minutes for the lunch rush, which is probably unacceptable for catering to high net worth individuals. The five-teller equivalent results in an average 3-minute wait at lunch. If service is to be really stellar, perhaps the 1½-minute wait of the six-teller equivalent would be

---

TABLE 14.6: *Basic Waiting Line Model*

Assumptions: 1 server, customer arrivals Poisson distributed, service time exponentially distributed

λ = Arrival rate (example: people per hour)
μ = Service rate (example: people per hour)

$1/\lambda$ = Average time between arrivals (example: minutes per person)
$1/\mu$ = Average service time (example: minutes per person)

Steady state calculations of managerial interest

ρ = Utilization = λ/μ (percentage of time the server is busy)

n_L = Average number in line = $\lambda^2/[\mu(\mu - \lambda)]$
n_S = Average number in the system = $\lambda/(\mu - \lambda)$

t_L = Average time in line = $\lambda/[\mu(\mu - \lambda)]$
t_S = Average time in the system = $1/(\mu - \lambda)$

P_n = Probability of n people in the system = $(1 - \lambda/\mu)(\lambda/\mu)^n$

Service rate necessary given a specific time in line goal:

$$\mu = \frac{\lambda t_L + \sqrt{(\lambda t_L)^2 + 4\lambda t_L}}{2t_L}$$

The formulas above are already programmed in an Excel spreadsheet on the Student CD called "queue.xls" under the "infinite queues" worksheet. This spreadsheet was written by John McClain, Johnson Graduate School of Management, Cornell University.

Access your Student CD now for the Queue.xls spreadsheet containing the formulas.

---

2. Technical considerations: The waiting line is from an infinite source of customers with an infinite potential line length, the number of arrivals per unit time is Poisson distributed, there is no balking or reneging, and service times are exponentially distributed. These distributions are used both because they are found to represent many business situations well, and they result in the simple equations found in Table 14.6. The results provided by the formulas used here are "steady rate" results; that is, the results that would accrue if these systems were run at the indicated levels indefinitely.

more appropriate. The important idea here is that using these methods provides managers with information about their potential choices. Table 14.7 assesses the potential choices.

Note that such solutions would result in enormous amounts of idle time throughout the day. Consequently, if high service solutions are desired, it is usually valuable to include in those job descriptions numerous duties that are not time dependent and can be done at the employee's leisure during the inevitable downtime between customers.

CENTRALIZING WAITING LINES: MULTIPLE SERVERS

An important strategic decision for many services is the level of centralization. For example, should an information systems group within a company be a separate, centralized unit that serves the whole company, or should each company division form its own information systems group? As an example that many consumers can relate to, should an airline operate a few large call centers or dozens of call centers located throughout the country? A separate call center in each major city would reduce telephone charges, but airlines find that with a few centrally located, large centers, often with 1,000 or more employees, the increased telephone charges are more than offset by the personnel cost benefits of centralization.

To see how this strategy might work intuitively, consider the following "social" situation: The "party problem." Consider a party with two bartenders. Should both bartenders be in the same room, perhaps next to each other, or should they be in separate rooms where the line at one cannot be seen by patrons in another? If the goal is to require guests to stand in line as little as possible, then the two bartenders' lines should be within eyesight of each other. If the two bartenders are together, it's not possible for one to have a long line while the other is idle. If they are in separate rooms, however, different line lengths could easily be the case. As is discussed in the additional quantitative material on the Student CD, putting two separated bartenders together can cut waiting in line by 30%.

The "party problem" seems to be somewhat trivial, but the role of queue centralization is a serious business issue. Table 14.8 shows a potential set of choices faced by those who wish to set up a telephone call center system. Consider a system that

Access your Student CD now for Table 14.7 as an Excel worksheet.

TABLE 14.7: *Average Minutes Waiting in Line at Jones B&T*

(single server calculations based on Table 14.6)

Time of Day	Number of Tellers*						
	1	2	3	4	5	6	7
8:00-9:00 A.M.	15.0	1.5	0.6	0.3	0.2	0.1	0.1
9:00-10:00 A.M.	15.0	1.5	0.6	0.3	0.2	0.1	0.1
10:00-11:00 A.M.	**	**	5.0	1.6	0.8	0.5	0.3
11:00-Noon	**	**	**	3.8	1.5	0.8	0.5
Noon-1:00 P.M.	**	**	**	18.8	3.0	1.4	0.8
1:00-2:00 P.M.	**	**	5.0	1.6	0.8	0.5	0.3
2:00-3:00 P.M.	**	7.5	1.7	0.8	0.4	0.3	0.2
3:00-4:00 P.M.	15.0	1.5	0.6	0.3	0.2	0.1	0.1

*Assumes a single teller with the speed of the number of tellers shown.

**"Steady state" averages cannot be reached. Workload greater than capacity. As time continues, waiting lines would continue to increase without end.

TABLE 14.8: *Centralization of Waiting Lines*

Example: Telephone Call Center
 Average handle time per call = 3 minutes
 Service level desired: Average seconds to answer = 10
 Call volume = 4,000 calls per hour

Facilities	Call Volume per Facility	Workload Hours per Facility	Staff Required per Facility*	Total Staff Required
20	200	10	14	280
8	500	25	30	240
4	1,000	50	56	224
2	2,000	100	107	214
1	4,000	200	209	209

*Staffing numbers based on the Erlang-C probability distribution, which are not shown in this text, but is the most common distribution used in practice for determining call center capacity.

receives 4,000 calls per hour with an average handle time of three minutes per call, or 4,000 × 3/60 = 200 hours worth of work to do in an hour. Given a service objective of taking an average of 10 seconds to answer a call, some choices on facilities are given in Table 14.8. At the extremes, one could have one large call center employing 209 people, or one could have 20 smaller centers that each employ 14 people. The mathematics of queue centralization cause the choice between hiring 209 or 14 × 20 = 280 people to provide the same level of service.

ADVANCED QUEUING MODELS

Quantitative material on advanced queuing modeling techniques can be found on the Student CD. The material includes:

- formulas for multiple channel queues
- adapting the formulas on Table 14.6 to constant service times
- the general system approximation
- priority queues

Access your Student CD now for quantitative material on advanced queuing models.

THE PSYCHOLOGY OF QUEUING

The famous philosopher Berkeley claimed that "perception is essence," which is clearly the case in waiting lines. How long customers wait in line matters far less than how long they *believe* they wait or whether they perceive the wait to be fair or unfair. The perception of waiting times can be drastically different from the waiting times that actually occurred. When people are asked how long they waited for a service, it is not unusual for their answer to be either half as much or twice as much time as actually passed. In one research project, a customer timed at waiting 90 seconds in line claimed to be waiting more than 11 minutes.

Researchers developed several rules concerning the management of the psychology of queues (e.g., Katz, Larson, and Larson, 1991).

- **Perception is more important than reality.**

Researchers found that the overall opinion of a customer correlates more highly with how long the customer thinks he waited than how long he really has been waiting. Consequently, being attuned to the psychological aspect of waiting lines can be vital.

- **Unoccupied time feels longer than occupied time.**

Operational Action: Distract and entertain with related or unrelated activity.

Time waiting with nothing to do feels longer. The hands of the clock appear to move more slowly when a customer is not occupied. In reaction, businesses should attempt to distract the customer.

One story in operations' lore tells of a large Boston hotel that received complaints about long waiting times for the elevators. Instead of installing more elevators, management changed the wall covering in the elevator lobby to mirrors, presumably to allow the guests to check out their hairdos while waiting. As the story goes, the number of complaints plummeted.

Many businesses adopt similar strategies. A cottage industry centers around songwriters who focus on small ditties played to customers on telephone hold. Southwest Airlines is legendary for its humorous approach to telephone holds. One time it ran a recording that asked customers a series of questions, only to tell the customer at the end of the session that the survey served no purpose other than to help her pass the time. A number of banks and hospitals attempt to deal with the psychology of waiting by installing televisions or newswires for waiting customers to view, but the results have been mixed, with some efforts actually decreasing customer satisfaction.

- **Preprocess waits feel longer than in-process waits.**

Operational Action: Communicate as soon as possible and get customers "in process."

Amusement park waiting lines can be long, hot, and dull. Disney, however, makes customers feel "in process" while waiting by having entertainment to view and listen to in the line. Restaurants can provide menus or drinks to waiting customers to make them feel in process.

Medical offices also practice this technique. Customers waiting in a large holding area do not know whether they will ever be helped, so the wait seems longer. However, when moved to a different waiting area—an examination room—patients realized that they were in process, so a 20-minute wait in the lounge and a 10-minute wait in the exam room seemed less than a 30-minute wait in the lounge.

- **Uncertain or unexplained waits feel longer than known waits.**

Operational Action: Communicate frequently.

Amusement parks are also adept at setting customer expectations as to how long their wait will be, thereby reducing anxiety. Seeing a line for the "Killer Koaster" stretch into the distant horizon is dispiriting not only for the certainty of a long wait, but the uncertainty of whether the wait may be 30 minutes, 90 minutes, or four hours. However, when one sees the sign stating, "Your wait will be 3 days, 9 minutes from this point," one finds some comfort from removal of the uncertainty. Further yet, many such signs deliberately overestimate the time required, so that when the front of the line is reached in only 2 days, the customers are actually happy that they beat expectations.

This psychological aspect of waiting is seen frequently in appointment situations. If a customer arrives at 1:45 for a 2:00 appointment, the first 15 minutes of waiting pass quickly psychologically because the customer is anchored to a 2:00 time frame. However, any unexplained wait after 2:00 is viewed as the work of an international conspiracy aimed at the customer. This is because the customer is no longer mentally anchored to a time. The customer lacks an expectation of when his or her wait will end to replace the original expectation of 2:00. The way to avoid this feeling is to continue to acknowledge the customer, provide a reason for lateness, and anchor the customer to another time that will be met.

Customers also form expectations due to a physical setup. For example, a West Texas bank experienced a rush of activity every Friday as a number of customers received weekly paychecks. To be sensitive to customer needs, the banker physically installed a dozen teller windows—up from the usual three—to be used solely on Fridays to accommodate the rush. Unfortunately, he reported that customer satisfaction declined the rest of the week when customers entering the branch saw a dozen teller windows available, but only three tellers behind them. This situation constituted an unexplained wait for these customers.

- **Unfair waits feel longer**.

  Operational Action: Physically segment different markets.

  Especially within the United States, any line that is not first-come, first-served is viewed as unfair. Unfortunately, to be successful, businesses must use the most-important-customer-first rule instead. This rule can be applied more easily in non-face-to-face situations such as telephone call centers. Software now available can recognize incoming telephone calls from important customers and push those calls to the head of the line. In face-to-face situations, the best method is to physically segment customers so that different customer classes no longer can view the service differential. This practice is prominent in banking, where high-end customers are often served outside the traditional bank branch system.

  Some examples of "unfair"—or not first-come, first-served—systems that are tolerated by customers include the separate check-in lines for first-class airline passengers, the "12 items or less" lines at grocers, and the "commercial accounts" lines at banks. The more businesses can move to these segmented line strategies, the more profitable they can become.

Summary

The waiting line problem is an important one for many services. It often forms the basis of the customer service quality judgment. Further, it is a problem that is inherently nonlinear and, therefore, difficult for managers to understand. Thoughtful, hard-working managers who are responsible for hiring decisions but do not understand this material can find themselves chronically short staffed and not know why.

Waiting line systems are not simply numbers, though. Marketing and operations must jointly attack the problem both through number crunching and by attacking the psychology components of waiting. Appropriately setting customer expectations and responding to unspoken customer needs for reassurance can be just as effective as adding expensive capacity.

Many waiting line situations are too complex for either the formulas discussed in this chapter. For those systems, simulation, rather than plugging in formulas, is the best way to discover answers to managerial questions. The simulation of complex systems is discussed in Chapter 9.

Access your Student CD now for information on advanced queuing models.

Review Questions

1. Why do waiting lines form even when more than enough capacity is available to handle customers?
2. What are the major cost trade-offs for managers to consider in waiting line situations?
3. What is the basic reason that centralizing waiting lines reduces wait times?
4. What are some techniques that can be used to manage customers' perceptions of wait times?

Problems

14.1. Mary Jane Smith, sole employee of The Office of Student Complaints About Operations Courses, has an irate visitor every 20 minutes on average, and the visitor takes an average of 15 minutes to handle. Assuming Poisson arrivals and exponential service times:
   a. What percentage of time is Mary Jane idle?
   b. How long is the line, and how much time do students spend waiting, on average?

14.2. If a server takes precisely 15 seconds to serve a customer and customers arrive exactly every 20 seconds, what is the average waiting line length?
   a. –5.3
   b. 0
   c. 2.25
   d. Infinite
   e. None of the above

14.3. If the customer arrival and service time numbers in problem 14.2 are not exact, but only averages conforming to the exponential distribution, what would be the average line length?

14.4. Due to its size, Incredibly Big Discount Store positions a service desk at both ends of the store, about a mile apart. John staffs the north entrance, where 18 customers arrive per hour. Marsha staffs the south entrance, where 12 customers arrive per hour. Both can serve a customer in three minutes. Assuming Poisson arrivals and exponential service times, how long is the line and how much time do customers spend waiting, on average?

14.5. (Appendix material) John and Marsha from problem 14.4 fell in love and petitioned management to move their service desks next to each other. Aside from the humanitarian benefits, what will be the effect on customer waiting?

14.6. Your summer internship takes you to a Southwest Airlines reservation center. The 1,000 telephone service representatives answer calls concerning flight times, book reservations, handle customer complaints, and so on. The following memo requesting additional service reps is on your desk.

"Worker utilization is getting too low. Our workers now average about 20% idle time. The average waiting time for our customers is now only five seconds. That is, they spend an average of only five seconds on hold before service reps can answer their calls. In keeping with our low cost philosophy, I recommend that we cut the work force by 10%. The increase in customer hold time to 5.5 seconds is a trade-off that I believe is warranted by the cost savings."

Is this analysis appropriate? Why or why not?

14.7. Eric Johnson started the Johnson Grocery Company after years of frustration in not being able to get good, fresh baked goods in Nashville. Johnson Grocery originally specialized in cakes, tarts, breads, and doughnuts sold from Eric's home. His success among the affluent, gourmet food crowd allowed him to expand to a second store within six months and to a half-dozen outlets within the first year. Due to customer requests, he expanded into bagels, ready-made salads, and other manufacturers' products such as gourmet ice cream and gourmet pet food.

Once Eric got beyond a dozen stores, the expense and administrative burden of overseeing all those kitchens caused Eric to maintain a central kitchen/supply location downtown that restocked all the stores. Currently, the distribution center is causing problems in the form of underutilized employees and long lines for truck loading.

The loading dock at the distribution center will accommodate only one truck for loading or unloading at a time. Company-owned trucks arrive according to a Poisson distribution with a mean rate of three trucks per day. At present the company employs a crew of three to load and unload the trucks, and the unloading/loading rate is Poisson distributed with a mean rate of five trucks per day. The company can employ additional (or fewer) persons in the loading crew and increase the average loading rate by one truck per day for each additional employee up to a maximum of six persons who can be utilized effectively in the process (for example, four workers could load/unload six per day, or two workers could load/unload four per day). The company estimates that the cost of an idle truck and driver is $40 per hour and the company pays $12 per hour (including benefits) for each employee in the loading crew.

Eric called in Luke Froeb, foreman of the loading crew, to his office to discuss the problem. Luke contends that they are overstaffed. He dislikes seeing idle workers, and is roundly feared by the loading crew. "We can be more profitable if we fire one of these so-called workers," Luke said. "They are always just sitting around waiting for trucks to come in."

Luke's comments seemed true enough, but the trucking supervisor, Bruce Barry, had earlier told Eric that the truckers' feelings were hurt by the long lines they had to sit in waiting to be unloaded.

   a. Advise Eric on the proper number of loading dock personnel to employ to minimize costs under the current system.

   b. Comment on his business plan. Also, note any operational changes that could be made to improve the situation.

14.8. The words of Big Boss echo in your head: "I don't want to see any of our customers on hold more than 20 seconds, but don't go crazy with the number of employees either."

One of your responsibilities is a small telephone call center. You receive 1,000 calls per hour, every hour, from 8 A.M. to 5 P.M. If all operators are busy the call is automatically placed on hold. Each call lasts an average of two minutes. Employees go to lunch at either 11:00 or 12:00 for one hour; no other lunch choices and no other breaks are offered. Use the adapted single server queuing models (Table 14.6) to determine how many employees you should employ.

14.9. What is better from a waiting line perspective: One employee who is twice as fast as a normal employee, or two employees?

14.10. After graduating with a degree in operations from Big State U., Joan found her job of a lifetime at Yukon Savings of Nome, Alaska, and she was put in charge of operations. A memo from her assistant, Dave, a classmate of hers at BSU, dealt with waiting lines at ATMs. "Recently, I heard customer complaints of intolerable waiting times at our ATMs. I suggest we study the matter further. I would like your approval to hire 50 data collectors to view waiting lines around the state. This entire process should be completed in three weeks at a cost of less than $100,000."

Joan sadly shook her head and thought, "If only Dave had paid more attention in operations class. We can get the information we need directly from the data we already have."

Each ATM logs a time entry for the beginning and end of each transaction. Analyze the following data for 1:00 P.M. to 3:00 P.M. and determine the extent of the problem.

Transaction Begins	Transaction Ends
1:00	1:01
1:01	1:03
1:03	1:10
1:10	1:14
1:14	1:22
1:22	1:23
1:30	1:31
1:31	1:33
1:33	1:44
1:44	1:47
1:57	2:02
2:06	2:08

Transaction Begins	Transaction Ends
2:08	2:18
2:18	2:21
2:21	2:22
2:34	2:38
2:38	2:39
2:39	2:41
2:49	2:50
2:55	2:58

14.11. (Appendix material) Your current facility employs six servers and has an average line length of 6.66. How long would the line be if a seventh server is added?

14.12. You landed a choice job as operations manager of a new fast-food chain, Continental Cuisine. Continental Cuisine plans to serve a large array of non-traditional fast foods to go, such as veal picata and steak diane, in a bit more time than is required to serve traditional fast foods. The operational key to success is the plan to have a number of mini-kitchens available to your servers.

As operations chief you must choose between four alternative service designs suggested:

- In design #1, customers enter the system, wait in one line for the first server to place an order, then the second server completes the service. At that point the next customer places an order.
- In design #2, separate waiting lines form in front of each server, where each server takes the orders from customers and processes them.
- Design #3 is similar to design #2, except that customers join only one queue.
- In design #4, customers form a single waiting line and are served by a service team consisting of two servers. One server takes the customer's order and then both servers work together to prepare the order. Due to the tasks involved in preparation, work can easily be split in half between the team.

Preliminary studies indicate that arrival and service times are appropriate for the use of queuing formulas. The average ordering time is small, averaging 30 seconds. Preparation time, on the other hand, is long, averaging 12 minutes. Which service design do you choose and why?

Selected Bibliography

Katz, K., B. Larson, and R. Larson. 1991. Prescription for the Waiting-in-Line Blues: Entertain, Enlighten, and Engage. *Sloan Management Review*, 32(2), 44–53.

Quinn, P., B. Andrews, and H. Parsons. 1991. Allocating Telecommunications Resources at L.L. Bean, Inc. *Interfaces*, 21(1), 75–91.

Randhawa, S., A. Mechling, and R. Joerger. 1989. A Simulation-Based Resource-Planning System for the Oregon Motor Vehicles Division. *Interfaces*, 19(6), 40–51.

CASE STUDY

Queuing Psychology and the Oregon Department of Motor Vehicles[3]

The news was shocking and, as usual, work ground to a halt in the Oregon Department of Motor Vehicles North Eugene branch. A memo with the governor's signature stated that their new mission was, "to serve the Oregon public." This new mission statement immediately replaced their prior mission, which seemed to many as, "to be personally amused by annoying the Oregon public."

It was clear that such a radical change in mission required a change in operational strategy. Currently, the DMV, staffed by five counter operators, one of whom also functioned as the manager, processed approximately 40 different types of transactions, each with separate forms and procedures. The Oregon public could enter one of four different lines, depending on the transaction type they needed.

Lines averaged a steady 10–12 people at each station. Whenever lines exceeded 20, the employee at that window closed the window and spent the next 15 minutes on a coffee break. The coffee pot and break room were positioned at the center of the office so that the DMV employees on break could get a good look at how angry their customers would become. Most amusing of all, 9% of the customers were in the wrong line and had to wait in a second line to complete their transactions. A loudly stifled guffaw from the employees alerted one another to such a customer. Another 18% had incomplete paperwork and were required to return another day. Combined, these groups of customers took virtually no time to wait on and, consequently, the productivity of the office (measured by customers served per employee) was one of the best in the state.

Questions:

1. What queuing psychology rules are being broken at the Oregon DMV and what should be done to fix the problems?
2. Although many of the behaviors in the Oregon DMV case are not true, these particular numbers are true and need attention: 9% of the customers were in the wrong line and had to wait in a second line to complete their transactions, and another 18% had incomplete paperwork and were required to return another day. What can be done to address this situation?

3. *Source*: Adapted in part from Randhawa, Mechling, and Joerger (1989).

CASE STUDY

Staffing and Scheduling
Bank Branch Tellers

Banking hours for your branch are from 9:00 A.M. to 5:00 P.M. Monday through Thursday, and 9:00 A.M. to 7:00 P.M. on Friday. The bank lobby area contains six teller spaces, and a drive-through facility offers three spaces. Due to the bank configuration, tellers cannot handle customers in both the lobby and drive-through.

Data were collected for both customer arrival patterns and service times. The average numbers of customer arrivals for both the drive-through and lobby are in Table 14.9. The average time it takes to serve a customer in both the lobby and drive-through averaged three minutes. An overall service goal for the bank was that customers should not have to wait more than an average of two minutes in line. Use the formulas provided in the text to determine staff requirements during the week.[4]

Translating staff requirements to an actual employee schedule can be a difficult task. Employees cannot be scheduled for more than 40 hours/week. Part-time employees are to be avoided, if possible, due to their higher cost. If part-time employees are used, they must be scheduled in at least four-hour blocks. Tellers are entitled to a paid 15-minute break each day, an unpaid one-hour lunch break, and an additional 30-minute break on Friday for supper. Regulations state that workers cannot work more than five-hour blocks without a meal break. Tellers were scheduled to work 8:30 A.M. to 5:15 P.M. Monday through Thursday and until 7:15 P.M. on Friday due to necessary prep and closing work.

The head teller at each branch takes on extra duties that require an hour per day away from the teller line, but these duties do not require a one-hour block.

Questions:

1. Determine the overall amount of work required in a week. If inventory could be used, how many tellers would be needed?
2. Determine the personnel requirements for each hour of the day using queuing formulas and taking into consideration the service goal.
3. If the purpose is to meet the requirements from the queuing model with the fewest number of staff, fill out Table 14.10 with your solution. Due to the different work hours required on Fridays, separate tables will be needed for at least Monday–Thursday and Friday. Table 14.10 contains room for eight personnel, although it is unlikely that you will need that many. Each employee schedule should contain a designation for the 15-minute break and lunch breaks. The head teller also requires administrative time off.

---

4. The one-server formulas in Table 14.6 are not technically correct for this multiple server problem. However, they may still be used and will provide an upper bound on the number of tellers needed. Alternatively, the formulas and tables in the appendix may be used to increase accuracy.

CASE STUDY

4. What would be the savings in personnel of rearranging the branch so that tellers would be able to handle both drive-through and lobby traffic?
5. Consider the effect of absent employees due to two weeks of vacation time per year, and a reasonable number of sick days per employee.

Access your Student CD now for Table 14.9 as an Excel worksheet.

TABLE 14.9: *Average Number of Customers*

Time	Lobby		Drive-Through	
	Monday–Thursday	Friday	Monday–Thursday	Friday
9:00-10:00 A.M.	6	15	5	10
10:00-11:00 A.M.	15	21	7	15
11:00-Noon	24	45	15	24
Noon-1:00 P.M.	36	63	19	30
1:00-2:00 P.M.	38	70	19	32
2:00-3:00 P.M.	31	52	8	18
3:00-4:00 P.M.	20	44	6	9
4:00-5:00 P.M.	13	36	9	10
5:00-6:00 P.M.		69		28
6:00-7:00 P.M.		75		25

TABLE 14.10: *Employee Schedule*

	Head Teller	Teller 2	Teller 3	Teller 4	Teller 5	Teller 6	Teller 7	Teller 8
8:30 A.M.								
8:45								
9:00								
9:15								
9:30								
9:45								
10:00								
•								
•								
•								
6:00 P.M.								
6:15								
6:30								
6:45								
7:00								
7:15								

Tools for Managing Services

Major operational decisions in service firms are often made on the basis of "gut feel." The instinct of grizzled veterans was often the only source consulted to make decisions such as granting a loan, locating a hotel, or determining employee requirements. The tide, however, is turning. As one executive of Southland Corporation (7-Eleven stores) put it: "Retailing used to be an art—now it's a science." The same can be said about services in general. In this section of the book we will look at some tools for aiding managerial intuition.

This section can add distinctive value to a business career. A business degree cannot confer the wisdom, connections, and practical know-how of 30 years' experience in a particular industry. What this section can deliver is new thinking and new methods those 30-year veterans have never seen—it brings new skills to old and important problems.

The business decisions discussed in this section represent high-impact and high-dollar decisions. Applying the methods discussed here to a business run primarily according to "gut feel" can create enormous benefits to both the business and an individual decision maker's career.

For example, deciding on the best location for a business (Chapter 16) can be THE key decision that forever limits or assists unit profitability, regardless of the unit's management. Likewise, developing a system for allocating resources to customers and determining which customer groups to target (Chapter 18) are not decisions made every day, but they profoundly affect a business.

The tools described here are quantitative in nature. This should not, however, be cause for alarm. None of the tools described here require higher-level mathematical preparation. Further, the chapters focus on using these tools, rather than creating them, leaving the mathematical complexities to more technical books. To a large extent, the purpose of Part 5 is to develop knowledge of when to use a tool, rather than attempting to create "mathematical masters." The goal is to give enough context so that, years from now, well after the details of this book recede from memory, a businessperson will know when to pick up the telephone and call for help.

CHAPTER

15

Real-World Project Management[1]

LEARNING OBJECTIVES *The material in this chapter prepares students to:*

- Understand and appreciate the characteristics and complexities of real-world project management.

- Identify factors that influence both success and failure in project management.

- Learn both qualitative and quantitative techniques critical to successful project management.

- Make qualified decisions related to time, cost, and performance trade-offs when managing projects.

- Develop, analyze, and interpret quantitative tools for managing uncertainty in project management.

In this chapter, we delve into the real world of project management not only to develop an understanding of leading-edge tools, methods, and techniques, but also to gain an understanding of what is required for success. The real world is complex, uncertain, messy, and often indeterminate with no clear right or wrong answer to the issues and problems organizations face. Perhaps nowhere is this reality more evident than in project management.

CHARACTERISTICS OF PROJECT MANAGEMENT

Projects constitute the most pervasive process of business administration. Whether in finance, marketing, management information systems, or any other functional area, projects are part of everyday business life and represent a principal means for getting work done. A project consists of an interrelated set of activities designed to achieve a set of business objectives with defined resources and within a specified timeline. A well-planned project specifies what needs to be done, when it needs to be done, and the resources required to do so. Many times, however, things are not so well specified.

Typically, project objectives are defined in terms of deliverables. Deliverables are the work products that are created during the course of a project. Tangible deliverables include financial reports, remodeled homes, or a spacecraft. Deliverables can also be intangible, nonphysical items that are nevertheless clearly defined achievements. Examples of intangible deliverables include software programs, user training,

---

1. This chapter was written by Michael Ketzenberg, Assistant Professor at the College of Business, Colorado State University.

and corporate mergers. The sheer plethora of deliverables and countless methods for producing them makes each project a unique undertaking. Even so, from small well-defined projects like painting a house to monumental endeavors like putting a man on the moon, many of the same methods and techniques for project management can be applied to achieve their disparate objectives. In fact, although projects clearly vary in degree with respect to their magnitude and complexity, they all share, to one extent or another, the following common characteristics.

Unique One-Time Focus

One of the difficulties inherent in successful project management results from its originality. It's a one-shot deal that has never been accomplished before. Whether a project is defined as the development of a new software program, as coordinating and planning the merger of two organizations, or as a project of any other type and size, a given project represents new challenges. Even though hundreds of thousands of software programs have been developed and a large number of corporations merged, each occurrence is distinct. There has only been one Windows 95 and only one R. J. Reynolds and Nabisco merger, for example. This important point helps clarify the common project characteristic in the following discussion.

Subject to Uncertainties

Often, unexplained and unplanned events arise during project implementation that can affect resources, objectives, and timelines. Because projects are unique and represent new business endeavors, they are subject to uncertainties. It may be unclear whether the project objectives can in fact be achieved. For example, most new product development projects fail. Even small-sized projects often require new combinations of skills and resources that create uncertainty with respect to project success.

Multiple Stakeholders

By stakeholder we refer to any person or entity with a vested interest in the outcome of a project. This vested interest can take the form of customers who use the project results, companies that pay for a project, and project team members themselves who are responsible for the outcome. Most projects answer to several stakeholders. Take, for example, a typical consulting engagement. A company (buyer) engages the consulting company to help implement a project. The consulting company forms a project team headed by a partner of the firm and comprised of various managers and associates. The same team formation occurs on the side of the purchasing company, meaning that often the two teams work together and take responsibility for the outcome. The set of stakeholders, however, is not necessarily limited to these two teams, the project managers, and the companies involved. Consider also that these companies may be publicly owned. Large-scale, highly visible projects that involve public companies also face stockholders as stakeholders in the project. A clear example came as the U.S. Defense Department awarded to Lockheed the largest-ever, $200 billion project to develop the Joint Strike Fighter.

The difficulty with multiple stakeholders arises from their different interests in both the processes and outcomes of a project. What a team member on a project values may be entirely different from what a stockholder values. As a consequence, multiple stakeholders induce an added level of complexity to project management.

Finite Lifetime and Limited Resources

A project is generally constrained by limited resources and a fixed period of time available for completion. As a result, mistakes, delays, poor communication, and problems with coordination seem more pronounced and may even be more difficult to overcome. Many times, second attempts are not an option.

No Clear Authority

In many projects, particularly those that involve people and other resources from multiple functional areas, or even those that span organizational boundaries, the chain of command in a project may conflict with the formal management structures of the participating organizational units. An often-heard expression is that project managers are "given all the responsibility, but none of the authority;" that is, the project manager is held accountable for project success, but is not necessarily in full control of project resources.

This type of situation often occurs in matrix organizational structures. A matrix structure arises when project teams are formed with individuals that span multiple functional areas (e.g., accounting, finance, marketing, and operations). Individuals in these functional areas typically report to an immediate boss or supervisor in their own area. As such, a project team member who works on a particular project may be responsible to a project manager who resides in another department, in addition to his or her immediate supervisor. In this type of situation, problems can arise, particularly when resources are tight and priorities conflict. What can the project manager do when a team member becomes unavailable due to the request of another supervisor? Difficulties are compounded when project team members work on multiple projects simultaneously. Not only is it clear that project managers do not fully control their resources, but it can be difficult for project team members to prioritize their work. Hence, when managers plan the timing of project activities, considerable uncertainty surrounds the availability of resources. Consider further the consulting engagement example discussed earlier. The consulting firm may be responsible for directing and coordinating the work of the client firm employees, but clearly issues arise over the authority of the consulting firm to direct the work of the client employees. Yet these instances are common and present a constant challenge to successful project management.

These characteristics, whether considered individually or collectively, help clarify impediments to success in real-world project management. Nevertheless, successful projects are completed all the time. Even when we talk about successful project management, however, the definition of success itself can prove elusive. How do we know a project is a success or failure? Sometimes the answer is self-evident. When a rocket explodes on the launch pad or an architectural firm wins a design competition for a new building, success or failure is palpable and clear. In many, if not most cases, however, the definition of success is considerably less clear.

Consider, for example, when a new computer operating system is introduced in the market place. Is success measured by a certain level of technological achievement, by revenues, by market share, by the level of critical acclaim, or perhaps by some combination of factors? If the definition of success itself is not clearly understood, then how will it be possible to be successful? In the next section, we provide a framework for qualifying success and failure in project management.

MEASURING PROJECT SUCCESS

Among other more notorious lies like, "the check is in the mail," is the adage that "successful projects are completed on time, within budget, and to specifications." Although it may seem reasonable on face value to make such a claim, by this definition of success, there would be no successful projects—certainly not for projects of any meaningful or significant size. Many, if not most projects, are delivered late, come in over budget, or do not satisfy all requirements specified at the project inception. Yet, many of these projects are still considered successful.

In the real world, with real project management, projects are fluid and dynamic processes, subject to change and uncertainty, such that (1) nothing goes as planned, and (2) nothing goes as planned. Implementing a project resembles a journey. The destination may be clear, but the process is uncertain. Detours and sidetrips are possible, and the destination itself may even change en route. With respect to project management, resource levels may change, so too requirements, along with timetables. Hence, when the actual and completed project is compared with what was planned, the inevitable and perhaps significant deviations would eliminate a determination of success according to the prior definition. Yet, even with changes, problems, and the uncertainties that arise in project management, there are many successful projects. Consider, for example, the release of Windows 95, which was not only delayed for several months but was shipped with several bugs, and many planned features were dropped from the initial release. Nevertheless, no one will deny that by obtaining a 90% share of the market for personal computer operating systems, the Windows 95 product launch (and its successors) proved to be a success. So, how do we know whether any given project is a success?

The answer is at once simple and complicated. It is simple because the best determination of success is by those with a vested interest in it—the stakeholders. We say that project success lies in the eye of the stakeholder. A significant complication arises, however, when multiple stakeholders hold different interests, values, and objectives, which can and do change over time.

Take the consulting engagement example we discussed earlier. Success for the client may be measured, say, in how much operating costs are cut after project completion. For the consulting company, success may be measured in terms of the revenue generated by the engagement. Are the two linked? Perhaps, but there is no reason that a given project will be successful under both measures. The complication does not end there either. Consider the project manager from the consulting firm. It may be that the project manager is using the client engagement as a platform for promotion. Now, add in the project team members' different measures for success. Which measure or measures are valid or most important? Which measures are conflicting?

The answer depends on the project in question and the stakeholders involved, but it clearly brings up an important and significant consideration. Not all stakeholders are created equal. It is absolutely critical, in managing a project, that the stakeholders are identified, prioritized, and their measures of success well understood. Hence, a critical factor to successful project management is a thorough understanding and dissemination of project objectives so that project results can ultimately be measured in a manner that delineates and rationalizes the vested interests of the stakeholders. In this way, it is then possible to focus on the methods for achieving the specified results.

Understanding that success is in the eye of the stakeholder, and hence, "we will know it when we see it," is but a first step. The next logical step is realizing the processes necessary to achieve the desired success. Because any project includes far greater opportunities for things to go wrong than to go right, a good starting point for understanding the factors critical to success is to address the common causes for failure.

QUALITATIVE METHODS FOR ACHIEVING SUCCESS

Experience is the great educator in life: Experience brings failure and through failure rises success. The United States did not launch a rocket to the moon on its first try. We might say mission control was very experienced. In a like manner, a successful project manager, unless extremely lucky, will have experienced prior failures and consequently perhaps knows more about what to do to avoid failure rather than what to do to generate success. From this perspective, we lay the groundwork for achieving success in project management as we discuss common causes for project failure and methods to avoid them.

Living in an Uncertain World

As we stated previously, the real world is subject to uncertainties, and real-world project management is no exception. The surest way to set a course for failure is to be unprepared for uncertainty. Stuff happens, problems arise, and plans must change. In other words, we can be absolutely 100% certain that the actual implementation of a project will *not* be done in accordance to the initial project plan. Hence, plans that do not account for uncertainty are considerably more likely to fail than those that do.

Uncertainty implies that the path to success lies in conservative planning. For example, resources should not be fully loaded at 100% utilization. If an employee is scheduled to work 40 hours a week, the project plan should not count on 40 hours of work. Although the precise number is hard to determine, a target of 80% for planned use of available hours is common, particularly in consulting. Lower utilization means flexibility to handle problems and issues as they arise during project implementation. It also means that planned work will take longer to complete, but it provides a conservative approach that also establishes the opportunity to exceed expectations—another critical issue to which we proceed.

Managing Expectations

Meeting the expectations of stakeholders is critical because the determination of project success resides with them. Managing expectations means monitoring and controlling them as they change over time. Hence, from the perspective of managing a project to success, it is important to not only understand those expectations, but to positively influence them over time as well.

To positively influence expectations means being positioned to exceed them. To do so requires a conservative approach to project planning. As we discussed, without conservative planning, the flexibility to handle problems or issues as they arise is absent. In turn, when problems do arise, the communication with stakeholders can only be negative—higher costs, extended deadlines, and other negative events. Conservative planning builds in a cushion to absorb issues and problems as they arise, which minimizes or eliminates negative communication. Furthermore, when things go right and problems are avoided, the project can be completed in less time, with fewer resources, and lower costs. Without conservative planning, the best that can be done is to meet expectations.

Conservative planning is but one example of managing expectations effectively. In fact, the need to manage expectations highlights a key set of skills required of project managers. Not only must a project manager be competent with respect to the technical skills and resources to do the project work and the managerial skills to plan and control the project implementation, she or he must demonstrate softer skills to effectively communicate and positively influence the variety of people who interact within the scope of a project. Certainly, the level of competence required in these three disparate areas of technical, managerial, and people skills is high, which explains why it is so difficult for organizations to find good project managers.

Scope Creep

Probably the most insidious and problematic issue to manage over the course of a project is scope creep. Scope creep refers to unplanned increases in project deliverables and hence increases in the workload of project activities. Scope creep arises from poor and inconsistent communication, fueled by mismanaged expectations. Generally, a natural tendency is for those who pay for a project or use the deliverables to want more than what is delivered. Without *clearly* defining work objectives in a written form that is communicated among everyone involved, it is possible for different people to form different expectations of the work to be completed and the objectives to be achieved. In other words, some people will be dissatisfied with the level of project work being accomplished. For consulting engagements in which these "some people" are paying clients, this expectation and failure to "meet" it can be particularly devastating.

Consider an example in which a software development firm is developing a computer system for a client company. The client company will have certain expectations about the functionality to be delivered, and so too will the developer. However, if the precise level of functionality is not written, communicated, and agreed upon, the client company may believe certain functionality is included where the developer does not. Virtually no good outcome is possible from this failure. Either the client will be disappointed when it becomes aware that desired functionality is missing or the developer, in order to placate the client, must do additional, unplanned work. Clearly, issues related to scope creep also tie in to effectively managing expectations of stakeholders.

In general, written communication and contracts that clearly spell out project scope and objectives will curtail scope creep and enable expectations to be managed appropriately. Probably just as important as it is to specify what is included in a project, is also to delineate specifically what is *not* included within the scope of a project. Because of the natural tendency for scope creep to occur over the course of a project, conservative planning (as already discussed) that allows for some scope creep also provides a way to positively influence expectations. In fact, planning for scope creep is similar to maintaining a capacity cushion that gives the project team flexibility to handle changes in project workload. In our software development example, even if the written scope and objectives document clearly shows that certain functionality is not included in the deliverables, the developer, with a capacity cushion, can include the additional functionality at no additional cost to the client and thereby exceed expectations.

So far, we have discussed qualitative factors that influence project success and failure. Although they are extremely important, so too are the more technical skills and methods needed to plan and manage projects to success. In the next section, we introduce quantitative tools for managing projects.

QUANTITATIVE TOOLS AND TECHNIQUES FOR PROJECT MANAGEMENT

Network diagramming offers one of the more versatile techniques for planning and managing projects. A network diagram is a graphic illustration of the activities in a project and the relationship among the activities. Recall that a project consists of a set of interrelated activities. The precedence relationships among activities identify which activities must be completed before other activities may start. A network diagram not only illustrates these precedence relationships, but is also useful for answering several questions important to effective project management. How long will the project take? What are the critical paths? What activities lie on the critical path?

Naturally, in order to draw a network diagram, it is essential to know the set of activities involved in the project to be diagrammed as well as the precedence relationship among those activities. Sometimes, however, projects are ill defined. Even with well-defined projects, it still may be unclear what activities are necessary to the project. For example, consider a project that involves buying a house. This project includes tasks such as viewing homes, preparing a contract, house inspection, obtaining a mortgage, and closing. Several other activities may or may not be included. Some activities such as surveys, engineering reports, or inspections can be conditional to any number of factors. Only during the course of such a project will the actual requirements become known. Alternatively, when not enough is known up front about the activities in a project, another project can be defined to better clarify the principal project requirements. It is important to note that omissions or errors concerning activities to be included or their relationships can significantly affect the likelihood of project success.

Once the activities for a project are clearly defined and their relationships determined, a work breakdown structure (WBS) can be developed. A WBS is simply a hierarchical organization of project tasks that decomposes project processes into subtasks and finally elemental activities at the lowest level. In Figure 15.1 we illustrate a WBS for the example project we use throughout the remainder of this chapter. The example project concerns the design, development, and implementation of an order/entry computer program.

Table 15.1 lists activities, their durations, and precedence for the nine activities displayed in the WBS. The labels A through I will be used to identify activities in the network diagram. Each label is associated with an activity description in the second column and an estimated duration, specified in weeks, is listed in the third column. Finally, the fourth column identifies activity relationships delineating the immediate predecessors for each activity. In our systems development example, activities A and B have no immediate predecessors. All other activities have at least one immediate predecessor and sometimes more. Consider activity C, Reports Design. This activity can begin only after the activities A and B are completed, where activities A and B are identified as immediate predecessors to C.

FIGURE 15.1: *Work Breakdown Structure for the Systems Development Project*

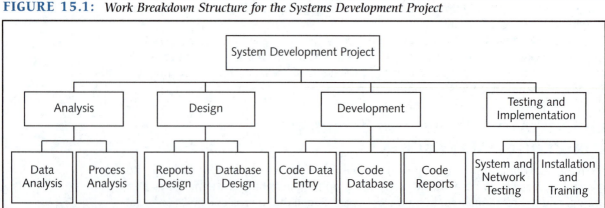

TABLE 15.1: *Activity Information for the Systems Development Project*

Activity	Description	Duration (weeks)	Immediate Predecessor(s)
A	Process analysis	4	—
B	Data analysis	3	—
C	Reports design	5	A, B
D	Database design	5	B
E	Code reports	4	C, D
F	Code data entry	3	D
G	Code database	4	D
H	System and network testing	3	F, G, H
I	Installation and training	1	H

CHOOSING A PROJECT NETWORK DIAGRAMMING TECHNIQUE

Two commonly accepted approaches to diagramming project networks include (1) activity on node (AON) method, and (2) activity on arrow (AOA) method. With AON, nodes represent activities and arrows represent precedence relationships. With AOA, nodes represent events, such as the beginning or end of an activity, and arrows represent activities.

Figure 15.2 illustrates both techniques with a small example of three interrelated activities. In this example, Activity A is the immediate predecessor of activities B and C. Note that even though the two techniques can yield different-looking diagrams, they relate the same information. Hence, the selection of one method over another method is principally a matter of personal choice. An AOA diagram, however, becomes a little more complicated due to the inclusion of dummy activities. Dummy activities are used in an AOA diagram whenever two activities would otherwise share the same starting and ending nodes. In effect, only one arrow is allowed between any two nodes. Dummy arrows help preserve the precedence relationships of the work breakdown structure, without violating the single arrow rule. Figure 15.3 provides further illustration of ways to diagram common relationships using both techniques.

CONSTRUCTING A PROJECT NETWORK

Using our example of the systems development project, we will proceed to construct a project network using the AON method. The steps for diagramming hinge on two

FIGURE 15.2: *Illustration of AOA and AON Diagramming Techniques*

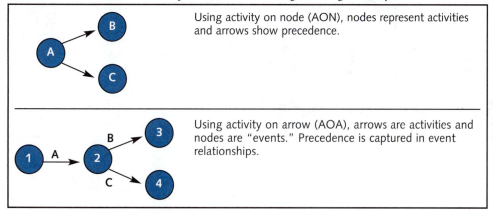

Using activity on node (AON), nodes represent activities and arrows show precedence.

Using activity on arrow (AOA), arrows are activities and nodes are "events." Precedence is captured in event relationships.

FIGURE 15.3: *Ways to Diagram Common Activity Relationships*

AOA	AON	Activity Relationships
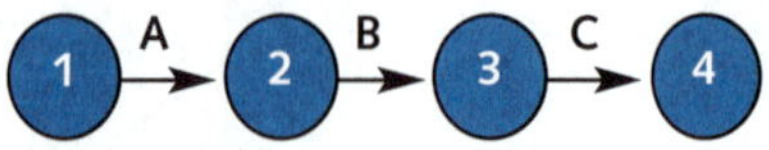 (a)	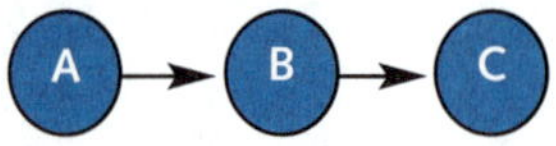	A precedes B, which precedes C.
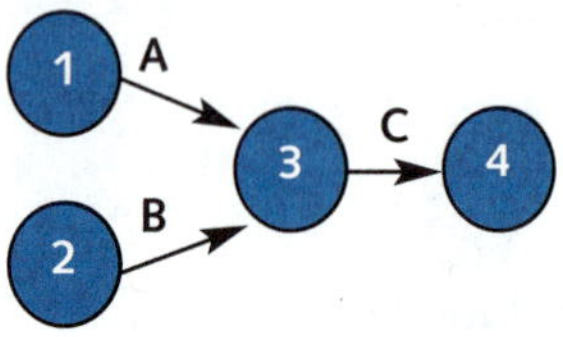 (b)	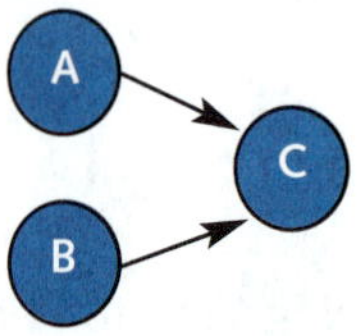	A and B must be completed before C can be started.
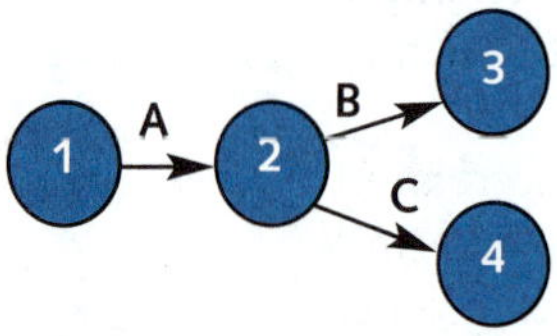 (c)	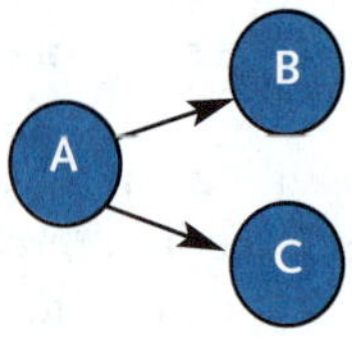	B and C cannot begin until A has been completed.
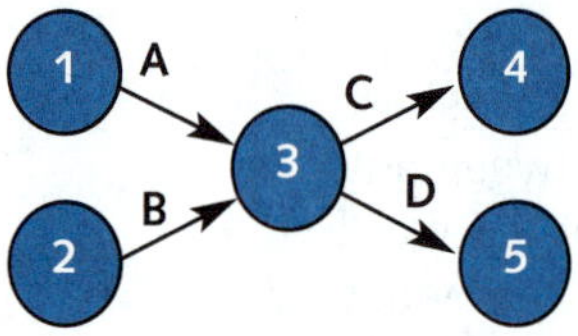 (d)	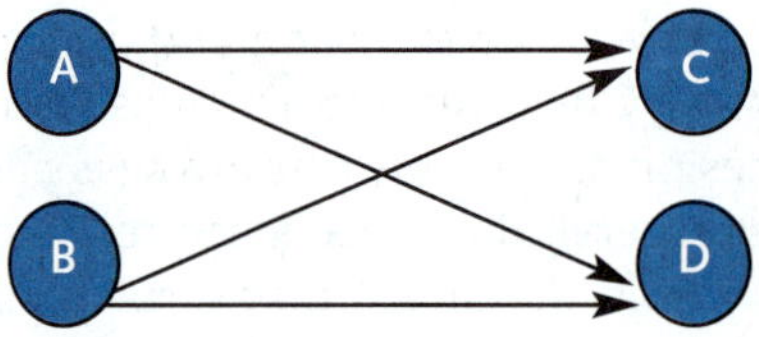	C and D cannot begin until both A and B have been completed.
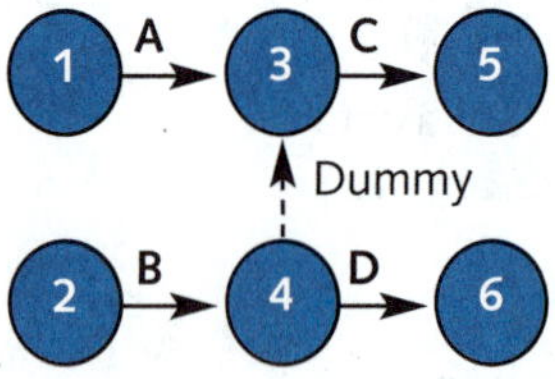 (e)	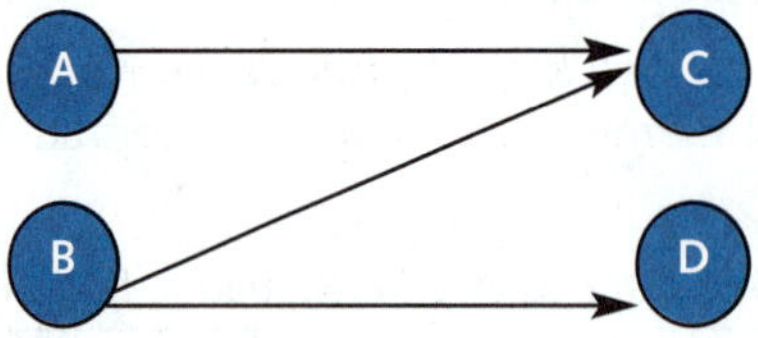	C cannot begin until both A and B have been completed; D cannot begin until B has been completed.
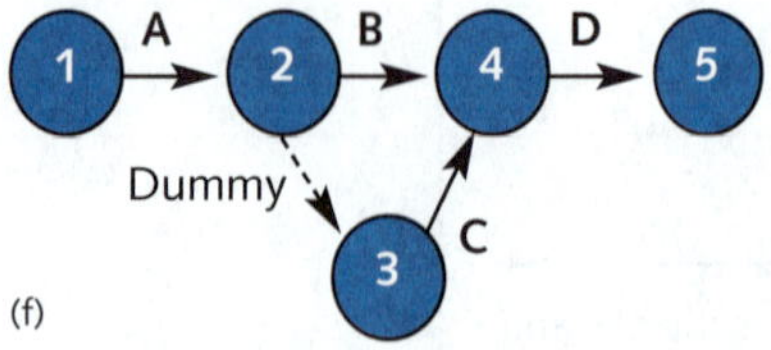 (f)	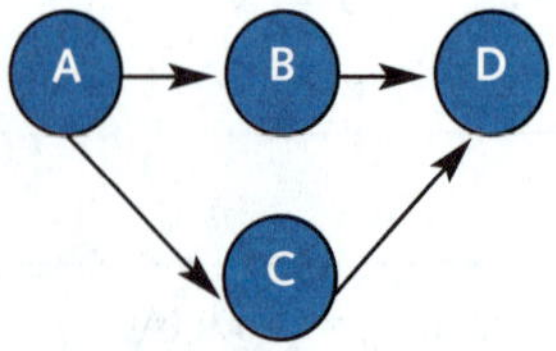	B and C cannot begin until A has been completed; D cannot begin until both B and C have been completed.

rules: Each activity is represented by a single node and the arrows indicate the precedence relationships. To begin, start with a node to represent an activity with no precedents. If the project requires more than one such activity, as in our example, then create a dummy activity labeled "Start" to serve as the predecessor for all the activities without defined predecessors. The "Start" node has no duration and may be diagrammed as a square for clarity of representation.

Build nodes and arrows as precedence relationships demand and continue in a logical fashion from starting node to ending node. If an activity is not a predecessor for any other activity, then it is an ending node. If more than one activity falls into this category, create a dummy activity for the ending node in the same fashion that we use a dummy "Start" node with multiple starting activities. Note that both dummy Start and End nodes may be desirable, if not required, to provide clear signals of the start and end of the project.

DIAGRAMMING THE SYSTEMS DEVELOPMENT PROJECT

As indicated by the work breakdown structure in Table 15.1, this system development project consists of nine activities. The project deliverable is an installed computer system with user training. To proceed to this mark, both process and data analyses must first be conducted. These activities identify what the system must accomplish and the data that the resulting system must maintain and utilize. Once these tasks are completed, then the different system modules can be designed and afterwards coded. Only after all activities are coded can the system be tested, and only after successful system testing can the entire program be installed and the users trained on how to use it.

The AON network for the system development project is shown in Figure 15.4. In this diagram, activities are shown as circles, with arrows that capture precedence and indicate the order in which activities are to be completed. Note that activities A and B are linked to a start node because they have no immediate predecessors. Then, observe the arrows that link both activities A and B to activity C, thereby indicating that C cannot begin until A and B are completed. Activity B is the only immediate predecessor of Activity D. The diagram proceeds, essentially translating the information of the work breakdown structure into the visual representation of the project network. Note that activity I is not the predecessor of any other activity and links to an ending node. In this case, the ending node is not required, but visually helps to clarify the end point of the project.

FIGURE 15.4: *Example Project Network Diagram*

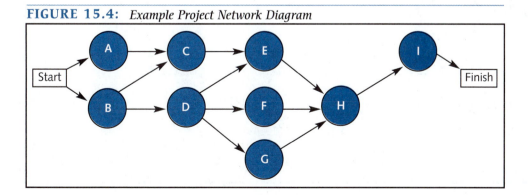

Of course, it (almost) goes without saying that there is a wide array of software and other technologies that can be used to facilitate project management. Microsoft (MS) Project ™ is one software tool that automates many tasks. Simply by entering tasks, task times, and precedence relationships, MS Project can generate a network diagram. Figure 15.5 shows the corresponding MS Project network diagram for our example project.

DEVELOPING A PROJECT SCHEDULE

A project network can be used to develop a project schedule or plan. The project schedule actually expands on the network by identifying the duration of the project and the start and end times for each activity in the project. A Gantt chart, like a network diagram, provides another way to develop and present a project schedule. In a Gantt chart, activities are listed vertically, and task times are denoted horizontally in bars that are mapped on a rolling calendar. The length of the bar corresponds to the length of the given task. Figure 15.6 shows the MS Project Gantt Chart for our example.

The project schedule identifies the due dates and timing of events within the project timeline. The duration of a project is equal to the longest path in the project network, where a path is represented by a unique set of activities that link start and end nodes. The length of a path is determined by the sum of the durations for activities on the path. Table 15.2 identifies the five paths for the example system development project.

The longest path in a project is also known as the critical path. Since the longest path is the critical path, a project cannot be completed in any time shorter than indicated by the sum of activity times on the critical path. In our example, the critical path is A-C-E-H-I. Activities on the critical path are also known as critical activities. The idea behind the term *critical* is that any delay of these activities will delay the entire project. Hence, these activities require focused management attention.

FIGURE 15.5: *MS Project Network Diagram for the Systems Development Project*

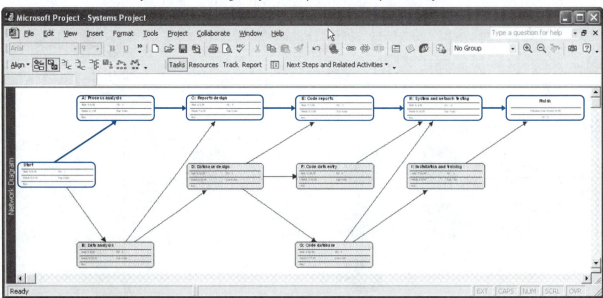

FIGURE 15.6: *MS Project with Gantt Chart for the Systems Development Project*

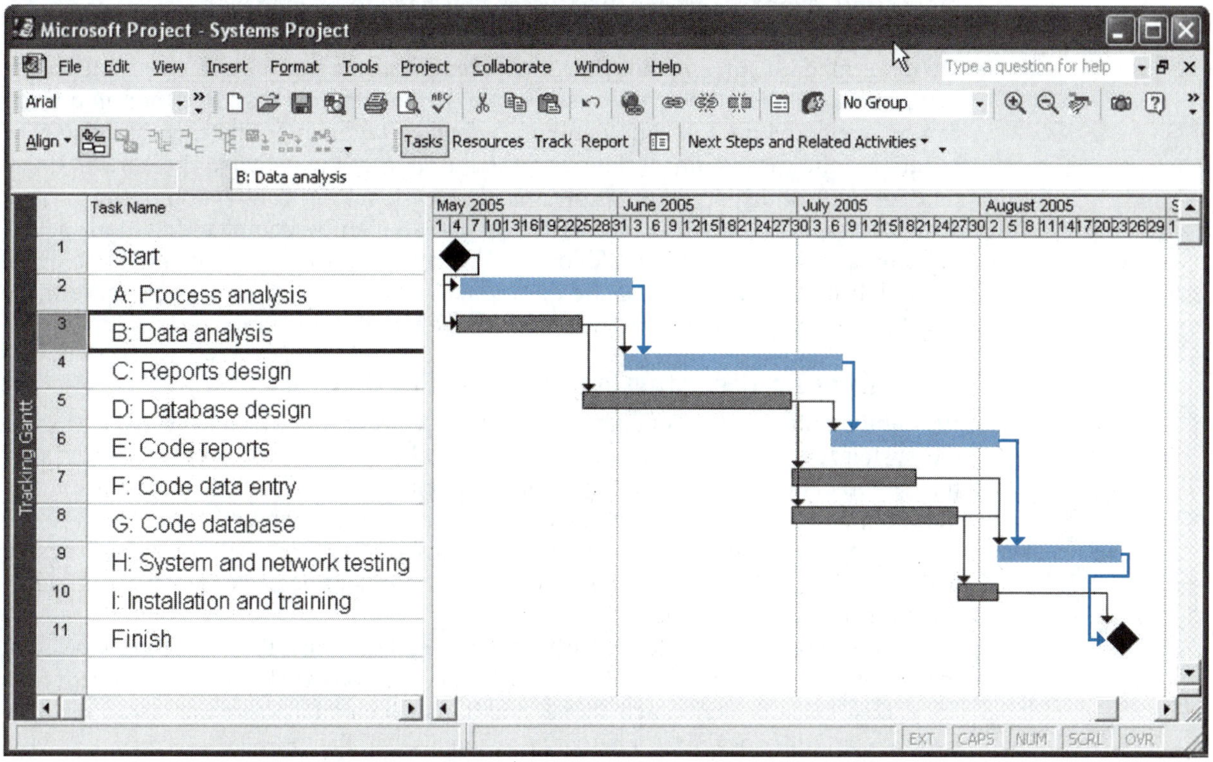

A project may include more than one critical path. This situation arises when two or more paths of the same length are also longer than any other paths. Our example contains only one critical path.

In small projects with only a few paths, it is a simple matter to manually identify each path and determine their lengths. Projects of any meaningful size may require hundreds if not thousands of paths. In these situations it is helpful to use any one of several available computer software programs like Microsoft Project™.

Even though careful management attention must be devoted to critical activities, noncritical activities should not be forgotten. Noncritical activities are, naturally, those activities that do not reside on a critical path and, as such, include activity slack. Activity slack is measured as the amount of time that an activity can be delayed before it becomes critical and delays the entire project. Because projects are plagued with uncertainty, activities with little and sometimes moderate levels of slack should also be carefully monitored. In fact, should delays occur, the critical path may shift

TABLE 15.2: *Paths in the Example Project*

	Path	Duration (weeks)
1	A-C-E-H-I	17
2	B-C-E-H-I	16
3	B-D-E-H-I	16
4	B-D-F-H-I	15
5	B-D-G-H-I	16

to one or more other paths in the project. This last point reemphasizes the notion the projects are dynamic, evolving processes that need to be managed.

Activity slack can be determined once the start times and end times for activities are determined. Four different time estimates are used: early start, early finish, late start, and late finish. The earliest start time denotes the earliest time that an activity can be started without violating any precedence relationship. The earliest finish time is equal to the earliest finish time plus the duration of the activity. The earliest finish time for the last activity in the project is also the length to completion of the project. The latest finish time is the latest time an activity can be completed without delaying one or more activities that follow it. The latest start time for an activity is equal to the latest finish time minus the duration. We now look at how to compute these four time estimates, beginning with earliest start and finish times.

Computing Earliest Start and Earliest Finish Times

We demonstrate the task of computing earliest start and finish times with our example system development project. We use the abbreviation ES to denote early start time, EF to denote early finish time, and D to denote an activities duration. Using this notation, $EF = ES + D$. The earliest start time for any given activity is equal to the maximum earliest finish time of any predecessor activities. With no predecessor activities, the earliest start time is zero. Figure 15.7 identifies activity times and durations for our example project.

To obtain the solution for earliest start and earliest finish times, one must begin at the starting node at time zero. The starting node itself has zero duration, so in effect its $ES = D = EF = 0$. Hence, activities A and B, which emanate from the start node have earliest start times of zero. For activity A where $D = 4$, then $EF = 0 + 4 = 4$. Likewise, for activity B where $D = 3$, $EF = 0 + 3 = 3$. Now, activity C can only begin once the last predecessor activity is completed, activity A with $EF = 4$. Consequently, for activity C with duration 5, $ES = 4$ and $EF = 5 + 4 = 9$. For activity D with duration 5, $ES = 3$ because activity B is its only predecessor and $EF = 3 + 5 = 8$.

Moving forward to activity E, its earliest start time is the maximum of the earliest finish times of its two predecessors, activity C with $EF = 9$. Hence, ES for activity E is 9 and $EF = 9 + 4 = 13$. $ES = 8$ for both activities F and G since activity D is their sole predecessor. For activity F, $EF = 8 + 3 = 11$ and for activity G, $EF = 8 + 4 = 12$. ES for activity H is determined in a similar fashion to activities C and E because it has multiple predecessors. The maximum EF of either activities E, F, or G is 13, so ES for activity H is 13 and its $EF = 13 + 3 = 16$. Finally, activity I has an ES of 16 and an $EF = 16 + 1 = 17$.

FIGURE 15.7: *Early Start and Early Finish Times*

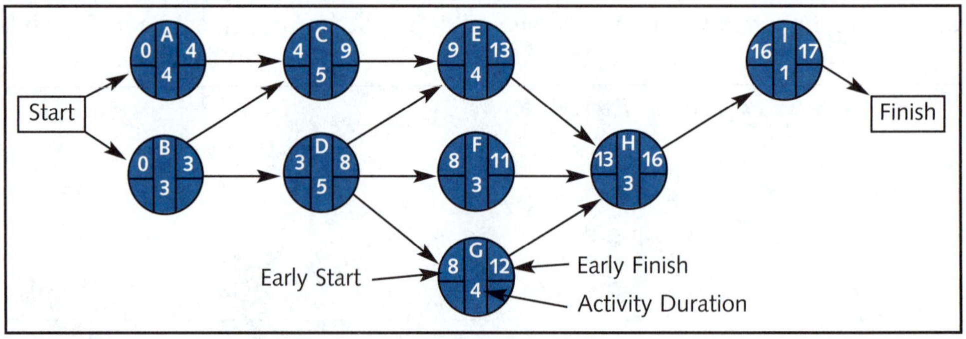

Computing Latest Finish and Latest Start Times

The process for computing latest finish and latest start times is the reverse of the process used for computing earliest start and earliest finish times. The latest finish time (LF) for any activity is equal to the minimum of the latest start times of any activities to which it is an immediate predecessor. The latest start time (LS) is simply the latest finish time minus the activity duration time, or, $LS = LF - D$. If an activity is not a predecessor of any other activity, and hence, is a final or ending node of the project, then the latest finish time is equal to the earliest finish time. Finishing any later than the earliest finish time would delay completion of the entire project.

We begin the process of determining latest start and latest finish times with the final or ending activity of the project. In our example, activity I is the final activity. Its earliest finish time is 17 weeks so its latest finish time must also be 17 weeks. Working backwards, $LS_I = 17 - 1 = 16$. Then, using the label of each activity as a subscript, the following computations can be made:

$$LF_H = LS_I = 16, \quad LS_H = LF_H - D_H = 16 - 3 = 13$$

$$LF_E = LS_H = 13, \quad LS_E = LF_E - D_E = 13 - 4 = 9$$

So far, we observed that the latest start and finish times are equal to the earliest start and finish times. This result will always be true for activities that reside on the critical path. Critical activities allow no slack and must be started and finished at the right time or the project as a whole will be delayed. Noncritical activities, however, may allow for slack. Slack is defined as the maximum amount of time that the latest start of an activity may be delayed beyond its earliest start time, without delaying the project. By definition then, slack $= LS - ES$. Because $LS - ES = LF - EF$, an equivalent measure of slack is latest finish time minus earliest finish time. Activities F and G contain slack because they are not on a critical path:

$$LF_F = LS_H = 13, LS_F = LF_F - D_F = 13 - 3 = 10, \text{slack} = LS - ES = 10 - 8 = 2$$

and

$$LF_G = LS_H = 13, LS_G = LF_G - D_G = 13 - 4 = 9, \text{slack} = LS - ES = 9 - 8 = 1$$

Activities C and A are on the critical path so we know that they have zero slack and that their latest finish and latest start times are equal to their earliest finish and earliest start times. Activity D is not a critical activity and to complicate matters, it is a predecessor activity to three other activities: E, F, and G. The rule applied here is that the latest finish time for activity D is equal to the minimum of the latest start times for the three activities. In this case, the minimum latest start time of activities {E, F, G} is 9. Hence, $LF_D = 9$ and $LS_D = 9 - 5 = 4$. The method for determining the latest finish time for activity B is the same as for activity D. Here, however, the latest finish time for each of the two activities that follow it {C, D} is the same. Hence, $LF_B = 4$ and $LS_B = 4 - 3 = 1$. Figure 15.8 shows the MS Project schedule for our example, with activity start and end times, as well as activity slack. The MS Project file for this example is on the Student CD.

In summary, a project network serves as an effective tool for managing projects. Using a project network, we can determine when activities should be started, when they should be completed, and where in the project slack resides so that resources may be properly shifted if necessary. The project network can also identify critical activities and critical paths so that management attention will be focused on what is important.

Access your Student CD now for the Microsoft Project file for this example.

FIGURE 15.8: *MS Project Schedule Table for the Systems Development Project Displaying Activity Slack Times*

	Task Name	Duration	Start	Finish	Late Start	Late Finish	Free Slack
1	Start	0 wks	Thu 5/5/05	Thu 5/5/05	Thu 5/5/05	Thu 5/5/05	0 wks
2	A: Process analysis	4 wks	Thu 5/5/05	Wed 6/1/05	Thu 5/5/05	Wed 6/1/05	0 wks
3	B: Data analysis	3 wks	Thu 5/5/05	Wed 5/25/05	Thu 5/12/05	Wed 6/1/05	0 wks
4	C: Reports design	5 wks	Thu 6/2/05	Wed 7/6/05	Thu 6/2/05	Wed 7/6/05	0 wks
5	D: Database design	5 wks	Thu 5/26/05	Wed 6/29/05	Thu 6/2/05	Wed 7/6/05	0 wks
6	E: Code reports	4 wks	Thu 7/7/05	Wed 8/3/05	Thu 7/7/05	Wed 8/3/05	0 wks
7	F: Code data entry	3 wks	Thu 6/30/05	Wed 7/20/05	Thu 7/14/05	Wed 8/3/05	2 wks
8	G: Code database	4 wks	Thu 6/30/05	Wed 7/27/05	Thu 7/7/05	Wed 8/3/05	0 wks
9	H: System and network testing	3 wks	Thu 8/4/05	Wed 8/24/05	Thu 8/4/05	Wed 8/24/05	0 wks
10	I: Installation and training	1 wk	Thu 7/28/05	Wed 8/3/05	Thu 8/18/05	Wed 8/24/05	3 wks
11	Finish	0 wks	Wed 8/24/05	Wed 8/24/05	Wed 8/24/05	Wed 8/24/05	0 wks

In addition, it should be noted that the process itself of putting together a project network before the project is scheduled to start facilitates learning about project details. At this time, project scope becomes clear, activity relationships are clarified, and resource requirements are established. In essence, it puts the project on the right track. One thing that any project manager can count on, however, is that the project plan as described by the initial project network is certainly not identical to what will be implemented.

As we discussed at the beginning of this chapter, projects are subject to risks and uncertainties such that what is planned will be changed, possibly many times over, before a project is completed. Project team members get sick, quit, or are required for (euphemistically, borrowed and never returned) other more critical projects. The work can take longer or shorter than planned. Additional work that was initially not considered may arise, the project deliverables can change, not to mention myriad other possibilities, all of which may affect the project. In other words, unplanned stuff happens, and usually not of the good variety. On any project of meaningful size and complexity, the project network that describes what actually happened on the project may show little resemblance to the project network as initially developed.

The importance of this last point is that projects and the networks that describe them are not static or frozen in time. They are dynamic and should be treated as such. Just because one project path is critical today does not mean that two other project paths will not be critical tomorrow. For this reason, the project network must be consistently updated to reflect its changing state. In the next section, we proceed with a statistical analysis approach to managing projects and show how project networks can be adapted to explicitly incorporate the elements of risk and uncertainty.

PROBABILISTIC PROJECT MANAGEMENT

The framework that we developed in the prior section for developing and using project networks can be adapted to consider the risks and uncertainties ever present in projects. Instead of treating activity durations as known, deterministic, and fixed, we can treat them probabilistically. With this approach, it is possible to answer questions such as, "What is the probability of completing the project in a certain amount of time?" In essence, we can treat activities as if they are random variables and assign probabilities to activity times to reflect the inherent uncertainties. Then, we can use these probabilities to calculate means and variances for activity times that, in turn, can be used to calculate project statistics.

The approach requires three time estimates for each activity. These include an optimistic time (*a*), a most likely time (*m*), and a pessimistic time (*b*). The optimistic time is the shortest time estimate and reflects the duration of an activity when everything goes nearly perfect. The most likely time estimate reflects the idea that bad stuff will happen (problems arise) and cause an activity to take longer than the optimistic time. The pessimistic time, the third time estimate, provides an activity time when just about everything that can go wrong does go wrong.

The statistical analysis approach assumes the probabilities for activity times are taken from the beta distribution. The choice of beta distribution arises because of its flexibility: The distribution can have any number of shapes that will allow the most likely time estimate to lie between the optimistic and pessimistic times. The most likely time estimate is the mode of the beta distribution with the highest associated probability. Because of its flexibility and ability to accommodate probability distributions of such variety and because projects and their activities themselves are so varied, the beta distribution is an ideal choice for accommodating uncertainty in project management.

The degree to which the three time estimates are close together or far apart is a direct measure of the uncertainty associated with an activity. It also presupposes that it is possible to assign three separate and reasonable time estimates. The three estimates may not be different values. For example, an activity may have the same optimistic time and most likely time, or the same pessimistic time and most likely time. In some cases, however, estimating activity times may prove difficult, particularly with new processes, methods, or techniques that provide no previous experience upon which to base those estimates. In essence, the activity times are a source of uncertainty. The task itself of estimating activity durations, then, is akin to forecasting. As such, judgmental forecasting methods may be particularly appropriate here, particularly those methods that can be used to generate a consensus forecast among all members of the project team.

With three time estimates, the mean time of an activity, denoted as t_e, can be estimated by

$$t_e = \frac{a + 4m = b}{6}$$

(15.1)

Note that the formula for t_e is a weighted average of the three time estimates in which the most likely time (*m*) is weighted four times that of either the optimistic or pessimistic times. The variance of the beta distribution, denoted as σ^2 is the square of the standard deviation σ and is given by

$$\sigma^2 = \left(\frac{b - a}{6}\right)^2$$

(15.2)

The variance provides a direct measure of the uncertainty with respect to activity durations. Notice that the variance increases as the difference between the optimistic and pessimistic times increases. Alternatively, when the pessimistic and optimistic times are identical, the activity duration is assumed known with certainty and consequently the variance is zero.

Calculating Means and Variances

Here, we use our example of the system development project to demonstrate how to calculate the mean and variance for an activity's time. For example, what would the mean and variance be for activity H if $a = 1$, $m = 2$, and $b = 9$? By plugging these values into the equations for t_e and σ^2 we find that

$$t_e = \frac{a + 4m + b}{6} = \frac{1 + 4(2) + 9}{6} = 3$$

and

$$\sigma^2 = \left(\frac{b - a}{6}\right)^2 = \left(\frac{9 - 1}{6}\right)^2 = 1.78$$

Note that the calculated mean for activity H is three weeks, while the most likely time estimate is two weeks. This example highlights the point that the mean and most likely time estimate will not necessarily be the same. The mode of a distribution and its mean will only be the same if the distribution is symmetric around the mean, such as the normal distribution. We show the calculated values t_e and σ^2 for all activities in the systems development project in Table 15.3.

Once activity statistics for a project are computed, they can be used to help determine where the greatest sources of uncertainty reside, and hence where management attention should be focused. The difference in time estimates for an activity are a measure of uncertainty, which can be captured in the variance of an activity. Therefore, it is a simple matter of finding those activities with the highest variances to indicate the highest level of uncertainty.

As shown in Table 15.3, activities B and H in the example project are associated with the highest level of uncertainty. The higher numbers for these activities do not necessarily mean that the level of uncertainty is out of line or that the uncertainty for the other activities is low enough. Management attention to the specific case can determine whether the uncertainty of a given activity is too significant and then focus efforts toward reducing that uncertainty or perhaps readjusting time estimates.

TABLE 15.3: *Time Estimates and Activity Statistics*

Activity	Time Estimates (weeks)			Activity Statistics	
	Optimistic (a)	Most Likely (m)	Pessimistic (b)	Mean (t_e)	Variance (σ^2)
A	3	4	5	4	0.11
B	1	2	9	3	1.78
C	3	5	7	5	0.44
D	2	5	8	5	1.00
E	1	4	7	4	1.00
F	2	3	4	3	0.11
G	1	4	7	4	1.00
H	1	2	9	3	1.78
I	1	1	1	1	0.00

ANALYZING PROBABILITIES

Uncertain activity times result in uncertain project duration. The main objective of the probabilistic approach to project management is to plan for uncertainty and to be able to assess those probabilities with respect to the project timeline. Evaluating the probability of meeting project due dates is an invaluable contribution of the probabilistic approach. To be able to calculate probabilities, however, we need to make a rather restrictive assumption about the relationship among activities.

We assume that the durations of all activities are independent of one another. Naturally, this assumption may not be valid. For example, if a specific project team member is assigned to multiple activities (a common occurrence), then activity durations are likely to be dependent. Nevertheless, the assumption allows us to draw upon the central limit theorem to compute project statistics. Recall that the central limit theorem holds that the sum of a group of independent, identically distributed random variables approaches a normal distribution as the number of random variables increases. With respect to project management, activity times are the random variables. By assuming activities times are independent, we can then use the sum of the expected times and sum of the variances for all activities that reside on a given path to assess the probability of completing the path by a desired completion time, where

$$T_E = \Sigma(\text{Activity times on the path}) \qquad (15.3)$$

and

$$\sigma^2 = \Sigma(\text{Variances of time on the path}) \qquad (15.4)$$

To illustrate how we can calculate the probability of completing a path by a given date, we return again to our example of the system development project. Here, we might ask the question, "If we assume the desired due date for the project is 19 weeks, what is the probability that the path with the longest expected completion time is finished within the desired time frame?" Before we begin, some additional notation is helpful. Let T = due date for the project and T_E = expected completion time for the path. With these values, then T, T_E, σ^2 can be used to compute a z-score, where the value of z is the number of standard deviations (of a standard normal distribution) that the project due date is from the expected completion time. Specifically,

$$z = \frac{T - T_E}{\sqrt{\sigma^2}} \qquad (15.5)$$

Now, in our example, $T = 19$. Because the path with the longest expected completion time is given by A–C–E–H–I, then

$$T_E = \Sigma(\text{Activity times on the path})$$
$$= 4 + 5 + 4 + 3 + 1 = 17$$

and

$$\sigma^2 = \Sigma(\text{Variances of activity times on the path})$$
$$= 0.11 + 0.44 + 1.00 + 1.78 + 0$$
$$= 3.33$$

so that

$$z = \frac{T - T_E}{\sqrt{\sigma^2}} = \frac{19 - 17}{\sqrt{3.33}} = 1.10$$

Using the Normal Distribution provided on the text's endsheet, the probability associated with a z-score of 1.10 is 0.8643. Hence, there is an 86.43% chance of completing the path on time. Note that we determined only the probability associated with the given path and not the entire project. Even though path A–C–E–H–I requires the longest expected completion time, due to the stochastic nature of activity times, any of the other four paths *may* take longer than 19 weeks. Hence the probability of completing the project within 19 weeks will be some value less than 0.8643.

To get a more accurate assessment of the probability for completing the project by a desired due date, we discuss two approaches. Our first alternative is to compute the probability that all paths are completed within 19 weeks. First, we calculate the probability that each of the other paths will be finished within 19 weeks, just as we did for path A–C–E–H–I. Then we obtain a joint probability by multiplying the individual probabilities. The joint probability provides an approximation of the probability for completing that project by the desired due date. Using the joint probability also depends on the assumption that path completion times are independent of one another. Naturally, if activities are common to more than one path, this assumption is no longer possible. Even so, path independence is generally an acceptable assumption when a project comprises a sufficiently large number of activities.

Alternatively, simulation can also be used to assess the probability of meeting project due dates. With this approach, a simulation software package such as SimQuick can be used to simulate project activity times and then compute statistics with respect to project completion times. The approach is akin to analyzing processes as we discussed in Chapter 9. Here, however, the project activities are the processes. For more specifics, please refer to Chapter 9.

The point of these exercises for any project is to determine the likelihood of meeting project due dates. If the resulting probabilities are unsatisfactory, the project manager can take action to increase the likelihood for success. Options available to do so include adding resources to reduce the project length, changing due dates, or changing project deliverables. In the next section we discuss these alternatives in more detail.

MAKING TIME, COST, AND PERFORMANCE TRADE-OFFS

Although a project network can be a useful tool for determining a project completion date, the date itself is generated in isolation of management expectations and may demonstrate virtually no relationship to what management or the various stakeholders desire for a given project. In the systems development project, the network we developed indicates an expected completion time within 17 weeks. However, management, or the customer who is purchasing the system, may want it much sooner than the date indicated by the project timeline. There is no magic here. Whenever a difference between expectations and the work required arises, either the amount of work must be adjusted or expectations changed. In effect, the project team will have to choose from several options that may include the following:

- Adding resources (people, money, equipment) to complete certain project activities in less time with more resources
- Reducing performance specifications of deliverables so that less work is required with the idea that the project duration should be shorter with fewer requirements
- Changing management expectations so that a later due date is acceptable, possibly by increasing performance specifications or perhaps by demonstrating problems associated with other alternatives
- Combining the previous alternatives

Making Time–Cost Trade-Offs

If a project falls behind schedule, or for that matter, whenever the planned completion date is later than a desired completion date, one alternative may be to add more resources to the project in order to increase the likelihood of achieving the desired date. Naturally, there may be the problem of too many cooks in the kitchen, such that adding more people to an activity may actually add complexity and increase project length. In many cases, however, project activities can be delegated among a larger group of people so that the work as a whole can be completed in less time. In effect, throwing more resources at a project to get things done more quickly essentially makes a trade-off between time and money: Spending more money (adding resources) will reduce the project length (buys time).

In this context, the cost of expediting certain activities to get a project done more quickly must be balanced against the potential benefits. For example, a firm may be penalized by delivering late on a project or may receive a bonus for coming in early. The process of making the time–cost trade-off is referred to as project crashing, and we discuss it next.

Crashing Costs

In order to make time–cost trade-offs, accurate estimates regarding the times and costs involved are necessary. From this perspective, two types of costs and two time estimates are needed for any activity that lies within the consideration set. These include

- Normal time (NT) = Expected activity duration without crashing
- Normal cost (NC) = Expected activity cost without crashing
- Crash time (CT) = Expected activity duration with crashing
- Crash cost (CC) = Expected activity cost with crashing

Although normal time is the longest expected duration for an activity, the crash time is the shortest possible expected duration. The difference, namely $NT - CT$, represents the time gained and traded for the cost: $CC -$ ~C. The basic idea is that the crash time for any activity will be less than normal time, but will come at a higher cost.

We make the assumption that costs are linear. Hence it costs proportionally the same to reduce an activity by one day as it does two days, or more. For example, consider an activity where $NT = 10$, $CT = 5$, $NC = \$1,000$, and $CC = \$5,000$. If a total of 5 crash days are possible for a total cost of $\$4,000$ ($CC - NC$), each of the five days comes at a cost of $\$800$. Therefore, reducing the activity's duration by two days will cost $\$1,600$, by three days will cost $\$2,400$, and so on. Another implicit assumption is that activities can be crashed any number of days between normal time and crash time. For any activity, the cost to crash an activity by one period is

$$\text{Per period crashing cost} = \frac{CC - NC}{NT - CT}$$

We also refer to the per period crashing cost as "bang for the buck." All else being equal, it is more desirable to crash activities with the biggest bang for the buck, which means reducing the greatest amount of time for the least amount of money. Nevertheless, we need to make a distinction between reducing a given activity's duration and reducing the duration of the entire project. Even though an activity's time may be reduced, the project duration may remain the same. In other words, a goal of crashing at minimum cost to achieve a shortened project timeline is more involved than simply selecting an activity with the biggest bang for the buck. Three factors must be considered.

First, it makes sense only to crash activities that are on the critical path. Crashing noncritical activities does not affect project length. Second, even crashing an activity on a critical path may not reduce the project duration. This situation arises when the project contains more than one critical path. In these cases, it will be necessary to crash selected activities that reside on all critical paths simultaneously. Finally, it is important to realize that the process of crashing may cause the set of critical paths to change. We now introduce a three-step process for crashing that accommodates these considerations. Starting with the set of project paths in normal time (i.e., without crashing),

1. Identify critical path(s).
2. Find an activity or set of activities that will reduce the length of all critical paths by one time period for the biggest bang for the buck.
3. Stop if the desired project length is achieved or no more activities can be crashed. Otherwise, go to step 1.

As described, the three-step process of crashing is iterative. Because the critical path may change, crashing should be performed (to the extent possible) one time period per iteration. It only makes sense to crash activities on the critical path, and all critical paths must be reduced simultaneously. We illustrate the process of crashing with our example systems development project.

Crashing at Minimum Cost to Achieve a Desired Completion Date

In the systems development project, the expected completion date is 17 weeks. How would we crash the project if management wanted an expected completion date of 14 weeks? To begin, it is helpful to list the full set of paths in the project and the durations for each one of them. The example contains the following five paths:

- A–C–E–H–I with duration 17 weeks
- B–C–E–H–I with duration 16 weeks
- B–D–E–H–I with duration 16 weeks
- B–D–F–H–I with duration 15 weeks
- B–D–G–H–I with duration 16 weeks

Table 15.4 contains the necessary crashing information for each activity in our example. Beginning now with step 1, we look first at the only critical path at this time, namely path A–C–E–H–I at 17 weeks. Proceeding to step 2, of the critical activities A, C, E, H, and I, activity A has the least cost for crashing at $500 per week as identified in the last column of Table 15.4. Hence, we crash activity A one week, which

---

TABLE 15.4: *Crashing Information*

Activity	Normal Time (weeks)	Normal Cost	Crash Time (weeks)	Crash Cost	Crash Days Allowed	Cost per Crash Day
A	4	$2,000	3	$2,500	1	$ 500
B	3	$3,500	2	$4,000	1	$ 250
C	5	$5,000	3	$7,500	2	$1,250
D	5	$8,000	4	$9,500	1	$1,500
E	4	$4,000	2	$6,000	2	$1,000
F	3	$2,500	1	$3,000	2	$ 250
G	4	$6,000	3	$6,400	1	$ 400
H	3	$3,000	3	—	—	—
I	1	$1,000	1	—	—	—

reduces both the critical path and project duration by one week to 16 weeks. After crashing, the path durations are:

- A–C–E–H–I with duration 16 weeks
- B–C–E–H–I with duration 16 weeks
- B–D–E–H–I with duration 16 weeks
- B–D–F–H–I with duration 15 weeks
- B–D–G–H–I with duration 16 weeks

We have not reached 14 weeks, so we proceed back to step 1. Of the five paths in the project, four of them are now critical. In order to reduce the project length by one week, it will be necessary to reduce the lengths of all four paths simultaneously. The following combinations are possible {C,B}, {C,D}, {E,B}, {E,D}, and {E,G}. Note that {A,B} would be possible and in fact provide the biggest bang for the buck, or least cost per crash day, except that activity A was already crashed by its one allowable day. Of the remaining choices, the combination of crashing activities {E,B} costs the least at a total of $1,250 for both activities. After crashing, the path durations are:

- A–C–E–H–I with duration 15 weeks
- B–C–E–H–I with duration 14 weeks
- B–D–E–H–I with duration 14 weeks
- B–D–F–H–I with duration 14 weeks
- B–D–G–H–I with duration 15 weeks

Now, only two paths are critical, with a length of 15 weeks. We need to crash one more week to reduce the project duration down to 14 weeks. Only the following combinations will work: {C,D}, {C,G}, {E,D}, and {E,G}. Of these possibilities, the combination of {E,G} for $1,400 is the lowest.

In summary, we required three iterations of crashing activities one week at a time in order to crash the project down from 17 weeks to 14 weeks. The cost of crashing would be $3,150, increasing the total estimated project cost from $35,000 to $38,150.

The crashing technique for managing projects reduces their durations by making a trade-off between time and money. Because time and cost are the only considerations in the process, many important qualitative aspects will be ignored if they are not explicitly considered. For example, project crashing can increase stress levels, increase the use of overtime or extend working hours, and generally affect employee attitudes and morale in negative ways.

Reducing Performance Specifications and Other Alternatives

Making time–cost trade-offs is one way to expedite project activities and reduce the duration of the project. As previously mentioned, however, other alternatives may be more attractive to pursue and, interestingly, these other alternatives are often ignored or at best given limited consideration. One of these is making time–specifications trade-offs. The basic idea is similar to making time–cost trade-offs. Here, however, project specifications generally indicate the amount of work involved in a project, and because the work involved and the time required are directly related, it is possible to make a trade-off between time and specifications. In essence, the project duration can be reduced by simply eliminating certain project deliverables. For example, in the systems development project, it may be more attractive to simply drop or postpone a certain number of the reports the computer program automatically generates. By dropping these project deliverables, it may be possible to shift the resources originally intended for them onto other activities that could reduce the project duration without increasing costs. Naturally, the opportunity to eliminate deliverables on any project depends on a number of factors, particularly how critical a given deliverable is to the overall project. For example, activity B, Database Design in the systems development project, could not be dropped without effectively crippling the project. But, as mentioned, if certain reports are not critical, they could be dropped or postponed to a later date. In fact, one method of rapidly implementing computer programs is to quickly develop a core system with just basic features and only later, through a series of "enhancements" or future mini-projects, does the full system evolve.

It should be noted that if the planned project completion takes longer than desired, perhaps an approach may be to revisit the desired date of completion. Where did the date come from? Many times, a project team will find that the date is not set in stone. Perhaps it was originally decided because it seemed "reasonable" at the time. But most often, dates and durations are generally thought of first and the work requirements second. Hence, when the due dates of project deliverables are based on a good reason, the work should fit the schedule. Otherwise, it may be better to let the schedule (due dates) fit the work that is required.

Finally, it is important to realize that within the alternative set, individual alternatives are not mutually exclusive. It may be possible, even desirable, to implement a combination of these alternatives. For example, it may make sense to crash a project a few time periods and eliminate some of the deliverables. Alternatively, the desired due date might be put off until later, while simultaneously crashing a few activities on the project.

Summary

Projects are complex and dynamic processes and ever-present parts of business operations. Although projects vary in size and importance, they share certain characteristics that make them difficult to manage. Projects are subject to uncertainty, often involve multiple stakeholders, are subject to finite lifetimes and limited resources, and in many cases provide no clear authority within the project's structure. Each of these characteristics adds to a project's complexity and makes success difficult to achieve. Project success itself is often difficult to determine because of multiple stakeholders who effectively determine success. Consequently, it is important to manage the expectations of stakeholders and provide constant and consistent communication among everyone involved.

Successful project management means avoiding the common causes for failure and using state-of-the-art tools and methods to plan and control work as it proceeds. Common causes for failure include not proactively managing uncertainty, improperly managing expectations among stakeholders, and scope creep. A critical success factor that arises from these observations is conservative project planning.

An exceptional tool for project planning is a network diagram. A network diagram helps determine the project schedule and answer questions pertaining to when activities will start and end. The process of planning never ends until the project is completed. Because of the dynamic nature of projects, planning, in effect replanning, must be repeated periodically to update project status and allow management to make appropriate adjustments when necessary.

Review Questions

1. What are the common characteristics of projects? How do these characteristics increase the complexity and difficulty of achieving success in project management?
2. How should project success be determined?
3. What is meant by conservative project planning? Identify examples of conservative planning.
4. What are some of the common causes for project failure? Identify ways in which these causes can be circumvented or otherwise managed.

Problems

15.1.   The following table outlines the activities, activity durations, and the precedence relationships of a project to be scheduled:

Activity	Duration (days)	Immediate Predecessors
A	3	—
B	2	—
C	6	A
D	4	A
E	5	A,B
F	2	C
G	8	D
H	2	E
I	5	F,G,H
J	10	E

a. Construct an activity-on-node network for the project.
b. Calculate the ES, EF, LS, and LF for each activity.
c. How long will it take to complete this project?
d. What is (are) the critical path(s)?
e. What is the slack for each activity not on a critical path?

15.2.   The following table outlines the activities, activity durations, and the precedence relationships of a project to be scheduled:

Activity	Duration (weeks)	Immediate Predecessors
A	3	—
B	6	A
C	4	A
D	3	B
E	2	B,C
F	4	C
G	2	D,E,F

a. Draw the project network for the project.
b. Calculate the ES, EF, LS, and LF for each activity.
c. How long will it take to complete this project?
d. What is (are) the critical path(s)?
e. What is the slack for each activity not on a critical path?

15.3   You receive the following project information for each activity, the time (in weeks) it takes to complete, the possible weeks by which that time can be reduced, and the cost per week to decrease the activity time. The cost to complete the project in normal time is $10,000.

Activity	Duration (weeks)	Predecessor(s)	Crash Weeks Possible	Crashing Cost per Week
A	3	—	1	$1,500
B	2	—	—	—
C	7	A,B	3	$1,750
D	4	B	1	1,000
E	5	B	2	$1,250
F	1	C,D,E	—	—
G	2	E	1	$1,250

a. Draw the project network for this project.
b. What is the minimum time duration of the project?
c. What is the critical path of the project?
d. What is the slack time, if any, for activity D?
e. How much will it cost to complete the project in 10 weeks? 9 weeks?

15.4   You receive the following project information for each activity, the time (in weeks) it takes to complete, the possible weeks by which that time can be reduced, and the cost per week to decrease the activity time. The cost to complete the project in normal time is $15,500.

Activity	Duration (weeks)	Predecessor(s)	Crash Weeks Possible	Crashing Cost per Week
A	4	—	1	$900
B	2	A	2	$500
C	4	A	2	$800
D	3	A	1	$250
E	4	B,C	1	$750
F	1	C,D,E	—	—

a. Draw the project network for this project.
b. What is the minimum time duration of the project?
c. What is the critical path of the project?
d. How much will it cost to complete the project in 12 weeks? 10 weeks?

15.5   If it is desirable to crash a project to shorten its time to completion, why not simply crash the activity with the lowest crash cost per period of time?

15.6   The following table outlines the activities, activity durations, and the precedence relationships of a project to be scheduled:

Activity	Duration (days)	Immediate Predecessors
A	3	—
B	2	—
C	6	—
D	4	A,B
E	5	B,C
F	2	A,D
G	8	D,E
H	2	F,G
I	5	G
J	10	F,H,I

a. Construct an activity-on-node network for the project.
b. Calculate the ES, EF, LS, and LF for each activity.
c. How long will it take to complete this project?
d. What is (are) the critical path(s)?
e. What is the slack for each activity not on a critical path?

15.7 A project has an expected completion time of 16 weeks, yet the desired completion times is 14 weeks. If the variance of activities on the path with the longest expected completion time sums to 636, then
a. What is the probability of completing all activities on the path within the desired time frame?
b. If the project includes other paths, albeit with shorter expected completion times, why would the probability of completing the entire project be less than the answer to part (a)?

15.8 Management decided to implement the project described in the following table:

Activity	Predecessor(s)	Optimistic Time (weeks)	Most Likely Time (weeks)	Pessimistic Time (weeks)
A	—	2	3	5
B	—	1	2	4
C	A	3	3	5
D	A,B	2	6	9
E	C	2	4	5
F	B,D	1	2	3
G	E,F	2	3	4

a. Draw the project network.
b. What is the expected completion time of the project?
c. If the path A–D–F–G has the longest expected completion time, why is it not necessarily the critical path?
d. What are the variances for each activity?
e. Assuming that the path completion times are independent, what is the probability of completing the project in 15 weeks?
f. Given the same assumption as in part (e), what is the probability of completing the project in 12 weeks?

15.9 You are chosen to take over the following project and finish it four days ahead of the time indicated by the critical path. The following AON diagram describes the little remaining work to be done on this overdue project. Note that the activity durations, in days, are shown in parentheses.

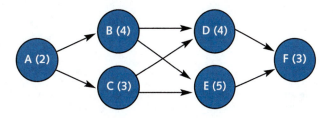

The following table outlines information available regarding crash costs and times for the remaining activities.

Activity	Crash Cost ($/day)	Crash Days Possible
A	—	—
B	350	2
C	200	2
D	100	2
E	300	2
F	450	1

a. Use the critical path method to determine the duration for this project.
b. What is the most economical way to crash the project duration by four days? How much will it cost?
c. What is (are) the new critical path(s)?

CASE STUDY

The Quick Course Preparation Case

Tom and Harry sat dumbstruck as Dick, the Chair of the Management Department, asked them if they would co-teach the new MBA elective in Services Operations this fall. The slack jaws and waggling tongues were a little disconcerting. Dick then added, "Ok, I know it's asking a lot, given the additional teaching load and that there's only 30 days (not counting today) until the start of the semester, but we've got to have some motivation for this class and so there you have it. With both of you to split the effort, however, I don't think it should be too overwhelming."

"Dick, you know the students generally and intensely dislike it when there are two instructors teaching the same course. This does not bode well for the program or our teaching evaluations. Not to mention the last time this happened," replied Harry.

"Last time?" asked Dick.

"I told you not to mention that," said Harry.

Dick sighed. "Naturally, lines of communication and responsibility must be clearly defined so that the students know the score and expectations are properly managed. For that matter, I suggest breaking up the course into two modules, with each of you being the 'de facto' instructor for one of them."

Now Tom got into it. "Perhaps that might work, but I think preparation time is the bigger issue, what with only 30 days to prepare. You know it's a new course—a completely new preparation, and since it has a distance teaching component, all the materials need to be ready by the first day of class. How can we even get the course materials, including book and course pack to the bookstore in time? First, you have to select the course materials that include the textbook, cases, and reading materials—five days at least. Then, the order lead-time of the book itself is another 20 days alone. Actually, it could take anywhere from 15 to 25 days."

Dick responded, "That sounds like less than 30 days to me, but then math was never my strong point. Besides, I've heard that the new edition of *Successful Service Operations Management* is great. It even has a book chapter on Project Management. Surely, that should cut down the time devoted to selecting a book, and anyhow, I'm sure we can expedite book delivery via FedEx, if necessary, for about $500. That would save another three days if needed. Even with a fiscal budget that is, for the lack of a better metaphor, tighter than your ability to give A's, I'm sure I can loosen up a few dollars to make it happen if necessary."

Harry chimed in at that point, "Ok, but I think the cases and other reading materials are going to pose a bigger problem. It takes five days for our selections to go through the copyright department. Then it's another ten days to wait until they are delivered, and that's being more charitable than saying that this case is challenging. I mean, really, the materials could take anywhere from seven to fourteen days to be delivered. Only then can the course pack be put together, assuming we've put together all the other material—the lecture notes, homework sets, case assignments,

CASE STUDY

and syllabus by that time. I mean, just putting the material together will take three days at least, then it's another five days until they are back from the printer and delivered to the bookstore."

"Ok, Ok, Ok," said Dick. "I realize you both did not expect this on your plate, particularly with the slack jaws, waggling tongues, and everything, but I have every confidence in the both of you to put together a bang-up course and save the day. I'm sure it won't go unnoticed by the Dean and it certainly won't by me. Moreover, I'll set aside some money so you have a graduate assistant that can help with the homework sets and the grading. I can also set aside some time to help. So why don't the both of you sit down, talk it through, and put together a plan. If there is something else you think of that I can do to help, just let me know."

Later, Tom and Harry met to discuss what they needed to do. Harry started. "Ok, as far as I can tell, the *very* first thing we need to do is figure out the course content. We should be able to hammer that out in about four days. Then we can select the course book, the cases, and supplementary reading materials as we discussed before. I think the estimate you stated earlier, five days, sounds about right. Although, if we get caught short on time, I know we can cut our search time for course materials via educational pay Web sites on the Internet. It would cost about $700, but then it should only take two days to select the materials."

"Well, that might be handy and as Dick mentioned, he can find some money if necessary," said Tom. "Once the materials are selected, we'll have to prep the lectures, create the case teaching plans, and of course, the syllabus. I'm sure we can draw on some material from our other courses, so I bet we can prep the lectures in about eight days, the case teaching plans should take about four days, and the syllabus two days at most. After we put together the lecture material, we can then put together the PowerPoint slides—say five days, and the lecture notes, afterwards, for the course pack in another day. What else?"

"Well, as I said before, the course pack should also contain both the case assignments and homework sets. Once the case teaching plans are completed, the case assignments should only take two days to put together. As for the homework sets, once we decide on the syllabus, I figure that should take another four days. I've got a lot of material already prepared that we can use."

"Since we will get a graduate assistant to help, we can have whoever that person is put together homework solution sets. I'd like to have it done before the start of the semester. That way, we can resolve any problems before they crop up during the course. But that means we have to hire the assistant and go through all that bother. Looking through a hundred resumes, well, I'd rather be a student assigned to this very case."

"Come on Tom, a graduate assistant will be a big help, and it won't be much of a bother," said Harry. "Look. It will take, say, five days to go through the hiring

CASE STUDY

process, probably another five days of training and on-the-spot education, but then that person will be able to put together the solution sets for us. It will probably take ten days for whoever we hire, but I'd gladly trade the effort of creating solution sets with the effort on hiring and training—particularly given that we later have a resource to help with grading."

"Yeah, I'm sure you're right," said Tom. "We can actually get started on the hiring process at anytime, and I'm sure it won't hold us up. Anything else we've forgotten? That is, is there any other information we can impart on our readership to enhance the learning experience of this case?"

"The only thing I can think of is that we need to remember to leave five days lead time for the course pack to be printed and delivered to the bookstore, once we've put it together. Although, I know they can expedite for a fee of $400 that will cut it down to two days. Otherwise, I think we've covered everything."

Questions:

1. Viewing course management from the perspective of project management, what do Tom and Harry need to do to help ensure success of the course? That is, what issues must they address as co-teachers that they would not otherwise need to address? Will separating the course into modules address these issues appropriately? If not, what else do you recommend?

2. Put together a network diagram for this project assuming deterministic task times (use mean expected completion times). The network diagram should identify all activities, precedence relationships, and task times.

3. From your network diagram, list all paths, identify path lengths, and those that are critical.

4. Without crashing and without regard to whomever actually does the work, will the project be completed in normal time? If not, what, if anything, can be done in order to complete the course preparation within the allotted 30 days?

5. Using your answer to question 4 and the probabilistic time estimates, what is the probability of completing the project on time? What would be the best means of ensuring that this probability is greater than 95%. *Hint:* You first need to compute the probability of completing each path that contains activities with uncertain times.

Site Selection for Services

LEARNING OBJECTIVES *The material in this chapter prepares students to:*

- Use factor rating systems and regression to find locations for demand-sensitive services.

- Use Geographic Information Systems.

- Understand methods for locating back-office services.

- Be able to create a mathematical model for locating a service network.

Selecting a site for most service firms is a fundamentally different problem than selecting a site for most manufacturing facilities. Consequently, even if the topic of "site selection" or "location" has been studied in a previous class in operations management, this chapter is still applicable. Selecting a site for a manufacturing plant is done infrequently, and the basis for the decision is often centered on reducing costs usually through tax concessions from local governments or exploiting inexpensive labor. For example, in the 1990s Hynix Semiconductor, BMW, and Mercedes-Benz received tens of millions of dollars in tax breaks to build plants in Oregon, South Carolina, and Alabama, respectively.

For service firms, however, the site selection problem can be a frequent one. It is not unusual for a "hot" retailing firm to add several hundred new stores in a year. For example, Dollar General, a 6,700-store chain, opened 600–700 new stores each year for the past few years. The location decision is often not based on lowering costs—and the vast majority of service outlets are too small for governments to give anything in the way of tax incentives. The decision usually centers on how the location will help generate revenue.

For many service firms, site selection poses the most important operational decision faced. A poor location can doom a facility to failure regardless of how well it is managed. Despite its importance, this decision is still one that most firms struggle with—a decision often made with far more "gut feel" and opinion than science and fact.

TYPES OF SERVICE FIRMS

Different types of services have very different needs regarding site selection and use radically different methods to attack this problem. Consequently, this chapter is organized by the type of service firm (see Figure 16.1).

Demand-Sensitive Services

The goal of site selection in a demand-sensitive service is to attract customers through location. Prominent examples include most of the service firms a consumer will visit, such as banks, restaurants, and retail stores. The problem of site selection is most critical in this type of business, since it is the customers who have to be enticed to travel to the service site, rather than employees being ordered to travel to the customer. The difference between the best site and a reasonably good site for delivered services or quasi-manufacturing services might reduce overall profits a few percentage points. The difference between the reasonably good and best site in demand-sensitive services is the difference between profit and loss.

Delivered Services

The goal in delivered services is to use multiple locations to cover a geographic area effectively. Examples in the public sector include fire and police protection, postal facilities, and emergency medicine. Private sector examples include food delivery, package delivery, private medical services (e.g., private ambulance services), and repair services (for example, business computer repair, where downtime represents lost customer orders). A retail "saturation strategy" that is used in many industries, such as grocers and convenience stores, also is helped by the methods covered in this section.

Quasi-Manufacturing Services

The goal in these services is to minimize the logistical cost of a multiple location network. Examples include the back-office processing centers of banks and insurance companies, warehouses, hotel reservation centers and other call centers, and many firms in the wholesaling industry.

Other types of service firm location decisions include locating a corporate headquarters, an Internet-based service, or finding a location for duplicate systems in case of a primary system disaster, for example. Those location decisions, however, are more idiosyncratic, and do not lend themselves as readily to the type of analysis that will be discussed here.

FIGURE 16.1: *Types of Service Firms and the Main Goal of Siting*

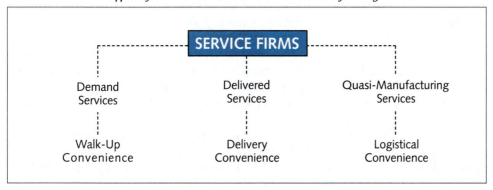

SITE SELECTION FOR DEMAND-SENSITIVE SERVICES

Consider finding a location for a mid-priced restaurant. A good site would be characterized by a long list of attributes: It would be good to be close to business offices, be easily accessed, be in an area with high traffic, include ample parking, room for expansion, good competitive factors, a nice local government for zoning variances and taxes, and be inexpensive to lease, among others. Even for those who never worked in retail, banking, or a restaurant, it is fairly simple to draw up a long list of characteristics that would make for good retail locations.

Unfortunately, just creating a list of criteria and getting the necessary data isn't enough. If a developer finds a potential site that is better than all the rest on all criteria, the immediate action to take is to wake up because it is only a dream. Among the sites scouted for a demand-sensitive service, one will be lower in cost, another have better access, and the third will be closer to customers. What is needed is a method to present and weigh the conflicting advantages of various sites—some way to determine whether, say, being a quarter-mile closer to downtown is better or worse than being a quarter-mile closer to a major university. Without some agreed-upon method, a firm must rely on the biased and often conflicting opinion of individuals.

Two methods that attempt to bring some order to the data are factor rating and regression. A third method for presenting location data that has become popular in recent years will also be discussed: Geographic Information Systems.

None of these methods can replace entirely the art of site selection. All three of the techniques discussed here are meant to augment, rather than replace, human judgment, because none of them are robust enough to take into consideration the full range of detail necessary. These methods are best put to use through data reduction; that is, the sites that score poorly on either a factor rating scheme or a regression analysis are eliminated from consideration, and the few top sites are then further scrutinized.

Factor Rating

In a factor rating system the key criteria for consideration are listed and subjectively assigned weights, then prospective sites are subjectively assigned values for the key criteria, and the assigned values are combined with the criteria weights to determine an overall score for the site.

Table 16.1 shows an example for finding a restaurant site in the Washington, D.C., area. First, important criteria are listed. To keep this example simple we consider only five criteria: "income of neighborhood," "proximity to shopping centers," "accessibility," "visibility," and "traffic." Table 16.1 presents two mathematically identical ways that these criteria can be given numerical rankings. The first method assigns a higher point total to more important criteria, the second method allows each factor to be judged on the same scale—a scale of 1–10 here—and then the score is multiplied by a corresponding percentage depending on the importance of the factor.

Four potential sites for our Washington, D.C., area restaurant are: Springfield, Tyson's Corner, Gaithersburg, and Alexandria. Here, they are ranked according to the second method on Table 16.1. Field agents visit the sites, collect data, and assign a ranking for each factor with each site. Multiplying each rating by the appropriate percentage, Gaithersburg tops the list with a $10(.40) + 10(.25) + 8(.15) + 7(.10) + 8(.10) = 9.20$ factor rating score.

As a site selection system, factor rating offers both advantages and disadvantages. The primary advantage is transparency and ease of use. The simplicity of the system allows everyone involved to easily understand how it works. Also, providing

TABLE 16.1: *Utilizing Factor Rating to Analyze Potential Washington, D.C., Restaurant Sites*

Factors	Range
Income of neighborhood	0–40
Proximity to shopping centers	0–25
Accessibility	0–15
Visibility	0–10
Traffic	0–10

OR

Factors	Scale	Multiplier
Income of neighborhood	0–10	.40
Proximity to shopping centers	0–10	.25
Accessibility	0–10	.15
Visibility	0–10	.10
Traffic	0–10	.10

Potential Sites:	Springfield	Tyson's Corner	Gaithersburg	Alexandria
Income	4	8	10	6
Shopping	2	7	10	4
Access	1	9	8	4
Visibility	6	9	7	6
Traffic	3	8	8	5

TOTAL SCORE:

Springfield	3.15
Tyson's Corner	8.00
Gaithersburg	9.20
Alexandria	5.10

numerical weights up front avoids the endless arguments over whether, say, one "visibility" point is worth one or two "income of neighborhood" points.

Among its substantial disadvantages, however, the weighting of the factors is highly arbitrary. Why is "income of neighborhood" four times more important than "traffic?" Because the "big boss" said so. In actuality, the relationship may be entirely different. The arbitrary nature of this process is compounded by the 1–10 ranking scale. One person may look at the situation and give it a 3, but someone else may call it a 5. Consequently, any ranking of sites that may come out of such a system is highly suspect. In the particular example given, the best use of the numbers at the end of the process is to narrow the field of competitors, rather than pick a winner. That is, look further at the Gaithersburg and Tyson's Corner sites, and perhaps drop putting any more resources into investigating the Springfield and Alexandria sites.

Another problem with factor rating systems, usually discussed in statistics courses, is multicollinearity. That is, several factors that are given weights might be correlated with each other. So instead of measuring different attributes, the factor rating system gives points to the same attribute. For example, if points are given for both the average income of the local area as well as the average housing value, then what is really happening is that income is being doubly weighted. Given the way factor rating systems are used, the best defense against this double weighting is common sense. In the next method discussed, regression, multicollinearity can be detected fairly easily by tests provided in any introductory statistics textbook.

Regression

Using regression as a site selection method is similar to factor rating. In regression, however, the weights that the factors receive are determined by their actual relationship to results, rather than by managerial whim.

The process in building a site selection regression model is different and more complex than factor rating. Because of these differences and the one-time nature of the project of putting together the initial model, calling in outside consultants to assist would be recommended.

One difference lies in the overall objective. In factor rating, the goal is to derive some overall score for a site. This score, however, provides no intrinsic meaning. Gaithersburg's score of 9.2 versus Tyson's Corner's score of 8.0 does not translate directly into 9.2 – 8.0 = 1.2 more in profits, market share, or customer satisfaction. The score from a factor rating model is an abstract entity. The function of a site selection regression model depends on a real objective (or *dependent variable* in regression-speak). Determining what the dependent variable should be is not the easy task it would appear, but the details of that issue are left for Chapter 17. For the purposes of this discussion, the dependent variable of interest will be "profits."

In similar fashion to factor rating models, an initial step in site selection by regression is listing the factors that influence profits. Some of the factors used by First American Bank in the mid-1990s in their site location model can be found in Table 16.2. The next step is quite time consuming; data for all the factors for each existing unit must be collected. The available data are then used in actually converting factors into independent variables that a regression model can use, a process usually called transforming the variables.

Note that the general factors of "age of population" and "income of households" are further broken out into three independent variables. The reason is based on the complexity of the relationship of many independent variables with profitability. As a hypothetical example, profits may be lowest serving a young population, high serving a middle-aged population, and moderate profits achieved serving an older population (Figure 16.2). But the output of a standard regression model is one weighting (the beta coefficient) for each variable. In this case, saying that profits increase, by say, 1% times the population age, is misleading. It may be the average relationship, but it understates profits for middle-aged customers and overstates profits for older customers. In Table 16.2, the "customer age" factor is broken into three independent

TABLE 16.2: *First American Bank Site Selection Independent Variables*

Factors	Independent Variables
Age of population	% of population 25–34 % of population 35–54 % of population 55+
Annual income of households	$20,000–$34,000 $35,000–$49,000 $50,000+
Street placement	1–10 rating
Pedestrian traffic	# pedestrians/5 minutes
Years facility open	years

FIGURE 16.2: *Transforming Variables: Hypothetical Relationship of Profitability and Customer Age*

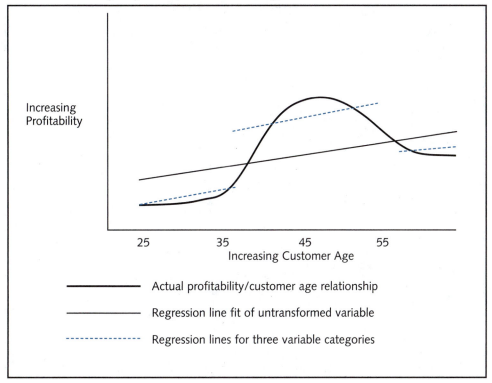

variables that provide a better fit for the true relationship. Here, First American determined three separate age categories would be best. Variables can be transformed, however, in an enormous number of ways. Perhaps four or five categories would have been better, or the upper limit on the "young" category should have been 39 instead of 34. Determining the best variable transformations is a large part of the art of creating regression models for site selection.

Another typical method for transforming variables to use in site selection regressions is to take some reasonable function of the variable. For example, consider the relationship between a restaurant and nearby office space (Figure 16.3). A restaurant located inside a large office building may serve a significant lunch crowd from the building, and the same restaurant located a half mile away would get significantly less traffic. However, if the restaurant were 5 miles away from the office versus 5½ miles away, the drop-off in customers from the extra half mile would be minimal. So, the first half mile is far more important than subsequent half miles. In this example, a simple regression of distance on customers yields the straight line shown, actually predicting a negative number of customers at a 6-mile distance. The regression performed on the function [logarithm(customers)] (that is, taking the logarithm of the number of customers, rather than just the number of customers) yields a better result, as shown by the curved line in Figure 16.3.

Note, however, in Table 16.3, that neither regression truly captured the real benefit of being inside the office building, with the regressions predicting 110 or 116 customers while the actual number is 200, which indicates a better way to view this

FIGURE 16.3: *Transforming Variables: Customer Patronage of a Restaurant and Distance from the Workplace*

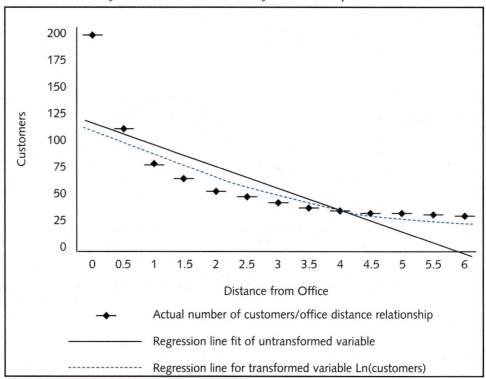

TABLE 16.3: *Transforming Variables in Restaurant Problem[a]*

Dependent Variable: Number of Customers	Independent Variable: Distance from Office (miles)	Regression: Predicting Customers with Untransformed Variable[b]	Regression: Predicting Customers Regressing Distance on Ln(Customers)[c]
200	0.0	116	110
110	0.5	106	95
70	1.0	96	82
60	1.5	86	71
49	2.0	76	61
42	2.5	67	53
37	3.0	57	45
33	3.5	47	39
30	4.0	37	34
28	4.5	27	29
27	5.0	17	25
26	5.5	8	22
25	6.0	−2	19

[a] More detailed data are available as a Microsoft Excel spreadsheet on the text CD.
[b] Regression $R^2 = 0.60$
[c] Regression $R^2 = 0.84$

relationship needs to be found. In this example, one can view the problem as two basic types of restaurants: Type 1—restaurants inside an office building; and Type 2—restaurants that require travel. It might be advisable to create two different regression models for these two different types. For example, Dollar General uses six different regression models for what they perceive as six different store types in their portfolio.

A type of variable needed in a regression model that is not needed in a factor rating model is a variable that explains the profitability of existing units but has no bearing on a new site. Note, for example, that the variable "years facility open" appears in Table 16.2 as a variable used by First American bank in selecting brand new sites. At first glance, it would appear that such a variable would be irrelevant. But consider the data in Table 16.4. If one were to look just at the relationship between "distance from downtown" and "profits," it would seem reasonable to say that new facilities should all be located downtown. However, if the "years facility open" variable is also considered, it becomes clear that being far from downtown may not doom a facility to low profitability, after all.

Even though it adds more science to the issue of site selection, regression also poses several drawbacks. A primary problem is a lack of education. Many longtime real estate employees are simply unaware of regression, so the output numbers seem to come from a mysterious "black box" and are not trusted. The level of statistical uncertainty in regression models also presents a problem. For example, Taco Bell's regression-based models predicted revenue for potential sites. However, the expectations of service personnel are that these predictions should have the accuracy of budget numbers—that is, these predictions should be within a few percentage points of what actually occurs. Because the revenue predictions can be different from actual results by 20% to 30%, real estate personnel felt they were of little value and discontinued their use. However, this assessment indicates a lack of understanding of how to use regression models. These models are best at displaying differences between potential sites, rather than accurately predicting what next year's revenue will be for a specific outlet.

Small chains or new ventures cannot readily use regression for this purpose. Regression requires that a history already be developed; that is, a regression model needs data, so a firm must already have several facilities in the field before they can be analyzed by regression. Further, the best that regression can do is look at how different factors affected last year's profits. It is a blind numerical technique that cannot feel upcoming trends.

TABLE 16.4: *Hypothetical Relationship of Facility Age and Profits*

Number	Profits	Years Facility Open	Distance from Downtown
1	High	10	1
2	High	10	1
3	High	10	1
4	High	10	1
5	High	10	10
6	Low	1	1
7	Low	1	10
8	Low	1	10
9	Low	1	10
10	Low	1	10

Geographic Information Systems

A Geographic Information System (GIS) is computer software that links location to information in an easy-to-use visual format. A GIS is more than just a map on a computer screen. The purpose of site selection GIS is to predict demand based on information stored in geographic databases. For any given point on a map, a GIS system can answer questions such as "How many households within a 5-mile radius have annual incomes over $50,000?" "What is the likely cannibalization effect on my network of stores by placing a store in this location?" "What potential sites in a region are zoned commercial, between 2 and 5 acres, and not in the 100-year flood plain?" "What market share among women, ages 35–50, will a new store located at a specific address take from the existing store network of competitors?"

The first GIS uses were in politics, geology, and environmental planning. For example, congressional redistricting is an exercise that occurs in the United States every 10 years. A possible goal in redistricting is getting as many favorable districts for one's political party as possible. For example, given 3 million Republicans and 3 million Democrats in a state with 11 House of Representative seats, one congressional district could be created with 550,000 Republicans and no Democrats, while the other 10 districts could have 245,000 Republicans and 300,000 Democrats, thus assuring 91% Democrat representation in an evenly divided state. The main tool used to create such political districts is a GIS system. For example, in 2001 in Texas, the state Redistricting Board approved maps that would change the Republican edge in the state house from 78–72 to 88–62.[1]

Due to both increasing computer power and a shift in the marketing programs of leading GIS firms, business uses of GIS grew significantly in the past decade. In addition to using GIS for site selection, other business uses include sales territory partitioning, vehicle routing, or target marketing campaigns. The leading firms in the industry include Tactician, ESRI, Intergraph, GDS, Strategic Mapping, and Mapinfo (a sample of firms using GIS systems is on Table 16.5).

A GIS provided by Tactician Corporation and available on the Internet at http://www.tactician.com is used here as an example. We are trying to find a good site for the new restaurant, MyPlace. Its target market is middle-aged households (ages 35–54) with annual incomes of $50,000–$75,000. We want to find an appropriate locale with a number of potential customers within easy walking or driving distance. The chosen site is the address of 975 Adair Avenue, Atlanta, Georgia. On the

TABLE 16.5: *A Partial List of Geographic Information System Users*

Ace Hardware	DuPont Merck
Anheuser Busch	Hilton Hotels Corporation
Arby's	JCPenney
AT&T	John Deere
Avis	Marks & Spencer
Banc One	McDonald's Corporation
BellSouth	Molly Maid
Blockbuster	OfficeMax
Chemical Bank	Safeway Stores
Chevron	Tesco Stores Ltd.
Coca-Cola	Wells Fargo
Dayton-Hudson	

---

1. S. Attlesey (2001), "New Maps Could Give GOP Large Minority in Both Houses," *Dallas Morning News*, July 25, p. A1.

MapScape screen (Figure 16.4), three different trade areas are chosen: within a quarter-mile, within a three-minute drive, and within a 10-minute drive.

Figure 16.5 shows the area within a quarter-mile, and Figure 16.6 shows that 49 households in that quarter-mile meet the criteria. (The numbers on figures16.6 and 16.8 are from the 1990 census. Tactician provides material from the 2000 census for a fee.) Figure 16.7 shows the area in which persons are capable of driving to this location within three minutes. Note that the area is irregularly shaped, because this software realizes that one can travel faster on main roads. Figure 16.8 shows that 770 households meet the criteria in this three-minute drive radius.

The software demonstrated here is available over the Internet at http://www.tactician.com. More sophisticated software from the same company contains imbedded mathematical models that can assist in determining the percentage of demand that may be expected from an area, depending upon the competitive environment. One such model is known as the gravity model.

Gravity Model of Demand

The so-called "gravity" models are a set of several variants of a basic theme that sounds quite logical: Given two similar stores, a customer is more likely to go to the closer one. A simplistic interpretation of this idea is that the attraction to a store j of the n stores in the neighborhood from a customer i is based solely on the travel time T_{ij}. So, given several similar stores nearby, the probability P_{ik} of customer i going to a specific store k is given by

$$P_{ik} = \left(1/T_{ik}\right)/\sum_{j=1}^{n}\left(1/T_{ij}\right)$$ (16.1)

FIGURE 16.4: *Tactician™ Report Choice*

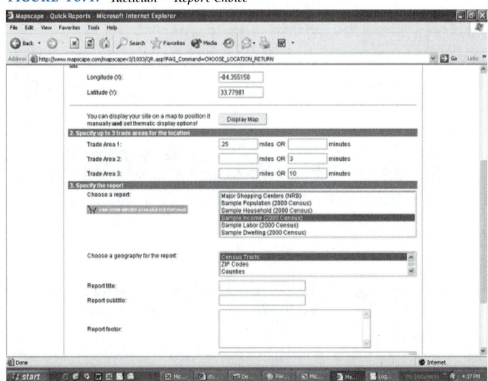

FIGURE 16.5: *Map of Area Within a Quarter-Mile*

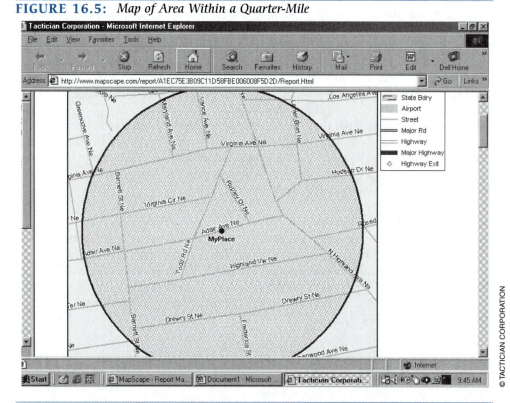

FIGURE 16.6: *Demographic Information of Area Within a Quarter-Mile*

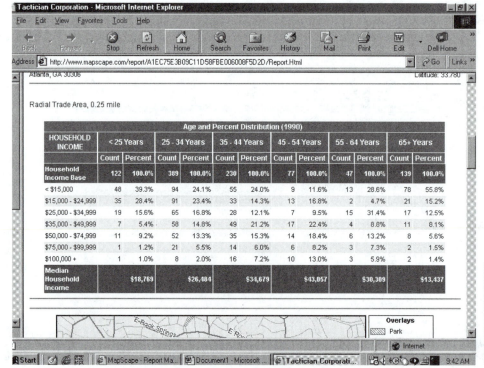

Radial Trade Area, 0.25 mile

HOUSEHOLD INCOME	< 25 Years		25 - 34 Years		35 - 44 Years		45 - 54 Years		55 - 64 Years		65+ Years	
	Count	Percent	Count	Percent	Count	Percent	Count	Percent	Count	Percent	Count	Percent
Household Income Base	122	100.0%	389	100.0%	230	100.0%	77	100.0%	47	100.0%	139	100.0%
< $15,000	48	39.3%	94	24.1%	55	24.0%	9	11.6%	13	28.6%	78	55.8%
$15,000 - $24,999	35	28.4%	91	23.4%	33	14.3%	13	16.8%	2	4.7%	21	15.2%
$25,000 - $34,999	19	15.6%	65	16.8%	28	12.1%	7	9.5%	15	31.4%	17	12.5%
$35,000 - $49,999	7	5.4%	58	14.8%	49	21.2%	17	22.4%	4	8.8%	11	8.1%
$50,000 - $74,999	11	9.2%	52	13.3%	35	15.3%	14	18.4%	6	13.2%	8	5.6%
$75,000 - $99,999	1	1.2%	21	5.5%	14	6.0%	6	8.2%	3	7.3%	2	1.5%
$100,000 +	1	1.0%	8	2.0%	16	7.2%	10	13.0%	3	5.9%	2	1.4%
Median Household Income		$18,769		$26,484		$34,679		$43,057		$30,309		$13,437

FIGURE 16.7: *Map of Area Within Three-Minute Drive*

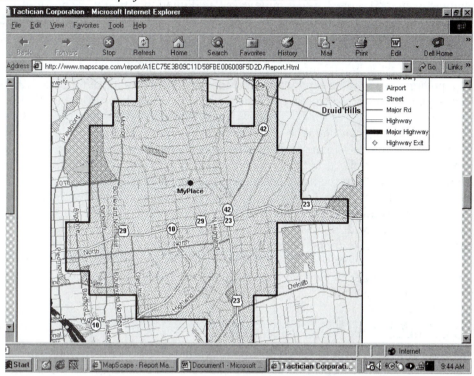

FIGURE 16.8: *Demographic Information of Area Within Three-Minute Drive*

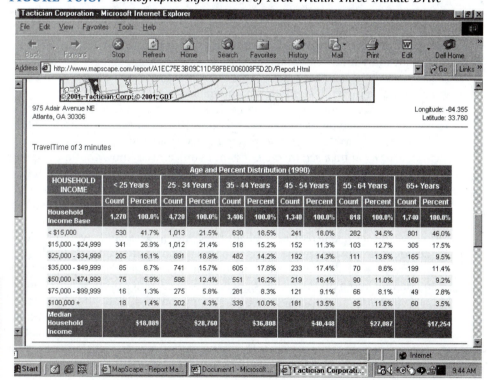

Consider the following three stores: Store A is five minutes away, Store B is 10 minutes away, and Store C is 15 minutes away. Equation (16.1) indicates that the probability of going to Store A = 0. 55, Store B = 0.27, and Store C = 0.18. Once a probability is determined, it can be applied to the group under study, such as the number of people in specific census tracts or zip codes.

This simplest of gravity models can accommodate many adaptations. For example, equation (16.1) can be expanded to include factors such as the differential attractiveness of different-sized stores, or particular exponents on the travel time that are industry specific.

Some criticisms can be made of the basic concepts of gravity models. The idea behind a gravity model is that stores that are closer are more attractive. If that is true, then why *ever* go to the more distant store? Simply showing increased probability seems to run counter to the basic argument. Also, most of these gravity models rely on the ratio of travel times. For instance, being 20 minutes away is twice as bad as being 10 minutes away. But is being two seconds away really twice as bad as being one second away, or at short distances, is there really any effect? Further, when a mathematical model is trying to predict patronage it bases the travel time on trips from home. However, consumers often "trip chain" and go to several stores on one trip or travel from the workplace, rather than from home, so the travel time from home may not be relevant.

Site Selection for Delivered Services

The usual goal for delivered services is to either minimize the costs of multiple sites or maximize the effectiveness of limited resources. Management must decide how many facilities to have and where to locate those facilities.

The steps to make these decisions include the following:

1. *Establish a service goal.* The goals can be simply stated. For example, everyone within a city boundary should be reached by ambulance within 10 minutes. Or they can be more complex, such as a primary ambulance within 10 minutes and a backup within 15 minutes.
2. *Mathematically represent a service area.* Even though a goal of "10 minutes to every home" may be desired, the mathematics behind these problems cannot handle that load—there are too many "homes." What is required is that customers are grouped by census tract, zip code, city section, or city, and the time from any facility to the customer grouping is considered.
3. *Determine demand from service area.* It is not sufficient to know that a computer repair technician can be dispatched to a downtown location in 20 minutes. If 40% of your customers are downtown, will the second caller be required to wait a few hours? Demand must be aggregated by customer grouping so that site capacity is set properly.
4. *List potential sites and determine relationship of sites to demand.* It would be ideal if one could simply determine demand and let a computer run wild finding the appropriate set of sites. However, that option is generally not feasible. A given area contains too many possible sites for most computer programs to handle. A computer may also choose one of too many inappropriate sites because of not enough land and improper zoning among other issues. Also, the relationships of the demand clusters and the potential sites need to be assessed. This decision generally takes a yes or no format: "Can site X meet the demand at customer grouping Y within the established service goal?"

EXAMPLE 16.1

Figure 16.9 depicts a small example for finding locations for an ambulance service. The goal is to have the fewest stations while still serving each area in 12 minutes or less. The 12 demand groups are labeled A through L and represent potential sites. Travel times are noted on the links between the demand groups. Note that the travel times do not always correspond with the physical distance between the points. Due to rivers and bridge placement, hills with no roads over the top, the speed of freeways versus surface streets, heavily congested areas, parks with no through roads, and several other aspects of any city's traffic patterns, 1 mile on a map may take one minute or 10 to travel.

This example is a relatively simple one, but the solution is typically not obvious at first glance. A more realistic problem would be several times this size, and would be more complex in terms of service standards (backup services required) and capacity (certain sites are subject to limited capacity).

FIGURE 16.9: *Example Problem for Delivered Services*

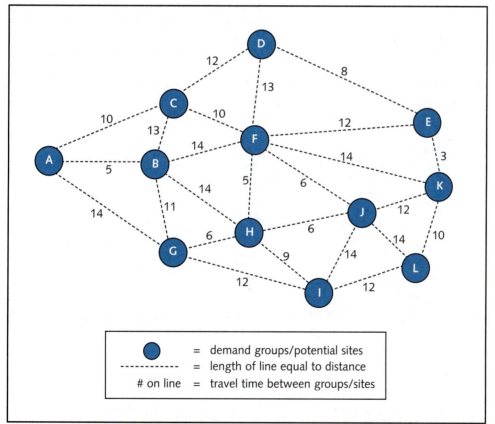

Expected Results

The four-step process outlined earlier will not provide a "perfect" solution. A perfect solution would require considering each household individually and consider every possible location. In the approach outlined, the grouping of demand points and the necessity of inputting possible locations means that the perfect solution will be found only by accident. What this procedure delivers is a good solution, which is more than can be accomplished without an appropriate method.

Consider a likely alternative to this process. Start with one store, which is placed in the best location, add another store placed in the second best location, and so on. (This method is called a "greedy" algorithm by management scientists.) This process can easily lead to the problem shown in Figure 16.10. Given a situation with two pockets of high demand and one store to locate, a greedy algorithm would want to locate right in the middle, so that both markets could be served. When a second store is added, it would make sense to locate it in one of the high-demand markets. However, if one was planning ahead of time, the third solution on Figure 16.10 is clearly the best: Have one store in both high-demand locations.

The methods involved become increasingly sophisticated. At American Medical Response, a nationwide, for-profit emergency medical service, their ambulances are not housed at a hospital or fire station. The squadron of ambulances is constantly shifted to different locations throughout the day as units are called on for emergencies. This system allows for faster response time in general, and allows for such shifts as moving most of the fleet from downtown during the day to the bedroom communities at night.

Mathematical Solution Methods for Delivered Services

A discussion and examples of these models can be found on the Student CD.

Access your Student CD now for information on mathematical solution methods for delivered services.

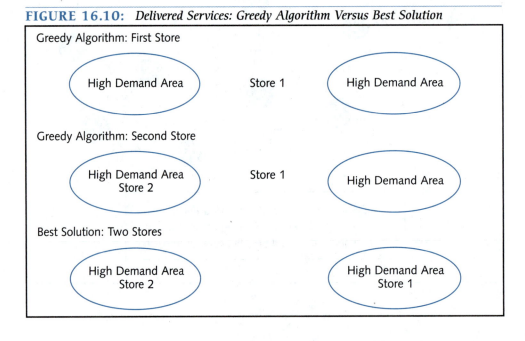

FIGURE 16.10: *Delivered Services: Greedy Algorithm Versus Best Solution*

Greedy Algorithm: First Store

High Demand Area   Store 1   High Demand Area

Greedy Algorithm: Second Store

High Demand Area
Store 2   Store 1   High Demand Area

Best Solution: Two Stores

High Demand Area
Store 2   High Demand Area
                                       Store 1

SITE SELECTION FOR QUASI-MANUFACTURING SERVICES

Many service facilities require little face-to-face contact with their customers. Perhaps largest in number are telephone call centers. An estimated 4 to 6.5 million people in the United States work in call centers. Also prevalent in this category are the back-office operations of financial services firms, such as banks and insurance companies. The industry of wholesaling also exhibits this characteristic. For these facilities, the main purpose in site selection is often to minimize costs, rather than attract customers. The managerial decisions to make are how many sites, the location of each site, and the staffing of the resulting facilities.

It would seem that these decisions would be made infrequently, but that is not the case. Warehouses in the wholesaling industry, in particular, are fairly easy to move. In a survey of wholesalers it was found that warehouse location decisions were reviewed annually by 63% of firms. Commercial software is available to help with this problem. At least 16 vendors of such software offer products ranging from $5,000 to $80,000 (see Ballou and Masters, 1993).

The extreme range in prices for software mirrors the complexity and robustness of the products. With all the software available, however, basic flaws remain. None of the packages can provide a truly optimal solution; that is, for a large national or multinational firm, no software can be expected to find the best number, location, and staffing of a network of facilities given only data about customers because the problem is too complex.

The software uses three basic types of methods. They are presented in order of lowest to highest price, and correspondingly, usually lowest to highest efficacy.

- *Heuristics:* A heuristic is a "rule of thumb," but often a highly complex rule. As a simple example, heuristics for warehouse site selection could be similar to the "greedy" algorithm presented earlier. If 10 warehouses are to be placed, start by locating the first warehouse in the best place as if it were the only warehouse; then locate the second warehouse as if only two warehouses were to be placed, and so on. Clearly, this method will not be optimal. Other heuristic approaches however, are more complex and are closer to finding the "best" solution.
- *Deterministic simulation:* In a deterministic simulation software package, costs are input into the software so that if the user chooses a set of locations, the software can provide the overall cost. The weakness results from the requirement that the user supply the specific list of locations.
- *Mixed integer/linear programming:* Linear programming can be used to find the best set of locations among a given list; that is, if the user gives the linear program 100 potential locations, it will pick out the best network of 10 among them. Again, however, the user must list the initial set of locations.

Mixed Linear/Integer Programming for Location Selection

A discussion and examples of these models can be found on the Student CD.

Access your Student CD now for information on mixed linear/integer programming for location selection.

Summary

The location decision is both a fundamental and frequent decision for many service firms. The success of any store is intrinsically linked to attributes of its location. We explored some methods used by several different types of services: demand-sensitive services, delivered services, and quasi-manufacturing services. Factor rating, regression, and GIS offer tools to service firms to determine how to generate demand through their location.

Firms wishing to cover a geographic area can use linear-programming-based tools. Through our ambulance service example, we showed that travel time is just one of many considerations in this decision. With real situations of a larger size, the decision becomes much more complex and can include such factors as service standards and capacity issues to attempt to determine the "best" solution.

Finally, a variety of tools are available for quasi-manufacturing firms that do not require physical contact with customers. These firms desire to minimize their costs by selecting the best location for new sites. Available software, offering a range of complexity and robustness, utilize heuristics, deterministic simulations, or mixed integer/linear programming to determine the most profitable location from the given alternatives.

Review Questions

1. In what ways are service location decisions different from manufacturing location decisions?
2. Services are delineated into three different categories in this chapter: demand-sensitive services, delivered services, and quasi-manufacturing services. Why?
3. Three general types of site location systems were discussed: an informal system, a factor rating system, and regression-based systems. Under what business conditions, if any, should each of these systems be used?
4. In many firms, numerical analysis merely supported a location selection system. Given, say, a bigger sample size for such models, or a model with a high R^2, or other conditions that make these models better, should such models replace, not just augment, "gut feel" managerial decisions? Under what conditions should regression-based models be used to choose specific locations?
5. What are the strengths and weaknesses of GIS systems?
6. What are the basic assumptions underlying the gravity model of demand?
7. What is meant by the phrase *mathematically represent a service area* when forming a plan for a network to deliver services?
8. Mixed integer linear programming is presented as a solution technique for the warehouse location problem. Heuristics are also commonly used. If linear programming provides optimal solutions, why are any other techniques used?

TABLE 16.6: *Data for Problem 16.1*

Site	Access (0.2)	Proximity to Customers (0.4)	Competition (0.2)	Traffic (0.2)
Allendium	7	4	5	9
Beatical	8	6	5	9
Canak	3	9	2	8
Delirouse	4	2	7	5
Everm	8	6	4	6
Fouirt	1	4	3	7
Guerney	7	4	8	4
Hiight	5	1	6	2

Problems

Access your Student CD now for Tables 16.6 through 16.9 as Excel worksheets.

16.1. In finding a location for a new restaurant, the eight sites listed in Table 16.6 were rated on a scale of 1–10 on four attributes. The weighting of each attribute is in parentheses in the column heading. What are the scores of each location? What decision(s) should be made?

16.2. Consider the restaurant location problem again. This time, the historical profitability of each location is listed in Table 16.7. Devise a regression-based system to predict the profitability of a new site, Zwderkan, that has a rating of 5 in every category.

16.3. In finding a location for a new bank branch the eight sites listed on Table 16.8 have been rated on a 1–10 scale on four attributes. The weighting of each attribute is in parentheses in the column heading. What are the scores of each location? What decision(s) should be made?

16.4. Consider the bank branch location problem again. This time, the historical profitability of each location is listed in Table 16.9. Devise a regression-based system to predict the profitability of a new site, Ysard, that has a rating of 6 on Office Space, 2 on Middle Class Population, 8 on Competition, and 1 on Visibility.

16.5. Using http://www.tactician.com, compare two locations in your city to determine which contains the most households with incomes over $50,000 in a half-mile radius, or some other relevant criterion.

TABLE 16.7: *Data for Problem 16.2*

Site	Access	Proximity to Customers	Competition	Traffic	Profit
Allendium	7	4	5	9	$464
Beatical	8	6	5	9	$509
Canak	3	9	2	8	$283
Delirouse	4	2	7	5	$535
Everm	8	6	4	6	$417
Fouirt	1	4	3	7	$259
Guerney	7	4	8	4	$600
Hiight	5	1	6	2	$406

TABLE 16.8: *Data for Problem 16.3*

Site	Office Space (0.25)	Middle Class Population (0.50)	Competition (0.15)	Visibility (0.10)
Ignatius	4	9	5	2
Jaedicom	5	5	3	2
Kalik	1	2	3	8
Laviat	8	2	6	3
Mortruse	4	8	1	4
Nurz	6	8	6	3
Poeatica	8	5	7	4
Quoos	2	4	3	3

TABLE 16.9: *Data for Problem 16.4*

Site	Office Space	Middle Class Population	Competition	Visibility	Profits
Ignatius	4	9	5	2	$396
Jaedicom	5	5	3	2	$276
Kalik	1	2	3	8	$220
Laviat	8	2	6	3	$436
Mortruse	4	8	1	4	$189
Nurz	6	8	6	3	$454
Poeatica	8	5	7	4	$543
Quoos	2	4	3	3	$233

16.6. The hunt is on: Rich's 13-year-old daughter Alexandra is going to give him an introductory trombone concert later in the day, and he wants to purchase earplugs before then. Three stores in the vicinity sell earplugs: EarsPlus, 10 minutes away; ICantBelieveYouBoughtHeraTrombone, 15 minutes away; and KidNoise, 20 minutes away. According to the gravity model, what is the probability Rich will go to each store?

16.7. The people in census track 013411 spend $100,000 in local dress shops, those in census track 013443 spend $80,000, and those in track 013422 spend $200,000. Consider only two dress shops: Ralph's and Lulu's. The travel time from each shop to each area is in Table 16.11. Adapt the gravity model to determine how much will be spent at each shop.

16.8. *This problem requires the quantitative content on the Student CD.* An area wishes to find a fire-fighting strategy that balances cost and response time. Table 16.11 presents a travel time matrix for 11 locations. Any of the locations may be used for a fire station.

TABLE 16.10: *Data for Problem 16.7*

Store	Track 013411	Track 013443	Track 013422
Ralph's	10 minutes	30 minutes	20 minutes
Lulu's	15 minutes	20 minutes	20 minutes

TABLE 16.11: *Data for Problem 16.8*

	1	2	3	4	5	6	7	8	9	10	11
1		39	49	46	45	48	15	24	21	25	26
2	39		13	10	11	12	40	15	20	18	15
3	49	13		3	5	3	35	29	35	30	28
4	46	10	3		2	5	33	26	32	27	25
5	45	11	5	2		3	30	29	34	29	27
6	48	12	3	5	3		33	32	37	32	30
7	15	40	35	33	30	33		33	32	26	28
8	24	15	29	26	29	32	33		3	8	5
9	21	20	35	32	34	37	32	3		6	7
10	25	18	30	27	29	32	26	8	6		3
11	26	15	28	25	27	30	28	5	7	3	

a. If the desired response time is 19 minutes, how many stations are needed and where should they be located? (*Hint:* Adapt equations [16.2], [16.3], and [16.4] and the associated Excel file on the Student CD.)

b. Determine a trade-off curve. Find out what the worst response time would be if only two fire stations could be built, then three stations, then four stations.

Selected Bibliography

Ballou, R., and J. Masters. 1993. Commercial Software for Locating Warehouses and Other Facilities. *Journal of Business Logistics*, 14(2), 71–107.

Plastria, F. 2001. Static Competitive Facility Location: An Overview of Optimization Approaches. *European Journal of Operational Research*, 129, 461–470.

Spencer, T., A. Brigandi, D. Dargon, and M. Sheehan. 1990. AT&T's Telemarketing Site Selection System Offers Customer Support. *Interfaces*, 20(1), 83–96.

Regression-Based Site Selection at La Quinta Hotels[4]

The old adage that says the three most important aspects of real estate are "location, location, location," is especially true in the transient hotel business. The physical site is an essential attribute of a new hotel. No amount of marble in the foyer can bring customers to a poor location, and a good location could profit under mediocre management.

Unfortunately, considerable disagreement can still arise over which sites are better than others. Everyone could agree that a Death Valley Hotel probably would be a poor choice, but it is difficult to determine exactly what makes for a good choice. To be considered beyond the most preliminary investigation, each potential site must have a number of positive aspects. Historically, selecting a site for new La Quinta Inns proved to be decidedly more art than science. Although objective data could be gathered, sifting through the data and finding a good site still requires "gut feel." And everyone's gut feel is a little different. With more difficult economic times and increased industry capacity squeezing La Quinta's profits in early 1987, location decisions required more scrutiny.

La Quinta decided to try a new approach to selecting sites: Using regression analysis of the current performance of their installed inn base to determine sites for new inns. The first test of the approach would be to select a site in the growing Dallas market.

The La Quinta Hotel Chain

Sam Barshop started Barshop Motel Enterprises, Inc., in 1962. In 1972, Barshop Motel Enterprises, Inc., became La Quinta Motor Inns, Inc. (LQM), with 30 inns, and started to expand rapidly. La Quinta grew steadily over the next decade, and by 1987 owned or operated 191 inns in 29 states (Table 16.12). LQM locations are centered in Texas, but LQM expanded throughout the Southeast, Southwest, and Midwest, employing 5,800 people, and showed a profit in the 10 years 1977–1987 (Table 16.13).

Motor inns operated and licensed by La Quinta are positioned in the mid-price, limited service segment of the lodging industry, between luxurious "full service" motor inns and "budget" motels. La Quinta Inns appeal to guests who desire simple rooms and convenient locations and whose needs do not include banquet facilities, meeting rooms, in-house restaurants, cocktail lounges, and room service. Specifically, La Quinta attempts to cater to the frequent business traveler.

---

4. *Source:* This case is based on the work of Sheryl Kimes and James Fitzsimmons, "Selecting Profitable Hotel Sites at La Quinta Motor Inns," *Interfaces*, 20(2), 1990, pp. 12–20. Information regarding the company background and the site location project for La Quinta Motor Inns, Inc. was obtained from published reports, but the proposed Dallas expansion is fictitious.

CASE STUDY

TABLE 16.12: *La Quinta Owned, Operated, or Licensed Inns*

ALABAMA
Birmingham
Huntsville (2)
Mobile
Montgomery
Tuscaloosa

ARIZONA
Phoenix (2)
Tucson

ARKANSAS
Little Rock (4)

CALIFORNIA
Bakersfield
Chula Vista
Costa Mesa
Fresno
Irvine
Sacramento
San Bernadino
San Diego
Stockton
Vista

COLORADO
Colorado Springs
Denver (7)

FLORIDA
Deerfield Beach
Ft. Myers
Jacksonville (3)
Miami
Orlando
Pensacola
Pinellas Park
Tallahassee (2)
Tampa (2)

GEORGIA
Atlanta (6)
Augusta
Columbus
Savannah

ILLINOIS
Champaign
Chicago (3)
Moline

INDIANA
Indianapolis (2)
Merrillville

KANSAS
Lenexa
Wichita

KENTUCKY
Lexington

LOUISIANA
Baton Rouge
Bossier City
Lafayette
Monroe
New Orleans (5)
Sulphur

MICHIGAN
Kalamazoo

MISSISSIPPI
Jackson

MISSOURI
St. Louis

NEBRASKA
Omaha

NEVADA
Las Vegas
Reno

NEW MEXICO
Albuquerque (3)
Farmington
Santa Fe

NORTH CAROLINA
Charlotte (2)

OHIO
Columbus

OKLAHOMA
Oklahoma City (2)
Tulsa (2)

PENNSYLVANIA
Pittsburgh

SOUTH CAROLINA
Charleston
Columbia
Greenville

TENNESSEE
Knoxville
Memphis (3)
Nashville (2)

TEXAS
Abilene
Amarillo (2)
Austin (4)
Beaumont
Brazosport
Brownsville
College Station
Corpus Christi (2)
Dallas/Ft.Worth (12)
Eagle Pass
El Paso (3)
Harlingen
Houston (12)
Killeen
La Porte
Laredo
Longview
Lubbock
Lufkin
Midland
Nacogdoches
Odessa
San Angelo
San Antonio (11)
Temple
Texarkana

Texas City
Tyler
Victoria
Waco
Wichita Falls

UTAH
Salt Lake City

VIRGINIA
Hampton
Virginia Beach

WASHINGTON
Seattle

WYOMING
Casper Cheyenne
Rock Springs

RODEWAY INN
San Antonio

ROYAL INN
Houston

**LICENSED
LA QUINTA INNS**
ARIZONA
Flagstaff

FLORIDA
Orlando

OHIO
Cincinnati
Dayton

TEXAS
Corpus Christi
Denton
Fort Worth
Galveston
McAllen

CASE STUDY

TABLE 16.13: *Selected Financial and Operational Data for La Quinta Inns*

($ millions)

	1987*	1986	1985	1984	1983	1982	1981	1980	1979	1978	1977
Revenue	$177	179	160	137	113	103	83	62	48	39	30
Net operating income	$32	44	40	39	37	NA	NA	NA	NA	NA	NA
Net earnings	$4.1	5.8	9.0	12.8	13.5	12.3	8.6	6.4	4.9	3.7	2.5
Long-term debt	$382	394	313	297	243	190	140	119	87	66	54
Total assets	$623	621	541	504	404	324	229	179	131	97	78
Inns owned or licensed	191	176	157	138	129	112	103	90	78	68	63
Rooms owned or licensed (in thousands)	24.1	22.0	19.6	17.0	15.9	13.6	12.3	10.6	9.1	7.8	7.1

*1987 financial results estimated. All other data as of fiscal year end May 31.

A customer survey in 1981 showed that 83% of La Quinta's guests were business travelers, approximately 80% were regular customers who stayed at La Quinta an average of 10 times a year, and approximately 80% of whom visited a local site within 4 miles of the hotel. The main reasons cited by customers for staying at La Quinta were convenient locations, clean rooms, courteous service, and reasonable rates.

Although La Quinta does not provide any food service at its inns, aside from a continental breakfast offered in its lobbies, it locates adjacent to restaurants or provides funds for construction of adjacent restaurants. La Quinta holds an ownership interest in 87 restaurants operated by third parties, such as Denny's or JoJos.

La Quinta's typical inn is located along an interstate highway or major traffic artery convenient to businesses, contains 100 to 175 guest rooms, provides 24-hour front desk and message service, same-day laundry service, a swimming pool, and in-room color televisions with "Showtime." La Quinta Inns are typically of masonry construction with a distinctive Spanish Colonial architecture.

Individual inns are usually managed by married couples who live on the premises. On a typical day shift they supervise one housekeeping supervisor, eight room attendants, two laundry workers, two general maintenance persons, and a front desk

CASE STUDY

sales representative. LQM fully owns about half of the inns that bear its name (Table 16.14). Some inns are 50% partnerships, others are just managed by La Quinta. For nine La Quinta Inns, only the La Quinta name was licensed, with no managerial direction from corporate headquarters. For the licensed and managed inns, LQM provides chain services such as bookkeeping, national advertising, and "teLQuik," a national reservation system.

The mid-price, limited service lodging industry is highly competitive, and La Quinta competes directly with other lodging establishments in all locations. Each of the inns competes with other major chains as well as with other hotels, motels, motor inns, and other lodging establishments not affiliated with any major chain. There is no small number of competitors that are dominant in the industry.

Site Selection at La Quinta

La Quinta considers the selection of sites for its inns to be among the most important factors in its business. Sites are chosen for guest convenience and are generally readily accessible to and visible from interstate highways and major traffic arteries.

TABLE 16.14: *Ownership of La Quinta Inns*

	1987	1981
La Quinta Inns owned by LQM		
Owned 100%	88	33
Owned 52–80%	7	5
Owned 50%[a]	54	44
	149	82
Inns of other names owned by LQM	2	7
Total company owned and operated	151	89
La Quinta Inns managed by LQM[b]	31	0
La Quinta Inns licensed to others[c]	9	14
	191	103

[a] Prudential Insurance has been a joint venture partner since 1971 and was a 50% partner in 28 inns and 16 restaurants in both 1981 and 1987. Metropolitan Life Insurance was a 50% partner in three inns and two restaurants in 1981 and eight inns and four restaurants in 1987.

[b] LQM sold 31 inns it owned 100% to La Quinta Motor Inns Limited Partnership in fiscal 1987. The sale improved cash flow, increased borrowing capacity, and allowed recognition of real estate appreciation.

[c] Licensing of the La Quinta name ceased in 1977. Since fiscal 1981, the company purchased five inns from licensees.

CASE STUDY

Other major site criteria include proximity to office centers, the central business district, commercial and industrial concentrations, medical and educational complexes, regional shopping malls, military bases, and airports. La Quinta's expansion strategy is guided by the concepts of (1) clustering, or building multiple inns in the same metropolitan area; (2) adjacency through locating new inns within approximately 300 miles of existing properties; and (3) filling in, or moving into smaller cities (populations less than 100,000) within existing market areas.

Eight people provided input in the site selection process: Four site evaluators physically toured each potential site and gathered information. Robert Moore, Executive Vice President and Chief Development Officer, Thomas Neilon, Vice President of Real Estate, and the Director of Marketing Research evaluated the data and opinions of the site evaluators and expressed opinions of their own. The company president, CEO, and chairman of the board, Sam Barshop, exercised the final say in all site selections.

Unfortunately, the key variables consulted by all those involved in site evaluation were based on "experience" and "gut feel." Everyone agreed that being close to a university, military base, hospital, or downtown led to additional guests at the hotel. What was less definitive was the relative worth of each of these factors. For example, what was better, a site within 1 mile of a moderately large military base or within 3 miles of a large university? The relative weighting of these factors was based strictly on intuition.

Site Selection by Regression

La Quinta desired a less haphazard approach to site selection. Further, the current process was both costly and produced too many disagreements, and the risk of choosing a poor site became more costly in the last half of the 1980s due to the weakening of the Texas economy.

For assistance in selecting sites, Barshop turned to the business school at the University of Texas, Austin. LQM and UT–Austin had a comfortable relationship, with both the president of the university and the business school dean sitting on the LQM board of directors.

The project was supervised by Professor James Fitzsimmons and performed by a doctoral student, Sheryl Kimes. After interviewing the eight individuals involved in site selection, Ms. Kimes compiled a list of the factors they thought affected the success of a La Quinta Inn (Table 16.15).

Although site selection committee members may disagree on which characteristics are more important for a successful hotel, they all agreed that the profitability of a hotel was based on proximity to local attractions. Because of the presumed dependence of profitability on known factors, Ms. Kimes decided to use regression analysis to model profitability and use the list of factors in Table 16.15 as the independent variables.

CASE STUDY

TABLE 16.15: *Variables Considered*

Category	Name	Description
Competitive	PRICE	Room rate for the inn ($/night)
	RATE	Average competitive room rate ($/night)
	RMS1	Hotel rooms within 1 mile
	RMSTOTAL	Hotel rooms within 3 miles
	ROOMSINN	Rooms in La Quinta Inn
Demand generators	CIVILIAN	Civilian personnel on base
	COLLEGE	College enrollment
	HOSP1	Hospital beds within 1 mile
	HOSPTOTL	Hospital beds within 4 miles
	HVYIND	Heavy industrial employment
	LGTIND	Light industrial acreage
	MALLS	Shopping mall square footage
	MILITARY	Military personnel
	OFC1	Office space within 1 mile (in 000)
	OFCTOTAL	Office space within 4 miles (in 000)
	PASSENGR	Airport passengers enplaned daily
	RETAIL	Scale ranking of retail activity (0 poor, 10 excellent)
	TOURISTS	Annual tourists (in 000)
	TRAFFIC	Traffic count (traffic/hour)
	VAN	Airport van (1 yes, 0 no)
Demographic	EMPLYPCT	Unemployment percentage
	INCOME	Average family income
	POPULACE	Residential population
	STATE*	State population per inn
	URBAN*	Urban population per inn
Market awareness	AGE	Years inn has been open
	NEAREST	Distance to nearest La Quinta Inn
	CLOSEST	The inn number of the closest La Quinta Inn (data for inn numbers 1-56 is on the Student CD.)
Physical	ACCESS	Accessibility (0 poor, 10 excellent)
	ARTERY	Major traffic artery (1 yes, 0 no)
	DISTCBD	Distance to downtown (miles)
	SIGNVIS	Sign visibility (0 poor, 10 excellent)
Success measures	OCC_83	Occupancy rate in 1983 (percentage)
	OCC_86	Occupancy rate in 1986 (percentage)
	PROFIT_83	Profit in 1983 ($ in 000)
	PROFIT_86	Profit in 1986 ($ in 000)
	OP_M_83	Operating margin in 1983 (percentage)
	OP_M_86	Operating margin in 1986 (percentage)

*Variables not included in data set

Reprinted by permission, S. E. Kimes and J. A. Fitzsimmons, "Selecting Profitable Hotel Sites at La Quinta Motor Inns," *Interfaces* (20)2, March–April 1990. Copyright 1990. The Institute of Management Sciences, now the Institute for Operations Research, and the Management Sciences (INFORMS), 901 Elkridge Landing Road, Suite 400, Linthicum, MD 21090.

CASE STUDY

Determining the dependent variable seemed more difficult than determining the independent variables. Exactly what is the appropriate measure for a "good" hotel? After discussion with the site selection committee, three candidates emerged that seemed plausible.

1. *Occupancy*. Occupancy is the ratio of average rented rooms to total rooms. It is a widely used statistic in hotel administration.
2. *Profit*. The bookkeeping methods used allowed each inn to be a profit center, so profit data were available.
3. *Operating margin*. Operating margin is a percentage measure that consists of adding depreciation and interest expenses to the profit of an inn and dividing by the total revenue.

The economics of the preceding few years whipsawed the profitability of the hotel industry in oil-producing states. Due to the turbulent economic environment, the project developers decided to gather data for two different years: a good year, 1983, and a poor year, 1986. Because of the unprofitability of new inns and the expense of data gathering, data only were collected on a group of 56 mature inns. (Data can be found on the Student CD.)

Access your Student CD now for data for this LaQuinta Inns case.

Dallas Expansion

The first test of utilizing regression for location analysis was to determine an appropriate location for expansion in the Dallas market. The population and real estate prices in the Dallas area were increasing rapidly. Dallas was touted as one of the top cities in the nation in which to do business, and the northern suburb of Plano was considered a boomtown due to the surge in population and corporate headquarters. Twelve inns were already in place and doing well in the Dallas/Ft. Worth metroplex.

The six candidate sites for expansion in Dallas were as follows:

A. *Dallas—Downtown*. The corner of Houston and Young Streets, three blocks from the convention center and two blocks from the Trinity River.
B. *Dallas—Oak Lawn*. 3000 Oak Lawn Avenue, located in a large retail shopping area.
C. *Dallas—Fair Park*. 3500 Cullum Boulevard, across from Fair Park, a large complex that holds a football stadium (the Cotton Bowl), the Starplex Amphitheatre, various exposition halls, and hosts the state fair.
D. *Dallas—Southern Methodist University*. Near Mockingbird and McMillan Streets, one block from the eastern border of the Southern Methodist University campus.
E. *Coppell—DFW Airport*. 1000 Sandy Lake Road, on property currently owned by Marriott but not yet built on.

CASE STUDY

F. *Plano—Legacy.* 5200 Legacy Drive in an area with a mostly finished office park near the offices of Electronic Data Systems, Texas Instruments, Raytheon, and other similar firms.

Purchase and development costs differ mildly for each of the potential sites. The data for each location are contained on the Student CD.

It was clear that the data from the 56 mature inns could be analyzed and put to use. What was not clear was the role any regression output should play. Should "gut feel" augment any regression model, or vice versa? Should the model be used to pick a site or just to eliminate poor choices? What were the strategic and tactical considerations that could not be modeled in a regression?

Questions:

- Which of the three success measures is appropriate? (Use both intuitive and data-driven arguments.)
- Are the variables considered (Table 16.16) appropriate for the decision at hand? What other variables might you want to consider?
- Determine appropriate predictors of operating margin through correlation and regression analysis. Comment on the variables both in and not in your predictive model.
- How should your model be used in site selection?
- Make recommendations concerning the Dallas expansion.

Advanced Models: Data Envelopment Analysis

The material in this chapter prepares students to:

- Understand the characteristics of a good evaluation system.

- Apply the basic evaluation systems and understand their shortcomings.

- Use Data Envelopment Analysis as an evaluation tool.

- Additional technical material is on the student CD.

A key difference between services and manufacturing is the number of the company's facilities and the nature of the work they do. Manufacturers tend to have a small number of facilities that usually make different products. Services often have a large number of units, where each unit does nearly the same task.

For example, General Motors, with year 2003 sales of $196 billion and 326,000 employees, operates 30 fabrication and assembly facilities in the United States and approximately 100 such facilities around the world, with most of those facilities making different types of cars. McDonald's has a similar number of employees, 418,000, but generates about one-tenth the revenues ($17 billion) spread over more than 31,129 sites, where each of those sites strives to produce the same burger and fries. As shown on Table 17.1, many service systems grow to enormous size in terms of units, even though they may not be well known.

The sheer size of many service systems, combined with their geographic dispersion, creates difficulties in assessing performance, which differs from manufacturers. The manufacturer Hewlett-Packard made "management by walking around" famous, a practice in which senior leaders literally walk around among employees to find out how operations are progressing. However, as the number of distinct units within many services increases, it is no longer feasible for a company leader to have first-hand knowledge of what goes on. Sam Walton was famous for his personal approach to management at Wal-Mart, but his firm grew so quickly that even his goals were scaled down to just visiting each Wal-Mart store once in his life.

TABLE 17.1:   *Service Companies with Multi-site Operations*

Many companies today operate a large number of retail facilities. Some of these will be familiar. Many will be unfamiliar, even though they have hundreds of outlets!

Company	Number of Sites	Company	Number of Sites
Auto-Related		McDonald's	31,129[c]
AAMCO Transmissions	more than 700	Subway	17,500
Budget Rent-a-Car	3,240		
Jiffy Lube	2,156	*Hair Styling*	
Meineke Car Care	891	Fantastic Sam's	1,350
Midas (brake/muffler repair)	2,777	Supercuts	1,778
Novus Auto Glass Repair	more than 2,200		
		Lodging	
Banks		Choice Hotels	more than 5,000[b]
Bank of America	4,495[a]	Marriott	2,600
Wachovia Bank	2,626[a]	Super 8 Motels	more than 2,000[b]
Cleaning		*Other*	
Coverall Cleaning Concepts	7,085	Carlson Wagonlit Travel Associates	1,121
Jani-King	more than 9,500	Dollar General (discount stores)	6,700[b]
Mitex Indoor Hygenics	more than 4,000	GNC (nutrition)	4,811
		Heel Quik! (shoe repair)	732
Desserts		Kumon Math and Reading Centers	1,272
Baskin-Robbins (ice cream)	3,460	Kwik Kurb (concrete services)	more than 1,250
Dunkin' Donuts	4,736	Merle Norman Cosmetics Studios	2,006
Tim Horton's (doughnuts)	1,893	Miracle Ear (hearing aids)	1,103
TCBY (frozen yogurt)	2,006	Pearl Vision (eyecare)	811
Yogen Fruz Worldwide, Inc.	more than 5,000	Radio Shack	7,113
		Snap-On (tools)	4,680
Fast Food		Wal-Mart (discount stores)	4,800[c]
Burger King	8,246		
Domino's Pizza	5,996		

Source: The Franchise Handbook (Spring 2004).

[a] *Source:* FDIC, April 2004.
[b] *Source:* Company Web site. Data as of year end 2003.
[c] *Source: www.fortune.com*, data as of year end 2003.

Typical performance reviews require human judgment. Without firsthand knowledge of the conditions under which a unit operates, however, the usefulness of informal judgment in reviewing performance is limited. Many types of performance review systems are employed in service firms. Within a business curriculum, detailed explanation of those systems is generally covered in a course on organizational behavior. Consequently, most systems will not be discussed in this book. Here, we focus on a relatively new method of performance appraisal and benchmarking used almost exclusively in service firms: Data Envelopment Analysis (DEA).

Formally, DEA is a linear programming technique for measuring the relative efficiency of facilities. However, detailed knowledge or even a comfort level with linear programming is not required to understand how DEA works or to run a DEA system in practice. Along with discussing the theory behind DEA, we will show how to use DEA in spreadsheet software (Excel) and discuss the software vendors available who provide easy-to-use DEA packages.

In managerial terms, DEA is a practical measurement tool for businesses with many different sites performing similar tasks when a single overall measure, such as profit or ROI, is not sufficient.

The next section will describe the general reasons for establishing formal performance review systems and discuss the drawbacks of common systems. Then, DEA will be explored in detail.

CHARACTERISTICS OF EVALUATION/ BENCHMARKING SYSTEMS

System Uses

Although the need for some kind of performance measure may seem obvious, the best type of system to implement depends on the goal. Several possible goals are listed in Table 17.2. It is not unusual for a corporation to use several independent performance measurement systems, each satisfying a different need.

A common goal of a performance measurement system is evaluation: determining the good from the bad, assigning pay raises, distributing bonuses, or deciding who gets the next promotion. Rather than the evaluation of subordinate employees within a unit, which is usually done by the unit manager, we are concerned here with evaluating entire units or the manager of a unit. One goal is to separate managerial performance from the performance of a unit. When looking at candidates to determine who gets the promotion to manage the flagship unit downtown, it's important to know whether a top-performing unit is performing well because of or in spite of the unit manager.

A less common but important use of a performance evaluation system is resource allocation; determining which unit gets extra personnel or equipment, which unit receives more or less budget money, or, when corporate needs require it, which units are closed.

Another use of performance evaluation systems is simply classification; determining the best units for either public recognition, or identifying better or worse performing units for finding best practices for the firm, or in order to send trainees to appropriate environments to learn good technique.

Common Performance Measures

At first glance, talk of which yardstick to measure unit performance by seems odd, when simple unit profitability seems the obvious choice. Of course, for nonprofit businesses, profitability is not a particularly good measure. But even in for-profit businesses, individual unit profitability runs into several problems as a measure.

For many businesses, true unit profitability is difficult to measure, on both the cost and revenue sides. Cost measurement can be difficult if many small service units

---

TABLE 17.2: *Characteristics of Performance Evaluation Systems*

Uses	Measures Commonly Used
Evaluation	*Profit*
Units	*Sales volume*
Employees	*Contribution margin*
Resource allocation	*Customer service*
Rationalize personnel/capital	*Market share*
Expense control	
Unit closure	**Methods**
Classification	*Comparison to negotiated goals*
Recognition/reward	*Outputs*
Identification	

of the same firm share employees, inventory, or equipment as needed. Although it is possible to parse out the costs between units, actually doing so requires detailed paperwork and does not send a team-oriented message to unit management. Many costs are temporary or provide unfair disadvantages. For example, due to alleged price manipulations by Enron and others, electricity costs in the summer of 2001 for a hotel in California were several times higher than for a hotel in New Hampshire. Therefore, to say the California hotel manager performed worse than the New Hampshire manager due to a temporary imbalance beyond managerial control would be inappropriate. Also, a large cost for many service units is occupancy or land/space rental. Due to the nature of long-term leasing agreements or the changes in price of purchased land, a unit may be highly profitable or unprofitable largely due to real estate values. This measure may tell a company that the land underneath the unit should be sold, but it does little to inform a company of the value of the manager of the unit.

Revenue measurement can also be difficult in industries that share customers between units. In banking, for example, the profitability of a checking account is customarily assigned to the bank branch that opened the account. The problem with this arrangement is that a given customer may, for example, open an account near her home, but use the branch closer to her office for bank services. Consequently, the branch of account gets all the revenue while the other branch gets all the expense. This problem is a significant one in banking. A First American Bank study indicated that, on average, only 20% of customer branch transactions occurred at the branch that opened the account.

Profitability also is problematic as the sole measure of performance because it fails to tell the whole story. If a unit is trying to build market share, current expenses are quite often higher because of this effort. Also, an easy way to manipulate current profit numbers is to skimp on service. Laying off or hiring low wage, inexperienced employees will help the current period financial results, but it can lead to poor customer service that will hurt the bottom line in the future.

Because of these difficulties with profitability as a measure, other considerations such as sales volume, contribution margin, customer service, or market share also are often considered in the evaluation process.

Common Evaluation Methods

Many common evaluation techniques exhibit several weaknesses that DEA does not share.

1. They rely on a comparison to negotiated goals, which can reward counter-productive behavior.
2. They involve just viewing results without a consideration of resources used to get those results.
3. The weights used to combine different measures are subjective.
4. Performance criteria do not adjust quickly to changing environments.

Managers are often compared to negotiated goals. A problem with this method is in how the goals are set. One way to set goals is to compare them to the previous time period: "Your goal for this year is last year plus 10%." Unfortunately, this approach encourages bad behavior, such as shirking and sandbagging. A poor performer who shirks her duties can increase output by merely shirking a little less next time around, while a great performer always has her bonus tied to her great performance last year. Further, once someone makes that "last year plus 10%" goal, an incentive to sandbag or cease working arises at that point, because an employee knows that having unusually good results today will only be penalized through higher goals tomorrow.

In a multi-site firm, service goals are often set for unit managers by regional or national staff. But staff members may meet unit managers infrequently and know only limited information about the difficulties of particular local neighborhoods. The two problems with this approach include a tendency to focus solely on results, rather than results per resource used, and the goal-setting process used to account for local problems.

If local differences are taken into consideration in goal setting, it is usually up to the unit manager to make a case for specific goals by pointing out local conditions and negotiating appropriately. Consequently, it can be the case that the successful unit manager is one who negotiated goals successfully, rather than managed a unit well.

To get around such biases in negotiated goals, it is tempting to look only at results: How much money was made, what market share is, and so on. Results alone, however, often do not truly reflect how well someone is doing her job. A mediocre manager might get good results from a unit in a great location, while a great manager may only get mediocre results from a unit in a bad location.

Finally, once performance measures and goals are agreed upon, another difficulty is figuring out how to combine them. Often, in the end, only a single decision needs to be made, such as whether to give a raise of 10% or 5% or whether a specific unit should be closed or kept open. The information, in the end, must be reduced to a single decision, but figuring out the formula is difficult. How much accounting profit is worth a 0.2 point increase in customer satisfaction? How much profit now is a 2% market share increase worth? In most performance evaluation systems, managers supply percentages of the overall evaluation to different categories, but those managerially supplied percentages often seem capricious, or fit one situation but not another. A manager who says, "I don't know how to weight these things, so I'm not going to weight them at all," only compounds the problem. The true meaning of "not weighting" items on a list usually means giving them all equal weight, which is, of course, a weighting system unto itself.

ADVANTAGES OF DATA ENVELOPMENT ANALYSIS

The purpose of this chapter is to introduce DEA as a performance evaluation method for multi-site services. The advantages of DEA over traditional, more subjective methods include the following:

- *Data reduction:* DEA output reduces multiple performance measures to a single number.
- *Objectivity/fairness:* The weighting of performance measures is carried out by a known algorithm.
- *Personalization:* The weighting of performance measures reacts to the individual unit; that is, weights are different from unit to unit depending upon their special characteristics. As described in more detail later, weights are chosen by DEA for each unit that will make that unit look the best.

Rather than comparing units to negotiated goals, DEA compares units to the actual results achieved and resources used by other real units. This aspect gives DEA the following advantages over goal-based methods:

- *Environmental change response:* If the economy, or any other important uncontrollable factor, unexpectedly goes up or down, goal-based measures must be readjusted, and readjusting someone out of his annual bonus is rather unpopular. Because DEA takes into consideration only actual results, factors affecting everyone will not affect results.

- *DEA doesn't reward sandbagging, nor does DEA punish superior performers:* Again, because one is compared to peers rather than a personal history, stellar management is not penalized for results that are great, but not as great as last year.

DEA is not suited to all multi-site firms. It is best suited to firms with "results ambivalence," result measurements that are not easily combined, and units that provide similar services and have similar competitive goals. These conditions are explained here.

If it is unquestioned that, for example, a unit profitability statement is clearly the only result that matters, DEA is probably not the best technique. If profitability, market share, customer satisfaction, among other factors, are all important, that is, if some ambivalence remains as to the specific results that are important, then DEA can be helpful.

DEA combines numbers that do not ordinarily add up well. For instance, DEA does well in combining that 0.2 customer satisfaction rating increase mentioned earlier with market share percentage information and financial results.

Also, DEA is best suited to comparing units with similar goals. DEA would not work well if the units being compared were plants that assembled Corvettes, SUVs, and minivans. As will be explained later, the math behind DEA works best when a large number of similar units share similar goals.

THE CONCEPT OF DEA

DEA can be applied to such diverse fields as public school educational programs, courts of law, hospitals, school busing, baseball player salaries, oil and gas production, vehicle maintenance, retail stores, mining, and bank branches. There have been over 1,800 academic publications regarding DEA (Gattoufi, Oral, and Reisman, 2004). Table 17.3 lists some firms that use DEA. Note the large number of consulting firms on this list. In addition to being a tool a corporation can use in a routine reporting manner, DEA provides an especially valuable tool for project consulting.

A number of prominent, successful applications of DEA testify to its many strong points. However, this chapter is not meant to be an advertisement for the

---

TABLE 17.3: *A Sample List of Corporate Users of DEA**

AMEC Offshore Development	Integrated Decision Systems, LDA plc
Ameritech	Libraries Unlimited
Banca Populare di Milano	Midlands Electricity Board
Bank of Scotland	Mitomo Co, Ltd, M2L
Boston Consulting Group	PricewaterhouseCoopers
British Gas Transco	S.H.C. (Switzerland)
CalEnergy Company Inc.	Securities & Exchange Comm. (Thailand)
Carlson Marketing Group	Strategic Leadership Sciences (Europe)
Commonwealth Bank (Australia)	Syndactics Inc.
CountryWide Banking Corporation (Australia)	The Boston Company
CREG (Colombia)	U.S. Air Force
DERA	USA Defense Logistics Agency
Direct Line Insurance	Whitbread plc
EIS, GSW	World Bank
Guy's Hospital (London)	Xuzhou Hospital (Peoples Republic of China)

*Partial list of Banxia "Frontier Analyst" software users.

technique. Because the technique can be a confusing one, a number of inappropriate applications are possible as well. Users of DEA must guard against its drawbacks. First, the technique will be explained, then extensions to the basic technique and problems will be discussed.

DEA combines numerous relevant *results obtained* (called *outputs* by DEA professionals) and the *resources* used to create those results (called *inputs*) into a single number that represents the *productivity* (called *efficiency*) of using resources to create results.

The basic thought that DEA is trying to project is:

$$\text{Performance} = \text{results obtained/resources used}$$

Or, in "DEA-speak":

$$\text{Efficiency} = \text{outputs/inputs}$$

A DEA report will show a single number ranging from 0 to 1 that rates the performance, or efficiency, of whatever is being reviewed. An efficiency rating of 1 means that the unit rated is fully efficient—the best among the group at what it does. A rating less than 1 means a unit is inefficient at producing results from the resources it has. As shown graphically, the amount of inefficiency can be physically and geometrically interpreted. An efficiency of 0.90 means that the performance of the unit is physically 90% of the way to being fully efficient.

For each unit that is being measured, a DEA program finds weightings for results and resources used to solve the following general problem:

$$\text{Maximize:}$$

$$\text{Results} \times \text{a weighting for each result for a specific unit}$$

provided that

$$(\text{results} \times \text{weighting})/(\text{resources} \times \text{weighting}) \leq 1$$

for all units in the system, and

$$\text{resources} \times \text{weighting} = 1$$

for the specific unit being rated.

Or, in the more typical language of those who use DEA, one of the linear programming formulations is[1]:

$$\text{Maximize outputs}_j \times \text{output weight (specific unit } j) \tag{17.1}$$

$$\text{s.t. (subject to)}$$

$$(\text{outputs}_i \times \text{output weight}) - (\text{inputs}_i \times \text{input weight}) \leq 0 \text{ for all units } i \tag{17.2}$$

$$\text{inputs}_j \times \text{input weight} = 1 \text{ for specific unit }_j \tag{17.3}$$

$$\text{input weight, output weight} \leq 0 \tag{17.4}$$

In plain English, what is meant to be done in DEA is to find the most favorable weights for every unit, given the results and resources used of all other units, so that the performance of a given unit will be as high as possible, with "1" being the highest possible performance.

---

1. Of the several different types of DEA formulations, the one presented here is called an "output oriented, primal" formulation because it maximizes outputs for a given level of inputs and relates to the linear programming "primal" formulation instead of the "dual" formulation. Similarly, one can have an "input orientation," where the formulation is to minimize the resources used for a given level of performance. A good reference listing a variety of DEA models is Charnes et al. (1994).

One of the intriguing aspects of DEA is that no a priori weighting of outputs or inputs is assumed. Every unit gets full credit for doing what it does best. The thinking is that if the "results ambivalence" assumption is true and all the results being measured are important to the company, it doesn't matter how a unit makes its contribution. An easy way to visualize this concept is through an example from the world of sports. A football team needs players who can pass, catch, run, tackle, and so on. But if they chose players on a strict weighting of, say, 30% passing, 20% blocking, 50% running, one can imagine that winning games would be a challenge. A team composed of people who are merely good at specific positions would easily defeat a team composed solely of the greatest quarterbacks to play the game.

PARK CITIES BANK AND TRUST:
A DEA EXAMPLE PROBLEM

Assume that the only relevant measure for a retail bank branch is profitability, and profit is entirely determined by loan and deposit balances. Unfortunately, even with that simplification the task of determining good and bad performers is not easy. Due to factors beyond the scope of this text, the actual amount of money earned every year on loan and deposit portfolios can vary widely. In some years, loans are highly profitable whereas deposits are marginally so, in other years the reverse is true. If measured on profit alone, branches that are good at generating checking accounts may be viewed as excellent branches one year and poor performers the next, even if they are performing at a sustained level of excellence in generating deposits. Consequently, a gross profit number based on specific profit margins that can change may not be appropriate.

DEA takes a different approach. Essentially, DEA combines the two balances (loans + deposits) using every possible ratio of profit margins and chooses the set of loan and deposit margins that are most complementary to the branch being evaluated. After choosing such a set of loan and deposit margins for each branch, the DEA program rates the efficiency of each branch on a scale of 0 to 1.

Table 17.4 shows five potential levels of the Park Cities Bank's branch performance, which are reproduced graphically in Figure 17.1. Table 17.4 lists identical inputs of 100 for each branch and separate outputs of loans and deposits. Inputs can be construed as personnel, total expenses, and so on. Branches A, C, and E show the highest efficiency rating of 1 and are deemed efficient; that is, no other branches outperform them on both measures. In terms of profits, the efficiency rating of 1 means that there is a pair of profit margins on loans and deposits on which each of those branches would be the most profitable branch in the system. Note that these are "relatively" efficient branches—relative to the other branches in the system. DEA defines which branches are the "best practice" branches in a system, which does not necessarily mean they can beat the competition.

TABLE 17.4: *DEA Evaluation of Park Cities Bank Branch Performance*

Branch	Inputs	Loans	Deposits	Efficiency
A	100	$10	$31	1
B	100	15	25	0.83
C	100	20	30	1
D	100	23	23	0.92
E	100	30	20	1

FIGURE 17.1: *Park Cities Bank DEA Efficient Frontier*

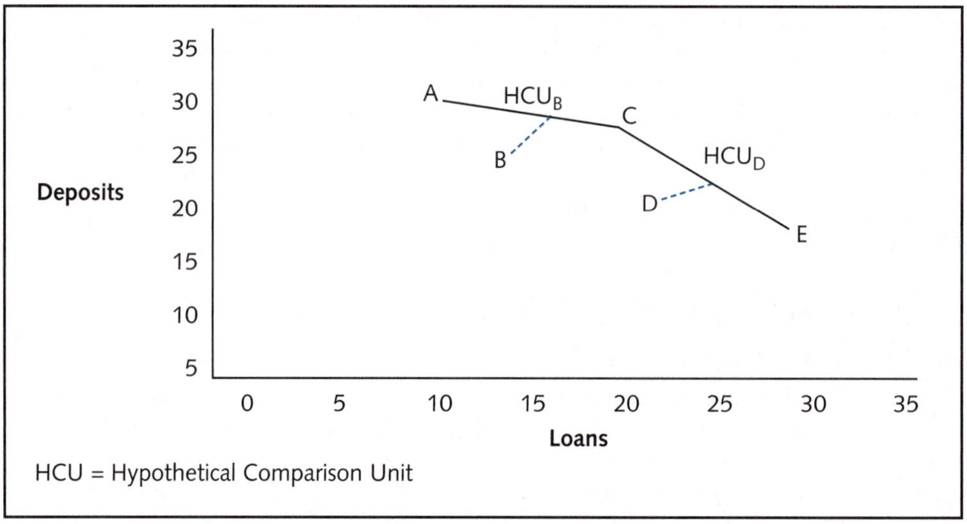

HCU = Hypothetical Comparison Unit

Note that branch A is deemed efficient even though it generated far fewer loans than branch C and only minimally larger deposits. Even more extreme, a branch with $1 more in deposits than branch A and a total of $0 loans would also have an efficiency of "1." It is efficient in the same sense that Pareto efficiency is viewed in traditional economic theory, where the efficient frontier represents the trade-off curve in the classic production function or consumer indifference curve. Consider how such a branch could be an "efficient" performer in practice: If loans were a "loss leader" and had a negative profit margin, a branch with lots of deposits and no loans would be a star.

For branches B and D, however, no possible loan/deposit margins would cause these branches to be the most profitable. For branch B this is easily seen, as it is "dominated" by branch C; that is, branch C performs better on both dimensions than branch B. As the number of outputs and inputs increases, a dominant relationship such as the one between branches B and C becomes less likely. Consequently, direct comparisons become less useful and the need to use DEA increases. Further, once a two-output scenario is exceeded, the intuition and graphical analysis that guide the preceding example fail and the data reduction afforded by DEA becomes more valuable.

The case of branch D demonstrates a nondominated unit. No other branch dominates branch D on both dimensions. For nondominated branch D, DEA creates a Hypothetical Comparison Unit (HCU) that is a linear combination of efficient units. In this case, the HCU_D is composed of a melding of branches C and E and would represent a point of (25, 25) on Figure 17.1. The HCU_D of (25, 25) is the point on the efficient frontier one would hit if a line were drawn from the origin, through branch D, to the frontier. A line with one endpoint is called a *ray*, consequently, it is known as radial efficiency. The efficiency measure is geometrically interpreted: Branch D is 92% of the distance from the point (0,0) to the HCU on the efficient frontier. The HCU corresponding to branch B is (18.1, 30.2), leaving branch B with an efficiency of 83%.

DEA gives more information than just efficiency scores. For inefficient units, merely being told that "your efficiency is 70%" is not particularly helpful. The typical output of a DEA model also provides information on what must be improved by how much to become efficient, and information that is called a *reference set* for a unit. The reference set of a unit is the group of efficient units that the inefficient unit is most like. For example, in Figure 17.1, the reference set for branch B would be branches C and A. In essence, this information gives a manager a list of mentors that are similar to that unit, but do a better job.

To show exactly how these calculations are made, the specific model of equations (17.1) through (17.4) for branch B follow. Recall, the variables solved for in the model are "loan weight" and "deposit weight." (The numbers in the following model come from Table 17.4.)

Branch B Analysis

Maximize 15 loan weight + 25 deposit weight	(17.5)

s.t.

10 loan weight + 31 deposit weight – 100 inputs ≤ 0 {Branch A}	(17.6)
15 loan weight + 25 deposit weight – 100 inputs ≤ 0 {Branch B}	(17.7)
20 loan weight + 30 deposit weight – 100 inputs ≤ 0 {Branch C}	(17.8)
23 loan weight + 23 deposit weight – 100 inputs ≤ 0 {Branch D}	(17.9)
30 loan weight + 20 deposit weight – 100 inputs ≤ 0 {Branch E}	(17.10)
100 inputs = 1 {Inputs = 1}	(17.11)

An Excel spreadsheet containing this example can be found on the Student CD.

Access your Student CD now for an Excel worksheet continuing this Branch B calculation.

DEA IMPLEMENTATION PROBLEMS

Many DEA implementations fail. Some general guidelines are helpful in utilizing DEA.[2]

Complexity

DEA is simply hard for many people to understand. Despite the graphical nature and interpretation of the output, and the ease of use of DEA software, practitioners find it confusing and are often uncomfortable when their raises depend on this inscrutable technology. For this reason, DEA is often better used simply as a means of classification, benchmarking, or finding reference sets and possible paths of improvement than it is for determining raises or bonuses.

Size Matters

At some point, when the number of outputs and inputs is large and the number of units being looked at is small, mathematically every unit will become efficient. Because of this excess of outputs and inputs, more than half of the branches obtained the highest efficiency rating in prior studies of bank branches. Although these studies may placate branch managers, they are not helpful to senior management for decision-making purposes. A judicious choice of outputs and inputs retains the power of DEA but limits the number of branches that will attain the highest rating. Consequently, a "rule of thumb" says that no less than twice as many units should be considered as there are inputs and outputs combined.

---

2. For a more robust and technical treatment of this issue, see Metters, Frei, and Vargas (1999), and Dyson et al. (2001).

Ambivalence Regarding Outputs

In the example given previously, DEA makes sense only in the case of ambivalence as to whether a branch generates deposits or loans. In the broader context, in a strong hierarchy of strategic goals, where one goal is clearly preeminent, DEA is not useful.

It would be highly unusual to be ambivalent among all strategic goals. Some goals are normally more important than others. In the DEA formulation used in the example problem, branch A was efficient even though its loan balances were far too low. The basic DEA formulation can be easily changed to reflect the reality that branch A is not a top performer. Limits can be placed on the amount of efficiency that can be generated from any one output. If say, a limit of 70% of the efficiency rating can come from any one output, branch A would no longer be deemed efficient. (See section "Adapting DEA to Managerial Concerns.")

Access your Student CD now for information on adapting DEA to managerial concerns.

Spurious Efficiency

DEA looks at every possible ratio of outputs to inputs to give a unit the highest efficiency possible. Sometimes this function results in a false, or spurious, efficiency. For example, consider a poorly performing bank branch that does a lot of transaction processing, but little else, and does that poorly. Because loan origination is not the strategic branch focus, only one loan officer works in the branch. Let us say the branch performs poorly on both transaction processing and loan origination, and that "transactions processed" is a DEA output and "loan officers" is an input. Despite poor performance, this branch might appear efficient because the ratio of transactions processed to loan officers is the best in the network, which is not a reasonable measure on which a firm would like to base performance evaluations.

Employee Gaming

DEA is susceptible to "gaming" by managers just as with many other performance evaluation systems. This vulnerability specifically relates to the previous point on spurious efficiency. Following the example in the prior paragraph, if a manager knows that the efficiency score can be influenced by nonsensical ratios, the manager may take action to manipulate those ratios.

Access your Student CD now for a description of how to do DEA in Excel as well as other DEA software.

TECHNICAL MATERIAL ON STUDENT CD

The following written material can be found on the student CD:

- a description of how to do DEA in Excel as well as other DEA software
- mathematically adding restrictions to the weights in a DEA problem
- more graphical interpretations of DEA (by Ken Klassen, Brock University)

Summary

This chapter focused on the more narrow topic of DEA formulation and implementation. In the broader view, DEA can be a useful managerial tool, but only under the proper circumstances. Foremost, applicability depends on numerous units that attempt roughly the same task where the firm has true goal ambivalence. If diverse units are input, the exercise will be futile because all the branches will appear equally efficient. For example, due to the mathematics of DEA, if only one branch made mortgage loans and mortgage loans were an output, that branch would be efficient regardless of its other characteristics.

The first uses of DEA were concentrated in the nonprofit sector. The multiple outputs and goal ambivalence inherent in the nonprofit sector appropriately fit the DEA methodology. Any transfer of this technology to the for-profit sector must also find an environment where a single measure of productivity or efficiency is not recognized. When multiple measures are appropriate, however, DEA is a superior technique to the standard business practice of analyzing ratios at an individual level. Performance reviews based on standard ratio analysis encourages managers to increase some measures at the expense of others. DEA—when performed properly—evaluates the entire package of inputs and outputs to assess unit performance.

Review Questions

1. What are the benefits and disadvantages of traditional evaluation measures such as unit profits or goal-based performance measurement?
2. What are the required business conditions for using DEA?
3. What are the benefits and disadvantages of DEA?
4. What is "results ambivalence," and why is it important?
5. What is the purpose of the "Hypothetical Comparison Unit?"
6. Why is the reference set a useful managerial tool?

Problems

17.1. University faculty are often evaluated and promoted based on two main criteria: Teaching and research. At many of the "research" schools, a rough weighting may be 80% research, 20% teaching. What would be the benefits or disadvantages of rewarding faculty based more on a DEA-like weighting of research and teaching? That is, allowing individual faculty to choose the weighting that suits them the best?

17.2. Consider a DEA analysis of many units of a firm with two outputs and two inputs. Unit A has outputs of 110 on Output 1 and 140 on Output 2 with inputs of 170 on Input 1 and 1,050 on Input 2. Unit B has outputs of 100 on Output 1 and 70 on Output 2 with inputs of 190 on Input 1 and 1,500 on Input 2. Even without knowing the data from the other units in the firm, could either of these units be efficient?

17.3. (This problem can be solved using pen and paper only.) The multi-site service units in Table 17.5 have two outputs, profit and a customer satisfaction rating, and one input called, well, "input." Which of the service units would be called efficient by DEA?

Access your Student CD now for data for Problems 17.4 through 17.7 in Excel worksheet form.

17.4. The data in Table 17.6 depict two outputs of "margin" and "market share" and one input of "payroll." Find the efficiencies of units 1–4.

TABLE 17.5: *Data for Problem 17.3*

Unit	Inputs	Profit	Customer Satisfaction Rating
A	10	14	8.2
B	5	9	3.8
C	10	−5	8.3
D	10	20	7.0
E	10	10	7.8

TABLE 17.6: *Data for Problems 17.4 and 17.5*

	Margin	Market Share	Payroll
Unit 1	18.0	14.1	125.9
Unit 2	12.2	15.9	136.4
Unit 3	14.1	19.2	132.8
Unit 4	16.5	14.2	132.3

17.5   For the data in Table 17.6, if "market share" were restricted to providing only 20% of the total efficiency, what would the efficiencies of units 1–4 be (i.e., "market share" × market share weight ≤ efficiency × 0.2)?

17.6.   Based on the three outputs and three inputs in Table 17.7, find the efficiencies of units A–J.

17.7.   For the data in Table 17.7, if "sales growth" were restricted to providing only 20% of the total efficiency, what would the efficiencies of units A–J be (i.e., "sales growth" × sales growth weight ≤ efficiency × 0.2)?

Selected Bibliography

Charnes, A., Cooper, W., Lewin, A., and L. Seiford. 1994. *Data Envelopment Analysis: Theory, Methodology and Applications*. Kluwer Academic Publishers, Boston.

Dyson, R., Allen, R., Camanho, A., Podinovski, V., Sarrico, C. and E. Shale. 2001. Pitfalls and Protocols in DEA. *European Journal of Operational Research*, 132, 245–259.

Frei, F., and P. Harker. 1999. Projections onto Efficient Frontiers: Theoretical and Computational Extensions of DEA. *Journal of Productivity Analysis*, 11(3), 275–300.

Gattoufi, Oral, and Reisman. 2004. DEA Literature, a Bibliographic Update. *Socio-Economic Planning Sciences*, 38, 159–229.

Metters, R., Frei, F., and V. Vargas. 1999. Measurement of Multiple Sites in Service Firms with Data Envelopment Analysis. *Production and Operations Management*, 8(3), 264–281.

TABLE 17.7: *Data for Problems 17.6 and 17.7*

	Outputs			Inputs		
	Margin	Sales Growth	Market Share	Logistics Cost	Rent	Payroll
Unit A	18.0	25.7	14.1	155.3	81.5	125.9
Unit B	12.2	20.6	15.9	174.8	78.1	136.4
Unit C	14.1	20.6	19.2	168.6	82.1	132.8
Unit D	16.5	22.2	14.2	162.9	82.5	132.3
Unit E	14.6	22.1	15.7	166.1	87.2	130.4
Unit F	14.0	20.1	14.0	169.4	87.2	132.9
Unit G	15.1	19.8	13.6	167.1	81.1	130.4
Unit H	17.2	21.3	15.3	160.7	83.2	129.2
Unit I	14.9	18.0	14.1	168.8	83.9	133.8
Unit J	15.6	14.4	16.0	169.8	81.8	129.9

Branch Performance at Nashville National Bank

Julie Moore, Senior Executive Vice President and Chief Operating Officer of Nashville National Bank (NNB), sat at the helm during a time of rapid expansion that saw NNB grow from three to ten branches in a few years. Unfortunately, that expansion is now responsible for some personnel problems. Many of the branch managers are complaining loudly about discrepancies in pay, titles, and resources. One older branch manager who recently received an unfavorable performance review threatened to sue NNB for age discrimination if he was fired.

The complaints focused on the branch performance appraisal process. Determining some measure of bank branch performance is essential. Without some agreed-upon performance measure, varied decisions such as branch expansion/ closure, managerial promotion, and resource allocation are left to the "feel" of senior management. Currently, Julie gave all branch manager performance reviews herself. Being a "hands-on" type of manager, she felt that she was in an informed position to pass judgment on each branch. She based her judgments on what she feels each branch should have accomplished during the past year, given their location and past performance, but used no particular benchmark.

During the mid 1990s, when the bank operated only three branches and she knew each manager well, her informal style seemed to work well. With the complexity of a larger branch network, combined with the political factions arising within it, she realized that a more formal approach was necessary. Under her informal evaluation system, many managers felt that the negotiating and presentation skills of branch managers can be a more important input to their performance appraisals than the actual performance of their branch.

Julie decided to compare the formal branch performance evaluation systems that peer banks use to see if one would fit at NNB.

Branch Growth at Nashville National Bank

NNB was founded in 1980 as a largely retail bank serving upper-middle class customers in Nashville. Nashville, Tennessee, has a population of 570,000, while the encompassing Standard Metropolitan Statistical Area has a population of 1.2 million, making it approximately 35th on a list of the largest metro areas in the United States. NNB had only three branches within Nashville when it merged with a failed thrift, Belle Meade S&L, in 2003, and gained three more branches. The Belle Meade area in Nashville is the wealthiest section of town. In 2004, NNB purchased another failing institution, Farmer's Bank, located in more rural Robertson County, which added one branch. Last year NNB and People's Bank, with three branches in suburban, middle-class communities south of Nashville merged, bringing the total branches in the NNB system to ten.

CASE STUDY

Each of the acquisitions was made because the banks were considered "good buys," rather than for strategic considerations. Outwardly the branches underwent few changes. The employees of the purchased banks were kept on at their current pay scale and title. Few procedural changes were made to make them conform to NNB's methods. For instance, loan application and review were different from branch to branch. At the extreme, only the former Farmer's Bank branch made agricultural loans.

The major changes at NNB occurred in the backroom operations. The most significant change was to the computer systems. Each of the disparate systems was integrated to ensure that accounts could be accessed in real time from any branch in the NNB system. This capability was greatly appreciated by their customers. Many customers preferred to process transactions at a variety of branches in the NNB system, not just the particular branch that opened their account.

The acquired branches catered to different market segments than NNB traditionally embraced. Belle Meade S&L focused on retail banking for the higher-income local customers. Farmer's Bank provided both retail and commercial services for agricultural purposes. As agriculture declined in importance in the local economy, the market share of Farmer's commensurately decreased. People's Bank provided retail services to a basically middle-class clientele.

Assessing Branch Productivity: Available Techniques

Although it is clearly necessary to implement some measure of branch performance, considerable disagreement surrounds what should be measured and how to measure it. A wide variety of measurement and reporting techniques are currently used by different banks to evaluate branches.

Julie narrowed the choice of alternatives to three commonly used techniques: branch profitability, branch ranking and branch goals, and one emerging technique used only recently—Data Envelopment Analysis (DEA).

- **Branch Profitability.** Many banks evaluate branches by fashioning financial statements for each branch. Interest and fee income from accounts is credited to the branch where the accounts originated. This income is netted against interest costs and noninterest expenses to determine a profitability level (Table 17.8).
- **Ranking Reports.** An alternative is to evaluate branches according to performance in specific areas separately, rather than using a single profitability number.
- **Goal Reports.** Preset goals are negotiated with each branch manager on a variety of topics. Performance evaluation is based on the percentage of goals attained. The categories used for goal reporting would be similar to those used in ranking reports.
- **Data Envelopment Analysis (DEA).**

CASE STUDY

TABLE 17.8: *Branch Profitability Financial Statement*

Sample Branch Profitability Statement
($ in 000)

	September 1999
Interest Income from Loans[a]	384.2
Federal Funds Sold[b]	0.0
Total Interest Income	384.2
Interest Expense from Deposits[a]	(185.5)
Federal Funds Purchased[b]	(23.0)
Total Interest Expense	(208.5)
Provision for Credit Losses	(26.5)
Net Interest Income After Provision for Credit Losses	149.2
Noninterest Income	
Deposit Account Fees	22.2
Loan Fees	12.1
Total Noninterest Income	32.3
Noninterest Expense	
Salaries	(35.0)
Benefits	(7.4)
Occupancy	(4.1)
Other Expense	(18.2)
Total Noninterest Expense	(64.7)
Net Income Before Support Expenses	116.8
Specific Support Expense[c]	(32.6)
Net Income Before General Expense	84.2
General Support Expense[d]	(22.4)
Net Income	61.8

[a] Income/expense from loan and deposit accounts initially opened by branch.
[b] If more deposits are taken in than loans given out, the excess is sold on the Federal Funds market. If excessive loans are granted, the money is borrowed from the FF market.
[c] Expenses of central administration directly related to branch activity.
[d] Expenses of central administration not directly related to any specific branch (e.g., president's salary).

CASE STUDY

Branch Managers Revolt

The problem of evaluating branches was brought to the forefront by the former People's Bank managers. They knew their titles were of lower rank than other branch managers, but they believed that it was due to the merger process and that salaries were relatively equal. When they inadvertently discovered the wide gaps in salaries between branch managers they were furious (Table 17.9). The former People's managers demanded that Julie bring their titles and salaries up to the level of the other managers.

John Semple, the president of NNB, was against any pay increases. He believed that the former People's branches were not producing as well as the others and that their managers should be paid accordingly. Realizing that his "feel" was not going to be good enough to placate the branch managers, he instructed Julie to come up with an objective method of determining how well the branches were doing.

Julie's Folly

Julie decided to use DEA to evaluate the NNB branch system. She used five outputs and three inputs. The outputs chosen were branch profit, a deposit transaction index, a new account index, an existing account index, and agricultural loan balances.

Branch profitability was calculated as shown in Table 17.8. Julie used the average monthly profit for the last three years. The other measures are combined indexes of many items. The transaction index multiplies the number of transactions handled at a branch by the standard time required to perform the transaction. For example, handling a routine deposit takes 20 seconds, but writing a cashier's check

TABLE 17.9: *Branch Manager Salaries*

Original Bank	Branch Number	Branch Manager Title	Branch Manager Salary
NNB	1	Vice President	$58,000
NNB	2	Vice President	$62,500
NNB	3	Senior V.P.	$75,000
Belle Meade	4	Vice President	$60,000
Belle Meade	5	Senior V.P.	$70,000
Belle Meade	6	Vice President	$56,000
Farmer's	7	Vice President	$62,000
People's	8	Assistant V.P.	$48,000
People's	9	Assistant V.P.	$46,000
People's	10	Assistant V.P.	$44,000

CASE STUDY

takes 3 minutes. The branch with the largest amount of standard time was given an index value of 100 and the other branches were indexed accordingly.

Similar procedures were used for new and existing accounts. A certificate of deposit for $10,000 at 5.5% interest is far less profitable than a regular savings account with a $10,000 balance at 3.0%. Consequently, indexes using approximate profitability ratings were used to weight new and existing account activity.

Finally, at the specific request of the Farmer's branch manager, Julie also included agricultural loan balances as an output.

For inputs, Julie used the average personnel and total branch expenses over the past three years. Also, some locations were clearly better than others and branches located in prime spots would reasonably be expected to perform better so a "location desirability" estimate was included as an input.

According to Julie's calculations, nearly every branch was perfectly efficient and of the three that had less than 100% efficiency, the lowest efficiency was 92% (a sample calculation appears in Figure 17.2, results are in Table 17.7). The inescapable conclusion was that the former People's branch managers were right: They were underpaid.

When Julie presented her method and conclusions at the next Executive Operating Committee meeting she was met with a less than enthusiastic response. When she finished, a stony silence ensued and Julie noticed that John was staring down at the desk with his head in his hands.

Vicente Vargas, senior vice president and head of the check-processing center, was the first to speak. "This is garbage. John, give me three days and I'll give you something you can use." When Julie began to protest, John interrupted, "Julie, leave the room. I'd like to hear what Vicente has to say."

Questions:

1. What are good characteristics of evaluation methods in general?
2. What are the strengths and weaknesses of each of the available techniques for measuring bank branches?
3. Specifically, is DEA a good choice for NNB?
4. Construct a superior DEA model. Report the efficiencies for each branch.

CASE STUDY

FIGURE 17.2: *DEA Example Calculation*

		Outputs					Inputs					
		Branch	Deposit Trans.	New Account	Existing Account Balance	Ag. Loan	Personnel	Total	Location			Right
Original		Profit	Index	Index	Index	Balance	Expense	Expense	Index	Total	Hand Side	Slack
Bank		======	======	======	======	======	======	======	======	======		
NNB	Branch 1	95	65	100	90	0	39	80	9	0.000	< 0	0.000
NNB	Branch 2	70	68	78	77	0	37	82	9	-0.233	< 0	0.233
NNB	Branch 3	108	75	80	100	0	41	92	8	0.000	< 0	0.000
Belle Meade	Branch 4	63	68	69	73	0	42	88	9	-0.351	< 0	0.351
Belle Meade	Branch 5	115	77	85	98	0	54	99	10	-0.017	< 0	0.017
Belle Meade	Branch 6	85	72	69	90	0	37	84	10	-0.129	< 0	0.129
Farmer's	Branch 7	12	17	12	34	25	45	92	7	-0.816	< 0	0.816
People's	Branch 8	45	93	40	52	0	65	125	7	-0.852	< 0	0.852
People's	Branch 9	39	94	45	58	0	73	109	8	-0.754	< 0	0.754
People's	Branch 10	50	100	38	65	0	79	118	9	-0.751	< 0	0.751
	Branch Inputs						54	99	10	1	= 1	0.000
	Branch Outputs	115	77	85	98	0						
	Variables	0.00855	0.00000	0.00000	0.00000	0.00000	0.00000	0.00964	0.00455	C23:J23 are variables		
	Input Weights (sum to 1)						0.000	0.955	0.045			
	Output Weights	0.983	0.000	0.000	0.000	0.000	(sum to objective function)					
	Maximize Outputs		0.983	D28 is the objective function cell.								

Access your Student CD now for the Branch 5 DEA Calculation Excel worksheet.

Advanced Models: Scoring Systems[1]

The material in this chapter prepares students to:

- Understand the value and prevalence of scoring systems.
- Complete a score card.
- Create a scoring system.
- Understand on an intuitive level which mathematical techniques can assist in scoring systems.

If you ever applied for a car loan, your application was probably "scored" by your bank or your car dealer's financial group. Home mortgage applications, infant health evaluation, customer call lists, and much more all rely on fairly recently developed methods known as "scoring systems."

Scoring systems are used in a variety of industries for a variety of purposes, including the following:

- Attracting customers
- Selecting which customers to take when too many want your service
- Allocation of resources (employee time) among customers
- Data reduction

Why haven't you heard much about these systems? It will become clear, in this chapter, why these systems are rarely discussed by corporations and are almost always considered as extremely confidential. Well-designed scoring systems can cut costs and make your decision making much more consistent.

HISTORY OF SCORING

The earliest scoring systems were developed in 1941 by David Durand for use by finance houses. A few more applications were reported through the 1960s, but the

---

1. This chapter is adapted from Metters, R. (2000). Models for Customer Selection. In Fitzsimmons and Fitzsimmons (eds.), *New Service Development*. Sage Publications, Thousand Oaks, CA. Reprinted by permission of Sage Publications, Inc.

use of scoring systems was not widespread and the few that were created were strictly used in the credit scoring arena. Customer solicitation and resource allocation scoring came later. In those early days, some people believed that "it is unlikely that credit scoring systems will be become widely adopted . . . [and] will be relegated to the academic world" (Harter, 1974).

The 1970s, however, saw an explosion of the use of scoring, especially credit scoring. Three factors converged to increase their use: advances in computing ability; the explosion of credit card use, which required a cheaper method of loan approval than for existing loans; and the passage of the Equal Credit Opportunity Act (ECOA) and Regulation B. The ECOA and Reg B prohibited discrimination in granting credit. Further, a legal case of discrimination could be shown statistically; that is, an individual did not have to show that a specific loan officer at a bank personally discriminated against him or her. Instead, showing statistically that a bank rejected the loan applications of a disproportionate number of minorities made a prima facie case of discrimination. The regulations stated that a defense for these charges is to make loans through a "statistically sound, empirically based" system of granting credit— or credit scoring. Scoring is now so widespread in retail banking and finance houses for approval for credit cards and auto loans that it would be unusual to find a U.S. retail bank that does not use scoring for this purpose.

Today creating scoring systems is a significant service business in itself. An acknowledged market leader in the field is The Fair, Isaac Companies in San Rafael, California, but the list would also include the European firms George Wilkinson Associates, Scorex Ltd. and CCN Systems. Some corporations, such as Merrill Lynch and GECC, however, developed their systems internally, as did several large commercial banks.

SCORING IN USE TODAY

Many large corporations depend heavily on cold-call sales by their associates to generate new business. New stockbrokers, for example, must pick up the phone to identify new clients. The key question, of course, is whom to call. Lists of individuals identified by net worth or income are not available, but brokers clearly should only call potentially profitable customers who can afford to buy large amounts of financial products. As the characters in a movie about salesmen, *Glengarry Glen Ross*, would say, "It's the leads. The whole thing is the leads."

Merrill Lynch's solution was to get the leads by developing a scoring system. Their system infers customer profitability by comparing demographic data of potential customers with demographics from its current customer base. Merrill Lynch uses this procedure to develop the calling lists for their brokers (Labe, 1994).

In similar applications, direct mail and telephone solicitation companies that use customer selection, or scoring models, report a 50% reduction in acquisition costs while facing only a small reduction in customer response. Specifically, the direct mail marketer Fingerhut mails about 340 million catalogs per year to 7 million customers, which means that some customers would get up to 120 catalogs per year. Applying scoring methods cut their revenue a small portion, but cut mailing costs significantly, increasing profitability by $3.5 million a year (Campbell et al., 2001).

When Durand (1941) began his work, loan officers used their considerable judgment acquired over many years to evaluate a customer's loan application and decide whether to underwrite the loan. Today, most banks select loan recipients by assigning points to demographic characteristics. A clerk adds up the points and a

SERVICE OPERATIONS MANAGEMENT PRACTICES

Scoring Systems Change an Industry

In the "old days," banks were the natural place to get a home mortgage. An applicant filled out a lengthy application and waited a month or more to find out whether she was approved. It was thought that the individual expertise of knowledgeable lenders was necessary to evaluate credit risks.

Now, credit scoring is prevalent in the process. Instead of requiring human judgment for loan approval, information is typed into a computer and a proprietary scoring system used nationwide accesses credit reports and gives the applicant a numerical score. These scores—called *automated underwriting* in the industry—offer such a reliable measure of credit risk that knowledgeable bankers are no longer necessary. The reliability of credit scoring led to large-scale selling of home loans; that is, someone who brought in the customer for a loan could sell that loan to another investor, based largely on the credit score. Making loans no longer requires a vault full of cash.

These two factors combined to change the industry of home mortgages. Now, mortgage brokers, who are not bank employees but who qualify prospective homeowners for mortgages for a living, are becoming the dominant force in the industry. According to a UBS Warburg analyst, traditional banks are becoming "a shrinking and increasingly irrelevant" part of the industry.

Source: Barta (2001).

loan is made if the point score exceeds a predetermined amount. Replacing or augmenting judgmental loan underwriting based on experience with customer selection by scoring reduced bad loan ratios by one-third. Banks could also cut costs through replacing higher-priced loan officers with lower-cost clerks. A third benefit comes from decisions that are more consistent. Under the traditional system—usually called a judgmental system because it relies on human judgment—an applicant can be turned down by one lender and accepted by another within the same bank.

The use of scoring models, instead of a more judgmental system, allowed GE Capital Corporation (GECC) to allocate resources more effectively. GECC faces the daunting task of collecting $1 billion of delinquent consumer loans each year. In order of decreasing expense to GECC, it can collect on a loan by initiating legal procedures, having a collector personally call, have a computer call the customer with a taped telephone message, send the customer a letter indicating he is delinquent, or do nothing and let the regular billing process inform the customer he did not make a payment. Scoring models allow GECC to target the appropriate method to a customer based on a computerized analysis of the customers' payment behavior. The scoring model allowed GECC to reduce loan losses by 9%, reduce costs of collection, and increase customer goodwill (Makuch et al., 1992).

These models are designed to replace individual expert judgment with a cheaper and more reliable method. Even when a score augments rather than replaces individual judgment, it is still useful in reducing the amount of communication and data needed.

An APGAR score was probably your first personal encounter with a scoring system. Every time an infant is born, one of the first tasks of hospital personnel is to determine its APGAR score. The APGAR score is helpful in describing a general level of health at a given moment by mentioning a single number rather than a long list of vital signs and movements of fingers and toes.

The use of scoring systems is widespread today. In Table 18.1 you can see the diverse use of scoring systems in industry. Although the creation of scoring models is itself a significant service industry, the nature of the scoring process lends itself to use in service firms rather than in manufacturing organizations. Scoring is most efficient and effective when evaluating large numbers of potential customers where statistical analysis can benefit from large sample sizes. The users of scoring systems,

---

TABLE 18.1:   *Partial List of Industries that Use Scoring*

- Auto Insurance
    Customer acceptance
- Brokerages
    Customer solicitation
- Education
    Nonneed (merit) based scholarships in colleges
    Improving "yield" (percentage of admitted students who choose to enroll)
- Health Care
    APGAR (score for infant health)
    APACHE (score for emergency medicine)
    Craniofacial Index (predicts sleep apnea)
- Mass Mail/Telemarketing and Retailers
    Target market identification (e.g., high incomes)
    Selecting solicitation targets (response rate prediction)
- Merchant Banks
    Corporate bankruptcy prediction
- Parole Boards
    Paroling prisoners
- Retail Banks and Finance Houses (e.g., Household Finance Corp.)
    Loan approval for
        credit cards
        auto loans
        home loans
        small business loans
    Solicitation for products (e.g., pre-approved loans)
    Credit limit settings and extensions
    Prediction of credit usage
    Prediction of customer retention
    Collection of bad debts
- Tax Collection
    IRS income tax audits
- Utility Companies
    Credit line establishment
    Length of service provision

Source: Adapted from Metters (2000), Models for Customer Selection, in Fitzsimmons and Fitzsimmons (eds.), *New Service Development*. Sage Publications, Thousand Oaks, CA, p. 293.

therefore, tend to be service firms with individuals as customers, rather than manufacturers whose customers are other companies.

SCORING METHODOLOGIES AND IMPLEMENTATION

Building a scoring system is simple in theory, but can be capricious and complex to implement. The five basic steps to building one are as follows:

1. Divide customers into two groups: "good" and "bad."
2. Determine risk score cut-off level.
3. Identify the variables associated with good/bad results.
4. Develop a numerical scorecard.
5. Score your customers.

Each of these steps is described in the following subsections.

Separating "Good" and "Bad" Customers

Because of the managerial decisions involved—often "accept" or "reject"—the outcomes of current customers (or "dependent variable") is usually either 0 or 1. For example, in scoring for credit acceptance, the two groups of data are those customers who paid off a loan and those who defaulted on a loan. The decision to make on prospective customers is accept or reject, or 0 or 1. Two categories are the most common number in practice, but more than two are possible with some techniques.

Numerical Risk Score

Step 2 also involves breaking current customer data into two categories. A profitability level is associated with each group, and an acceptable risk level is established. For example, consider a retailer planning a direct mail campaign. Combining mailing, printing, and other costs, we might assign a loss of $0.45 for a piece of mail that lands in the trash and an average profit of $20 for a direct mail customer who responds. If mail is sent to 100 potential customers that all have a 1% chance of responding, the profitability of the mailing will be $99 \times (-\$0.45) + 1 \times \$20 = -\$24.55$, or a net loss. However, if mail is sent to 100 potential customers that all have a 3% chance of responding, the profitability of the mailing will be $97 \times (-\$0.45) + 3 \times \$20 = \$16.35$, or a net profit. The equation which brings profits and losses into balance can be derived algebraically by considering the following rule: Approve a mailing until

$$\text{Expected Profit} = \text{Expected Loss from marginal account.}$$

Working through the algebra (not included here), we derive the following relationship: Probability threshold = loss from a bad account/(loss from a bad account + gain from a good account). Or, in this case 2.2% = 0.45/(0.45 + 20).

The mass mailer, therefore, doesn't want to waste money mailing to those who won't respond, but will send mail to anyone with a 2.2% or greater chance of responding.

The mass mailer, therefore, would like to find some assessment of the "odds" of responding and send mailings to homes only with larger odds than 2.2%.

Variables Associated with Good/Bad Results

Clearly, we would like some method to assess the odds of a response for each potential customer. The general idea of scoring is to generate those odds by establishing statistical relationships based on a company's own customer base. That is, extrapolate the known outcomes of the company's current customers to demographic information of potential customers.

The difficult task is to assess the odds of customers who have conflicting demographic information. For example, a company may realize that their best customers are 35- to 50-year-old married female homeowners with incomes between $35,000 and $50,000. But given a choice of a 30-year-old married female homeowner with a $30,000 income and a 40-year-old single female renter with an income of $45,000, who should be chosen? Scoring models assign specific points to each demographic characteristic that make such trade-offs easy to see.

Developing a Numerical Scorecard

Unfortunately, the most widely practiced statistical technique, multiple regression, is insufficient for this task. Consider the "perfect" data set in Figure 18.1. Everyone under 35 years of age defaulted on loans and all those over 35 years paid their loans.

FIGURE 18.1: *Fitting Categorical Data*

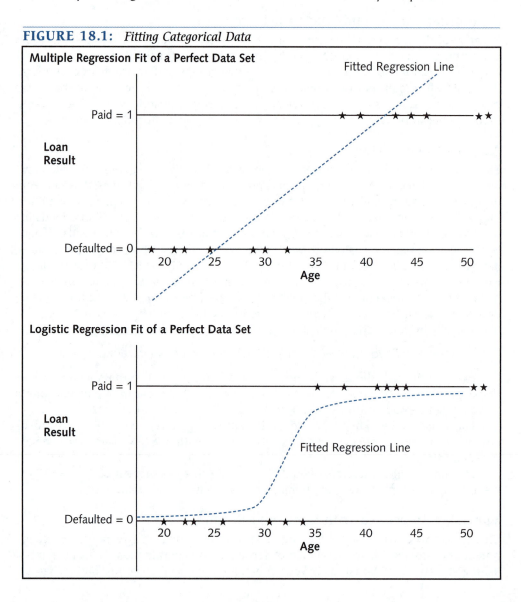

The results of standard regression appear in the first drawing, where the traditional straight line minimizing mean squared error is depicted. The numerical result of a regression on these data is the equation Y = –0.87 + 0.04 × age. An Excel file with this equation is on the Student CD. This regression yields the odds of a 20-year-old paying back a loan to be negative (–0.07) and the odds of a 50-year-old to be far greater than 100% (1.13). Neither of these results makes sense in our general understanding of probabilities.

Access your Student CD now for an Excel file of this equation.

Mathematical techniques useful in scoring include discriminant analysis, decision trees, and, less commonly, logistic regression, integer programming, and neural networks.[2] For a visual example of how these techniques work, the trend line for logistic regression is shown on the second graph of Figure 18.1. Instead of fitting a straight line to data, logistic regression fits the function:

$$\text{score} = \ln[\text{odds}/(1 - \text{odds})] \qquad (18.1)$$

Using the logarithm (ln) function sets bounds on the score at 0 and 1. Using some algebra on equation (18.1),

$$\text{odds} = e^{\text{score}}/(e^{\text{score}} + 1) \qquad (18.2)$$

where $e \cong 2.718$.

This calculation gives an analyst more realistic results. For example, for the perfect data represented in Figure 18.1, the curve hugs the data nearly precisely. The fitted function is score = –376.092 + 10.901 × age. An SPSS file with this equation is on the Student CD. So, a 34-year-old has a 0.4% chance of a good account, a 34½-year-old a 49.8% chance, and a 35-year-old has a 99.6% chance of being a good account.

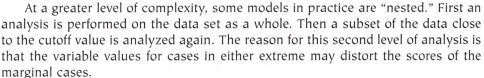

Access your Student CD now for an SPSS file of this equation.

At a greater level of complexity, some models in practice are "nested." First an analysis is performed on the data set as a whole. Then a subset of the data close to the cutoff value is analyzed again. The reason for this second level of analysis is that the variable values for cases in either extreme may distort the scores of the marginal cases.

The way in which a scoring system is implemented affects the method of data analysis. In some firms, a score is calculated directly from a computer system without any human intervention. In others, however, a score is calculated manually using a physical score card like the one depicted in Figure 18.2.

Assume the monetary relationship between good and bad accounts were such that a probability of a good account needed to be 90% for approval. Then the cutoff score of ln[.9/(1 – .9)] = 2.20 would be appropriate. In the example of Figure 18.2, the fitted equation uses application data such as home ownership and age. The actual score card used by the clerk mimics the fitted equation by starting each applicant with 80 points (the constant for the fitted equation) and assigning points for each characteristic, such as adding 50 points for those age 56 or older and subtracting 20 points for those between 26 and 35 years. Those who score more than 220 points are approved.

Note that the point scores within a category are additive, not multiplicative. For example, a 56-year-old and a 75-year-old both get 50 points because they are in the same category: age ≥ 56. The reason for an additive score card is its simplicity: A clerk merely checks boxes and adds a column of numbers. The implication for an additive card on the modeling process is that each of the *independent* variables must

2. See Rosenberg and Gleit (1994) for a detailed review of the mathematics behind these techniques in the context of credit scoring.

FIGURE 18.2: *Score Card Fitted by Logistic Regression*

Required Odds of a Good Customer: 90%

Cutoff score for logistic regression: Ln [0.9/(1 − 0.9)] = 2.20

Fitted equation

.80 + 1.30 Own Home	− .05 Other	
+ .85 S + C w/bank	− .05 Checking	
+ .50 (56 + yrs. old)	+ .15 (36–55)	− .20 (<25)
+ .33 Retired	+ .25 Manager	− .26 Laborer
+ .53 (10 + yrs. job)	+ .25 (5–10 yrs.)	

For convenience, multiply all values by 100.

Everyone starts with 80 points.*

Residence	Own home + 130		Other –5
Bank Accounts	Savings and checking with bank + 85		Checking only –5
Age	56+ years + 50	36–55 years + 15	26–35 years − 20
Work	Retired + 33	Manager + 25	Laborer − 26
Time on Job	10 years or more + 53	5–10 years on job + 25	

Accept if score greater than 220.

*Score in blue for a renter (–5), with savings and checking with the bank (+ 85), 62 years old (+ 50), and retired (+ 33). Everyone starts with 80 points so the total point score is 243.

also be coded as (0,1); that is, each explanatory variable must be transformed by segmentation. For example, one continuous variable such as income could be transformed into three variables such as income less than $40,000, income between $40,000 and $80,000, and income greater than $80,000, each with a 0 or 1 as data, as in Table 18.2. This segmentation creates some modeling difficulties, however, because no general rules guide for the number of segments or for the location of segment borders (should it be age ≥ 56 or age ≥ 57?). Finding the best break points and

TABLE 18.2: *Variable Parsing in an Additive Scorecard: Example of an Income Variable*

Actual Variable Value	Variables Used in Scorecard		
	0 to 25	26 to 80	81 and above
20	1	0	0
33	0	1	0
110	0	0	1
19	1	0	0
55	0	1	0
86	0	0	1
147	0	0	1

the proper number of categories is an art as well as a science. In general, though, an easy way to determine whether one break point is better than another is whether the overall fit of the model is improved.

Accept/Solicit/Apply Resources to Customers over the Set Score

Use of credit scoring scorecards is straightforward. Those who score above the predetermined score pass this test and those who don't either are declined credit or some type of exception analysis is required by a lender to move an application forward.

Other types of scorecards, however, can proceed differently. Thus far the examples shown focused on scoring demographic factors, such as age and zip code. Another important and related technique is called *behavioral scoring* and relates to the performance of a customer within a system. The most common example of behavioral scoring is in the collection of delinquent loans. Earlier, we gave an example from GECC, but the practice is becoming fairly common.

As related earlier, a number of approaches are available for collecting on a delinquent loan. Prior to using a scoring system, many companies used a standard practice of sending a letter first, then a telephone call at a designated interval. A scoring system, however, scores behavior such as how recently the debtor made a payment, how much was paid, the percentage of minimum payments made, previous history of missed payments, and other factors to determine a method to minimize the combined costs of collection and bad debt.

Figure 18.3 illustrates another type of score card often seen in practice. This type of card stems from the decision tree or recursive partitioning approach. Operationally, the applicant's demographic characteristics are followed down the tree until either an acceptance or rejection ends a branch.

PROBLEMS WITH SCORING SYSTEMS

Scoring systems clearly mark an improvement over judgmental systems in both fairness and cost, but they are not a panacea. Problems with scoring systems can be divided into two categories: methodology problems and implementation problems.

FIGURE 18.3: *Decision Tree Example of a Score Card*

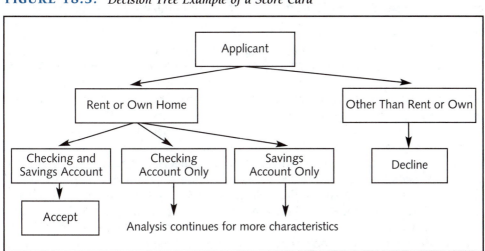

Methodological Problems

The "good" versus "bad" account may make intuitive sense for a Yes or No decision, but from a managerial standpoint this coding neglects the underlying differentials in customer profitability. In the context of line-of-credit approval, for example, one account can lose $100,000 and another only $10, yet they are all coded 0. Conversely, a line-of-credit that is never used (and, therefore, does not generate revenue) and a highly profitable line of credit are both coded 1. An ideal system would take profitability into account, rather than just a simple Yes or No. The odds of defaulting or paying off are different from the odds of being a very profitable or unprofitable customer. One can imagine a more complex scoring system that does not merely make Yes or No decisions, but gives everyone credit with a corresponding interest rate that reflects his or her risk and profitability.

Scoring systems also suffer from "screening bias." As stated by Rosenberg and Gleit (1994, p. 596): "The best credit system would grant credit to every applicant during some time period to gain credit information for the entire population." Unfortunately, many scoring systems rely on the currently installed customer base. If some groups are systematically excluded prior to implementing a scoring system, therefore, the system contains no data by which to judge them.

A third methodological problem focuses on the life of a scoring system. Any scoring system is only valid for as long as the customer base remains the same. Entering or targeting new markets or changes in mores or economic conditions may render a scoring system useless. A general rule of thumb is that a scoring system needs to be recalibrated every three to five years.

Myers and Forgy's (1963) research provides a good example of the shelf-life problem. They found that the presence of a telephone in a household was an indicator of someone who would pay debts. In their study, 8% of households did not have a telephone, and those households were an astounding 10 times more likely to default than households with a telephone. Today, only an extremely small number of U.S. citizens do not have telephones, which means the telephone criterion should no longer apply. Yet, in the mid-1980s some banks still awarded score card points for the presence of a phone number on an application.

Implementation Problems

Scoring systems face some criticism for how they are used and because employees and shrewd customers can subvert them if they are not implemented properly.

Fairness

Despite the fact that credit scoring systems arose partly to equalize access to credit, some minorities feel that scoring systems lock them out of obtaining credit. The Federal Reserve says the data agree with them, but industry disputes that finding. It is believed that minority applicants face a higher hurdle, because of the manual override procedure at many banks. It is alleged that most banks allow a lender to ask for an exception to an insufficient score for marginal customers, but some feel that those exceptions strongly favor nonminority customers.

As another example, many universities are concerned about their "yield," or the percentage of students who are accepted by the school who eventually enroll. University rating organizations like *U.S. News & World Report* use the yield statistic to rank schools, so a better yield may increase a school's ranking. Firms like Noel-Levitz and George Dehne & Associates create scoring systems for schools to improve their yield. For many schools, however, increasing yield means turning down excellent students and admitting inferior ones. A student with a 1600 SAT score, a 4.0 GPA, and who is captain of the basketball team may be denied admission to a school, because the school's yield model indicates that such a student would be unlikely to enroll. Denying that student admission increases both the yield rate and rejection rate, both measures that are used to rate universities.

Impersonal Decision Making

By their nature, scoring systems are impersonal, which can lead both to comic errors and customer irritation. In a celebrated case, a Federal Reserve governor with a spotless credit record was denied a Toys "R" Us credit card, because the scoring system negatively weighted a large number of recent inquiries on his credit report. Scoring cannot evaluate factors such as political ramifications and extenuating circumstances effectively. Consequently, some manual review often is desirable.

Face Validity

Scoring systems often find patterns in the data that appear nonsensical or are difficult to explain. For example, auto insurance companies sometimes base the decision to insure motorists on their credit records, rather than on their driving records.

Misuse/Nonuse of Scoring Cards

When implementing scoring systems care must be taken with both employees and potential customers. If scoring system parameters become public knowledge, potential customers can "game" a system. It became known, for example, that Johns Hopkins University was less likely to offer students scholarships if they came to an on-campus interview. Scoring systems revealed that if students were interested enough to go to an on-campus interview, a scholarship, instead of a loan, would not be further inducement to enroll, whereas a scholarship changed the enrollment probabilities more drastically for students who showed less initial interest.

Consider, also, that banks never check certain information provided by credit card applicants, yet it contributes to a score. If potential customers discovered that, they could inflate their scores.

Employees can help applicants increase their scores by "guiding" them through an application process. If the incentives for employees are based on the number of accepted applications that they generate, employees have a stake in making their clients look as good as possible.

A solution to these problems is to hide the scorecard from employees and customers. For example, the national U.S. scoring system for mortgage loan approval is a proprietary system of the system developer, The Fair, Isaac Companies. Mortgage brokers are unaware of the point totals given to specific customer attributes, thereby making it difficult for mortgage brokers to take unfair advantage of the system. Similarly, the IRS has steadfastly refused to divulge the algorithm that decides which tax returns get audited.

Scoring also has human resource implications. Employees often see scoring systems as a denigration of their experience and talent and a threat to their jobs. The idea that their years of experience can be replaced by a score card is not generally embraced enthusiastically. Consequently, when first replacing or augmenting a judgmental system with a scoring system, efforts must not focus on employee reduction. To do so would invite subtle sabotage through incorrect scoring or to a more open refusal to use the system.

Summary

Scoring techniques are applied in a wide variety of industries and for a number of different functional uses, including customer selection, customer solicitation, and resource allocation among customers. The construction of scoring systems is a service industry in itself, and because of the nature of the techniques, they are much more useful to service providers than to manufacturers.

The use of scoring systems is likely to increase. A large drawback to their use in the past was the need to collect data, which meant entering data from customer files manually into a computer system. Today, most customer data is held electronically, so the costs of implementing scoring systems continue to decline. Further, as scoring contributes more to financial successes, those companies that do not use scoring systems will be at a considerable competitive disadvantage. Although scoring systems do suffer from some methodological problems, proper implementation of a well-designed scoring system can contribute to building and maintaining a successful business.

Review Questions

1. Give some examples of industries that could or do currently use scoring systems and discuss how this practice impacts their business profitability, their strategic focus, and their costs.
2. What are some ethical considerations in using scoring systems?
3. Name some industries that should be particularly sensitive to charges of discrimination in the use of scoring systems. Discuss ways to lessen these occurrences and strategies for coping with such charges.
4. Why can't standard regression models be used for many scoring models?

Problems

18.1. Based on the following information, decide whether the applicant scores sufficiently to receive an account.

- Average profit for a successful account is $500
- Average loss for an unsuccessful account is $4,500
- A fitted equation is as follows

$$0.75 + 0.82 (25 < age < 45) + 1.10 (age > 45)$$
$$-0.35(time\ on\ job < 2\ years) + 1.22(time\ on\ job > 5\ years)$$
Applicant: 37 years old, 7 years at the current job

Determine the applicant score and the appropriate cutoff point.

18.2. Based on the following information, decide whether this person should be the target of a telephone solicitation.

- Average profit for a successful call is $50
- Average loss for an unsuccessful call is $1
- A fitted equation is as follows

$$-0.15 + 0.28(25 < age < 45) + 0.10(age > 45)$$
$$-0.35(time\ on\ job < 2\ years) + 0.22(time\ on\ job > 5\ years)$$
Applicant: 37 years old, 7 years at the current job

Determine the applicant score and the appropriate cutoff point.

TABLE 18.5: *Data for Problem 18.5*

Observation	Age	Good (1), Bad (0)
1	25	1
2	31	1
3	34	0
4	37	1
5	45	1
6	46	1
7	49	1
8	52	0
9	53	0
10	55	1
11	59	0
12	63	0
13	66	0
14	70	0

Access your Student CD now for data for Problem 18.5.

18.3. What are the odds of a customer being a good one if the output score from a logistic regression model is 1.55? Use equation (18.2).

18.4. What are the odds of a customer being a good one if the output score from a logistic regression model is 0.89? Use equation (18.2).

18.5. For the data in Table 18.5, find the relationship of age to being a "good" account by traditional linear regression and by logistic regression. What is the probability of a 26-year-old being a good account measured by traditional regression and by logistic regression?

Selected Bibliography

Barta, P. 2001. Why Big Lenders Are So Frightened By Fannie and Freddie. *The Wall Street Journal* (April 5), A1.

Campbell, D., Erdahl, R., Johnson, D., Bibelnieks, E., Haydock, M., Bullock, M., and H. Crowder. 2001. Optimizing Customer Mail Streams at Fingerhut, *Interfaces*, 31(1), 77–90.

Durand, D. 1941. Risk Elements in Consumer Installment Financing, *Studies in Consumer Installment Financing*, Study #8, National Bureau of Economic Research, New York.

Harter, T. 1974. Potentials of Credit Scoring: Myth or Fact. *Credit and Financial Management*, 76, 27–28.

Labe, R. 1994. Database Marketing Increases Prospecting Effectiveness at Merrill Lynch. *Interfaces*, 24(5), 1–12.

Makuch, W., Dodge, J., Ecker, J., Granfors, D., and G. Hahn. 1992. Managing Consumer Credit Delinquency in the U.S. Economy: A Multi-Billion Dollar Management Science Application. *Interfaces*, 22(1), 90–109.

Myers, J., and E. Forgy. 1963. The Development of Numerical Credit Evaluation Systems. *Journal of the American Statistical Association*, 58(303), 799–806.

Rosenberg, E., and A. Gleit. 1994. Quantitative Methods in Credit Management: A Survey. *Operations Research*, 42(4), 589–613.

CASE STUDY

MBA Savings and Loan[3]

It was a Friday afternoon in late April when the officers' meeting of the Goizueta Business School Savings and Loan officially convened. In attendance were the two outgoing second-year officers, Julee Carucci and Jim King II, and the two incoming first-year officers, Nancy Toland and Leonard Beren.

"If we're going to expand over to Divinity and Law, our manual processes are going to be too much work. We're going to need more efficient systems," said Julee. "We can start with the loan approval process. Poring over loan applications is time consuming, but worse than the time is the aggravation. People take it so personally when they're turned down. Anyway, we have enough data now to use a scoring system for loan approval. With a scoring system we can shift the credit approval responsibility away from the loan officer."

"Agreed," noted Jim. "A scoring system would also cut out a lot of training time every year for the outgoing lenders. Nothing against you two first-years, but I certainly don't have a lot of enthusiasm for training right now."

The MBA Lending Program

In 2000 a supplemental loan program was established for the MBAs. Unlike loan funds set up for education expenses, this program loaned money for nontraditional student needs such as vacations, moving expenses, and furniture purchases. The program was initiated by the dean as an auxiliary student service. The dean believed it provided another way to improve the relationship between the school and its students. The original funding was derived from the school endowment. Loans could be made for up to $5,000. Repayment terms varied from three months to three years, depending on circumstances. The program was intended to be profitable, with the proceeds retained by the student association.

The program was administered each year by two second-year students who were elected by their classmates the year prior. These students had the responsibility of credit approval, setting interest rates and payment schedules, payment processing, and bad debt collection.

By 2003 the MBA lending program had become an accepted institution. More than 700 loans were made, and the program showed a small profit. Due to the program success, the program would be expanded to lend monies to students in the nearby schools of law and divinity in the next academic year. It was expected that demand would be as strong in those schools as in Goizueta.

---

3. *Source:* The subject of this case is fictitious. Data for the cases is contained on the CD that accompanies this text.

CASE STUDY

Credit Approval

Students applied for loans in a fashion similar to that of bank loans. A formal application was submitted (Table 18.3) and the application was reviewed by both officers. A credit report was also obtained for each potential borrower (Figure 18.4). The application was sent to the admissions office for comparison to admissions data, but the rest of the information provided by the applicant was accepted at face value and with no attempt at corroboration.

Both officers had to agree on granting the loan for credit to be extended. Approximately 80% of the students who applied received credit. For about 85% of the applications both lenders agree on acceptance or rejection. "Most applications are fairly clear," said Jim. "There are obvious good risks and bad risks." Of the remaining 15%, after lengthy debate, about half were eventually accepted.

"The ones we turn down seem to react in three ways," said Julee. "About half seem to get mad about it. Occasionally there are heated words, but usually it's more of a seething look they get. Some folks just sort of withdraw. They feel like a credit denial is a scarlet letter or something. Then there are those who shrug it off, probably because they never expected to get it in the first place. We do get some outlandish requests." The MBA lending program officers replaced the Operations Management professors as the favorite target at the annual dunk tank.

The methods used for credit approval were a combination of experience, lessons learned from the past officers, and hunches. At base, though, Julee and Jim differed in their views on credit approval. Julee felt that character, more than financial status,

TABLE 18.3: *Credit Application Information*

Demographic Data	Financial Data
Name	Annual salary at last job
Social security number	Checking account number
Date of birth	Savings account number
Current address	Total indebtedness
Home phone	Other credit accounts
Previous address	
Time at last address	
Nearest relative	
Previous employer ("none" if coming directly from undergraduate institution)	
Time on last job ("none" if coming directly from undergraduate institution)	
Undergraduate institution	
GPA at undergraduate institution	

CASE STUDY

FIGURE 18.4: *Credit Report*

Applicant Name	Spouse Name
Present Address	Years at address
Previous Address	Years at address
Social Security Number	Spouse Social Security Number

Employer	Position	Hire Date

_____/_____ $_____
Verified/Date   Income

Spouse Employer	Position	Hire Date

_____/_____ $_____
Verified/Date   Income

Public Records: [   ] None Learned   [   ] See Below

Court records checked for judgments, foreclosures, tax liens, and bankruptcies through:

[   ] Direct Search/Repositories   [   ] Repositories

Trade Name Account Number	Opened/ Updated	High Credit	Balance Owing	Terms	Mths. Rev.	Past Due	Account Status 30/ 60/ 90
Bank of America I139272	06/97 03/02	5000	00	—	48	00	Rev 00/000/00

Inquiries:	no inquiries in the past 90 days

CODES:
Acct. Desg.:	Account Designation of I for Individual or J for Joint.
Opened/Updated:	Date account opened and date latest information posted to account.
High Credit:	Credit limit for revolving debt or initial loan amount for installment loans. "R-1" indicates loan type and worst payment. "R" indicates a revolving loan versus I for installment. "1" indicates that there has never been a late payment. "2" would indicate a previous 30-day late payment, etc.
Terms:	Number of months on an installment loan.
Mths. Rev.:	Number of months account has been reported to credit bureau.
Past Due:	Current past due status.
Account Status:	Total number of times account has been 30, 60, 90 days late.
Inquiries:	Number of times account has been checked recently. An indicator of other credit being applied for simultaneously.

CASE STUDY

was a better guarantee of loan repayment. She balanced the information on the credit application with a personal judgment of the applicant's integrity. Jim, however, relied solely on the information contained in the credit application.

Both were somewhat critical of the other's selection criteria. "Jim is always muttering, 'If we would lend only to Harvard grads we wouldn't have any collection problems.' He went to Harvard himself and he's got a real hang-up about where someone went for undergrad," said Julee as she rolled her eyes. "That's not just me, that's a few years of experience talking," replied Jim. "The folks who taught us told us that the people who went to the better schools tended to pay up. Besides, you seem to have a fondness for people with high undergrad GPAs."

The amount of credit extended was not always a fixed amount. Applicants were encouraged to make one application for a total credit limit rather than apply many times for specific funds. The amount of credit limit given was more a source of contention than the approval process. Both Julee and Jim accorded a higher limit to those applicants they felt were better risks. Due to their difference in perceived risk between applicants they rarely agreed initially on a total credit limit.

Bad Debt Collection

A nagging problem of the MBA lending program was bad debts. Approximately 10% of the borrowers did not repay the entire amount of their loan and another 10% repaid only after litigation was started. It was estimated that a successful account contributed an average of $200 to the MBA association, but a bad account cost an average of $700. Because debt collection was carried out by the officers, the methods of collection varied significantly depending on the particular officer. Julee and Jim each handled half the accounts.

Julee believed that early and vigorous actions deterred bad debts. If a borrower was 10 days late with a payment, Julee sent a strongly worded letter to the borrower. If the delinquency persisted another week, she telephoned to remind the borrower. If the borrower continued to be a month late and was still in school, a large red poster was placed high on the wall above the student mailboxes with the word "Deadbeat" and the offender's name in 200 point type. For borrowers not still in school, Julee would advise relatives and employers of the payment delinquency. Julee would continue to contact the borrower by phone and letter up to 180 days delinquency. At this point the loan was declared in default and, on principal, Julee would instigate legal proceedings to recover the loan no matter the amount in default. For borrowers still in school and more than a few months late, she was known to greet them in the hall as "the defendant."

Jim found the collection part of the job distasteful and his style differed considerably from Julee's. He would send out a written "reminder" notice for someone a

CASE STUDY

TABLE 18.4: *Variables for Data Collection*

Variable	Description
AGE	Age in years
SALARY	Annual pay at last job
T_JOB	Time on last job in years
U_G	B.A. at most competitive school = 1; competitive school = 2; less competitive = 3 (school ratings according to Barron's)
GPA	GPA at undergraduate school
SAVE	Presence of savings account (0,1) variable
CR_NONE	No credit on file: 1, otherwise: 0
CR_GOOD	No worse than three 60-day lates on credit report (0,1) variable
CR_BAD	Worse than one 90-day late on credit report (0,1) variable

month or two months late. Once every few months he would dedicate the afternoon to calling borrowers more than a few months late.

Although Jim found Julee's methods uncivilized, her default rate was the lowest the program had seen in its five year history: 13% compared to Jim's 22%.

Credit Approval Training

Access your Student CD now for data in Excel worksheet form.

Despite Jim's reluctance, a credit approval training session was scheduled for a few days later. The same five completed applications (data on disk) that Julee and Jim had been taught from the prior year were brought along. Further, Jim brought along the data on 500 past borrowers to help Nancy and Leonard start the credit scoring process. (Variables collected are described in Table 18.4. Data are on the accompanying CD in both Excel and SPSS format.)

Questions:

1. Create a scorecard derived from the data on disk, score each of the five test applicants, and designate whether to accept or reject.
2. Is the MBA lending program a good idea?
3. How should credit limits be established?
4. How should bad debts be collected? How do various collection methods correspond to the overall strategic issues of running a school?

Name Index

Subject Index

Q

R